RESEARCH IN THE HISTORY OF ECONOMIC THOUGHT AND METHODOLOGY

A RESEARCH ANNUAL

RESEARCH IN THE HISTORY OF ECONOMIC THOUGHT AND METHODOLOGY

Founding Editor: Warren J. Samuels

Series Editors: Jeff E. Biddle, Ross B. Emmett and Marianne Johnson

Recent Volumes:

RESEARCH IN THE HISTORY OF ECONOMIC THOUGHT
AND METHODOLOGY   VOLUME 28-A

RESEARCH IN THE HISTORY OF ECONOMIC THOUGHT AND METHODOLOGY

A RESEARCH ANNUAL

EDITED BY

JEFF E. BIDDLE

*Department of Economics, Michigan State University,
East Lansing, MI 48824, USA*

ROSS B. EMMETT

*James Madison College, Michigan State University,
East Lansing, MI 48825, USA*

United Kingdom – North America – Japan
India – Malaysia – China

Emerald Group Publishing Limited
Howard House, Wagon Lane, Bingley BD16 1WA, UK

First edition 2010

British Library Cataloguing in Publication Data
A catalogue record for this book is available from the British Library

ISBN: 978-0-85724-059-0
ISSN: 0743-4154 (Series)

Awarded in recognition of
Emerald's production
department's adherence to
quality systems and processes
when preparing scholarly
journals for print

INVESTOR IN PEOPLE

CONTENTS

v

LIST OF CONTRIBUTORS

Humberto Barreto	Department of Economics and Management, DePauw University, Greencastle, IN, USA
Daniele Besomi	Centre d'études interdisciplinaires Walras-Pareto, University of Lausanne, Switzerland
Joe Blosser	University of Chicago, Chicago, IL, USA
Cécile Dangel-Hagnauer	University of Nice-Sophia Antipolis and CNRS-GREDEG, Valbonne, France
Stewart Davenport	Department of History, Pepperdine University, Santa Monica, CA, USA
Ross B. Emmett	James Madison College, Michigan State University, East Lansing, MI, USA
Giampaolo Garzarelli	IPEG, School of Economic and Business Sciences, University of the Witwatersrand, Johannesburg, South Africa
Willie Henderson	Alworth Institute for International Studies, University of Minnesota, Duluth, MN, USA
John F. Henry	Department of Economics, University of Missouri-Kansas City, MO, USA
Kevin D. Hoover	Department of Economics and Department of Philosophy, Duke University, Durham, NC, USA

Steven Horwitz   Department of Economics, St. Lawrence
                           University, Canton, NY, USA

Subbu Kumarappan   Department of Agricultural, Food and
                           Resource Economics, Michigan State
                           University, East Lansing, MI, USA

Nicholas Mercuro   Michigan State University College of
                           Law, East Lansing, MI, USA

Robert E. Prasch   Department of Economics, Middlebury
                           College, Middlebury, VT, USA

Thomas A. Stapleford   Program of Liberal Studies, University
                           of Notre Dame, Notre Dame, IN, USA

Paul B. Trescott   Department of Economics, Southern
                           Illinois University, Carbondale, IL, USA

EDITORIAL BOARD

ACKNOWLEDGMENTS

The editors wish to express their gratitude for assistance in the review process and other consultation to the members of the editorial board and to the following persons:

Philippe Le Gall
Vivianna Di Giovinazzo
D. Wade Hands
Perry Mehrling
Ed Noell
Rachel Penn
Warren J. Samuels

WESTERN ECONOMIC ADVISERS IN CHINA, 1900–1949

Paul B. Trescott

In 1895–1900 China suffered two serious humiliations. The first was defeat by Japan in the brief but decisive Sino-Japanese War in 1895–1896. The second was the invasion by international military forces in response to the Boxer Rebellion of 1900. These accelerated efforts by Chinese leaders to enlist western assistance in upgrading China's educational and economic systems. Enhanced freedom for missionary activities led to inflow of western economists to teach in China's Christian colleges. Remission of the Boxer indemnity by the United States government led to the creation of Qinghua College in 1911 with the purpose of preparing Chinese for study in the United States – many of whom became economists (for details, see Trescott, 2007).

Successive Chinese governments also drew on a significant number of western economists as advisers. The largest proportion provided advice concerning monetary and fiscal affairs. Best known among these was Edwin Kemmerer's Commission of Financial Experts. The 17 members spent most of 1929 in China, and produced a set of important reports on financial policy. Several members remained in China as continuing advisers. These have been described in detail earlier (Trescott, 1995).

The American advisers described here came in response to invitations from agencies and organizations in China. With the inception of the League of Nations in 1920, however, there came into existence an institutional source for international economic advisers. The League established a

A Research Annual
Research in the History of Economic Thought and Methodology, Volume 28-A, 1–37
Copyright © 2010 by Emerald Group Publishing Limited
ISSN: 0743-4154/doi:10.1108/S0743-4154(2010)000028A004

significant advisory presence in China, which included economists Carlo Dragoni (Italy) and Sir Arthur Salter (Britain).

SOME CONTEXT

China around 1900 was an enormous domain with approximately 400 million people, almost all of them desperately poor. Most were farmers, working intensively on small tracts of land using relatively primitive technology. It was in many respects a Malthusian economy, with high death and birth rates and many residents living close to the subsistence level.

Social stratification was extreme, encouraged by the wide acceptance of Confucian doctrines which counseled submission to authority. The upper classes supported an extraordinary extent of high culture – art, music, drama, literature, philosophy, and calligraphy. Chinese arts and crafts were world-famous, notably fabrics and porcelains – "China," after all. Chinese farmers, while backward in many respects, had been quick to respond to market incentives in developing production of cotton and soybeans, as well as traditional rice and wheat.

Before the 1840s, China had been relatively isolated from the West – a deliberate policy of the Manchu rulers. Beginning with the Opium Wars around 1840, the British forced China to open to interaction with the West. Unlike the Japanese, who had a similar experience and emerged as a strong modernizing power, the Chinese Qing (Manchu) monarchy was weak, corrupt, and incapable of effectively defending the country. A series of "unequal treaties" steadily widened opportunities for westerners to come to China to trade, to invest and conduct business, and to establish missionary enterprises such as churches, schools, and colleges. China's customs service, the chief source of government revenue, came under western domination, with import duties not to exceed five percent. Chinese government officials struggled to strengthen the country and the Manchu regime. Following the humiliation of the war with Japan, modern colleges and universities began to appear. Prominent Chinese intellectuals began to discover and publicize the ideas of western economics. In 1911–1912, the Qing monarchy was overthrown in a relatively bloodless coup led by military commander Yuan Shikai.

Meanwhile in the West two important trends were overlapping. One was the professionalization of economics and the development of graduate-level instruction. The second was the widespread popularity of the Christian Social Gospel. The overlap was personified in the activities of Richard T. Ely, a strong adherent of the Social Gospel, who returned from doctoral study in Germany to help develop graduate economics at Johns Hopkins and Wisconsin and was one of the founders of the American Economic Association in 1885 (Church, 1974; Bateman, 1998). Three of our early China advisers, Jeremiah W. Jenks, Henry C. Adams, and Frederic E. Lee, were strongly influenced by the Social Gospel. John Lossing Buck, who contributed advice on the silver question, was a Presbyterian missionary.

Many of the western advisers (notably the Kemmerer group) had no institutional sponsorship, but were recruited at the initiative of Chinese persons who had studied in the West. And of course, some early economic advisory roles were played by the western diplomatic staff in China. China's most influential "foreign expert" at the turn of century was Sir Robert Hart, the administrative head of the Chinese customs service, directing the primary source of government tax revenue (Ganschow, 1976). Hart engaged former British missionary Joseph Edkins, who translated William Stanley Jevons's *Primer on Political Economy* into Chinese in 1886 and published a series of monographs on Chinese financial matters (Edkins, 1901, 1903, 1905; Yih, 1985, p. 4.)

MONETARY ADVISERS: J.W. JENKS

In the late 19th century, China's monetary system was very nearly a laissez-faire system-based primarily on silver. Chinese mints coined silver coins roughly equivalent in size and fineness to Mexican dollars.[1] Copper cash, bank notes, and other forms of money fluctuated in value in relation to gold and to each other.

Between 1880 and 1902, the market value of silver in terms of gold fell by half. This brought a corresponding decline in the foreign-exchange value of the Chinese currency. This trend helped make Chinese exports cheaper on world markets, thus promoting larger sales. But the instability of the exchange rate was a major deterrent to foreign lenders considering loans to China – unless those were explicitly contracted in terms of gold. Foreign-exchange instability also caused difficulties for Chinese customs administration. China was pressuring for autonomy in setting tariff policy. The Western powers were reluctant to grant autonomy until China's foreign exchange rate was stabilized.

In several areas, long-standing silver-based monetary systems were being transformed into some form of gold-exchange standard.[2] To economize on gold reserves, the country's monetary reserves would be held mainly in the form of deposits in the major international financial centers. China was urged to adopt a gold-exchange system by a few high-ranking Chinese officials and by Sir Robert Hart (Kann, 1926, pp. 82–96).

In January 1903, the governments of China and Mexico petitioned the United States government to stabilize the value of silver in terms of gold. The issue of the monetary standard had been a major topic of controversy in the U.S. Bryan's defeat in the presidential election of 1896 had slain the dragon of "free silver," and its demise was embodied in the Gold Standard Act of 1900. The United States created a Commission on International Exchange, consisting of Jeremiah Whipple Jenks, Charles A. Conant, and Hugh H. Hanna. Jenks was designated to go to China. He was then Professor of Economics at Cornell, holding a doctorate from Germany (Kemmerer, 1993, pp. 12–14).[3]

Jenks arrived in China in January, 1904, to present a proposal for a gold-exchange system. As the Commission described it:

> a pamphlet was prepared setting forth the main points of its plan ... with the reasons for making the suggestions. This pamphlet, printed in both English and Chinese ... was widely distributed among the officials and most important business men of China. Some of the Chinese papers reprinted the pamphlet in full, while other papers there ... reprinted extracts from it as well as brief articles covering special points which were especially prepared for this purpose by the commissioner. (Jenks, 1904, p. 14)[4]

Jenks traveled extensively in China, remaining until August 1904. He observed monetary practices in different areas and assessed the problems of government administration of monetary affairs. An English-language newspaper described Jenks as "the suave, unassuming but thoroughly earnest professor of Cornell University, with his unexcelled mastery of facts and figures" (Jenks, 1904, p. 19). There was general support for the gold-exchange proposal among western governments, eager to facilitate investment in China. For the U.S. government, the Jenks proposal can be seen as an extension of the 1900 adoption of the gold standard at home.

However, the Chinese government did not adopt the proposed gold-exchange system. Two obstacles were probably decisive, as follows:

1. China would need to maintain a monetary reserve, partly in gold in China and partly in deposits in Western banks. Lacking money, the Chinese government could acquire such a reserve only by borrowing. Managing the reserve, particularly if it were becoming depleted, would be challenging.[5]
2. To maintain the proposed subsidiary silver (and copper) coinage would require limiting the quantity of coins issued. China's mints operated on the principle of unlimited coinage of silver. Owners of silver initiated

coinage, bringing in silver and receiving coins. If the monetary value of the coins were set above the bullion cost, there would be a flood of silver into the mints.[6]

However, according to Wei Wen-pin (1914, p. 101), the Jenks proposals were doomed by opposition from Chang Chih-tung, a prominent official, stemming from misunderstandings reflecting defective Chinese translations.

The Jenks report gave Chinese readers a relatively sophisticated introduction to monetary analysis. The report described the economic and financial adjustments which would occur if the monetary reserve were significantly increasing or decreasing (in response to disequilibrium in the balance of international payments) (Jenks, 1904, pp. 98–100, 112–113).

The issues raised by the Jenks report remained in active discussion for many years. In 1910, the Chinese government was close to adopting a program to create a simplified and uniform coinage system, as part of a plan to acquire loans abroad for economic development purposes. In developing these plans, they had engaged Dr. G. Vissering, who was serving as head of the Javasche Bank in the Netherlands East Indies (Indonesia).

Any plans for Chinese monetary reform were overturned when the monarchy was overthrown in the 1911 Revolution (Cameron, 1931, pp. 170–171; Field, 1931, pp. 55–60). However, Vissering continued his work and produced a two-volume study. He proposed that the government create a gold unit of account, with no coins or notes involved at first. The Central Bank would accept deposits of gold or equivalent foreign exchange. The arrangement would be voluntary and would gradually build a gold reserve and phase out the old disorderly forms of money (see Salter, 1934a, pp. 107–109).

Many of Jenks's ideas resurfaced in the proposals of the Kemmerer Commission in 1929 – not surprising, since Kemmerer had been Jenks's protege. Jenks himself maintained an interest in China and wrote about its affairs on numerous occasions.[7] He visited China again in 1916 and campaigned vigorously for increased American investment in China (Jenks, 1916a, 1916b).

HENRY CARTER ADAMS AND CHINA'S RAILROADS

Railroads developed very slowly in China. At the end of 1896, China had only 370 miles of track.[8] After the Boxer hostilities, construction expanded rapidly. The Chinese government discovered that owning and operating rail lines could be an important source of revenue, and proceeded eagerly to encourage foreign involvement. However, Chinese public opinion was violently opposed to so much foreign influence, and the issue contributed to the revolution in 1911.

By 1920, China had 7,000 miles of railway in place, about half owned and operated by the government (Spence, 1990, pp. 328–329). Railroad economics became a popular subject for Chinese students in the United States.

Henry Carter Adams came to China in 1913 to advice the Chinese government on railroad accounting. Officials wanted to strengthen the revenue-producing role of the railroads and improve the chances to obtain foreign investment. Adams had been serving as chief statistician for the U.S. Interstate Commerce Commission since its creation in 1887. He also held a professorship at Michigan, where he organized the department of Economics. He had a deep Christian faith and had studied theology before turning to Economics and obtaining a PhD from Johns Hopkins. He had written extensively on public finance and labor. In 1895, he was chosen President of the American Economic Association (Coats, 1968, 1992).

One of the Adams's major achievements at the ICC had been to get the railroad companies to provide uniform accounting reports. In China, Adams's task was more daunting, for accounting itself was in its infancy. He worked closely with Dr. Wang Ching-chun, who had completed a doctorate at Illinois with a specialty in railroad economics (see Trescott, 2007).

Adams commenced work in Peking in November 1913, riding on horseback to work at the Ministry of Communications. He noted that

> of the 18 foreign advisers I am about the only one not here for ornamental purposes ...
> I have met the Chinese members of the Commission and I am trying to teach them the fundamental principles of classification, for all the world as tho [sic] they were students in the University. The difficulty here is, that the gov. [sic] does not have men who know enough to stand up against the blasted foreigners, so that, if we work out a form of records for the railways, it may or it may not be used intelligently. (H.C. Adams to [children] Teddy and Carter, Peking, November 28, 1913, H.C. Adams Papers, Box 13)[9]

Adams soon came to realize that his work "is assuming an importance I never dreamed of ... . Things are in a very bad way here, financially ... . My work *may* prove of great assistance in giving the country credit. That is why the bankers and railroad men are so favorably impressed" (H.C. Adams to [son] Carter, Shanghai, December, 21, 1913, H.C. Adams Papers, Box 13).

Adams was soon distressed by the corruption and lack of work discipline. "This government is wholly inefficient ... and there is no hope in them ... .

Meanwhile the foreigners are sucking the lemon dry ... ."[10] "The commercial incapacity of the Chinese impresses me more than before. It seems useless to work for efficiency for that means just so much more squeeze to other officials. If China had a little of the habit of commercial honesty, the sense of official trusteeship, there is nothing she could not do." "Why do these children try to play with live steam engines?" (H.C. Adams to Carter, January 27, 1914; September 8, 1915, and Nov. 24, 1915; H.C. Adams Papers, Box 13).

Despite his pessimism about China, Adams persisted in his work until 1917. Besides railroad matters, he provided advice on policies regarding currency, banking, and workmen's compensation (H.C. Adams to Carter, March 10 and 31, 1914, H.C. Adams Papers, Box 13). Besides his direct influence on the individuals he worked with, he composed a 140-page monograph on Chinese railway accounting which was ultimately published in both English and Chinese (Adams, 1928). Some samples:

> The modern railway accountant is no longer a clerk whose duty it is to keep records according to rules laid down by the general manager; on the contrary, he has become a critic, responsible for detecting unnecessary wastes in operation, and for testing the efficiency of current administration.

> [E]stablished rules of accounting are generalizations for the guidance of business conduct a disregard of which is a step in the direction of business disaster.

> An accounting rule which requires that adequate repairs, replacements, and depreciation should be made current charges against revenues, is a business law of self-preservation.

> The funds for railway undertakings in China have been obtained in large part from private sources. These funds have been made secure by mortgages on the railway property ... . To preserve to the government the revenues from its railways to which it is entitled, and at the same time to preserve to the bondholders the full measure of the security for their loan, places the Chief Accountant of Chinese railways ... in the position somewhat of serving two masters. (Adams, 1928, pp. 6, 9–10, and 12, respectively)

At the time of Adams's death in 1921, the Chinese Ministry of Communication presented a tribute (see Hollander, 1922, pp. 415–416). In 1933, Alfred Kaiming Chiu praised the quality of China's railway statistical data, crediting Adams for their excellence (Chiu, 1933, p. 16).

Unfortunately, the disruption of national authority after 1911 led to serious interruption of railway building.[11]

OTHER ADVISERS IN THE EARLY REPUBLIC

One of the Adams's acquaintances in Peking was William F. Willoughby, a Princeton professor. After graduating from Johns Hopkins in 1888, Willoughby joined the U.S. Department of Labor and published extensively on topics related to labor conditions and social legislation (Willoughby, 1898, 1899, 1901a, 1901b, 1905). He taught economics at Johns Hopkins and Harvard in 1901. From 1901 until 1909 he held several high positions in Puerto Rico, then served as assistant director of the U.S. Census. These latter experiences shifted his interests to public administration, particularly in relation to economic policies. He became professor of jurisprudence and politics at Princeton in 1912. He served as constitutional adviser to China's President Yuan Shikai in 1914–1916 (Chih, 1981, p. 212; *Who's Who in America, 1920–21*, p. 3096).

Frederic Edward Lee was, like Jenks and Adams, an economist with strong Christian convictions. He completed a doctorate at Yale in 1916, having received a Bachelor of Divinity degree there in 1914. He spent two years studying at the London School of Economics, then taught in Japan for two years before joining the U.S. War Trade Board in 1918. In 1920, he became economist consul for China, serving in Shanghai and Peking, a position he held until 1922. While there he gathered material for his book *Currency, Banking and Finance in China* (Lee, 1926), an admirable summary of monetary conditions at that time. It was informational and did not advance policy proposals. Lee subsequently taught at the universities of Maryland and Illinois (*Who's Who in America 1948*, p. 1446). Lee's time in China overlapped with that of E. Carlton Baker, who served as economic adviser to northern warlord Chang Tso-lin in 1920–1923 (MacCormick, 1977, pp. 61, 276).

Scott Nearing was another economist who was strongly influenced by Christian ideals of concern for the poor. Nearing earned a doctorate at Penn in 1908 and remained there as a faculty member. He was a popular teacher and wrote several textbooks. From early times, his concern for labor conditions and social welfare led him to a radical stance, particularly in his opposition to child labor. He was an exceptionally prolific writer – his bibliography fills 10 pages in 1 biography (Saltmarsh, 1991, pp. 321–330). Nearing was dismissed from Penn in 1915 for his radical views. Two years later he was dismissed from the University of Toledo for his opposition to World War I.

Nearing gravitated to New York, where he lectured in many venues as part of the radical community. He became an extremely popular lecturer at the Rand School of Social Science, visited the Soviet Union in 1925 and joined the American Communist Party in 1927. In his New York lecture activities, Nearing became acquainted with Chen Kung-po, while Chen was studying Economics at Columbia. Chen had become a member of the Central Executive Committee of the Kuomintang in 1926. He was able to arrange an invitation for Nearing to come to China as an economic adviser to the Chinese Railway Administration (Whitfield, 1974, pp. 160–161).[12]

In preparation for his visit, Nearing (assisted by Harry Freeman) composed a monograph which he entitled *Whither China? An Economic Interpretation of Recent Events in the Far East* (Nearing, 1927). Much of the monograph presented a Marxist view of China's situation. It was a competent piece of library research, which ended with a candid recognition of the rightward turn taken by the KMT in 1927, when the Communist elements were purged. That rightward turn disrupted plans for Nearing's activities in China, and although he went there in 1927 as planned, he did not apparently do any advising to the railway authorities.[13] His biographies and autobiography tell little of his China visit, except for a bizarre lecture at (Christian) Yenching University.[14] After three months he moved on to the Soviet Union in November 1927. Chen Kung-po weathered the political disruptions and continued to play a prominent role in the KMT until the 1940s.

Soon after, the Chinese railways engaged another adviser in the early stages of a career which would take him to the Nobel Prize – Wassily Leontief. Leontief left the USSR in 1925 to study in Berlin, where he assisted Werner Sombart and studied with Ladislav Bortkiewicz. In 1928, he published an article on the balance of the Soviet economy which contained the germs of input–output analysis which earned him Nobel honors (Leontief, 1928). He moved to Kiel where he completed a doctorate with a dissertation which developed a dynamic general-equilibrium model.

In 1928, Leontief accepted an offer to advice China's Ministry of Railways and spent a year there. One task was negotiating with China's creditors who were, as he put it, "in a weak position, since their property could be expropriated." As Leonard Silk described it:

> Leontief also worked on the planning of new rail lines. He had only the most scrappy data for planning purposes, so he decided to create his own. He persuaded his minister to get an airplane; he had cameras mounted on it and sent it out to photograph the crops. He used these pictures, on a sampling basis, to make estimates of farm production by regions as a basis for planning rail lines. (Silk, 1976, p. 144)

Soon after returning to Kiel, Leontief came to the United States to join the National Bureau of Economic Research, and shortly afterward, to become a member of the Harvard faculty. He was elected President of the AEA in 1970 and received the Nobel Prize in 1973.

THE KEMMERER COMMISSION, 1929

When the new KMT government took power, Sun Fo became Minister of Railways. He had completed a master's degree in economics at Columbia in 1917. He was the son of Sun Yat-sen (died in 1925), who had published a grandiose plan for China's economic development, emphasizing transport improvements (Sun Yat-sen, 1928). Sun Fo was committed to a program of externally financed transport development following the lines of his father's proposals. To facilitate such financing, Sun Fo engaged Edwin W. Kemmerer to bring a team of financial experts to China in 1929 to advise on a wide range of national issues (see Trescott, 1995).

Kemmerer was then a professor at Princeton, with a doctorate from Cornell. His mentor J.W. Jenks had helped him secure a position to supervise the introduction of the gold-exchange system in the Philippines in 1903–1936. Beginning with a visit to Mexico in 1917, Kemmerer became very involved in international advisory work and earned a reputation as the "Money Doctor" for persuading countries to adopt sound, conservative monetary systems (Drake, 1989). Kemmerer was President of the American Economic Association in 1926.

When the Commission of Financial Experts set up their operations in Shanghai in February 1929, the group included 16 Americans besides Kemmerer. Six of them had been Kemmerer's students. Prominent among them were Arthur N. Young and his brother, John Parke Young (both Princeton PhDs), Frederick A. Cleveland (PhD finance, Penn), Oliver Lockhart (PhD, Cornell), Benjamin Wallace (PhD political science, Wisconsin), and Frank Whitson Fetter (PhD Princeton, son of Frank A. Fetter, a distinguished economist).

As anticipated, the Commission recommended that China adopt a gold-exchange monetary standard similar to the Jenks proposal. Circulating money would consist of silver and copper coins and banknotes, all kept at par with the standard gold unit by full convertibility. The silver coins would contain metal worth less than their monetary value. No gold coins would be produced. Rather, domestic money would be convertible into gold bars or into foreign exchange. Most of the government's monetary reserve would be held as deposits in international money centers.

The proposed system would stabilize the exchange rate between Chinese money and the principal monetary units of other countries. One of the Kemmerer's favorite arguments was that the system would cause China's domestic money supply to rise or fall in a manner which would contribute to balance-of-payments equilibrium.

The Kemmerer proposal was not adopted. It encountered many of the same objections as the Jenks proposal. Assembling the reserve would be costly, and there were still doubts that government officials could manage it honestly and competently. As the world slid into the Great Depression, China's silver system protected the country against the extreme deflation engendered by the international gold standard (see Fong, 1934).

However, the Commission's work had two important effects. First, the Chinese government did significantly reduce the disorder of the monetary system, closing down some of the local mints and curbing banknote issues. More important, in 1930, the government adopted Arthur Young's recommendation that the valuation of Chinese currency for customs duties (the chief source of government revenue) be fixed in terms of gold. The Chinese customs gold unit (CGU) was given a gold valuation equivalent to U.S. $.40. The government then arranged for the creation of CGU paper currency and bank deposits. Adoption of the CGU helped raise customs revenue from $244 million in 1929 to $388 million (Chinese dollars) in 1931 (Young, 1997, p. 73).

It is appropriate to review here the follow-up to the Kemmerer report provided by Sir Arthur Salter (below), who came to China under the auspices of the League of Nations in 1931. By 1931, Salter (1934a) could argue that "if the eastern countries which ... had currencies based on silver ... had retained that system, it would have been better for them and for the world" (p. 92). He expressed alarm about the potential fall in the world market price of silver if it were relegated to secondary status under the Kemmerer plan, and felt this might cause trouble in introducing the new system, requiring a relatively large gold reserve (Salter, 1934a, pp. 94–95). With these qualifications, Salter endorsed the Kemmerer proposal but noted reasons to delay its implementation until the loan markets were more favorable for borrowing the needed reserve.

Salter proposed that the government abolish the tael as a unit of account. He urged extending the use of gold unit bank deposits (already begun with the CGU). If a new gold-exchange system was definitely announced, these gold unit deposits could be created in exchange for silver at the official parity. Banknotes and token coins could be issued, convertible into the gold unit. Initially, the Central Bank should hold 100% reserves in gold or equivalent foreign exchange (Salter, 1934a, pp. 109–112).

Just as the fall in value of silver undermined much of the Kemmerer proposal, so the events of September 1931, undermined Salter's version of a gold-exchange standard. Britain severed the link between sterling and gold, allowing the pound to fall and the pound price of gold to rise. Thus deposits held in British banks by overseas monetary authorities were correspondingly devalued. However, correspondent deposits in New York City banks did not take a comparable shock until early in 1933.

The Kemmerer Commission presented extensive reports on numerous other areas of financial policy, including banking, fiscal policy and taxation. Some significant policy recommendations were adopted, particularly in regard to banking. Economic issues were prominently featured in the Commission's "Report on revenue policy" ([Kemmerer] Commission of Financial Experts, 1929). The report noted that "The realization that taxes are in fact a contribution to collective purposes, not a mere 'one-sided' compulsory exaction of wealth by the Government (or ... by officials largely for their own private and personal benefit) must be gradually built up through the devotion of public funds to useful public purposes." The Commission felt that China was not ready for taxation of incomes and inheritance, but should rely on existing revenue sources (chiefly customs and excise) to use existing administrative capabilities. They suggested taxing increments of land values resulting from urban public improvements.[15]

The report warned against "excess burden": "the yield to the government should be commensurate with the burden it [taxation] imposes upon taxpayers, and not dry up the sources of revenue, as it may do if it unduly burdens ... industry and business" ([Kemmerer] Commission of Financial Experts, 1929, p. 2). They urged abolition of the notorious *likin*, under which taxes were repeatedly imposed on the same goods moving through internal trade channels.

In its consideration of import duties, the Commission strongly opposed protectionism. Tariff policy was a very sensitive issue, for the Chinese government was just beginning to secure the power to set its own tariff rates. The "unequal treaties" of the 19th century had required that Chinese import duties not exceed 5 percent. The Commission recommended a modest general increase in rates to increase revenue. But they noted the danger that higher tariff rates on luxury products might stimulate their production.

Not surprisingly, the Chinese government took advantage of tariff autonomy to raise rates, a policy which initially increased both revenues and protection (Wright, 1938, pp. 601–651). Collection of nuisance levies (likin, coastal trade) was phased out. Tariff rates, which averaged only approximately 4 percent before 1929, went above 25 percent after 1934. However, the Japanese occupation of Manchuria in 1931 greatly impaired customs enforcement in northeast China.

When Kemmerer left China in December 1929, he was clearly not pleased with China or with what his group had accomplished.[16] His proposals did not receive the large-scale rapid adoption they had experienced in Latin America. Any chances Kemmerer's influence would stimulate capital inflow to China was destroyed by the world depression. China was probably fortunate that the gold-standard and central-banking recommendations were not followed, because of their deflationary tendencies.

However, Curti and Birr (1954, p. 176) introduced their discussion of the Kemmerer Commission in China with the comment that "American technical and advisory work proved to be of far greater importance in China than in many smaller countries." Much of this influence occurred because so many of the Commission members remained in China. Arthur Young remained until 1947. Frederick Cleveland, despite his advanced age, stayed in China until 1935. Officially he was one of the administrators of the Salt Revenue; he also continued to advise on budgeting and financial control. Oliver Lockhart remained in China until 1941. His chief work was advising on tax matters. Arthur Young credited Lockhart with "the development of a respected service to operate the consolidated taxes on factory products" (Young, 1971, p. 339). In 1935, Lockhart replaced Cleveland in the Salt Revenue. Arthur Young, Lockhart, and Fenimore Lynch (another member) were all involved in the turbulent changes in China's monetary system taken in response to U.S. silver policy. These are discussed later. On the whole, the Kemmerer experts were involved more in helping improve the honesty and efficiency of financial administration rather than in economic policy-making. They became a part of the administrative structure, participating in daily operations and not merely offering advice from outside.

When serious floods ravaged central China in 1931, Arthur Young had a major role in administering the relief program. He helped carry out the program to borrow wheat in the United States (where the market was seriously depressed) and sell it in China where food supplies were scarce, and use the proceeds for flood relief and reconstruction. Young was also the principal architect of a 1932 program of rescheduling China's payments on the national debt to take advantage of declining interest rates. In 1933, Young traveled to Washington to negotiate another loan, this one to buy cotton and wheat for resale in China, with the proceeds going for economic development purposes (Young, 1997, pp. 51–59).[17]

LEAGUE OF NATIONS ADVISERS

Contacts between the Chinese government and staff members of the League of Nations and its subsidiaries began in the mid-1920s. Ludwig Rajchman, Director of the Health Section of the League Secretariat, visited China in late 1925. In 1927, Albert Thomas, Director of the International Labor Organization, came to China to inquire into labor conditions. When the KMT had gained political domination, they invited Rajchman to return, which he did in late 1929. Soon after there followed visits by Sir Arthur Salter, Director of the Financial and Economic Organization, and Dr. Robert Haas, head of the Transit and Communications Organization. Accompanying Salter were staff experts Maurice Frere and Elliott Felkin (Hoe, 1933).[18]

Salter had studied Economics and many other things at Oxford, 1899–1904 (Salter, 1961, pp. 31–32). He joined the British Civil Service, where the World War I catapulted him into important responsibilities for international shipping policy. When the League of Nations was formed at the end of the War, Salter became director of the Economic, Financial and Transit Section. One of his close colleagues was Jean Monnet (Salter, 1961, p. 147). Salter was intimately involved in problems of German reparations and the financial reconstruction of many of the new-formed nations in Europe. Salter (1961) later remarked "When I came to Geneva I brought some knowledge of finance and economics, as I had ever since my undergraduate days read widely in this field and had afterwards ... found them closely interwoven with the practical work in which I was engaged" (p. 189).

Rajchman, Salter, and Haas met with finance minister T. V. Soong in April, 1931.[19] The Chinese government then undertook to create a new National Economic Council (NEC), to be a focal point for an ongoing program of cooperation with the League for economic development and for health and education. In November 1931, Chiang Kai-shek himself sketched out an ambitious program for the new NEC. This included public works for transport and water control, public health programs, and educational reform. Industrial development and financial policy were to be studied. Particularly interesting was a section on "Land Reform and Agricultural Improvements," instructing the NEC to base a coordinated plan on the work of "those institutions which are engaged in surveys and studies of this subject throughout China" (Hoe, 1933, p. 15).

In August 1931, the Chinese government announced a "Ten-Year Plan," formulated with the aid of the League. Barely an outline, its 14 subject areas bore a strong resemblance to Sun Yat-sen's proposals.[20]

Sir Arthur Salter stayed in China for several months. He recounted a conversation with Chiang Kai-shek, in which Chiang was seeking

> some method of improving China's financial resources and arresting the depreciation of the currency ... It was not easy, especially through an interpreter, to expound the economics of the problem. What he understood most clearly of what I said he liked least. I told him there was only one quick and simple solution. If the budget was unbalanced, he would be forced to meet current expenses by printing notes, and that must bring inflation; and his budget could only be quickly balanced if he could make a settlement with the Communists which would save him the expense of fighting them. (Salter, 1947, p. 216)

Salter worked closely with T.V. Soong (who had studied economics at Columbia) and was very impressed by him (Salter, 1947, p. 221). But he was keenly aware of the political and administrative obstacles to economic improvement. However impressive were China's material and human resources

> the indispensable basis [for improvement] was peace, external and internal, and reasonably good government. Without this all financial and economic schemes were useless. And to this the technician could contribute nothing. The first step must be political and military; economic reconstruction might then consolidate; but it could not initiate. (Salter, 1961, p. 220)

Salter returned to England, just in time to be confronted by the British decision, in September 1931, to sever the link between gold and the pound sterling. He became a member of the Economic Advisory Council "and was on a small economic committee with [Sir Joshua] Stamp, [John Maynard] Keynes, G.D.H. Cole, and Walter Citrine among its members and with Hubert Henderson as Secretary. This met frequently and reported upon the main issues of policy at the time" (Salter, 1961, p. 230). Salter was much impressed with Keynes's macroeconomic ideas and supported efforts to expand money and expenditures (see Salter et al., 1932; Salter, 1967, pp. 86–87). He was to return to China in 1933.

OTHER LEAGUE ACTIVITIES

In October 1932, the League sent Dr. Carlo Dragoni to advise on agricultural conditions. He was professor of agricultural science at the

University of Rome. Selskar Gunn of the Rockefeller Foundation interviewed Dragoni in Shanghai in March 1933, and reported as follows:

> He has traveled quite a bit and is a man of considerable ability and acute observation.
> He considers that the three outstanding immediate problems in the agricultural field in
> China are:
>
> 1. A thorough-going study of land tenure.
> 2. Development of crop statistics.
> 3. The establishment of a central agricultural experimentation station.
>
> D[ragoni] was particularly impressed with the work being done under the direction of
> Professor [John Lossing] Buck at Nanking and Professor Franklin Ho at Nankai. He
> also thinks well of the efforts at Yenching University in Rural Sociology. What is needed
> most of all, in his opinion, is a good organization of the Central Government and he
> believes that the National Economic Council, although a weak affair at the present time,
> is capable of being developed.
>
> His experience with peasants in China leads him to believe that they are not bound up
> with tradition and that they are always willing to adopt new methods or grow new crops
> if they can be shown the benefits ... [Dragoni] is much impressed with the development
> of cooperatives in some places in China and in the advance in rural credit
> organizations ... Where you have owner-farmers, as is particularly true in the north,
> you have practically no communism, but in the central regions of China, and in large
> sections of the south, where the land is owned by the so-called gentry and rented out
> under conditions to the peasants, communism and banditry are rife.
>
> D. does not believe that the agricultural methods studied by Chinese in foreign countries
> have very much value in China ... . (Gunn, "Travel diary," March 8, 1933, Rockefeller
> Foundation Archives, Record Group 1, Series 601, Box 12, Folder 129)

The League delegated five European engineers to come to China to advise
on public-works construction projects. They also sent a sericulture expert,
two public health experts to aid in flood relief in 1931, a German expert to
aid improvement of the telephone and telegraph service, and two experts
concerned with civil service reform. The League's Financial Section sent
Rene Charron to work on improving the Chinese Postal Savings Bank,
arriving in January 1933 for six months (Hoe, 1933, pp. 18–23). In April, he
talked with Selskar Gunn, who reported:

> RC is very frank concerning the present L. of N. program in China and its lack of
> success ... He feels it must be altered. Many of the experts who come stay too short a
> time and little or no good arises from their visits. Some scheme must be worked out so
> that the men who come out from the League will have some authority and not be merely
> advisers. (Gunn, "Travel diary," April 13, 1933, Rockefeller Foundation Archives,
> Record Group 1, Series 601, Box 12, Folder 129)

This comment puts into perspective the work of Arthur Young, Cleveland, Lockhart, and Lynch, who did have "some authority" and had a significant role in policy-making and execution. The public health program did display significant achievements, and in July 1933, Ludvig Rajchman was chosen as the League's technical liaison officer attached to the NEC (Hoe, 1933, pp. 23–30). Rajchman, unlike the League short-timers, became an insider and a particularly close confidant of T.V. Soong (Salter, 1947, p. 220; Young, 1971, pp. 342–347). By that time, the plans of the NEC and the advice of the League were being implemented with funds from the cotton and wheat loan negotiated by Arthur Young.

Sir Arthur Salter came to China for his second visit, a three months' stay in late 1933. A major part of his task was to comment on the monetary situation with particular reference to silver. We discuss this later. In January 1934, he participated in a study of economic and financial conditions in Chekiang Province as part of a group which included professors Franklin Ho (Ho Lien) and H.D. Fong of Nankai University (both of whom had received doctorates in economics from Yale). Their report was strongly critical of the land tax and many other aspects of the public finances of the province. "The farmer's case is the harder because so much of the [government] expenditure brings him no visible benefit"(Salter, 1934a, p. 131).

Salter ended his 1934 report with some cogent comments on economic development plans for China. He warned that "the rest of the world is full of disastrous examples of wasteful experiments in State assistance to the wrong industries by the wrong methods"(Salter, 1934a, p. 139). Protective tariffs could be an example. He urged improvement of highways and railroads, a priority consistent with Sun Yat-sen's original proposals. Second, he recommended expanding technical education, specifically mentioning not only civil engineering and railway construction, but also "accountancy, book-keeping and the common elements of business management." Third, he favored "establishment of institutions which would, for each class of article, secure proper testing and grading of quality" (Salter, 1934a, pp. 143–144). This last was already under way in programs for cotton and silk. Salter closed with further warnings about over-extending government enterprise.

In April 1934, Rajchman presented a lengthy report on the collaborative work between the League and the NEC. The most striking features were a set of proposals for rural reconstruction in Kiangsi Province, where Mao Zedong and the Communists had recently enjoyed some success before being driven out by Chiang's military. The proposals included the following:

> the conversion of the tenant-farmer into an owner-farmer, with the full legal property in the land he tills ... any large properties ... being abolished, and tenancy itself being an

exceptional arrangement arising only out of special conditions ... [give] each tenant a
prima facie ownership, put upon every owner who is not tilling or managing the whole of
his property the onus of proving his claim to continue his ownership as a small owner.
(League of Nations, 1934, p. 18)

This proposal, with its close resemblance to Sun Yat-sen's "land to the
tillers" slogan, has a very radical cast – depending, of course, on how the
"large properties" were to be "abolished" – by purchase, or by confiscation.[21]

The report went on to recommend progressive taxation of land, backed
up by a comprehensive system of registering land ownership. Other
proposals would improve access to credit, and provide rural social services,
particularly relating to education and health.

Sir Arthur Salter and other League representatives provided input to the
deliberations of land policy (League of Nations, 1934, p. 23).

League representatives also helped with the Commission for the
Rationalization of the Cotton Industry, which was created in October
1933, giving attention both to cotton farming and to cotton manufacture.
They noted the very low productivity in cotton farming and urged the
adoption of improved seeds. They encouraged the formation of cooperatives
to improve product quality and marketing efficiency – goals already
embodied in the Hebei Cotton Improvement Commission (Reynolds, 1975,
p. 459). Quality improvement was also the focal point of a program for the
silk industry, aided by Dr. Benito Mari, an Italian sericulture expert (League
of Nations, 1934, pp. 23–25).

In 1934, Salter cited these sectors as promising areas for industrial
development. But he argued that "the increase of the production of the
average agriculturalist remains the fundamental problem of China's
economy," and that this increase "must be the essential foundation on
which industrial development must be built." He warned against imitating
the development programs of other countries (such as Russia), and stressed
the importance of railway extension (Salter, 1934b, pp. 94–99).

Robert Haas came to China in 1935 on behalf of the League and
reported in very positive terms. He was particularly impressed by highway
construction – these were roads he had driven on himself – and by the
development activities carried on by the governments of individual
provinces (League of Nations, 1935). However, from this point, League
activities related to China's economy faded away. Rajchman's appointment
as Technical Delegate was not renewed after July 1934, although he
continued to have a close connection with T.V. Soong.[22]

The eroding of League influence was related to the coming of Jean
Monnet. He had been a colleague of Sir Arthur Salter working for the

League. After leaving the League, Monnet was invited in November 1932, by T.V. Soong, to come to China, on the recommendation of Rajchman.[23] Monnet arrived in China in November 1933, undertaking to organize the China Development Finance Corporation. During his eight months' stay, Monnet persuaded Shanghai bankers to provide capital and management for the new organization, which was designed to float bond issues overseas and use the proceeds to finance development projects. An implicit purpose was to by-pass the potential monopolistic influence of the China Consortium, a cartel of American, British, French, and Japanese banks (Field, 1931). The Japanese were angered at this maneuver, which added to their hostility toward Rajchman. They enlisted the aid of the British, who helped undercut Rajchman and the League (Duchene, 1994, pp. 52–56).

As Monnet explained it to James Harvey Rogers, the Corporation "will in general supervise the rehabilitation of debts now in default, and the placing of new foreign credits in China" (Rogers diary, April 17, 1934). The Corporation was making a promising start, particularly in aiding railroad construction, when the outbreak of war with Japan brought its operations to a halt.[24] Monnet went on to achieve outstanding success as one of the architects of European economic unification after World War II (Young, 1971, pp. 364–371). Rajchman, although suspected to be a Communist, and often viewed as a shady character in wartime Washington, went on to become a founder of UNICEF.

THE SILVER CRISIS OF 1934–1935

During the first two years of the world-wide economic downswing which followed 1929, China was relatively insulated. The market value of silver fell roughly in proportion to other commodities, so China's domestic price level was not under deflationary pressure from the international economy. After Britain's departure from gold in August 1931, however, deflation became increasingly severe in China. Sir Arthur Salter warned against devaluing the yuan or cutting it adrift from silver (Salter, 1934b, p. 54).

In March and April 1933, the Chinese government followed advice from Kemmerer, Salter, and others and abolished the tael as a unit of account. Minting began of a new silver dollar (yuan) bearing Sun Yat-sen's likeness (Leavens, 1939, pp. 202–205). When the United States in 1933 adopted a policy of trying to purchase silver and raise its price, China experienced serious deflationary effects. Arthur Young engaged in frantic diplomatic efforts to moderate U.S. policy, but in vain (Young, 1971, pp. 212–214).

In February 1934, Minister of Industry Chen Kung-po created a Committee for the Study of Silver Values and Commodity Prices. The chair was Leonard Hsu (Hsu Shih-lien) a sociology professor at Yenching University. Hsu had studied economics at Stanford before shifting to Iowa for a doctorate in sociology. He was well connected politically. The membership included three members of the Nanking University College of Agriculture and Forestry, namely John Lossing Buck, Ardron Lewis, and Chang Lu-lwan.[25] The Committee presented a lengthy report in December 1934, which was published in 1935. The report was largely an application to China of the monetary ideas of George Warren and Frank Pearson, agricultural economists at Cornell. Lewis had been their student and had clearly become a fervent advocate of their viewpoint (see the report of three of Warren and Pearson's articles in Ministry of Industry, 1935, pp. 168–224).

Warren and Pearson based their analysis on inspection of data, without any significant monetary theory.[26] They concluded there was a close connection, in the United States and Western Europe, between commodity prices and gold. "The central idea is that there is some definite proportion between the increase of the supply of gold ... and the growth of production ... which will result in stable prices; when the rate of growth of the gold supply is above this ratio to the growth of production, prices will rise, and in the converse case they will fall" (Hardy, 1935; Warren & Pearson, 1935, pp. 94–95).

In April 1933, President Roosevelt had suspended the convertibility of dollars into gold at the previous price of $20.67 an ounce, allowing the price of gold to fluctuate. In July, Professor Warren was invited to Washington as an adviser to the President on financial matters, and it was widely assumed that his ideas were guiding administration policy.[27] His emphasis shifted to the price of gold, indicating that commodity prices would rise roughly in proportion to an increase in the price of gold. Eventually the price of gold was set at $35 an ounce in January 1934, at which price a vast amount of gold flowed into the United States and into the Treasury. Warren triumphantly noted a significant rise in commodity prices.

To apply this analysis to China, Lewis stressed the connection between the value of silver and commodity prices. He found that between 1890 and 1936, the purchasing power of silver in China was closely correlated with the purchasing power of silver in England and in the United States (Ministry of Industry, 1935, pp. 5, 8).[28] Thus "the general level of wholesale prices in China has apparently been determined, over a period of years, by the purchasing power of silver in the world" (Ministry of Industry, 1935, p. 9).

Following his mentors, Lewis argued that "the total supply of silver in the world should increase as fast as the production of basic commodities if the value of silver in terms of commodities is to remain stable" (Ministry of Industry, 1935, p. 101). Silver production had not maintained such growth, however. The Committee report predicted dire consequences if silver continued to rise in value and nothing were done to offset the attendant deflationary effects.[29]

Ultimately the Chinese government nationalized silver while disconnecting the Chinese currency from it and allowing its price to rise – replicating what had been done in regard to gold in the United States. We return to that topic shortly.

JAMES HARVEY ROGERS

The silver question became a focal point for much foreign expert opinion. The U.S. Treasury sent Yale Professor James Harvey Rogers of Yale to China for a monetary reconnaissance, arriving in April 1934.[30] He was one of the country's most brilliant young monetary economists.[31] He was accompanied by Dickson Leavens, who had spent many years at Yale-in-China, Changsha, and was gathering material for his forthcoming book on silver. Rogers was not there to advise the Chinese, but some of his conversations had an advisory aspect.[32] The U.S. Treasury Department had also appointed Nanking's Professor John Lossing Buck as a special investigator of monetary conditions in China. Buck met with Rogers in April 1934, and shared information he was collecting on the use of various kinds of money in the farming districts (some of which appeared in Ministry of Industry, 1935, pp. 68–87). Rogers noted that Buck "was sure of the connection between falling agricultural prices and the high price of silver, he was also equally clear that a further rise in the price of silver would aggravate the difficulties of the farmers" (Rogers' diary, April 14, 1934, Rogers Papers). Rogers also met with Arthur Young, Lockhart, and Lynch, who were all very involved with the issue.

Later that month Rogers went to Nanking and spent more time with Buck and with Ardron Lewis. Rogers was thoroughly familiar with the Warren–Pearson monetary analysis, having shared an office with George Warren in Washington when both were simultaneously appointed as advisers to President Roosevelt. Rogers reported that he discussed with Lewis

the lack of relationships between imports and exports and the price of silver. His response was that if I would compare instead the purchasing power of silver with

imports and exports a much closer relationship would be found ... . He was quite clear
that prices in [of?] foreign products in general would drop in case the price of silver were
raised artificially. (Rogers' diary, April 28, 1934, Rogers Papers)

Rogers was clearly skeptical about Lewis' view. On May 21, he had an
opportunity to discuss these matters further with Buck: "I think, that at the
end, he was inclined to accept my point of view as opposed to that of Lewis
or Warren."[33]

Rogers met Chiang Kai-shek on April 30. Chiang spoke strongly about
the harm that raising silver prices would do to Chinese agriculture. In May,
Rogers had a lengthy discussion with H.H. Kung, Minister of Finance,
which could well have constituted an "advisory" interchange:

J.H.R. explains to Kung the advantage to China in being on the silver standard, which
acts as a stabilizing influence. K. agrees to this statement.

R: "Rise in the price of silver will increase imports, at least temporarily. Prices of
agricultural products have been decreasing as silver has been increasing recently.
As most of the exports are agricultural products, higher silver will hurt exports."
(Rogers' diary, May 13, 1934, Rogers Papers)

They speculated (inconclusively) about the connection between silver
price and emigrant remittances and short-term capital movements.[34] Rogers
wondered if China was politically in a condition to borrow abroad.
"If China borrows abroad, higher silver will be advantageous." He
continued "President [Roosevelt] wishes to know actual effect of changes
in silver price upon China itself. A program for borrowing in the near future
is very important. Higher silver ... will aggravate agricultural distress. But
borrowing abroad is necessary in order to develop transportation, etc."
(Rogers' diary, May 13, 1934, Rogers Papers).

Rogers reported back to Washington, his telegrams calling attention
to agricultural distress, and warning that further rise in silver prices
would aggravate China's misery (Young, 1971, pp. 204–205). He traveled
extensively in Manchuria before leaving China in early July 1934. By then
FDR had given in to pressures from silver interests, and accepted the Silver
Purchase Act of June 1934, which committed the U.S. Treasury to buy silver
on a large scale, and its price began to rise.

In October 1934, the Chinese government imposed an export tax on silver
intended to capture any premium between its Chinese monetary value
and its (higher) international market price (Leavens, 1939, pp. 293–304).
However, continued large-scale smuggling of imported commodities
brought a steady deflationary outflow of silver. By 1935, it became evident
that trying to operate a silver-based domestic system at a different value

from the world price was not viable. In November 1935, China went off the silver standard. The Chinese government required that silver be sold to the government at the relatively unfavorable (prior) official price.[35] Banknote currency was declared to be legal tender. The international value of the Chinese currency was to be stabilized in relation to a combination of U.S. and British money. To obtain the needed reserves of foreign currency, the Chinese government was able to sell part of the nationalized silver to the U.S. Treasury. The new program, with its emphasis on "managed currency," was a far cry from the simple automatic monetary system envisioned in the Kemmerer report. However, the new system did bring China closer to a fixed exchange-rate system.

The silver crisis thus involved a confluence of a large number of western economic advisers. Lewis and Buck were based in Nanking and were linked primarily to the Ministry of Industry, whereas Young, Lockhart, and Lynch were based in Shanghai and were close to H.H. Kung and the Ministry of Finance. According to Arthur Young

> Britain then sent to China Sir Frederick W. Leith-Ross, Economic Adviser to the British Government. His coming galvanized China into action.
>
> For months before he arrived plans for comprehensive monetary reform had been ready. Lynch, Lockhart and I worked on these with close cooperation with Kung and Soong. These plans proved to be substantially what was finally put into effect. I welcomed Leith Ross' coming and had a high regard for his ability ... When he arrived in Nanking in September [1935], I met him at the railway station. I spent part of the day with him, giving him my analysis of the financial situation and explaining what I thought should be done. His ideas were similar and we found ourselves in accord. (Young, 1997, p. 81)

By implication, the confluence of British and American influence led to the November actions.

Once China dropped silver from its monetary base, it could benefit from the higher silver value by selling it to the U.S. Treasury on advantageous terms, using the funds to add to Chinese international reserves. Young was involved in negotiating this transaction. Lynch played an important part in arranging the relationships with overseas banks which were involved in creating a foreign-exchange reserve to back the Chinese currency.

After all the excitement surrounding silver, the next two years were years of prosperity and progress in China's economy. With the League eclipsed, emphasis shifted to the link with Germany as a way of financing programs for the NEC (Young, 1971, pp. 366–376). Much of Arthur Young's work centered on reorganizing China's national debt. With the more optimistic economic outlook came a firming of financial markets. Interest rates fell and government debt could be refunded at lower interest rates, helping to hold down government deficits.

WAR WITH JAPAN

The outbreak of war with Japan in 1937 greatly weakened the Chinese government's fiscal position. The Japanese soon gained control over China's major port cities, and disrupted or seized revenue sources. Arthur Young found himself involved in discussions which led to suspensions of principal and interest payments for Chinese public debts secured by customs revenue and revenue from the salt service. Government deficits widened and the money supply increased as the government borrowed from the banks. Inflation slowly accelerated, and the Chinese yuan declined on foreign-exchange markets. Foreign-exchange controls were imposed in 1938 over Young's objections (Young, 1963, p. 175).

During the period 1937–1941, the United States was officially neutral regarding Japan. Young devoted much of his energy in trying to elicit financial aid for the Chinese government in the United States. This began with loans from the Export-Import Bank (Young, 1963, p. 83). Young was in the United States from August to November 1939, and for about a year beginning in the middle of 1940. Part of his effort was to persuade the U.S. government to help support the international value of China's currency.

Oliver Lockhart remained with the Chinese salt service until illness obliged him to leave the country late in 1940. By then he and Young were struggling to oppose a government monopoly planned for salt and a number of other commodities (Young, 1965, pp. 34–35). Young also tried in vain to block the government's resolve to maintain the foreign-exchange value of China's currency higher than its market value or purchasing-power parity. After the U.S. entered the war (December, 1941), this rate provided a very unfavorable basis for acquiring yuan for dollars. The demand for dollars at the controlled rate greatly exceeded the supply, and people who could get the dollars at such rates could obtain large profits. This was a major element in wartime corruption and a source of bitterness by the Americans against the KMT.

LAUCHLIN CURRIE

Another major contributor to monetary economics became involved with China during the War. This was Lauchlin Currie, who had completed a doctorate at Harvard in 1931. Currie pioneered in the measurement of M1 (currency plus checking deposits) and its income velocity (Sandilands, 1990, pp. 31–53; Trescott, 1982, pp. 76–81). He also became a supporter of Keynes's emphasis on aggregate demand and on fiscal deficits as a way to stimulate aggregate demand. These views were not popular with his Harvard colleagues, and in 1934 he moved to the U.S. Treasury, and then to the Federal Reserve. After numerous research reports on fiscal policy, Currie became in July 1939, a personal economic adviser to President Roosevelt.

In January 1941, the Chinese government invited Currie to investigate China's problems relating to inflation and foreign exchange. "Thinking that his mission was to be concerned with purely technical economic issues, especially inflation, Currie took with him Emile Despres from the Federal Reserve. However, it became clear that his visit was being used for broader political purposes," (Sandilands, 1990) particularly as evidence of U.S. support for Chiang and the KMT. And the Chinese did their best to lobby Currie to help them obtain financial assistance from the United States.

The chief outcome of his visit in February 1941, was to persuade Chiang to take over collection of the land tax from the provincial governments. The tax would, Currie felt, rest mainly on wealthy landowners and was consistent with "the lines of social justice and equality laid down by Dr. Sun [Yat-sen]" (Sandilands, 1990, p. 111).[36] On his return, Currie persuaded President Roosevelt to include China as a beneficiary of the new Lend–Lease program. And Currie was appointed chief administrator of the Lend–Lease program for China.

Once the United States entered the war, there developed many interactions between the Chinese government and American economists. By this time, the war in China was a relatively stagnant holding operation, much to the dismay of General Joseph Stilwell and others who hoped for more. Currie went to China again in July 1942, for three weeks, this time primarily to try (without much success) to achieve better relationships among Chiang, Stilwell, and Ambassador Clarence Gauss. Many Americans were disgusted with the ineptness and corruption of the Chinese government. A focal point for bad feelings was gold. In 1942, the Chinese proposed, with Arthur Young's endorsement, that some U.S. funds be provided in the form of gold which could be sold for local currency in China as a method of slowing money growth and curtailing inflation. The U.S. Treasury agreed to this in December 1942. But after their initial support and early shipments in 1943, the Treasury slowed shipments to a virtual halt, contradicting their expressed commitments. Even 20 years later Arthur Young wrote about the incident with great bitterness. He singled out

Treasury official Harry Dexter White as the person chiefly responsible. White, who held a PhD in Economics from Harvard, was later accused of improper Communist involvement (Young, 1965, pp. 281–298).[37] Similar accusations were unfairly directed against Currie, creating employment difficulties for him after the war's end.

In the summer of 1944, Arthur Young was a member of the Chinese delegation at the Bretton Woods Conference which created the World Bank and International Monetary Fund.[38] His brother John Parke Young participated as part of the U.S. representation. Arthur Young played a major role in drafting China's request for assistance from the United Nations Relief and Rehabilitation Administration (UNRRA), which was created in 1943. In the spring of 1944 UNRRA sent economists Owen Dawson and Eugene Staley to China as consultants (Young, 1963, p. 368). A formal China program began in 1945 and was developed in connection with a Chinese counterpart agency CNRRA. Harry Price, veteran of the Kemmerer Commission and the Yenching University faculty, was a high administrator of UNRRA.

UNRRA and CNRRA provided support for a number of grass-roots programs to promote rural development. These included the Industrial Cooperatives program, the Joint Commission on Rural Reconstruction, and James Yen's Mass Education movement. UNRRA sponsored formation of the Agricultural Industry Service (AIS), dedicated to promoting "appropriate technology" for rural China. AIS was largely the creation of Harry Clement, an economist in the Washington UNRRA office.[39] In China, AIS utilized the services of Carl Hopkins, who had a PhD in Economics from Harvard. He designed and administered a number of socioeconomic surveys (Stepanek, 1992, pp. 168–169).

Economist Irving Barnett spent 18 months working for UNRRA in China, mostly in the program to rebuild the dikes on the Yellow River and rehabilitate the large area which had been flooded when the dikes were breached on Chiang Kai-shek's orders.[40] He wrote his dissertation on UNRRA in China. He felt the Yellow River project was relatively successful as a combination of relief and rehabilitation (Barnett, 1955, p. 313). However, much of the UNRRA program was ineffective. It was begun in haste and forced to close prematurely in face of the Communist take-over. There was relative success in restoring the railway system, but other ventures involving farm tractors and fishing vessels failed dismally. UNRRA gave supplies rather than cash, a practice which encountered major obstacles of transport and storage. Chinese handling of the supplies was sometimes corrupt or incompetent.

At the end of war in Europe in 1945, Arthur Young prepared a memo urging the Chinese government to give priority to financial rehabilitation, restraining government deficits and monetary growth (Young, 1965, pp. 378–383). But this advice went unheeded. The government commenced grandiose projects, both civil and military. The re-establishment of Chinese government control over the former Japanese-occupied areas was badly handled, especially in Taiwan. Frustrated and ill, Arthur Young resigned in February 1946. However, he returned in August 1947, to aid in managing foreign-exchange rates. He was instrumental in helping arrange a U.S. government loan to China in 1948. After that, he finally severed his China connection.

The KMT government of Chiang Kai-shek collapsed in 1949, losing a civil war to the Communists led by Mao Zedong. Many Chinese followed Chiang to Taiwan. Under the leadership of Chiang Kai-shek and, later, his son Chiang Ching-kuo, Taiwan achieved rapid economic growth and successful democratic government. An endowed professorship honoring Arthur Young was established at Soochow University in Taiwan.

SUMMARY AND OVERVIEW

Western economists provided China with valuable assistance in many areas. It is impressive that four on-site advisers had been or would be presidents of the American Economic Association.

Why did they come? An impressive number were motivated by Christian values and altruism. Concern for social welfare was a pervasive character-istic of the economics profession in the Progressive era. Professionalism as such is probably the best interpretation of the Kemmerer Commission and the League representatives. No doubt there was an element of opportunism as well. Kemmerer became a rich man from his advising. The members of his commission who remained in China may have done so in part because the job markets in the United States were weak in the 1930s.

There was wide diversity in the sponsorship of our advisers. Jeremiah W. Jenks and James Harvey Rogers were sent by the United States government to promote objectives of national monetary policy (and the Treasury engaged John Lossing Buck for the same goal). Frederic Lee was a consular official. Chinese initiative brought Henry Carter Adams, William Willoughby, E. Carlton Baker, Scott Nearing, Wassily Leontief, the Kemmerer commission and (initially) Lauchlin Currie. The creation of the League of Nations opened the way for extensive advisory activities, notably those of Sir Arthur Salter.[41] After World War II, this kind of sponsorship was taken up by UNRRA.

The period under study witnessed extensive study of economics in the West by Chinese – this is the focus of our earlier work (Trescott, 2007). Often western-educated Chinese were the chief contacts for the western advisers. We have mentioned Wang Ching-chun (PhD Yale), Sun Fo, T.V. Soong and Chen Kung-po (graduate economics study at Columbia), Leonard Hsu (undergraduate and graduate economics at Stanford), Ho Lien and H.D. Fong (both Yale PhDs).

The League of Nations helped create elements of an integrated economic development program, advancing public health, waterways, and programs for quality control and production increase for cotton and silk. Although economic development had not coalesced into a respected academic specialty, the western advisers provided highly sensible advice on many development-related topics. These extended from sound money through infrastructure, promoting foreign investment, improving education, and above all, improving domestic and international law and order. Failing the last-named, the other recommendations could not do much good.

On the specific issue of the monetary standard, the western advice appears in retrospect to have been misdirected. The consistent efforts to put China on the gold-exchange standard, from Jenks to Kemmerer, might have improved the inflow of foreign capital but would have exposed China to more severe deflation after 1929.

The Chinese government also generally overruled the recommendations of Arthur Young and his colleagues for sound financial management during the War. The artificial over-valuation of Chinese currency was a source of corruption and ill-will. Western advisers also cautioned against the extension of government authority into economic production which became so extreme during and after the War. But of course it is impossible to judge what would have happened had their counsel been better followed.

NOTES

1. Although the silver coins were sometimes termed "dollars," they were more commonly referred to as "yuan" (meaning round). "Yuan" remained the preferred term for the Chinese monetary unit (Jenks, 1904, p. 196).

2. Several of these are described in Kemmerer (1916). Kemmerer, who was Jenks's student at Cornell, was directly involved in creating the Philippine program and went to other countries as an observer.

3. Jenks was influenced by the Social Gospel: "Under the direction of the noted economist Johannes Conrad at the University of Halle, he imbibed historical

economics from its source" (Wunderlin, 1992, p. 16). He taught at Cornell 1891–1912, then moved to New York Univesity. He was chosen President of the American Economic Association in 1906. His work is reviewed by Wunderlin (1992, pp. 15–22, 170–171).

4. The text of the pamphlet was reproduced in Jenks (1904, pp. 75–175).

5. China's fiscal situation, then and for many years afterward, was extremely shaky. There was a well-justified fear that a monetary reserve could easily be stolen or diverted to fiscal uses (see Jenks, 1904, pp. 92–93).

6. Jenks quoted opinions of some observers that stabilizing the rates of exchange among different forms of money would eliminate opportunities for "squeeze" profits for some officials (Jenks, 1904, pp. 63–64). Jenks noted that Chinese "business men have little confidence in the good faith of the Government, or in the ability of the Government officials" (Jenks, 1904, p. 66). The Jenks report is a near-treatise on Chinese monetary practices.

7. Jenks (1905) paid tribute to the "marked intelligence, the untiring vigilance, the mental acuteness" of Chinese people, and cited the reforming efforts being made by the Imperial government. He was particularly impressed by communications media – the telegraph and postal system – and the prospective development of railroads. This essay is one of the first to sense the prospective importance of the bicycle. The *Readers Guide to Periodical Literature* noted four China items by Jenks in 1905–1906, one in 1911, and six in 1915–18.

8. "Many Chinese considered railways disruptive to the harmony of nature and of man; they sliced across the land, disturbing its normal rhythms and displacing its benevolent forces; they put road and canal workers out of jobs and altered established market patterns" (Spence, 1990, pp. 249–250).

9. Adams decided that, despite the multiplicity of national accounting systems, "the arrogance and embarrassment suffered by the various accounting offices are so great owing to the everchanging and inconsistent orders coming down from the various departments of the general government, that all are willing to compromise if only a stable and authoritative procedure can be built up" (H.C. Adams to Dr. Reeve, Jan. 2, 1914, H.C. Adams Papers, Box 13).

10. Adams also reported that "the chairman of the Commission for which I am adviser paid $18,000 for a new mistress, two weeks ago, and levied on the Station agents of the government railway, to foot the bill" (H.C. Adams to Dr. Reeve, January 2, 1914, H.C. Adams papers, Box 13).

11. A League of Nations study (1934, p. 45) indicated there were only 7,000 miles of track, of which 2,000 were unimportant branch lines.

12. Nearing's autobiography incorrectly identified Chen as a former student at Penn (Nearing, 1972, p. 141). Chen's biography is in Boorman (1967–1971, Vol. 1).

13. It is not fanciful to believe Nearing could have given useful advice. He was very knowledgeable (if moralistic) about labor relations. The Chinese railways did in fact develop a substantial social-welfare orientation toward their employees (see Lou, 1937).

14. "On the evening of his lecture, Nearing was picked up and taken to the university where he was led unto an unlit room and told that his audience was waiting in the dark. They would hear Nearing's ideas but could not jeopardize themselves by revealing their identities. In total darkness, Nearing delivered his talk,

hearing only his voice and breathing in the crowd. When he finished he was let out of the building and taken back to his room" (Saltmarsh, 1991, p. 223).

15. On this point the interests of Arthur Young (who had written his dissertation on Henry George's single-tax proposal) joined those of Sun Yat-sen, who had been influenced by Henry George (see Young, 1917a, 1917b; Sun, 1928, pp. 36, 40–41, 44, 49, 56–57, 75, 81).

16. His diary (in the E.W. Kemmerer Papers) for December 7, 1929, recorded: "These people have no capacity for enduring group action and cannot cooperate for any length of time. Individual and family selfishness too strong and bitter and no national patriotism or sense of obligation above family obligation."

17. Ultimately China borrowed approximately $17 million, paying 8.6 percent. It was used for such development activities as "water conservation, public health, education, and rehabilitation of areas recovered from the Communists. About a fourth went to build highways" (Young, 1997, p. 60).

18. Of Frere: "later to be a financier and banker of world-wide fame," "an economist of high quality." Frere, who subsequently became president of the Bank of Belgium, was head of the Intelligence Service of the League division which Salter headed (Salter, 1961, pp. 109, 161, 208, 215).

19. One outcome was a 1931 League mission on education in China which included the prominent economic historian Richard Tawney from the London School of Economics (Trescott, 2007, p. 196).

20. "It is planned to build a merchant fleet of 8,000,000 tons, the industrial power plants of 20,000,000 horse power; to produce 120,000,000 tons of iron and steel, 2,200,000,000 tons of coal; to reclaim 300,000,000 acres of arable land; and to install 36,000,000 new spindles" (Hoe, 1933, p. 18). To put these in perspective, the iron and steel figure was approximately achieved in 1984 (though I am adding pig iron and steel; this may involve double counting). The 1985 output of coal was 872 million tons (aproximately 40 percent of the 1931 target), and there were a total of 23 million spindles in cotton production in 1985 (*Encyclopedia of New China*, 1987, pp. 311, 324, 341).

21. The Land Act of June 1930 contained similar provisions. "[W]here a tenant had cultivated his land for ten years, and the landlord was an absentee, the tenant would apparently without any form of payment become an owner. Moreover, the provincial authorities are given power ... to impose a limit on the amount of land to be owned by any one person, and to expropriate, with or without compensation, all owners whose possessions are in excess of this limit" (League of Nations, 1934, p. 20). These programs were never carried out.

22. There was strong Japanese opposition to Rajchman and, apparently, to the League involvement generally. Rajchman had strongly assisted T.V. Soong in urging the League to act against Japan's seizure of Manchuria in 1931 (Young, 1971, pp. 342–345).

23. Monnet had been involved in the investment banking business in Europe beginning in 1926, and helped negotiate loans to Poland, Rumania, Yugoslavia, and Bulgaria (Duchene, 1994, pp. 45–46).

24. Its various railway projects are reviewed in Chang Kia-ngau (1975). Fong (1942, pp. 80–82) suggested the Corporation as a model for a much broader China Reconstruction Finance Corporation to play a central role in post-war investment.

25. Buck was an agricultural economist and agronomist with a PhD from Cornell, where he had studied under George Warren. He was also the first husband of noted novelist Pearl Buck, who divorced him in 1933 (Trescott, 2007, especially Chapter 9). In 1934, Buck was appointed as a special agent of the U.S. Treasury, with a vague general assignment to gather information about monetary conditions and the status of silver in China. His assignment (which included office space in Washington) had some similarities with those of George Warren and James Harvey Rogers.

26. A referee suggested that Warren and Pearson were simply using a modification of the quantity theory of money. Their thinking is expressed across pages 64–126 in their *Prices* (1933), often in a very diffuse manner. Three salient points may be noted:

a. On p. 70, they say that the price of wheat may be expressed as:

$$\frac{\text{Supply of gold and demand for wheat}}{\text{Demand for gold and supply of wheat}}$$

b. The conventional equation of exchange, $MV = PT$, is mentioned, but Warren and Pearson deny their approach corresponds to those terms (1933, p. 81, n. 2).

c. They reproduce a lengthy list of price forecasts from 1918 through 1930, mainly by Warren, "based on the supply of and demand for gold" (1933, pp. 117ff).

27. There was even talk of Warren going to China as an adviser, but Morganthau vetoed the idea. I am grateful to Professor William Hogland, biographer of Warren, for this information (personal communication, March 5, 1991).

28. This did not hold during World War I when Britain imposed on embargo on silver exports. Lewis (Ministry of Industry, 1935, pp. 87–91) found a similar correspondence using the value of gold in and outside China.

29. In 1933, Lewis and Chang had recommended a form of Irving Fisher's "compensated dollar," but this proposal did not appear in the report (Fong, 1934, p. 517).

30. Treasury Secretary Morganthau was quoted as indicating there were "two schools of thought on silver. One is that an increased [dollar] price for silver will mean greater exports from the United States for China. The other is that if the price of silver is increased, China will have to curtail her imports. Professor Rogers will find out which school is right" (Leavens, 1939, p. 261).

31. Rogers was in many ways a monetarist long before that term was used. He originated the term "monetary base" for the special configuration of Federal Reserve and Treasury accounts, and was one of the first to stress its causal impact on the money holdings of the public (Trescott, 1982).

32. Treasury Secretary Morganthau told Rogers that the administration opposed further increase in silver prices. The implication is that they hoped Rogers's report would buttress this position (Young, 1971, pp. 203–204).

33. Rogers was more concerned that U.S. policy would lead (as it did) to an outflow of silver from the Chinese monetary system, causing a decrease in the money supply and deflation within China. Lewis was probably looking more at the likelihood that the rise in the value of the Chinese monetary unit would make imports cheaper and exports more expensive. Whether that would worsen China's

balance of trade would depend on the familiar comparison of price elasticities of supply and demand.

34. There is a close parallel between this conversation and an undated formal memo by Rogers, "The relation between the price of silver and China's balance of international payments" (Rogers Papers, Box 50, Folder 719).

35. Before this time the Chinese government as such did not hold silver reserves. The Chinese banks held silver reserves to maintain their banknotes and deposits at parity with silver. Rawski (1993) argues that the deflationary influence of U.S. silver policy on China was not great. Brandt and Sargent (1989) present evidence that the disestablishment of silver was undertaken to enable government and its cronies to profit from the difference between the compulsory purchase price and the world market value. Recent studies of these episodes include Lai and Gau (2003) and Burdekin (2005).

36. Sandilands (1990, p. 111) goes on to report that Currie "believes that Chiang was not in the slightest bit interested in his views on economic matters."

37. White was certainly guilty of some bad economics. In October 1944, he blamed the Chinese inflation primarily on "shortage of goods." He stated that "it was cheaper for the [Chinese] government to print fapi [the current paper money] than to absorb fapi in exchange for gold ... " (quoted in Young, 1965, p. 289). The purpose of gold sales was to withdraw fapi from circulation. Both gold and paper currency had to be flown in from outside. In 1944, the purchasing power of a ton of gold was 28 times as large as that of a ton of the most common denomination of paper money (Young, 1965, p. 291, 1963, pp. 371–375).

Besides White, other Treasury officials involved with China were accused of Communist involvement, notably Frank Coe and Solomon Adler. Both left the United States in the 1950s and went to work for a Chinese Communist government intelligence unit (Yu, 1997, p. 281; Boughton, 2001, pp. 227–228; Rittenberg & Bennett, 1993). However, Arthur Young stated that "In years of working with Sol [Adler] I never had occasion to suspect his loyalty" (Young, 1997, p. 224).

Young also gave a clean bill to health to Chi Chao-ting, who became Secretary General of China's Stabilization Board in 1942 (Young, 1963, pp. 187–188). Chi's Communist affiliation became known after 1949. During the postwar hunt for Communists, an anonymous informant alleged that "Chi Ch'ao-ting, with Sol Adler's knowledge and acquiescence, may have deliberately promoted the collapse of the Nationalist regime's currency through a variety of ill-advised monetary policies" (Klehr & Radosch, 1996, p. 159).

38. As early as July 1943, Young prepared a memo analyzing the international monetary plans associated with Keynes and White. He noted that "neither plan adequately recognizes the need for monetary rehabilitation as preliminary to longer-term stabilization." The pressure on individual countries to establish exchange rates seemed premature for countries like China. Young also noted that the plans could only succeed if members avoided wide disparities in inflation rates (Young, 1965, pp. 375–377).

39. Joseph Stepanek, who headed the AIS program in Hunan Province, said of Clement, "My admiration for him grew as I recognized that the roots of the AIS lay in his motivation to help the poor, first at a Quaker work camp in West Virginia, in the early Farm Security Administration, and then as the founder of a

program in Central America ... to assist the manufacture of consumer goods no longer available from the United States because of World War II" (Stepanek, 1992, p. 69).

40. Roger Evans of the Rockefeller Foundation visited China in 1947. He wrote: "The dyke was finally closed and the Yellow River returned to its old course on March 15, 1947, but there remains the vast problem of 'bringing back' the inundated and ravaged areas ... into which people are pouring back at the rate of over 2,000 a day" (Evans, "Travel Diary," April 23, 1947, Rockefeller Foundation Archives, Record Group 1.1, series 601, Box 51, Folder 430).

41. However, according to Selskar Gunn, most of the League-sponsored advisers were paid by the Chinese government (Gunn to Max Mason, November 18, 1933; Rockefeller Foundation Archives, Record Group 1, Series 601, Box 10, Folder 101).

ACKNOWLEDGMENT

Special thanks go to Cheng-chung Lai, Lyric Hughes Hale, Ardron Lewis, A.W. Bob Coats, Arthur Young's children Elizabeth Roulac and Allen Young, and three now-deceased members of the Kemmerer Commission: Harry Price, Donald Kemmerer, and Whitson Fetter.

REFERENCES

Adams, H. C. (1928). *Manual of railway accounting*. Peking: Ministry of Communications.

Barnett, I. (1955). *UNRRA in China: A case study in financial assistance for economic development*. Ph.D. dissertation, Columbia University, Columbia.

Bateman, B. W. (1998). Clearing the ground: The demise of the Social Gospel movement and the rise of neoclassicism in American economics. In: M. S. Morgan & M. Rutherford (Eds), *From interwar pluralism to postwar neoclassicism* (pp. 29–52). Durham, NC: Duke University Press.

Boorman, H. L. (1967–71). *Biographical dictionary of republican China*. New York: Columbia University Press.

Boughton, J. M. (2001). The case against Harry Dexter White: Still not proven. *History of Political Economy, 33*(2), 219–239.

Brandt, L., & Sargent, T. (1989). Interpreting new evidence about China and U.S. silver purchases. *Journal of Monetary Economics, 23*(1), 31–51.

Burdekin, R. C. K. (2005). US pressure on China's currency: Milton Friedman and the silver episode revisited. Unpublished manuscript.

Cameron, M. (1931). *The reform movement in China 1898–1912*. Palo Alto, CA: Stanford University Press.

Chang, K.-N. (1975). *China's struggle for railroad development*. New York: DaCapo.

Chih, Y.-J. (1981). Goodnow's mission to China, 1913–1915. *Tsing Hua Journal of Chinese Studies, 13*(1 and 2), 197–219.

Chiu, A. K. (1933). *Recent statistical surveys of Chinese rural economy 1912–1932*. Ph.D. dissertation, Harvard University, Harvard.

Church, R. L. (1974). Economists as experts: The rise of an academic profession in the United States, 1870–1920. In: L. Stone (Ed.), *The university in society* (Vol. 2, pp. 571–609). Princeton, NJ: Princeton University Press.

Coats, A. W. (1968). Henry Carter Adams: A case study in the emergence of the social sciences in the United States, 1850–1900. *Journal of American Studies, 1*(1), 1–21.

Coats, A. W. (1992). Henry Carter Adams (1851–1921): Religion and the making of an American economist. Unpublished manuscript.

Curti, M., & Birr, K. (1954). *Prelude to point four: American technical missions overseas 1838–1938*. Madison: University of Wisconsin.

Drake, P. W. (1989). *The money doctor in the Andes: The Kemmerer missions 1923–1933*. Durham, NC: Duke University Press.

Duchene, F. (1994). *Jean Monnet: The first statesman of interdependence*. New York: W.W. Norton.

Edkins, J. (1901). *Chinese currency*. Shanghai: Presbyterian Mission Press.

Edkins, J. (1903). *The revenue and taxation of the Chinese empire*. Shanghai: Presbyterian Mission Press.

Edkins, J. (1905). *Banking and prices in China*. Shanghai: Presbyterian Mission Press.

Encyclopedia of New China. (1987). Beijing: Foreign Languages Press.

Field, F. V. (1931). *American participation in the China consortium*. Chicago, IL: University of Chicago Press.

Fong, H. D. (1934). Bibliography on silver and China. *Monthly Bulletin on Economic China, 7*(12), 513–524.

Fong, H. D. (1942). *The post-war industrialization of China*. Washington, DC: National Planning Association.

Ganschow, T. (1976). Review of Fairbank, J.K. et al., The I. G. in Peking: Letters of Robert Hart; Chinese Maritime Customs, 1868–1907. *Journal of Economic History, 36*(4), 956–958.

Hardy, C. O. (1935). *The Warren-Pearson price theory*. Washington, DC: Brookings Institution.

Hoe, Y. C. (1933). The programme of technical cooperation between China and the League of Nations. Paper presented at the Institute of Pacific Relations Conference, Banff, AB, Canada.

Hollander, J. (1922). Memorial to former president Henry C. Adams. *American Economic Review, 12*(3), 401–416.

Jenks, J. W. (1904). *Gold standard in international trade: Report on the introduction of the gold exchange standard*. Washington, DC: Government Printing Office.

Jenks, J. W. (1905). The progress China is making. *American Monthly Review of Reviews, 31*(5), 595–598.

Jenks, J. W. (1916a). China's vital question. *Journal of the American Asiatic Association, 15*(12), 358–362.

Jenks, J. W. (1916b). China, America's silent partner. *World's Work, 33*(2), 165–171.

Kann, E. (1926). *The currencies of China*. Shanghai: Kelley and Walsh.

[Kemmerer] Commission of Financial Experts. (1929). Report on revenue policy. December 10, in *Taxation, Tariff and Railway Finance*, Vol. 4. Box 76, E.W. Kemmerer papers.

Kemmerer, D. L. (1993). *The life and times of Professor Edwin Walter Kemmerer, 1875–1945.* Champaign, IL. The Author.

Kemmerer, E. W. (1916). *Modern currency reforms.* New York: Macmillan.

Klehr, H., & Radosch, R. (1996). *The Amerasia spy case.* Chapel Hill: University of North Carolina Press.

Lai, C.-C., & Gau, T. J.-S. (2003). The Chinese silver standard economy and the 1929 Great Depression. *Australian Economic History Review, 43*(2), 155–168.

League of Nations. (1934). Report of its technical delegate on his mission to China. Council Committee of Technical Collaboration with China, April 1, Geneva.

League of Nations. (1935). Report by the director of the section for communications and transit on his mission to China. Council Committee of Technical Collaboration with China, Geneva.

Leavens, D. H. (1939). *Silver money.* Bloomington IN: Principia Press.

Lee, F. E. (1926). *Currency, banking and finance in China.* Washington, DC: Government Printing Office.

Leontief, W. (1928). Die Wirtschaft als Kreislauf. *Archiv für Sozialwissenschaft und Sozialpolitik, 60,* 577–623.

Lou Y.-W. [Lu, Y.-w.] (1937). *Les Oeuvres Sociales dans les Chemins de Fer Chinois [Social Work of Chinese Railways].* Paris: P. Bossuet.

MacCormick, G. (1977). *Chang Tso-lin in Northeast China 1911–1928.* Palo Alto, CA: Stanford University Press.

Ministry of Industry. (1935). *Silver and prices in China.* Shanghai: Committee for the Study of Silver Values and Commodity Prices, Commercial Press.

Nearing, S. (1927). *Whither China: An economic interpretation of recent events in the Far East.* New York: International Publishers.

Nearing, S. (1972). *The making of a radical: A political autobiography.* New York: Harper and Row.

Rawski, T. G. (1993). Milton Friedman, silver, and China. *Journal of Political Economy, 101*(4), 755–758.

Reynolds, D. R. (1975). The Chinese industrial cooperative movement and the political polarization of wartime China, 1938–1945. Ph.D. dissertation, Columbia University, Columbia.

Rittenberg, S., & Bennett, A. (1993). *The man who stayed behind.* New York: Simon and Schuster.

Salter, A. (1934a). *China and the depression: Impressions of a three-month visit.* Nanking: National Economic Council.

Salter, A. (1934b). *China and silver.* New York: Economic Forum.

Salter, A. (1947). *Personality in politics.* London: Faber and Faber.

Salter, A. (1961). *Memoirs of a public servant.* London: Faber and Faber.

Salter, A. (1967). *Slave of the lamp.* London: Cox and Wyman.

Salter, A., Keynes, J. M., Stamp, J., Blackett, B., Clay, H., & Beveridge, W. (1932). *The world's economic crisis and the way of escape.* New York: Century.

Saltmarsh, J. A. (1991). *Scott Nearing: An intellectual biography.* Philadelphia, PA: Temple University Press.

Sandilands, R. J. (1990). *The life and political economy of Lauchlin Currie*. Durham, NC: Duke University Press.
Silk, L. (1976). *The economists*. New York: Basic Books.
Spence, J. (1990). *The search for modern China*. New York: W.W. Norton.
Stepanek, J. E. (1992). *A town called Shaoyang: Introducing industry appropriate to China*. Boulder, CO: Gold Hill Publications.
Sun, Y.-S. (1928). *The international development of China*. London: Hutchinson.
Trescott, P. B. (1982). Discovery of the money-income relationship in the United States, 1921–1944. *History of Political Economy, 14*(1), 65–88.
Trescott, P. B. (1995). The money doctor in China: Edwin Kemmerer's commission of financial experts, 1929. *Research in History of Economic Thought and Methodology, 13*, 125–158.
Trescott, P. B. (2007). *Jingji Xue: The history of the introduction of Western Economic ideas into China, 1850–1950*. Hong Kong: Chinese University Press.
Warren, G. F., & Pearson, F. A. (1933). *Prices*. New York: Wiley.
Warren, G. F., & Pearson, F. A. (1935). *Gold and prices*. New York: Wiley.
Wei, W.-P. (1914). *The currency problem in China*. New York: Columbia University Press.
Whitfield, S. J. (1974). *Scott nearing: Apostle of American radicalism*. New York: Columbia University Press.
Willoughby, W. F. (1898). The French Workmen's compensation act. *Quarterly Journal of Economics, 12*(4), 398–418.
Willoughby, W. F. (1899). The study of practical labor problems in France. *Quarterly Journal of Economics, 13*(3), 270–291.
Willoughby, W. F. (1901a). Labor legislation in France under the Third Republic. *Quarterly Journal of Economics, 15*(3 and 4), 390–415, 551–577.
Willoughby, W. F. (1901b). The integration of industry in the United States. *Quarterly Journal of Economics, 16*(1), 94–115.
Willoughby, W. F. (1905). Employers' associations for deal with labor in the United States. *Quarterly Journal of Economics, 20*(1), 110–150.
Wright, S. F. (1938). *China's struggle for tariff autonomy*. Shanghai: Kelly and Walsh.
Wunderlin, C. E., Jr. (1992). *Visions of a new industrial order: Social science and labor theory in America's progressive era*. New York: Columbia University Press.
Yih, M.-H. (1985). Some notes on the influx of western economics into China by the end of 19th century and at the beginning of 20th century. Unpublished manuscrupt.
Young, A. N. (1917a). The single tax. *Bulletin of the University Extension Division, University of California, 3*(17).
Young, A. N. (1917b). The possibilities and limitations of special taxation of land. *National Conference of Social Work Report*, (101).
Young, A. N. (1963). *China and the helping hand 1937–1945*. Cambridge, MA: Harvard University Press.
Young, A. N. (1965). *China's wartime finance and inflation, 1937–1945*. Cambridge, MA: Harvard University Press.
Young, A. N. (1971). *China's nation-building effort, 1927–1937*. Stanford, CA: Hoover Institution.
Young, A. N. (1997). *Cycle of Cathay*. Vista, CA: Ibis.
Yu, M.-C. (1997). *OSS in China: Prelude to Cold War*. New Haven, CT: Yale University Press.

PRIVATE PAPERS

E.W. Kemmerer Papers, Public Policy Papers, Department of Rare Books and Special Collections, Princeton University Library, Princeton, NJ, USA.

H.C. Adams Papers, University of Michigan Archives, Bentley Historical Library, Ann Arbor, MI, USA.

J.H. Rogers Papers, Manuscripts and Archives, Sterling Memorial Library, Yale University, New Haven, CT, USA.

Rockefeller Foundation Archives, Rockefeller Archive Center, Sleepy Hollow, NY, USA.

MONSIGNOR JOHN RYAN ON THE ETHICS AND ECONOMICS OF MINIMUM WAGE LEGISLATION

Robert E. Prasch

A BRIEF OVERVIEW OF PROGRESSIVE ERA MINIMUM WAGE LEGISLATION IN THE UNITED STATES

In the US minimum wages were initially enacted by individual states, beginning with the Commonwealth of Massachusetts in 1912. These laws were modeled on legislation enacted over the previous two decades in Australia, New Zealand, and England (Fisher, 1926, chap. 8; Hammond, 1915, 1913; Hobson, 1915; Hart, 1994, chaps. 2 & 3; Morris, 1986). From 1912 to 1923, the legislatures of 16 states, Puerto Rico, and the District of Columbia passed minimum wage legislation, although not all of them were operational by the end of this period (Brandeis, 1935, p. 501; Clark, 1921; Millis & Montgomery, 1938, chap. 6; Morris, 1930, chap. 1).

Although some state legislatures such as Arkansas and Utah set their minimum wage at a fixed rate, most states empowered a commission such as California's Industrial Welfare Commission to manage its minimum wage policy. This commission would appoint "Wage Boards" for each industry

A Research Annual
Research in the History of Economic Thought and Methodology, Volume 28-A, 39–70
Copyright © 2010 by Emerald Group Publishing Limited
All rights of reproduction in any form reserved
ISSN: 0743-4154/doi:10.1108/S0743-4154(2010)000028A005

made up of representatives of industry, labor, and the public. These boards were authorized to conduct investigations of wages, hours, cost of living and, depending on the conditions they uncovered, to calculate and set a minimum wage appropriate to the specific conditions of a given industry. It followed that under this wage board system different industries operating in the same state could be required to adhere to different minimum wage rates (Douglas, 1919; Hutchinson, 1919, chap. 4; Kelley, 1911; Ryan, 1923b, 1910a). Wage boards were favored by reformers, and virtually all economists, because they were more flexible, could be modified to fit different locations and industries, and took more detailed information into account in the setting of minimum wage rates (Clark, 1921, 1913; Ryan, 1910a, 1913, p. 586, 1915, p. 636, 1923b).

These initial American experiments in minimum wage legislation differed from some, but by no means all, other nations in one important respect: in deference to the "Liberty of Contract" doctrine then hegemonic in the American judiciary, Progressive-era reformers felt obliged to restrict coverage of minimum wage legislation to women and children (Brandeis, 1935; Broda, 1928; Skocpol, 1992, chap. 6). Most of the leaders in labor market reform, such as Florence Kelley of the National Consumers' League, believed that minimum wage legislation should, and eventually would, be extended to include men. However, they nevertheless defended minimum wage statutes that exclusively covered women and children as both a necessary reform and the initial step of a broader strategy to reform what they perceived to be an inherently unequal wage bargain (Kelley, 1912; Ryan, 1927, chap. 6, 1913, pp. 582–583, 1906, chaps. 4–6; See also Storrs, 2000, chap. 2; Skocpol, 1992, chap. 6; Zimmerman, 1991). This pragmatic strategy, despite its deference to the political and judicial realities of the day, ultimately failed when the United States Supreme Court overturned a District of Columbia minimum wage statute in 1923 [*Adkins v. Children's Hospital* 261 U.S. 525 (1923)].

In the wake of the Court's five-to-three *Adkins* decision, no state's minimum wage statute was able to withstand a challenge in the US Supreme Court until Washington State prevailed in *West Coast Hotel Co. v. Parrish* [57 U.S. 578 (1937)].[1] As with the overturned statutes of 20 years earlier, Washington's minimum wage law was limited to women and minors. However, the grounds for the Supreme Court's reversal in *West Coast Hotel* clearly paved the way for the Fair Labor Standards Act, which enacted a minimum wage for women and men in 1938 (Nordlund, 1997, chaps. 1–3; Perkins, 1946, chap. 21; Paulsen, 1996, chaps. 4–7). Since 1938, political debate has largely focused on the level and breadth of minimum wage legislation, rather than its legitimacy.

THE ORIGINS OF MONSIGNOR JOHN A. RYAN'S IDEAS ON SOCIAL REFORM AND MINIMUM WAGE LEGISLATION

Monsignor John Augustine Ryan (1869–1945) was one of America's earliest and more important proponents of minimum wage legislation. As a prominent intellectual and moral figure, he emerged as an influential reformer whose career spanned both the Progressive and the New Deal Eras. Through his writings in a wide variety of outlets, including several books, the popular Catholic and secular press, his service with the National Conference of Catholic Charities, the National Consumers' League, and his testimony before, and service on, several state minimum wage hearings and committees such as those in Minnesota, Wisconsin, New York, Ohio, and Pennsylvania, John Ryan played an instrumental role in the early theorizing and enacting of this once-controversial policy (Broderick, 1963, pp. 39–45, 80–86; Curran, 1982, chap. 2; Gearty, 1953, pp. 31–58).[2]

As both a student and a faculty member at both St. Paul's Seminary (MN – now the University of St. Thomas) and the Catholic University of America, Ryan "wanted to examine economic life in the light of Christian principles, with a view to making them operative in the realm of industry." To Ryan, "the salvation of millions of souls depended largely upon the economic opportunity to live decently, to live as human beings made in the imagine and likeness of God" (Ryan, 1941, p. 59).

Ryan dated his early commitment to these ideas to Pope Leo XIII's Encyclical Letter, *Rerum Novarum* ("On the Condition of Labor"). Indeed, this text was central to his thinking, and he referred to it as "the greatest pronouncement made by any of the Popes on the social question" (Ryan, 1920b, p. 57, n.1). In his autobiography, Ryan presented a more detailed description of the origins of his ideas. There he describes growing up in a household where the ideas and issues of the day were read and discussed. According to Ryan, many of the ideas and positions that he held and promoted in later life could be traced to his childhood in rural Minnesota. This is significant since, by almost any measure, late-nineteenth-century Minnesota was brimming with political and social unrest, charismatic political leaders, and many new and unconventional ideas. Across the upper midwest populism, anti-monopoly agitation, public ownership of utilities, and the economic theories of Henry George were being presented and debated as alternatives to the status quo (Dorfman, 1934, chap. 2).

Ryan spends several pages of his autobiography discussing the populist firebrand, novelist, and politician Ignatius Donnelly (Ryan, 1941, pp. 12–18). Donnelly, who moved to Minnesota from Philadelphia, emerged from the abolition movement deeply committed to economic and social justice issues. He left the Republican Party to join the Farmer's Alliance (Populists) and served as a Minnesota State Assemblyman, Lieutenant Governor, Congressman, and State Senator. Donnelly was widely known, and either admired or reviled, as a passionate and articulate populist orator and major force in reconfiguring the ideas, passions, and ballots of Minnesotans – especially those from the more rural areas (Anderson, 1980; Broderick, 1963, chap. 1; Ryan, 1941, chaps. 1–2). In his autobiography, Ryan reports that he was in the habit of attending state assembly debates during his youth and met Donnelly on several occasions. The lasting importance of the Populists and Donnelly to Ryan is underscored by his own reflection, made late in his life, that "If election day of 1892 were somehow to return tomorrow and I were to go into the polling booth with the added knowledge and experience that I now possess, I should again and with greater confidence vote the Populist ticket" (Ryan, 1941, p. 18; General James B. Weaver was the candidate of the People's Party that year).

In the midst of this upheaval, the Social Gospel movement emerged as a sympathetic and important, if not always welcome, response from a number of prominent Protestant clergy and lay intellectuals. The Social Gospel argued for the rejuvenation and reconstitution of American religious life in concert with the reform of society. Richard Ely, John Commons, Henry Carter Adams, Samuel Lindsay, and John Bates Clark were, along with many others, each initially drawn to economic analysis to advance the social goals suggested to them by their Christian faith (Danbom, 1987, chaps. 2–3; Everett, 1946; Fine, 1964, chap. 6; Gonce, 1996). The core idea of this movement was the proposition that the successful salvation of individuals would be facilitated by a mitigation of the oppressive economic and social conditions that precluded so many people from having an opportunity to consider the revealed truths of religion. Josiah Strong, an early leader in this movement, "repeatedly urged the churches to recognize that they could not save people's souls without at the same time changing their environment." The implications of this thinking were profound, "In Strong's opinion, both the individual and society had to be transformed at the same time" (Muller, 1959, p. 196; for a fuller exposition of this argument by one of its most prominent thinkers, see Rauschenbusch, 1908). The power of these ideas for the emerging younger generation of economists is suggested by the following quotation from one of John Commons' early books:

> The primary and fundamental right is the right to life. If the state guarantees this in its fulness (sic), the state must furnish the individual, not only with protection against the unlawful violence of his fellow-men, but also with a share of the social product equal to his minimum of subsistence. (Commons, 1893, p. 66)

In parallel, although separate and distinct development, several prominent leaders within the American Catholic Church such as Archbishop John Ireland of St. Paul, Cardinal James Gibbons of Baltimore, Bishop John Keane of Richmond, and Bishop John Lancaster Spalding of Peoria were rethinking the relationship of practicing Catholics to the idea of being American, along with the need to more fully engage the civic life of the nation. These Church leaders advanced a new, and somewhat controversial, position that "saw no basic incompatibility between being Catholic and being American, urging strong Catholic participation in American life and espousing cooperation with non-Catholics in areas of political, social, and economic life" (Curran, 1982, p. 5). Fundamental issues were at stake in this rethinking of Catholic life, including the relationship of Catholics to those non-Catholic groups and organizations espousing what were, for the day, radical social reforms. These included the union movement led by the Knights of Labor and the single-tax agitation associated with the name of Henry George (Curran, 1982, chap. 1; Ryan, 1941, chap. 2).

Of course, these discussions represented only one aspect of several changes then taking place within the larger Catholic Church. Many scholars, within and without the Catholic Church, credit Bishop Wilhelm Emmanuel von Ketteler (1811–1877) as the founder and initial proponent of the ideas and propositions now known as Catholic Social Thought (Murphy, 1991; O'Brien, 1968, p. 11; Ryan & Husslein, 1920, chap. 3). Consider Monsignor William Murphy's summary of Ketteler's contribution to Catholic thinking on economic issues:

> he went beyond the phenomenon of sin to confront the philosophies and ideologies that controlled the economy: they were unable, he said, to respond to the fundamental needs and rights of the workers. Ketteler offered a set of doctrinal principles by which to judge these prevailing ideas and to present a fuller understanding of man and society. That set of principles became the basis of the Christian social movement, (Murphy, 1991, p. 10)

The importance of Ketteler's ideas is best conveyed by the leader of the Church and the author of *Rerum Novarum*. His Holiness Pope Leo XIII described Bishop von Ketteler as "my great predecessor, the man from

whom I learned" (cited in Murphy, 1991, p. 9). According to the historian
David O'Brien:

> Catholic social thought combines a powerful emphasis on natural rights with a view of
> society as an imperative of nature itself, indispensable for the full development of man's
> personality and the attainment of his salvation. The individual, endowed with rights
> independently of society, is simultaneously bound to pursue the good of society, which
> he depends on for the provision of those conditions necessary for his own self-
> development. (O'Brien, 1968, p. 7)

Another important influence on Ryan came from several of his teachers at
the Catholic University of America. Ryan and his biographer specifically
mention Fathers William J. Kerby and Thomas J. Bouquillon, each of
whom was rearticulating Catholic theology in light of the new realities of the
industrial era and the widespread demand for social reform (Broderick,
1963, chap. 2; Ryan, 1941, chap. 4). Bouquillon's influence is mentioned in
the preface to Ryan's first book, *The Living Wage* (1906). Ryan identifies
another important inspiration, along with a glimpse into what would
emerge as his pragmatic and result-oriented strategy for reform, when he
dedicated *The Living Wage* to Richard Ely – an economist and highly
visible figure within the Protestant Social Gospel movement. However, from
what we now know of his education and early inspirations, Ryan's
dedication was overly generous in crediting Ely with initially moving him to
investigate economic problems. But it was smart from a strategic sense
(Ryan, 1906, p. v).

Ryan's early effort to find common ground with a prominent non-
Catholic reformer such as Ely provides an insight into his politically
pragmatic approach to achieve social reforms. Although there can be no
doubt that Ryan took his calling as a practicing Catholic and priest to be the
center of his life's inspiration and work, he actively sought out alliances and
common ground with non-Catholics to pursue social goals that he believed
were in the interests of all humanity, Catholic and non-Catholic alike. As a
consequence, Ryan was an important and influential figure in Progressive
era reform and politics. But it must be emphasized that this influence was
not as a figure of mass appeal, rather it was exercised through his influence
and reputation among the Catholic and non-Catholic intellectuals, lawyers,
labor leaders, and other prominent activists and opinion makers who
collectively made up the leadership of the Progressive movement. With
hindsight, it is evident that Ryan's copious writings were carefully crafted to
appeal simultaneously to a national and pan-Christian audience while

remaining grounded in, and consistent with, the Catholic principles of theology, ethics, and vision of a just social order.

Ryan's earliest writings, which appeared during his years of graduate study, were concerned with the ethical dimension of economic activities and demonstrated his developing interest in fundamental social reform. An early example is "The Ethics of Speculation," an article based on the thesis he presented for his first graduate degree, the Licentiate in Sacred Theology (S.T.L.) (Ryan, 1902b). But it was the dissertation that Ryan presented for his Doctor of Sacred Theology (S.T.D.) that was to become his first and perhaps most important book. The full title of this dissertation was *A Living Wage: Its Ethical and Economic Aspects*. This highly original work represented the first effort by an American scholar to construct a complete analysis of the ethical and economic issues raised by minimum wage legislation. Although it drew upon some important precedents and writings from New Zealand, Australia, and the United Kingdom, Ryan's book was published several years before wage legislation was on the American political horizon (Ryan, 1906).

For several decades after the publication of *The Living Wage* and in numerous popular and academic articles, sermons, and organizing activities, Ryan argued for a range of labor legislation including, but not limited to, minimum wages. Throughout his career, he consistently maintained that a legislated living wage was both a moral necessity and good social policy. What separated Ryan's proposal from the charge of utopianism was his argument that such a policy was neither incompatible with nor overly disruptive to the smooth operation of a property-based market economy. To establish these several conclusions, Ryan based his ethical arguments on the idea of human dignity found in the Catholic, and philosophical, natural rights tradition (Beckley, 1988). Simultaneously his economic analysis was, for the most part, closely grounded in the economic analysis of his day.[3] Drawing upon these dual foundations, Ryan became an important and useful ally of those prominent Progressive era intellectuals and reformers working for labor legislation in general, and for minimum wage legislation in particular. In the words of Father Joseph Husslein, "It was a Catholic priest – be it said to the glory of the Church – the Rev. John A. Ryan, D.D., who first effectively championed the minimum wage legislation in the United States, and it is another Catholic priest, the Rev. Edwin V. O'Hara, whose name, as Dr. Ryan himself remarks, 'is written in the annals of the United States Supreme Court as the official upholder of the first minimum wage law' " (Husslein, 1919, p. 91).[4]

MONSIGNOR JOHN A. RYAN AND
THE ETHICS OF A LIVING WAGE

Ryan always stated that his primary inspiration came from the Church. And there are reasons for this claim. In his Encyclical Letter of 1891, Pope Leo XIII had forcefully articulated the ethical basis of a living wage (Although, as is self-evident, it leaves open the question as to how such a wage is to be achieved):

> Let it be granted, then, that, as a rule, workman and employer should make free agreements, and in particular should freely agree as to wages; nevertheless, there is a dictate of nature more imperious and more ancient than any bargain between man and man, that the remuneration must be enough to support the wage-earner in reasonable and frugal comfort. If through necessity or fear of a worse evil, the workman accepts harder conditions because an employer or contractor will give him no better, he is the victim of force and injustice. (Pope Leo XIII, 1891, from the translation reproduced in Ryan & Husslein, 1920, p. 83)[5]

Ryan's primary ethical argument for minimum wage legislation was derived jointly from the Christian tradition and natural rights theory. It proposed that people are imbued with human dignity, and for that reason, able-bodied persons are entitled to meet their basic needs through their own labor – even under modern conditions where so many workers lack access to productive resources other than their own labor. To Ryan,

> Natural rights are the moral means or opportunities by which the individual attains the end appointed to him by nature. For the present it is sufficient to say that this end is right and reasonable life. The exigencies of right and reasonable living, therefore, determine the existence, and number, and extent of man's natural rights. (Ryan, 1906, p. 44)

A "right and reasonable" life requires that a person have access to the necessary means to live a life consistent with human dignity and the opportunity to achieve their potential as a human being. This includes the recognition and respect of the other members of society (Ryan, 1902a, pp. 163–165). It follows that the required minimum standard cannot be fixed in some immutable fact of nature, such as the biological requirements of life, which can be measured as so many grains of rice or loaves of bread per day. Rather socially determined standards of propriety and respectability necessarily play a role.[6]

Like the classical economists, Ryan thought that the level of subsistence was a socially determined minimum contingent upon social norms and a given society's state of development (Ryan, 1906, p. 68). For example, modern societies place demands on people with regard to personal grooming, dress, and presentation that have evolved into virtual mandates for anyone hoping to qualify for a job or standing within the community. Accordingly, a living wage must be one set at a level consistent with "right and reasonable living." Once such a standard of living has been achieved, each of us can begin our primary ethical task – to develop our unique personality. This task is at the core of Ryan's conception of natural rights, "Right and reasonable life, the welfare of the person, consist in the development of man's personality through the harmonious and properly ordered exercise of his faculties" (Ryan, 1906, p. 48; Beckley, 1988).

Ryan fully understood that the natural rights theory he advanced was in opposition to the individualism and utilitarianism of nineteenth-century English political economy, to say nothing of the legislation inspired by that perspective. "For those who maintain that the supreme end of life and rule of conduct is one's own happiness, there can, of course, be no such thing as a right in the *moral* sense of the term" (Ryan, 1906, p. 54, italics Ryan's). Indeed, as a consequence of their widespread acceptance at this time, Ryan often had occasion to criticize the principles of individualism and utilitarianism (Ryan, 1906, chap. 1, 1916, chap. 22, 1923a, 1927, chap. 1). First, he argued that the intellectuals who initially developed these ideas did not accept them in their pure form. Although Ryan did not explicitly state to whom he was referring, we might surmise that it was John Stuart Mill, who in his famous essay *Utilitarianism* acknowledged that people derived more pleasure from intellectual than sensual experiences, and for that reason, educated tastes were more fully human (Mill, 1863, chap. 2). Second, Ryan maintained that the principles of strict individualism and utilitarianism were at variance with widely held social norms that operated as checks on self-seeking. With approval, he observed that these principles were rejected by "the overwhelming majority of men and women who live outside of lunatic asylums" (Ryan, 1906, pp. 54–55).

Ryan has been criticized for failing to ground his arguments in scripture (Curran, 1982, pp. 84–91). Ryan was undoubtedly aware that he could have taken a more scriptural approach as the Christian tradition presents several justifications for the idea of a living wage. For example, Adam was excluded from the bounty of the Garden of Eden with the following condemnation, "In the sweat of thy face shalt thou eat bread" (Genesis, 3:19). In the *Book of Matthew* we are told that "the workman is worthy of his meat" (Matthew, 10:10). And in *Psalms* we are told, "For thou shalt eat the labour of thine hands: happy shalt thou be, and it shall be well with thee" (Psalms 128:2). Nevertheless, Ryan decided to base his reasoning on natural law arguments. We do not know, and likely will never know, the reason for this emphasis. Perhaps he had calculated that this form of argument would appeal to more people, especially among the educated classes, additionally, he may have thought that such arguments would stand a better chance in an American court of appeal.

Ryan argued that because man is enjoined to earn his bread through his own labor, a just society must provide him with an opportunity to accomplish this end. It follows that "The primary natural right from which the right to a Living Wage is deduced, is the right to subsist upon the bounty of the earth" (Ryan, 1906, p. 68). To Ryan, a corollary of the previous statement is that the private property rights of individuals, while essential to a well-ordered society, must be secondary to our primary right to earn a share of the earth's bounty adequate to sustain a standard of living consistent with human dignity. "For the right to live decently by one's labor is as important as the right to life and more important than the general right to property" (Ryan, 1910b, p. 473; see also Ryan, 1902a, pp. 164–165). To Ryan private property was a means and not an end in itself, so it followed that society had a legitimate say in its disposal by private individuals. To the extent that private property promoted the dignity of individuals, it was both just and valid. To the extent that its use or scope impeded this end, the law of property should be modified:

> Private property is morally legitimate because it is the method that best enables man to realize his natural right to use the gifts of material nature for the development of his personality. It is, therefore, merely a means, and its scope is determined and limited by the end which it promotes, and which is its sole justification. (Ryan, 1906, p. 72)

Ryan stressed that the ethical foundation of the living wage was the dignity of mankind and not the greater good of society, whether measured in productivity or total wealth (Beckley, 1988, pp. 66–68). Ryan reasoned that a utilitarian foundation for a minimum wage such as the "social good" would constitute an inadequate defense of the ethics of a living wage in the event that a situation emerged where a greater social good could be achieved with a lower wage (Ryan, 1906, pp. 82–85). As a Catholic priest and natural rights theorist Ryan maintained, throughout his writings, that human dignity took intellectual and ethical priority over the utilitarian standard of the "greatest good." Drawing from a long tradition of Catholic teaching on natural law, Ryan argued that human dignity must be considered as an end in itself (Ryan, 1902a, 1906, chap. 4, 1910b, pp. 461–462, 1913, 1916, chap. 23,1920a). "For Ryan human dignity is grounded, not in autonomy, but in the universal and natural capacity of humans for excellence" (Beckley, 1988, p. 67). Being a core principle of natural law it followed that, with few exceptions, rights based on our human dignity could not be superseded by the needs of society. Although these social needs might be compelling or even pressing, short of a crisis such as our collective defense against an aggressor, they must remain secondary. To Ryan the principle that the ends of society or the state were before the dignity of the individual was the basis of a political philosophy he loathed – that of Fascism (Ryan, 1927, chap. 5).

Consistent with the earlier arguments, Ryan thought that each worker's right to a living wage could be derived from the first principles of natural law:

> The thesis to be maintained in this volume is that the laborer's claim to a Living Wage is of the nature of a *right*. This right is personal, not merely social: that is to say, it belongs to the individual as individual, and not as a member of society; it is the laborer's personal prerogative, not his share of social good; and its primary end is the welfare of the laborer, not that of society. Again, it is a natural, not a positive right; for it is born with the individual, derived from his rational nature, not conferred upon him by a positive enactment. In brief, the right to a Living Wage is individual, natural and absolute. (Ryan, 1906, p. 44)

In sum, to Ryan the principles of human dignity and natural law dictate that each and every person is entitled to an opportunity to fully develop their personality. Anything less would denigrate the worker by denying him or her the means to become a full member of society. "The true formula is, that the individual has a right to all things that are essential to the reasonable development of his personality, consistently with the rights of others and the complete observance of the moral law" (Ryan, 1906, p. 65). To maintain any other position would, according to Ryan, suggest that it is reasonable or valid to treat another person as merely an object or means:

> Now, since a reasonable life and the reasonable development of personality are of equal intrinsic importance in all human beings, the fruits of the earth, the common heritage, ought to be distributed in such a way that this end will be realized. Consequently when any person is hindered from obtaining access *on reasonable terms* to this minimum of material goods his dignity and rights are violated, and some other man or men, or some social institution, has committed an act of injustice. (Ryan, 1906, p. 74)

RYAN'S CRITIQUE OF THE "LIBERTY OF CONTRACT" DOCTRINE

During the late nineteenth century and continuing into the Progressive era, labor legislation was challenged, and frequently overturned, by both state

and federal courts (Tribe, 1978, chap. 8; Fine, 1964). Not surprisingly many
progressive activists, social scientists, and legislators criticized the intellectual underpinning of the courts' reversals – the late-nineteenth-century
doctrine of "Liberty of Contract" (Pound, 1909; Powell, 1924). To support
his reform agenda Ryan contributed to this literature (Ryan, 1927, chap. 1,
1923a, 1906, chaps. 1–2).

But providing an effective criticism would not prove to be easy. Besides
business interests, the liberty of contract doctrine was supported by a
powerful intellectual tradition – the English political economists of the
nineteenth century:

> To a very large extent this notion, as well as the attitude of those who quietly ignore the
> moral aspect of the rate of wages, is the result of practical deductions from the teaching
> of the earlier English political economists. ... Now if political economy warrants this
> popular conclusion it creates at once a presumption of some value in favor of the
> justness of wages that are determined by the method of unlimited bargaining. The
> method is apparently sanctioned by the authority of science. (Ryan, 1906, pp. 5–6)

Ryan thought that the English political economists had overemphasized
the essentially a priori proposition that individual liberty, combined
with enlightened self-interest, would bring about a just human order.
This metaphysical claim was supported by a naive and equally a priori,
"faith in the beneficent and leveling influence of competition" (Ryan, 1906,
pp. 14–15). Like so many of the American economists of his era, Ryan
thought that the English political economists were wrong on both counts
(Clark, 1913, 1902; Ely, 1884; Power, 1999; Rodgers, 1998, chap. 3; see also
Prasch, 2000, 1999, 1998).

To Ryan, the experience of England under the regime of *laissez-faire*
revealed the tendency for free labor markets to undermine the living
standards of unorganized workmen, even as great wealth was created for the
privileged classes. To make his case, Ryan drew upon the authority of some
of the most important of the new generation of British economists, including
Thorold Rogers, Sidney and Beatrice Webb, and John Hobson, to
demonstrate that an unregulated market system featured structures and
tendencies that undermined the proposition that unfettered competition
worked for the benefit of all (Rogers, 1890, chap. 19; Webb and Webb,
1920/1897; Hobson, 1906, 1900).

The basic flaw that Ryan identified in the liberty of contract approach to
wage determination was its implicit premise that "competition was free and
general among both laborers and employers" (Ryan, 1916, p. 329). He
thought that the material circumstances of the individuals engaged in a

bargaining process often modified its outcome, with adverse effects for those who could least afford them:

> When a labourer is compelled by dire necessity to accept a wage that is insufficient for a decent livelihood, his consent to the contract is free only in a limited and relative way. It is what the moralists call *"voluntarium imperfectum."* It is vitiated to a substantial extent by the element of fear, by the apprehension of a cruelly evil alternative. The labourer does not agree to this wage because he prefers it to any other, but merely because he prefers it to unemployment, hunger, and starvation. (Ryan, 1916, p. 329)

Ryan rejected the idea that anyone whose bargaining power is strengthened by monopoly, or the ignorance or distress of another, is acting ethically when they draw upon such advantages to achieve a favorable bargain. He argued that the notion that the prevailing market wage, even when determined under free contract, was somehow a just wage ignored "the moral claims of needs, efforts, or sacrifices" (Ryan, 1916, p. 332). From this, it followed that a purely formal conception of law, one that applied a single standard to all persons in all situations, was often unjust when applied uniformly to persons in different situations. "[W]hile legislation should treat all individuals and classes equally in so far as they are equal, it ought just as surely to treat them unequally in those respects in which they are unequal" (Ryan, 1910b, p. 468).[7]

Ryan concluded, along with Pope Leo XIII and the emerging Catholic social thought tradition, that inequalities in bargaining power meant that free market outcomes could not and should not be society's final arbiter of economic justice (Husslein, 1919, chaps. 9, 21, 23; Curran, 1982, chaps. 1–2). Instead, Ryan argued that human dignity, as that is understood in the natural rights tradition, presents us with a substantial criteria for a just distribution that is not contingent on the outcome of unrestricted bargaining in the marketplace. Ryan also claimed that his perspective would not be controversial as most people have an intuitive and reasonably accurate understanding of natural rights (Ryan, 1906, pp. 43–66). From this he observed, correctly, that the worker's right to a living wage was a principle that enjoyed a broad consensus within American society (Glickman, 1997). Ryan summarized these sentiments as follows, "Indeed, it may be said with confidence that the common sense and unbiased convictions of the community not only repudiate the theory that free contracts are always just, but maintain that when the laborer is compelled to accept less than a certain decent minimum of remuneration he is in truth defrauded" (Ryan, 1906, p. 37).

THE LIVING WAGE: A "PERSONAL LIVING WAGE" OR A "FAMILY LIVING WAGE"?

Ryan argued that the lowest wage paid for labor should be a living wage. Yet he also recognized that this wage level could mean different things to different people – including differences between the several philosophers, theologians, and economists who agreed with the principle of a living wage. To establish a more concrete standard for the living wage, Ryan tried to identify the conditions, and thereby the level of income, that would allow a working person to achieve their full human potential – what he repeatedly called "a right and reasonable life." His name for such a wage level was the "Personal Living Wage" (Ryan, 1906, chap. 5).[8]

After developing the qualities of, and the need for, a personal living wage, Ryan argued that it was insufficient for the majority of the manufacturing workforce. The reason was that a personal living wage would be inadequate for male workers since Ryan believed that a man could only realize his full human potential as the head of a family (Ryan, 1906, pp. 116–120). After reviewing some statistics on average family size, Ryan presented his criteria for a "family living wage" – a wage that would enable a man, his non-working wife, and four-to-five children under the age of 16 to live a dignified life. He proposed that the standard for a family living wage be calculated as follows: "the cost of maintaining himself and wife until death and the children until they are of an age to be self-supporting, divided by his working time as an adult in full vigor, will give in terms of money the family Living Wage" (Ryan, 1906, pp. 119–120; see also Ryan, 1902a, p. 173).

Clearly such a standard of living, and the wage rate necessary to support it, was higher than the personal living wage. Indeed, the estimate that he proposed, $600 per year, was comparable to the living wage previously proposed by John Mitchell, the head of the United Mine Workers, whose estimate Ryan quoted with approval (Ryan, 1906, pp. 130–131). Ryan calculated that if we set aside the agricultural sector (which was then extensive), approximately 60 percent of all non-professional, non-farm, adult male workers earned less than his proposed family living wage in 1895 (Ryan, 1906, p. 162).

Ryan's two wage standards, the personal living wage and the family living wage, did leave him with a potential quandary: If the latter was exclusively for the support of persons (men) with families, should employers pay their employees in accordance with the sex or the personal circumstances of each laborer? Obviously such a policy would be administratively complex. It would also present firms with a clear incentive to exclusively hire persons without families. Such a result would be disastrous as every society has a compelling interest in the welfare of the next generation. Finally, would it be just if all men, as potential heads of families, were paid a family living wage, whereas the pay of all women remained at the (lower) personal living wage? Ryan fails to provide complete answers to such questions. He does, however, present some principles that we can use to at least partially resolve them.

The first principle was that those who provide equal work are entitled to equal pay, independently of the worker's sex or age, "Distributive justice requires that equally competent workers be rewarded equally" (Ryan, 1906, p. 108). A second principle was that men should not be priced out of any occupation by legislation. "Unless we hold that an increase in the proportion of women workers is desirable, we must admit that social welfare would be advanced by the payment of uniform wages to both sexes for equally efficient labor" (Ryan, 1906, p. 108).

These two principles enable us to address some aspects of the discrepancy between the personal living wage that adult women workers were entitled to as a matter of right, and the higher family living wage that Ryan considered to be rightfully owed to adult men. Nevertheless, this discrepancy remains a problem when viewed from today's perspective on sex equality. That said, Professor Alice Kessler-Harris has, in her well-regarded book on the subject of women's wages, misunderstood Ryan's position on what constitutes a living wage for working women. Specifically, she states that Ryan was of the opinion that when it came to calculating a living wage for women, "it seemed fair to reduce women to the lowest levels of bestiality" (Kessler-Harris, 1990, p. 11). As demonstrated earlier, Ryan's principle for setting the minimum wage was "a right and reasonable life." This, in turn, was grounded in a fundamental right to "human dignity." It follows that setting the living wage equal to biological subsistence – "bestiality" in Kessler-Harris' words – is inconsistent with Ryan's stated views. Indeed, Ryan might more plausibly be criticized for insisting on his second principle of "equal work for equal pay" since a sexist society would be unlikely to *perceive* a woman's contributions to be equal to a man's, independently of the facts of the case. It follows that this latter principle would tend to exclude women from certain positions if employers were mandated to pay them the same wage as their male colleagues. Finally, Ryan had occasion to act on his views, and his actions consistently reflected a more generous understanding of a women's wage than Kessler-Harris credits him for. One example is the actual wording, mentioned earlier, of the minimum wage legislation he helped draft for the State of Minnesota. Ryan's biographer provided, as typical, another important instance. He notes that when Ryan served as the Chairman of an advisory committee to the wage board of the State of Minnesota, he "wanted the minimum wage set on the assumption that a women lived in a home of her own, but he could not carry his board on this issue" (Broderick, 1963, pp. 83–84). Additional evidence comes from the not inconsequential fact that Ryan periodically worked with major feminist organizations, such as the National Consumer's League, on labor legislation.

I suspect that the source of Professor Kessler-Harris' condemnation of Ryan is his assignment of a lower minimum wage to women workers than their male peers *as a matter of natural right*, even though he simultaneously upholds, but as a secondary principle, the idea of an equal wage for equal work. Since feminism has a long-standing concern with the equality of rights between the sexes, there are legitimate grounds to be concerned with the logic of Ryan's argument.[9] In light of the above, I believe that the historical record affirms that Ryan was in the forefront of those who made it their life's work to improve the wages and livelihoods of working women and that his contributions were recognized and appreciated by the leading feminists and social reformers of his era.

In addition to women, Ryan extended his two principles of wage equality to the many children then in the workforce. In general he thought that it was safe to assume that children were members of a household. He concluded that the minimum wage that employed children were entitled to *as a matter of right* should be lower than that allowed to adults. But, as in the case of women workers, Ryan also thought that children should be paid the equivalent of a family living wage if they worked as efficiently as adult men. Nevertheless, the legitimate earnings of children remained a secondary concern since Ryan was among those pushing for more restrictive child labor laws, including a constitutional amendment to ensure that the courts would uphold such legislation (Broderick, 1963, pp. 97–98; Ryan, 1918; 1920b, pp. 116–119, 1927, chap. 21).

RYAN ON THE ECONOMICS OF WAGE DETERMINATION AND MINIMUM WAGE LEGISLATION

Ryan's theory of wage determination drew from both the economics of what we now remember as the Institutionalist tradition and that which came to constitute the emerging Neoclassical school. With regard to the latter, Ryan subscribed to both the "supply and demand" theory and the recently articulated marginal productivity theory of wages (Ryan, 1906, chap. 14).

This dual heritage is important as some commentators have mistakenly suggested that Ryan rejected economic theory altogether. To comprehend Ryan's economic thought, it must be understood that during this era a commitment to the marginal product theory of distribution was not inconsistent with maintaining a broader "Institutionalist" perspective. The latter's contribution was to stress the relative immobility of labor, the importance of imperfect competition, and the role of bargaining power in the setting of wages and prices. It was for these reasons that the growing popularity of the marginal product theory of distribution did not, at least initially, undermine the nearly unanimous support of Progressive Era American economists for minimum wage legislation. For example, three of Columbia University's most prominent economists, John Bates Clark, Henry Rogers Seager, and Edwin Seligman all simultaneously held a broadly Neoclassical theory of wage determination even as they each supported some variant of minimum wage legislation for both men and women (Clark, 1913; Prasch, 2000, 1999, 1998; Seager, 1917, chaps. 15, 29, 30, 1913; Seligman, 1923, pp. 650–654, 1915).[10]

What set Ryan apart from most of his contemporaries was not his support for minimum wage legislation, rather it was his call for a relatively high minimum wage in conjunction with his belief that this "living wage" should be exclusively determined by the needs of the worker, rather than by reference to their needs in conjunction with the financial condition of industry or with the state of the labor market. Among the many proponents of minimum wage legislation in the American academy, Ryan's position was clearly that of a minority. However, we should note that Ryan's perspective did attract substantial political support since a majority of the state laws that authorized minimum wages made no mention of broader economic conditions in their enabling legislation (the exceptions were Colorado, Nebraska, and Massachusetts, see Brandeis, 1935, p. 523, n. 64). In contrast to Ryan, a more moderate proponent of minimum wage legislation, John Bates Clark, explicitly rejected a minimum wage that solely considered the needs of workers, and argued that market conditions should be taken into account when a state's Industrial Welfare Commission or Wage Board set the minimum wage for a particular industry (Clark, 1913; Prasch, 2000).

Although he was certainly aware that different industries faced different circumstances, Ryan argued that wage boards should not be bound by current labor market conditions when making wage determinations because (1) the level of the minimum wage was an ethical question, and (2) the labor market was subject to several structural distortions that lowered both the wages and productivity of many workers, especially those – such as women – with low levels of experience and unionization. Ryan believed that with the passage of reform-oriented legislation, including a minimum wage set at the level of a living wage, many of these problems would be corrected. As to those firms that could not pay a living wage, he thought that they did not have a right to subsist off of the implicit subsidy provided by the low wages of their employees – he preferred that they surrender their share of the market to more effective and efficient firms that could make a profit while paying a living wage. Although Ryan's position may have been relatively extreme, many economists of substantial standing shared it, including Arthur Holcombe of Harvard University and George Gorham Groat of Ohio Wesleyan University and later of the University of Vermont (Holcombe, 1912, p. 34; Groat, 1913, pp. 108–109; Prasch, 1998, pp. 169–171).

Another reason why Ryan rejected the current condition of industry when calculating the minimum wage was that he believed that a minimum wage set at a living wage would increase aggregate output. Specifically, he anticipated higher efficiency from labor remunerated at the level of a living wage. He also anticipated that minimum wage legislation would induce other adjustments such as the greater use of machinery, improved management techniques, lower monopoly profits, and perhaps a modest increase in the price of some non-wage goods. In short, Ryan believed that living wage legislation could induce enough additional output for everyone to enjoy a living wage and the potential for a dignified life (Ryan, 1906, chaps. 8–9, 1910b, pp. 468–473, 1913, 1915).

With regard to levels of employment, Ryan was less confident of the outcome, but remained cautiously optimistic. He concluded that "Nevertheless, experience, analogy, and all the available indications would seem to justify the assertion that the sum total of employment both within and without the affected industries would not necessarily be diminished, and would not improbably be increased" (Ryan, 1910b, p. 471).

It is worthwhile to note that most minimum wage statutes of this era reflected a concern for disemployment effects by allowing the less capable or the less experienced to work for a set period of time at a reduced rate. For example, inexperienced adult women in Oregon could be employed for up to one year at the wage rate allowed for minors (Bureau of Labor Statistics, 1915, p. 20). Section 8a of the California statute was typical of state legislation in its wording:

> For any occupation in which a minimum wage has been established, the commission may issue to a women physically defective by age or otherwise, a special license authorizing the employment of such licensee, for a period of six months, for a wage less than such legal minimum wage; and the commission shall fix a special minimum wage for

such person. Any such license may be renewed for like periods of six months. (from State of California, Acts of 1913, chap. 324, reproduced in Clark, 1921, pp. 239–244)

Similar exemptions can be found in the enabling legislation of Arkansas, Colorado, the District of Columbia, Kansas, Massachusetts, Minnesota, North Dakota, Puerto Rico, Texas, Utah, Washington, and Wisconsin for various classifications of people including the disabled, minors, or apprentices. In many cases rules were promulgated as to what percentage of the workers at any given establishment could work under these special wage rates – for example in Minnesota and Colorado it was 10 percent, and in California it was left open to the commission to set the percentage as they saw fit on an industry-by-industry basis (Brandeis, 1935).

RYAN ON THE ECONOMICS OF CONTEMPORARY LABOR MARKETS

Ryan identified five structural features of contemporary labor markets that he thought were responsible for the inadequate wages of so many workers. Although none of these arguments originated with Ryan, he developed his own assessment of the importance of each of them, and whether they could be offset by economic policy, specifically minimum wage legislation.

First, although Ryan subscribed to the supply and demand theory of wage determination, and thought that in a competitive market wages would tend to equal the marginal product of labor, he did not think that the labor market should be thought of as a single entity featuring an equilibrium price. Appealing to our collective experience, and the authority of the British economist John E. Cairnes, Ryan proposed that the labor market was composed of several non-competing sub-markets:

> Competition among laborers is not nearly so immediate nor so extensive as among the owners of capital. Locomotive engineers have no fear of being displaced by "section-hands." The world of labor is divided into a series of "non-competing" groups which rise one above another, from the lowest grade of common labor to the highest form of special ability and skill. Within each group there is competition, more or less immediate and unlimited; but among the various groups it is indirect in action and restricted in extent. (Ryan, 1906, p. 223)

Ryan understood that competition between subgroups of workers did occur. But he also argued, again on the authority of Cairnes, that because job skills took time to acquire and were not fully transferable between lines of work, labor market adjustments would be gradual (Ryan, 1906, pp. 223–225). Cairnes described intra-market labor mobility in the following terms:

> What we find, in effect, is not a whole population competing indiscriminately for all occupations, but a series of industrial layers, superposed on one another, within each of which the various candidates for employment possess a real and effective power of selection, while those occupying the several strata are, for all purposes of effective competition, practically isolated from each other ... We are thus compelled to recognize the existence of non-competing industrial groups as a feature of our social economy; and this is the fact which I desire to insist upon. (Cairnes, 1874, pp. 66–68)

To Cairnes, the adjustments that did occur were largely a consequence of a disparity between the entry of new workers into a particular sub-market and the gradual retirement of older workers. He observed that movements between industries and locations in mid-life were relatively rare. This lack of movement between jobs could be attributed to various obstacles such as training costs, ignorance, inertia, and monopoly. To Cairnes and Ryan it followed that conventional market signals such as the inequality of wages between industries would be relatively ineffective in reallocating labor over the short- to medium-term (Ryan, 1906, p. 225, n. 1; Cairnes, 1874, pp. 63–73).[11]

The second problem Ryan identified was that of monopoly. Consistent with the then prevalent theories of monopoly, such as that advanced by John Bates Clark and John Maurice Clark, Ryan believed that the effects of monopoly were evident in both the output and labor markets (Clark & Clark, 1912). In this analysis, monopolies drove up prices by restricting output. It followed that their initial effect was to reduce the real wages of their customers by raising the cost of commodities. Since monopolists raised prices by restricting output, they also employed fewer people. The indirect consequence was a release of surplus labor into related labor markets, and a reduction in the real wage offered for that particular class of labor.

> The result is that men are thrown out of employment, to enter into competition with their fellows both within and without the combinations, and thus bringing down the wages of all. On the other hand, the increased cost of living which follows a monopolistic organization of industry affects the laborer precisely as it affects other consumers. (Ryan, 1906, p. 166)

In their analysis of this same phenomena, John Bates Clark and John Maurice Clark assumed that labor was homogeneous, so that when monopolies diminished output, and therefore reduced their payrolls, it would crowd the entire labor market of the region in which the monopoly operated. The consequence would be lower wages for all laborers, including those on the monopoly's payroll, unless the workers that remained employed by the monopoly could bargain collectively. Ryan differed from portions of the Clarks' analysis since he believed, with John E. Cairnes, that labor markets were segmented. Hence the relative crowding of one or several sub-markets would not induce many workers to leave those markets. Each sub-market could feature its own wage, one that could be expected to persist. In short, Ryan believed that in the presence of widespread monopolization, one could anticipate that a range of wages would be paid for the same quality of labor.

Third, Ryan argued that under modern conditions labor faced a continuous threat of displacement by new machinery. This tendency, on its own, should be unobjectionable since many if not most economists – then and now – have insisted that the introduction of machinery simultaneously opens up new opportunities elsewhere in the economy. For this reason, economists have traditionally maintained that the introduction of machinery does not imply a sustained lack of demand for labor in the economy taken as a whole. Ryan's economic heresy was to challenge this last claim:

> Up to the present the substitution of machinery for hand processes does not seem to have caused any permanent increase in the proportion of unemployment. The number of idle men is probably no greater, relatively to the whole working population, than it was before the coming of the machine regime. And yet, it must be borne in mind that this result is a mere accident, for there is no necessary connection between the introduction or extension of machine production and the continuity of employment. (Ryan, 1906, p. 167)

Ryan was aware that his contention went against a core proposition of Classical Political Economy, one known as Say's Law. This latter proposition was most clearly articulated by a young John Stuart Mill who confidently stated that:

> Nothing can be more chimerical than the fear that the accumulation of capital should produce poverty and not wealth, or that it will ever take place too fast for its own end. Nothing is more true than that it is produce which constitutes the market for produce, and that every increase of production, ... creates, or rather constitutes, its own demand. (Mill, 1844, p. 73)

Of course, Ryan's position on the relationship between the introduction of machinery and the level of employment and wages was and remains a proposition almost instinctively rejected by most economists. But before dismissing Ryan's statement as the preoccupation of an over-zealous reformer, let us note that he was careful not to overargue this particular point. He did not claim that machinery invariably leads to less employment – he only claimed that economists cannot guarantee, on the basis of pure theory, that it would not. Furthermore, let us also recall that no less a figure than David Ricardo, in the third edition of his *Principles of Political Economy and Taxation*, dismayed his friends and supporters by allowing that he saw some merit in the notion that the introduction of machinery could be detrimental to the interests of labor (Ricardo, 1821, chap. 31; Prasch, 1997). If Ryan overreached on this point, he had excellent company.

As it was, Ryan based his analysis of the effects of new machinery on the work of the British economist John Hobson. Hobson argued that the introduction of machinery may, or may not, have a detrimental effect on the absolute level of employment, although he was confident that it would lower the share of manufacturing in total employment. To Hobson, the actual outcome depended on several offsetting forces, so the net effect of machinery on employment would necessarily be an empirical question. Hobson was more certain that the evidence indicated that machinery would tend to make industrial employment "more unstable, more precarious of tenure, and more fluctuating in market value" (Hobson, 1906, p. 334). He was also convinced that machinery had a "leveling" tendency on the skills of those who worked directly with it. "Though the quality of intelligence and skill applied to the invention, application, and management of machinery is constantly increasing, practical authorities are almost unanimous in admitting that the proportion which this skilled work bears to the aggregate of labour in machine industry is constantly diminishing" (Hobson, 1906, p. 345). In sum, machinery was detrimental to the bargaining power and consequently the wage security of the industrial workforce.

Fourth, as noted earlier, Ryan agreed with John Bates Clark's general proposition that in a competitive labor market workers were paid their marginal product. Indeed, Ryan refers to Clark as an authority on the economics of distribution and wage determination. However, in contrast to Clark, Ryan did not believe that a distribution according to the marginal productivity of each factor was either just or unique (Clark, 1899, chap. 1). Specifically, Ryan thought that in many sub-markets the causal relationship between the marginal product of labor and the wage was the inverse of that which was typically supposed. In other words, at the lower end of the labor market, it was the wage that determined the productivity of labor:

> The fact is that the amount of energy expended by the laborer who is wholly dependent upon his wages, is always limited by his wages, can never be in excess of them. The subsistence received by the men and women employed in sweat shops does not repair a large amount of energy, but, on the hypothesis that they continue at work, it replaces all that they actually expend. (Ryan, 1906, pp. 85–86)

Fifth, was an argument that Ryan built upon the supposition that a modern capitalist economy chronically over-invests its savings in productive capacity that is often underutilized, thereby inducing financial distress, economic depression, and unemployment. Although several important economists of this era proposed such a theory of the business cycle, Ryan attributed its most advanced formulation to John Hobson (Ryan, 1941, pp. 64–69). Following Hobson's line of argument, Ryan believed that a tendency to overinvestment was a core flaw of the modern economy (Hobson, 1906, chaps. 11–13; Ryan, 1906, pp. 168–175). Perhaps optimistically, Ryan believed that minimum wage legislation could offset some of the consequences of the structural tendency of free market economies to overproduce capital goods:

> This theory is at variance, obviously, with one of the common-places of the older political economy. We have been assured very frequently that general over-production is an absurdity, since a supply of goods always means a demand for goods, and since the wants of men are never fully satisfied. Undoubtedly the existence of goods implies the power to purchase other goods, and the existence of unsatisfied wants means a desire to purchase; but what Adam Smith called "effective demand," the only kind of demand that will take the surplus goods off the market, requires that the purchasing power and the desire exist in the same persons. ... The very excess of productive power relatively to the needs that are combined with purchasing power, means an excess of supply of labor, which in turn means unemployment and low wages. (Ryan, 1906, pp. 174–175)

By subscribing to Hobson's underconsumption theory of generalized unemployment, Ryan was at his most unorthodox with regard to economic theory and method. At the time that the above paragraph was written, Hobson's work had not yet achieved the wider degree of acceptability that it was to gain with the onset of the Great Depression and John Maynard Keynes' macroeconomic explanation of its origins.

Finally it should be noted that Ryan explicitly rejected the labor theory of value and both the scientific and the ethical lessons that socialists and Marxists derived from it. This was, of course, in keeping with the views of Pope Leo XIII and the long-standing position of the Catholic Church (Hillquit & Ryan, 1914; Ryan, 1906, chap. 10, 1916, chap. 22; Husslein, 1919, chap. 21; Curran, 1982, chap. 2). Ryan consistently and repeatedly maintained that a legitimate return was owed to both land and capital, but only after the owners of these productive factors had satisfied the ethical priority of paying their employees a living wage. In other words, returns to inanimate assets were legitimate, but should be subordinate to the claims of employees, whose right to a living wage was of a higher ethical priority (Ryan, 1906, chap. 4).

Ryan concluded, as did many other reformers and economists of the Progressive era, that the asymmetric structure of bargaining power meant that a significant portion of the labor force would be denied full remuneration for their skills and effort. Although many economists thought that the marginal productivity theory of distribution provided a reference point for the value of labor under perfectly competitive conditions, many of them, including John Bates Clark, Henry Rogers Seager, and John Ryan, thought that the highly specific conditions of perfect competition were, at best, a partial representation of the reality of the American labor market – and that this fact was critical to analysis and policy formulation (Clark, 1913; Prasch, 2000). From this perspective, the wage level that we actually observe is the consequence of a large number of unequal bargains. On the one side is capital – increasingly organized into large corporate units – and on the other is the mass of individual workers, who have to contend with the relatively immediate needs of themselves and their families, and for that reason cannot readily endure a lengthy spell of unemployment or even a protracted negotiation.

That the contingencies of bargaining power played an important role in the process of wage determination was confirmed, for these reformers, by the large variance in wages that were observed among persons possessing similar labor skills and living in the same location. Even for those economists who were least disposed, on theoretical grounds, toward minimum wage legislation this latter fact was of crucial importance. As an example, consider Frank Taussig of Harvard University. After an article that featured a lengthy *theoretical* presentation of the futility of minimum wage legislation under competitive conditions, Taussig concluded that a plausible case could be made in support of such legislation for women. The reason had to do with the contingencies of the bargaining process under non-competitive conditions:

> It may well be that there is need of regulating and protecting the wages of women, and of prescribing minimum rates for those in the lowest group. The conditions of their employment are such as to lead easily to "unfair" wages – wages kept low by taking advantage of timidity, ignorance, lack of mobility, lack of bargaining power. The lack of standardization, and the divergent rates of pay under similar conditions, point strongly to haphazard influences of this sort. (Taussig, 1916, p. 441)

Economic theory, in conjunction with the labor market statistics that were increasingly available at this time, led the overwhelming majority of American economists, including John Ryan, to conclude that some variety of minimum wage legislation was both necessary and desirable. The conclusion that firms had undue discretionary power over the wage bargain and could employ that discretionary power to the detriment of their workers and society as a whole, pointed to some form of minimum wage legislation as an inescapable conclusion (Prasch, 2000, 1999, 1998; Power, 1999).

CONCLUSION

To John Ryan, the ethical and economic case for a minimum wage set at the level of a living wage was overwhelming. Ryan also maintained that there was nothing particularly novel or radical about such an idea since the era of "free contract" was a relatively recent innovation in labor market law and practice (Ryan, 1910b, p. 466; Steinfeld, 1991). After a short survey of wage doctrines, Ryan drew the following conclusion, "Either explicitly or implicitly men have always been virtually unanimous in the conviction that the standard for determining wages should be a moral standard" (Ryan, 1906, p. 40). On this basis, he surmised that those who remained opposed to legislation supporting labor's legitimate claim to a living wage based their erroneous arguments on either self-interest or false ideas. "The practical recommendations of the economists and ordinances of the legislators can be traced to false principles, false reasoning, incomplete analysis of facts, and the selfishness of the dominant industrial class" (Ryan, 1906, p. 22). In light of the economic analysis of his day, the ethics of natural law doctrine, and the emerging theology of several Christian churches, including his own Catholic Church, it was evident to Ryan that the tyranny of a pure *laissez-faire* regime should be overturned. Ryan was optimistic that with intelligent legislation an economy based on private property and market exchange could result in a well-ordered, prosperous, and free society.

At the conclusion of a recent book on the politics of the minimum wage, Jerold Waltman made the following observation:

> The Progressives who imported and built the minimum wage house carried a view of political economy that was partly influenced by civic republicanism. They did not detach economic analysis from the public good, broadly conceived ... It [the minimum wage] was built on a feeling that people who worked had a dignity as people that was eroded by sweatshop conditions and the lives generated by substandard wages. A minimum wage was a way to give worth and dignity to individuals. (Waltman, 2000, p. 141)

Waltman accurately summarizes an important element of the ideas and ideals shared by Monsignor John Ryan and most of his colleagues within the Progressive movement. The legislated living wage they proposed was part of a larger vision of economic justice, one based on the conviction that everyone was entitled to earn a living through their own labor. It followed that a just social order, including the modern industrial state, had to ensure that a person's labor could provide them with the material conditions necessary for, in Ryan's words, "a right and reasonable life." As argued earlier, the Progressives, and not just the Catholics among them, generally shared this perspective, along with the belief that such a goal could be readily achieved through intelligent state action. To these reformers, the living wage was more than simply a legislative measure designed to alleviate poverty. It was about the dignity of work and constructing a society in which productive and remunerative work could be the basis of a just, democratic, and sustainable social order (Danbom, 1987; Skocpol, 1992, chaps. 6–7; Hofstadter, 1955). This vision was nicely summarized by Henry Rogers Seager, a Columbia University economist and co-founder of the influential American Association for Labor Legislation, "Thus it (the minimum wage) is a reform that should appeal to all classes of reformers. It will strengthen the foundation, a vigorous and independent citizenship, on which all must build. On these grounds, I commend it to your consideration" (Seager, 1913, p. 12).

NOTES

1. Massachusetts' minimum wage statute was widely thought to be exempt from this ruling as its decrees were not mandatory. Under the Commonwealth's statute non-complying employers faced a penalty of adverse publicity as the Massachusetts Minimum Wage Commission was authorized to publish the fact of their non-compliance in newspapers across the state. Although this may appear to be a light penalty, proponents and adversaries each reported that the Massachusetts minimum wage was effective in raising wages for the lowest paid workers (Dewson, 1924; Brown, 1917).

2. Ryan was also active in child labor and civil liberties causes, among many others. He was also a co-founder of the Catholic Economics Association, which in 1970 became the Association for Social Economics.

3. Remarkably, American economists of the Progressive Era were close to unanimous in their support for minimum wage legislation, at least in the form that it then took, that is to say administered by a wage board and covering women and minors exclusively (Prasch, 1999, 1998).

4. Ryan's influence is also evident in the fact that virtually every minimum wage ordinance passed during this period directed wage boards to focus on the needs of the worker when setting minimums in various industries (Brandeis, 1935; Douglas, 1919; Dewson, 1924; Clark, 1921). The Minnesota ordinance speaks directly to a "reasonable life" that is not surprising since Ryan had a hand in writing it.

Additionally it was a student of Ryan's – Father, later Archbishop, Edwin O'Hara – who as the Chairman of the Oregon Industrial Welfare Commission, and thereby responsible for administering Oregon's minimum wage. In that role O'Hara was named in the lawsuit, *Stettler v. O'Hara* (243 U.S. 629, 37 Sup. Ct. 475), that initially upheld the constitutionality of minimum wage legislation in 1917, albeit by a slim 4-4 decision (O'Hara, 1914; Clark, 1921, pp. 33–42). A consequence of this close vote was that the US Supreme Court would have an opportunity to revisit the issue. In 1923 it did, finding against the District of Columbia's minimum wage by a vote of 5–3.

5. Professor A. M. C. Waterman kindly alerted me to the fact that the above translation, as reproduced from Ryan and Husslein's text, is somewhat idiosyncratic (unfortunately, Ryan and Husslein neglected to identify whose translation they were using). For this reason, it is constructive to contrast the above with the text as it appears in the Vatican's approved 1943 translation. The differences, while subtle, constitute a statement that is less forceful than that presented earlier:

> Let it be granted then that worker and employer may enter freely into agreements and, in particular, concerning the amount of the wage; yet there is always underlying such agreements an element of natural justice, and one greater and more ancient than the free consent of contracting parties, namely, that the wage shall not be less than enough to support a worker who is thrifty and upright. If, compelled by necessity or moved by fear of a worse evil, a worker accepts a harder condition, which although against his will he must accept because the employer or contractor imposes it, he certainly submits to force, against which justice cries out in protest. (Pope Leo XIII, 1943, para. 63).

6. If biological subsistence were to be selected as the reference point, the minimum wage could be set at a remarkably low level, as was once illustrated by George Stigler (Stigler, 1945). In such a case, there would be really little need for such legislation, a fact that probably did not escape Stigler as he made his calculations.

7. Compare Ryan's statement in the text with Aristotle's observation that, "If the persons are not equal, their (just) shares will not be equal; but this is the source of quarrels and recriminations, when equals have and are awarded unequal shares or unequals equal shares" (Aristotle, 1962, bk. 5, p. 118).

8. Over the next decade many estimates of the cost of living were published. These studies were often spurred by legislative mandates requiring minimum wages to constitute a "reasonable" or "living" wage. These cost of living studies were designed to estimate the level of income that would constitute a minimally acceptable quality of life in different locations (cf. Ogburn, 1919; Packard, 1915; Persons, 1915a, 1915b).

9. Of course, Kessler-Harris is correct to ascribe to Ryan the belief that a women's role was primarily that of a homemaker. However, we should note that at this time the rhetoric and practice of many women reformers, feminist leaders, and trade unionists suggests that they shared this perspective. Since Ryan also supported women's suffrage, his most significant break with his colleagues in the feminist movement was over the issue of birth control. This should not come as too much of a surprise since he was, after all, a Catholic priest (Ryan, 1927, chap. 27). We also know that he was highly critical of the National Women's Party who, in

their quest for an Equal Rights Amendment to the Constitution, opposed much of the labor legislation that Ryan and his allies had worked to enact (Ryan, 1927, chap. 6). However, this latter contest was much bigger than Ryan and reflected a fundamental, and ultimately destructive, conflict within the larger feminist movement (Zimmerman, 1991; Butler, 2002).

10. What is, from today's vantage point, a clear distinction between the Neoclassical and Institutionalist schools was neither an obvious nor an important distinction to most American economists of the Progressive era. What these economists were conscious of, and sensitive to, was a distinction between inductive and deductive methods in economics, and they were especially anxious to distance themselves from what they perceived to be the *a priorism* of the English tradition within economics (Prasch, 1996). The idea that Institutionalism was an independent school of economics only emerged toward the latter part of the period covered in this chapter (Rutherford, 2000).

11. Cairnes' and Ryan's belief that labor was a relatively immobile factor of production has an important intellectual pedigree that includes Adam Smith, "Such a difference of prices, which it seems is not always sufficient to transport a man from one parish to another, would necessarily occasion so great a transportation of the most bulky commodities, not only from one parish to another, but from one end of the kingdom, almost from one end of the world to the other, as would soon reduce them more nearly to a level. After all that has been said of the levity and inconstancy of human nature, it appears evidently from experience that a man is of all luggage the most difficult to be transported" (Smith, 1976, p. 84).

ACKNOWLEDGMENTS

I thank Falguni A. Sheth, A. M. C. Waterman, Patrick Welch, Rebecca Edwards, and the archivists and librarians at Catholic University Library Special Collections, Vassar College and St. Michael's College for their assistance with this project. I also thank the audiences who heard earlier versions of this paper, including the History of Economics Society and my colleagues in the Department of Economics at Middlebury College.

REFERENCES

Anderson, D. (1980). *Ignatius Donnelly*. Boston, MA: Twayne Publishers.
Aristotle. (1962). *Nicomachean ethics* (M. Ostwald, Trans.). New York: Macmillan.
Beckley, H. (1988). The legacy of John A. Ryan's theory of justice. *American Journal of Jurisprudence, 33*, 61–98.
Brandeis, E. (1935). Labor legislation. In: J. R. Commons (Ed.), *History of labor in the United States, 1896–1932* (Vol. 4). New York: Macmillan.

Broda, R. (1928). Minimum wage legislation in the United States. *International Labour Review, 17*(1), 24–50.

Broderick, F. (1963). *Right reverend new dealer: John A. Ryan.* New York: Macmillan.

Brown, R. (1917). Oregon minimum wage cases. *Minnesota Law Review, 1,* 471–486.

Bureau of Labor Statistics. (1915). *Effect of minimum-wage determinations in Oregon.* Bulletin no. 176. Government Printing Office, Washington, DC.

Butler, A. (2002). *Two paths to equality: Alice Paul and Ethel M. Smith in the ERA debate, 1921–1929.* Albany, NY: State University of New York Press.

Cairnes, J. (1874). *Some leading principles of political economy newly expounded.* New York: Macmillan.

Clark, J. B. (1899). *The distribution of wealth.* New York: Macmillan.

Clark, J. B. (1913). The minimum wage. *The Atlantic Monthly, 112,* 289–297.

Clark, J. B., & Clark, J. M. (1912). *The control of trusts.* New York: Macmillan.

Clark, L. (1921). *Minimum wage laws of the United States: Construction and operation.* Bureau of Labor Statistics Bulletin no. 285. Government Printing Office, Washington, DC.

Commons, J. (1893/1963). *The distribution of wealth.* New York: Augustus M. Kelley.

Curran, C. (1982). *American Catholic social ethics: Twentieth-century approaches.* Notre Dame, IN: University of Notre Dame Press.

Danbom, D. (1987). *The world of hope: Progressives and the struggle for an ethical public life.* Philadelphia, PA: Temple University Press.

Dewson, M. (1924). The minimum wage law in Massachusetts. In: F. Frankfurter, M. Dewson, & J. Commons (Eds), *State minimum wage laws in practice.* New York: National Consumers' League.

Dorfman, J. (1934). *Thorstein Veblen and his America.* New York: Viking Press.

Douglas, D. (1919). American minimum wage laws at work. *American Economic Review, 9*(4), 701–738.

Ely, R. (1884). *The past and present of political economy.* Johns Hopkins University Series in Historical and Political Science, 2nd Series, Vol. 3, pp. 5–64.

Everett, J. (1946). *Religion in economics: A study of John Bates Clark, Richard T. Ely, Simon N. Patten.* New York: King's Crown Press.

Fine, S. (1964). *Laissez-faire and the general welfare state: A study of conflict in American thought.* Ann Arbor, MI: University of Michigan Press.

Fisher, A. (1926/1966). *Some problems of wages and their regulation in Great Britain Since 1918.* New York: Kelley.

Gearty, P. (1953). *The economic thought of Monsignor John A. Ryan.* Washington, DC: Catholic University of America Press.

Glickman, L. (1997). *A living wage: American workers and the making of consumer society.* Ithaca, NY: Cornell University Press.

Gonce, R. (1996). The Social Gospel, Ely, and Commons's initial stage of thought. *Journal of Economic Issues, 30*(3), 641–665.

Groat, G. (1913). Comment on Seager. *American Labor Legislation Review, 3,* 106–109.

Hammond, M. (1913). The minimum wage in Great Britain and Australia. *The Annals of the American Academy of Political and Social Science, 48,* 22–36.

Hammond, M. (1915). Where life is more than meat: The Australian experience with wage boards. *The Survey, 33*(19), 495–502.

Hart, V. (1994). *Bound by our constitution: Women, workers, and the minimum wage.* Princeton, NJ: Princeton University Press.

Hillquit, M., & Ryan, J. (1914). *Socialism: Promise or menace?* New York: Macmillan.

Hobson, J. (1900). *The economics of distribution.* New York: Macmillan.

Hobson, J. (1906). *The evolution of modern capitalism: A study of machine production* (Rev. ed.). New York: Macmillan.

Hobson, J. (1915). The state and minimum wage in England. *The Survey, 33*(19), 503–504.

Hofstadter, R. (1955). *The age of reform: From Bryan to F.D.R.* New York: Vintage.

Holcombe, A. (1912). The legal minimum wage in the United States. *American Economic Review, 2*(1), 21–27.

Husslein, Rev. Joseph. (1919). *The world problem: Capital, labor, and the church.* New York: P. J. Kennedy & Sons.

Hutchinson, E. (1919). Women's wages. *Studies in History, Economics and Public Law, 89*(1), 1–179. New York: Columbia University Press.

Kelley, F. (1911). Minimum-wage boards. *American Journal of Sociology, 17*(3), 303–314.

Kelley, F. (1912). Minimum-wage laws. *Journal of Political Economy, 20*(10), 999–1010.

Kessler-Harris, A. (1990). *A woman's wage: Historical meanings and social consequences.* Lexington, KY: University Press of Kentucky.

Mill, J. S. (1844/1948). *Essays on some unsettled questions of political economy.* Reprinted by the London School of Economics and Political Science, John W. Parker, London.

Mill, J. S. (1863/1979). *Utilitarianism.* Indianapolis, IN: Hackett.

Millis, H., & Montgomery, R. (1938). *Economics of labor: Labor's progress and some basic labor problems* (Vol. 1). New York: McGraw-Hill.

Morris, J. (1986). *Women workers and the sweated trades: The origins of minimum wage legislation.* Brookfield, VT: Gower.

Morris, V. (1930). *Oregon's experience with minimum wage legislation.* New York: Columbia University Press.

Muller, D. (1959). The social philosophy of Josiah Strong: Social Christianity and American progressivism. *Church History, 28*(2), 183–201.

Murphy, W. (1991). Rerum Novarum. In: G. Weigal & R. Royal (Eds), *A century of Catholic social thought: Essays on "Rerum Novarum" and nine other key documents.* Lanham, MD: University Press of America.

Nordlund, W. (1997). *The quest for a living wage: The history of the federal minimum wage program.* Westport, CT: Greenwood.

O'Brien, D. (1968). *American Catholics and social reform: The new deal years.* New York: Oxford University Press.

O'Hara, E. (1914). Protective standards for women workers in Oregon. *Proceedings of the 41st annual national conference of charities and correction.* Fort Wayne, IN: Fort Wayne Printing.

Ogburn, W. (1919). Measurement of the cost of living and wages. *Annals of the American Academy of Political and Social Science, 81*, 110–122.

Packard, E. (1915). Just getting along. *The Survey, 33*(19), 514–515.

Paulsen, G. (1996). *A living wage for the forgotten man: The quest for fair labor standards, 1933–1941.* Selinsgrove, PA: Susquehanna University Press.

Perkins, F. (1946). *The Roosevelt I knew.* New York: Harper & Row.

Persons, C. (1915a). Women's work and wages in the United States. *Quarterly Journal of Economics, 29*(2), 201–234.

Persons, C. (1915b). Estimates of a living wage for female workers. *Journal of the American Statistical Association,* New Series, no. 110, pp. 567–577.

Pound, R. (1909). Liberty of contract. *Yale Law Journal, 17*(7), 454–487.

Powell, T. R. (1924). The judiciality of minimum-wage legislation. *Harvard Law Review, 37*(5), 545–573.

Power, M. (1999). Parasitic-industries analysis and arguments for a living wage for women in the early twentieth-century United States. *Feminist Economics, 5*(1), 61–78.

Prasch, R. (1996). The origins of the *a priori* method in classical political economy: A reinterpretation. *Journal of Economic Issues, 30*(4), 1105–1125.

Prasch, R. (1997). International trade, machinery, and the remuneration of labor: A reexamination of the argument in the third edition of Ricardo's *Principles of political economy and taxation.* In: J. Henderson (Ed.), *The state of the history of economics* (pp. 68–80). New York: Routledge.

Prasch, R. (1998). American economists and minimum wage legislation during the Progressive Era: 1912–1923. *Journal of the History of Economic Thought, 20*(2), 161–175.

Prasch, R. (1999). American economists in the Progressive Era on the minimum wage. *Journal of Economic Perspectives, 13*(2), 221–230.

Prasch, R. (2000). John Bates Clark's defense of mandatory arbitration and minimum wage legislation. *Journal of the History of Economic Thought, 22*(2), 251–263.

Rauschenbusch, W. (1908). *Christianity and the social crisis.* New York: Macmillan.

Ricardo, D. (1821/1973). In: D. Winch (Ed.), *The principles of political economy and taxation* (3rd ed.). Rutland, VT: Charles E. Tuttle.

Rodgers, D. (1998). *Atlantic crossings: Social politics in a progressive age.* Cambridge, MA: Harvard University Press.

Rogers, J. (1890). *Six centuries of work and wages: The history of English labor.* New York: G.P. Putnam & Sons.

Rutherford, M. (2000). Understanding institutional economics: 1918–1929. *Journal of the History of Economic Thought, 22*(3), 277–308.

Ryan, J. (1902a). The laborer's right to a living wage. *Catholic University Bulletin,* 156–174.

Ryan, J. (1902b). The ethics of speculation. *International Journal of Ethics,* 335–347.

Ryan, J. (1906). *A living wage: Its ethical and economic aspects.* New York: Macmillan.

Ryan, J. (1910a). Minimum wages and wage boards. *The Survey, 24,* 810–820.

Ryan, J. (1910b). A minimum wage and wage boards: With especial reference to immigrant labor and woman labor. *Proceedings of the National Conference of Charities and Correction,* Boston: George H. Ellis.

Ryan, J. (1913). Minimum wage legislation. *Catholic World, 96,* 575, 577–586.

Ryan, J. (1915). Statement of John A. Ryan. Fourth Report I, Appendix III, State of New York Factory Investigating Commission Albany, NY.

Ryan, J. (1916). *Distributive justice: The right and wrong of our present distribution of wealth.* New York: Macmillan.

Ryan, J. (1918). The supreme court and child labor. *Catholic World, 108*(November), 212–223.

Ryan, J. (1920a). A living wage. In: J. Ryan & J. Husslein (Eds), *The Church and labor* (pp. 259–271). New York: Macmillan.

Ryan, J. (1920b). *Social reconstruction.* New York: Macmillan.

Ryan, J. (1923a). *The supreme court and the minimum wage.* New York: The Paulist Press.

Ryan, J. (1923b). *Minimum wage administration.* United States Bureau of Labor Statistics Bulletin no. 323, Misc. Series 30. Government Printing Office, Washington, DC, pp. 132–135.

Ryan, J. (1927). *Declining liberty and other papers.* New York: Macmillan.

Ryan, J. (1941). *Social doctrine in history: A personal history.* New York: Harper & Bros.

Ryan, J., & Husslein, J. (Eds). (1920). *The Church and labor.* New York: Macmillan.

Seager, H. R. (1913). The theory of the minimum wage. *American Labor Legislation Review, 3,* 81–91.

Seager, H. R. (1917). *Principles of economics* (2nd Rev. ed.). New York: Henry Holt.

Seligman, E. (1915). Testimony on wages and wage legislation. Fourth Report. New York State Factory Investigating Committee, Vol. 5, J.B. Lyon, New York, pp. 2764–2769.

Seligman, E. (1923). *Principles of economics: With special reference to American conditions* (3rd ed.). New York: Longmans, Green & Co.

Skocpol, T. (1992). *Protecting soldiers and mothers: The political origins of social policy in the United States.* Cambridge, MA: Harvard University Press.

Smith, A. (1976). *An inquiry into the nature and causes of the wealth of nations.* Chicago: University of Chicago Press.

Steinfeld, R. (1991). *The invention of free labor: The employment relation in English and American law and culture, 1350–1870.* Chapel Hill, NC: University of North Carolina Press.

Stigler, G. J. (1945). The cost of subsistence. *Journal of Farm Economics, 27*(2), 303–314.

Storrs, L. (2000). *Civilizing capitalism: The national consumers' league, women's activism, and labor standards in the New Deal era.* Chapel Hill, NC: University of North Carolina Press.

Taussig, F. (1916). Minimum wages for women. *Quarterly Journal of Economics, 30*(3), 411–442.

Tribe, L. (1978). *American constitutional law.* Mineola, NY: Foundation Press.

Waltman, J. (2000). *The politics of the minimum wage.* Chicago: University of Illinois Press.

Webb, S., & Webb, B. ([1897] 1920). *Industrial democracy.* New York: Longmans, Green & Co.

Zimmerman, J. (1991). The jurisprudence of equality: The women's minimum wage, the first equal rights amendment, and *Adkins v. Children's Hospital,* 1905–1923. *Journal of American History, 78*(1), 188–225.

HISTORY OF ECONOMICS AND HISTORY OF SCIENCE: A COMPARATIVE LOOK AT RECENT WORK IN BOTH FIELDS

Ross B. Emmett

Margaret Schabas' (1992) "Breaking away" manifesto called for the historians of economics to identify themselves more with their colleagues in the history of science and less with those in the discipline of economics. Her "Coming together" update (2002) assessed what historians of economics had been doing since 1992, showing that some progress has been made toward her goal, but that much remained to be done. Central to Schabas' efforts is the claim that the history of economics needs to stop being simply the vindication of the discipline of economics (economists do not need it, so why chase after them?); implicitly her argument is that the history of science stopped providing a vindication of modern science some time ago. My own contribution to the debate over Schabas' manifesto (Emmett, 1997) did not examine the existing literature on the history of economics in light of Schabas' manifesto, but instead focused on how one's understanding of the relation between the community of historians of science and scientific communities could assist with reconstructing the relation between the community of historians of economics and the scientific community of economists. Like Schabas, I argued that historians of economics, qua historians, share more with historians of science than they

A Research Annual
Research in the History of Economic Thought and Methodology, Volume 28-A, 71–94
Copyright © 2010 by Emerald Group Publishing Limited
All rights of reproduction in any form reserved
ISSN: 0743-4154/doi:10.1108/S0743-4154(2010)000028A006

do with economists, although I simultaneously suggested the relation was
more nuanced than Schabas suggests, given that the rational reconstruction
of past arguments may be part of economic thought today[1] and that just
as historians of science have used sociology and are beginning to use
economics to explain the history of science, historians of economics may end
up using the discipline they study to explain its own history.

The philosophical and methodological vision behind Schabas' manifesto
was fleshed out in Wade Hand's (2001) *Reflection without Rules*, which won
the Joseph Spengler award for the best book in the history of economics
from the History of Economics Society (HES) in 2002. Why did a book on
economic methodology win the prize for the history of economics? If the
rules regarding what constitutes scientific knowledge are contested, then,
Hands argues, communities of scientists cannot turn to the philosophers of
science to tell them what constitutes scientific knowledge or progress. They
construct the rules themselves in their communities' theories and practices.
Indeed, economists, like most scientists, do not spend their days wondering
if their models constitute "good science" – they spend their days using and
improving their models, which also means they spend time finding data,
improving the tools they use to evaluate the models and data, teaching,
seeking grant monies, persuading others that their improved models work
well, and so on. Contemporary science theory reminds us that scientists
engage in the same types of activities we do and have no special access to the
progress of knowledge.

Historians of science and economics are also freed, because Hands' story
allows us to stop telling the story of how and why scientific advancement
occurred by the rules set by some undefined standard. Historians can focus
on historical reconstruction – sorting out and telling how scientists and
economics in particular time and places worked, what tools they developed
to assist them with their activities, why they considered the products of
their work to constitute contributions to knowledge, and how others were
persuaded of the scientific status of their work. What were the rules by
which "science" survived and thrived in the past? Such an endeavor is
illuminating, even if we cannot say that the rules were correct, or even that
the conclusions scientists in the past reached helped us to understand better
what the correct rules for scientific knowledge are. As Hands reminds us
at the end of his introduction, a viewpoint such as the one he identifies,
and which I will argue underlies much of the work currently being done
in the history of science (if not always in the history of economics), "is not
inconsistent with the basic Enlightenment commitment to science as a
uniquely worthy form of life" (Hands, 2001, p. 8). And I might add that it

does nothing to deny that the historical study of scientific and economic knowledge in the past remains a worthy act of appreciation for that unique form of life.

One way to evaluate whether the history of economics has moved toward the history of science is to compare recent work in both fields. To narrow the comparison in two rapidly expanding publication areas, I decided to examine two corresponding sets of literature in each field: the articles and books to which the HES and the History of Science Society (HSS) awarded their best article and best book prizes. An older organization, HSS has been awarding prizes for the best book in the field since 1959 and has awarded a prize for the best article since 1979. HES started in the mid-1970s and began awarding its best article award in 1995.[2] The HES best book award was initiated in 2004, which provided the starting point for my comparison. The winners of the awards from both societies over the period from 2004 to 2008 form the basis for my comparison.[3] We have already met one of those winners – Hand's *Reflection without Rules*. Despite the appropriateness of the choice of Hands' book for the first HES Spengler Award because it identifies the historiographic vision that underlies recent work in the history of science, his book itself is not a history; not even a history of the recent developments in science studies. But if we cannot place it among the other studies, we can use the questions Hands raises for us as we examine the other winners. What do the new studies in the history of science and economics look like? Do they look increasingly alike as they depart from the quest to judge the growth of scientific and economic knowledge by some set of external standards? Are these fields, as Schabas desires, becoming unified? These questions will be addressed, but first, let us look at the authors.

THE AUTHORS

The history of science prizes have been awarded to 12 individuals (8 individual authors and 2 sets of coauthors). The history of economics prizes have been awarded to 10 individual authors (no coauthored papers). Seven of the 10 economics prize winners are located in economics departments; the others are in history;[4] business history (McCraw); and the history of political thought (Hont). Six of the 12 history of science prize winners are located in history of science programs;[5] four more are in history departments;[6] one is in a classics department;[7] and one is in a geography department. Among the prize winners, then, the history of science is almost exclusively practiced by historians of science, whether they are in history of science departments or in history/classics departments, whereas the history of economics is primarily, but not exclusively, practiced by those in economics departments.[8] Although departmental affiliations can be deceiving and ever-changing, clearly Schabas has not convinced historians of economics to abandon the discipline of economics.

The geographer K. Maria Lane (Price/Webster Prize, 2006) comes the closest among the history of science prize winners to a typical historian of economics: She operates out of a geography department, teaching regular geography courses, but her research is in the history of the field. Ironically, the one economist in our group of authors who now teaches in a history department is the only author in either group whose award-winning article was published in a leading journal in a scientific field – the *Journal of Political Economy*.[9] However, two of those who have won HES book prizes do not actively participate in the field: Thomas McCraw is a business historian at Harvard,[10] and Istvan Hont is a historian of Enlightenment political theory and political economy at Cambridge.

Two of the most prominent programs in the history of science are responsible for more than half of the HSS prize winners: 7 of the 12 winners either received their Ph.D. from, or are employed by, the history of science and technology programs at Harvard University and Johns Hopkins University. If one looks back over the entire history of the HES's best article award, one would say that Duke University and Cambridge University are both well-represented among the winners of the Society's prizes, with four each.[11] But the more obvious division among the winners of the history of economics prizes we are considering is that more than half are from outside the United States – Europe (four), Australia (one), and Brazil (one). In fact, only four Americans have won the best article award since its inception (and two of those were coauthors), and no member of an American economics department has won the award since 2002.[12] In the group we are considering, the only HSS prize winner outside North America is in Europe (Marc J. Ratcliff).

Two of the best article award-winning authors won their respective prize for the second time during the five years we are looking at here. Thomas Hankins of the University of Washington won the Price/Webster Price in its second year – 1980 (Hankins, 1977). And Mauro Boianovsky of the University of Brasilia won the HES best article award in 1999 (Boianovsky, 1998). Only one author has won both the best article and the best book prizes from either society: Deborah Harkness (1997, 2007).[13]

Among historians of any ilk, books are the signature achievements. But the pressure from other disciplines for tenure and promotion criteria to reflect primarily the number of articles one produces may work against junior faculty who focus on book-length treatments. So how do junior and senior faculty among our prize winners compare in terms of articles versus books? Among our prizewinning best article authors, 8 of the 11 could be classified as junior faculty, and the one coauthored article was written by a former graduate student and his thesis supervisor. Among the best book authors, only two of the authors could be considered junior faculty; most are senior fellows who are well-known for their previous work.[14]

Finally, none of the past five prizewinners of either the Spengler or the HES best article prizes was a woman. Two women have won the Pfizer Prize in the past five years, and one woman the Price/Webster Prize.

A SIMPLE FRAMEWORK TO GUIDE OUR COMPARISON

I struggled to find an appropriate means by which to compare these works. Despite their commonalities, they are a disparate lot. They cross centuries: Although most examine the economics or science of the mid-nineteenth to mid-twentieth centuries, one winner of an article prize examines optic science in the ancient Greeks, and several book awards have gone to histories covering the sixteenth and the seventeenth centuries. Does geography matter? We not only have different parts of Europe at times when the differences mattered more than they do even today but also some studies focused on urban life and other focused on rural life. One could even argue that changes in modes of transportation matter to the histories being told for both the communication among scholars and the location of scientific endeavors. Our studies cross topics: from alchemy and chemistry to international trade, ethology, the combination of geography and astronomy, biology, mathematical economics, optics, equilibrium theory, physics, innovation and economic development, as well as graphs and diagrams of several types. One article even covers the location and design of corporate research facilities.

Several studies emphasize beginnings: the creation of a science, the initiation of a research program, new ways of envisioning natural and social phenomena, and the invention of a graphing technique or a diagram. Others challenge claims to origins: Are the claims for various revolutions in scientific and economic knowledge really valid? Who really was revolutionary? Who is responsible for a particular diagram? And some stories even record deaths – not only of people but also of sciences and ways of doing science.

Philosophical and methodological concerns abound: The role of induction and empirical research in the creation of knowledge appears frequently, as do what we today often refer to as boundary concerns – where does one discipline end and another begin, what is the difference between science and nonscience? There are biographies, and even some autobiographical material, but while most use biographical materials, their focus is usually not biographical. They also employ different types of historiographic approaches. Most of the studies fall under the rubric often described as historical reconstruction – the situating of theory, scientists, and their tools in their contemporary environment. However, we have several studies that focus more on representational or rhetorical strategy, and at least one rationally reconstructs the work of the past for the purpose of improving our treatment of issues today.

One thing they all share is historical sources: with one quite understandable exception,[15] every winner uses primary source materials other than published texts in their research. Personal correspondence, unpublished drafts of papers and reports, oral history, diaries, scientific journals, laboratory reports, and so on all find their place among the award winners.

So how can these award-winning books and articles be organized for comparative purposes that would be useful for the purpose of considering the progress of Schabas' call for historians of economics to become like historians of science? In the end, I decided on a simple heuristic that will allow me to address that purpose.

Imagine, if you will, a long table. Draped across the table is an even longer cloth. At one end of the table is a little sign that reads "Ideas." A similar sign at the other end reads "Practices." Halfway between the two is a third sign – "People." Admittedly crude, this imaginary table allows us to place the books relative to each other along a spectrum running from a primary focus on ideas to a primary focus on practices (Fig. 1). The table also allows us to see that movement away from the ends inevitably moves us toward a consideration of people. The central role of people is also indicative of the role that people play as the mediators between ideas and practices; thus, studies that focus exclusively on ideas will seldom deal with practices (and vice versa), but those that do incorporate personal material regarding the scientist(s) will often do so in the process of describing how ideas and practices intersect. Finally, the heuristic raises the interesting question of whether the history of practices might not have more in common with the history of ideas than it does with biography. Or, to put it positively,

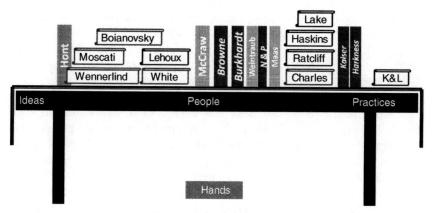

Fig. 1. The Books and Articles Arranged.

to the extent that histories of ideas begin to incorporate the people thinking about the ideas, they may look similar to the histories of practices that also incorporate material about the people undertaking them. Words are deeds, as Wittgenstein said.

So much for the organizing heuristic, now let us use it to see if it helps work through the differences among our award-winning books and articles.

IDEAS ↔ PEOPLE

At the core of the old approach to the history of science and economics was the assumption that what mattered were the theories and ideas of scientists and economists and that the history of scientific/economic knowledge was story of the development of better theories to replace previous ones through a rational process. A common heuristic device was the association of theories with particular people or groups, and historical information about those individuals or groups was accepted as useful background knowledge for historians to employ in constructing the sequence of theoretical development. The transition from Smithian "absolute advantage" to Ricardian "comparative advantage" and then to the Heckscher/Ohlin emendations of Ricardo, leading to the Heckscher–Ohlin–Samuelson model, provides a common economic example. Problematize that model by introducing the Leontief paradox and challenge it with Krugman's geography of trade and you have a nice heuristic for remembering the development of international trade theory, capped at each post-1950 point by a Nobel prize winner. If the people behind the names were relevant to that development, the story often focused on how they came to their ideas, often against great odds. But this personal history, as George Stigler (1965, 1982) argued, was incidental ultimately to the history of ideas, which were science itself.

A quick look at Fig. 1 will show that the "Ideas" end of the table is less occupied than the "Practices" end is, and most of the works are arranged toward the middle of the table. But we will start with the clearest example of a "history of ideas" approach among our award winners: Istvan's Hont's *Jealousy of Trade*. Hont tells us right up front that the purpose of his study is "to identify political insights in eighteenth-century theories of international market rivalry that continue to be relevant for the twenty-first century" (Hont, 2005, p. 4). He goes on to remark that intellectual history is most useful when "it unmasks impasses and eliminates repetitive patterns of controversy" (Hont, 2005, p. 4). *Jealousy of Trade*, he tells us, has its "eyes firmly fixed on the challenges of today" (Hont, 2005, p. 5). Here is a history congruent with Cristina Marcuzzo's (2008) argument that the history of economic thought is (to quote a historian of scientific thought) "one long argument" (Mayer, 1993) and that a study of the essential components of the argument at some point in the past can illuminate our concerns today. In his essay on the "Rich-Country-Poor Country" debate (Hont, 2005, pp. 267–322), for example, he rationally reconstructs David Hume's argument in a 12-step process that those engaged in similar debates today over outsourcing and international trade could easily use to defend a nuanced version of the free trade argument. Using historical documents unavailable to most of Hume's contemporaries,[16] Hont shows that the argument was indeed coherent and makes sense in the context of contemporary debate. Furthermore, he shows why the contributions of Scottish political economy (especially Hume and Adam Smith) ended the prospects of meaningful discussion of commercial society within the confines of the language of civic humanism. In other words, Hont's argument is built on the assumption that the Enlightenment project remains an integral part of modern discourse and that rationally reconstructing the work of its earliest proponents can illuminate contemporary (in both senses of the word!) discourse.

Even though Hont's book is firmly in the "history of ideas" camp, you will notice that it is not at the extreme end of the table. Hont's work is in the Cambridge tradition of historiography (Skinner, [1969] 1988; Tully, 1988; Pocock, 2009), which seeks to interpret work in the context of available meanings at the time, before seeking to consider how its ideas may be transplanted to today. Inevitably, then, Hont has to consider the thinker – in his case, usually David Hume or Adam Smith – and the context in which Hume and Smith operated. The Cambridge tradition has, in fact, prided itself on examining the meaning of ideas in their context. At the same time, the context Hont uses is more narrowly defined than it will be in the case of the other works at this end of the table.

Similar to Hont's historical concerns are those of two of the best article award winners, one each from the history of science and the history of economics. Careful textual analysis and awareness of the context of surrounding arguments distinguish the essays by Daryn Lehoux (2007) and Carl Wennerlind (2005) from other efforts to settle questions about the meaning of central themes in their respective subjects' work (for Lehoux, Gallen, and Ptolemy; for Wennerlind, Hume). Yet, both authors also have concerns about how contemporary theorists might appropriate their interpretation of past theorists. Lehoux begins and ends his essay with a discourse on the problem (optical and perspectival) of what we see when we look in the mirror. Wennerlind published his essay on Hume in the journal of the economics department at the University of Chicago, the foremost articulator of the quantity theory of money in recent times. Although Wennerlind makes no comment about the connection between Hume's treatment of inflation and the quantity theory in the paper, the fact that he sought to publish the paper in the *Journal of Political Economy* makes the statement for him!

One other work deliberately makes a connection between the history of ideas and their present day use. Thomas McCraw's biography of Joseph Schumpeter, otherwise devoted to the historical reconstruction of a person's life and ideas, also focuses on the contribution of a past thinker to present problems. The title *Prophet of Innovation*, of course, is forward-looking, and McCraw tells us right at the beginning that "the phenomenon of capitalist innovation" is as much the subject of his book as Schumpeter himself is (McCraw, 2007, p. ix). He also concludes the book with a chapter on Schumpeter's legacy for both modern economists and modern innovators/ entrepreneurs. However, his biographical focus, as we will see later, more often keeps his attention elsewhere. On our table diagram (Fig. 1), McCraw sits on the "Ideas" side table in recognition of this dual focus.

The other three items on the left side of Fig. 1 are placed between "Ideas" and "People" for slightly different reasons. Like Wennerlind, the articles by Mauro Boianovsky (2006) and White (2004) focus on the interpretation of specific portions of the work of a past economist – Don Patinkin and William Stanley Jevons, respectively. Although the primary focus of their work remains the historical reconstruction of the meaning of specific texts, they have no direct concern for the consequences of their findings on contemporary theory.[17] In Boianovsky's case, the problem is accounting for Patinkin's efforts to explain involuntary unemployment as a disequilibrium phenomenon as he struggled to write two key chapters in his *Money, Interest and Prices* (Patinkin, 1956). Bioanovsky considers Patinkin's correspondence with other theorists, his reflections on Keynes and on the Chicago tradition of monetary theory, and his use of standard tools in monetary theory as he tells the story of Patinkin's writing task. White shows how apparent confusions in Jevons' marginal analysis can be clarified by considering changes in his understanding of the conservation principles in physics.[18] White's analysis requires careful comparison of the breadth of Jevons' scientific work, not only his economic concerns, over a multiyear period.

The other work included in this space is the article on consumer demand theorists by Ivan Moscati. Moscati's article is difficult to categorize for two reasons. On the one hand, his purpose is to provide an account of the economists' indifference to the early experimental findings regarding consumer demand that turns on their desire to protect their theory from attack, especially attacks that appear as weak as they see the experimental findings to be. Moscati's purpose could imply the need for a richly textured examination of the theorists' professional lives, the nature of the evolving relations between disciplines from the interwar to the postwar period, and the type of epistemological claims that economists were willing to accept. He does provide accounts of the experiments the psychologists ran and how the experiments arose from the psychologists' interactions with the economists. However, although he admits that "the meager influence of the experimental research *may* be explained by bringing into play academic, social, political, or economic factors" (emphasis added), Moscati goes on to suggest a "purely epistemological" rationale: "empirical evidence contrary to a scientific theory can be always imputed to the failure of some auxiliary assumption" and "a scientific theory is rejected only if it can be replaced by a practical alternative" (Moscati, 2007, p. 393). Thus, the explanation he provides, on the other hand, is the evolution of ideas by logical progression, stripped of any role for the people involved. Although the epistemological claim may be logically sufficient, one wonders if the economists themselves ignored the experimental research on epistemological grounds or whether an appeal to other factors would strengthen the argument made. Caught between an account that points to the role of the personal, but ends up considering only the logical relation of ideas to each other, I placed Moscati in the middle of the "Ideas" side of the table.

PEOPLE

At the center of the table are two biographies: McCraw's biography of Joseph Schumpeter and the second volume of Janet Browne's two-volume biography of Charles Darwin. As we have already seen, these two books are not the only works that have biographical material, but they are the only Spengler or Price/Webster prize winners, which are full-length biographies. However, for all the reasons that the tension between context and progress are present in the histories told among our prize winners, biography is both welcomed and avoided. After all, historians and biographers have always had an on–again, off–again relationship. When intellectual development is emphasized, biography is denigrated, except to the extent that people like to hear stories about great heroes they admire.[19] When the context of people and ideas is emphasized, the role of an individual scientist's life seems too unique to matter; we want general trends, networks, tools and techniques, and institutional explanations. Is the biographer merely serving as champion or executioner, thereby setting up the present as judge of the past?

Despite these reservations, a recent conference, and subsequent supplement to the *History of Political Economy* journal, made the case for the use of biography and other forms of life-writing by historians of economics. Biographers seem to be helping restore the relationship as well, if our award winners can be taken as representative of their fields. Browne and McCraw are two very good examples of biographies that may aid historical interpretation. Surprisingly, these biographies are of two individuals who have, in many ways, resisted "the turn to the personal" as part of the interpretation of their work. After all, Charles Darwin stands as one of the two iconic figures of modern science – everyone knows the names Darwin and Einstein, even if they do not know much about evolutionary biology or physics. And Joseph Schumpeter's theory of capitalism as "creative destruction" has long survived what waning interest there may be in the titillating details of the life of a man who once said his three goals were to be the greatest lover, the greatest horseman, and the greatest economist in the world.

Browne and McCraw make the details of these two central figures of the nineteenth and twentieth century respectively not only come to life but also become crucial to the interpretation of their work. In the concluding volume of Browne's two-part biography of Charles Darwin (2003; the first volume was Browne, 1996), she makes Darwin's own attachments to a life lived in a particular place and to the social necessity of detailed correspondence that his time and location required, integral to the interpretation of not only the theory of evolution but also the central role of the theory of natural selection in it. The garden in Darwin's home, and his vast correspondence, become the settings in which "he transformed his daily activities into scientific knowledge" (Browne, 2003, p. 202).

In McCraw's (2007) biography of Schumpeter, the story of his relationship with women does occupy a large amount of the book, but rather than just being the revelation of the details of his reputation as a womanizer, *Prophet of Innovation* portrays Schumpeter's relationships in a more complex, and hence more human, fashion. Although seemingly unconnected with his economic ideas, these relationships end up defining key elements of the development of his intellectual life, making biography essential to under-standing the meanings Schumpeter gave to his theoretical work: "Under a burden of almost unbearable grief [Schumpeter's mother, wife and newborn son all died within the space of two months in 1926], he again took up his mission of trying the unravel the enigmas of capitalism and human society. And over the next twenty-three years, often in the face of severe despondency, he produced a vast and incomparable body of work" (McCraw, 2007, p. 140).

If our lives, our tools, and our practices, even the warp and woof of our daily life, matter to the development of science, then studies of crucial junctures in that development, even though often misunderstood at the time or in our standard histories, can re-enliven our sense of how science moves forward. Put differently, biography reminds us that our histories are not clinical trials or reconstructed logical arguments, but narratives, with both a strong sense of plot and a keen desire to admire the richness of life as the stories move along.

PRACTICES ↔ PEOPLE

The most succinct statement of the historiographic vision behind the work at the "Practices" end of the table is provided by David Kaiser's history of the Feynman diagrams in postwar theoretical physics. In contrast to work focused on the historiography of the progress of scientific "Ideas" – the other end of the table – Kaiser argues that

> a rival vision of how to analyze work in theoretical sciences has begun to take shape. Building upon these studies, this book begins with a simple premise: since at least the middle of the twentieth century ... most theorists have not spent their days ... in some philosopher's dreamworld, weighing one cluster of disembodied concepts against another, picking and choosing among so many theories or paradigms. Rather, their main task has been to calculate. ... They have accomplished [this task] by fashioning theoretical tools and performing calculations ... These tools have provided the currency of everyday work. (Kaiser, 2005, pp. 8–9, emphasis in original)

The histories on this side of the table in Fig. 1, then, historically reconstruct the practices and tools of scientists and economists in their own settings. Just as tools and practices appear in the studies at the other end of the table as means by which to communicate ideas, ideas here provide the opportunity for scientists to engage in the tasks of measurement, calculation, persuasion, model-building, grant-writing, corresponding with others, and even teaching, and also appear as the consequence, often fleeting, sometimes unintentional, of those tasks.

Kaiser's history of the Feynman diagrams is a wonderful representative of what a focus on practices can achieve. Feynman himself makes few appearances in the book, because beyond the first chapter, it is not about his creation of the diagrams. Rather, Kaiser tells the story of how the diagrams were dispersed across the theoretical physics discipline and how they were adapted by others in the process, sometimes for the own purposes, and sometimes in ways that clarified or standardized them. In fact, the book is almost the biography of a tool. The people who appear in Kaiser's book are those responsible for the dispersion of the diagrams: Freeman Dyson, Tomonaga Sin-itiro, and Geoffrey Chew, to name just a few of the young theorists in whose hands the Feynman diagrams were put to use. But Kaiser's focus remains on the diagrams, almost as if the people become the instruments by which the diagrams take on a life of their own as they are passed around the world and across time. Much like Darwin's garden in the hands of Janet Browne, the physicists' lives and seminar rooms become the setting in which Kaiser displays the tool at work.

Another example will help strengthen our sense of the distance the literature at the "Practices" end of the table stands from, not only from a focus on "Ideas" but also from the biographies located at the middle of our table. Deborah Harkness's *The Jewel House* examines scientific and medical practice in London at the beginning of the "Scientific Revolution." In a particularly effective chapter, Harkness points out that Elizabethan projects share some similarities with "Big Science" today – the royal promotion of "all good sciences and wise and learned inventions tending to the benefit of the commonwealth of our said Realm and Dominions, and serving for the defense thereof" (Harkness, 2007, pp. 143–144). Her real purpose in talking of "Big Science," however, is to goad us into realizing that Elizabethan projects did not stand at the beginning of a continuous line of scientific progress leading to "Big Science" today. Instead, they were the consequence of their context – the city of London. London provided the means and context within which the various tensions between the private profits and the common good were worked out, often in unexpected ways involving the interests and actions of "vernacular practitioners" who have often been overlooked in constructing the history of science (Harkness, 2007, p. 260). Scientific progress, if we can even use that term, occurs in her account quite decidedly outside the realm of research laboratories we know from traditional histories of science.

In Harkness' book, the scientists of our usual stories hold a backseat to the "vernacular practitioners" she concentrates attention on, but they do remain actors. Slightly to the right of her book on our table lies an article that is the only work on the table in which scientists or economists matter almost not at all for the story. Scott Knowles and Stuart Leslie's (2001) examination of Eero Saarinen's corporate research campuses focuses on an architect who was commissioned by GM, IBM, and AT&T to design research facilities in the postwar period. In each case, the facility designed by Saarinen is more of a statement about the perceived status of scientific knowledge in society than it is a setting in which scientific knowledge can be pursued. Ironically, where a "nonscientific" setting assists the progress of science in Harkness' account of Elizabethan London, the "industrial Versailles" of Saarinen's research facilities hinder it in Knowles and Leslie's account. Turns out scientists do not work the way Saarinen imagined they did!

Between Kaiser's biography of the Feynman diagrams and the center of the table lie two groups: one of four books, and one of four articles. They are not grouped that way to keep the books (or articles) together but rather because the two groups have somewhat different mixtures of practices and people. The books lie closer to the middle because they also show how a treatment of practices can intersect (through people) with our understanding of ideas.

All of the books are boundary stories concerned with transitions between types of scientific activity. Newman and Principe (2002) have a story about the birth of the Scientific Revolution that is similar to Harkness', although somewhat narrower in focus and breadth of vision. They focus on the origins of modern chemistry, complicating the usual story by looking in detail at George Starkey's alchemical experiments and Boyle's metaphysical speculations to argue that the process of transition from alchemy to chemistry is far more complicated than many scientists would wish. Who really was revolutionary anyway?

Richard Burkhardt (2005) tells us the story of the emergence of the science of ethology by Niko Tinbergen and Konrad Lorenz in the 1930s. For Lorenz and Tinbergen, animal behavior was best studied in natural settings; their ethology was a radical departure from animal studies based on physiological investigation. Among other things, the ethologist had to go to the animals, rather than have dead specimens brought to them; ethologists, therefore, pioneered the creation of field stations and the practices of animal observation associated with them. But they also had to defend their science, both within biology and in the general public. Burkhardt's story, therefore, tells us not only of the practices that Tinbergen and Lorenz adopted but also the justifications they provided to defend their new science and the conclusions they arrived at. His book is the closest of this group to a full-length biography (and located on our table that way), but all of the books in this group incorporate elements of biography.

Roy Weintraub (2002) examines how twentieth-century economists' use of mathematics reflected their understanding of what mathematics was becoming and how different approaches to math infiltrated economics and econometrics. Gerard Debreu's mathematical economics was shaped by the prominence of Nicholas Bourbaki in French mathematical education when Debreu was trained at L'École Normale Supérieure. The mathematician Cecil Phipps and the economist Don Patinkin reached an impasse in regard to the econometric evaluation of Patinkin's work because they worked from different assumptions regarding the use of mathematics in economics. Sidney Weintraub (nonmathematical economist) asked his brother Hal (mathematician) for assistance in finding a mathematical means of expressing Sidney's economic theories. That collaboration (never quite successful) led Hal to suggest some ways in which new models of economics could be elaborated using work he was doing in physics. Through all these stories, Weintraub shows how the intersection of economics and mathematics was not as clearly marked as standard histories would suggest. Weintraub's book incorporates one other element that is not present elsewhere in the award winners: autobiography. His own story of how he came from mathematics to economics provided a fitting conclusion both to the story of his father's and uncle's uneasy relations over economics and mathematics and to the story of how economics came to mathematics. What had been an uneasy relationship for those educated before World War II became easy for those educated in the 1950s and 1960s, because economics "had become a science of building, calibrating, tuning, testing, and utilizing models constructed out of mathematical and statistical-econometric materials" (Weintraub, 2002). Sounds a lot like Kaiser! (Snide remark: if theoretical economists calculate like theoretical physicists, calibrate like theoretical physicists, and test like theoretical physicists, are they theoretical physicists?)

We have already met William Stanley Jevons in White's award-winning article on Jevons' use of the conservation principles in his treatment of marginal principle. Harro Maas (2005) takes up the larger task of examining the philosophical and scientific background of Jevons economics. Frequently, such a contextual work would be placed on the other side of the table in Fig. 1: we would see Jevons' economic work in its intellectual context. But Jevons was a participant in scientific work in several fields during his lifetime, and Maas tells us a story that enriches our knowledge of Jevons' intellectual context with detailed consideration of his scientific practice and its relation to his thinking about induction, the mind, and the world in which we live, including the economy.

The four articles form a separate group from the four books in this area of the table in Fig. 1 because they all deal, in one way or another, with the problem of representation, a common theme today in science studies and the humanities. K. Maria Lake (2005) explains the role that geographers with experience in cartography had in creating astronomy's common perception of the surface of Mars in the late nineteenth century. Inexperienced in astronomical observation, but well-equipped with the cartographic techniques that had shaped the way people, including astronomers, understood the relation of geographic forms on the Earth's surface, the geographers were given the opportunity to assist with charting the surface of Mars at a particularly advantageous moment in the two planets' orbits around the Sun. Although the geographers' drawings did not exactly match those of the astronomers, familiarity with the geographers' forms and public admiration of the geographers' exploration of unknown places on Earth led to their adoption, which shaped the way we saw Mars for most of the twentieth century. Lake's primary interest, therefore, is in the way the representation of Mars played a rhetorical function in social and scientific persuasion.

Similar types of argument are found in the studies by Marc Ratcliff (2004) and Hankins (2006). Ratcliff's study of Abraham Trembley's generous dissemination of living specimens of polyps for others to observe and experiment on through dissection. Ratcliff argues that Trembley's generosity created widespread knowledge, among both the scientists and the public, of a poorly understood creature, a willingness to allow experiments that had previously been viewed with some suspicion and new techniques of both transportation of living specimens and experimentation. Thomas Hankins' most recent award-winning article uses various biographical materials and correspondence to explain John Herschel's defense of graphical methods in debates during the 1830s with the likes of William Whewell. Back in the late 1970s, when the history of science was firmly in the "history of ideas" camp, Hankins opened the door for the development of historiographic methods with his defense of biography in the history of science (Hankins, 1979).

His new article is similar in style to history of economics articles that lie on the other end of the table, except that his focus is not on an idea but rather on a graphical method. Hankins uses Herschel's defense of his graphical method for finding the orbit of double stars to bring together the common story about Herschel's place in the history of astronomy and his less well-known participation in the philosophical debate over the nature of induction and scientific knowledge. The interest of Herschel and other natural philosophers in graphs, Hankins argues, came despite their disagreement on the nature of scientific method and nature of induction, because "graphs brought the hand and the eye to the aid of the mind. They gave shape to the numbers, shape that pictured the regularities hidden in them" (Hankins, 2006, p. 633). Herschel's place in both the theoretical and the philosophical stories was secured, Hankins argues, because of his graphical methods. Thus, Hankins' article shares similarities with both Kaiser and Maas and joins the other representational articles between them.

Loic Charles' (2003) article on Quesnay's *Tableau Economique* was awarded the best article award after a virtuoso performance at the HES meeting. How appropriate that his article is the closest, among the history of economics award winners, to the science studies focused solely on practices. And yet ideas are not lost here but illuminated by his overturning of the quest for the key to how Quesnay used his *Tableau* as a model (after Hankins and Kaiser and White and so on, might one not be forgiven for assuming that if it is a graph it must be a model? Charles response, no, not if you had bothered to figure out how images like the *Tableau* were used in France!). Charles (2003, p. 544) argues that "the creation of the Tableau was of paramount importance in the development of Quesnay's economic thinking. It gave concrete shape to Quesnay's intuition of the economy as a set of economic variables interrelated by arithmetical ratios on the basis of which he was able to build a whole model." But the *Tableau* itself was not the model: it was the representation of the economy that allowed Quesnay to begin.

IS THE HISTORY OF ECONOMICS DRAWING CLOSER TO THE HISTORY OF SCIENCE?

If we return to the table in Fig. 1, we can make a preliminary response to question that introduces our conclusion.

Suppose you and I stand on opposite sides of the table in the middle and take hold of the cloth at the mid-point, right between McCraw's biography of Schumpeter and Browne's biography of Darwin. Now let us lift the cloth up as if we were creating a pyramid, allowing the books and papers that had been sitting on the cloth to tumble toward either end of the table. What would be the result?

On the "Ideas" end of the table, we would find Hont, Lehoux, Wennerlind, Boianovsky, White, Moscati, and McCraw. Seven items in all: six of the nine history of economics award winners (remember, Hands was already off the table), and only one of the history of science award winners. On the "Practices" end, we would find Weintraub, Knowles and Leslie, Harkness, Browne, Kaiser, Newman and Principe, Lake, Charles, Ratcliff, Maas, and Hankins. Twelve items in all: 9 of the 10 history of science winners, and only 3 of the history of economics award winners.

The conclusion of our study of the award-winning works themselves is as clear as our result when we looked at the authors: Just as historians of economics are not leaving economics departments to join Schabas in a history or history of science department, the works they are writing remain, by and large, histories of ideas. Although historians of science now predominately write about scientific practices, historians of economics continue to write predominantly about ideas.

For those who would like to see the history of economics begin to move toward the history of practices, some hope can be seen in the increasing attention paid by historians of ideas to the role that the economist plays in the creation and dissemination of ideas and to the interaction between economists and others (in our award winners, it is usually other social scientists or mathematicians) in the process of creating, defending, and disseminating their theories. And, of course, they could also simply go out and write better histories, thereby winning the best book and article awards themselves!

NOTES

1. Is rational reconstruction a part of the history of science? The evidence of the books and articles covered in my comparison suggests that it is not. Perhaps here, we come to a difference in our perception of the history of social thought and the history of natural science: Many people, both in the social sciences and in society generally, believe that the ideas of past social and economic thinkers have relevance today, whereas few believe the same about past scientists. Whatever the relation of our recovery of their ideas may be, we all may be Keynesians once again, but we are unlikely to ever again be followers of Helmontian chymistry.

2. One difference between the societies' respective best article prizes is that while the HSS limits its selection to articles published in the Society's journal *Isis*, the HES accepts nominations of articles published in any journal.

3. See appendix for a list of the award winners and more about the prizes.

4. Carl Wennerlind, who has a Ph.D. in economics, is located in the history department of Barnard College, Columbia University.

5. Two of the historians of science – David Kaiser and Laurence Principe – share their appointments with departments in the natural sciences (Kaiser in physics; Principe in chemistry). Kaiser, however, is the only active scientific researcher.

6. Two of the historians have Ph.D. in the history of science: Richard Burkhardt, Jr., and Scott Knowles.

7. Daryn Lehoux – the classicist – has a Ph.D. in the history of science and technology.

8. The author of this article has a Ph.D. in economics and has been appointed in economics departments but currently is appointed in an undergraduate liberal arts college of public affairs located in Michigan State University (James Madison College). I have adjunct status in the economics department.

9. Wennerlind also happens to be Schabas' coeditor of a volume of essays on David Hume's political economy (Wennerlind & Schabas, 2007).

10. Winner of the Pulitzer Prize in 1987 for *Prophets of Regulation* (McCraw, 1986). Note the similarity in title to his book on Schumpeter.

11. If we add Boianovsky (2006), which was written while the author was visiting in Duke's economics department, we have to give Duke the nod.

12. In fact, the only members of American economics departments to win the best article prize since its inception are David M. Levy (2002) and Craufurd Goodwin (1998). Goodwin's coauthor was a student who has become the partner of an investment firm.

13. Lest one suspect that the HSS granted Harkness both awards for the same work, her earlier work on the Dee family plays only a small role in *The Jewel House* (Harkness, 2007, pp. 222–223), although it did become the basis for another book (Harkness, 1999).

14. The latter group includes the two coauthors of the 2005 Pfizer prize: William Newman and Lawrence Principe.

15. Daryn Lehoux only uses extant texts from Greek philosophy.

16. Anticipating a point yet to be made, the use of archival materials is not enough to identify an author as a practitioner of the new history of economics/science.

17. Although White does use the opportunity to criticize a current, widely known, analysis of the history of economics (Mirowski, 1989), which contains the particular interpretation of Jevons, which White claims to be incorrect.

18. Part of the support for his argument comes from early versions of the work encapsulated in Maas' award-winning book (2005), which is placed elsewhere in Fig. 1.

19. Even George Stigler, for all his antipathy to biography, wrote memoirs (Stigler, 1988) and probably read early versions of the Friedman's *Two Lucky People* (Friedman & Friedman, 1998) with delight!

ACKNOWLEDGMENT

The author would like to thank the participants at the "History of Economics as History of Social Science" workshop, L'École Normale

Supérieure de Cachan, France, June 19, 2009 for comments on the figure and my comparison.

REFERENCES

Boianovsky, M. (1998). Wicksell on deflation in the early 1920s. *History of Political Economy*, *30*(2), 219–275.

Boianovsky, M. (2006). The making of chapters 13 and 14 of Patinkin's *Money, Interest, and Prices*. *History of Political Economy*, *38*(2), 193–249.

Browne, J. (1996). *Charles darwin: Voyaging*. Princeton, NJ: Princeton University Press.

Browne, J. (2003). *Charles Darwin: The power of place*. Princeton, NJ: Princeton University Press.

Burkhardt, R. W., Jr. (2005). *Patterns of behavior: Konrad Lorenz, Niko Tinbergen, and the founding of ethology*. Chicago, IL: University of Chicago Press.

Charles, L. (2003). The visual history of the *Tableau Économique*. *European Journal of the History of Economic Thought*, *10*(4), 527–550.

Emmett, R. B. (1997). Reflections on 'breaking away': Economics as science and the history of economics as the history of science. *Research in the History of Economic Thought and Methodology*, *15*, 221–236.

Friedman, M., & Friedman, R. D. (1998). *Two lucky people: Memoirs*. Chicago, IL: University of Chicago Press.

Hands, D. W. (2001). *Reflection without rules: Economic methodology and contemporary science theory*. Cambridge: Cambridge University Press.

Hankins, T. L. (1977). Triplets and triads: Sir William Rowan Hamilton on the metaphysics of mathematics. *Isis*, *68*(2), 175–193.

Hankins, T. L. (1979). In defence of biography: The use of biography in the history of science. *History of Science*, *17*(1), 1–16.

Hankins, T. L. (2006). A 'large and graceful sinuosity': John Herschel's graphical method. *Isis*, *97*(4), 605–633.

Harkness, D. E. (1997). Managing an experimental household: The Dees of Mortlake and the practice of natural philosophy. *Isis*, *88*(2), 247–262.

Harkness, D. E. (1999). *John Dee's conversations with angels: Cabala, Alchemy and the end of nature*. Cambridge: Cambridge University Press.

Harkness, D. E. (2007). *The jewel house: Elizabethan London and the scientific revolution*. New Haven, CT: Yale University Press.

Hont, I. (2005). *Jealousy of trade: International competition and the nation-state in historical perspective*. Cambridge, MA: Belknap Press.

Kaiser, D. (2005). *Drawing theories apart: The dispersion of feynman diagrams in postwar physics*. Chicago, IL: University of Chicago Press.

Knowles, S. G., & Leslie, S. W. (2001). 'Industrial versailles': Eero Saarinen's corporate campuses for GM, IBM, and AT&T. *Isis*, *92*(1), 1–33.

Lake, K. M. D. (2005). Geographers of mars: Cartographic description and exploration narrative in late Victorian representations of the red planet. *Isis*, *96*(4), 477–506.

Lehoux, D. (2007). Observers, objects, and the embedded eye: Or, seeing and knowing in Ptolemy and Galen. *Isis*, *98*(3), 447–467.

Maas, H. (2005). *William Stanley Jevons and the making of modern economics.* Cambridge: Cambridge University Press.

Marcuzzo, M. C. (2008). Is history of economic thought a 'serious' subject? *Erasmus Journal for Philosophy and Economics, 1*(1), 107–123.

Mayer, E. (1993). *One long argument: Charles Darwin and the genesis of modern evolutionary thought.* Cambridge, MA: Harvard University Press.

McCraw, T. K. (1986). *Prophets of regulation: Charles Francis Adams, Louis D. Brandeis, James M. Landis, Alfred E. Kahn.* Cambridge, MA: Harvard University Press.

McCraw, T. K. (2007). *Prophet of innovation: Joseph Schumpeter and creative destruction.* Cambridge, MA: Belknap Press.

Mirowski, P. (1989). *More heat than light: economics as social physics, physics as nature's economics.* Cambridge: Cambridge University Press.

Moscati, I. (2007). Early experiments in consumer demand theory, 1930–1970. *History of Political Economy, 39*(3), 359–401.

Newman, W. R., & Principe, L. M. (2002). *Alchemy tried in the fire: Starkey, Boyle, and the fate of Helmontian chymistry.* Chicago, IL: University of Chicago Press.

Patinkin, D. (1956). *Money, interest, and prices: An integration of monetary and value theory.* Evanston, IL: Row, Peterson.

Pocock, J. G. A. (2009). *Political theory and history: Essays on theory and method.* Cambridge: Cambridge University Press.

Ratcliff, M. J. (2004). Abraham Trembley's strategy of generosity and the scope of celebrity in the mid-eighteenth century. *Isis, 95*(4), 555–575.

Schabas, M. (1992). Breaking away: History of economics as history of science. *History of Political Economy, 24*(1), 187–203.

Schabas, M. (2002). Coming together: History of economics as history of science. In: E. R. Weintraub (Ed.), *The future of the history of economics* (pp. 208–225). Durham, NC: Duke University Press.

Skinner, Q. ([1969] 1988). Meaning and understanding in the history of ideas. In: J. Tully (Ed.), *Meaning & context: Quentin Skinner and his critics* (pp. 29–67). Princeton, NJ: Princeton University Press.

Stigler, G. J. (1965). Textual exegesis as a scientific problem. *Economica n.s., 32*(November), 447–450.

Stigler, G. J. (1982). The scientific uses of scientific biography, with special reference to J.S. Mill. In: *The economist as preacher and other essays* (pp. 86–97). Chicago, IL: University of Chicago Press.

Stigler, G. J. (1988). *Memoirs of an unregulated economist.* New York, NY: Basic Books.

Tully, J. (1988). *Meaning & context: Quentin Skinner and his critics.* Princeton, NJ: Princeton University Press.

Weintraub, E. R. (2002). *How economics became a mathematical science.* Durham, NC: Duke University Press.

Wennerlind, C. (2005). David Hume's monetary theory revisited: Was he really a quantity theorist and an inflationist? *Journal of Political Economy, 113*(1), 223–237.

Wennerlind, C., & Schabas, M. (Eds). (2007). *David hume's political economy.* London: Routledge.

White, M. V. (2004). In the lobby of the energy hotel: Jevons's formulation of the post-classical 'economic problem'. *History of Political Economy, 36*(2), 227–271.

APPENDIX A. BEST BOOK AWARD WINNERS

	Pfizer (HSS)	Spengler (HES)
2004	*Charles Darwin: The Power of Place* Janet Browne (Princeton University Press, 2003)	*Reflection without Rules: Economic Methodology & Contemporary Science Theory* D. Wade Hands (Cambridge University Press, 2001)
2005	*Alchemy Tried in the Fire: Starkey, Boyle, and the Fate of Helmontian Chymistry* William Newman and Lawrence Principe (University of Chicago Press, 2002)	*How Economics Became a Mathematical Science* E. Roy Weintraub (Duke University Press, 2002)
2006	*Patterns of Behavior: Konrad Lorenz, Niko Tinbergen, and the Founding of Ethology* Richard W. Burkhardt, Jr. (University of Chicago Press, 2005)	*William Stanley Jevons and the Making of Modern Economics* Harro Maas (Cambridge University Press, 2005)
2007	*Drawing Theories Apart: The Dispersion of Feynman Diagrams in Postwar Physics* David Kaiser (University of Chicago Press, 2005)	*Jealousy of Trade: International Competition and the Nation State* Istvan Hont (Belknap Press of Harvard University Press, 2005)
2008	*The Jewel House: Elizabethan London and the Scientific Revolution* Deborah E. Harkness (Yale University Press, 2007)	*Prophet of Innovation: Joseph Schumpeter and Creative Destruction* Thomas K. McCraw (Belknap Press of Harvard University Press, 2007)

History of Science Society (HSS): The Pfizer Prize is awarded annually to the author(s) of a book that is viewed by the selection committee as an outstanding contribution to the history of science. The book must have been published in English during the three years before the year in which the Pfizer Prize is awarded. Although books that contribute to the history of medicine or the history of science and technology may be considered, preference is given to books in the history of science because the Society for the History of Technology and the American Association for the History of Medicine each award their own prizes. The Pfizer prize is funded by Pfizer, Inc. The first Pfizer prize was awarded in 1959.

History of Economics Society (HES): The Joseph J. Spengler Best Book Award is awarded annually to the author(s) of a book that is viewed by the selection committee as the best recent book in the history of economics. The book must have been published in English during the two years before to the Society's annual meeting at which the award is given. The Spengler Award was first bestowed in 2004.

APPENDIX B. BEST ARTICLE
AWARD WINNERS

	Price/Webster (HSS)	Best Article (HES)
2004	"'Industrial Versailles': Eero Saarinen's corporate campuses for GM, IBM, and AT&T" Scott Knowles and Stuart W. Leslie (*Isis*, Vol. 92, No. 1, 2001, pp. 1–33)	"The virtual history of the Tableau Economique" Loic Charles (*European Journal of the History of Economic Thought*, Vol. 10, No. 4, 2003, pp. 527–550)
2005	"Abraham Trembley's strategy of generosity and the scope of celebrity in the mid-eighteenth century" Marc J. Ratcliff (*Isis*, Vol. 95, No. 4, 2004, pp. 555–575)	"In the lobby of the energy hotel: Jevons's formulation of the post-classical 'economic problem'" Michael V. White (*History of Political Economy*, Vol. 36, No. 2, 2004, pp. 227–271)
2006	"Geographers of Mars: Cartographic inscription and exploration narrative in late Victorian representations of the Red Planet" K. Maria D. Lane (*Isis*, Vol. 96, No. 4, 2005, pp. 477–506)	"David Hume's monetary theory: Was he really a quantity theorist and an inflationist?" Carl Wennerlind (*Journal of Political Economy*, Vol. 113, No. 1, 2005, pp. 223–237)
2007	"A 'large and graceful sinuosity': John Herschel's graphical method" Thomas L. Hankins (*Isis*, Vol. 97, No. 4, 2006, pp. 605–633)	"The making of chapters 13 and 14 of Patinkin's *Money, Interest, and Prices* Mauro Boianovsky" (*History of Political Economy*, Vol. 38, No. 2, 2006, pp. 193–249)
2008	"Observers, objects, and the embedded eye: Or, seeing and knowing in Ptolemy and Galen Daryn Lehoux" (*Isis*, Vol. 98, No. 3, 2007, pp. 447–467)	"Early experiments in consumer demand theory, 1930–1970" Ivan Moscati (*History of Political Economy*, Vol. 39, No. 3, 2007, pp. 359–401)

History of Science Society (HSS): The Pfizer Prize is awarded annually to the author(s) of an article in *Isis* (the journal of the History of Science Society) that is viewed by the selection committee as a contribution of the highest standard to the history of science. The article must have been published in English during the three calendar years before the year in which the Price/Webster Prize is awarded. The Prize was known as the Zeitlin-Ver Brugge Prize from 1979 (when it was first awarded) to 1989, when it became the Derek Price Prize. In 2002, the name was changed again to honor Rod Webster.

History of Economics Society (HES): The Best Article in the History of Economics is awarded annually to the author(s) of an article that is viewed by the selection committee as the best recent article in the history of economics. The article must be published in English during the calendar year before the Society's annual meeting at which the award will be bestowed. The first Best Article award was bestowed in 1995.

SYMPOSIUM ON
CLÉMENT JUGLAR

JOSEPH CLÉMENT JUGLAR
1819 - 1905

Photo by E. Pirou, reproduced from P. Beauregard, *Notice sur la vie et les travaux de M. Clément Juglar* (Paris: Firmin-Didot), 1908

CLÉMENT JUGLAR ON COMMERCIAL CRISES: THE DICTIONARY ARTICLES

Cécile Dangel-Hagnauer

Recent events have stirred renewed interest in the works of past authors who attempted to explain the emergence and the recurrence of economic crises. One of the most important economists to have thoroughly and systematically analyzed the periodical return of crises is the French economist Clément Juglar (1819–1905).[1]

Strangely, general acquaintance with Juglar's works is rather poor, although his name is familiar to many, even outside the economics profession. As we know, Juglar owes much of his fame to Schumpeter. In *Business Cycles*, Schumpeter developed the idea of a "three-cycle schema" formed by the superposition of "Kondratieffs," "Juglars," and "Kitchins." He also regarded Juglar as the "great outsider who may be said to have created modern business-cycle analysis" (Schumpeter, 1950) and as the first economist to have understood the importance of combining theory, statistics, and history in the field of economic analysis, a method he himself advocated (Schumpeter, 1954).

Although Juglar's writings themselves have given rise to little investigation, even in France,[2] which contrasts with the constant reference to Juglar by early-twentieth-century French economists writing on the business cycle, all of whom emphasized the importance of Juglar's contribution, the innovative nature of his method, which they themselves sought to apply,[3]

A Research Annual

Research in the History of Economic Thought and Methodology, Volume 28-A, 97–113

Copyright © 2010 by Emerald Group Publishing Limited

All rights of reproduction in any form reserved

ISSN: 0743-4154/doi:10.1108/S0743-4154(2010)000028A007

while also distancing themselves from Juglar.[4] With the emergence of the mathematical theories of the cyclical behavior of economic activity, the so-called national schools disappeared and, as a result, Juglar became a mere reference in books on economic history.

In the English-speaking world, Juglar's contribution has been almost completely ignored.[5] A curious piece of work is Thom's 1893 "translation" of Juglar's (1889) *Des crises commerciales et de leur retour périodique en France, en Angleterre et aux Etats-Unis*. Actually Thom's book is entitled *A Brief History of Panics* (1893) and bears the subtitle "Englished and edited with an introductory essay." It turns out the author "unhesitatingly rendered the French very freely" and, more importantly, only translated the passages in Juglar's book referring to the United States, entirely omitting his theoretical discussion, and even adding a brief account of the panics that occurred after 1890.

This raises the question as to why Juglar's works have not stimulated more attention among historians of economics. Actually, Juglar writings were abundant (some 191 entries), as he contributed many articles, in particular to the *Journal des économistes*. His interests were numerous and his writings on crises appeared in scattered articles, before he brought them together in the two editions of *Des crises commerciales*. Regrettably, the book has several drawbacks, especially in its lengthy (560 pages) and repetitious second edition, as it lacks rigorous organization, its style is tedious, and the wording often ambiguous. Hence, trying to make sense out of it is quite a challenging endeavor.

Fortunately, there was a strong tradition in France in the eighteenth and nineteenth century of synthesizing knowledge within encyclopedia and dictionaries. As Juglar was considered an authority in the area of crises, he was asked to write articles for several dictionaries, in particular two articles that appeared shortly after the publication of each of the two editions of *Des crises commerciales*.

Unlike the two editions of the book (Juglar, 1862, 1889), these articles are reasonably clear, concise, and focus on the main line of argument developed by Juglar in his writings on crises. They show quite straightforwardly the continuity of the method he applied, based on the analysis of the balance sheets of issuing banks and on price series. They also show how his analysis evolved over the years.

In the two articles, Juglar insists his sole focus is on "commercial" crises, although there are many sorts of crises, including "monetary" crises. The view he defends is that there are no monetary crises outside commercial crises. Conversely, commercial crises, which periodically disrupt the course of business and exchanges, are always accompanied by monetary disturbances, as appears visibly in banking statistics. In effect, Juglar's main contribution is in providing a careful examination of the banking statistics he has at hand. They allow him to provide evidence that crises are recurrent events and they enable him to bring to light several series of "prosperities," "crises," and "liquidations." However, though he succeeds in accounting for the relationship he finds between these banking statistics and cyclical phenomena, he fails to build a theoretical explanation of what he observes. Yet, these articles show that Juglar's goal is to build this theory. Accordingly, in 1863, Juglar begins by blaming speculation, fueled by credit, for the periodical outbreak of crises. By 1873, in the article's second edition, foreign exchanges are introduced as an additional factor. By 1891, credit plays the leading role, along with the capital market. There is especially an attempt in the second article to show how phases are connected to one another and to explain why prices increase during prosperity, why they stop increasing at the outbreak of the crisis, why they decrease during liquidation, and why they start increasing again at the end of the liquidation. Missing, however, is a theory of the determination of prices that would have provided a basis to the definition of the crisis – the stoppage in the increase in prices – that Juglar suggests in his last writings.

The evolution of Juglar's thought over this important period in the history of theory of business cycles is expounded in the following two sections, devoted to presenting the articles.

CRISES COMMERCIALES: THE 1863/1873 ARTICLE(S)

Juglar's entry on "commercial crises" appeared in Maurice Block's *Dictionnaire général de la politique ... avec la collaboration d'hommes d'État, de publicistes et d'écrivains de tous les pays.*[6] The dictionary went through two editions – in 1863 and 1873 (with a reprint of the second edition in 1884). One of the most remarkable features of these articles is that they sum up the 258 pages of the first edition of Juglar's *Des crises commerciales* in only 13 pages. Although they are not numerous, the changes that Juglar introduced in the second edition are important, as they testify to the work he did in that decade on banking and foreign exchanges.

The article begins with a rather long (one page) introduction and is then divided into two main sections, ending with a short conclusion. Only the second section bears a title, "Former Opinions on Crises."[7] The first section is subdivided into seven subsections: "Causes of Crises," "On discounts,"

"On the Metallic Reserves," "Circulation of Banknotes," "Deposits and Various Current Accounts," "On Advances by Banks on Government Securities, Railroad Stocks and Bonds," and "Duration and Liquidation of Crises." The second section only includes three subsections: "Political Causes of Crises," "Monetary Crises," and "Opinions of the Main Economists." This enumeration indicates that Juglar's main goals in this article consist in presenting his position with regard to the debates on crises at the time he was writing, in particular concerning the causes of crises. It also reveals Juglar's methodology, the use of statistics, chiefly banking statistics describing the items of the balance sheets of the Bank of France and the Bank of England, with a view to providing factual evidence of the recurrence of crises and an estimate of the duration of the three "periods" that succeed each other: prosperity, the crisis, and the liquidation.

The Crisis: What It Is, How It Occurs, and What Happens Before and After

Juglar does not use the term "cycle" to designate the time interval during which the three periods unfold and there is some ambiguity in what the word "crisis" denotes. Actually, going through the article the reader picks up three definitions of the crisis: (1) "a commercial crisis is a disruption to the course of business;" (2) "crises are the natural reactions that occur as a consequence of efforts made to raise even further production that has already been carried to excess proportions;" and (3) "a crisis is ... a general liquidation."[8] So, although Juglar is one of the authors to have underlined the periodicity of crises, thereby making an important step towards producing a theory of cycles by distinguishing three phases within the cycle, we see him confusing the liquidation with the crisis itself. This is most striking in the final sentence that closes the article, where, speaking of the "temporary torpor" that prevails during crises, Juglar's punch line is: "in a word, [the crisis] is a general liquidation."[9] This ambiguity disappears in the second dictionary article.

To say the least, the list of subsections that compose the entry does not strike the reader as being the support of a well-structured argument. Juglar's paper does lack organization. However, the introduction of the article is quite clear and it introduces the ingredients that make up the contour of the crisis. First, the three phases of the cycle are described: (a) the six or seven years of prosperity and their rising prices; (b) the crisis and the sudden upsurge in the demand for discounts, the withdrawal of specie, and the hike in the discount rate; and (c) the liquidation and its price cuts, the decrease of discounts, the reflux of specie, and the return of the discount interest rate to its "ordinary" level. Second, Juglar provides a succinct account of what happens in the short interval of time during which the crisis is wreaking havoc: disrupted business causes imbalances in the clearing of credit instruments, so agents appeal to banks for more discounts. As financial conditions become harsher, businesses have no other choice than to cut prices, leading to a slowdown of activity in workshops, with its consequences on people's lives, on consumption, and on demographics.

The starting point of the crisis is thus the increased discounts. This happens because there is a need for ready cash, as credit instruments fail to clear as a result of difficulties incurred in transactions.[10] As a result, crises are all the more serious as credit is more relied upon, which is the case in countries where industry and trade are highly developed. Crises also tend to spread from one country to another, as business and credit cross borders increasingly over time. Thus, at this stage of the argument, it is the widespread reliance on credit that is the main condition for crises to occur.

Banking Statistics

Thus, banking statistics provide the raw materials that enable Juglar to perform his observations. More than three and a half pages (out of 13) are devoted to analyzing the balance sheets of the Banks of France and of England, with additional references to these items at the end of the article. Discounts, metallic reserves, banknotes in circulation, deposits and current accounts, and advances on securities are presented in 9 out of the 11 tables the article contains, and are closely inspected, but it is the evolution of discounts and metallic reserves that help portray the three phases of the cycle. Accordingly, discounts rise during prosperity, hit a peak at the time of the crisis, and fall back during the liquidation. This sequence was observed 10 times between 1799 and 1864, which provides evidence that crises return periodically. In addition, Juglar draws up a table of the price of wheat in an attempt to show the evolution of prices over the three periods.

Of interest is the method used by Juglar to bring to light the movement of discounts. Focusing on three periods 1844–1849, 1850–1857, and 1858–1864,[11] he notes the *minimum* and *maximum* level reached each year by discounts (and also by reserves and banknotes in circulation). Then, he constructs a huge table setting in parallel the evolution of the *minima* and *maxima* reached by these items for the Bank of France and the Bank of

England. Examining these figures leads Juglar to show that in both countries discounts increase during the prosperity, exhibit a sharp rise when the crisis breaks out, and decline sharply during the liquidation.

Reserves move in the opposite direction, which produces a drain of specie when the crisis breaks out and a reflux during the liquidation. As regards the circulation of banknotes, Juglar's main goal is to show that crises are not caused by excess issues. Similarly, the examination of deposits and current accounts provide evidence that withdrawals are not related to crises.

What Causes Crises to Occur Periodically?

The fact that prosperities, crises, and liquidations are accompanied by observable movements in banking statistics provides Juglar with a tool for detecting the movements of economic activity but does not explain these phenomena, which is why half of the article is about "the causes of crises." The long introduction is followed by a lengthy subsection entitled "Causes of Crises;" the entire second section discusses other economists' opinions on the subject.

In "Causes of Crises," Juglar dismisses the causes usually cited, like food shortages and wars, as his objective is to account for the fact that crises occur repeatedly and in very different contexts. So he rejects the usual explanations, basing his reasoning on the argument that the plurality of alleged causes is a sign that none of these explanations is "determining." Using a distinction he borrows from medicine, the area in which he had begun his professional career, Juglar appeals to the opposition between "predisposition" and "determining cause." A patient will become ill with pneumonia if he is predisposed to catching it. Otherwise he can stand in the cold and yet remain in good health. Likewise, a declaration of war can resound, but it will have no effect unless there is a social predisposition to causing a crisis to break out. So it is the social predisposing cause of crises that Juglar seeks to uncover.

A plausible candidate is speculation. Speculation is part of human nature. It induces agents to overproduce. Hence, it is very tempting to see in speculation the predisposing cause of crises. Indeed, Juglar does insist on speculative behavior being typical of humans, on the role it plays during the upswings of business activity, on the necessity to recreate confidence for activity to pick up at the end of the liquidation. At the same time, Juglar emphasizes the role played by credit. In other words, speculation seems to play a leading part, but it is fed by credit. Where credit is little relied upon, speculation has a minor impact. The gradual development of credit over the nineteenth century and its diffusion across national borders, caused crises to have far-reaching effects, in particular by creating an interdependence between nations (which Juglar labels *solidarité*), thereby causing crises to spread from one country to another.

Hence, Juglar's purpose is certainly "to determine the *circumstances* in which crises develop and specify the causes that lead to their outbreak," but what is more important still is to identify "the *conditions* that are indispensable for them to exist, ... the phenomena that are then constantly observed regardless of the so numerous and so diverse causes that are mentioned depending on the need of the moment" (emphasis added). These conditions are the division of labor, the development of great industry, commerce and foreign trade, and the reliance on credit. Speculation is certainly part of the picture, as in its absence, credit would not have the adverse effects we witness; but, conversely, in the absence of credit, speculation would not wreak havoc the way it does.

If anything, the cause of crises is prosperity itself: "The determining cause is elsewhere. It is the consequence of a previous state that must be studied carefully," Juglar writes.[12] We shall see that Juglar will pick up this lead in the 1891 article.

In the second section of the 1863/1873 entry, Juglar devotes a subsection to showing that crises do not have political causes, simply because they do not coincide with critical political events (wars, in particular), breaking out before uprisings and revolutions, or occurring in periods of political tranquility. And there are no "monetary" crises: although frequent, monetary disturbances are mere incidents that have little or no impact on business; whenever monetary crises are serious enough to merit the label "crises," they are actually "commercial" crises.

In the final subsection on the "Opinions of the Main Economists," Juglar cites those of J.B. Say, Senior, Wilson, Tooke, Coquelin, and du Puynode. This selection may appear odd, unless the reader bears in mind that Juglar's goal is to dismiss excess issues of banknotes, as well as the withdrawals of deposits, as the causes of crises. In particular, Juglar goes at great length to bring up facts that contradict Coquelin's position in favor of free banking. More generally, Juglar refers here to the debates on central banking and the conduct of monetary policy. Thus, he alludes to the criticisms opposed to the Peel Act of 1844 and insists on the restrictions imposed upon the Bank of France (in the use of its capital), on the monopoly the Bank enjoys in the issuing of banknotes, and on the discount rate policy. The question of the Bank of France's privilege is discussed at length. Visibly, Juglar is siding here with Wolowski (1864) in the ongoing debate on free banking,[13] and devotes nearly one page to refuting the theory according to which the freedom of banks would be the adequate way of preventing speculation and thus crises. Taking up again the method relied upon earlier, Juglar examines the minima and maxima of deposits. He points to their erratic oscillations, disconnected with crises and unrelated to the oscillations of reserves, and notes that the countries where free banking prevails are not better protected from speculation than those where monopoly reigns. Finally, Juglar discusses the position of the proponents of a fixed discount rate, only to show that history provides evidence that such a policy is inefficient.

Juglar ends the article by stating that there is no remedy to crises, except perhaps in better governance of banks, and by mentioning that other indicators (economic, demographic, financial) move in step with discounts and reserves. The article closes with a comparison of the business standstill that is caused by the crisis with a "prelude to more beautiful destinies."

The Evolution of Juglar's Thought over the 1863–1873 Decade

For the translation, the 1873 edition has been used as a copy-text and Juglar's alterations to the 1863 version are indicated in the footnotes. Among these changes, some concern wording and are designed to convey greater clarity.[14] For similar reasons, in his discussion on the opinions of other economists, Juglar adds a paragraph where he comments on Say's opinion. Naturally, several tables have been updated, even though Juglar forgets sometimes to bring the corresponding changes to the text. There is also a reference to an institutional change brought to the Bank of France.[15]

More interesting are the additions to the text. Many sentences are completed with references to movements in the foreign exchange market. For instance, in the following sentence, the passage in italics is added to the initial 1863 version: "At the same time, the banknotes issued in exchange for discounted mercantile paper are instantly presented for reimbursement, and *under the influence of unfavorable foreign exchanges the metallic reserves* diminish as swiftly as portfolios build up." Also added to that same paragraph is "the exchange rate returns to par, and the reflux of specie begins," with which the paragraph ends.

These additions are easy to explain. As a matter of fact, Juglar, along with Paul Coullet, was entrusted by the Bank of France with publishing in French the *Extraits des Enquêtes anglaises sur les questions de banque, de circulation monétaire et de credit*, which appeared in 1865. Three years later, in 1868, Juglar published his second book, *Du change et de la liberté d'émission*.

The purpose of the book is to discuss whether a limit should be set on the amount of banknotes issued by banks. In other words, should a rule be applied to the Bank of France similar to the one stipulated in the Peel Act of 1844. Juglar argues that the real question to be raised is not this one, as it reveals the ignorance of the role played by foreign exchanges. He asserts that it is ineffective to impose restrictions on the amount of banknotes that are issued, as business is chiefly conducted on credit, essentially trade credit, and that banknotes are not used in transactions, except for retail trade and for balancing credit operations. Moreover, the role of banks is mainly to ensure the clearing of commercial bills. This is so in any case in France, in the absence of the clearinghouses that perform this task in England and in the United States. All the while credit operates smoothly, credit instruments are easily cleared, and business and transactions can follow their course. Unfortunately, the reliance on credit tends to produce a rise in prices, so that at some point some failure occurs and disrupts the workings of the clearing system. This is when the crisis breaks out.

In fact, Juglar describes a succession of 12 phases, 9 of which lead to the crisis and three to its liquidation. Interestingly, at the center of the process we have the foreign exchange market. As long as credit instruments issued by residents are compensated by claims on foreign countries, business can go on as usual. But as soon as the clearing process is interrupted as a result of an excessive increase in prices, the ensuing deficit causes the drop of the foreign exchange rate and an outflow of specie. In other words, the reduction of metallic reserves is the result of unbalanced trade, both domestically and abroad. This is when issuing banks increase the discount rate to preserve their reserves.

Having written *Du change*, Juglar quite naturally incorporates the role of foreign exchanges into the 1873 edition. And the role of foreign exchanges will remain an essential link in the chain of events that build up till the explosion of the crisis in the second edition of *Les crises commerciales* and thus in the 1891 dictionary articles.[16]

CRISES COMMERCIALES: THE 1891 ARTICLE

Although this article also went through two editions, the 1900 edition is a mere reprint of the entry on "commercial crises" that appeared in Léon Say and Joseph Chailley's *Nouveau dictionnaire d'économie politique* that was first published in 1891.[17] Compared to the 1863/1873 entry, this one is shorter (less than 10 pages) and better structured, as it is neatly divided into five sections, and is followed by a short bibliography that includes works by Juglar, along with books by authors such as Tooke, Lord Overstone, Briaune, and Wirth, among others.

The Three Periods

The title of the first section, "Outline of a Crisis: Three Periods," is a bit confusing. However, even though Juglar still does not use the term "cycle," the three "periods" are each attributed a denomination, which is an improvement over the 1863/1873 article. They are "the explosion of the crisis," "the liquidation of the crisis," and "prosperity."

Juglar underscores that the crisis per se, its explosion, is very short, whereas the liquidation lasts much longer. As to the prosperity, it consists in several years of bustling activity, easy credit, and rising prices. However, as time passes, the conditions for the crisis to break out slowly build up. Interestingly, Juglar indicates that the interest rate goes up, as a result of funds available for investment becoming scarcer. Thus, the capital market is now part the explanatory framework.

As prices rise, sales become harder to realize, leading to growing difficulties to meet financial commitments. The instability that, by then, characterizes the situation is such that any incident will cause the explosion. The section ends with the single table the article contains: its purpose is to show that crises (1) break out at the same moment in the different countries, and (2) are periodical, as evidenced by their recurrence throughout the nineteenth century.

Prices

The second section is by far the longest (three and a half pages) and bears the title "Definition of a Crisis; Causes of Crises." Here, Juglar seeks to provide a single unequivocal definition of the crisis, which is also an improvement compared to the three definitions of the crisis that appeared in the 1863/1873 article. Accordingly, Juglar defines the crisis as the moment when the rise in prices, which is characteristic of prosperity, stops. The crisis *is*, thus, the "stoppage" in the increase of prices.

All the other developments that can be observed are consequences brought about by this event. Credit instruments no longer clear as well as before, agents begin scrambling for cash, so the banks are besieged with demands for discounts.[18] The banks are soon confronted with "unfavorable foreign exchanges," meaning that the unbalanced payments are experienced within the country, and also across borders, so foreign creditors will also require to be paid in specie. The depletion of metallic reserves is actually what signals the explosion. To protect their reserves, the banks raise the discount rate.

The increase in the discount rate is thus a consequence and not the factor that triggers the crisis. On the other hand, it has a specific purpose, that of increasing the price of precious metals. Indeed, because their value is intrinsically more stable, during the period of rising prices, their market value increases less than that of other commodities. As a result, to face their commitments, holders of commodities will seek to borrow precious metals to pay off their debts. However, the increase in the discount rate will bring the price of precious metals in line with the price of the other commodities. It then becomes more rational for agents to cut prices, leading to the general price decline that is characteristic of the liquidation.

The second part of the section deals with the causes of crises. Stating the opinions of several economists, ranging from Robert Peel, John Stuart Mill, and Max Wirth, to Coquelin, Leroy-Beaulieu, Bonamy Price, and others, Juglar criticizes them for focusing exclusively on the liquidation, and not on the three phases. Juglar's own opinion is that crises are caused by the increase in prices that occurs during the prosperity: so "why not," Juglar writes, "point to the *rise that preceded* [the crisis], as there lies the primary cause that emerges from these observations?"

So, in this article, Juglar proposes one single definition of the crisis and identifies a sole cause. He affirms there is, at the time he is writing, a consensus on what characterizes crises, namely the three "accidents" that succeed each other: the rise in prices that precedes them, the depletion of reserves, and a fall in prices. The rise in prices is typical of the prosperity that precedes the crisis; the fall in prices is the distinctive feature of the liquidation.

He then sets out to explain how the periods are connected to one another, noting that authors disagree on what causes prices to move according to this pattern. In particular, he expresses his disagreement with the "old doctrine" according to which prices increase when the quantity of money becomes larger. Again, business is chiefly financed by credit, so the quantity of money is of little importance and the relevant concept is the "rapidity" of the circulation of money. Here Juglar also reasserts his rejection of the explanation according to which crises are caused by accidents. The *variety* of causes invoked, he argues, is sufficient proof that such explanations are fallacious.

The third (two-page) section of the entry, which bears the title "Mechanism of Crises," is where Juglar provides his tentative explanation. His starting point is the situation of the economy when it is about to recover. Once the liquidation has been completed, all the conditions are present for the revival to occur: low interest rates, abundant capital seeking employment. All that is needed is the awakening of the entrepreneurial spirit for project makers and ... speculators to arrive on the scene. If prices start rising at the beginning of prosperity, it is because capital seeking employment is abundant.

This is when credit enters the picture. Its major effect is to stimulate demand. Hence prices increase, which provides additional credit, and so on and so forth. The price increase is, thus, accounted for by a cumulative process that sets in motion.

What stops the rise? The fact that, suddenly facing supply, there is a lack of demand. Why is that? Because of overproduction? Juglar does contemplate this possibility, but only for a moment, leaving it unexplored, unsurprisingly, as Juglar does not provide a theory of the production process.

Why then is demand insufficient? Is it for lack of wants? Is it because prices are too high? Certainly not because of a lack of wants, Juglar asserts. So, because prices are too high? Juglar's answer is yes, indicating that his reasoning has become circular.

However, Juglar tries to separate what is happening in the retail market from what is going on in the wholesale market. Prices are too high for consumers, so the retail market does not clear. Why do then merchants not reduce their prices? Basically, because they think they can postpone the reduction, by increasing their reliance on credit. All the while the banks respond positively to their requirements, the holders of goods let their inventories pile up. So in the wholesale market, there is a growing amount of unsold stocks facing an escalating quantity of discounted bills. So what Juglar is depicting is some kind of price rigidity, created by the existence of credit, which can explain why prices remain high for a while, before the decline sets in. It is only when credit becomes unaffordable (the cost of specie too high) that agents have no other choice than to sell off their goods. Equilibrium is thereby restored and the two stocks vanish into thin air.

However, why prices will continue their descent during the liquidation is not accounted for.

In conclusion, what is obviously missing is a theory of the determination of prices. Juglar is definitely not a theoretician. In passing, this lack of a theory of prices is perhaps the reason why Juglar considers that prosperity is "the normal state of the market," whereas it is a period of rising prices.

Crises and Wealth – Crises and Society

A few words on the two final sections of the entry. In the fourth section, which is one page long, Juglar discusses the effect of crises on the development of wealth, repeating that crises will tend to be more serious and violent in countries where progress is swifter. Conversely, countries that are shielded from the damage caused by crises are also those that experience little or no progress. Interestingly, Juglar indicates that crises are all the more severe as one moves closer to the foreign exchange markets, displaying his continued interest in the issues that have led him to write *Des changes*.

Along the way, Juglar reaffirms that crises recur periodically, but not at regular intervals.

In the one and a half pages of the final section, Juglar discusses the works of economists and statisticians concerned with the measurement of the "social and moral state of human societies at a determined period of time in the various countries." He emphasizes the difficulties faced when conducting international comparisons. He goes on to suggest that the best way to overcome them would be to measure the intensity of exchanges, notably through the examination of the balance sheets of great banks. So, once again, Juglar defends his method consisting in the scrutiny of banking statistics, although other statistics can be used to complete the picture, like the issues of securities, imports and exports, government revenue, etc. Other indicators, he adds, like demographic indicators can be used to describe the "manifestations of social life." These statistics, he reminds the reader, are granted considerable space in the two editions of *Les crises commerciales*.

This presentation would be incomplete without our mentioning Juglar's belief that the periodicity of crises and the ability to follow their evolution in the balance sheets of banks could help predict crises, as he affirms in the final footnote, referring the reader to places in his book where he has undertaken to do so.

CONCLUDING REMARKS

The two dictionary articles are very different and bear witness to the maturation of Juglar's conception of the "oscillations" of economic activity. They differ in the way they are organized: although it is repetitious, the second entry is more rigorously constructed. They do not provide the same definition of the crisis: the hesitations that mark Juglar's attempt to define the crisis in the first entry contrast with the position he takes in the second entry, where he seeks to provide a single definition.

Although, in the 1863/1873 dictionary article, the movement of economic activity is painstakingly scrutinized through the evolution of central banks' reserves and discount portfolios, Juglar truly tries to provide an explanation for the way prices evolve over the three phases that make up the cycle, in the 1891 entry. So, while great emphasis is placed on causation in the first paper, Juglar is more adamant in seeking to explain how the economy moves from one phase to the other in the second one.[19]

The first entry contains numerous tables; only one is included in the second entry, where the methodology used by Juglar to identify the movements of the different balance sheet items is not even mentioned. This contrasts with the improved quality of the statistics that Juglar relies upon in the second edition of his book, which includes a list of prices of commodities and presents a refined utilization of the maxima/minima methodology.

This indicates that the scholar whose interest in Juglar's contribution to economics has perhaps been roused by the reading of these two articles could usefully examine the contents of the two editions of *Les crises commerciales*. To begin with, he or she could conveniently refer to Besomi's article in the present volume. Besomi provides an in-depth discussion of all the themes merely alluded to here, including Juglar's intensive use of statistics; the relationship between speculation, credit and prices; crises and progress, equilibrium and the natural state, the meaning of "periodicity"; and of course the central question of causality. Furthermore, Juglar's developments on money, credit, and banking are worth looking into, and are perhaps more relevant than those that deal strictly with crises and cyclical economic behavior.[20]

NOTES

1. Following in the footsteps of his father, Juglar took up medicine and became a physician at the age of 27. A witness of the events of 1848, he soon became interested in social and economic issues (see Beauregard, 1908).

2. In France, only two articles had been dedicated to Juglar since the 1990s (Gilman,1991; Pellissier, 2000) before the publication of the special issue of the *Revue européenne des sciences sociales* (Bridel & Dalpont-Pont Legrand, 2009). This publication followed a conference organized by Jean de Mathan, Juglar's great-grandson, and held in Paris at the *Institut de France*, the seat of the *Académie des sciences morales et politiques* (of which Juglar became a member in 1892), in celebration of the centennial of Juglar's death in December 1905.

3. Typically, Albert Aftalion (1913) proposes to follow Juglar's method, i.e., the examination of stylized facts, the demonstration of predecessors' inability to account for such facts, before suggesting his own explanation.

4. Aftalion (1913), in particular, attempts to provide a theoretical account of economic fluctuations, a task Juglar fails to accomplish.

5. A notable exception is Niehans (1992).

6. The second edition of the *Dictionaire* (Block, 1873) included 2,324 printed pages and was published in two volumes (A–G and H–Z).

7. In the 1863 edition, the title is *Influence of Political Causes, Opinion of the Main Economists, Means of Preventing Crises, Proposed Remedies*.

8. Juglar provides no description, let alone a theory, of the process of production.

9. The ambiguity is not specific to Juglar, as even today, in French, there is a tendency to use the word "crisis" when referring to a recession or a depression, for instance in the phrase "*la crise des années trente*."

10. In fact, the credit instruments that Juglar refers to are "effets de commerce." We have used the expression "mercantile paper" to avoid the use of "commercial paper" which is often found in the nineteenth century literature.

11. 1861 in the 1863 edition.

12. This assertion is probably the one that comes closest to Schumpeter's erroneous quote "the only cause of depression is prosperity" (Schumpeter, 1954, p. 1124), a statement Juglar never articulated.

13. Wolowski authored the report read before the *Académie des sciences morales et politiques* following the prize attributed to Juglar's contribution to a competition opened in May 1860 on the subject of commercial crises. Juglar's memorandum was later published as the first edition of *Des crises commerciales*.

14. Also, as a result of the change in the title of the second section from "Influence of the Political Causes. Opinion of the Main Economists. Means to Avoid Crises, Proposed Remedies." to simply "Former Opinions on Crises," Juglar inserts a sentence of transition at the end of the section's introduction: "Let begin with the most generally admitted causes; afterwards, we will discuss the particular opinions of several economists."

15. For some mysterious reason, an entire passage referring to the Crimean war is scrapped in the subsection on "political causes." This was probably to keep down the article's overall length, as it is noteworthy that the 1863 version ends with a bibliography that is also missing in the 1873 edition, doubtless for the same reason. This war, often considered to have caused the crisis of 1864, is mentioned in the 1891 article.

16. This article was well received, as witnessed by the review that appeared in *The Economist* (December 19, 1863), which speaks in terms of a "scientific demonstration of commercial crises." The reception of the 1891 article was even

more favorable, as it gave rise to an English translation in the *Rhodes Journal of Banking*, May, 1894. All things considered, despite some misinterpretations and although the ambiguities present in Juglar's text are not dealt with adequately, the translation provides a fair account of Juglar's entry.

17. The first 1891 edition of the *Nouveau dictionaire* included 2,513 printed pages and was published in two volumes (A–G and H–Z). A supplementary volume (277 pages) was published in 1897 and added to the otherwise unchanged edition in 1900 (Say & Chailley, 1900[1891]).

18. In passing, it is noteworthy that "Banks" is written, throughout the greater part of the article, with upper-case *b*, which indicates that Juglar is referring, in the case of France and England, exclusively to the central banks. In contrast, Juglar writes *banque de France* in the 1863/1873 entry.

19. Hence, the opposition between predisposing and determining cause is not mentioned in the second article, although Juglar repeats that the multiplicity of causes that are called upon to explain crises is sufficient to dismiss the corresponding explanations given the recurrence that characterizes crises. He has, thus, not abandoned the argument underlying the use of the medical metaphor, as evidenced by its replication in Juglar (1889, p. 28).

20. Juglar's style is not particularly elegant. It frequently lacks rigor and is sometimes ambiguous, thereby requiring some interpretation. Footnotes in French have been included when meaning is uncertain. Whenever possible, punctuation, sentence structure, and the vocabulary used by Juglar have been reproduced as faithfully as possible, provided meaning is clearly conveyed and reading reasonably easy. One problem that needed to be dealt with was the use Juglar makes of long sentences (sometimes a full paragraph long), composed of clauses separated by colons, semicolons, or even commas. When feasible, Juglar's punctuation has been respected. When necessary, commas and/or linking words have been added or omitted.

ACKNOWLEDGMENT

The author would like to thank Daniele Besomi for reading the first drafts of these translations, for his helpful comments, and for indicating useful references. The usual disclaimer applies.

REFERENCES

Aftalion, A. (1913). *Les crises périodiques de surproduction.* Paris: Marcel Rivière.

Beauregard, P. (1908). *Notice sur la vie et les travaux de M. Clément Juglar.* Paris: Institut de France.

Block, M. (Ed.) (1873). *Dictionnaire générale de la politique, avec la collaboration d'hommes d'Etat, de publicistes et d'écrivains de tous les pays, édition entièrement refondue et mise à jour* (2nd rev. ed., Vol. 1). Paris: O. Lorenz, Libraire-éditeur.

Bridel, P., & Dalpont-Pont Legrand, M. (Eds). (2009). Clément Juglar (1819–1905): Les origines de la théorie des cycles. *Revue européenne des sciences sociales, 47*(143).

Gilman, M.-H. (1991). Clément Juglar 1819–1905 analyste des crises. In: Y. Breton & M. Lutfalla (Eds), *L'économie politique en France au XIXème siècle* (pp. 277–302). Paris: Economica.

Juglar, C. (1862). *Des crises commerciales et de leur retour périodique en France, en Angleterre et aux Etats-Unis.* Paris: Guillaumin.

Juglar, C. (1863). Crises commerciales. In: M. Block (Ed.), *Dictionnaire général de la politique* (1st ed., Vol. 1, pp. 615–627). Paris: O. Lorenz.

Juglar, C. (1868). *Du change et de la liberté d'émission.* Paris: Guillaumin.

Juglar, C. (1873). Crises commerciales. In: M. Block (Ed.), *Dictionnaire général de la politique* (2nd rev. ed., Vol. 1, pp. 586–598). Paris: O. Lorenz.

Juglar, C. (1889). *Des crises commerciales et de leur retour périodique en France, en Angleterre et aux Etats-Unis* (2nd ed.). Paris: Guillaumin.

Juglar, C. (1891). Crises commerciales. In: L. Say & J. Chailley (Eds), *Nouveau dictionnaire d'économie politique* (2nd ed., Vol. 1, pp. 641–651). Paris: Guillaumin.

Niehans, J. (1992). Juglar's credit cycles. *History of Political Economy, 24*(3), 545–569.

Pellissier, D. (2000). Clément Juglar: héritage et actualité de sa théorie des cycles. In: P. Dockès, L. Frobert, G. Klotz, J.-P. Potier & A. Tiran (Eds), *Les traditions économiques françaises 1848–1939* (pp. 273–285). Paris: CNRS Editions.

Say, L., & Chailley, J. (Eds). (1900[1891]). *Nouveau dictionnaire d'économie politique* (Vol. 1). A-H, Paris: Guillaumin.

Schumpeter, J. A. (1950). Wesley Clair Mitchell 1874–1948. *Quarterly Journal of Economics, 64*(1), 139–155.

Schumpeter, J. A. (1954). *History of economic analysis.* New York: Oxford University Press.

Thom, D. W. (1893). *A brief history of panics and their periodical occurrence in the United States.* New York: G.P. Putnam's Sons.

Wolowski, L. (1864). *La question des banques.* Paris: Guillaumin.

COMMERCIAL CRISES (1863/1873) [*]

Clément Juglar
Translated by Cécile Dangel-Hagnauer

In the first half of this century and up to the present day, attention has been directed, at various epochs, to what we agree should be called "commercial crises" or "monetary crises," without people being very much aware of the difference that is seemingly attached to these two denominations.[1] What then is a commercial crisis? Can a commercial crisis exist without there being a monetary crisis, and vice versa? In what circumstances are crises observed?

After a period of great prosperity – of six to seven years on average – and a continuous rise of all securities and commodities, whereas judging by outside appearances nothing seems to have changed, suddenly, due to the needs of trade and to an immobilization of capital greater than savings could have provided, the demands for bank discounts succeed each other in an unusual fashion and bank portfolios inflate before our very eyes. At the same time, the banknotes issued in exchange for discounted mercantile paper are instantly presented for reimbursement, and under the influence of unfavorable foreign exchanges, the metallic reserves diminish as swiftly as portfolios build up.[2] To restrain this movement, the banks raise the discount

---

[*] Translation based on Juglar, C. (1873). Commercial crises. In: M. Block (Ed.), *Dictionnaire générale de la politique, avec la collaboration d'hommes d'Etat, de publicistes et d'écrivains de tous les pays, édition entièrement refondue et mise à jour* (2nd ed., Vol. 1, pp. 586–598). Paris: O. Lorenz, Libraire-Éditeur. The first edition of Block's dictionary was published in 1863; Juglar's entry covered pp. 615–627.

A Research Annual
Research in the History of Economic Thought and Methodology, Volume 28-A, 115–147
ISSN: 0743-4154/doi:10.1108/S0743-4154(2010)000028A008

rate with such haste that there is an increase of general anxiety.[3,4] Finally, as demands remain strong, not only the higher discount rate but also the difficulties opposed by banks make it impossible for both business and further speculation to continue.[5] One must liquidate and sell by cutting prices; immediately, bankruptcies and suspensions occur, the exchange rate returns to par, and the reflux of specie begins.[6]

As a result of this forced liquidation, the banks' portfolios shrink, reserves are replenished, and the discount rate returns to its ordinary conditions almost as quickly as it had departed from them.

This sudden interruption in the course of business produces a general disturbance that precludes any recovery until a fairly complete and serious enough liquidation has allowed the return of confidence, until it has become possible to recognize the firms that have resisted the turmoil, or those whose credit has not been affected.

A commercial crisis is therefore a disruption to the course of business, a failure of mercantile paper to clear across the various world markets – which requires the intervention of metallic specie[7] – followed by the downgrading and the depreciation of commodities, and by the suspension, the bank-ruptcies, and the collapse of imprudently engaged commercial firms. The upheaval is felt far off in the distance and is reflected in all aspects of peoples' lives, such as in the movement of population, marriages, births and deaths, and public revenue. The increase in the price of money, as a result of unfavorable foreign exchanges, causes government securities to decline. Workshops interrupt their activity, prices drop and, in this general atmosphere of disarray, consumptions decrease.

All these phenomena are temporary. Were they to last longer, they would result in the ruin of nations. They have become more visible since the beginning of the century, but that they affect more especially modern societies is due to the more extensive use of credit. In the past, these phenomena unfolded more slowly and had more enduring effects. It is chiefly in recent times that the periodic return of crises has been observed and that their concurrence in France, England, Germany, and the United States has attracted attention. There is indeed an apparent interdependence among the large trading and industrial countries. In earlier times, commercial ties were weaker, and business was not undertaken on so great a scale as to require the support of credit. We produced for markets we knew well and for buyers with limited needs. Today, we do so for the whole world, and despite the first-sight impression that demand is unlimited, there are nonetheless times in which production is insufficient, others where there are gluts, poor sales, owing to the continuous and too rapid rise in prices. This is due to general industrial conditions, to the power of machines, to the immobilization of the capital needed to face competition, and to the impossibility of interrupting a process in which one is engaged, for fear of making considerable losses. In times past, although these conditions were wanting, there were episodes of distress and turmoil, as there are even now; but as credit was practically unheard of, there were none of those terrifying suspensions, which, in the course of reestablishing price equilibrium, give rise to an exaggerated reaction and bring down everything with them. Wars, food shortages, and epidemics were once very powerful scourges. Today the abuse of credit seems to have become an even greater evil. In England, it is especially since the frequent intervention of credit that crises have occurred more regularly.[8] Understandably, business conducted in cash can never produce crises.

When credit plays a great role in transactions,[9] there comes a time when, after having faced a few difficulties in carrying out exchanges, some hesitation appears, and as mercantile paper no longer clears, indicating a stoppage in the trading of goods, foreign exchanges become unfavorable, which calls for the intervention of metallic specie.[10] To defend their reserves, banks raise the discount rate, that is, they increase the price of metal up to the price level of goods;[11] which is when the crisis is said to break out. The greater the amount of credit in a country and the more active the circulation, the more crises are serious. Credit disappears completely in such moments; only the ordinary transactions in cash remain. But does this mean these disturbances occur without there being some apparent cause, without commerce having been disrupted by some external factor? This is what the study of the causes will help us understand.

CAUSES OF CRISES

The symptoms that precede crises are utterly undistinguishable from the signs of great prosperity; ventures and speculations of all sorts proliferate; the price of products, the value of land and houses rise; the demand for labor increases and wage rates augment, interest on the contrary diminishes. Add to that a gullible public – whose doubts vanish at the sight of the first successful undertaking – and a taste for gambling, which spreads as prices continue to rise and as the hope of becoming rich in a short time takes hold of people's imagination. Finally, increasing luxury leads to excess spending, fueled less by greater income than by the higher value of capital estimated at market prices.

Crises appear only in nations whose commerce is well developed. There cannot be crises in countries where there is no division of labor and no foreign trade. The more credit is restricted, the less crises are to be feared.

Food shortages, wars, revolutions, tariff changes, loans, fashion variations, new trade openings, these are the main causes of crises that have in turn been put forward. However, the real test would be to see these causes reproduce, in similar circumstances, the same effects. Unfortunately, when we consider social phenomena and everything that concerns life, this relationship between causes and effects is rarely prominent. In this state of uncertainty, the most dissimilar causes are called upon to explain the same facts. We have good reason to be surprised by the lack of judgment of the human mind and the facility with which it accepts anything it is presented with; it is so hungry for an explanation that, when it finds nothing better, it is satisfied with words. Indeed, the multiplicity of the causes that are suggested is sufficient, in our opinion, to prove their little effectiveness, since, whereas a single one should suffice, a great number are accumulated; now, as they are not always simultaneously present, it is natural to think, as we eliminate them one by one, that none is a determining cause, since its intervention is not indispensable to produce the result ascribed to it.

The determining cause is elsewhere. It is the consequence of a previous state that must be studied carefully. In medicine we call it a predisposition. Cold weather, for instance, is the cause of many illnesses: in one patient it causes rheumatism; in another, pneumonia; in still another, pleurisy. Although the cause is the same, the result differs. The individual predisposition is what tips the scales in one or the other direction, the proof being that, in its absence, cold weather produces no illness in a healthy individual. The same applies to crises; this is what we will seek to demonstrate. We will endeavor to determine the circumstances in which crises develop and specify the causes that lead to their outbreak. However, we will mainly insist on the conditions that are indispensable for them to exist, on the phenomena that are then constantly observed notwithstanding the so many, the so diverse causes that are mentioned depending on the need of the moment.

To sum up in a single proposition the result of our studies on this subject, we may say that crises are the natural reaction that occurs as a consequence of efforts made to raise even further production that has already been carried to excess proportions,[12] and if crises are more intense today than they were in the past centuries, it is because we now have at our disposal means of production unknown to our forefathers. Therefore, we will need to get used to the idea of the periodical return of these commercial turbulences that, at least up to now, appear to be one of the conditions for the development of big industry.

The impetus given to activity is such that, for a certain number of years, raw materials are barely sufficient for factories to operate, imports and exports are constantly increasing; then, without expecting it,[13] all conduits are full, no further outflow is possible, all circulation ceases, and a crisis breaks out. Speculations stop; money, so abundant several months before, becomes scarcer; reserves are what disappear next;[14] calls for funds continue; they cannot be satisfied; floating stocks enter the market: hence, all securities depreciate, forcing liquidation in the worst possible conditions. These speculative follies, these excesses, are too much part of human nature for us to succeed in preventing them in any way.

When we study the official reports published by the government and the large public administrations, we are struck by a very salient fact that the figures themselves reveal at first glance: we see periods of rise and fall that follow each other with the greatest regularity.[15] The same applies to customs tables, the average price of grain, the records of population movement, and the prices of government securities. Everywhere, the same phenomenon appears, and there is, everywhere, a perfect correspondence with banks' statements.

If one examines the official statements describing the situation of the banks of France, England, and the United States, little time is needed to recognize, among the numerous divisions of their assets and liabilities, several items that are worthy of the greatest attention:[16]

1. The development of discounts and advances;
2. The metallic reserves;
3. The circulation;
4. The deposits and current accounts.

The first two, especially, display so identical and regular a course, in periods of both crisis and prosperity, that they will serve as a guide for recognizing those periods and indicate whether danger is impending or distant. The last two items, the circulation and the deposits, do not exhibit the same regularity; their oscillations are not of the same kind; their variations, much smaller in size, can occur in the absence of crises, owing to some particular and local needs, without any influence on the general course of business.

We shall thus proceed to examine the facts we have just mentioned.[17]

ON DISCOUNTS

The level of discounts follows a steadily increasing course for a certain number of years, usually six or seven, by which time it has tripled or quadrupled; then there is a pause, discounts stagnate for one or two years, before resuming their course and reaching an often sky-high figure when the crisis breaks out. A glance at Table 1 will provide us with convincing evidence.

From 1799 to 1804, discounts rise from 111 to 510 million in the most prosperous year (1802), drop to 503 million, reach 630 million at the time of the crisis, and fall back to 255 after the liquidation.

The same phenomenon occurs six or seven times in the first half of the present century and coincides perfectly with all the revolutions, wars, and epidemics that recur periodically in our country.

Let us now compare the price of wheat in times of crisis and prosperity (Table 2).

The maximum price for wheat always precedes and accompanies crises, as the preceding table bears out. The minimum does not always occur in the prosperous years, as in 1814 and 1849; but prices are always moderate in the years of prosperity, there is no exception.

As a result, by simply examining *discounts* and the *price of wheat*, over a period of at least five to six years, one can recognize whether a crisis is nearing or is still far-off, and, instead of attributing the commercial distress to unrest and revolutions, its cause and origin should be sought in the excesses of speculation, the overstocking of factories and the rise of prices.[18]

Every six or seven years, a general liquidation seems to be necessary for trade to start expanding once again.

Liquidations are what produce crises, which are the true touchstones of the value of commercial houses. All those that have embarked on undertakings that are beyond their means succumb. The others, robust enough to resist, resume the course of their operations with new vigor, freed as they are from the obstacles of imprudent speculation. But then, how could an industrialist, whose products are in demand, be wise enough to limit his production to the needs of the market? He is inevitably led to incessantly extend his operations as long as demands succeed each other. Then, all of a sudden, speculation, which has run out of steam, ceases; production, having reached high levels, is compelled to slow down, to subside; it becomes necessary to reduce wages and even to dismiss part of the workers one employs, which awakens among them those feelings of hate that manifest themselves so violently during the revolutions brought on by this discontent and this general distress.

Table 1. Discounted Bills.

	1799–1804 (million)	1805–1810 (million)	1805–1813 (million)	1814–1818 (million)	1820–1826 (million)[b]	1820–1830 (million)	1832–1839 (million)	1832–1847 (million)	1849–1857 (million)	1859–1864 (million)[a]
Starting point	111	255	255	84	255[b]	253	150	150	256	1,414
Years of prosperity	510	557	557	547	638	638	760	943	951	2,122
Pauses	503	545	545	"	"	"	756	749	907	2,066
Crises	630	715	640	615	688	617	1,047	1,329	2,085	2,881
Liquidations	255	391	84	253	407	150	847	256	1,414	2,448

Translator's notes: Table number and caption have been added during translation.
[a] Column absent in the first (1863) edition;
[b] For the period 1820–1826, the amount of discounts at the "starting point" is changed in the 1873 edition, from 253 to 255.

Table 2.   Average Price Per Hectoliter.

	Years of Abundance		Years of Shortage	Crises[a]
1799	16^{f}20^c	1803	24^{f}55^c	1804
1809	14 86	1812	34 34	1813
1814	17 73	1817	36 16	1818
1822	15 49	1829	22 59	1830
1834	15 25	1839	22 14	1839
1841	18 54	1847	29 01	1847
1849	14 15	1855	29 32	"
1859	16 74	1856	30 75	1857

Translator's note: Table number and caption have been added during translation.
[a]In the first edition, the ditto mark in the last column is missing.

Understandably, these periodical disturbances to which labor is subjected disrupt the living conditions of the working class and impose upon it harsh and painful deprivations: of this the movement of marriages, births, and deaths provide evidence, barring some exceptions that are easily observed when a great war is threatening or breaks out. In such circumstances, marriages (hence births) increase excessively, to allow young men to escape from being called up again.

There is thus a regular succession of prosperous periods, crises, and liquidations. All we need is a quick look at the annual, monthly, and weekly statements of the banks of France and England to show that their development can be followed step by step, almost month after month, or, at any rate and very clearly, year after year. The figures will tell us whether a crisis is nearing or way off, and, once the storm has blown over, they will allow us to perceive the moment of business revival.[19]

It is the simultaneous examination of the *maxima* and *minima* of the numerical records that will provide this remarkable result, whose constant recurrence since the beginning of the century, in France and in England, proves that we are not faced with a fortuitous relationship, with one of those accidents brought about by simple coincidence. Actually, once the *movement has begun* in one direction or the other, *upwards or downwards*, it continues uninterruptedly until there is a complete turnabout, which does not mean that every month the discounts, for instance, will be higher than the month before; there will be some oscillations; but each year's *maxima* and *minima* will always be higher and lower than those of the previous year, except for some rare and very slight exceptions, which perhaps we would not meet if we had the year's true extreme figure, whereas the official publication only depicts the situation on a single day.

Table 5 summarizes the operations of the two big institutions that exhibit the largest variations, depending on whether the general situation is prosperous or critical.[20] Our preference has been to choose, to bring out such variations, the following periods: 1843–1847, 1850–1857, and 1858–1861.[21]

Examination of the table of discounts (Table 1) shows that, from 1799 to 1855, the minimum reached by discounts varied within very narrow limits, from 84 million to 256. After having dropped to 84 million in 1814 and to 150 in 1832, the minimum fell, in 1849, to the same level as in 1805 and 1820.

In the years of crisis, discounts nearly always display the same figure between 1804 and 1830 (Table 3).

It is as if it were an inevitable figure; there is but one exception, that of the year 1810. Since 1830, discounts have increased in proportion to the intensity and the size of speculation (reaching the figures described in Table 4).

This figure, when it is compared to those reached in previous and subsequent years, is a clear indication that speculation is the cause of this artificial overexcitement of trade. It can thus be feared that we will see crises become more and more serious as industry develops.

Thus, in 1801, discounts drop back from 630 to 256 million; in 1830, from 617 to 155; in 1847, from 1,329 to 256; in 1857, from 2,081 to 1,414; in 1864[22], from 2,881 to 2,448.

In 1847, discounts fall back to 256 million, their level at the beginning of the century; this can give some idea of the extent of commercial distress (Table 5).

Table 3. Discounts, 1804–1830.

1804...	630 million	1826...	688 million
1813...	640 million	1830...	617 million
1818...	615 million		

Translator's note: Table number and caption have been added during translation.

Table 4. Discounts, Since 1830.

1839	1,047 million	1857	2,085 million
1847	1,329 million	1864[a]	2,881 million

Translator's note: Table number and caption have been added during translation.
[a] In the first edition, Juglar provides the figure for 1861 (2,123 million).

Table 5. Bank of France and Bank of England, 1844–1864.

		I. Portfolio, Discounts						II. Metallic Reserves				III. Notes in Circulation			
		France[*]		England		Total annual discounts		France		England		France		England	
		Max	Min	Max	Min	France	England	Max	Min	Max	Min	Max	Min	Max	Min
		fr.	fr.	p. st.	p. st	fr.	p. st	fr.	fr.	p. st	p. st	fr.	fr.	p. st	p. st
1st period	1844	101	73	11	7	749	2.6	273	236	15	14	215	242	21	19
	1845	164	88	16	8	1,003	18.5	268	193	16	13	262	257	22	19
	1846	180	135	23	12	1,290	34.2	197	110	16	13	311	258	21	19
	1847	192	167	21	14	1,327	38.3	89	66	14	8	255	229	20	17
	1848	252	57	16	10	692	8.8	137	53	15	12	383	263	19	16
	1849	57	41	11	9	256	4.5	289	145	17	14	413	359	19	17
2nd period	1850	144	100	14	9	1,175	7.4	475	432	17	14	492	449	20	18
	1851	150	93	15	11	1,240	15.2	622	470	17	13	563	503	20	18
	1852	273	106	14	10	1,824	7.7	608	510	22	17	671	552	23	19
	1853	394	231	19	12	2,847	25.9	533	316	20	14	685	628	23	20
	1854	410	241	16	13	2,947	22.6	497	280	16	12	642	582	22	19
	1855	479	310	19	12	3,745	22.1	440	210	18	10	662	592	20	18
	1856	511	382	21	13	4,419	30.9	285	163	13	9	638	594	21	18
	1857	608	501	31	15	5,596	49.1	288	188	11	6	612	531	21	18
3rd period	1858	543	348	25	14	4,561	''	593	250	19	12	690	562	22	20
	1859	534	440	19	16	4,947	''	644	523	19	16	754	669	23	21
	1860	562	437	24	19	5,083	''	548	431	16	12	787	709	24	20
	1861	608	444	21	16	5,329	''	431[b]	285[c]	14	10	778	713	21	19
	1862	682	446	21	17	5,217	''	431	285	18	14	869	723	22	19
	1863	681	475	25	17	5,512	''	406	196	15	13	864	739	22	19
	1864	791	562	23	17	6,449	''	367	152	14	12	839	720	22	19

Note: Movements of the portfolio, of the metallic reserves and of the circulation of notes, on the basis of the monthly and weekly statements, in France and England, in the three last periods[a].

Original note: [*]For Paris only until 1850; for Paris and branches, from and including that year. The amounts are in millions of francs (fr.) for the bank of France, and in millions of pounds sterling (p. st.) for England.

Translator's notes: Table number and caption have been added during translation.

[a]In the second edition, "movements" replaces "developments." In addition, Juglar provides the figures for years 1862, 1863, and 1864;

Each of the periods that serve as a basis for this table encompasses the years of prosperity and the extreme year in which the crisis breaks out. The two following ones are those of the liquidation. Following these two years, the movement resumes its course and goes through the same phases.

The similarity and the simultaneity of this movement, in France and England, clearly indicate that there is nothing particular or local about it and that it does not undergo the influence of the country's institutions or laws.

The Metallic Reserves

The metallic reserves are the counterpart of the discounts.[23] In the banks' monthly statements, it is striking to notice the movement, in the opposite direction, of the portfolio and the reserves. While one is constantly increasing, the others are quietly decreasing, flowing out little by little in a continuous fashion, and the dearth of specie is especially visible in times of crises, each of which reveals itself, to the careful observer, a long time in advance through the decline of the monthly and weekly *maxima* and *minima*.[24]

The reflux of specie is observed immediately after the crises, in the two or three following years, when the suspension of business comes to an end or at the time of the revival. By recovering so quickly, the reserves, like the discounts, display a higher maximum than in the previous period.

This dual movement of discounts and metallic reserves is therefore not specific to one single year, the year of the crisis, as it is seemingly believed, for we see it unfolding very visibly in one direction and in the other. The crisis appears and breaks out when, on both sides, the movement has reached its extreme limits, which proves that, even if external causes can trigger the outbreak, it must be recognized that everything was ready for this outcome to occur and that a little bit sooner, or a little bit later, liquidation was necessary; for a crisis is but a general liquidation that allows business to resume its course on a solid footing, and not by relying on credit conditions that are so tight that, under the burden of accumulated charges, collapse is inevitable.[25]

The situation of the metallic reserves differs from that of the discounts and the circulation of banknotes; its minimum is always observed in the year when the crisis breaks out and its maximum in the years of prosperity, contrary to what is noted for the two other items.

The reserves' maximum varied from 25 million (first period, 1799–1804) to 626 million, 1847–1856; 646 million, 1857–1864, and 1,318 million, 1864–1871 (Table 6).[26]

Table 6.   Bank of France Metallic Reserves.

Periods	Minima at the beginning of the period	Maxima	Minima at the end of the period
1799–1804	5	25	1
1804–1810	1	83	32
1810–1813	1	124	5
1814–1818	5	118	34
1820–1826	34	218	86
1826–1830	86	238	104
1830–1836	104	181	89
1836–1839	89	249	169
1840–1847	169	279	57
1847–1857	57	626	152
1857–1864	152	646	152
1864–1871	152	1,318	398

Note: Variations of the metallic reserves in Paris, and from 1848 including the branches and department banks[a].
Translator's note: Table number and caption have been added during translation.
[a]The data for 1857–1864 and for 1864–1871 are added in the second edition. Also, Juglar modifies figures for 1847–1857 (49, 626, and 72 in the first edition). "Departments" (*départements*) are the administrative divisions of France.

From 1814, the reserves' minimum remains very close to its 1818 level (34 million), 57 million in 1847, 49 million in 1848;[27] since the merger of the departmental banks, the movements of ebb and flow are even greater although the level of the reserves has been declining slightly less.[28]

Each time reserves reach their lowest level, specie flows back more abundantly than ever to the bank's coffers.

Thus

	Paris only (millions)	Paris and branches (millions)
1805–1807	1–89	
1825–1828	86–238	
1836–1838	89–298	
1848–1851	49–626	91–622
1857–1858	72–287	163–644[29]
1864–1868	38–937	152–1,314[30]

The preceding figures show clearly enough this twofold movement of ebb and flow.

CIRCULATION OF BANKNOTES

The circulation of banknotes exhibits much smaller oscillations than the discounts and the metallic reserves. Its maximum is always observed in the years that follow the crises, in France as well as in England, whereas the maximum of the metallic reserves has already been reached.[31] When appeals to the bank are the most pressing, the circulation has already fallen; when they diminish, it declines to a lower minimum than that of all previous years, before it picks up again.

For the period 1840–1847, the maximum reaches 311 million on December 31, 1845. On January 15, 1847, the reserves having fallen to their minimum level, the circulation amounts to only 271 million and by September 17, 1847, it has dropped to 217.

So there has been no excess issue, since the total amount is 40 million below the maximum already observed before.

Likewise, in England, the circulation's maximum, from 22 million pounds sterling reached in 1845, had declined to 18 million by October 1847, whereas the discount rate was at 6 percent; on the 25th of the same month, when it was brought to 8 percent, the total sum of issued banknotes did not exceed 20 million pounds sterling.

The circulation is affected but very weakly by the variations of the current accounts, for while the latter diminish by 83 million (1845–1847), the former only drops by 24, and this decline is probably not the effect of this one single cause, as the maximum circulation, 311 million in 1845, corresponds to only 95 million in the current accounts; in 1844 already, it stood at 245 million, and they did not exceed 39 million. From 39 million, they rise to 120 million (1844–1845), and yet the circulation varies only from 245 to 260 million, by roughly 15 million. The upward and downward oscillations are not comparable in size.

DEPOSITS AND VARIOUS CURRENT ACCOUNTS[32]

The deposits and the current accounts do not display the regular movements of the metallic reserves and of the discounts. Their oscillations are sudden, related to some quickly satisfied specific wants, which do not affect the general course of business. They are observed during prosperities and crises alike. Their amplitude can vary by as much as a factor of two; over the year, a drop or a rise of 50 percent is commonly observed. One must not be surprised to see such oscillations also occurring when banks are facing difficulties, but they are of little importance, as this is but the natural repetition of the movement observed in previous years, during which there was no noticeable influence on either metallic reserves or on discounts.

In both France and England, we note the same evolution. From 1840 to 1848, in France, deposits and current accounts varied from 32 million (1842) to 120 million (1845), reaching 37 million on July 24, 1847, whereas the reserves had already climbed back to 81 million. On January 15, 1847, when reserves were at their lowest, deposits and current accounts still stood at 64 million. Hence their minimum does not coincide with that of the metallic reserves; but, what is more, the former appears to be completely independent of the latter. For, if we have a quick look at the *minima* of the previous years, we find the same decline if not a greater one in 1844–1843– 1842–1841 (37, 34, 32, 35 million). For the period, these are years of prosperity.

From 1844 to 1857, we observe the same pattern.[33] The current accounts' maximum falls from 197 million to 150 million (1852–1857). The minimum that had been noted in 1855 (92 million) is not reached again; by the time the reserves had dropped to 184 million (January 3, 1857), they still totaled 131 million. On November 15, the interest rate was at 9 percent and the reserves were at their lowest (181 million), whereas there were still 125 million in the current accounts: that is, an amount 25 to 30 million in excess of the minimum ever reached in all previous years.

In England, as well, private deposits, varying from 3 to18 million pounds sterling between 1841 and 1846, fall back to 7 million in 1847, a minimum already observed in 1843, 1844, and 1845.

From 1848 to 1852, they vary from 8 to 15 million; in the following years and into 1859, they do not fall below 9 million; *this minimum is not even reached* during the crisis.

With the discount rate at 9 and 12 percent, from November 4 to November 18, deposits remain at 12 and 14 million pounds sterling. In December, amidst the difficulties of a very dreadful liquidation, they had already returned to their maximum, 15 million pounds sterling.

We insist on these variations, because some very authoritative writers claimed that crises were most often caused by withdrawals from banks' current accounts, causing a quick decline of metallic reserves; factual evidence proves the opposite.[34]

THE ADVANCES BY THE BANKS ON GOVERNMENT SECURITIES, RAILROAD STOCKS, AND BONDS

The increase and decrease of advances do not follow the same course in England and France. In our country, where their development only began in 1852, we do not observe the continuous up-and-down movements that struck our attention so forcibly in the case of discounts and metallic reserves;[35] in contrast, in England, the maximum figure is the result of an, so to speak, uninterrupted sequence, and during crises, it coincides with that of discounts. The immoderate increase in the amount of advances in difficult times, their decline or rather their nearly complete disappearance during liquidations, everything truly indicates that advances are linked to the movement of trade.

In France, on the contrary, we observe sudden oscillations, unrelated to each other, that result instead from a special need that is easy to recognize (when borrowings and conversions are issued, in the case of advances on government securities, when railroad-building activity is being given a great boost, in the case of advances on stocks and bonds).

The total amount of annual advances on government bonds, which, in Paris, reached 262 million in 1852 (conversion of the 5 percent bond), decreases to 68 million in 1854. The Eastern war loan raised their level to 452 million, and in 1857, the year of the crisis, it did not exceed 124 million.[36] The same holds for advances on railroad stocks and bonds: estimated at 395 and 326 million, in 1853 and 1855; they do not exceed 102 million in 1857.

DURATION AND LIQUIDATION OF CRISES

Generally crises do not last very long, if we consider only the most critical moments, that is, those during which the demands for discounts, the decline of metallic reserves, and the unfavorable foreign exchanges induce banks to raise the rate of interest several times in quick succession.[37] As long as confidence creates the conditions for credit to be granted, the rest follows. The facilities credit provides allow the undertaking of large-scale transactions without having to worry about prices; is it not the role of credit to support you and to help you meet your commitments? But there comes a time when, because of trading difficulties, it becomes necessary to fall back upon metallic reserves. This is when crises break out, panics take hold of the public, transactions come to a standstill and suspensions occur. Credit vanishes into thin air. Its absence points to how useful it is, but actually what is lost is only a small fraction of what was owed.[38] This state does not persist for more than six weeks or two months, and then comes the crisis' liquidation, which lasts between 18 months and two years. The previous years' bustling activity is succeeded by sluggishness of trade, merely confined to cash operations. The continuous rise in prices of the preceding years, replaced by a rapid decline, brings to a halt all business whose main support was provided by credit.

The excesses of domestic and foreign trade, carried out at prices inflated by speculation and not at natural prices, these are the main cause of all the difficulties. As products cannot be sold at ever increasing prices, all trade comes to a standstill. As merchandise is for sale, the price decrease is quick: it reaches 25–30 percent within a few months, thereby wiping out, in an instant, the rise of several years. This is when the so brilliantly constructed credit structure collapses,[39] and premiums have disappeared: as securities no longer find buyers, one must liquidate and abandon one's dreams, face losses, whereas a year earlier one expected to make a fortune. Yet it must not be inferred that credit and speculation are harmful, for whereas commercial embarrassments last a fairly short time, at most one or two years, prosperous times extend over several years in a row, six or seven on average. During this period there is widespread progression. The market is supplied very abundantly with cheap money, interest falls below 3 percent; demands for funds are immediately satisfied; offerings for securities are greatly oversubscribed, so they must be reduced, and all this takes place whatever the obstacles that might get in the way. At this moment, a great war would not slow down the movement; resources are so plentiful that they can meet all demands, even the hugest borrowings. Government funds can be affected, but the movement of trade does not decelerate, carrying on instead until the bank's portfolio becomes glutted with amounts of discounts even greater than in the previous crisis. This fact alone, observable before any restrictive measures are taken, clearly points to the needs, to the embarrassments of trade, which requires, to continue its course, even greater reliance on credit. In view of these disruptions, the development of societies, their intense activity and their power, are all the more surprising. As to the periodical return of crises, it stands out clearly in the enumeration of the crises that have been occurring since the beginning of the century, as we see in Table 7.

Table 7. Commercial Crises: France, England, and the United States.

France	England	The United States
1804	1803	"
1810	1810	"
1813	1815	1814
1818	1818	1818
1826	1826	1826
1830	1830	"
1836	1836	1837
1839	1839	1839
1847	1847	1848
1857	1857	1857
1864[a]	1864	Civil war

Translator's note: Table number and caption have been added during translation.
[a]The last row of the table is added in the second edition.

A simple inspection of this table shows that these three countries are interdependent, as we find them in the same situation within an interval of just a few months.

There is no regular development of the trade and of the wealth of nations without pain and without resistance. Temporary halts occur during which society as whole seems completely paralyzed, resources appear to have vanished; the country looks as if it were about to disappear into an abyss or at least to be entering a state of general bankruptcy.

The more we observe commercial crises, since the official statements of the banks have been at our disposal in France, England, and the United States, that is, since the beginning of the century, the more we remain convinced that their course, their accidents are becoming increasingly simultaneous,[40] so that, as soon as some difficulty is felt on either side of the Atlantic, rarely is there no corresponding event on the opposite one. If we narrow the scope of our investigation, we note that since 1800, in England and France, crises have followed a regular and parallel course, breaking out and ending in liquidation at almost always the same time.

That, in America, crises were less observed in the first few years is due to the weak development of its relations and of its trade, but they quickly acquired the same importance and standing as the commercial disruptions that distress the world periodically, yet without impeding the development of the country's prosperity. It can even be said that the severity of crises is proportionate to the development of the wealth of the country. A crisis is a temporary halt that, after a rise of several years during which speculation had eventually gained the upper hand, enables regular trade to recover its normal course after having rid itself of imprudent speculation. Thus, at no time does one see greater enthusiasm, easier business conditions, more confidence and security than after the liquidation of crises. As their name indicates, crises are distressing accidents, but, as in diseases, they prepare a better condition by expelling all impurities.

Despite the large number of bankruptcies that accompany crises, rarely do we see good houses going bankrupt. Those that have let themselves be dragged into mad speculations are liquidated, which rids the market of an incessant cause of turmoil and ruin. As long as the rise persists, products are traded and no one loses. But woe betide the last buyer! The decline is so quick that, without the credit facilities that had hitherto engaged him and supported him, his ruin is inevitable; like so, trade returns to its natural path.

Bad harvests, the high price of grain, food shortages often accompany the glut of banks' portfolios in our country, and they complicate all the more an already bad situation; however, this coincidence is not required for a commercial crisis to take place; evidence of this is provided by observing what is happening in America, where, despite low prices of grain, the development of discounts and, to some extent, the abuse of credit, cause crises to break out slightly earlier than in Europe, the situation being equally embarrassed on both sides.

If the food shortage coincides with already glutted portfolios, the crisis will undoubtedly be more serious, but it will still be a mere accident, causing all the more trouble as, the pyramid of credit having been overturned, at the smallest shock, everything collapses and tumbles down. The extent to which discounts decline clearly indicates whether the liquidation has been drastic and far-reaching, in which case a vigorous and long-lasting revival of business can be predicted. If, on the contrary, there is only a temporary halt, a small reduction of discounts, in a word, a semi-liquidation, there will be a slight recovery, soon followed by a relapse.

FORMER OPINIONS ON CRISES[41]

In every country, in France, England, and the United States, a particular opinion on the causes of crises has predominated, and this opinion has varied according to times and circumstances. Whatever the case, nonetheless, we are rather inclined to accuse our neighbor and to put the blame on him. We affirm that we have been led almost despite ourselves, so as to absolve ourselves in advance. We keep repeating that, were it not for outside complications, we would be in a good position! And yet crises occur everywhere in similar circumstances and at the same moment, as we have indicated. The only difference is the starting point, which is sometimes in France (1818), sometimes in England (1825), and other times in the United States (1836). But as soon as the shock is delivered, like the flame running along a gunpowder train, crises spread with lightening speed in the main marketplaces of the world. So – to pursue our comparison – since the mine blows up everywhere at the same time, it must have been prepared and loaded everywhere, waiting only for an accident that sooner or later, in one place or another, would produce the explosion.

Because they were unwilling to admit that crises are not a contemporary fact but the result instead of profound alterations in credit operations and in society's methods of production, most authors, more concerned with the epoch in which they were writing, sought to explain the origin and the nature of crises by suggesting causes that were very special and specific to circumstances. In all epochs, the dominant event of the period was taken as the cause of all evil. Sometimes, it was an internal or external disturbance; and it was so convenient to blame the inadequate charter of the issuing banks, notably the artificial limit, so they say, that banks impose on their operations by making them depend on their metallic reserves. People liked to forget that the essential requirement when issuing banknotes is that *money* be *readily available* as nothing else can replace it: the removal of the obligation of redeeming them in specie upon presentation is what causes in no time their unavoidable depreciation. This is what experience has shown in France, England, and the United States; it has been conclusive everywhere.

It must not be forgotten that a banknote is merely a liability, a commercial bill, a simple commitment, a simple promise; it replaces neither gold nor silver, although the ease with which it circulates economizes on their use. Promissory notes, bills of exchange, notes issued by bankers, checks, and letters of credit, even though they do not have the same advantages as banknotes, also enter the circulation and make it impossible to confuse the metallic circulation with the fiduciary circulation. In England, in the past few years, although the bank's circulation reached 30 million pounds sterling, the total amount of bills of exchange was estimated at more than 130 million pounds sterling (Tooke, Newmarch), and it is reckoned that this paper circulates one-third more quickly than money. The huge quantity of checks that are traded in the *Clearing House* (150 million francs per day and more) also perform the functions of the banknote.[42]

As, in the midst of embarrassments, credit institutions remain the main hope, the only source of assistance, their charter has been carefully examined. Each of the items of their balance sheet, their privilege, their monopoly, their nominal capital, realized and available, the circulation, the metallic reserves, the current account deposits, the variation of the rate of interest, all have in turn been criticized and blamed; according to their supporters, had these criticisms been given credit, crises would have disappeared forever. The variety of the causes and of the means proposed to prevent or to cure a pain whose symptoms and effects are similar casts some doubts as to their effectiveness.

The decline of the metallic reserves, the suspension of banknote redemption, the difficulties of discounting, not to mention the high rate that is then demanded, these are the most serious difficulties that must be fought.

So let us examine the opinions on this topic of the main economists and inquiry committees. First of all, the blame was laid on the most obvious causes, namely wars, revolutions, food shortages, borrowings, and so on. But crises occur extensively without there being any such complications, whose harmful influence must not however be ignored. Let us begin with the most generally admitted causes; afterwards, we discuss the particular opinions of several economists.[43]

POLITICAL CAUSES OF CRISES

Although political causes play a secondary role in producing commercial crises, they should not be disregarded. All the complications, unrest, and ruin they involve are so strikingly obvious that, for whoever does not scrutinize the origins, this is where is to be found the most convenient, the simplest, and the easiest to grasp, explanation of all commercial disturbances. The delusion is all the greater as events are what are blamed for the embarrassments, for the seriousness of a critical position in which, with the greatest imprudence, one had not feared to engage.

However, a glance at events in England and in the United States shows us that the most serious crises, in these two countries, broke out in the absence of any political complication (crises of 1825, 1837, 1847, and 1857).

But let us reconsider the whole string of crises and political events since 1800, let us seek whether they coincide, not only abroad, but also at home in France, with the so many and various political events that, like a series of changes of scenes in a show, have one after the other contradicted all the predictions and upset the schemes of the most shrewd politicians.

The crisis of 1804 breaks out only one year after the Amiens peace treaty. The crisis of 1810 occurs at the time of the establishment of the continental blockade, which was expected, according to its instigator's predictions, to provide us with undisputable commercial supremacy. In contrast, the wars with Austria, Prussia, and Spain did not impede the course and the expansion of business. Recovery had been quick, and it was only after the disasters of 1813 and of 1814 that the liquidation was thoroughly achieved.

The crisis of 1818 breaks out in the middle of peacetime, following a period of feverish excitement and boundless, or so was it believed, subscriptions of all the loans that were issued.

The French and foreign governments drew upon them extensively to settle their expenses and to constitute the debt that the wars of the Revolution and the Empire had left as a souvenir across Europe, among both the victors and the vanquished.

The crisis of 1825–1826 was only felt three years after the Spanish war, and in England and the United States, the crisis was much more intense than in France.

The crisis of 1830 alone coincides with the July Revolution. However, the development of industry and trade throughout 1829 and into 1830 already indicated how fraught with tension the situation was, how difficult business conditions were. It was the straw that broke the camel's already over-burdened back, and it forced a liquidation that had been only partial in 1826. But then, how quickly industry and trade developed until 1836! At that moment the English and the American crises hit France and led to a temporary halt, activity resuming nonetheless its course until 1839; but then embarrassments were felt everywhere, although to various extents, with no political accident that could provide either an explanation or a rationale. The Eastern question, which threatened to disturb peace in Europe in 1840, arose after the crisis and did not precede it.[44]

The period from 1840 to 1847 elapses without the occurrence of any important political events. In the absence of any disturbance, the wealth of nations develops at a quicker pace. The crisis of 1847 had already struck France and England with all its great intensity when the revolution broke out on February 24, 1848. After a prosperous period, the smallest sufferings are unbearable, and restless populations, like ours, seek in internal revolutions a remedy to their distress, or at least a distraction, and an outflow of the excess population in external wars with all their raging consequences.

There is no better proof of the influence and the action of commercial crises on the life of nations and on the variations of public opinion in difficult times and in prosperous years, as the latter is determined almost entirely by one or the other of these situations. Tooke observes that the war declared in 1793 was not what initiated the lack of confidence and the discredit that brought trade to a standstill at that time. It worsened an already bad situation, which had become so under the effect of the worldwide expansion of the system of credit and of paper circulation. Bankruptcies appear in the autumn of 1792: consols were still quoted at 90. *The decline of prices is not the consequence of the war, but the result of the liquidation of the great operations undertaken two or three years before.*

The last crisis of 1857, so dreadful in England and the United States, affected France only weakly in the beginning. A few light wounds were silently healed, and an attempt was made to get started again; but from this moment up to 1860 the movement was held back, and until the natural evolution, in the form of a serious liquidation, had not run its course, the recovery was quite difficult;[45] everyone, "the departments, the cities and individual companies [had] embarked upon very huge expenses" (according to Mr Fould in his report of 1861).[46,47]

In other countries, a crisis can break out without the government being held responsible for its consequences; it is also true that, in prosperous years, people are less prone to render thanks to their government as if it were the originator and the single source of all prosperities. The government is more willing to let good be merely the result of the fair and fruitful competition of all engaged interests.

In France, as it must sadly be admitted and as it is unfortunately confirmed by our numerous revolutions, our attachment to the government is scarcely chivalrous. We support and praise it as long as it acts in accordance with our own interests, or even better, provided it lets us conduct our business as we wish; whenever, most of the time because of our own mistakes, business becomes difficult and embarrassed, we withdraw our trust. After having taken an awkward position, we enjoin the government to act, or, tossing restlessly in our bed of pain, we ask for reforms that are sometimes irrelevant, always regarded as panaceas to all our pains, and our demands are but a means of expressing our discontent.[48] From this disastrous and dangerous habit of being grateful for all good in years of prosperity, there results, through the reverse effect, that one charges and blames it for all evil in times of crisis. Hence this ebb and flow of public opinion in France, which now establishes a dynasty, now overturns it.

MONETARY CRISES

In line with the investigation we have just made, can it be admitted that monetary crises exist independently of commercial crises, that they are special crises, characterized by the diminution of metallic reserves, by the outflow of specie for the purpose of balancing certain domestic or foreign payments, and that they end spontaneously when these temporary needs have been met? If under this heading we consider the mere decline of reserves, followed by a slight increase of the discount rate, it is certain that such movements are not rare, but nor do they ever cause any serious disturbance to business and, more often than not, they cease very quickly. They are periodical movements required by the necessities of trade; but they are not crises, for we see them recurring regularly every year. The recourses to metallic reserves are moderate and never a threat; a mere 1 percent increase of the discount rate, often even no change whatsoever, and everything ceases. We do not find here the glutted portfolio, the rushed demands for discounts, the unfavorable foreign exchanges, which drain simultaneously the specie at such a speed and in such proportions that, for fear that the sight repayment of banknotes might be at risk, the discount rate is increased several times in quick succession, maturities are reduced, and credit is even completely cut off.[49] These are the only cases when a monetary crisis can be said to be occurring, but then what we are really witnessing is a commercial crisis. In all other circumstances, a monetary crisis, if one still wants to call it so, is only a minor accident that is improperly referred to as a crisis.[50]

OPINIONS OF THE MAIN ECONOMISTS

J. B. Say thought that the public's haste, in times of crises, to claim the redemption of banknotes – in a word, a *run* on the bank, to use the English expression – was due to their excess issue, which reduced the value of gold and caused it be exported to where it retained its full value.[51] By multiplying the circulating medium for discounting purposes, business was thus extended to a size disproportionate to that of capital.

J. B. Say was wrong in blaming the excess issue of banks. The cause of all evil is the excess issue of mercantile paper, of bills of exchange, which do not clear upon maturity, because the products, whose price has increased, circulate more slowly; to close the gap, it is necessary to resort to specie.[52]

Senior notes that, in 1825, exports of precious metals totaled 4,400,000 pounds sterling. From 1855 to 1857, in France, judging by the purchases of bullion, the sum exported exceeds 1,300 million francs!

Wilson attributes crises to a simple speculative fever erupting at a certain moment, due to the enticement caused by certain operations. But what provokes this fever? This he does not say.

Tooke seeks to establish a link between crises and the rise of grain prices, which also recurs periodically. He insists on the variations of exchange rates and with much sagacity points to their importance in the balancing of payments with foreign countries. In a very curious table, he points to the coincidence of favorable foreign exchanges with the reduction of overseas expenses (war, purchases of grain, etc.). These two causes need not always interfere, for, in 1825, whereas they had no role to play, the decline of foreign exchanges was such that the drain on metallic reserves went on for the greater part of the year.

One cannot estimate whether there is an excess or a shortage of circulation by comparing the number of banknotes issued to the size of metallic reserves. Only exports or imports of precious metals, in other words, *only foreign exchanges provide the proper estimate.*

In England, the exaggerated issue of banknotes and excess speculations of all sorts have especially been the concern of the authors who have studied commercial crises. In France, Mr Coquelin, in his book on credit and banking expresses the same opinion as J. B. Say,[53] but instead of blaming the mere reimbursement of banknotes, he believes it is rather the deposits in current accounts that are withdrawn in specie.[54] The privileged banks would be the cause of all evil. Their monopoly creates an overabundance of savings funds and an overflow of such funds seeking employment. Mr du Puynode, in his book, *De la Monnaie, du Crédit et de l'Impôt*, totally shares the opinions already expressed by Mr Coquelin.[55]

We have stated the objections that have been raised concerning the banks' present charter and indicated the methods that are recommended for supporting trade, even speculation, by means of devices so well-designed that they would never be the victims of their excesses and would be able to brave any danger with impunity.

The most simple observations will show us to what extent factual evidence contradicts these attractive theories.

An excess issue of banknotes is especially noticeable only where free banking prevails, for, if we examine the circulation of banknotes issued by the privileged banks in France and England, we observe that, since the resumption of payments, it is not at all excessive in times of crises.

It is subject to yearly variations and never reaches its maximum during embarrassments, which is when the metallic reserves are at their lowest.

Table 8 describes the variations of the circulation in England and France during the last four crises.

The maximum always precedes the crises; by the time they break out, it has already fallen.

The ratio of the metallic reserves to the paper circulation is much more variable, ranging from one-third to one-seventh. In the United States, the latter proportion is the one most often observed. In 1837, there were six paper dollars for one metal dollar in the banks' coffers; in 1857, eight paper dollars for one metal dollar.

The privileged official circulation is nothing, so to speak, compared to the private and free circulation, which, under the heading of bills of exchange, letters of credit, promissory notes, money orders, and checks, performs the functions of the banknote in a way that is so useful to society. According to Messrs Tooke and Newmarch, it has not fallen below 180 or 200 million

Table 8.   Paper Circulation During Crises.

	England			France	
	Millions of £ st.			Millions of fr.	
	Max	Min		Max	Min
1st period					
1820...	26	22	1820	171	122
1822...	20	16	1824	251	194
1825...	26	19	1825	243	179
2nd period					
1832...	19	16	1831	238	200
1834...	20	16	1835	241	207
1837...	20	16	1836	231	196
3rd period					
1840...	18	15	1840	251	200
1845...	22	19	1846	311	243
1847...	20	17	1847	288	217
4th period			Paris and branches		
1846...	19	16	1848	415	272
1853...	23	20	1853	685	628
1857...	21	18	1857	649	529

Translator's note: Table number and caption have been added during translation.

pounds sterling in recent years, whereas the overall circulation of the banks of England, Scotland, and Ireland did not exceed 41 million.[56] This is where excesses can be found when, promises to pay having matured, products not having been sold, or proceeds not having been collected, the bank is called upon, and when also, not only for credit, but also for settling certain payments, the metallic reserves are dug into.

It is these liabilities, most of which are unsuitable for acceptance by banks, that cause the suspensions, the forced liquidations, the bankruptcies, in other words, the whole train of events that ordinarily characterize crises.

Indeed, why would the banks enlarge their circulation so as to absorb the floating promises to pay and the least secure of them all, those which not only have not been honored, but for which extension has been requested?

In each period we face the succession of the same accidents: a quick increase of discounts, unfavorable foreign exchanges, a decline of reserves, and a drain on the coffers of the bank, in conjunction with an almost unchanged circulation.[57]

Thus, in 1804, 1813, 1847, and 1857, defensive measures, that is, the increase in the discount rate, the shortening of discount maturities, the limitation of redemptions, even their suspension, are taken only when the crisis, having reached its peak, is about to end and to subside: this is so very true that money flows back immediately, which would not happen, if needs were the same as before. For it is easy to understand that these restrictions avert the outflow of specie but that they cause its return, demand remaining unchanged, is less easy to grasp, unless we recognize that the forced sale of the products, which the speculators did not want to relinquish earlier at a loss, is the only single way of ending the reliance on *specie* for the *clearing of exchanges*.

In France, as the blame could not be put on the Act of 1844, great efforts were made to look elsewhere for the cause and the remedy to crises. Capital, deposits in current accounts, and the fixity of the discount rate, these were the most seriously discussed issues.

We will not mention the rasher and more unscientific opinions of those who did not fear to propose a more or less disguised return to paper currency.

At all epochs, the bank has always supplied the circulation with an amount of paper currency much greater than its capital, accepting the temporary sacrifices that its position imposed upon it, but that were more than compensated in years of prosperity by the interest earned on the capital invested in government securities. Its capital itself, which in compliance with its charter always remains available, would not protect the reserves in difficult times. The statement of the bank's operations shows us, in effect, that the purchases of bullion added up to an amount of 1,300,000,000 francs, from 1855 to 1857, which represents nearly 15 times its capital.

As to the deposits and the current accounts, we have expounded the opinion of Mr Coquelin, supported by Mr du Puynode. Unfortunately, whereas it is attractive at first glance, it soon appears that it does not fit the facts, when one takes the pains to seriously check whether it is borne out by the official figures.

In France and England, their considerably large oscillations – since they vary *every year* by about 33 percent in England and by 50 percent in France – are not, as it might be thought, at their minimum in times of greatest business embarrassments and when all available capital is called back.[58]

In the last two periods, in 1847 and 1857, the deposits' minimum is observed in the years that precede the crisis in France and England.

The maximum, which is noticed in the years of greatest prosperity, is often reached the very year when the minimum is met.

Table 9 provides a portrayal of the situation.

The most cursory examination shows us the considerable variations that recur annually and form what can be called the normal movement of deposits.

What must especially be noted is that, in England, the minimum and the maximum vary only very slightly. In France, only the maximum presents large differences, but the *minima* have not varied within each period.

In both countries, the same minimum is observed during prosperity and during crises.

What is more, the minimum does not even coincide with that of the metallic reserves.

Table 9.   Deposits and Current Accounts.

Bank of England (in millions of pounds sterling)			Bank of France (in millions of francs)		
Year	Max	Min	Years	Max	Min
1845...	11	8	1844...	60	37
1846...	18	8	1845...	120	42
1847...	11	8	1847...	69	37
1852...	15	9	1852...	157	104
1856...	14	9	1855...	167	92
1857...	15	9	1857...	150	104

Translator's note: Table number and caption have been added during translation.

In England, in 1857, the minimum, 9 million pounds sterling, is reached on June 27, whereas reserves are still at 11 million. When they declined to 6 million (November 18), with a discount rate at 10 percent, private deposits had already climbed back to 13 million and even to 14,900,000 pounds sterling, on November 25, with reserves still at a low of 7 million.[59]

The same can be said of public deposits. The minimum, observed in July 1857 (3 million), had risen in October (8 million), dropped back to 5 million, and then barely varied from November 11 to 25, before moving slightly upwards (6 million on December 2).[60]

In France, on March 13, 1857, the current accounts' minimum (104 million) coincides with metallic reserves still standing at 219 million.

By November 15, when the latter reached their minimum, current accounts had already climbed back to 125 million.

Nor does the minimum figure of the Treasury's current account coincide with the trough of the metallic reserves. It is reached in March (68 million); in September, on the eve of the crisis, it hits its maximum (121 million), and finally, in November, when the reserves are threatened, it only drops to 72 million. Besides, the Treasury does not withdraw its deposits in specie; it is the first to be concerned with bringing relief to the bank, and the banknotes that serve to settle the accounts of the various public utilities are not amongst those that are presented for redemption in order to make payments abroad.

The careful examination of the way deposits evolve over time does not confirm Mr Coquelin's otherwise so ingenious views. This is a case where practice refutes theory.

In the United States, the rapid development of deposits, which, from 109 million, rose to 230 million dollars in 1857, was yet surpassed by that of discounts and advances, which from 364 had reached 684 million, while the so dangerous and altogether artificial ratio of the metallic reserves to the paper in circulation, a ratio of 1 to 8, remained a threat.[61] The last two causes alone were to bring on the suspension that the withdrawal of deposits further precipitated.

Now, what is there to be said about free banking, as this is the solution that Messrs Coquelin and du Puynode advocate? Can it seriously be considered as a practical means of averting the excesses of speculation? The compared history of crises in the United States, Scotland, England, and France, countries subjected to a regime of either free banking or monopoly of note issue, will exempt us from dwelling on this matter.[62]

Left to be examined now is the last method that has been recommended: the fixity of the discount rate. An anonymous writer believes that fixity would provide a benefit that is desirable to everyone, namely the invaluable advantage of a perfectly secure, always regular and smooth, circulation of the liabilities representing realized exchanges. But is this condition, *of utmost importance* to the system, always fulfilled? Whereas speculators are attracted by the profits resulting from regular and prosperous business activity, they lose no time, when they have run out of resources, in resorting to anything that can support them by increasing the paper circulation; thence the issue of accommodation bills.[63] To obtain funds, whose access is charged a very high price, many houses do not hesitate to create for themselves, through a system of sham credit, fictitious resources, and to circulate sums that have no raison d'être. Here is the first source of error. The second one is to think that, when discounts are cheap, banks are less exacting, less strict in the scrutiny of discounted bills, hence an unwarranted extension of trade credit. However, the total value of discounted bills is never as low as at such times.[64] Besides, what is advised has already existed in the past without producing the awaited beneficial effects.[65] Those who recommend fixed discount rates or an increase in the circulation of banknotes as remedies have certainly forgotten the crises of 1804, 1810, 1813, 1818, 1826, 1830, 1839, and 1847, during which neither the fixed discount rate maintained at 5 percent nor the free issue of banknotes that was entirely unrestricted in several countries were able to prevent disaster.[66]

Crises, like illnesses, appear to be one of the conditions for the existence of societies where trade and industry dominate. We can anticipate crises, alleviate their effects, partially protect ourselves from them, facilitate business recovery; but eliminating them is something, despite having resorted to the most diverse devices, so far no one has managed to achieve. To propose a remedy ourselves, having recognized the little effectiveness of those recommended by others, is impossible, even less since, as a result of a natural evolution, equilibrium reestablishes itself and prepares a firm ground on which one can fearlessly take foot and cover a new period.[67] Knowing the nature and the seat of the pain is already a great achievement; changing the system does not suffice to prevent or eliminate it; only the experience and expertise of those entrusted with the government of credit institutions can diminish or mitigate its adverse effects.

We can only mention, here, the interdependence and the perfect correspondence that exist between the clearly observable oscillations of discounts and metallic reserves and the other phenomena, manifestations of the life of peoples, such as commercial transactions (imports and exports), the movement of the population (marriages, births, and deaths), public revenues, direct and indirect taxes, Treasury deficits, the floating debt, and so on:[68] everything moves together under the effect of mutual interdependence, subjected to the same influences, as if responding to the same power of expansion and contraction. The constant repetition of the same accidents, in the three countries where credit and business are the most developed, provides accordingly the best scientific confirmation of what we wanted to demonstrate.

Thus, the steady development of the wealth of nations does not take place without pains and without resistances. During crises, everything is temporarily at a standstill, society seems paralyzed; but this is only a passing torpor, the prelude to more beautiful destinies: in a word, it is a general liquidation.[69]

NOTES

1. [*Translator's note:*] In Juglar (1863), the opening sentence begins as follows: "For several years, attention has been directed by the circumstances towards what we agree should be called...."

2. [*Translator's note:*] In Juglar (1873), "notes" is replaced by "banknotes" and "and under the influence of unfavorable exchanges" is added.

3. [*Translator's note:*] It is important to note that Juglar refers exclusively to banks that issue banknotes. In other texts, Juglar writes "Bank(s)" using upper-case *b*, as he is in fact referring to the Bank of France, the Bank of England, etc.

4. [*Translator's note:*] In Juglar (1863), this sentence is completed by "without noticeably diminishing the requirements of trade," which Juglar deleted in the second edition.

5. [*Translator's note:*] In Juglar (1873), the author replaces "complete refusals" by "difficulties."

6. [*Translator's note:*] In Juglar (1873), "the exchange rate returns to par, and the reflux of specie begins" is added.

7. [*Translator's note:*] In Juglar (1873), addition of "a failure of mercantile paper to clear across the various world markets, thereby requiring the intervention of metallic specie."

8. [*Translator's note:*] In Juglar (1873), the author replaces "its intervention" by "the frequent intervention of credit." To be noted: the wording in French is more ambiguous, as Juglar writes "les crises se sont régularisées."

9. [*Translator's note:*] In Juglar (1873), "When credit operates actively in transactions" is replaced by "When credit plays a great role in transactions."

10. [*Translator's note:*] In Juglar (1873), addition of "and as mercantile paper no longer clears, indicating a stoppage in the trading of goods, foreign exchanges become unfavorable."

11. [*Translator's note:*] In Juglar (1873), addition of "that is, they increase the price of metal up to the price level of goods."

12. [*Translator's note:*] In Juglar (1873), "already" is added.

13. [*Translator's note:*] In Juglar (1873), the author replaces "tout à coup" by "sans qu'on s'y attende."

14. [*Translator's note:*] In the first edition, Juglar writes "la reserve disparaît même," which is replaced by "la reserve disparaît à son tour" in the second edition.

15. [*Translator's note:*] In the 1873 edition "que les chiffres font ressortir d'eux-mêmes à première vue" replaces "que les chiffres offrent d'eux-mêmes tout d'abord."

16. [*Translator's note:*] In Juglar (1863), the list is introduced by "Ce sont."

17. [*Translator's note:*] Replacement, in Juglar (1873), of "porter notre attention sur l'étude" by "procéder à l'étude."

18. [*Translator's note:*] In Juglar (1873), "and the rise of prices" has been added.

19. [*Translator's note:*] In the first edition, Juglar writes "The figures will speak for themselves better than anything we could add. They will allow us...."

20. [*Translator's note:*] In Juglar 1973 edition, the author replaces "The table that follows" by "The table below."

21. It will be easy to complete this study by examining the tables that trace the movement back, in the case of France, to the beginning of the century, and even further back, in the case of England. One would thus find, in the past, confirmation of the present and valuable indications for the future. We provide these tables in our book on commercial crises and on their periodical return in France, England, and the United States, awarded the prize of the *Institut*, Paris, Guillaumin. (*Translator's note*: the "Institut" that Juglar is referring here is the *Académie des sciences morales et politiques*.)

22. [*Translator's note:*] In the first edition, Juglar provides the data for 1861 (2,122 to ").

23. [*Translator's note:*] In Juglar (1863), the wording is: "The metallic reserves being the counterpart of the discounts, we must study them here."

24. [*Translator's note:*] Juglar does not begin a new paragraph here in the first edition.

25. [*Translator's note:*] Juglar writes: "car une crise n'est qu'une liquidation générale pour permettre aux affaires de reprendre sur un base solide, et non sur les ressorts d'un crédit trop tendu, que les charges accumulées finissent par rompre."

26. [*Translator's note:*] In the first edition, Juglar only provides figures for two "periods" (1799–1804 and 1847–1856).

27. [*Translator's note:*] In Juglar 1963, the author adds "in 1857, 70 million."

28. [*Translator's note:*] "since the merger ... slightly less" is added by the author in Juglar (1873). The adjective "departmental" refers here to the French *départements*.

29. [*Translator's note:*] In Juglar (1863), the figure for 1857 (Paris only) is 70.

30. [*Translator's note:*] The author adds the figures for 1864–1868 in Juglar (1873).

31. [*Translator's note:*] The author has substituted "follow" (*suivent*) for "precede" (*précèdent*) in the second edition.

32. [*Translator's note:*] Juglar provides no table here for this item. See, however, Table 9.

33. [*Translator's note:*] Juglar writes "1844 to 1857" in both editions, whereas it would have been natural for Juglar to carry on with the study of 1850–1857. In fact, he is implicitly referring to the table included at the end of the article. However, the figure he cites in this passage in reference to 1852 (197) differs from the one that appears in the table (157). The other figures are consistent.

34. [*Translator's note:*] There is a slight difference in the wording used in the two editions. Juglar replaces "de là, diminution rapide" by "ce qui entraînait une diminution rapide."

35. [*Translator's note:*] In the first edition, Juglar writes: "In our country, their development only began in 1852. We...."

36. [*Translator's note:*] Juglar is referring here to the Crimean war (1853–1856).

37. [*Translator's note:*] Interestingly, "the unfavorable exchanges" appears in both editions. This is the only reference to the role of exchange rates in Juglar 1963.

38. [*Translator's note:*] Juglar's wording here is "mais en réalité on ne perd qu'une faible fraction de qu'on lui [credit] devait."

39. [*Translator's note:*] Juglar writes: "Alors l'échafaudage si brillant du crédit s'écroule...."

40. [*Translator's note:*] In the second edition, Juglar replaces *solidaires* (interdependent) by *simultanés* (simultaneous).

41. [*Translator's note:*] In the second edition, Juglar has changed this subtitle from: "Influence of the Political Causes. Opinion of the Main Economists. Means to Avoid Crises, Proposed Remedies."

42. [*Translator's note:*] The specification within parentheses (150 million francs per day and more) is added in Juglar (1873).

43. [*Translator's note:*] This sentence is added by Juglar in the second edition.

44. [*Translator's note:*] The "Eastern question" (*la question d'Orient*) refers to problems raised in Europe by the decay of the Ottoman Empire. See, for instance: Lane-Poole, S. (1899), review of Driault, E., La Question d'Orient depuis ses Origines jusqu'à nos Jours, *English Historical Review*, *14*(56), 805–806.

45. [*Translator's note:*] In the first edition, Juglar uses the future tense: "has not taken place, the recovery will be quite difficult."

46. [*Translator's note:*] Juglar is referring here to Achille Fould's report to Napoleon III (September 29, 1861). In his report, Fould criticizes the accumulation of public debt and advocates the increase of taxes. Convinced by Fould's arguments, the emperor ordered the official publication of the report and Fould was appointed minister of finance. For details, see *The New York Times* (November 30, 1861).

47. [*Translator's note:*] The following passage, which appears in Juglar (1863), is deleted from the second edition: "The Crimean war was over, the peace treaty signed, and whereas there was widespread hope for a revival of business and for industrial and commercial activity greater than ever before, the crisis came as a surprise to all those who did not realize that the good business situation resulted from the exaggerated development of discounts."

48. [*Translator's note:*] In Juglar 1963, the author writes: "nous réclamons de lui des réformes ... qui ne sont qu'un prétexte pour manifester notre mécontentement." In the second edition, the latter clause is changed to: "et nos réclamations ne sont qu'un mode de manifester...."

49. [*Translator's note:*] In the second edition, Juglar adds "the unfavorable exchanges."

50. [*Translator's note:*] In Juglar (1873), "que l'on désigne improprement de crise" is substituted for "que l'on désigne improprement ainsi."

51. [*Translator's note:*] Juglar switches from the present to the past tense after "English expression –" in the 1873 edition.

52. [*Translator's note:*] This paragraph is added by Juglar in the second edition.

53. [*Translator's note:*] Juglar does not cite the exact of title of Charles Coquelin's book, "*Du crédit et des banques*" (published in 1848) in either edition.

54. [Translator's note:] In the second edition, Juglar replaces "admettre" by "accuser" in "mais au lieu d'admettre/accuser le simple remboursement des billets...."

55. [*Translator's note:*] The title of du Puynode's book can be translated as "*On Currency, Credit and Taxes.*"

56. [*Translator's note:*] This sentence remains unchanged in Juglar (1873), whereas "in these recent years" (*dans ces dernières années*) is inappropriate here, as the period studied by Tooke and Newmarch is 1792 to 1856.

57. [*Translator's note:*] "unfavorable foreign exchanges" is added in Juglar (1873).

58. [*Translator's note:*] Juglar writes "*puisqu'elles peuvent varier,*" "elles" referring to "*les oscillations,*" whereas it would have been more rigorous to refer to "*les dépôts*" and write "*puisqu'ils peuvent varier.*" In English, this ambiguity disappears with the use of "they." However, the problem appears later in the sentence as it is obviously the deposits that are at their minimum, as confirmed by what Juglar writes in the following paragraph.

59. [*Translator's note:*] In this sentence, "they" seemingly refers to "the reserves," although this is not clear, as Juglar uses "il," which cannot stand for "l'encaisse" in the previous sentence or "la reserve métallique" in the previous paragraph. What might be lingering in his mind is "that of the metallic reserves," "celui [le minimum] de la reserve métallique." This is the only way for the sentence to make sense, although this solution does not solve the grammatical problem which still remains.

60. [*Translator's note:*] A problem similar to the one raised in the preceding footnote is found here, as it is not the "minimum" that had risen to 8 million pounds, but the "public deposits" themselves.

61. [*Translator's note:*] There is a slight difference in wording between the two editions. In the first edition, Juglar writes "which from 364 had also climbed to 684 million, and finally [surpassed] by the so dangerous and altogether artificial ratio of the metallic reserves to the paper in circulation, a ratio of 1 to 8."

62. [*Translator's note:*] The wording in the first edition is as follows: "The history of crises in the United States, in Scotland, in England, and in France, where free banking and monopoly exist, will exempt us from insisting any further."

63. [*Translator's note:*] Juglar replaces "the circulation" by "the paper circulation" in the second edition.

64. [*Translator's note:*] Juglar adds "however" in the second edition.

65. [*Translator's note:*] This sentence is introduced by "mais" in both editions, despite the introduction of "however" in the previous sentence. We have chosen to use "besides" instead of "but."

66. [*Translator's note:*] In the first edition, Juglar ends this sentence as follows: "during which the discount rate, maintained at 5 percent, and the free issue of banknotes were unable to prevent any disaster."

67. [*Translator's note:*] In the first edition, Juglar writes: "their [crises'] natural evolution reestablishes equilibrium."

68. For the tables, see our aforementioned book, *Commercial Crises, etc.* (Guillaumin, Paris).

69. [*Translator's note:*] At the end of his article in the first edition of Block's dictionary, Juglar provides a bibliography including references to books by Coquelin, Courcelles-Seneuil, du Puynode, Gautier, Faignet, as well as by Doubleday, Tooke, Wilson, Macleod, Ayr, and Carey.

COMMERCIAL CRISES (1891) ☆

Clément Juglar
Translated by Cécile Dangel-Hagnauer

There are a good many sorts of crises. Attempting here to deal with them all would require more than a volume; we will confine our study to those that concern economic matters; even so, it will not be possible for us to consider either agricultural crises or financial crises, or at any rate the crises of the latter category which, although they affect business, only involve Treasury operations in the form of partial liquidations or large borrowings.

Our chief focus will be on commercial crises, all of which are made more complicated and are accompanied by monetary embarrassments, which give them their essential character, although they may not be called financial crises.

All crises doubtlessly disturb the course of business as a whole and consequently the movement of exchanges, but no crisis interrupts it like commercial crises. The stoppage is abrupt, seems to break out like a peal of thunder, as if it were caused by some unexpected accident, always a new one in each crisis, and which cursory observation takes for the cause of all evil, whereas this accident has only precipitated the outcome.

☆Original publication: Clement, J. 1900[1891]. Crises commerciales. In: L. Say & J. Chailley (Eds.), *Nouveau dictionnaire d'économie politique* (Vol. 1, pp. 641–651). Paris: Guillaumin.

A Research Annual
Research in the History of Economic Thought and Methodology, Volume 28-A, 149–167
Copyright © 2010 by Emerald Group Publishing Limited
ISSN: 0743-4154/doi:10.1108/S0743-4154(2010)000028A009

1. OUTLINE OF A CRISIS: THREE PERIODS

As in diseases, a commercial crisis is a critical moment to go through. As soon as embarrassments arise, the question is whether one will resist or one will succumb. A crisis is the touchstone that allows us to gauge the soundness of commercial houses, the size of their commitments and of the resources they possess, in capital or in credit, to face up to them. Thanks to the crisis the market operates a sort of selection; the houses that have lost their balance collapse; the others resist. This is how crises indicate the firms that are dubious and those we can trust. Carried away as people were on the wings of credit, they now regain a foothold, although, alongside the businesses that are still afloat, a large number are now under water.

Thus the crisis is very brief, if we consider only its *explosion*, that is, the acute state, the moment where all credit having disappeared, the movement of trade having been interrupted, all business stops and great houses collapse. But not all of them fail on the very same day: there are some that are only wounded and that, with great efforts, manage to remain on their feet and will succumb only later. We then enter the *period of liquidation*, a long and painful one, during which, due to the fall in prices of all the products and of all movables and real estate, everything is at a standstill. As by now this price decline allows only very limited and forced sales, production and trade are carried out for the sole purpose of not letting equipment remain idle, because, although a few small profits may be made, losses are the most frequent outcome. This is a state of despairing languor and is still depicted using the *word crisis*; but it is no longer the crisis, it is the *liquidation of the crisis* which, depending on the volume of business and the situation of markets, lasts two to three or even four years.

There are thus two well-marked periods: the explosion of the crisis, a very short period; the liquidation of the crisis, a longer period; but there is a third period to consider, the one that precedes the crisis. How can it be characterized? It is a period of great business activity and consequently of great prosperity. Capital, at the beginning, is abundant and cheap; easy credit allows people to engage in business that is liquidated with the greatest facility, thanks to sustained and rising prices that accelerate trade all the more. Such trade generates profits and provides manufacturers and businessmen with additional capital, which further increases the volume of operations and quickens their pace. This state of affairs goes on for several years, roughly 7–10 years, as experience shows. But if prices keep on increasing or remain high, in the end the market situation differs from what is was initially. Capital has become scarcer:[1] from 2 percent, the discount rate has risen to 3, 4 or even

5 percent; the prices of carryovers are at their highest level; the impression is that there are many buyers who would like to get rid of part of their purchases but are unable to find new acquirers at current prices. Products no longer circulate and remain in store or warehouse, in the hands of the same people who are keeping them, after having paid the cost of carrying them over, or, in the case of real estate, at the cost of ruinous expedients, hoping that the rise in prices that has always been hitherto favorable will not let them down. This is when the situation becomes critical; the crisis is about to break out, it is a matter of months only and all that is needed is the demise of a large company or of a large credit institution for all business, leaning on so fragile a basis, to collapse.

Such is the crisis, such is its explosion, and along with it, *the stoppage of all business with the stoppage of the increase in prices*. And this occurs not only in one market, but in all the markets of the world that operate with the help of credit: they are thus interdependent.

Indeed, if we go back no earlier than to the beginning of the century (and we could go much further back, in the case of England), we find that, in the three countries of the world greatest for their industrial and trading activity, the explosion of these crises is observed at the same moment, and so are the periods that precede and follow them. Thus, we observe here indeed the whole set of circumstances that accompany commercial crises – which indicate that markets are interdependent – and also the recurrence of the same accidents in the same conditions – which reveals to us their periodicity. A glance at the table below will be sufficient to prove this Crises:

France	England	United States
1804	1803	–
1810	1810	–
1813–1814	1815	1814
1818	1818	1818
1825	1825	1826
1830	1830	–
1836–1839	1836–1839	1837–1839
1847	1847	1848
1857	1857	1857
1864	1864–1866	Civil War
–	1873	1873
1882	1882	1882

Having thus raised and delimited the question of crises, even though it involves the world's business as a whole, we now turn to the study of its causes and manifestations.

2. DEFINITION OF A CRISIS; CAUSES OF CRISES

For quite some time already attention has been directed, due to the disturbances it causes, toward what we agree should be called a commercial crisis or a monetary crisis, without really realizing the difference that is seemingly attached to these two denominations.

When this word "crisis" is articulated, is there a complete agreement on what is meant or what is understood by this very commonly, too commonly, used term?[2] For some people, the slightest accident is a "crisis." For others, as soon as there is a little trouble, a slowdown in business, we are in a state of crisis. Even so, the word crisis denotes a state of distress or suffering. A crisis can affect one or several industries or all industries; agriculture itself is not safe from it (V. AGRICULTURAL CRISES).[3] The crisis can be labeled industrial, commercial, monetary, or financial, depending on whether one of these characteristics is predominant in the eyes of the public. For the observer, the term crisis should only apply to a very well-defined collection of accidents, the collection that are always met with when the crisis breaks out. A crisis never occurs unexpectedly, it is always preceded by a period of great prosperity and great business activity that could not have taken place without, as it were, a continuous progression of the price increase.

The crisis is therefore the *stoppage* in the *increase of prices*, that is, the moment when *new buyers* are no longer to be *found*. Trading activity, hitherto very brisk and very profitable, is suddenly brought to a standstill; those who were hoping to make sales, and especially the last buyers, no longer know what to do with their goods; neither domestically nor abroad can they be placed, and yet commitments must be met. There is a rush for the Banks to obtain new means of credit, to postpone redemption dates by asking for renewals; to meet the demands, the bankers' portfolios of discounts, already inflated during the period of rising prices, take on more and more considerable proportions.

For the home market, extensions are therefore obtained, prices are maintained artificially without there being any new business; but for the foreign market, this cannot be done. Buyers of raw materials must pay for them, and as manufactured products are no longer accepted at the prices they are offered, after having used up all possible means of credit, these products must nevertheless be replaced, in order to settle business obligations. Now, there remains but one commodity, a commodity like the others, which, due to the greater stability of its value and its easy transportation, is still accepted in all markets: that is, the precious metals, gold and silver. Precious metals will thus be called upon extensively, causing a change in the role they usually play, namely when they only serve for the balancing of large commercial operations or for carrying out transactions in cash. Banks are no longer requested to provide credit instruments, banknotes or an account opened to perform transfers or clearings, they are asked to supply metallic coins or rather bullion for making remittances abroad.

The Banks' metallic reserves, which since the beginning of the prosperous period have been continuously declining, are already so much at risk and so low that the suspension of payments is imminent and inevitable unless measures are taken to protect them. Formerly for the lack of better knowledge the suspension of payments was unavoidable; of late we know how to avert it by raising the *discount rate* (q.v.).[4] It is this increase that is accused of being the cause of all the embarrassments, whereas it only indicates the seriousness of the situation and the imminence of a suspension of payments. To avoid this ruinous extreme, which in the past could not be escaped, it is often necessary, if action is taken too late, to raise the discount rate to 7, 8, 9, or even 10 percent.

Deprived of credit, or able to secure it still only on so very hard terms, badly engaged speculation must be liquidated and the products that were bought at rising prices must be sold off. Hence an extremely critical situation: everything has been shaken and nothing seems to be standing firmly anymore; not only have the imprudent been knocked over, but also the more prudent themselves do not know how they will come out of the squall. All credit, all trust, has vanished: there is a general scramble for safety. Business on credit is no longer conceivable; cash is what is demanded to wind up positions; and as all cash receipts are by now uncertain, everyone is seeking ways to generate liquidity, which further increases the number of demands with which the Banks are besieged. Consequently they have to raise the discount rate to preserve their reserves, the whole while the latter are being drawn upon, indicating that not all positions have been liquidated.

This acute state, which seals the fate of the greater number of speculators, cannot last more than 10 or 15 days; it is the acute state of the crisis, like the critical period in diseases that we call by the same name; this indicates how short-lived it is. Once this inevitable liquidation of all the liabilities that exceeded the speculation's capacity has been achieved, calm returns, the discount rate falls almost as quickly as it had risen, the period of liquidation begins and lasts several years.

As always, in the understanding of crises and in distinguishing these successive periods, theory moved ahead faster than practice; it is therefore not surprising that, 25 years ago, this theory was considered as one of the most obscure of political economy. Each author, looking from his own viewpoint, pointed to the cause of crises that tallied best with the system he had conceived or had founded, by referring to a practice that had been previously abused but that, at the time he was writing, was usually no longer current.

Robert Peel accused the abuse of the issue of banknotes whose disastrous effects he had witnessed during the episode of forced currency; Tooke, who came later, was of an opposite opinion, but the President of the United States, Jackson, placed in a situation similar to the one that had left its mark on Robert Peel, shared his opinions. Ch. Coquelin, a proponent of free banking, accuses monopoly of being the cause of all evil. As funds accumulate and take unproductive refuge in current accounts, reserves grow; to find a way to employ them, the Banks encourage discounts with a view to raising their dividends. Then suddenly these deposits are withdrawn and the crisis breaks out. Unfortunately, with the balance sheets right in front of our eyes, not only do we find no trace of this theory, for which free banking is the remedy, but we also notice that in the United States, where such freedom exists, these accidents are as frequent as elsewhere and even more violent.

Stuart Mill is also concerned with the issuing of paper, but it is in the form of mercantile paper, bills of exchange and checks; in a word, it is the abuse of credit, purchases concluded in exchange for a promise to pay, that he considers solely responsible.

For Mr. de Laveleye, it is the scarcity of specie and credit, that is, of means of exchange, which bring about crises.

Mr. Bonamy Price explains crises not by overproduction, but by the diminution of purchasing means; money being but a mere instrument of exchange, it is not what is lacking. So, what causes commercial depression? The simple fact that there are few commodities that can be exchanged, or rather that commodities which can be accepted in exchanges are wanting.

For Mr. Leroy-Beaulieu, what should be called a crisis is the interval that is needed for carrying out the transformation that, by lowering prices, is likely to attract new consumers. There is no permanent excess production. Low prices act as stimulants that bring in new classes of consumers.

All these explanations err in that, of the three periods of the crisis, they only focus on the last one, the period of liquidation.

As we see, it is always excess production that is, according to these theories, the primary cause of crises. Demand has been over-anticipated, a stoppage is needed, a reduction of prices is felt to be necessary; but then why not point to the *rise that preceded*, as there lies the primary cause that emerges from these observations?

A new cause (a mere accident for us) has recently been added to the previous list by Mr. Leroy-Beaulieu, who points to the termination of free-trade treaties. Governments, by applying protectionist and socialist policies, are the architects of crises. For him, the best remedy for preventing these terrible accidents seems to be in the conclusion of long-term free-trade treaties and the adoption of *ad valorem* rather than specific duties.

Max Wirth points to the disruption of equilibrium between production and consumption and observes that selling one's goods is difficult. Doubtless, this is the source of all embarrassments; but for the origin of the disruption he provides no explanation.

Finally, according to Mr. Yves Guyot, crises would result not from excess production but from excess consumption; as evidence, he points to the food shortages that sometimes accompany them, although more rarely nowadays.

The views on the causes have varied considerably among circles and across time. Thus, during the liquidation of the crisis of 1873, when there were complaints about the slowing down of business, the sluggishness was attributed to the series of wars that had disturbed the world, to the standing armies, to uncertainty, to general anxiety, to the return of the protective system since the abandonment of the free-trade treaties.

Thus, these opinions on the causes of crises come in many varieties; but all of them emphasize the suspension of exchanges; so there lies the main trouble. Why are the exchanges suspended? As a result of abusing the issue of paper, which drives out specie, according to Robert Peel, Jackson, and Laveleye; because of the diminution of means of purchasing, for Bonamy Price, who hastens to add that, money being but a mere instrument of exchange, it is not money itself that is lacking, but commodities that *have the power to buy*; now, are the latter not wanting because of the high prices at which they are maintained?

Notwithstanding Bonamy Price's reservation, we see that what is lacking during crises, whatever the cause may be, is metal, gold and silver accepted at par. What are threatened in these circumstances are the Banks' metallic reserves; what is dreaded is the suspension of payments; what catches everyone's eye is the everyday greater decline of the level of metallic reserves. This displacement of specie takes place under the influence of unfavorable foreign exchanges, which people in the past preferred to disregard, attributing it to other causes, a fallacious opinion remarkably refuted in the *Bullion Report* of 1810 (V. Enquêtes financières),[5] although the conclusions of that celebrated Report were rejected by Parliament.

Of late, the same error was still spreading, some 20 years ago, and has not yet completely disappeared. Ignoring the importance of this serious symptom, Coquelin claimed that unfavorable foreign exchanges, far from being the sign of a crisis, were a sign of prosperity.

Recently, since 1857, the drain of specie has been understood to be an extremely serious matter, and after having sought the best way of tackling it, it has been recognized in England that there was no method more quickly efficient than the increase of the discount rate; was it then not claimed that this increase was the main cause of crises?

In this quick review of the theories put forward, notwithstanding their diversity and their frequent disagreements, there are three accidents that are recognized as succeeding each other during crises: (1) the increase in prices that precedes them; (2) the drain of metallic specie that causes the explosion and (3) the decrease of prices that allows and facilitates the liquidation.

Thus the three periods of prosperity, crisis, and liquidation always succeed each other in the same order, despite displaying different features depending on the epoch. The more wealth increases, the greater the amplitude of movements, the oscillation being always in the same direction.

These three periods having been recognized, it is now necessary to explain how they relate to each other and what causes make them to succeed one another.

The prosperous period always follows a period of distress, of business slowdown, and of declining prices; it is announced by the resumption of business under the influence of rising prices. This price increase itself is brought about by the abundance of capital, resulting from the accumulation of old reserves and annual savings, which have barely been dipped into, despite the losses they have suffered. This capital, increased by the working capital of all the industries that decelerated their production during the liquidation of the crisis, is already offered in the market a few months only after the explosion, in search of employment in temporary investments on the Stock Exchange, artificially raising the prices of government stocks, whereas all other prices are decreasing.

Before seeking employment once again, these funds await the completion of the liquidation, that is, that the price decline has ended.

Once this result has been obtained, the prosperous period begins; it is impossible indeed for conditions to be better. Each house, having no commitments, has not only all its working capital at its disposal, but all its credit as well; in these circumstances, the resources of commerce and savings are huge. As the interest rate is very low, the public is on the lookout for investments and is seeking new ways to use its capital; to respond to its wishes, the Banks, and the bankers whose livelihood entirely depends on issues, are ceaselessly bustling about creating new projects, both real and sham. Before, stocks were issued at par; today they are issued at a premium; syndicates are formed for launching the issues and shoring up value, and then, as everybody is involved, everyone pushes in the same direction. One rise chases the other until not only has all of one's capital, but all of one's credit been used up as well.

It is in explaining this process that authors' opinions differ.

What causes the firmness and the rise of prices in prosperous times?

The abundance of capital, one might say, but in what form? In the form of money, mercantile paper, banknotes, checks? For these are the means used to facilitate the exchange of products without resorting to barter.

It has been claimed that prices depend on the quantity of money in circulation or on the amount of circulating instruments that replace it: banknotes, mercantile paper, bills of exchange, and checks.[6]

As regards money, we see the old doctrine always returning, the one which asserted that, if it were doubled, all prices would be doubled; now, the services of money as an instrument of exchange depend not on its quantity, but on the rapidity of its circulation.

The quantity of capital in the form of commodities is completely independent of specie. Yet, as they say, money albeit a commodity, is not like other commodities; its scarcity acts on all transactions, whereas this is not the case with iron, cotton, etc. Just because it serves as a means of exchange, does this imply there are no others? Banknotes, government notes, all forms of promises to pay, mercantile paper, bills of exchange, money orders, and checks: do they not achieve the same purpose? Money is said to intervene incessantly in exchanges; that is only true for retail trade, for small quantities; indeed, even in cash operations, as soon as the sum to be paid is large, it is banknotes and checks that intervene. Besides, in these daily exchanges, the quantity of money is of little importance, it is above all the rapidity of its circulation that indicates the services it provides and not at all the coined amount, which remains idle in the coffers of the Banks or in the tills of individuals.

For each crisis, one always tries to find a special cause: for the crisis of 1825, mad commercial speculations; for the one of 1847, a bad harvest; for that of 1864, large imports of cotton to be paid for in specie. But as these forms may *vary* infinitely, they do not lie within the scope of commercial crises; they are accidents that can disturb one of the social mechanisms, without stopping the general movements of exchanges and business, as is observed in commercial crises. Besides, a commercial crisis is always a monetary crisis, since it is the reduction of the Banks' metallic reserves that signals the explosion. Aside from this diminution of the reserves, we may be *in the midst of a monetary crisis*, like at the present time, as a result of the depreciation of silver, without general prosperity having suffered from it. Such was the case with the last food shortage and the high prices of grain in 1878–1880;[7] nonetheless nothing was able to *stop* business activity until the crash of January 1882.

Therefore, the explosion of crises is not due to an accident; there would be no explosion if everything were not prepared and if the mine was not loaded.

3. MECHANISM OF CRISES

Let us observe the facts: everything will then be clear. What do we see during the liquidation of crises? Business on credit has disappeared, the Banks' discount portfolios are empty, even business carried out in cash has slowed down considerably, and factories are at a standstill. As working capital lies idle, it is offered on the Stock Exchange; hence, a noticeable decrease of the interest rate and a semblance of great ease. Capital is offered at a very low price, like commodities. Outside of the houses that have been affected by the crisis, although there are no earnings in the form of capital gains, there are still savings; the large annual savings of civilized nations are still continuing and tend to lower profits. To raise the latter, new combinations are attempted, and the large mass of capital seeking investments reawakens the entrepreneurial spirit. Project makers appear; anyone, it seems, can report a new one; there is no limit to public gullibility.

Speculation benefits from this, establishes companies, issues stocks and, adding a premium on the commodities offered, over-excites the demand for securities still further with this sort of outbidding.

After each crisis and when the liquidation has been completed, there is thus a period of calm. The country licks its wounds and the industrial and commercial slowdown, combined with the power of savings, generates a large mass of capital that in no time gives a new boost to society, of which some parts were earlier more or less paralyzed.

This is the starting point of the revival of business; once there is a demand for capital, credit soon enters the picture.

What is credit? It is simply the power to buy in exchange for a promise to pay. But then, to what extent can it be used? All those who have credit will be able to buy; this power to purchase in exchange for a simple promise will increase the demand for products and, as a result, an increase in prices will follow, which, at first will concern only a few products and will soon spread and become generalized; prosperity will reign in the country, everyone will be wealthier. The hope of realizing a profit with purchases on credit, by throwing new classes of buyers all in the same direction, will further speed up the rise, all the more as credit increases with the upsurge of prices.

With such a driving force, affluence spreads, and no one wants to believe that so perfect a mechanism will ever stall. However, while the increase in prices provides new sources of credit and brings about a new rise, will there always be new purchasers? Will liquidation always be possible thanks to the mere circulation of paper and without resorting to specie? For, if money played a far greater role, the rise would not follow the same continuous upward movement, as the displacement of metal would attract attention.

Although it does not strike public opinion, this drain is nonetheless noticeable from the beginning of the increase in prices. A quick look at the banks' metallic reserves is enough to realize that, immediately after the reflux of specie, during the liquidation of crises, as soon as the maximum reserve level has been reached, the *downward movement* begins at once; slow and barely perceptible at the beginning, it escapes notice; but the proportion of the loss compared to the reserves increases every year, and finally the persistence of unfavorable foreign exchanges shows clearly the danger that is threatening the market. The increase in prices has slowed, even stopped, the exchange of products; they are for sale and find no buyers. To avoid selling at a loss, mercantile paper is renewed at redemption date; this is why, at the approach of the crisis, the portfolio of the Banks is swollen not only with all the bills presented to them, but also with all those for which renewal has been requested. If there were only domestic commitments, this could still go on; but to meet foreign liabilities, something must be delivered in lieu of the commodity whose price is too high for it to be accepted abroad.

What are the products that can be delivered? Those that are subject to the smallest price variations and are accepted in all markets: the precious metals. Where can they be obtained? From the circulation? That would be too difficult; it is considered simpler to draw on the Banks' metallic reserves, the depletion of which is instantly distinguishable; this seriously disrupts the equilibrium of the circulation of credit. Even before the directors have taken any measure to protect their threatened metallic reserves, the *increase in prices has stopped*; at once, there is a change in outlook; all that the public now wishes is *to sell*. As soon as commodities are offered rather than demanded, the price decline is *already looming*; the Banks are called upon more and more, until they set up obstacles by *raising* the discount rate, by *increasing* the *price* of the metallic specie – since it is what is in demand – in the same *proportion* as the price of commodities.

As there is no alternative other than to submit to this increase or to deliver one's goods at the price of the day, the liquidation begins. The decline, confined at first to the products in which there had been speculation, soon spreads to all transactions and even to cash operations.

According to the foregoing, that is, from factual observation, it can be inferred that the great annual savings of civilized nations, by constantly increasing their wealth, is continuously fueling an increase in prices proportionate to the size of these savings; this is *the normal state of the market*, the prosperous period. The crisis is approaching when the movement *slows down*, it *breaks out* when it *ceases*.

In a word, the main, it could be said that the only cause of crises is the *stoppage* of the *increase in prices*.

From the heights to which they had risen, we see them falling to their minimum levels, sometimes below their starting point.

And this is so true that often a crisis breaks out quite some time after the *accident* that caused the first tremor, which only checks the *increase in prices*. Thus, without going further back than modern times, the Crimean war was over and peace signed, when the crisis of 1857 broke out. Likewise regarding the grain shortage of 1879; the crisis broke out in 1882,[8] when all payments to foreign countries had been settled.

Similar price oscillations in the great business nations do not have enough time to spread and balance one another over the world; hence one of the first results of crises is to place considerable sums in the hands of foreigners. A large mass of capital moves around, goes abroad and gives rise to competition on the part of countries that are less elevated in the scale of civilization.

In short, any rapid and continuous increase of business that lasts a certain number of years is the harbinger of a crisis.

The crisis breaks out when there are more people wishing to sell than to buy.

The crisis results from a lack of purchasers; but what should be blamed? The price increase or the excess production?

Does the absence of buyers result from the absence of wants or from the increase of prices?

Is it retail or wholesale buyers that are missing?

As to the absence of wants, we cannot admit this cause is effective in the presence of the continuous development of consumptions. What *stops* them, what *limits* them, *is prices*, and when the latter have risen for a series of years, there comes a time where, in wholesale trade, exchanges are more difficult. As a result, there is so much supply that the unstable equilibrium of credit capsizes.

Commodities circulate more slowly or stop circulating altogether, mercantile paper is no longer easily cleared, it accumulates in the Banks' portfolios, is not even redeemed on due date and is rediscounted, that is, even bills non longer circulate. It is nonetheless necessary for something to *circulate* in the stead and place of *commodities* and *paper*, and this *something* is the specie and bullion that are *drawn* from the Banks' metallic *reserves*.

The decline of the level of reserves under the influence of unfavorable foreign exchanges is sufficient proof that the paper issued by credit and trade institutions no longer circulates as usual and the increase of the discount rate is only a violent means, in the absence of gentler ones, to make it resume its *customary* role. There is a stock of commodities represented by a *stock of paper*, and neither one nor the other can circulate anymore. It is therefore necessary, before producing anything more, to clear out this floating stock, in order to restore the equilibrium of prices. To reach this goal, it is first necessary to restore the *circulation* of paper and, for that purpose, to set its price and the price of specie in accordance with that of *products*, so that there is no resort made to *metal*, whose *market* value has not *varied*.

4. RELATIONSHIP OF CRISES WITH THE WEALTH OF COUNTRIES

Commercial crises are not observed in all countries, as it might be thought. Doubtless, embarrassments, business slowdown can be experienced anywhere, but these accidents should not be mistaken for what we call commercial crises. Thus, countries where most business is conducted in cash are not exposed to crises; whereas they do not reap the benefits of commercial vigor, they are not subjected to its setbacks. For a country to be confronted with them, a great development of credit transactions is necessary. It is in England, the United States, France, Germany, and in the main industrial cities that we have seen crises occurring and reoccurring for many years. Where industrial activity is weaker and slower, these commotions are not noted. Thus, parts of Germany, Russia, and Spain, although not entirely protected, are only subjected to their distant repercussion. It can even be added, though this may appear paradoxical, that the wealth of nations can be measured by the violence of the crises they undergo. Not to mention England and the United States, to cite a single fact that everyone has been able to observe: never has public fortune made greater progress in France than since 1848, and at the same time, never before has there been more discussion about commercial crises. According to some voices, since 1854, we would have been having one fall after the other, always getting back on our feet, but inevitably falling again soon. These people were mistaking mere accidents for commercial crises whereas they had none of their characteristics nor any influence on the development of public wealth; and it was to study them that the *Enquêtes sur les Banques* were opened in 1865.[9] Whatever may have been the obstacles, the stoppages, the losses, and even the ruin of which they were the consequence, the development of public wealth, which is self-evident to everyone, has never been, at any other time, more rapid nor more considerable.

Since the beginning of the century we see crises recurring at rather close, although by no means regular, intervals, and that depend on how fast business is increasing and on the conditions in which it is taking place. If in earlier times crises were less noticed, it was because the relations of nations with one another were less easy, more limited and, as a result, commercial activity and the development of wealth were slower, less exposed to such painful jolts: one may fall only if one has climbed up high. Reaction being everywhere only the counterpart of action, the former will always be closely related to the latter; so there need be no fear, when it is realized that crises do not last very long and that, before arriving there, one probably went through a series of years during which the earnings obtained from profitable operations made savings possible, while the crisis destroys and upsets all the combinations of the most recent years. However great the disaster, it cannot be admitted that it causes all the prosperous years' profits to disappear. Crises can occur and reoccur without entailing, as one sometimes likes to imagine, the ruin of nations. Undoubtedly stoppages and losses mark the movement of business, but the development of wealth runs its course nonetheless; this explains that, in spite of their periodicity, not only can a country exposed to commercial crises not become poorer, it might actually become wealthier much more quickly than those that are shielded from crises, that is, than those whose business is sluggish and are, it is true, protected from turbulence but left with really no hope of making large profits. A few less chances of loss diminish in a huge proportion the chances of gain.

The extent of relations, the nature of operations, the kind of products determine the intensity of crises in each country; they will even be felt all the more painfully as we come closer to the main centers where we perform the operations of foreign exchange, that powerful device for channeling the precious metals,[10] that great economic process whose purpose is to restore equilibrium and harmony in the various markets. So they follow step-by-step the development of the wealth of nations and their intensity is measured by its extent and by the rapidity of its progression; where it is slow and moderate, crises will be very short and barely perceptible; where it is quick and feverish, deep and violent crises will apparently disrupt for a time the whole business world. Either one or the other of these conditions has to be chosen, and the latter, in spite of the risks that accompany it, still appears to be the more favorable to the markets of civilized countries; it is the one that is observed in England, in the United States and France.

On the basis of these findings, should we envy the fate of the nations where transactions have that tranquility that keeps them sheltered from storms?

5. INFLUENCE OF CRISES ON THE ECONOMIC STATE OF SOCIETIES: HOW TO OBSERVE IT AND MEASURE IT

The influence of crises on the economic state of societies is quite obvious. There is no need to demonstrate it. But admitting this influence is easier than observing and measuring it.

Leading modern economists and statisticians have concerned themselves with searching for the distinctive sign that characterizes, at a determined period of time, the economic, social, and moral state of human societies in the various countries.

At the Hague Congress, in 1869, it was advised to focus especially on the budget of the working classes. Owing to the difficulty in achieving an accurate estimate of incomes, the question was raised whether it would not be easier to reckon expenses, which would lead to the same result. So consumptions should be observed. But they do not embrace all the manifestations of social life.

To move a step further, Mr. Neumann-Spallart extended the scope of his observations to all the branches of production that rely not only on nature, but mostly on labor and capital. The evolution of production must be considered as one of the surest indicators of the economic situation. Thus, in each country, he examined the industries that employ the largest number of workers and require the greatest amount of capital: coal, iron, and cotton, for Great Britain; coal, pig-iron, iron, and silk, for France; and so on for each country. He observed the intensity of trade, the circulation of men and things by land and by sea, *Clearing Houses* transactions, etc. Production and commerce indicate only one manifestation of material well-being; to complete the picture, it is necessary to add the consumption of foodstuffs and beverages, the deposits of savings banks, the number of banks, emigration, and bankruptcies. Still left is the moral state, of which crime, marriages and births records, etc., can give an idea.

In the first edition of our work in 1862, we ourselves had drawn up, and placed face to face with commercial crises, all those tables that economists compose so carefully for the present period. Our observation did not focus only on a few series of years; it went back to the beginning of the century where, doubtless in smaller proportions, we see the same oscillations recurring as they do in present times. In the past, like today, these oscillations corresponded to those we detected in the great banks' balance sheets. There was a coincidence that we pointed out and that, since then, has been overlooked.

All these documents having been brought together, the close relationship linking them to the movements of the banks' balance sheets caught the eye. We held the vital lead that would guide us through the business world and would indicate, at all times and in all countries, the period and the moment of the period where we are placed, so that we could find our bearings, unfurl the sails or take them in.

Up until now, the question that has been asked, and is still being asked, is: what variations are the most appropriate measure of the movements of public prosperity? To this question, M. Korosi did not hesitate to respond that the characteristic signs of the economic state of a nation were unknown, owing to the difficulty of comparing international consumptions; but, if instead of consumptions we consider the movements of exchanges, everything becomes simple and comparable.

Life is movement; business is the circulation of products or of that which represents them, mercantile paper, bills of exchange. Where can their passage be recognized with greater certainty than in the balance sheets of the great banks? By relying on them, there are no errors to be feared from double-counting or false estimates; all measures are correct and accurate. Every piece of mercantile paper indicates that an exchange and often even several exchanges have taken place. Now, barring crises or a situation of embarrassment, a product is not traded at a loss; every exchange gives rise to a profit, no doubt a variable one, but a profit nonetheless, and it is these successive profits, when circulation is easy and secure, that are the main source of the incomes of nations. We thus embrace commercial transactions as a whole, all of which eventually take the form, at a given moment, of mercantile paper or of a bill of exchange. We operate on large numbers, on a very large variety of products, and accordingly we diminish the chances of error. Although they are less marked and of shorter duration, we see the same ascending and descending series appear, moving in step, in the same or in the opposite direction, with those of the banks' balance sheets.

These successive and regular periods, which appear and stand out so clearly, have been deliberately ignored until now because we did not have figures covering a long series of years; now that we have them for nearly a century, their value cannot be disputed.

If the movements of exchanges are to be our guide and if banks' balance sheets portray their main features, which statistical documents should be chosen to complete the picture? First of all the items that are typical of the market: the prices of products, raw materials and manufactured goods, carryover rates, and exchange rates. Then, if we want to push our observation further and show the extent and the rapidity of exchanges, the transactions of *clearing-houses* allow us to capture them in the making. The issues of securities in the main commercial markets enable us to appreciate the abundance or scarcity of available capital, the eagerness or reluctance of investors to enter and immobilize their capital in the newly issued securities. Finally, we can observe the movements of exchanges in the records of imports and exports, the outcomes of which, measured in value, are greatly disturbed by the rise or the fall of prices.

These are the gauges and the indicators of the vigor or the slackening of business. All social positions are subjected to its favorable influence or to its adverse repercussions. There is but one step from private riches to public fortune. We will observe its situation in prosperous times and in times of crises in the budgets of governments and cities. The Treasury's revenue will carry its trace: excellent and continuously on the rise in times of prosperity, mediocre, and constantly declining during the liquidations of crises.

The receipts of city tolls, of railroads, of urban public carriages do not escape the common rule; in this way we track the variations of consumptions in these different forms.

To these declines in expenditures, which clearly indicate a decrease in incomes, there corresponds a diminution of savings: purchases of government stocks by Treasury paymasters, deposits in savings banks.

To all these manifestations of social life, the movements of population, marriages, births, and deaths cannot remain unrelated; accordingly we observe with interest in the official registers the trace of all the movements that accompany the periods of prosperity and liquidation.

Together with the balance sheets, there is thus a whole set of facts that are consistent with them, highlighting and showing that we are carried along in a general movement governing the entire social mechanism, with the Banks like simple manometers only indicating the pressure.[11]

BIBLIOGRAPHY[12]

COULLET and Clément JUGLAR, *Report from the committee on the circulating paper currency coin and exchange of Ireland*, 1804. – *Rapports sur la Banque d'Angleterre, en particulier le Bullion Report – Extraits des enquêtes parlementaires anglaises sur la question des Banques, de la circulation monétaire et du crédit*, 9 vol. 1865. – Tooke, *Bank charter*, 1844. – GILBART, *Causes of the pressure of the money market*. – Lord OVERSTONE, *Tract on the currency*. – HORSELY PALMERS, *Causes of money crisis* – BRIAUNE, *Crises*, in-8, 1840. – DUPONT de Nemours, *Banque de France: causes de la crise de* 1806. – MURET de Bort, *Banque de France, crise monétaire*, 1847, *coupures de 500 francs*. – TROCHET, *Crise financière de 1848, moyens de la faire cesser*. – SMITH, *The recent depression of trade, its nature, its causes, its remedies*, 1879. –MANZI, *Crisi agrarie e commerciale presso i romani*. – Wirth MAX, *Geschichte der Handel Krisen*; 3rd edition, 1883. – *Die quellen der Reichtum und Rucksticht auf Geschaftstockungen und Krisen in internationalen Geld Kapital und Waren Markt.* – *Banks crisis, Dictionary of political economy*, Mac Leod, 1863. – Clement JUGLAR, *Du change et de la liberté d'émission*. – *Des crises commerciales et de leur retour périodique en France, en Angleterre et aux Etats-Unis*, 2 édition, 1889.

NOTES

1. [*Translator's note*]: Juglar writes "le capital immobilisé est devenu plus rare". What he seems to mean by "capital immobilisé" is the funds available for immobilization (for investment).
2. Mr. de Foville has very rightly observed that our tongue confuses under a single denomination, "crisis," very different phenomena. The English has two words: *inflation* and *depression*; and even that is insufficient.
3. [*Translator's note*]: Juglar refers here to the corresponding entry in the dictionary.
4. [*Translator's note*]: Juglar refers to the corresponding entry on the discount rate.
5. [*Translator's note*]: Juglar refers here to the corresponding entry in the dictionary.
6. During the liquidation of crises, capital in the form of money is very abundant and yet prices are at their lowest.
7. Whereas 600 million francs of grain were imported.
8. In the United States in 1884; but by 1882 the rise in prices had ended.

9. [*Translator's note*]: See the bibliography at the end of the chapter.

10. [*Translator's note*]: Juglar's wording here is: "ce puissant moteur des métaux précieux."

11. By taking these indications into account, it might become possible to anticipate and predict crises, and to determine, with the help of the balance sheets of the Banks, in which of the three periods mentioned earlier we are at a given moment. This is what I attempted to do in the second edition of my book, *Des crises commerciales*, pp. 98, 113, 165, 497 and sq.

12. [*Translator's note*]: The bibliography has been reproduced exactly as it appears in the original.

"PERIODIC CRISES": CLÉMENT JUGLAR BETWEEN THEORIES OF CRISES AND THEORIES OF BUSINESS CYCLES

Daniele Besomi*

Crises have been occurring for a long time at more or less distant intervals; yet none of the theories that have been advanced to explain them has been accepted. (Juglar, 1889, p. 166)[F1]

1. INTRODUCTION

Business cycle theory is normally described as having evolved out of a previous tradition of writers focusing exclusively on crises. In this account, the turning point is seen as residing in Clément Juglar's contribution on commercial crises and their periodicity. It is well known that the champion of this view is Schumpeter, who propagated it on several occasions. The same author, however, pointed to a number of other writers who, before and at the same time as Juglar, stressed one or another of the aspects for which Juglar is credited primacy, including the recognition of periodicity and the identification of endogenous elements enabling the recognition of crises as a self-generating phenomenon. There is indeed a vast literature, both primary and secondary, relating to the debates on crises and fluctuations around the

A Research Annual
Research in the History of Economic Thought and Methodology, Volume 28-A, 169–283
Copyright © 2010 by Emerald Group Publishing Limited
All rights of reproduction in any form reserved
ISSN: 0743-4154/doi:10.1108/S0743-4154(2010)000028A010

middle of the nineteenth century, from which it is apparent that Juglar's book *Des Crises Commerciales et de leur Retour Périodique en France, en Angleterre et aux États-Unis* (originally published in 1862 and very much revised and enlarged in 1889) did not come out of the blue but was one of the products of an intellectual climate inducing the thinking of crises not as unrelated events but as part of a more complex phenomenon consisting of recurring crises related to the development of the commercial world – an interpretation corroborated by the almost regular occurrence of crises at about 10-year intervals.

The present chapter aims at examining Juglar's contribution in the context of the transition from the theories of crises to the theories of business cycles, focusing less on his specific theoretical contribution than on his, and his contemporaries', conceptions of cycles and crises. In the (scanty and sparse) literature on the history of economic thought on this topic, it is recognized that *some* of the ideas necessary to pass from crises to cycle theories were (or, at least, were becoming) common at the time, in particular, the notion that crises were recurring approximately in a regular way, following a common path and in stages systematically following one another. The truth of such statements, however, needs to be assessed, and it is necessary to examine whether other ingredients of what later became business cycle theories were already present. There are, moreover, some related and equally fundamental aspects of the same issue, the exploration of which has not so far been systematically pursued: what are the methodological premises for the examination of the "new" phenomenon of cycles? How are the alternative approaches – those interpreting crises as disconnected and accidental events – disposed of, methodologically and rhetorically? What role do crises and the cycle play in the working of the economic system? And how do they relate to the "normal" state of the system?

The more appropriate form I have found to deal with these problems is that of a (somehow Juglar-centered) partial thematic survey – unavoidably partial, because of the very nature of the materials at hand. Most writings were housed in pamphlets, ephemera, and articles in commercial, financial, or general-purpose journals, or even in newspapers, which today are not always easy to retrieve. Only very rarely those early contributions found place in books or articles in professional journals, in part because professional journals were not numerous at the time and in part because, as Schumpeter observed, "not much to their credit, the scientific leaders of the profession were not conspicuous" among the participants in the debates on crises (1954, p. 742). It will not, however, be a hunt for Juglar's forerunners: ideas only make sense in their context, and seemingly similar ideas taken in isolation may not prove fecund of further illumination. What matters here is the context, consisting in writers of different sorts (from lawyers to merchants, politicians to financiers and bankers, laypeople of various extraction, and occasionally economists as well[1]) fiercely debating the causes of crises, and their possible remedies.[2] This will be more the story of a set of *problems* than an account of the *answers* – also because in some cases, the answers were formulated without full awareness of the generality of the problem. The picture that emerges is that Juglar was not alone in taking up some of the above-mentioned problems, while he left untackled other important issues his contemporaries were instead discussing.

The subject of this chapter, moreover, is not only Juglar and his contemporaries. It is also the very transition from the explanation of crises as disconnected events – the dominant view in the first half of the nineteenth century – to the emergence of the modern notion of cycles toward the end of the century. Although this was to a certain extent gradual, certain intermediate steps are clearly recognizable. In the second quarter of the century, a number of writers were concerned with the alternation of good and bad times, of high and low prices, and were concerned with the appropriate policies to prevent these natural fluctuations from amplifying and degenerating. Throughout the nineteenth century, several writers shared a view of crises as related events characterized by a common morphology and recurring with some regularity, but retained an emphasis on crises and stopped short of thinking in terms of self-generating and self-sustaining cycles. This suggests that a proper historical interpretation of this era should recognize and characterize at least four distinct approaches, partly overlapping in time, and fundamentally different in terms of their understanding of the role of crises and for their way of explaining them: the theories of "crises," "oscillations," "recurring crises," and "cycles." Juglar, it is argued in this chapter, was an eminent representative of the "recurring crises" approach.

The chapter is structured as follows. Section 2 singles out the main components of Juglar's view on recurrent crises, beginning from his early writings and concluding with his more mature work (in separate subsections, as the changes were, in places, rather drastic).[3] The timing is important, for in the almost three decades between Juglar's two editions, numerous contributions on the subject were published. In Section 3, these constituent parts of Juglar's approach to crises are contextualized and further examined in the light the state of the debate before and at Juglar's time, with particular respect to the recurrence and concatenation of phases, the interpretation of causation, the relationship of growth and cycles, the use of statistics and of diagrams, the ingredients of Juglar's analytical construction, the implications of the usage of medical metaphors, and the relationship of crises to equilibrium and its stability. Section 4 investigates the different approaches to the problem of crises and cycles, in particular with respect to their interpretation of the relationship between normal and pathological states of the system. Section 5, the concluding section, evaluates Juglar's contribution and approach with respect to their context.

2. JUGLAR'S VIEWS ON PERIODIC CRISES

2.1. Laying Out the Premises

Juglar's argument was first developed at length in an article on "Des Crises Commerciales et Monétaires de 1800 à 1857" in the *Journal des Économistes* (Juglar, 1857) and elaborated in detail in the first edition of *Des Crises Commerciales et de leur Retour Périodique en France, en Angleterre et aux États-Unis* (1862), and later taken up in the entry on "Commercial crises" for Block's *Dictionnaire général de la politique* (1863).

2.1.1. Repetitious Facts and Recurring Crises
Juglar's explanation of crises is simple enough. Historically, commercial crises (*crises commerciales*) are always accompanied by monetary crises (*crises monétaires*). Juglar thus[4] analyzed long series of banking statistics (discounts, metallic reserves, circulation of banknotes, and deposits), at first only for France (1857) and later also for England, the Unites States, and to a lesser extent for Prussia and Hamburg (1862), which he compared with variations in population,[5] price of corn, import and exports, rents, and public revenue. He noted strict relationships in the movement of some variables (especially in the variations of discounts and reserves) and observed that changes systematically go through specific phases and are in concordance in the countries where commerce and industry are more developed. From this regularity, Juglar inferred[6] that the common premise to all crises lies in the excesses of speculation and in the inconsiderate expansion of industry and trade:

> Crises return with such consistency and regularity that one must take a stand and see them as the result of intemperate speculation and of a reckless development of industry and of large commercial enterprises. (1857, p. 36; 1862, pp. 6, 164)[F2]

The exuberance of speculation and enterprise is rooted in human nature (1857, p. 37, 1862, p. 7), which is liable to become overexcited (1857, p. 37) and to fall prey of the passion for gamble (1862, pp. 205–206) during the prosperous phase of activity when "everything seems to conspire to stimulate business like never before; all newly founded ventures find the capital they need. Securities are snatched and bought with unlimited confidence in the future" (1862, pp. 6–7, 1857, p. 36).[F3] Expenditure can, for a time, exceed receipts only thanks to credit (1862, p. 164). Excesses are thus nothing else than abuse of credit (1862, pp. 34, 38).[7] But this cannot last: a crisis will intervene, bad credits and other excesses will be liquidated, the system is brought back to its normal course of development, which it will be able to follow for a few years, before new abuses again shatter its foundations.

The theoretical apparatus is admittedly scanty: as Juglar himself pointed out in the second edition of his book, looking back at his original statement, the "law of crises and of their periodicity"[F4] was derived "without appealing to any theory or hypothesis,"[F5] but only by means of the observation of facts (1889, p. xv).[8,F6] Moreover, he was also wary of generalizations that could be drawn from his observations as to the cause of crises: "although the examination of the statistical documents we shall present may lead to deduce and recognize an economic law, prudence suggests not to jump to conclusion" (1862, p. 6).[F7] Juglar's purpose, indeed, was not the development of an analysis of the causes of crises, but stressing that these follow a common path and are related to each other:

> The return and the succession of the same facts, in *special circumstances*, at all *epochs*, in all *countries* and under any *regimes*: this is what had to be brought to notice. (1862, p. xiii)[F8]

Juglar's book was an answer (indeed, the winning answer) to a competition launched by the Académie des Sciences Morales et Politiques in 1860,[9] challenging the entrants to

> Inquire into the causes, and indicate the effects, of commercial crises[10] that took place in Europe and North America during the nineteenth century. These crises have been frequent at any epoch; but, as commercial relations knew new developments, the perturbing action brought [crises] bring with them are also touching more and more regions. (Académie des Sciences Morales et Politiques, 1860)[F9]

Juglar's approach consisted in relying on a large collection of data referring to long periods rather than on disputable assertions.[11] It was a precise methodological choice, which he pursued at the price of producing a tedious book:

> The consistent repetition of the same facts gives our history a true monotony. We are always led through the same phases in the same order of succession, annoying the

inquiring mind always eager for variety and novelty. But is this not the best evidence of what we wanted to prove? (1862, p. xii)[12,F10]

2.1.2. Causality and Rhetorics

Having laid this premise, in the next stage of his reasoning, Juglar moved to an epistemological ground. If crises are not to be taken as disconnected individual occurrences but share some features and tend to recur cyclically, there must be a common explanation of the phenomenon, in spite of the different circumstances affecting different economic systems at different times. In most of the literature of the time, however, crises were attributed to a number of different causes. Juglar was aware that he had to play two games at once if he wanted to win his case. On the one hand, he had to subsume all crises under the same scheme in spite of the objective differences between each special occurrence by reinterpreting the role of the special events and of the general premises of crises. On the other hand, he had to counter all his opponents' arguments at once and convince his readers of the rationality of his approach.

Juglar handled this challenge very effectively. The first edition of his book began with a discussion of the term "cause."[13] He elaborated upon a distinction routinely used by medical writers who divided the remote causes of disease into predisposing and exciting (or occasioning) causes, the former making the body liable to become ill, while the exciting cause immediately produces the disease in a body predisposed to it. This is ilustrated, for instance, in the entry on "causes" in the *Dictionnaire de Médecine Usuelle*, published only three years after Juglar completed his medical dissertation on the influence of heart diseases on the lungs:

> Let us then confine ourselves to the main distinction or classification of the causes of diseases. Some of them pave the way to diseases, most of which pertain to the organisation [of the organism]; they are called *predisposing* causes. Others, most of which are external, trigger the predisposition and produce the disease. They are called *determining* or *occasioning* causes. Let us consider as an example a man with a voluminous heart, abundant blood and a short neck; such a complexion is the predisposing cause of apoplexy. If, following an explosion of rage, this man undergoes an attack, his emotion is the occasioning cause. Without predisposition, the influences that could bring about a disease are powerless. But the indicators that would reveal the predisposition are often hidden. It would be difficult to diagnose *a priori* what would happen to the four unwise people who lie on humid ground while coated in sweat: one would catch a rheumatism, another would get catarrh in his lungs, a third diarrhea, and the fourth would get up perfectly healthy. A preliminary examination of the organization of each of them would surely help the diagnosis, but before the experiment is actually performed the result would often remain uncertain. (Lagasquie, 1849, p. 313)[F11]

In the medical literature up to the 1860s, diseases were understood as the result of individual combinations of remote causes: each case of a disease was ascribed to a different cause (or combination of causes), and the disease itself was defined in terms not of it etiology but its symptoms. Although there were earlier studies ascribing diseases to specific, universal, and necessary causes (fungi, parasites, etc.), only with the studies of Pasteur (late 1850s to 1870s) and Koch (1870s and 1880s), the nosological approach to diseases was substituted with an etiological understanding of them. In the previous literature, neither predisposing nor occasioning causes were seen as necessary, sufficient, or universal; the literature abounds with provisos to this effect, such as the following (extracted from another dictionary):

> sometimes the predisponent cause, by continuing long, may arrive at such a height that it alone, without the addition of any exciting cause, may produce a real disease. The exciting cause also, though it should not be able immediately to bring on a disease: yet if it continues long, will by degree destroy the strongest constitution, and render it liable to various diseases; because it either produces a predisponent clause, or is converted into it, so that the same thing may sometimes be an exciting cause, sometimes a predisponent one, or rather a cause of predisposition; of which the inclemence of the weather, sloth, luxury, &c. are examples.[14] (Jamieson, 1829)

Juglar took up the distinction between "occasional cause" and "predisposition,"[15] but radically departed from the interpretation of his medical mentors[16] by explicitly claiming that the explanation of crises must rely on relevant causation nexuses both necessary and universal, thus capable of description in terms of scientific laws. Without at first mentioning crises (thus remaining at the level of general principles of explanation), Juglar pointed out that when we look for the deep cause of what surrounds us, we are "under siege by a crowd of occasional causes" that "impair our view and often induce us to mistake the accident for the very origin of the affliction" (Juglar, 1862, p. 1). The following passage is a rhetorical masterpiece, as it expounds the principle that will subvert the adversaries' approach while at the same time very subtly ridiculing them:

> Food shortages, wars, revolutions, tariff changes, loans, fashion variations, new trade openings, these are the main causes of crises that have in turn been put forward. However, the real test would be to see these causes reproduce, in similar circumstances, the same effects. Unfortunately, when we consider social phenomena and everything that concerns life, this relationship between causes and effects is rarely prominent. In this state of uncertainty, the most dissimilar causes are called upon to explain the same facts. We have good reason to be surprised by the lack of judgment of the human mind and the facility with which it accepts anything it is presented with; it is so hungry for an explanation that, when it finds nothing better, it is satisfied with words. Indeed, the multiplicity of the causes that are put forward is sufficient, in our opinion, to prove their

little effectiveness, since, whereas a single one should suffice, a great number are accumulated; now, as they are not always simultaneously present, it is natural to think, as we eliminate them one by one, that none is a determining cause, since its intervention is not indispensable to produce the result ascribed to it. (Juglar, 1873, p. 587, translated by C. Dangel-Hagnauer in this volume, p. 118; 1862, p. 2)[F12]

Juglar concluded that one should study the "preceding state ... in the absence of which even the seemingly more powerful causes fail to operate. It is what in medicine is called predisposition" (1862, p. 2).[17,F13] Accordingly, when we pass to crises (which in Juglar's argument only appears at this point), we have to identify "the conditions necessary to their existence among the phenomena that are constantly observed, beyond to the so many and various causes that are invoked, depending on the needs of the moment" (1862, p. 3).[18,F14] Juglar could thus successfully contrast his unifying perspective to his opponents' special views, and indeed, he took every chance to do so (e.g., 1862, pp. iii, ix–xi, 1–2, 5–6, and passim; he further insisted on this in the second edition of his book, 1889, pp. 5, 27–29, 36, 43, 165, 197).

2.1.3. Instability, Periodicity, and the Morphology of Crises

Juglar's emphasis on the predisposing causes has two consequences. One is that in the absence of predisposition, a cause that could bring havoc would instead be ineffective (1862, p. 2). During prosperity, when people are over-excited, even "a big war could not halt the progression" (1857, p. 57).[F15] The second is that the causes actually occasioning the crisis are not that relevant, as it would have happened anyway. When everything is predisposed for the crisis, any accidental cause would precipitate it, like the last drop overflowing a full glass of water (1862, p. v). "During their periodical returns to our country, bad crops, expensive wheat and famines frequently co-occurred with the gluts of bank portfolios, and have introduced further complications to an already bad situation. Yet their presence is not necessary to produce a commercial crisis" (1862, p. x).[19,F16] These causes are thus reinterpreted as explaining not the actual crisis but its specific character. The interpretation of crises as individual events, each with its own specific cause, is thus turned on its head: the occasional circumstance only determines the specificity of each crisis, the difference with other similar events, while the general pattern is determined by the way in which the predisposing cause determines the unstable state of the system at certain points.

Two aspects deserve to be stressed in this connection. The first regards the notion of "periodicity." If accidental circumstances affect the actual course of crises, they can make them more or less intense but also anticipate or retard them. In Juglar's view, there is no room for strict periodicity.[20] The adjective "periodic" occurring in the title of Juglar's book thus refers to a different conception, which (not surprisingly) again happens to be more akin to the medical than to the astronomical one. The emphasis is not much on the duration of the period,[21] but on the return of the various phases that succeed one another in precisely the same order with similar character-istics.[22] The notion is thus related to the recurrence in general terms, to the idea that crises are not disconnected individual occurrences but part of a chain of events implying the return of disturbances after some conditions are fulfilled, rather than to the specific kind of cycles that repeat themselves with strict regularity.

Juglar identified three phases: prosperity, crisis, and liquidation (1862, p. 164) and discussed how they succeed each other.[23] The presentation, as well as the round of course through which they run, is asymmetric. The focus is on crises: their origin, their nature, their outbreak, and their liquidation. As anticipated early in this section, during prosperity, people become unduly optimistic (1862, pp. 202, 205–206) and start overspeculat-ing. The keywords, recurring in a long string, are "imprudence," "abuses," and "excesses."[24] "It is characteristic of human nature never to remain within appropriate limits" (1862, p. 20)[F17] and become overexcited (p. 167). The result is excess of speculation (pp. 16, 20, 24, 88), "extravagant application of floating capital" (Juglar 1862, p. 25, reporting Wilson's opinion on the 1847 crisis), "speculative folly" (pp. 6, 164, 199), foolish or imprudent speculation (pp. 25, 142, 208) "beyond their means" (p. 142),[F18] exaggerated expansion of discounts (pp. 27, 31, 209), abuse of credit (pp. 29, 34, 38, 88), overtrading (p. 29), fictive (p. 34), doubtful (p. 172) and artificial credit (pp. 57, 163), exaggerated prices (p. 37), and inconsiderate develop-ment of industry (p. 164).[25,F19] Some of these exaggerations and excesses refer to the credit market and the stock exchange; others affect production and goods markets. In particular, expenditure exceeds receipts, and investment runs ahead of saving: often among the results of the excess of speculation, there is "also the use and immobilization of an amount of capital larger than what could be sustained by the ordinary resources of the country, that is, by its savings" (1862, p. 164; see also pp. 38, 154).[F20]

So far as it goes, such a situation remains in an increasingly insecure balance: "So long as the rise persists, products are exchanged and nobody is losing. But unlucky the last holder!" (1862, p. 14).[F21] As speculation is carried on, tension accumulates (1862, p. 176),[26,F22] and the credit and trade relationships become extremely unstable. Although in the early stage of prosperity, the system could remain unaffected even by a war (1857, p. 57), toward the end it becomes like a basin about to overflow (1862, p. v) or like explosive ready to blast (1862, p. 176, 1863, p. 623), so that any occasional cause can set it off leading to "serious disturbances in consequence of small causes" (1862, p. iv).[F23] Juglar describes the failure of the system by means of the hydraulic metaphor of pipes becoming engorged: "all of a sudden, all channels seem glutted, there is no further vent, the circulation is halted and a crisis breaks out. All speculations stop. Money, which was so abundant a few months before, diminishes, becomes tight, or even disappears" (1857, p. 37).[F24]

How can these pipes be unblocked? The system must get rid of the unhealthy speculation, and here, the medical man emerges again. Commercial crises "are distressing accidents, but, as in diseases, they prepare a better condition by expelling all impurities" (1862, p. 14, 1863, p. 622).[F25] The diseased parts have to be suppressed (p. 208): during the liquidation, the less solid businesses[27] fail "and clear the market of a persistent cause of troubles and ruin" (1862, p. 14; see also p. 208).[F26] Eventually, the system is brought back to its healthy, normal state (1863, p. 623),[28] a stable (1862, p. 208) equilibrium (pp. v, 172): "a crisis is but a general liquidation from which business can resume its course on a solid footing" (1862, p. 176, 1863, p. 619).[F27]

2.1.4. Prosperity as the Normal State of the System

From these passages, Juglar's conception of the nature of capitalist accumulation emerges rather clearly. Prosperity is the normal state of the system and consists in the "regular development of the wealth of nations" (Juglar, quoted in Wolowsky, 1862; in Juglar, 1862, p. xiv).[F28] In its early stages, this is a self-sustaining state of moving equilibrium, where one's expenditure covers someone else's costs. Credit is a necessary premise to the increasing number of exchanges and therefore to accumulation. At this junction, credit does not create any problems, for everybody is confident that it can be liquidated easily. Yet, the instinct for gambling brings to overspeculation, which is by its nature cumulative: credits become more and more doubtful, and at some point, the system turns extremely unstable. The crisis explodes: excesses and abuses are wiped out, and the system is brought back to its normal track. In this view, periodical crises are a necessary inconvenience: they are "a disruption to the course of business" (1863, p. 615),[F29] but a disturbance intrinsic[29] to the accumulation process, and actually helpful, for economic advance contains and develops the germs of growing instability which have to be cleared. The resulting crisis is conceived as the undesirable product of accumulation itself and the premise for its recovery:

> Crises, like illnesses, appear to be one of the conditions for the existence of societies where trade and industry dominate.[30] We can anticipate crises, alleviate their effects, partially protect ourselves from them, facilitate business recovery; but eliminating them is something, despite having resorted to the most diverse devices, no one has managed to achieve so far. To propose a remedy ourselves, having recognized the little effectiveness of those recommended by others, is impossible, even less since, as a result of a natural evolution, equilibrium reestablishes itself and prepares a firm ground on which one can fearlessly take foot and cover a new period. (1863, p. 627, 1862, p. vii)[F30]

Although the endogenous/exogenous distinction was conceptually well within Juglar's reach, for it is strongly implied in the distinction between occasional cause and prédisposition (as witnessed by Lagasquie's 1849 dictionary entry cited above), he did not make that step. This apparently curious situation is due to the poverty of his theoretical and analytical apparatus: the concepts of endogenous and exogenous refer to internal and external with respect of the theoretical system, but Juglar's line is so ill-defined that an analytical classification would not be possible. A first problem in this respect, which Juglar tackled in the second edition, is that the mechanism declenching the crisis is not clear. Intuitively, one grasps that instability increases as speculation proceeds, so that at some point anything can act as the occasional cause. But the specific mechanisms explaining how instability grows are absent: the explanation relies on the public's enthusiasm, furor (1862, p. 205), infatuation, and frenzy (pp. 201–202)[F31] in subscribing to any new enterprise.[31] At this point of Juglar's analysis, the society's disease is thus explained by individual madness.

The second problem is more troublesome. The "normal state" is not defined. Prosperity is said to be an equilibrium, a state of regular progression supporting itself, but it is not clear how this happens; its driving force is never specified, nor are its equilibrium conditions. A notion uniquely based on the *absence* of "abuses" and "exaggerations" is, of course, circular reasoning. The tendency to accumulate thus remains unexplained, and so is the lower turning point: it is not enough to say that bad credits are liquidated and excesses eliminated if what drives the recovery is not specified. This has obvious implications on the exogenous/endogenous distinction: if the endogenous forces driving growth are not specified, one cannot define by contrast what is exogenous.

But there is also an implication regarding the conception of the succession of phases. Some inklings in the book suggest that Juglar seems to think that phases do not simply follow one another in a regular fashion, but that each one breeds the following: prosperity contains the germ of disorder (1862, p. 121; see also p. 172), the crisis is by necessity followed by a liquidation. "Once the *movement has begun* in one direction or the other, *upwards or downwards*, it continues uninterruptedly until there is a complete turnabout" (Juglar, 1863, p. 618).[F32] The point is precisely that one needs to explain the turnabout, but in Juglar's book, how prosperity gives rise to crisis is only intuitively clear, while it is fully unclear how and why liquidation gives place to prosperity.[32] A full explanation of the cycle is still wanting, but Juglar can offer a *description* ("we want to show here that we can follow *step by step the development* [from prosperous periods to crises and liquidations], almost month after month, or, at any rate and very clearly, *year after year*" (1862, p. 164),[F33] and even a diagnostic (1862, pp. 197–198). But at any rate, he laid out the principle that an explanation of a cyclical process requires that phases are linked to one another.

2.2. Revising, Adding, and Deepening

The second edition of *Des Crises Commerciales* was published in 1889. It is almost three times as long as the first edition, obviously containing many new materials, in particular, further statistics (Juglar brought up to date his previous series, to confirm and give more strength to his results: 1889, p. xv) and some graphic elaboration, additional considerations on the lines already expounded in the first edition, and a shift of emphasis in the argument giving more weight to monetary issues[33] and to the role of prices in Juglar's mechanism.

2.2.1. The Causal Chaining of Phases
Juglar insisted more than he did before, and with much more clarity, on some significant points in the transition from crises to cycle theories.[34] The most interesting one concerns the linkage between phases. Whereas in the first edition, the emphasis was on the *succession* of phases in the same relative order, in the new version, Juglar stressed the *causal chaining* of phases; in the first edition, the approach was more descriptive, in the second Juglar more clearly aimed at developing a causal explanation. It is no longer enough to record that "periods are linked to each other and follow each other with an ever surprising regularity" (1889, pp. 9, 48, 164).[F34] One must move a further step: "after these three periods had been identified, it has been necessary to look for their possible mutual relationships and for the causes under the influence of which they follow each other" (pp. 21, 4);[F35]

one has to understand how each phase results from "the reaction following the action" (p. xvi).[F36] Although Juglar's solution still relied on some unexplained entrepreneurial spirit and therefore was not fully satisfactory, having laid the methodological principle that each phase should contain the germ of the succeeding one was an extremely important step toward trade cycle theorizing.

The basic idea as to how each phase is characterized remained the same as in the first edition, although the connection between phases now worked through changes in the price level.[35] Prosperity, at least in its early stages, is a stable equilibrium of advance;[36] it corresponds to the system's normal, healthy state. As opposed to crisis as a diseased condition,[37] "In common parlance, the prosperous period does not have a name. It is what is regarded as the normal state, it is not even talked about. As it is the case for health, nothing appear more natural than prosperity" (p. 16): "it is the normal state of the market, it is the prosperous period" (p. 33).[F37] It is characterized by an equilibrium in prices (p. xvi), which is only broken when credit gets out of hand (pp. 53–54).[38] Credit itself is necessary to permit growth and thus prosperity.[39] Yet, its "exaggerated extension" and "abuse" (pp. 5, 47, 56, 168)[40] to pay for "excessive expenses" (p. 4) is driven by the "gambling attitude" of the public (p. 4), fed by the price hikes generated by these same expenses, in a speculation spiral eventually destabilizing the system's mode of advance.[41] This happens when purchases are no longer in proportion with the available capital (p. 53); "the equilibrium of prices is broken" (pp. 54, 34, 35, 165).[42,F38] Juglar resorted again to the analogies of the loaded explosive charge (pp. 30, 43, 165; see also 1900b, p. 646) and the overfull water basin (pp. 48, 165), that can explode or, respectively, overflow, due to any occasional cause, to stress the methodological point that the "predisposition" to crises lies at a deeper level than the accidental causes (see also p. 197).

Although "the term 'crisis' indicates a state of illness or suffering" (p. 13),[F39] Juglar repeats (citing Overstone) that crises imply "some down sides," but are "in other respects extremely salutary and beneficial" (p. 6);[F40] they are useful, and indeed, a necessary premise to the beginning of the recovery (p. 6), for they eliminate the excesses and bring the system back to equilibrium.[43] Contrary to the first edition, now Juglar offers a mechanism triggering the recovery: during the liquidation phase, no investments are taking place. Some savings, however, are still coming forward seeking productive use and lowering the interest rate[44] until the enterprising spirit[F41] is awakened again (Juglar, 1889, pp. 30–31, 21, 126).[45] When there is request of capital, credit intervenes again, and the cycle can recommence. The explanation, however, still relies on the "esprit d'entreprise," on the "natural" (and unexplained) tendency to accumulate;[46] the accumulation of loanable funds only plays a subsidiary role.[47]

It should be noted that Juglar is more concerned with credit by traders, in the form of promises to pay (pp. 57, 69, 71, 73), rather than with banking credit. The *request* for such credit between traders grows with increasing prices, but also the traders' willingness to accept promises as a form of payment growth with rising prices, and both in turn further increase prices.[48] Having shifted the emphasis on prices, Juglar supplied a new definition of crisis: "The crisis is then the *stoppage* of the *price rise*, that is, the period when no *new buyers are found*" (p. 14).[F42,49]

2.2.2. Miscellaneous Observations

An interesting feature of the second edition consists in Juglar's continuous confrontation with the doctrines of other authors on crises. This inaugurates a tradition that continues today, with many treatises on cycles expounding, for critical or contextualization purposes, the competing or the similar approaches.

Commenting on the progress of Juglar's thought between the first and the second editions of his book, Niehans commented that "the content was finally living up to the title," as the 1889 edition constituted a massive treatise on business cycles, whereas the previous version was just "a detailed chronicle of crises as reflected in bank balance sheets, with a few fragmentary statistics from other sources and very little economic analysis" (1992, pp. 549–550). The above dicussion suggests that this judgment does less than justice to the first edition. Already in the first version, there was a description (albeit intuitive only) of the mechanism of crises resulting from the gradually increasing tension due to the abuses of credit triggered by speculation. The crisis would be followed by a liquidation, setting the premises for a new recovery, thanks to the elimination of the previous excesses. On the contrary, Niehans perhaps credits too much to the second edition, where the mechanism of expansion is still dependent on an unexplained tendency to accumulate. At any rate, in the second edition, Juglar clearly stated the principle that phases should be causally chained to one another and did something toward filling the gap of the missing explanation of the lower turning point.

3. CRISES AND CYCLES AT JUGLAR'S TIME

Historical inquiries have already stressed that some of Juglar's proposition were not only anticipated by others but were also even commonplace. Other aspects, however, have not yet been the subject of research. My aim is not to hunt for Juglar's forerunners but to gather enough evidence on the diffusion, at his time, of a number of the ingredients that characterize his approach. This cannot claim to be a complete reconstruction of the context in which Juglar was operating, because it strictly remains within the field of the construction of economic theories of cycles and crises, leaving out for instance the political component of the debate – which would deserve a dedicated study – and its social implications. Nevertheless, portraying the state of the art at around Juglar's time is useful not only for assessing the originality of his contribution but also for identifying some landmarks in the history of the transition from crises theories to cycle theories.

3.1. Statistical Tables and Diagrams

One of the most distinctive features of Juglar's approach is the extensive use of historical and statistical analysis in connection with the cycle.[50] Juglar proudly claimed that he based his observations on facts rather than on theories or hypotheses (1889, p. xv; see Section 2.1.1), vaguely bringing to mind Petty's methodological statement in the Preface of his *Political arithmetik* (1690) and more precisely the declarations of intent by Playfair and Morier Evans. The former maintained that "I have grounded all my calculations and arguments on *facts*; I have studiously avoided those theories which, though sometimes useful guides, do not infrequently lead to grave errors" (1821, p. iii). Evans echoed him, "Studiously avoiding attempts at dissertation and strictly eschewing theories, [the author] has endeavoured to confine himself to a description of 'Facts and Figures' which while they may prove serviceable to most parties connected with mercantile pursuit, can be looked upon as offensive by few" (Evans, 1848, p. v).[51]

Before Juglar, there have been a few attempts to anchor the discussion of crises to a factual basis. Brand (1800) argued that the price of wheat is lower in times of war than in times of peace by tabling the annual prices of the previous 106 years and grouping them in years of peace and war. Playfair (1821) was mostly concerned with agricultural distresses, but Tooke's chronicle of prices (1823, 1838–1857) aimed precisely at examining the extent of price fluctuations.[52] Malthus commented that in the pursuit of his

inquiry into the causes of the fluctuations which have occurred during the last thirty years in the prices of corn and other commodities, [Tooke] adduces a large and interesting collection of facts. This mode of considering his subject we consider as peculiarly judicious. At all times an extensive collection of facts relative to the interchange of the various commodities of the commercial world, which is more within the reach of intelligent merchants than any other class of men, cannot but be of great importance to the science of political economy; but it is more particularly required at the present moment, when it must be acknowledged that some of our ablest writers in this science have been deficient in that constant reference to facts and experience, on which alone it can be safely founded, or further improved. (*Malthus, 1826, p. 214)

"Collections of facts" were indeed produced. Morier Evans published in 1848 an analysis of the commercial crisis of 1847–1848 and in 1859 a massive analysis of the 1857–1858 crisis, which he compared to those having occurred from 1825. His volumes (especially the latter) include plentiful of data of various kinds, especially balance sheets but also banking statistics, numbers of stores and of failures, prices, stocks, debts, production, and so on, enabling him to observe that "Each separate panic has had its own distinctive features, but all have resembled each other in occurring immediately after a period of apparent prosperity, the hollowness of which it has exposed," and even to stress that the uniformity is so striking that whenever fortunes can be rapidly accumulated "otherwise than by the road of plodding industry," one can safely predict that a panic is at hand (1859, p. 1).[53] Max Wirth also produced a voluminous body of historical analysis of crises,[54] beginning from the consequences of John Law' system in France. Although peppered with data, the nature of this work is historical, rather than statistical. On top of these volumes, a number of authors cited brief series of data or (more rarely) drew diagrams (e.g., Langton, 1857).

These contributions, however, were more illustrative than analytically significant. As Niehans stressed, Tooke's data were assembled more as a chronicle rather than with a theoretical purpose; Evans's data needed to be further distilled if anything was to be done with it.

In this context, Juglar's data marked some progress, as they were subject to some statistical analysis (rough as it was at times: Pellissier, 2000, pp. 274–276, 284) that could actually support some inductive process. His book contributed toward filling the scarcity of statistical analysis of economic fluctuations lamented by Jevons in a paper delivered before the British Association on the same year in which Juglar's first edition appeared.[55] But while Juglar's treatment of data did not go much beyond their listing in tabular form, Jevons and others were beginning to make extensive usage of diagrams.[56] Juglar only seems to have fully appreciated in the early 1880s that graphs enable "the eye to embrace at once a long series of yearly data and to perceive the recurrence of the same incidents" (Juglar, 1882, p. 5).[57] At the end of the 1870s, he started arranging his tables in a graphical way, listing maxima and minima of his series in separate columns, giving the impression of a zigzag movement (Juglar, 1877, pp. 375–376).[58] The zigzag lines connecting them were eventually explicitly added in several tabular presentations in the second edition of *Crises Commerciales* (1889).[59] He started incorporating time series diagrams in 1882 and 1886 articles, and he attached a number of them to the second edition of *Crises Commerciales*, but rather than depicting the entire series, he only listed maxima and minima and connected them with straight lines. This only slightly improved on the zigzag lines by illustrating whether and how much the successive maxima and minima were higher or lower than the previous ones. Juglar's procedure thus clearly reveals that graphs were intended as a means to illustrate his point, rather than accurately depicting data. This is confirmed by the only diagram including, besides the usual medium-period maxima and minima, also the yearly maxima and minima, drawn in a thinner line (Fig. 1). Although at most times, his medium-period maxima and minima actually correspond to the local maxima and minima of yearly figures, on a few occasions he cherry-picked his dates as to fit them with the observed crises or phases of prosperity. For instance, he chose as the beginning of prosperity year 1895, while the actually maximum of the gold and silver reserves of the Bank of France was recorded in 1893. Similarly, he chose his minimum for gold and silver reserves (indicating a crisis) in 1873 while the actual minimum was recorded in 1871.[60] These manipulations illustrate that Juglar's graphs were constructed starting from his argument, rather than the argument being based on raw data, as Juglar claimed he had done, and as Jevons (1874, p. 492) suggested would be the correct procedure.

If Juglar's diagrams were latecomers and at first rather primitive, his important contribution lies in having based his discussion of crises on the systematic collection and rudimentary statistical elaboration of facts and figures, in particular, regarding banking data. In this, Juglar was soon followed by Jevons (who, being a far better statistician, was more influential than Juglar) and later Tugan (1901, 1913), Bouniatian (1922), Aftalion (1913), Lescure (1907), Robertson (1915), and finally Mitchell (1913, 1927),[61] to cite only the main contributors.

3.2. The Periodicity of Crises

Early recognitions of some regularity in the occurrence of crises, attempts to evaluate an average period, and the distinction of phases and their concatenation have been discussed in the literature. Bergman's history of the theories of crises (the first and still the most complete and detailed

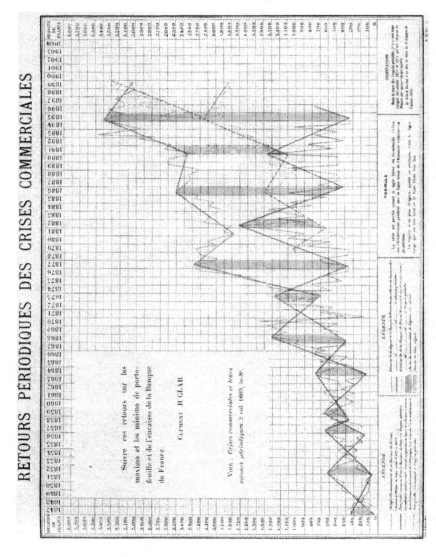

Fig. 1. Juglar's Periodic Commercial Crises Diagram (with yearly data). *Source:* Juglar (1900c).

account of the subject up to the end of the nineteenth century) indeed places the section on Juglar in the chapter on periodicity (von Bergmann, 1895, pp. 255–260). Nevertheless, this and other historical accounts of the early debates on the periodicity of crises (Miller, 1927; Schumpeter, 1954; Hutchison, 1953) only singled out a few milestones and a limited number of minor writers having observed that crises recur with some regularity, giving (especially Schumpeter) the false impression that Juglar was an outstanding pioneer. On most counts – as we shall see in the following sections – this is only partly true. And so far as the problem of periodicity is concerned, this idealization is completely false. Some writers had started moving in this direction at least seven decades before Juglar, and by the time he published his first writings, the idea that crises recur with some regularity was well rooted in a solid tradition of thought.

The first identification of an alternation of good and bad times in production (albeit agricultural) seems to be due to William Petty, exactly two centuries before the publication of Juglar's book:

> Suppose a man could with his own hands plant a certain scope of Land with Corn, that is, could Digg, or Plough, Harrow, Weed, Reap, carry home, Thresh, and Winnow so much as the Husbandry of this Land requires; and had withal Seed wherewith to sowe the same, I say, that when this man has subducted his seed out of the proceed of his Harvest, and also what himself hath both eaten and given to others in exchange for Clothes and other Natural necessaries; that the Remainder of Corn is the natural and true Rent of the Land for that year; and that the medium of seven years, or rather of so many years as makes up the Cycle,[62] within which Dearths and Plenties make their revolution, doth give the ordinary Rent of the Land in Corn. (Petty, [1662] 1899, p. 43)

Although this may not seem relevant in the context of industrial fluctuations, one must remember that a number of authors later took agricultural production as the starting point of their reflections (Briaune, 1840), for instance, but also numerous French scholars at the time of Juglar's writing).[63] Indeed, this passage is doubly scored in Jevons's copy of Petty's book (Foxwell, 1884, p. 361).

Observations regarding the recurring of commercial crises are scattered through the literature of the late eighteenth century, appeared with increasing frequency in the first decades of the nineteenth century, and by the 1850s were fairly common. Among the very early writers, one may cite Adam Anderson's reference to "fluctuations of commerce which happen frequently in the best of times" (1789, p. 243), William Anderson's opinion that "there is no doubt that, while this nefarious system [of trading on credit] is continued, as no bounds can be set to speculation, distresses and embarrassments will be felt at irregular periods" (1797, p. 39), and James

Currie's judgment that the distress caused by overtrading "is a disease which has a constant tendency to arise in seasons of great prosperity," "every sixth or seventh year of peace" (Currie, 1793, pp. 19, 16).

At the time of the Bullion debate, William Huskisson supplied a very detailed explanation of a credit-speculation crisis (see Besomi, 2010a); although he did not go as far as claiming periodicity for such events, he reminded his readers of "many recent occurrences" (1810, p. 137). His critic John Sinclair, instead, pointed out that if the medium of exchange fails to increase in proportion to the increase of commerce, commerce must experience frequent checks and the country undergoes "periodical returns of commercial distresses" (1810, pp. 57, 64).

After the approval of the corn laws, some writers worked out the first verbal models of economic fluctuations based on a cobweb-like mechanism. Malthus, among the first propounders of such a view (1815, pp. 25–27, 45–46), did not directly claim periodicity. But McCulloch went further and wrote of "ascending and descending progression" and of "a constant alternation of oppressively high and ruinously low prices" (1822, p. 454). Torrens was more explicit: in a *Letter to the Earl of Liverpool on the State of the Agriculture of the United Kingdom*, he explained that "the present distress is not the result of a casual glut, or of a temporary loss of confidence; but, on the contrary, is the consequence of an artificial and forced state of things, and that it must, under our existing laws, be of frequent and periodic recurrence" (1816, p. 11; see also p. 32), which will cause capital to "melt periodically" (pp. 16, 23, 31) and determine "periodical fluctuations in the value of produce" (p. 18).

Shortly later, John also resorted to a cobweb-like mechanism to explain price fluctuations, but extended it from the agricultural to the commercial world. He analyzed the crises of 1763, 1773, 1793, 1811, 1815–1816 and 1825–1826, which he described as "commercial vicissitudes, which, like a plague or a pestilence, visit the country at regular intervals of five, seven or nine years" (1826, p. 39). In 1833, he revised his estimate of the period arguing that "the commercial cycle is ordinarily completed in five or seven years, within which terms it will be found, by reference to our commercial history during the last seventy years, alternate periods of prosperity and depression have been experienced" (1833, p. 211; for a discussion, see Besomi, 2008c).

Meanwhile socialist writers also stressed the periodical character of crises. William Thompson pointed out that "as long as the present principle of action remains, *crisis* will succeed to *crisis*, at interval more or less distant" and insisted that "The *periodical* periods of crisis, recurring at irregular intervals, inseparable from the present principle of action, strike every vulgar eye" ([1827] 1971, p. v). Robert Owen argued that after 1810, an excess of production owing to machinery produced "periodical distress among the industrial classes" (Owen, 1836). In his comment on Owen's piece, Bray stressed that "the productive power had latterly been so greatly in excess of the powers of demand, that gluts of merchandise in all foreign markets were of periodical recurrence ... Wages had been reduced in consequence, which still more lessened the demand" (Bray, 1836).

On another front, in 1823, Thomas Tooke discussed price fluctuations, which, however, he attributed mainly to exogenous events: bad seasons, by causing price increases, encourage the development of credit which in turn feeds back on prices.[64] Later, in his *History of Prices*, Tooke (1838–1857) also incorporated endogenous elements, describing some phases (crises, in particular) as a reaction to the previous development.[65] The idea, however, that depressions are somehow related to the previous phase of prosperity, had already circulated for some time. During the Parliamentary debate in December 1792, Mr. Sheridan ironically denied it, indicating that a suggestion to the contrary must have been already advanced. He said that "to assert that the distress of commercial credit was owing to the greater prosperity of the country might make for a very sonorous period, but would not be much relished in the city. It would be considered as but a poor compliment to congratulate a man on his having proved himself one of the most industrious manufacturers, or enterprising merchants, by getting into the Gazette as a bankrupt." Mr. Rose, however, countered, "That the time of the greatest prosperity of a country might be the time of greatest distress to commercial credit, appeared from what happened in this country in 1772" (Great Britain, House of Commons, 1793, pp. 31, 33). Later, William Huskisson supplied an endogenous explanation of how an extraordinary incentive to commerce turns into excessive speculation, this being consistent with both the motives of the creditor and the debtor to expand credit beyond its boundaries, and of the reasons why such a condition is unstable and bound to collapse. This was not a fully endogenous explanation of the entire commercial cycle, as the starting point was an external impulse to trade, but it moved a good way toward it (Huskisson, 1810). Huskisson's view that prosperity contains the seeds of its own reversal gave rise to surprise and bewilderment not dissimilar from the one expressed by Sheridan two decades earlier. John Raithby, for one, could not believe that the very spirit of enterprise that guided the splendor of the British mercantile establishments could be productive of "mercantile delusion, wild adventures, and abuse of credit," which he attributed instead to "individual imbecility" and "individual calamities" (Raithby, 1811, pp. 96–101).

The cobweb-like mechanisms cited above also supplied semiendogenous explanations of price fluctuations relying on corn laws as the threshold amplifying natural price fluctuations in agricultural products, or (as in the case of Wade, 1826, 1833) even fully endogenous mechanisms. Similarly, James Wilson (1839) propounded a semiendogenous explanation of the alternation of high and low prices of agricultural products, in terms of a cobweb-like concatenation of states: low prices of agricultural products discourage production; the less fertile fields are abandoned, and after some time, production actually diminishes. This determines a price rise, which induces to cultivate again the less fertile fields, and after a lag production increases.[66] The mechanism is not entirely endogenous as it is fed by the false expectations in prices created by changes in the Corn Laws. Later, Wilson also suggested that these fluctuations extend to the whole productive system (1840; see Link, 1959, pp. 103–126). Thomas Corbet also relied on a cobweb-like mechanism to explain oscillation in each single trade (1841, pp. 33–36). He maintained them to be relatively innocuous and compensating each other, except that when they happen to grow too much, they involve most other businesses and turn into a general cyclical movement (pp. 102–106).

In truth, such attempts to construct theoretical explanations of cyclical fluctuations or of the recurrence of crises were rather rare. This, however, did not prevent writers from observing the phenomenon. By the end of the 1820s, descriptions of the alternation of prosperities, with rising prices and speculation, and depressions accompanied by falling prices, were already commonplace (Miller, 1927, p. 193).[67] At this time, we find further attempts to estimate the period: an anonymous American reported in 1829 that "an opinion is entertained by many" that the average period of these "fluctuations" (the term is used several times) that "do take place, and ... always will take place in countries, where paper money has been extensively introduced" is about 14 years (*Raguet, 1829a). In 1838, Hyde Clarke was under the impression that cycles – the term he used – in nature and society (without, however, specific reference to economic cycles) are subject to an elementary mathematical law (Clarke, 1838). Clarke considered not only 10-year cycles but also 54 years long waves, but he did not actually publish his reflections on the subject until 1847 (Clarke, [1847]1999; see Black, 1992; Henderson, 1992; and, for early appreciations, Jevons, 1878; von Bergmann, 1895, p. 239). Briaune, in an 1840 pamphlet on *Des crises commerciales. De leurs causes et de leurs remèdes* (note the word in the plural)[68] explicitly wrote about the "périodicité des crises commerciales" (p. 2), referring only to their return, without any reference to a more or less strict period. In 1848, Coquelin wrote that "commercial perturbations" "have become in certain countries in some degree periodical" (Coquelin, 1848, cited from the 1850 translation, p. 219; Coquelin, 1852a, p. 528), and Lawson wrote that examining the English panics, "we shall find these periods of commercial distress regularly and periodically recurring in cycles of from five to seven years" (Lawson, 1848a, p. 2).[69] Within a couple of decades, most writers agreed on a period of about 7–11 years, culminating of course in Jevons' claim that the phenomenon is strictly periodical (see Section 3.4).[70]

"Crises,"[71] "panics," "revulsions," and "convulsions" began to appear, in the plural, in the titles of books, articles, and pamphlets,[72] witnessing that such incidents were becoming to be understood as instances of the same phenomenon rather than disconnected events. Moreover, still along the same line, the issue of crises was deemed ready to become the subject of historical books (Bell, 1850; Anonymous, 1857a; Wirth, 1858; Evans, 1859); a historical sketch of previous financial panics was even published by a newspaper (*New York Herald*, 1857).

3.3. The Phases of the Commercial Round of Course

As a certain frequency and regularity in the occurrence of crises was acknowledged, commentators started to recognize some common pattern.[73] In the early decades of the nineteenth century, it was common to counterpoise "prosperity" and "depression" or "distress," or similar expressions,[74] such as Currie's contrast between "our late unexampled prosperity" and "our present unparalleled distress" (1793, p. 3), Attwood's "advancing or declining prosperity of the country" (1817, p. 11), Dupont de Nemours's "disturbance or prosperity" and "times of inactivity and happy times" ([1806] 1811, pp. 65–66), Tooke's "spirit of speculation and over-trading on the one hand, and to stagnation and despondency on the other" (1823, p. 87), Carey's "comparison between the extraordinary prosperity of Great Britain, and the general depression in the United States" (1823), Western's alternation of "distress and prosperity, depression and specula-tion" (1826, p. 224), Huskisson's "alternation of extravagant excitement and fearful depression, which this country has so often experienced of late years" (1826, p. 784), Scott's "Proposed measures for the removal of national distress and establishment of permanent prosperity" (1827), or Wade's "alternate periods of prosperity and depression" (1833, p. 211).

By 1830, Huskisson supplied a fairly clear-cut description of the various phases through which trade passes, beginning from a state where "supply and demand would continue in the same relation to each other," followed by "speculative purchases" causing an advance of prices at an accelerated rate, after which demand become languid and a pause ensues while goods continue to be offered for sale: in such conditions, "a glut or super-abundance of goods is said to exist." This begins a time of distress, during which prices fall and the bills of exchange are reduced in amount, until the goods in excess of demand are eventually sold (*Huskisson, 1830, pp. 446–452). Whereas Huskisson did not stress the division in phases to focus on the overall movement, Overstone presented a well-known neat parceling of the "cycle"[75] in 10 phases:

> The history of what we are in the habit of calling the 'state of trade' is an instructive lesson. We find it subject to various conditions which are periodically returning; it revolves apparently in an established cycle. First, we find it in a state of quiescence, – next improvement, – growing confidence, – prosperity, – excitement, – overtrading, – convulsion, – pressure, – stagnation, – distress, – ending again in quiescence. (Overstone, 1837, p. 31)

This account is quite illustrative of the "circular course" through which trade progresses, but Overstone did not elaborate further and these phases remained empty of analytical content. More suggestive is Longfield's representation in 10 phases of the "fluctuations of trade": a detailed description of the banks' discounts and their effects upon trade is illustrated with the 10 phases (caution, confidence, liveliness, overtrading, great apparent prosperity, sudden cessation, paralysis, distrust, panic, and bankruptcies) written in a circle, the period of which is said to be about five years. The account is not only descriptive: each stage of the process, although not easily linked to a specific phase in the list (thus witnessing the lack of analytical precision), is described in detail as following consequen-tially from the preceding one (Longfield, 1840, pp. 222–223). Briaune boiled down the number of phases to three ("crise," "reprise des affaires,"[76] and "développement commercial"), but like Overstone, he only used them in a descriptive way, without trying to specify an analytical content (1840, p. 13). Corbet discussed – also descriptively – a five-phases cycle: when "over-production, or as it is generally called over-trading, takes place in the community, it is generally followed by exhaustion, relaxation, depression, and distress – which again, after a time, are succeeded by a period of unusual briskness and activity" (1841, p. 105):

that such alternations or periods of activity and relaxation, or prosperity and depression, must [...] be at all times in operation or progress, so as to return periodically, independently of war or any other cause than the irregular or unequal exertion of human industry – the overdoing of things in particular class of the community, which again produces revulsion; – one excess, like the high and low or hot and cold fits of a fever, always giving birth to and generating another. (1841, pp. 105–106)

Seen in the context of these contributions, it is apparent that Juglar's emphasis on the succession of crises rather than on their singularity did not constitute a novelty but was rather the product of the atmosphere of his time. True, the writers cited above albeit numerous were still exceptions rather than the rule,[77] as most commentators, "in America as elsewhere, regarded a commercial crisis, not as a phase of a business cycle, but as the unhappy interruption of a normal trend of business that might have continued indefinitely had it not been for the unfortunate circumstances that brought on its collapse. Their observation of the cycle centered upon its most conspicuous phase – the crisis. Accordingly, the first attempts to explain crises sought the origin of each in some particular incident of the time. No general explanation common to all crises was offered; some writers explicitly denied that one could be formulated" (Miller, 1927, p. 187).[78] But commentators were not only increasingly aware that crises (or panics) come in "waves,"[79] but also identified some regularities, looked for common paths, and started to look for a unifying explanation, one that tells of a coherent story of phases succeeding one another in the same order and treated crises as members of a class of events (see Section 3.8 for more details). The 10-phase classifications were certainly too clumsy, and Juglar's three phases not only provided a welcome simplification and a morphological description closer to what was later found useful (Schumpeter 1954, p. 1124) but also gave (or, rather, attempted to give) an analytical specification to each phase. But by 1862, Juglar had only indicated that he *intended* to show how phases succeed one another; one of these causal linkages, however, was still left hanging in the air, and the other was only hinted at (see Section 2.1.4).

3.4. Again on the Periodicity of Crises: Recurrence versus Regularity

If at the time of Juglar's first edition a large number of commentators were aware that crises return with some regularity, as evidence accumulated the belief spread further. This is not to say that everybody accepted the idea of more or less periodical crises: some kept arguing (up to the 1930s, and with renovated vigor in the 1960s and especially from the 1980s) that crises are essentially unrelated phenomena triggered by some external event. Juglar himself reported, in his second edition, that his claims on periodicity had been subject to criticism – without, however, specifying by whom (1889, p. 3). By the 1920s, however, most authors would have subscribed to the periodic character of capitalistic accumulation, with an emphasis on the return of phases in the same relative order and admitting that the period is not strictly respected and can be affected by various events.

Some writers, however, went further than Juglar and most of his contemporaries and successors and claimed that cycles are strictly period-ical. The experience of the crises that occurred in Britain in 1815, 1825, 1836–1839, 1847, 1857, 1866, and 1878 (Jevons 1878b, p. 231) seemed to suggest a fairly precise decennial period, and to some authors, the problem of the recurring of crises presented the additional issue of explaining the causes of the regularity in the period. Among these writers, Jevons is of particular interest, as he was a contemporary of Juglar, as Juglar commented precisely on this aspect of Jevons's work, and as their opposite stands were for a while contrasted in the literature.[80]

Jevons accepted the psychological explanation of the cycle offered by John Mills. He stressed, however, that although Mills recognized the regularity of fluctuations, he did not explain their period. Jevons's well-known theory based on the recurrence of sunspots[81] was precisely an attempt to solve this problem:[82]

> It is a well-known principle of mechanics that the effects of a periodically varying cause are themselves periodic, and usually go through their phases in periods of time equal to those of their cause. (Jevons [1875], in 1884, p. 194)[83]

> When we know that there is a cause, the variation of the solar activity, which is just of the nature to affect the produce of agriculture, and which does vary in the same period, it becomes almost certain that the two series of phenomena, credit cycles and solar variations, are connected as effect and cause. (Jevons, 1878a, in 1884, p. 216)

> Taken altogether, the historical facts concerning the periodic recurrence of crises appear to me too strong to admit of doubt, and it is only the nature of the explanation of that recurrence which is a matter of speculation. (Jevons, 1878a, in 1884, p. 219)

Juglar contested Jevons's (and Cobden's[84]) excessive faith in strict periodicity:[85] "crises do not recur at fixed times" (Juglar, 1889, p. 163).[F43] He also implicitly rejected the methodological premise of the periodicity of causes: "this [...] does not imply that there are regular cycles of abundance and scarcity. Joseph's prediction of seven years of prosperity and seven years of distress itself proves that such a fact was an exception"

(p. 162).[86,F44] Juglar took the occasion to stress again that the outbreak of a crisis is only possible when equilibrium has become unstable: before that, any famine or war would not excessively derange the economic system, while if equilibrium is unstable any event can trigger the explosion (p. 165). The issue at stake was the two writer's interpretation of the causal nexuses, with Juglar's medical notion of causality (see Section 2.1) opposed to Jevons's mechanical (or even astronomical) one. Both writers discussed them quite openly. Juglar had in mind a continuously operating cause, building up tension in the system until it becomes sufficiently sensitive to accidental events that trigger the crisis. Jevons thought instead of periodical impulses, admitting nevertheless that secondary causes could anticipate or delay the event. At first, Jevons thought that the periodical impulses would act on the system by resonance. He could not, however, find any internal rhythmical cause of fluctuations synchronous with the external cause, and eventually, his sunspots operated purely as external causes, transmitted through the system by internal forces.

The contrast between Jevons's and Juglar's positions illustrates well three issues opened by the periodicity of crises.[87] The first concerns the regularity in the timing *versus* the recurrence of the same pattern at irregular times. By the 1860s, several writers had estimated the frequency of crises to be about 10 years, and the actual timing suggested indeed some regularity. This was clearly important in terms of business forecasting, which would be very much facilitated by strictly periodic recurrence of crises. Nevertheless, the first attempts at devising business barometers in the late 1880s (Siegfried, 1886; Numann-Spallart, 1886; de Foville, 1888) moved from Juglar's line of research rather than from Jevons's approach, gaining Juglar the nickname of "prophet of crises" (Neymarck, in Société d'Économie Politique, 1893, p. 7; Passy, 1905, p. 421).[F45] Interestingly, the idea of strict periodicity of crises raised a logical objection precisely in connection with predictability: if crises were subject to an iron law of periodicity and could be forecasted, they would be discounted in advance and therefore would not occur at all (Courtois, in Société d'Économie Politique, 1893, p. 13; Targe, 1902, p. 203). Yet, the opposite opinion was advanced by another adversary of the thesis that crises recur periodically: "a belief in a decennial period tends not only to produce one at the period fixed through groundless alarm, but at other times through groundless confidence in the unconditional remoteness of danger" (*Leslie, 1864, p. 1578).

The second issue concerns the nature of the first cause of crises. Juglar's position reflects the tradition of the overtrading view of crises (see Section 3.5). An excess of credit needs time to build up. Once trade starts accelerating, rises in prices, inducement to further speculation, and request for further credit are not instantaneous and must proceed for some time before the system is sufficiently unstable to be easily toppled. What matters here is the cumulation of effects over time, rather than the occurrence of a specific event. This was not the only tradition relying on continuously operating causes. Marx, for instance, saw crises as the temporary resolution of the contradictions intrinsic in capitalistic production, in particular (but not exclusively), the constant tendency to increase productivity by substituting capital for labor (in Marxian terminology, to increase the organic composition of capital), which negatively affects profit rates until eventually production is no longer profitable and requires to be interrupted, thereby suddenly interrupting the payment chain and bringing to a halt almost the entire productive system.

The idea that the rythmical nature of crises is determined by a periodically recurring cause can hardly rely on an *internal* antecedent, for otherwise, the primary phenomenon to be explained would be the periodicity of the antecedent itself. Indeed, the only attempt in this direction seems to have been the attribution of periodicity to the succession of entrepreneurial generations. Some writers argued that crises are allowed to return after the generation of entrepreneurs who has seen a crisis is substituted by a new generation, which has to learn the hard way how to resist the temptations offered by seemingly easy and profitable business opportunities. Consistently, one of these writers rejects as the "most baseless of the many extravagances which have been committed in the attempt to induce arithmetical formularies on economic science" the idea that "panics are governed by some mysterious law of periodicity" (Rogers, 1879, p. 224; see also Noyes, 1908; and a writer for *The Nation* in 1873, cited by Jones, 1900, p. 139).

The most suitable option for the holders of the thesis of periodical causes was then to resort to external antecedents, and the astronomical world was a natural choice (indeed after Jevons, we had Moore's (1908) phases of Venus). But – and this is the third issue relating to periodicity – this makes this approach a special case of the traditional way of explaining crises as the result of accidental, and essentially exogenous, events. This group of believers in periodicity and the larger party of nonbelievers shared a view of the economic system as self-adjusting, unless disturbed by some interference. The difference lied in the interpretation of economic data as showing a true periodicity, and in the recognition of a unique primary cause, so that Jevons would recognize a law of periodicity that was instead denied by the opposite faction. The debate focused indeed on the lawfulness of crises. The disparaging comment cited in the previous paragraph was not alone. The first all-round attack was published as an anonymous letter dated November 15, 1864, to *The Economist* (the author was later identified as Cliffe Leslie by his friend de Laveleye, who endorsed his argument by translating it in full in his *Le Marché Monétaire et ses Crises*, 1865, pp. 290–301).[88] Its very title, *Alleged Commercial Decades or Cycles*," indicates that the idea that crises come in waves about 10 years apart was beginning to be widespread enough to need to be countered. Leslie seems to have been worried not only by its endorsement by Jevons (1863) but also by politicians who had started to plan their policy having in mind the decennial recurrence of panics and argued that "besides the irregularity in our harvests, there are obviously many other uncertain vicissitudes which make it in the highest degree imprudent to reckon securely upon an easy money market and commercial prosperity throughout any year, and absolute madness to base trading speculations on the assumption of such a state of things for several years to come in succession" (*Leslie 1864, p. 1428). Leslie contested that crises could be interpreted as having the same origin and argued that even if decades of alternate rises and falls of prices could be identified in the past, "it would be altogether fallacious to infer that the same order of things would recur periodically for the future" (*ibid.*).

A debate held at the Société d'Économie Politique, in Juglar's presence, on the subject "Is there law or accident in the periodicity of crises?" is interesting in this connection. After he illustrated his theory affirming that there is a law in the periodicity of crises, Alfred Neymark specified that one could equally well claim that "there is casuality in the periodicity of crises," as crises are often the consequence of rumors or political accidents, amplified by the contagion of fear (Société d'Économie Politique, 1893, p. 8). Courtois pointed out that there is a huge difference between periodicity and recurrence of crises and that while Juglar could claim the latter, he could not claim periodicity which, in the definition given by the Littré dictionary, indicates a "revolution in a *given* number of years." "A period, then, implies a fixed timing, without uncertainty or probability. Periodicity is a specific feature of exact sciences. What depends on human acts cannot be bound by it. The duration of human life, for instance, is not a period, as it is subject to variation. Periodicity is the expression of a law, without periodicity there is no law. As Neymarck said, "an accident is not necessarily periodic" (Société d'Économie Politique, p. 12). Can crises be deemed to be periodic? Courtois denies it, summarizing Juglar's position as holding that crises must cease that year, unless they cease on that other year and must begin after so many years unless it is more or less than that. "Therefore there is no periodicity, and thus no law. All there is is probability, tempered by accidents" (p. 13).

The issue at stake was not simply whether or not crises occur with chronometric precision but was the interpretation of the phenomenon and of the very working of the economic system. These writers were themselves aware of this. Ferrara argued that the emphasis on crises was misplaced, for what should be stressed is the underlying state of progress, regardless of the accidental interruptions. He even maintained that before the periodicity of crises is proved beyond doubt, bowing to it would be for political economy an act of cowardice ([1864] 1890, pp. 274–279). Similarly, Leslie argued that

> For cynics who deride all proof of human progress, the notion of cyclical movement of things and recurring disaster, has obvious attractions; but it commends itself also to a better order of minds, since it has its brighter side in the ascending period of prosperity. ([1864] 1890, p. 1578)

3.5. Credit, Speculation, Prices, and Overtrading

All the analytical ingredients used by Juglar to explain how prosperities build up the premises to crises had been extensively advocated before him, often in similar combinations. Although the explanations Juglar rejected, based on mismanagement of the currency or on specificities of the banking system, were quite popular at the time (as witnessed by the debate between currency and banking schools, which echoed well beyond England), credit was one of the favorite culprits for a number of writers (and an accomplice even in the view of most participants in the debates on currency and banking). As aptly summarized by Miller in his study on banking theories in the United States before 1860:

> Credit was believed to play a threefold part in producing crises. First, it enabled men to 'overtrade' in periods where mutual confidence was high. Secondly, it formed a network of interrelations through which the insolvency of a few merchants embarrassed a great many others. [...] Finally, some emphasized the fact that the use of credit instruments in normal times furnishes a substitute for money, so that, when in troublous times cash payments are insisted upon in lieu of credit formerly extended, the financial stringency becomes all the more acute. (Miller, 1927, pp. 189–190)

Miller supplies a number of references from American writers, of which Gallatin (1831) is particularly notable, and to which Walker, in a discussion with Homer Stansfield (Walker & Stansfield, 1860), should be added, but it would be easy to list writers from other countries who held similar views. Among the publications fairly recent at the time of Juglar's writing, there are, for instance, Garnier (1845), Coquelin (1852a, 1852b), Société d'Économie Politique (1854), Courcelle-Seneuil (1858), Rey (1862), and Bonnet (1865) for France; Tooke (1823, Pt I, section VII), Langton (1857), Williams (1858), and MacLeod (1863, p. 626) – with his emphasis on "misused credit [as] the cause of those terrible mercantile catastrophes which periodically sweep over the world" – for England; and Ferrara ([1864]1890) for Italy.

Strictly related to credit are speculation and the psychology of the public, which were also often (but not exclusively) advocated in connection with credit. Credit permits speculation beyond one's own means, and manias feed the process. Psychology was also called to play a part in the reversal of the movement, as indicated by the very word "panic" used to indicate (and also characterize) the financial aspect of crises. Here again, a few examples will suffice: Lawson (1848a, p. 3) cites a 1825 writer who described the causes of contemporary panic "in words which might be stereotyped as applicable to all similar occasions":

> In all these speculations, only a small instalment, seldom exceeding 5 per cent. was paid at first, so that a very moderate rise in the prices of the shares produced a large profit on the sum actually invested. This possibility of enormous profit, by risking a small sum, was a bait too tempting to be resisted; all the gambling propensities of human nature were constantly solicited into action; and crowds of individuals of every description – the credulous and the suspicious, the crafty and the bold, the raw and the experienced, the intelligent and the ignorant, princes, nobles, politicians, placemen, patriots, lawyers, physicians, divines, philosophers, poets, intermingled with women of all ranks and degrees, spinsters, wives, and widows, hastened to venture some of their property in schemes of which scarcely anything was known but the name. (Anonymous, 1825, p. 3)

Credit and speculation figured prominently as the causes of the depression identified by the House of Lords secret committee on the causes of distress: "those which are connected with the Extension of Commercial Speculation, encouraged or checked by the Facility, or the Difficulty, of obtaining Credit" (Secret Committee on Commercial Distress, 1848b, p. iii). Emphasis on psychological contagion is found, for instance, in Langton (1857), J. S. Mill ([1826]1967; cited and discussed by Link, 1959, p. 151), and Longfield (1840). Authors stressing the role of speculation are, for instance, Tooke (for a discussion, see Link, 1959, pp. 131, 133–135, 139–141, 145–147, 157), J. S. Mill (Link, 1959, pp. 53–69, 149, 166–169, 171, 175, 177–178), Wilson (Link, 1959, pp. 112, 114, 119–120, 124), Ganilh (1826), *Raguet (1829a), Coquelin (1852a), Wilson (1859), and *Courcelle-Seneuil (1860). Emphasis on speculation must have been quite popular at the time; Guthrie reports that "The favourite doctrine of the *Times* and its followers is, that the mania for speculation is a disease to which human nature is subject, and which can be removed or alleviated only by moral appliances" (Guthrie, 1864, p. 5).

Juglar's belated shift of emphasis on prices also was not a novelty (see Section 2.2.1).[89] In the last decades of the eighteenth century, the debates on the "distress of the country" were associated with the price of provisions, whether because of wars (Brand, 1800; Duthy, 1801), famines, or the operation of the poor laws (e.g., *Malthus, 1800) or – toward the turn of the century – to banking policy and practice (e.g., Anderson, 1797; Boyd, 1801; Baring, 1801; Frend, 1801; Surr, 1801). A few years later, the controversy on the price of bullion – which gave rise to some interesting contributions to the theory of crises, such as Huskisson's – implied as a counterpart that the determinants of the general price level were examined. The cobweb-like verbal models mentioned in Section 3.2 were formulated in terms of fluctuations of prices. Tooke's discussion of fluctuations was entirely in terms of prices, rather than quantities,[90] and the debates on banking policy also concerned their effects on prices. A number of writers characterized the state of distress as one of low or falling prices (e.g., Horsley Palmer's testimony before the Secret Committee on Commercial Distress, 1848a).

By the 1880s, when Juglar incorporated price fluctuations in his mechanism explaining how credit and speculation fuel each other into excess, we already had Jevons's statistical investigations and a number of writings explicitly inquiring into the relationship of prices and fluctuations: among the most recent at the time, we may quote Giffen's "Trade depression and low prices" (1885), an anonymous "Depression of trade and prices of commodities" (1886), Leroy-Beaulieu's "La baisse des prix et la crise commerciale dans le monde" (1886), Foxwell's *Irregularity of Employment and Fluctuations of Prices* (1886), Marshall's "Remedies for fluctuations of general prices" ([1887] 1925), and Wasserrab's (1889) *Preise und Krisen* (for a survey that takes Juglar as its starting point, see Williams, 1919). Although a number of reflections on prices took as a starting point their relationship to the quantity of money, suggestions as to the link between prices, credit, and speculation could easily be found in the literature: Cobden, for instance, prefacing Chevalier's argument, wrote that "The tendency to a general rise of prices would lead to an expansion of credit, and an increase of speculation, which would be followed by panics and convulsions" (Cobden, 1859, p. x; Juglar might have been aware of this passage: see note 84).

Most of these writings rely on a tradition with roots deep in the eighteenth century. A detailed account of overtrading is found, for instance, in Defoe's *Complete English Tradesman*, where a chapter is dedicated to the dangers of a constant temptation to trade beyond one's credit (1726, letter VI, pp. 72–73). Smith could take the subject almost for granted, as he incorporated it without much discussion in the *Wealth of Nations* as the cause of the scarcity of money (Smith, [1776]1979, IV.i.16). Whereas the early treatments explored the moral side of the issue relating to traders not being able to face their commitments, by the end of the century, some writers had realized that overtrading contains a potential of instability capable of bringing the entire system of credit to the toppling point (see, e.g., Roscoe, 1793; *Anderson, 1797; Anonymous, 1796; also see Section 3.10). The credit – speculation – price-rise cumulative chain is eventually found in a fairly articulated way in Huskisson's pamphlet on the bullion report (1810, pp. 131–144). A measure of the success of this argument is given on the one hand by the taking up of the term in the daily press (see, e.g., *American Beacon and Commercial Diary*, 1816; *New-York Spectator*, 1826, 1840; *Daily Herald*, 1837; *Richmond Enquirer*, 1837; *The Atlas*, 1837) and on the other by the endorsement given by J. S. Mill in the discussion of commercial crises in the *Principles*. The passage is worth citing at length as it contains an admirably concise form of all what Juglar would have said four decades later:

There is said to be a commercial crisis, when a great number of merchants and traders at once, either have, or apprehend that they shall have, a difficulty in meeting their engagements. The most usual cause of this general embarrassment, is the recoil of prices after they have been raised by a spirit of speculation, intense in degree, and extending to many commodities. Some accident which excites expectations of rising prices, such as the opening of a new foreign market, or simultaneous indications of a short supply of several great articles of commerce, sets speculation at work in several leading departments at once. The prices rise, and the holders realize, or appear to have the power of realizing, great gains. In certain states of the public mind, such examples of rapid increase of fortune call forth numerous imitators, and speculation not only goes much beyond what is justified by the original grounds for expecting rise of price, but extends itself to articles in which there never was any such ground: these, however, rise like the rest as soon as speculation sets in. At periods of this kind a great extension of credit takes place. Not only do all whom the contagion reaches employ their credit much more freely than usual; but they really have more credit, because they seem to be making unusual gains, and because a generally reckless and adventurous feeling prevails, which disposes people to give as well as take credit more largely than at other times, and give it to persons not entitled to it. In this manner, in the celebrated speculative year 1825, and at various other periods during the present century, the prices of many of the principal articles of commerce rose greatly, without any fall in others, so that general prices might, without incorrectness, be said to have risen. When, after such a rise, the reaction comes, and prices begin to fall, though at first perhaps only through the desire of the holders to realize, speculative purchases cease: but were this all, prices would only fall to the level from which they rose, or to that which is justified by the state of the consumption and of the supply. They fall, however, much lower; for as, when prices were rising, and everybody apparently making a fortune, it was easy to obtain almost any amount of credit, so now, when everybody seems to be losing, and many fail entirely, it is with difficulty that firms of known solidity can obtain even the credit to which they are accustomed, and which it is the greatest inconvenience to them to be without; because all dealers have engagements to fulfil, and nobody feeling sure that the portion of his means which he has entrusted to others will be available in time, no one likes to part with ready money, or to postpone his claim to it. To these rational considerations there is superadded, in extreme cases, a panic as unreasoning as the previous overconfidence; money is borrowed for short periods at almost any rate of interest, and sales of goods for immediate payment are made at almost any sacrifice. Thus general prices, during a commercial revulsion, fall as much below the usual level as during the previous period of speculation they have risen above it: the fall, as well as the rise, originating not in anything affecting money, but in the state of credit; an unusually extended employment of credit during the earlier period, followed by a great diminution, never amounting, however, to an entire cessation of it, in the later. (Mill, [1848] 1965, Book III, Ch. 12, § 3)

The upshot of this story is that the ingredients of Juglar's account of the cycle were far from new at the time of his writing and actually were rather commonplace; nor was Juglar's combination of these ingredients particularly original. His first version was actually rather primitive, as it did not incorporate the price mechanism as the fuel of the speculative movement, and only in 1889, we find a more compete formulation (Section 2.2.1). The novelty of Juglar's contribution, then, cannot certainly lie in his specific theory of crises, and indeed, it is not to this that he owes his fame.

3.6. The Medical Metaphor and the Mysterious Tendency to Self-Adjustment

The use of medical metaphors to describe crises was quite widespread before and after the time of Juglar's writings, and the citation of a few instances may suffice. The most common examples consist in unspecific references to one or another cause of crises as "a canker," "an internal ulcer" (Cory, 1842, p. 3), or to revulsions in commerce as "a sort of periodic epidemic in our times" (*Turner, 1844, p. 50) or as a "maladie" (Chevalier, before the Société d'Économie Politique, 1854, p. 430), or to the various occurrences of panics as a "melancholy list" (Evans, 1859, p. 1).[91] This kind of comparison of crises to a disease simply meant to emphasize that something wrong is going on in the economic system, preventing it from working normally. It thus reflects the view that a crisis is a disturbance to some "normal," "healthy" state of the system, but does not carry us much further.

Two more specific comparisons of crises and disease are more of interest. One related to the spreading and amplifying of disturbances. Longfield, for instance, wrote that the crisis "is like an epidemic ... like the plague, or any other infectitious disease which may cease of itself" (1840, p. 222); similarly, Condy Raguet began an article "On the principles of banking" with the following words: "When a community is in the full enjoyment of health, few persons are to be found willing to listen to the warning of the cautious; and it is not until the destroying epidemics appears, and when relief would come almost too late, that the public mind is in a state capable of receiving the truths, a previous acquaintance with which might have saved them from disease. What is true of physical evils, is equally true of the moral evils" (Raguet, 1829b, p. 1). Similarly, we have Wade observing that "The spirit of speculation is often epidemic" (1833, p. 209); Dupin, writing of the "fever of speculation" (1846, p. 309); the anonymous writer of the short entry on commercial crisis in Meyers *Grosse Conversations-Lexicon* (1849a), who wrote of crises occasionally spreading like epidemics through the entire country; a Boston Cashier, observing that "speculative spirit is contagious" (Anonymous, 1850, p. 1); and Guthrie, stating that "Physicians seek, with more or less success, to explain the recurrence of epidemics; and shall economists despair of accounting for the periodicity of this widespread frenzy?" (1864, p. 6). In such a usage, the emphasis is on the contagious character of crises. Although Juglar did not use this specific analogy in the first edition, while there is only a passing remark in the second ("cette spéculation est contagieuse": 1889, p. 166), it is interesting to record such occurrences in the literature for they indicate a belief that crises are the result of some kind of instability (see Section 3.10). Other analogies, of course, could and did do equally well, such as the suggestive "down go prices like an avalanche" (Williams, 1858, p. 55).

The second connotation of the medical analogy is the comparison of crises to a disease, intended as an anomaly in the "normal" development of the economic system. We find it, for instance, in Say who, after listing "wars, embargoes, oppressive duties, the dangers and difficulties of transportation," social unrest, increasing uncertainty, arbitrary exactions, jobbing, and speculation as causes of obstruction to circulation, added, "No sooner is the cause of this political disease removed, than the means of production feel a natural impulse towards the vacant channels, the replenishment of which restores activity to all the others. One kind of production would seldom out-strip every other, and its products be disproportionately cheapened, were production left entirely free" (Say 1803, cited from the 1880 translation of the 4th edition, Book 1, Chs. 15 and 16).

Blanqui wrote of commercial crises as "truly periodical diseases" (1836, p. 258). Tocqueville referred to the return of industrial crises as "an endemic disease of contemporary democratic nations, which can be made less dangerous but cannot be cured, because it does not originate in an accident, but in the very temperament of these people" (1840, Part 2, Vol. 1, Ch. 11, p. 66).[F46] Briaune wrote that "the social body, like the human body, is subject to diseases, some of which originate from external accidents and only temporarily trouble the vital functions, while others are caused instead by organic defects and, on becoming chronic, affect the constitution and development of individuals and societies."[F47] Commercial crises belong to this second sort (Briaune, 1840, p. 1). Lawson wrote of commercial panics as "diseases to which the body politic is subject – not chronic diseases, but epidemics as regular in their recurrence as influenza itself, though only at longer intervals" and contrasted the regular natural function to the effects of "some interference either from the government or ourselves deranged the usual course of things" (1848a, p. 2). Roscher referred to crises as disturbances of equilibrium "belonging to the most dangerous shocks, diseases of the body of the economy, so to speak" (1849, p. 723) and as a "politico-economic disease" ([1877] 1882, p. 204). The Boston Board of Trade treated crises as "diseases which afflict the commercial system" (1858, p. 851). Boccardo discussed crises as "a disability of the modern social world; political economy is not only physiology, but also pathology and clinical practice" (1879, p. 126).[F48] These kinds of references to diseases clearly contrast the "natural" and "healthy" state of the system to the evil consequences of some disturbance, whether internal or external, the disease *is* the trouble.

The medical doctor in Juglar emerges again here: he – following his Paris mentors, as pointed out by Frobert and Hamouda (2008) – interpreted the disease not as a functional damage but rather as the *consequence* of such a damage.[92] An early commentator clearly understood that Juglar's argument reversed the perspective of the writers listed above: "Crises, according to Dr. Juglar, result from the abuse of high health, and not from a low state of the system" (McCulloch, 1867, p. 278). Whereas in the view of the these writers, the emphasis is on the *lack* of health, revealing a purely negative conception of crisis as a derangement of the natural state of the system, in Juglar, there is also a positive connotation: the crisis and the subsequent liquidation play a specific role in the elimination of the excesses and abuses that give rise to the disease. Their role, like crises in the critical stage of a disease, is to bring back to "health" and equilibrium. Driven by an unspecified self-rightening tendency (the consequence of the absence of specification is the lack of an explanation of the trough of the cycle, especially in the first edition of Juglar's book), similar to the "healing power of nature," the crisis is

> a healthy reaction of the organism against the disease and a struggle against its evil results. This force, designated as the healing power of nature, can be compared to the antidote to a poison. It continuously tends to re-establish the calmness and equilibrium in the organisation. (Hardy, 1849, p. 389)[F49]

Here is the sense of de Foville's recollection, according to which Juglar "is the only person I have ever heard praise the benefits of fever, and he once did it with such poetic eloquence that the passers-by stood still to listen" (1905, p. 293).

In this field, Juglar was better equipped than most other users of medical metaphors.[93] Whereas other writers only had a generic understanding of the nature of diseases, Juglar's medical training enabled him to understand the function and role of diseases in the physiology of the human body. His metaphors could thus play a heuristic function, as pointed out by Frobert and Hamouda (2008). This is not an isolated case: sometimes, metaphors are only used to illustrate an argument, but often, they help in transferring a way of thinking from one domain to another. The history of the theories of economic fluctuations offers other examples, such as the waves of the ocean (suggesting gravitation around a "mean sun")[94] or the pendulum – the metaphor that eventually displaced references to the physiology of the system to emphasize its mechanics: the choice of the analog, whether for illustrative purposes or as a heuristic device, is never neutral. As we shall see in Section 4.2, the transition from the nineteenth-century notions of crises as anomalies to the early twentieth-century view of cycles as the normal form taken by capitalistic relationships was indeed accompanied by a shift from "disease" as a preferred metaphor for crises to mechanical analogies of oscillating systems.

3.7. Crises and Progress

Juglar's idea that crises as painful but inevitable and necessary to growth was also not new at the time he formulated it. Its far origin lies in the comparison of the merits of the diffusion of credit with the danger of overtrading stimulated (or at least permitted) by credit (see Section 3.5). Without climbing too far back in time, we find, in 1800, Charles Long arguing that although credit and fictitious capital may have been pushed too far and in some instance can have done harm, "it has done great good; that a great part of the substantial wealth of this nation has been obtained by the credit of the British trader, enabling him to add fictitious capital to real capital; and to make profits, the result of the employment of both" (p. 20). More interestingly, in a comment on the Bullion Report, a writer contrasted the *collective* benefit of speculation supported by credit to the *individual* ruin that this may involve. Samuel Cock argued on similar lines that while conservative merchants wait for trade to be commissioned to them, young adventurers engage in speculation and seek new channels of commerce, often with scarce capital. Although this may lead to their personal "irretrievable embarrassment," "the country at large has derived an important benefit from their exertions" when the "rage of speculation" has ceased and new channels of commerce are opened up for everybody. This could not have happened without "confidence and credit to support and give effect to the energies of these spirited merchants" (Cock, 1810, p. 73).

An untitled leader in *The Times* argued that "good may result from the present crisis, and that the commercial horizon may be purified for the future" provided that creditors learn the lesson and show firmness and stern integrity:

> We have always asserted, that the present commercial embarrassments, severe as they may be, will have a beneficial result; and that it was well for the country that an impediment was thrown in the way of the existing method of conducting business: for if that system, which had already continued too long, had continued longer, the crash would have been more fatal. (*The Times*, 1826)

As we get closer to Juglar's times, the point of view that crises have a useful function to perform becomes better articulated, such as, in Garnier's entry on "Commercial crises" in the *Dictionnaire universel théorique et pratique du commerce et de la navigation*. He maintained that commercial crises are inescapable, they "are part of the nature of things" rather than being due to exogenous factors, but are temporary and necessary to permit growth, being the outcome of the "overexcitement of entrepreneurial spirit":

> They are inevitable. But the inconveniences are far from balancing the immense advantages that people gain from the vast development of their business. [Commercial crises] are crises of growth, and it is far better to have activity and wealth accompanied by commercial crises (were they necessary in the permanent nature of things) than idleness and poverty. Rich and prosperous countries are sometimes in a crisis; poor countries are permanently in a crisis.

> Moreover, commercial crises are in their nature temporary. The sudden drops in the value of goods attract buyers, facilitate consumption, unblock the glut and induce the liquidation of badly directed business. In these events, the producers or holders of goods undergo losses, but at the same time the buyers or holders of circulating capital gain

from them. The wealth of some people is destroyed, but that of others increases. There are individual sufferings, but from the social point of view there is no such an impoverishment, and the inconvenience related to the crisis is made up by the disappearance of the rotten enterprises. This is why shortly after the crisis business is seen to recover with more vigor and briskness than ever. (Garnier 1859, p. 925)[F50]

R. Hare, in "an effort to refute the opinion, that no addition is made to the capital of a community by banking," admitted that "the facility of getting credit, by multiplying purchasers," may contribute toward "great elevations and depressions in the prices of real estate," making people "alternatively rich or poor, according as greater or less confidence exists with respect to our national prosperity, and the consequent prospective demand for farms, plantations, or building lots, increases or diminished." But maintained that

> Judging from experience, it may be a question whether the ultimate, or average accumulation of national wealth, is less in consequence of the fluctuations of prices to which I have alluded. Such fluctuations rouse men to extraordinary exertion, and by a reaction after each subsiding wave, cause business to revive with a renovated and accumulated force. It is in consequence of the stimulus and reaction which accompany or follow great catastrophes, such as are produced by floods or fires, that after a few years, communities which have been subjected to them, will appear to have made advance even greater than might have been anticipated, had no such deteriorating accident occurred. (Hare, 1852, pp. 705–706)[95]

John Francis (the author of *History of the Bank of England*) described how crises are the necessary "result of some previous and prosperous period" out of which also numerous improvements in the institutional structure of the country and in her capital equipment follow, thus concluding that in spite of the evils panics have created, they have also been "productive of much good in their ulterior result" (*Francis, 1853, p. 471):

> If, then, I be correct in the conclusions I have drawn, our commercial crises have, at all events, produced certain good effects. A brief digest of these will give mercantile introduction to new countries, exclusive commercial privileges, new ideas in banking, the Bank of England itself, the advance and development of the principle of life assurance, hospitals to receive the sick and suffering, canals, docks, bridges, railways, joint-stock banks, mechanics institutions – all owing to such eras. These were some of the special advantages derived by the public from financial excitements; but there are more general and collateral benefits which spring during these periods. It is then that if a man has a new idea he will produce it, that if he has a new machine he will patent it. It is then that the inventor can find capital to perfect the invention which may add to a people's comfort, or stimulate their greatness. Nor is it one of the least of these benefits, that the excitement which precedes a commercial crisis changes the proprietorship of the good things of this world. Were it not for such great epochs, England would have been yet more nation of millionaires than she is; we should have been yet more like old Rome

when fallen on evil day, a people of extreme rich and extreme poor, instead of being, as I believe we are, a proof of the truth of Lord Bacon's wise aphorism, that money is like manure, and to do good requires to be spread. I believe that these crises are for good. They are the necessary consequences of a high productive power. We are eminently a nation of tradesmen, and that this is no reproach, let the republics of Italy in their palmiest days bear witness. But being good tradesmen, our capital is constantly increasing, and so long as this continues, we must find some mode of getting interest for it. (*Francis, 1853, p. 477)

Such views were not isolated. Critics of this opinion indeed felt that it was spread enough to deserve an explicit rebuttal. Thus in 1850, Ledru-Rollin, discussing "The periodical return of commercial crises which have occurred in England since the peace of 1815," indicated that "A theory has been invented ... assuming that these interruptions are necessary to trade; and according to these theorists, crises are an advantageous means of liquidation, which enable the principal houses to rectify their accounts" and commented that "This is a truly strange remedy; it must finish by destroying the patient, under pretence of eradicating the disease" (p. 283). In 1864, Ferrara pointed out that the linkage between credit and crises induced many[96] "enamored with the industrial miracles credit permits to make real" to accept crises as the price of growth. Besides Garnier's entry, he also referred to Coquelin (without giving a precise reference) and explicitly interpreted Juglar's statement that the return of crises is a condition of progress in industry as belonging to this tradition (Ferrara, [1864]1890, p. 274).[97] Similarly, a few years later, Hoyle stated that "there is an opinion prevalent, and it has obtained somewhat general acceptance, that the panics and depressions in trade are the natural outcome, and, indeed, I may say an essential result of the operations of trade: that they are needed to restore the languid commerce of a country to healthy action again" (1877, p. 14). Juglar himself referred to Overstone in this respect (1889, p. 6; see Section 2.2),[98] and Langton (1857) also deserves a place in this connection (for a discussion, see Ashton [1934]1977, pp. 71–72).

3.8. Proximate Causes and Vera Causa of Crises

Juglar's break with the multicausal understanding of crises (Section 2.1.2) was not isolated. Albeit in different contexts and with different terminology, the distinction between "occasional" cause and "predisposition" was available on both sides of the channel,[99] and it is not surprising that some authors applied it to the return of crises precisely in the same way as Juglar did, that is, both for its methodological implications and as a rhetorical device. Other writers, in fact, were looking for a unifying explanation of crises and accordingly sought a common cause for all instances and at the same time rejected the interpretations of crises as unique events, each having its own cause or set of causes.

3.8.1. Epistemology and Rhetoric

On the constructive side, these writers all introduced an epistemological break with respect to the (then mainstream) approach consisting in attributing a different cause to each crisis and argued that the observed similarity of such events implies the presence of a unique cause. They sometimes differed among one another as to the nature of such cause, but all tackled the problem of the existence of different circumstances at the time of each crisis by introducing the distinction between "occasional" (or secondary, determining or proximate) causes and a "true" (or remote, or primary) cause of crises, the former being specific to each event whereas the latter is common to the entire series.

At the same time, however, these writers had to gain acceptance for their own interpretation and reject the opposite thesis. The constructive side of their argument was thus accompanied by a rhetorical apparatus counter-posing the rationality and logical consistency of their own argument and disparaging at the same time the competing approach by stressing its epistemic inadequacy. Some simply argued that their hypothesis of a unique cause is more reasonable; others referred to the principles of science suggesting that the opponents failed to comply with them, and others ridiculed the adversaries. It is remarkable that their rhetorics focused precisely on what these writers thought to be the correct way of thinking about these problems rather than on some specific fallacy of the opponents. The issue at stake was not much this or that cause of the crisis (and the corresponding policy to remedy it), but the general way of approaching the problem of the recurrence of crises. They explicitly chose as battlefield the possibility of understanding the laws of crises, as opposed to the writers who emphasized instead their unsystematic nature. This epistemological revolution is thus the counterpart of the coming of age of a different way of interpreting the working of the capitalist system.

3.8.2. Robert Cockburn

The first two instances of the new approach of which I am aware date from 1840. Opening a pamphlet (published anonymously) titled *Remarks on trade and credit*, Robert Cockburn pointed out that whatever the proximate cause of crisis, it could only operate provided that the system was predisposed for a crisis. His terminology, like Juglar's, is explicitly medical:

> In former times, we heard the exclamations – "a dull trade;" "trade flat;" "business not brisk;" &c. Since the year 1824, the trading-world has altered its tone, beginning, at stated periods, with a cry of loud complaint, but ending with one which indicates little less than the agony of mind at approaching ruin. It matters not from what cause, whether from a deficiency in the harvest, excitement in domestic politics, dangers of wars threatening us from abroad, the speech of an American President against the Banking system of the United States, or the revulsion of monetary difficulties from those States, – each is productive of a serious effect throughout Great Britain, varying alone in intensity, according to the morbid degree of mercantile activity by which one of these occurrences may have been preceded. A very slight reflection must convince us that the causes enumerated could not produce the effect upon a sound system of trade. Infection is not easily communicated, where the body is not pre-disposed by weakness or ill-health. (*Cockburn, 1840, pp. 1–2)

Cockburn attributed the "primary cause [of] these periodical panics" "to the overtrading of all classes, – whether traders of property, or persons who possess nothing: to the principle and facility of credit; and last, though not least, to that vile system which gives currency to credits, and creates a feverish circulation, upon a rotten foundation" (p. 3). Although the distinction between proximate and primary causes is quite explicit, the criticism to the theories elevating the proximate causes of crises to a full explanation remained implicit. His contemporary economist-agriculturalist Briaune focused instead precisely on the epistemic implications of such a distinction.

3.8.3. Jean-Edmond Briaune

In his discussion of the "periodicity of commercial crises" (p. 2), Briaune suggested that crises are not to be discussed as disconnected individual events but are better understood as a succession of related occurrences. He therefore had to face the problem of rejecting the predominant individual explanation of crises emphasizing in their stead a common explanation. He did so by mocking the adversaries and bringing home an epistemological point at once. One of the points of view to be rejected was the "popular preconceptions" ("préjugés populaires" – shared, in reality, by renowned economists) ascribing crises to "political causes." In Briaune's view, the political and institutional setting can only be a secondary cause,[100] making things worse or better,[101] while the fundamental cause must be sought elsewhere, on the ground of the "general principle that seeks the same cause for a series of similar effects." The destructive part of Briaune's argument consists of a long list of political causes that should be expected to have produced precisely the opposite effect as the one actually observed: for instance, "one should profess that the prosperity from 1820 to 1827 was due to the changed electoral law, to the suspension of the freedom of the press and of individual freedom; to the riots in the schools, to the Paris, Saumur, Bedford and La Rochelle conspiracies that were its consequences; to the Spanish war, to the compensation laws, to the primogeniture rights, and to sacrilege, which were its continuation and complement."[F51,102] The other point of view to be rejected was the ascription of the last crisis to an excess of production, or to credit, or to stock market speculation. Criticizing these views, Briaune expounds the positive principle that should guide the reflection on the causes of crises:

> If these were the true causes, they would have had impact on the crises of 1811, 1817 and 1827, for the periodical return of the same affliction necessarily implies the existence of identical and permanent causes. However, nobody would assign to past crises the supposed origin of the present crisis; it is indeed rather illogical that similar effects, obviously linked to each other, are always attributed to different accidents. Against the general principle that for a series of like effects the same cause must be sought, one should bring irrefutable evidence; but such a proof is still missing. (Briaune, 1840, pp. 3–4)[F52]

The common premise Briaune identified was a sudden halt in consumption, the cause of which he thought to be the periodical increase in the price of cereals, which hits workers first, diminishing their consumption of other goods; successively, "the illness grows in geometrical proportion"[F53] by spreading to other branches of trade because of the solidarity of commerce (pp. 5–13).

3.8.4. Isaac Preston Cory

A similar view on causality is outlined in the opening passages of a pamphlet by Cory (a barrister and Lecturer of Hebrew at the University of Cambridge, 1801/2–1842):

> A variety of causes has been assigned to account for this depression, and as many remedies have been proposed to obviate it. The national debt, taxation, the currency, the unlimited power of the Bank of England over its issue, the excess of population, the corn laws, the oppressions of the millowners, have each their advocates, who would fain persuade us, that an alteration of some one or more of these would give relief and restore prosperity.
>
> It is not my intention to deny, that each and every one of them have their effect, and may, in some degree, influence the state of trade: but in the following pages I propose to avoid, as much as possible, the discussion of any of these subjects which have been worn threadbare, and upon which every one has made up his mind; while I would direct attention to what I humbly conceive to be a preliminary evil, much more extensive than

all of them put together – a canker in the very heart of our trading prosperity, which is
ever and anon producing the same recurrences of distress – temporary they may seem,
but which, I fear, are rather of a periodical nature, like the returns of the shivering fits
which precede the dissolution of the body by an internal ulcer. (Cory, 1842, p. 3)

Cory is thus advocating a common premise to all crises, more fundamental
than the various circumstances that may intervene and are capable of
altering the course of the panic but cannot be deemed to be ultimately
responsible for them.

3.8.5. James Anthony Lawson

A terminologically more accurate exposition is found in a paper "On
Commercial Panics" read by James Anthony Lawson before the Dublin
Statistical Society (of which he was the Secretary at the time), printed as a
pamphlet by the Society (Lawson, 1848a), and partly reprinted in the
Bankers' Magazine (1848b) and in *Hunt's Merchants' Magazine* (1848c)[103] –
this magazine, interestingly enough, is one of the few sources cited by Juglar
in his 1863 Dictionary entry.[104] Lawson was stuck by the fact that the
alleged causes of a number of the panics (of which, as cited above, he
recognized the periodicity and interconnectedness) could not have been
large enough to explain the havoc wrought by the panic themselves: "for
instance, the breaking out of the war in 1793, that alone never could have
occasioned commercial embarrassment if commercial affairs had been in a
sound state up to that time – it might have limited the future operations of
trade, or checked its advance, but it could not entail the universal ruin which
ensued." He concluded,

We must therefore look beyond the proximate cause or the occasion of the panic to find
its true cause; and I think from the details I have given you, you will be prepared to
anticipate the conclusion to which I have arrived, namely, that it is not attributed to a
sudden check *given to an extensive and long continued trade upon credit* – this check may
proceed from the various causes which we have seen gave occasion to the panic, or by
any other circumstances which cause a revulsion in the public mind, or cause a
disinclination to continue to give credit; and it will be found that when the system of
trading on credit has been extensively pursued, a very slight obstacle is sufficient to
overturn the entire system. (Lawson, 1848c, p. 284, 1848a, p. 4)

Lawson's distinction between "proximate cause" and "true cause" is thus
used to distinguish between a cause common to all events and the occasional
circumstances that actually give rise to the panic; this, however – as was the
case for Juglar – is prepared by the vera causa having generated enough
instability in the system so that a small event can give rise to disproportionate effects. Lawson also argues (the passage, however, does not

appear in 1848b and 1848c) that "If we have any faith in the truth or certainty of science, we must feel fully persuaded that the truths are of universal application; that they cannot be true at one moment and false at the next; that they are not to be taken up in smooth seasons, and laid aside in rough ones," to reject the "fallacy of [the] reasoning" involved in all the explanations of panics advocating the extraordinary nature of the case and thus blaming some exception to the ordinary rules (1848a, p. 1).[105]

3.8.6. Charles Coquelin

Another instance is found in the writings of Charles Coquelin. He starts from the observation that in the first half of the nineteenth century, crises have become "almost periodical"[106] and have acquired a character of suddenness they did not have before. Whereas in the past, crises were always due to famines, wars, or revolutions, and it was therefore easy to understand their causes, modern crises can arise "spontaneously," so to speak (1852a, pp. 527, 528, 533), and therefore require a different kind of explanation: the cause of the disorder is "obviously not external, but inherent to the very operations of commerce or to the intimate nature of credit" (pp. 527, 528, 533). The development of credit, which in the most advanced countries supports most commercial operations, is indeed the common circumstance permitting the occurrence of these crises. It also explains the suddenness of crises, as it makes the system intrinsically unstable: credit, in fact, requires mutual confidence, and if "for any reason"[F54] doubt arises as to the future respect of obligations, the whole system of commerce suddenly collapses; "the evil spreads like wildfire"[107] and envelops in little time the whole commercial world. The notion of a "spontaneous" insurgence of crises, made necessary by the observation of their almost periodical return, calls for an endogenous explanation based on some mechanism giving rise to instability.[108]

Similarly to credit, speculation and misdirected production can also be the occasional causes of crises. Deeper down, however, crises and their shared features must have a "general and common cause," and it is this "first cause" (pp. 530–531), or "originating cause" (p. 533),[F55] that must be sought, as opposed to the "determining cause" (p. 530) commencing each crisis. Coquelin maintained that this ultimate cause is the existence of privileged banks and their way of operating: this cause operates constantly, so that its effects (a glut of capitals) slowly but regularly cumulate so that after a time the effect produced (the crisis) is the same, whether the determining cause is an excess of speculation or an abuse of credit (p. 533).

Coquelin uses this argument to reject two alternative explanations of crises, Say's and Wilson's, who both blamed the 1825 crisis on speculation. To Say, he objected, "this explanation is obviously not sufficient, for one still has to ask what was the primum mobile, the original cause of this abuse [an excessive emission of banknotes] and of the adventurous speculations that followed" (p. 529). Against Wilson's explanation based on different causes of speculative manias (exploitation of foreign mines, on land property at home, on various companies, etc.), Coquelin argued,

> It will be agreed that it is hardly possible that the same disposition became manifest in so many different directions at once, if it was not aroused by a general and common cause. It is therefore this prime cause that has to be specified, and [Wilson's argument] fails to do this. There is no doubt that abuses of credit became apparent at the approaching of each of the crises broken out since the beginning of the century, and that they are a determining cause. There is also no doubt that excessive speculations have characterized each of these epochs and played an important part in the disorders that have erupted. But where the abuse of credit comes from, and why the speculative mood at some point takes possession of all minds, still remains to be explained. To say these are erupting frenzies tells us nothing and is a mere use of words. It is not natural that this kind of disease breaks out without being provoked. And the existence of a hidden cause, operating constantly, is finally demonstrated here by the almost periodical return of these calamities. (p. 530)

3.8.7. John Mills

Juglar's masterful piece of rhetoric (Section 2.1) needed some complements to fully convince fellow economists that the appropriate way to look at crises is in their interconnection with one another and with the other phases of the system. The challenge was taken up in Britain, independently of Juglar, by John Mills, a Manchester banker. In a paper read in December 1867 before the Manchester Statistical Society – which published it in its *Transactions*: Mills (1868) – a few years after the publication of Juglar's first edition, Mills took up issues of both the universality of laws and the uniqueness of crises. Mills cites Langton, Jevons, Coquelin, J. S. Mill, and Tooke's *History of Prices*, but neither Cory, Juglar, or Lawson.[109] Mills begins his argument by discussing the variegated literature of pamphlets flourishing after each crisis and discussing their causes:

> One feature these productions have in common: they deal with proximate causes only, or with mere antecedents as causes; each crisis appearing to be the result of its own separate accident, – usually some event lying on the surface of commercial history. The highest attempt at generalization does not ascend beyond the fact – unquestionable in itself – that over-trading, in some form or other, is the common forerunner of Panic. Overtrading, however, is not an ultimate fact, and its regular recurrence claim explanations quite as importantly as the tragic events which follow it. (Mills, 1868, p. 11)

Mills explains that he intends to apply "the method by which modern science brings physical and even social phenomena within the region of causation and law," which requires to identify the "uniformities of sequence" from which to generalize (p. 12). The first of such uniformities is that crises are so "numerous, regular, and persistent" that "whatever we may at present think of its cause, of its practical importance, or of its probable continuance, the periodicity of commercial crisis is at any rate *a fact*" (Mills, 1868, p. 14). This enables Mills to exclude that the proximate causes can be at the origin of the "facts of a new order" (1868, p. 13):[110] panics recurred with regularity even if the institutional conditions under which trade takes place have considerably changed in the previous 60 years and in spite of the immediate antecedents being bewilderingly varied in nature (pp. 14–15). Although some of the antecedents "in a subordinate sense ... may indeed have assigned to them the dignity of causes," "it is evident that these incidental causes do not account for the feature we have noted as *common to the whole series*, that of regularity of occurrence." Mills even noted that some events, grave in character, have occurred without culminating in a panic, or only slightly anticipating it with respect to the customary decennial rhythm, "showing how little the action of the normal causes of Panic could be accelerated by so vast an addition of external force" (p. 15). Not only does this argument echo Juglar's claim that even a war would not break a prosperity if no abuses of credit had previously predisposed the crisis, but goes one step further, by qualifying the proximate cause in question as an "external event" or "incidental disturbances" (p. 18), thus coming close to introducing the distinction between exogenous and endogenous causes.

Mills's argument is slightly different from Juglar's. While the latter was trying to identify the vera causa common to *each* crisis, Mills aimed at singling out the cause of the cycle *as a whole*. But the distinction between proximate and primary cause plays the same role in their criticisms to *individual* explanations of crises by appeal to general epistemic principles. Both authors linked this argument to the idea that if conditions are not fulfilled,[111] even grave events, that would otherwise determine a crisis, would be ineffective and, conversely, that at the right time, a small determining cause could trigger a panic (e.g., Mills, 1868, p. 38).

3.8.8. William Stanley Jevons

Jevons, who at Manchester had several occasions for discussion with Mills, felt the same urge. He immediately appreciated Mills's appeal to reject explanations based on proximate causes to inquire into the common causes of all cycles: "Mr. Mills has proved that such fluctuations have a deeper cause which we can only describe as the *mental disposition* of the trading classes" (Jevons, 1869). Later, he ridiculed,

> the variety of the explanations offered by commercial writers concerning the cause of the present state of trade. Foreign competition, beer-drinking, overproduction, trade-unionism, war, peace, want of gold, superabundance of silver, Lord Beaconsfield, Sir Stafford Northcote, their extravagant expenditure, the Government policy, the Glasgow Bank directors, Mr. Edison and the electric light, are a few of the happy and consistent suggestions continually made to explain the present disastrous collapse of industry and credit. (Jevons, 1878b, in 1884, p. 221)

Jevons, like Juglar, coupled the rhetorical purpose with a methodological objection to the search of specific causes for each crisis. Although depressions are often "apparently due to exceptional and accidental events, such as wars, great commercial failures, unfounded panics, and so forth" (Jevons [1875], in 1884, p. 203), the mechanical principle that periodical effects must have periodical causes (see Section 3.4) forbids that these are the ultimate causes: "so long as these causes are various and disconnected, nothing emerges to explain the remarkable appearance of regularity and periodicity which characterises these events" (Jevons, 1878b, in 1884, p. 222).[112] Again like Juglar, Mills, Lawson, and Cory, Jevons turns the interpretation of these exceptional events on its head: from causes of the crises, they are downgraded to causes of the irregularities in the period. When commerce is disturbed by wars, tariffs, or similar extraneous events, "it can be no matter of wonder that the regular march of the decennial variation was somewhat broken"(Jevons, 1878a, in 1884, p. 208).[113]

These writers' recognition that crises have a common, fundamental cause, while possibly being generated by different specific occasional causes, was a cornerstone in the transition from the emphasis on crises to the stress on cycles. Most earlier commentators saw crises as individual events, each with its own cause and with no connection to the preceding or following crisis. In this perspective, crises could be seen as accidents, as disturbances to an economic order that would otherwise give rise to fairly regular economic progress. Juglar and the writers listed in this section were instead laying the premises for an altogether different interpretation of crises, no longer seen as *disconnected events* but as members of the same *class of events*. This, in turn, was the premise of the recognition of general *laws*, applicable to the entire series of events. Other writers before them or contemporary to them were, as a matter of fact, offering the same explanation for all crises. But the important contribution of the authors considered in this section is on the epistemic level, as it highlights their awareness of working toward the construction of an explicitly unified explanation.

3.9. Equilibrium and the "Natural" State of the System

Not only the issues Juglar explicitly discussed must be examined but also at least one of his omissions. Among the problems Juglar was not aware of, the most important is the failure to discuss the equilibrium conditions. He clearly denoted prosperity as the normal, healthy, and equilibrium state of the economy, but never specified how such an equilibrium is characterized (Section 2.1.4). The relevance of this omission is twofold.

3.9.1. Crises and Equilibrium
Historically, one of the main theoretical problems to be solved in studies on crises and cycles has been the relationship of economic distress to equilibrium or normality. It was generally accepted, from the gluts debate at least to interwar years, that crises are disequilibrium situations, and one had to reconcile this fact with theoretical approaches describing economic systems as tending toward equilibrium. The mainstream approaches have tried to interpret cycles and crises as partial and temporary exceptions to the theoretical norm, due to frictions, exogenous events, miscalculations, mismanagement, or some other impediments or accidents. The critics, on the contrary, rejected the idea that the system is self-equilibrating and either introduced some form of systematic instability or suggested to switch altogether to a different theoretical setup (e.g., a dynamic one, see Besomi, 2006b).

The better known branch of this debate concerned Say's Law. On one side, there was the Say–Mill–Ricardo position, according to which production is undertaken with the purpose of consuming, and what is not immediately consumed is accumulated. In such conditions, general overproduction is logically impossible, although there may be temporary partial overproduction in some markets, caused by mismanagements, or political interferences or other disturbances, compensated by underproduction elsewhere. On the other side, the "heretics" (the qualifier is Keynes's[114]) stressed that due to various reasons (such as technological progress or the bad distribution of the product), part of the income generated in the production process may not be spent, therefore generating a general excess of production. In this view, crises are the outcome and the means for the resolution of such excesses, as they violently halt production bringing with them destruction and misery. The early champions of this view were

Malthus and Sismondi, who, however, lost their battle with the Ricardians. In France and England, the debate quickly petered out, although several "underground" writers kept thinking in terms of overproduction or underconsumption. In Germany, however, a number of writers kept discussing crises in terms of disturbances in the equilibrium of supply and demand and with explicit (sometimes critical) reference to Say's Law (see, e.g., Roscher, 1849, pp. 723–724; Schäffle, 1859, p. 638). The most important contribution in this line was Marx's, who carefully explored the various possibilities of crises opened by several specific aspects of the production process and especially, in most general terms, by the separation of the acts of buying and selling made possible by the use of money as an intermediary.[115] The latter point was anticipated by J. S. Mill, who at the same time also maintained that general gluts are logically impossible.[116] For all these writers, equilibrium, and the system's tendency to settle on such a state, was the focus of the debate. The culminating point in this tradition was Marx's precise statement of equilibrium conditions through his reproduction schemes,[117] which at once showed how the flux of exchanges could both satisfy the material needs of the productive process and generate a satisfactory profit, but also how these conditions could fail to be satisfied for various and intrinsic reasons making it necessary, from time to time, to interrupt the production process. The discussions on Marx's approach eventually gave rise to various theoretical views, including some that can be seen as the first true examples of business cycle theories in the modern sense – Tugan-Baranowsky (see Besomi, 2006a), Spiethoff, and Schumpeter.

The second approach to fluctuations in the early nineteenth century, based on cobweb-like mechanisms (see Section 3.2), implicitly took equilibrium as a reference point. These verbal models assumed a tendency of disequilibrium prices or quantities to ingenerate a set of economic forces tending to redress the situation. But the operation of these forces is delayed or hindered by slow reaction or institutional factors, so that the correction overshoots the mark, and the position is reversed. These models describe oscillatory motion, rather than dealing with crises and panics. In some sense, they anticipate some of the (proper) business cycle theories of the early twentieth century (the cobweb models, but also Aftalion's, Bouniatian's, Kalecki's, and Tinbergen's models), but they were not concerned with explaining the phenomena discussed by most of their contemporaries, namely, the violent and sudden upheaval caused by the total disruption of trade and finance.

The third line of approach, surely the most popular toward the middle of the century and at Juglar's time, focused on some form of the overtrading mechanism, to which different causes could be attributed (Section 3.5). A feature common to almost all writers sharing this view was that the excess of trade or of credit or of emission of banknotes was rarely qualified. It was assumed that there was some "correct" amount of trade or credit or issue, respectively, corresponding, for example, to one's capital, one's capacity to repay debt, and the real value of titles, but this was rarely defined with precision, also due to circumstances varying as a consequence of trade, credit, or issue being extended; accordingly, the "excess" was not defined either, and if referred to the "correct" amount, the reasoning became circular (Laidler, 1987).

In the writings belonging to this group, the equilibrium in the credit market is thus an implicit reference. However, neither its conditions nor its stability properties are analytically characterized. The consequences of this are not too dramatic for the possibility of explaining crises. A number of these writers, including Juglar, maintained that once the economy starts growing, there is a constant temptation to push trade and credit faster and faster, until this becomes excessive and the system collapses (see Section 3.10). It is not clear "excessive" with respect to what, but the accelerated pace of growth guarantees that, wherever the limit is, it will be overtaken.

3.9.2. The Onset of Recovery
The other side of the coin is more troublesome. If equilibrium is not well defined, it is more problematic to explain how the recovery sets in. These writers interpreted crises as the liquidation of bad debts, or more generally as the elimination of the "excesses." This was seen (explicitly, in the case of Juglar) as a return to the equilibrium state. But neither its conditions nor its features (except for the vague assumption that it consists in a state of progress) or the path by which it is reached are specified by most of these writers. As a matter of fact, then, the transition from liquidation to recovery remains unexplained. It is assumed as a matter of course, but not really accounted for. The causal chain is interrupted, making a complete theory of the cycle, with all phases growing out of the previous one and generating the following, impossible to establish.

3.9.3. Some Early Attempts to Identify the Conditions for a Self-Sustained Advance
Juglar does not seem to have realized that this is a serious problem for his stated programme of chaining all phases to one another (Section 2.2.1). Other writers, however, were aware that this aspect was problematic and attempted to tackle it. The earliest endeavor along this line of which I am

aware was offered by John Sinclair in 1810. He listed three conditions for prosperity to remain uninterrupted: that labor and goods necessary for internal consumption or for exports increase; that the price of goods is sufficiently high to stimulate production, but not high enough to hinder consumption; that the medium of exchange increases in proportion to the increase of commerce, so as to secure a market and a rapid sale of the goods produced, but also as to increase their price (Sinclair, 1810, pp. 60, 57). The latter condition "is by far the most material" (p. 60). If it is not satisfied, commerce experiences, and must experience, frequent checks (p. 57), and the country undergoes "periodical returns of commercial distresses" (p. 64). The reason why distresses return periodically is not explicitly stated but seems to be due to the banking system failing to supply currency at the appropriate pace. In other words, distress is seen as the result of the failure to fulfill the conditions for what today we would call a "moving equilibrium."

A later attempt to state the problem was by James Wilson. In spite of not having been able to solve it, he clearly saw this was a necessary step to take:

> In order to go into the investigation proposed, it is obvious that we must discover, that we must condescend to some given sum which, could it be maintained steadily, would be the correct amount of the means of the country absorbed for this particular purpose annually, namely, the purchase of wheat. (Wilson 1840, p. 19)[118]

Wilson admitted he knew of no principle to determine this point, and as a first approximation, he took the average price of corn, in analogy with the symmetrical movement of a pendulum fluctuating around it middle point. He took, however, equilibrium as its starting point, by imagining a given distribution of the capital of the country among various sectors bearing "the exactly proper proportion to each other to supply the wants of the community" (p. 21) and examined the consequences of a shortage of wheat throughout the system.[119]

More elaborate is John Mills's argument. Whereas Juglar swiftly avoided discussing the relationship of cycles and equilibrium, Mills precisely saw that there lies the main theoretical problem. Mills, as well as Juglar, considered prosperity to be the "healthiest" phase of the cycle (Mills, 1868, p. 24) and attributed to credit a "normal tendency to grow" (p. 32) and a "normal rate of growth." Mills also left this tendency unexplained, assumed as a matter of fact, but specified that credit "can only grow under the stringent condition of paying a discount proportioned to the degree in which growth outruns the supply of loan capital" (p. 32). Credit has thus a price, and this price is subject to the "economic law of supply and demand," "tending to preserve the necessary equilibrium" between credit and capital.

"I say 'the necessary equilibrium' because, in fact, Credit cannot long exist without it. Belief is founded upon evidence, and must be kept in contact with it" (p. 31). The growth of credit is thus kept in check by the stabilizing forces acting upon the rate of interest; yet, it is also subject to the destabilizing effect of speculation fostered by excesses of confidence (p. 27 and passim). Instability is thus limited by the stabilizing force (which sums its effects[120] to, and "applies an effective break to[,] the dangerous velocity with which a too facile Credit would multiply transactions" and "tends to preserve the natural and ... that vitally important equipoise between the growth of bill-making Credit, and the supply of Capital from accumulated profits and savings," p. 32). But in the speculative stage of the cycle, credit

> grows under such stimulating conditions, that any weighting of *that* side of the scale is quite out of question. The time comes too soon when our two laws, while they continue to be correlative, tend to become less and less *coefficient*. The adjusting principle is still at work, but under the influences now gathering, it becomes by degrees overborne, and at last overwhelmed. The Credit end of the beam is too far depressed to be raised again until lightened of its load by a violent process. As this, however, is owing to the relative default of Capital, it is clear that no amount of paper promises, *now* placed in the opposite scale, would redress the balance. (p. 35)

In such conditions, the set of psychological factors affecting credit "either neutralises the economic law of demand, or, reversing the poles of the magnet, it exerts a repellant instead of an attractive influence" (p. 34). After the panic, the law of supply and demand cannot immediately exert its effect for while gold and notes (after some caution on the part of lenders) flow back into the bank, borrowers do not find motive to invest, in spite of being "tempted by a low rate of interest," due to the restrictions in purchasing power (and therefore in demand) felt by most people as an effect of the crisis (pp. 20–22). But slowly confidence will return and will find good conditions in the "great accumulation of unused Capital and the ruling of an excessively low rate of interest" that established in the postpanic period and bring back to the normal time of revival, where credit continues to grow in an healthy fashion, kept in check by the law of supply and demand (pp. 22–24).

The contrast with Juglar is striking. Mills has clearly understood that the problem of crises cannot be severed from reflections on their relationship to equilibrium. In Juglar, by contrast, we only find the assumption that, by simple elimination of the excesses, the crisis will bring the system back to a state of stable (momentarily, at least) equilibrium. Juglar did not feel the need to discuss why such an equilibrium acts as an attractor to the system, while most of his contemporaries were discussing the aspects of this problem

in the context of Say's law, and later, the problem was clearly perceived to
be at the heart of trade cycle theorizing.

3.10. Instability

In spite of the difficulties intrinsic to the relationship between crises
and equilibrium (Section 3.9), some writers realized very soon that if
equilibrium is stable, crises can only be conceived as the result of temporary
disturbances external to the proper working of the economic system;
accordingly, they started arguing that crises are related to the instability of
the credit system. This was at first expressed in intuitive rather than
analytical terms, but toward the middle of the nineteenth century, these
reflections were beginning to be coupled with epistemic arguments on the
nature of the explanation of crises, especially on the part of the writers who
had been discussing the application to crises of the principle of causality
(Section 3.8).

I have already anticipated (Section 3.5) that toward the end of the
eighteenth century, some writers belonging to the "overtrading" tradition
started to stress that credit and speculation may destabilize the entire
system. William Roscoe had argued that the expansion of trade at the same
time requires and permits the expansion of credit. But credit is based on
trust, and if anything shakes confidence, progress becomes unsustainable
(1793, p. 11). Roscoe resorted to vivid metaphors to stress the instability of
such a state, qualifying prosperity as "undoubtedly of a very precarious and
inflammable nature," so that a spark suffices to dissipate confidence in the
air (p. 6). He also stressed that the wide extent of British trade makes the
country more vulnerable than others to sudden loss of trust, increasing "the
probability of the explosion," and rendering "the consequences of it, when it
once [takes] place, more general" (p. 25). Although he saw the cause shaking
confidence in an external event, namely, the outbreak of the war with
France, his interpretation of the unfolding of events was endogenous: "our
very prosperity becomes our misfortune" (p. 5). Also William Anderson,
writing in 1797 under anonymity, and an "Old merchant" writing in 1796,
stressed the instability of the credit system using the metaphor of a "baseless
building ... absolutely built upon quicksand" (Anonymous, 1796, p. 9;
Anderson, 1797, pp. 45–46). Anderson maintained that when credit and
speculation prevail, any serious shock to the credibility of credit would start
a run on the banks, so that "the whole paper system will tumble to the
ground; and all those concerned will inevitably lose their property" (1797,

pp. 45–46), and predicted that while the current monetary system was in force, "no bounds can be set to speculation, distresses and embarrassments will be felt at irregular periods" (p. 39). The old merchant emphasized that the "artificial credit" based on the emission of paper money under conditions of inconvertibility, together with the speculation it would permit, would cause "in times of even moderate distress, ... a fatal depreciation of public credit" (Anonymous, 1796, pp. 8–15).

Better elaborated was Huskisson's argument, that the explosion of the credit-speculation system was entirely consistent with the interest of both creditors and debtors. He maintained, in fact, that,

> The business of a merchant is to buy cheap and sell dear. His general wish is to be able, for this purpose, to command as large a credit as possible. He must consequently, upon abstract principle, be favourable to any system which is likely to give facility to the discount of commercial securities. His interest, therefore, appears to be the same as that of the banker; whose profit increases with the extension of such discounts. (1810, pp. 141–142)

The nature of the cumulative movement is therefore not exogenous (although the original impulse is normally given by the opening of new channels of trade or some similar event) but is determined by the proper logic of the system itself. Yet, its result is not stable, for any change in the banker's policy or any systematic (due to overstocking) or accidental (due to misfortune, imprudence, or extravagance) interruption of the chain of payments would bring the whole scheme to collapse.

Huskisson's emphasis of the consistency of the occurrence of crises with the "abstract principles" of political economy by means of the instability of equilibrium anticipates the arguments of Lawson, Coquelin, Juglar, and, later, John Mills. These writers were not content with pointing at the cumulative and fragile character of the speculative phase. They placed this aspect at the heart of their theories of crises and brought it at the center of their reflection on how crises should be explained. As we have seen in Section 3.8 (and Section 2.1.2 for Juglar), these writers maintained that all crises have a common, primary cause in spite of being occasioned by specific accidental events. They distinguished themselves from the authors believing that crises are individual events, each caused by a specific circumstance, in maintaining that the causes evoked as individual generators of crises only play a secondary role. More specifically, they argued that these causes, alone, would not be able to generate a crisis, while when the stage is set for a crisis, any small perturbation would start it off.

Lawson expressed this point as follows. First, he argued that the antecedents invoked as causes by other writers could not have occasioned the havoc that followed them:

> Now what strikes one in looking at all these panics is this, that the circumstance which immediately gave rise to the pressure is always wholly inadequate to account for its long continuance, and for the loss sustained by it. For instance, the breaking out of the war in 1793 never could of itself have occasioned much commercial embarrassment, if commercial affairs had been in a sound state up to that time; it might have limited the future operations of trade, or checked its advance, but it could not have entailed the universal ruin which ensued. In like manner, the fall of the prices of leading articles, which immediately preceded the panic of 1809, never alone could have caused it: nor could the circumstance of a deficient harvest alone; that would generally only entail a loss of one or two millions: but where the panic takes place, failures to many times more than that amount ensue; for instance, the general deficiency of food in 1846 never could of itself have occasioned the panic which ensued. We must, therefore, look beyond the proximate cause or the occasion of the panic to find its true cause. (Lawson, 1848a, p. 4)

Then, he argued that *any* disturbance to the credit system occurring in a situation of extended overtrading and intense speculation would cause a panic (Lawson, 1848a; the passage is cited in Section 3.8). In Lawson's view, each of the specific but accidental events that release the panic, its proximate cause, is not essential to its actual outburst, although it can help explaining the specific feature of each crisis. Proximate causes are interchangeable. It does not matter whether a war, a revolution, or a famine occurs, *any* of these circumstances would overturn the entire system. The true cause of crises, common to all events, is the tendency of the credit system to overexpand. It acts by making the system unstable.

Coquelin also emphasized that the outbreak of the crisis can be determined by any occasion, when the operation of the credit and banking mechanism has been building up enough tension. The primary cause of the crisis is the factor generating this tension, while the occasioning event plays a subordinate part and is a secondary cause. Coquelin stopped short of reaching the conclusion to which similar arguments brought Lawson before him and Juglar later to argue that the system of credit relationships becomes unstable and that it is precisely this instability that makes for the endogenous generation of crises. The expression used by Coquelin, a "débordement quelconque" (1852a, p. 532), that is, "any overflow," anticipates the metaphor later used by Juglar, who compared the accumulation of tension to the overfilling of a glass of water, when a single drop of water (the secondary cause) would determine the spillage.

4. CYCLES OR RECURRING CRISES?

A few decades after Juglar's first edition, toward the turn of the century, business cycle theories became a mature and relatively autonomous field in the discipline. The existence of cyclical fluctuations was almost universally admitted, and correspondingly, there was a flowering of theories and models produced in the interwar years by almost anyone who counted for anything in economics. This contrasts with the understanding of the phenomenon a century earlier, when crises were interpreted as disconnected phenomena of local significance. In the previous sections of this article, I have shown, with special reference to Juglar's writings, how some important steps in the transition have taken place. In the present section, I attempt to draw the broad picture.

4.1. From Crises to Cycles

The passage from the theories of crises prevalent in the first half of the nineteenth century to the theories of cycles dominating the scene by the outbreak of World War I was gradual but not linear and cumulative. Some writers took some of the intermediate steps but not others, and only a few of them were fully aware of what they were doing. Yet, the cycle theorists at the turn of the century felt they could easily characterize the essential features of the transition they helped to complete. Aftalion, for one, liquidated the old approach as misplaced emphasis and prepared the ground for the complete dismissal not only of the theories of crises but also of the very notion of "crisis":

> The earlier inquirers into the phenomenon, impressed by the devastation following crises, focused only on crisis itself, on the violent break of equilibrium that is observed for a brief time only. They ignored what precedes it and what follows it. Today we know, especially thanks to Juglar, that crisis is but one of the moments – in truth, the most distressing one – of an entire cycle taking place periodically ... Crisis is the point of intersection between prosperity and depression, the culmination of one phase and the beginning of the other ... What happens during the crisis cannot be understood or explained without examining the whole of the cycle: the prosperity preparing the crisis, and the depression which ensues from it and which prepares the return of good times. When the subject will be better known, writers will use less the expression *overproduction crises* and will use instead *economic cycles*. In scientific writings, the latter expression will tend to substitute the former. (Aftalion, 1913, Vol. I, p. vi)[F56]

Similarly, Mitchell summarized very effectively the evolution from crises to cycle theories as follows:

> Wide divergences of opinion continue to exist among competent writers upon crises; but in recent years substantial agreement has been reached upon two points of fundamental importance.
>
> Crises are no longer treated as sudden catastrophes which interrupt the 'normal' course of business, as episodes which can be understood without investigation of the intervening years. On the contrary, the crisis is regarded as but the most dramatic and briefest of the three phases of a business cycle – prosperity, crisis, and depression.[121] Modern discussion endeavor to show why a crisis is followed by a depression, and depression by prosperity, quite as much as to show why prosperity is followed by a crisis. In a word, the theory of crises has grown into the theory of business cycles.
>
> The wider grasp of the problem has discredited the view that crises are due to abnormal conditions which tempt industry and trade to forsake their beaten paths and temporarily befog the judgment of business men and investors, or to misguided legislation, unsound business practices, imperfect banking organization, and the like. As business cycles have continued to run their round decade after decade in all nations of highly developed business organization, the idea that each crisis may be accounted for by some special cause has become less tenable. On the contrary, the explanations in favor today ascribe the recurrence of crises after periods of prosperity to some inherent characteristic of economic organization or activity. The complex processes which make up business life are analyzed to discover why they inevitably work out a change from good times to bad and from bad times to good. The influence of special conditions is admitted, of course, but rather as a factor which complicates the process than as the leading cause of crises. (Mitchell, [1913] 1941, pp. 5–6)

Aftalion and Mitchell are not only recording the main features of cycle theories as opposed to crises theories but are passing a judgment on their relationship, from a less advanced stage of theorizing to a more advanced one, from a less general understanding of the phenomenon to a more general one. Yet, things were not that simple, for the transition also brought with it a shift in the general approach to the problem that cannot be considered as a smooth and unconditional "progress," but is more like a switch to an altogether different understanding of the problem. The relationship of crises to "normal," which Mitchell correctly placed at the center of his characterization, was more articulate than the two extremes of the specter depicted by Mitchell.

It is true that the "crises" approach (as I shall call it for brevity) treated crises as anomalies with respect to the "normal" state of advance, caused by some external factor, and that the "cycles" approach considers instead the "normal" development of the system to be cyclical.[122] There were, however, two intermediate conceptions, sharing some features of both approaches while remaining autonomous from both. One of them, which I shall call the "alternations" approach, included several writers sharing an interest in price fluctuations, in particular between the mid-1810s and the 1850s. This group includes, among others, those who developed cobweb-like mechanisms giving rise to alternations of high and low prices in response to agricultural fluctuations under the constraints of international exchanges due to the Corn Laws (for reference, see Section 3.2) and some of the writers taking part in the debates between the Banking and Currency schools, whose interests were focused on the relationship between prices and banking policy. These writers were essentially interested in the alternation of good and bad trade and in the policy to smooth out the effects of such fluctuations, rather than in crises or in the rhythm of the alternation.

The 'recurring crises' approach, also alternative to Mitchell's and Aftalion's extremes, is so denoted for the emphasis of its adherents to the recursiveness of these phenomena. It was coeval with both the crises and the cycles approaches, as it occupied most of the ground during the second half of the nineteenth century, with tail end on both sides. Its main feature is that these writers gave a special emphasis on crises, but insisted on their recurring character. Most of them considered crises as disturbances (or as the consequence of disturbances) of the production or exchange processes, as diseases with respect to the normally healthy state of the system, but at the same time, they thought that crises are periodically brought about by the very features of the accumulation process, to which they are therefore intrinsic. Among these writers, Clément Juglar occupied a preeminent position. Other writers – of which Marx is the most eminent representative – considered crises as the recurring outbreak of the contradictions of capitalist accumulation. Both groups maintained that crises are inevitable and necessary to temporarily reharmonize the accumulation process. But Juglar emphasized the positive character of accumulation in the long run, whereas Marx emphasized its constant tendency to grow in an increasingly conflictual way. The production process, in Marx's view, reproduces at ever higher levels the contradiction between the tendency to accumulate capital and its consequence on the profit rate as unemployment is absorbed and exerts increasing pressure on wages. Both Juglar and Marx thought that crises are a remedy to the excesses (or, respectively, the contradictions) of the economic system. But whereas for Juglar the temporary distress associated with crises was the price to pay for the system to continue progressing at ever higher levels, for Marx the temporary survival of the system brought with it a deepening of its inherent contradictions.

In spite of these very relevant differences, the writers of the "recurring crises" approach have in common the understanding of crises as related to some deep-seated disorder periodically bursting out, and in this, they differed from the "crisis" approach. They also differed from the "alternations" approach in considering crises as a phenomenon intrinsic to the accumulation process and focused on how such events are generated and run their course rather than on the amplification and generalization of some small and local fluctuations in prices and production. The "recurring crises" approach also differs from the "cycles" approach. The writers belonging to the first group were mostly interested in crises, not just as a matter of emphasis (as suggested by Aftalion's remark, cited above, that crises are the most dramatic phase of the cycle) but because they thought that crises were *the* phenomenon to be explained, whether as a deviation from the norm or as a culmination of the contradictions intrinsic in the accumulation process, in terms of both its causal relationships and the role they play in the capitalistic process.

These differences concerning the interpretation of crises and fluctuations manifest themselves in the way in which the writers of the "crises," "alternations," "recurring crises," and "cycles" approaches identified, understood, and explained the phenomena they were examining. The "crises" writers were essentially interested in explaining crises away as temporary anomalies to an intrinsic tendency to a more or less smooth progress. They considered them as disconnected events, and their procedure accordingly consisted in looking for special incidents or circumstances capable of explaining each of them.

Instead of focusing on the "normal" state of the system, the "alternations" writers took for granted that prices are sometimes above and sometimes below their "natural" level, due to chance fluctuations in agricultural production or due to frictions and maladjustments that are intrinsic in any adjustment process. This was the starting point of their analysis, which consisted in examining whether the existing institutional arrangements would amplify and smooth out such "waves." These writers were not much interested in describing the building up of a period of low or high prices but only in their alternation.

For the writers in the "recurring crises" tradition, crises were the primary facts and starting points for the analysis. They recognized crises as events belonging to the same class, thereby requiring a common explanation that could acquire the status of law. They examined how the conditions for their occurrence were set, how they exploded, and how they were liquidated. Their detailing of the phases preceding and following them was instrumental in explaining their occurrence, and their uniformity was instrumental in explaining their recurrence. Not only the explanation, but also the description, was centered around the crisis. Yet, their story can repeat, after events have run their full course from prosperity to crisis and liquidation, thanks to the fact that prosperity is seen as the "normal" state of the system; the "automatic" resumption of business kick-starts a new building up, explosion, and liquidation, without needing a special explanation as it belongs to the nature of things.

Finally, the explanation offered by cycle theorists instead takes as starting point the rhythmical dance of economic life. In this view, crises do not have any special role to play and are treated either as phases of the cycle (none of which is privileged but is the necessary outcome of the preceding one and the cause of the following) or as anomalies to its smooth course. The problem to be explained, for the cycle theorists, is the circular succession of phases; what matters is the repetition of the process and the conditions for this to be possible.

The relationship between crises and fluctuations in the four approaches lies on the epistemic domain even before having analytical implications. "Crises" writers could not have conceived of a cycle; indeed, such a notion did not occur to them, and when it became the subject of debate in other circles, they tried to deny the existence of such a phenomenon, interpreting the apparent periodicity as the result of more or less accidental circumstances of no theoretical significance. The "alternations" writers also did not think in terms of cycles: they considered disconnected ups and downs, some of the latter possibly accompanied by panics, without anyway exploring possible causes of the recurrence of such events. In the "recurrent crises" approach, the explanation of the "cycle," in the sense of recurrence of events in similar patterns, is a by-product of their inquiry on crises, on the assumption that crises are instances of a same class of events. In the "cycles" approach, on the contrary, the explanation of crises is subsumed under the enquiry on the rhythmical repetition of the process.

While the contrast between "crises," "alternations," and "recurring crises" approaches is apparent, there are two aspects of the contrast between "recurring crises" and "cycles" approaches that deserve further discussion. The first consists in the different relationship between crises and theoretical norm, a problem clearly at the heart of the entire history of the attempts to explain these phenomena (Besomi, 2006b). The second concerns the different emphasis by "recurrent crises" and "cycle" theorists on the automatisms guiding the course of events. These will be discussed in Sections 4.2 and 4.3, respectively.[123]

4.2. The Normal and the Pathological

Juglar's view of the relationship between crises and the "normal" behavior
of the economic system can conveniently be taken as the starting point for
discussing the difference between the "recurrent crises" and the "cycles"
approaches to the problem of crises. Some of the various aspects of this issue
can be illustrated by examining his terminology, his choice of metaphors,
and his morphological characterization of the succession of phases. He was
adamant, in both the first and the second editions of his book (see Sections
2.1 and 2.2), that he understood prosperity to be the normal, healthy state of
the system, whereas crises are unwelcome but unavoidable ways for bringing
back the system to its healthy state by clearing the morbid excesses
generated by the prosperous phase itself.

4.2.1. Prosperity as the "Normal" or "Healthy" State of the System

The "recurring crises" view shares with the "crises" approach the
interpretation of growth as the normal state of the system.[124] But while
the latter understood the anomalies as accidental and essentially extraneous
to the working of the system, Juglar and those who shared his viewpoint
admitted them as part and parcel with the very working of the system itself.
Before the periodicity of crises became an undeniable fact, the idea that they
could be independent events caused by unrelated antecedents was tenable.[125]
But after the crisis of 1847, and even more so after the one occurred in 1857,
harmonizing the view that progress is the natural state of the system with the
fact of recurring crises required a switch in the perspective.[126] The
disruption of the normal state of progress and its subsequent restoration
were therefore placed at the center of the inquiry, which accordingly focused
on the building up of the excesses bringing to the crisis and the subsequent
liquidation. Crises, as the negation of prosperity, are therefore at the heart
of a theorization aiming, however, to explain why the normal course of
business may be temporarily disrupted and then restated. These interruptions of the ordinary progression of trade follow a common pattern, which
repeats itself after having run its full course. At this point, the focus is on the
characterization of the pattern, not on its repetition.[127] Indeed, most of the
explanations offered for the phenomenon (in particular those belonging to
the "overtrading" tradition, see Section 3.5) gave full accounts of the
cumulation of tension during prosperity, its explosion, and eventually the
liquidation of bad debts, but did not bother to explain how business resumes
its usual course. Their view, in fact, was that this is the natural course that
trade would resume if undisturbed, and as such, needs no specific

explanation. As soon as crises have performed their function of eliminating the excesses perturbing credit, exchanges, and production, the conditions for prosperity would be automatically reinstated, and the system would be able to restart, in virtue of either the "healing force of nature" (as assumed by Juglar) or of any kick received from outside, such as the opening of a new market. The liquidation does not itself cause or launch the prosperity, it only sets its conditions. It is therefore not surprising that the characterization of the morphology of the cycle included an odd number of phases (Juglar's and Briaune's three and Corbet's five), usually centered around the "crisis" (see Section 3.3).[128]

Crises are obviously the most notable events in this decennial pattern of trade. The first commentators focused on the suffering related to crises.[129] At a later point, some writers observed that crises perform the useful function of clearing up all excesses, unsound credits, and speculations. The description became somewhat paradoxical, as it found good in what was commonly perceived as an evil. It thus became necessary to convey the message by means of an appropriate analogy. We have seen (Section 3.6) that Juglar resorted to the medical metaphor. This was not, however, the only possible choice for expressing the idea (itself widespread in the "overtrading" tradition: see Section 3.5) that crises are the consequences of the cumulation of previous excesses. Another metaphor widely used at the time was that of the storm clearing the skies overcharged with electricity and creating the premises for a return of good weather.[130] Kinnear, for instance, wrote that the public has grown accustomed to seeing monetary storms, "passing away after a few months, and all things restored to their wonted order and regularity – that the public seem almost to have come to the conclusion that these periodical tradequakes are phenomena inherent in our commercial system – the storm by which an overcharged atmosphere is restored to its proper equilibrium and purity" (Kinnear, 1847, pp. i–ii). Another writer diagnosed that the ongoing "storm will gradually pass off, having purified the atmosphere of commercial credit during its disastrous passing through it" (Anonymous, 1875, p. 2).

The explanation of crises in terms of recurring disturbances gradually gave way – without, however, totally disappearing – to the encompassing of crises as a phase of the cycle. This shift implied a very different view as to the operation of the capitalistic system and took place through an overall change in the very conception of crises, in the relationship of normal and pathological, in the division of phases, and in the choice of metaphors. And, above all, it implied a reversal of the way of explaining crises and cycles in their relationship.

A good starting point for examining this transition is the movement of the line between what is physiological and what is pathological. As we have seen in Section 3.5, in the early decades of the nineteenth century, there was no doubt that crises were pathological phenomena disturbing the normal course of business. With Juglar, crises and the following liquidation were seen as the system's response to unhealthy exaggeration born from within the economic system as a consequence of people's tendency to exuberance and passion for gamble (see Section 2.1). Crises still belonged to the field of pathology, but the medical conception at the time reduced the pathological to a quantitative excess (or deficiency) with respect to the norm in the intensity of the stimulations (whether internal or external) to which an organism is subject. On the one hand, the adherence to such a notion implied that the pathological should be studied using the same methods applied to physiology, that is, to the normal behavior of the system.[131] The extension of this principle to the analysis of economic crises was clearly a big step from the old approach to the problem, which treated instead crises and progress on totally distinct grounds. The clearest statement to this effect is perhaps due to Lawson, who rejected the argument of those who maintained that the laws of political economy cannot be applied to times of commercial crises by referring to the universality of scientific laws.[132] On the other hand, however, this methodological unification of pathology and physiology (and, similarly, of the theorization of crises and of the "normal" state of an economic system) "would make sense only if, first, the normal could be defined in a purely objective way as a fact and second, all the differences between the normal state and the pathological state could be expressed in quantitative terms" (Canguilhem, [1966]1991, p. 57).[133] The first of these conditions is precisely where Juglar, and most of his contemporaries, failed, for they did not provide a theoretical definition of the "normal" state of the system and thus found themselves running in circles.[134] The situation only changed after the 1870s, when equilibrium was defined in rigorous terms and could substitute generic references to Say's law. Only at that point, deviations from the norm became calculable and could be expressed in analytical terms (De Vecchi, 1983, pp. 263–272), thereby satisfying the second of the above-mentioned conditions. This lay the ground for a new kind of understanding of the phenomenon.

4.2.2. The Normality of the Cycle and the Euthanasia of the Notion of Crises
Within a few decades, the "cycles" approach had reformulated the problem in completely different terms. The idea that progress is the normal state of the system was substituted with the idea that the cycle is the norm. Some

statements to this effect will suffice to illustrate the new conception. Hawtrey wrote that "Trade is never normal; in times of average prosperity it is always on either the upward or the downward path; when it ceases to improve it is on the verge of collapse, when it ceases to slacken it is beginning to recover" (Hawtrey, 1913, pp. 75–76); Veblen, ([1904]1958, pp. 88–89) maintained that "Crises, depressions, hard times, dull times, brisk times, periods of speculative advance, 'eras of prosperity', are primarily phenomena of business ... The true, or what may be called the normal, crises, depressions and exaltations in the business world are not the results of accidents, such as the failure of crops. They come in the regular course of business." Mitchell wrote that "the 'normal state of trade' [is] a figment,'" for business annals show that "the only normal condition is a state of change" while "the theorist's 'normal state' ... is not to be looked for in an historical record[, n]or can we take for granted the existence of a moving 'normal state of trade' of such a nature that departures from it tend to correct themselves" (Mitchell, 1927, p. 376). Similarly for Spiethoff, "The 'normal state' is neither the upswing, nor the downswing, nor, least of all, the crisis. What is normal in a free, highly capitalist market system based on money, is the business cycle" (Spiethoff, 1953, p. 166). Finally, Robertson (1915) formalized the notion of "normality" of the cycle by considering a fluctuating equilibrium. He pointed out that, besides errors of judgment and miscalculations, the conditions determining the optimum level of investment change in the course of the cycle, being subject to both unidirectional change (as a consequence of technological progress) and of fluctuations in the degree of productivity during the cycle. Equilibrium is thus not stationary, but itself oscillatory. This notion was further specified in *Banking Policy and the Price Level* (1926), where Robertson distinguished between "justified fluctuations," that is, the fluctuations due to changes in the equilibrium conditions, and ampler fluctuations attributed to errors and frictions and to mistaken banking policies. This paved the way for the interpretations that saw the cycle no longer in terms of a deviation from equilibrium (or an oscillation around equilibrium), but in terms of what we would today call an attractor, a state toward which the system tends.

In this new conceptual setting, the theoretical gap left by Juglar was filled in. As aptly summed up by Mitchell in the passage cited in Section 4.1, inquirers aimed at understanding not only how prosperity degenerates into a crisis and is followed by a depression, but also how this depression in turns gives rise to prosperity.[135] With this, causality became fully circular, with each phase causing the following one, thus breaking away from a conception based on the cause of periodic disruptions of a cumulative process to give way to a new one encompassing the movement as a whole. The new phase so introduced deserved a name: "recovery,"[136] which was thus added to Juglar's three phases[137] to give rise to the now canonical division in four phases.[138] The asymmetry in the description of the phases of the cycle was to give way to a symmetrical theorization of the cycle. As Aftalion argued, "logics requires that prosperity, one of the phases of the cycle, is explained is the same way as crisis and depression, which constitute the other phase" (1913, Vol. I, p. 282). Strictly speaking, this only implies inverting the direction of the operation of the causal nexuses. But after a short time, the cyclical behavior itself was also described as symmetrical: the suddenness and violence of the crisis gave place to a gentle downturn, specular to the revival. The process was completed with the birth of the mathematical theories of the cycle, based on functional equations whose solution is a sine curve combined with an exponential term (Tinbergen, Kalecki, and Samuelson). In this formulation, the term "crisis" did not make any sense, and the stage was set for its disappearance. The first step was the downgrading of crisis from the center of the stage to a name for the cycle's peak. It was due to Lescure, who defined the crisis as "the point of intersection between a period of advance lasting three to five years and a period of depression of a similar length" (1932, pp. 2–3). Lescure was quickly followed by Aftalion (1913, Vol. I, p. 6) and Mitchell ([1913] 1941).[139] With this, crises quickly lost the main feature that was recognized by the writers of the "recurring crises" approach, namely, their suddenness and violence, and were reduced to a smooth transition.

At this point, the metaphors of the disease and of the tempest proved inadequate and were substituted by a mechanical analogy, the pendulum – which, like the disease for Juglar, was not only a nice descriptive devise but also played a heuristic role in guiding the foundation of cycle theorizing in terms of economic dynamics (for a brilliant discussion, see Louçã, 2001; for comment on the transition from one metaphor to the other, see Besomi, 2006b, and 2011).[140] This led to a description in terms of functional equations, resulting in sine waves where even the violence and the suddenness of the crisis were turned into a smooth and gently declining curve,[141] precisely symmetric with the phase of recovery. As, however, in the real world, crises stubbornly kept recurring, they were eventually again treated as anomalies: no longer with respect to a line of progress, but with respect to the cycle.[142] Accordingly, the cycle's upper turning point eventually had the name changed, and crises reappeared as aberrations. As stated by Baudin, "the cycle is a collective, physiological, vital phenomenon, extraneous to the monetary domain; the crisis is a pathological phenomenon of dissociation of the economy, which is boosted by the violence of cyclical oscillations and is more or less strictly related to monetary phenomena" (1936, p. 574).[F57] With this, the transition was completed.

4.3. The Necessity of Crises and the Automatism of Cycles

What are the implications of this shift in perspective on the understanding of the phenomenon? Although Aftalion and Mitchell claimed that the new view (the "cycles" approach) is just a generalization of the old "recurring crises" one, the differences are much deeper than they thought.

4.3.1. The Rhythm of Economic Life

Firstly, the cycles approach substitutes the idea of a rhythmical, continuous development to a notion based on repeatedly interrupted progress. These are different ways of conceiving the relationship between present, past, and future. In Juglar, the present is a continuation of the recent past[143] and is going to be projected in the future: every peak of development before a crisis has been, and will continue to be, higher than the previous one. True, crises will temporarily interrupt this progress, but they are also the means by which progress can continue. In the cycles approach, what matters is instead the repetition (which can be, but is not necessarily, coupled with a secular trend[144] and can be characterized by the coexistence of cycles of different frequencies). As radically put by Åkerman, "the pendulum movement may be regarded as a universal law which, in greater or less degree, governs the mutability of economic life" (Åkerman, 1932, p. 9). In such a view, time has a cyclical structure, thereby giving a different perspective to the interpretation of both history and economics (Pomian, 1977, and 1978; Wallerstein, 1991).

4.3.2. Economic Liberalism and the Automatism of Crises and Recovery

This leads to the second aspect. The cycles approach is accordingly more prone of falling into a mechanical understanding of the alternation of good times and bad times. This is particularly apparent in the dynamic approach of the early "econometricians," as indicated by Frisch's definition of "dynamics" (which quickly became canonical) as "a theory that explains," by means of functional equations, "how one situation grows out of the foregoing" (Frisch, 1933, p. 171; for acceptance of his definition, see Schumpeter, 1934 and Kalecki, 1935, p. 327). But, more generally, such an attitude is part of the deterministic spirit that pervaded economics (and indeed almost the entire scientific community) at the turn of the century. Among the several comments on this aspect, Myrdal's is particularly interesting:

the purely mechanistic attitude towards the business cycle [...] emphasizes that prosperity is 'necessary' in order to stimulate economic life, and that the crisis and depression are 'necessary' for a liquidation of the investment errors that arise in prosperity. This mechanistic attitude has many nuances. On the whole it represents, in terms of business cycle and monetary theory, a rationalization of economic liberalism, which erects its own fatalistic, negative attitude towards planned economic control into a doctrine. This peculiar attitude has its psychological basis in the habit men have of thinking in terms of rhythms and cycles. We walk, they reflect, by first advancing one leg and then the other; after the flood comes the ebb, after the sunshine comes the rain, after the day comes the night; and in the same way good and bad time must naturally follow one another. Cassel, [1932, p. 76] once jestingly remarked that perhaps the whole attitude was ultimately based upon a primitive Puritanism;[145] happiness is somehow evil, something immoral, which should be accompanied by a purifying misery now and then in order that those who have experienced it may be redeemed; and so it is only proper, right and natural that after the upswing, with all its sad mistakes, bad times should follow. (Myrdal, 1939, pp. 201–202)

The reference to the cycle as rationalizing the viewpoint of economic liberalism is worth emphasizing. Interestingly, Juglar took part in the debate within the Parisian Liberal circles on the implications of crises, where two views where clashing. As summarized by Leroy-Beaulieu, some of the participants in the debate "see [in the recent crisis] merely one of those periodical jerks, one of the diseases accompanying growth which are the companion and the ransom of all progress and which, brought by the natural course of things giving them an almost fatal character, eventually disappear on their own" (Leroy-Beaulieu, 1886, p. 386).[F58] Other writers thought instead that this specific crisis was different from the previous ones and that it had a character not natural but artificial, which they attributed to government mismanagement (Leroy-Beaulieu, 1886, p. 386). While the more traditional approach wanted to convey the impression that all goes well, except for some evil external factors disturbing the harmony of the system, the effect was easily the opposite, for the disturbances were generally being perceived (as is apparent if one reads the comments in the press) to be too regular and systematic to be mere accidents. Their ad hoc explanations sounded more and more like excuses. The writer relying on the recurrence of crises could instead bring into accord the idea that the system has a normal tendency to progress while having to eliminate, from time to time, the exaggerations due to excessive frenzy. Crises, with the suffering accompanying them, were a possibility, but were guaranteed to be temporary hindrances only and to launch progress again at a higher level. Some of the mechanistic features described by Myrdal were thus already present in the "recurring crises" approach. The idea that after good times a reversal must necessarily occur (through exceedingly good times) characterized the writings of Juglar and his contemporaries. Indeed, adjectives such as "inevitable" or "necessary" were frequently used to qualify the occurrence of crises, even if their purpose was more often to stress the endogeneity of the causal nexuses than to project the recurrence of crises in the future.[146] Correspondingly, a number of criticisms to the view that crises are periodical precisely attacked the determinism implied in such a view.[147]

There is, nevertheless, a sharp difference between the "necessity" of crises as discussed by most writers in the recurring crises tradition, and the fully determined automatism intrinsic in the sine curves resulting from the systems of functional equations that dominated the scene from the early 1930s to the 1970s.[148] In the second half of the nineteenth century, writings on crises were full of provisos and qualifications. Although they pinned down the cause of crises to a primary cause, they never denied the counteracting (or aggravating) effect of secondary causes (see Section 3.8) and were accordingly rather circumspect in their statements. As we have recalled at the end of Section 3.4, there were not only skeptics criticizing the "recurring crises" writers for excesses of determinism, but there were also those criticizing them, so far as they denied that the periodicity of crises is strict, for lack of determinacy: "The crisis must terminate in that year, unless this happens in that other year, depending on what happens. A new crisis will come at that time, unless it will come at some other time; this depends on what the future has in stock" (Courtois, in Société d'Économie Politique 1893, p. 13).[F59]

4.3.3. Back to "Recurring Crises"

The determinism of the "periodical crises" school was moderated by the importance they attributed to the human factor. Political interference, or the outbreak of wars, were events whose importance could not be denied in the causation of crises: not at all times, perhaps, but surely when the economy was so predisposed (see Section 3.8). What prepares the crisis is, in the view of the "overtrading" current, the irrational spirit of speculation (see Sections 2.1 and 3.5). Some writers also blamed the institutions (e.g., Coquelin). While in later years, the human component, even in its irrational aspects, was rendered by most writers in the field in a mechanical way, a counterexample dating from the 1930s is illustrative not only in this specific respect but also for emphasizing the epistemic character of the distinction between the "cycles" and the "recurring crises" approach.

Keynes treated crises not as the result of some logical necessity but of the psychological and conventional character of specific human actions. We normally live "in an intermediate situation which is neither desperate nor satisfactory" (Keynes, [1936]1973, p. 250), from which the system does not go too far, thanks to the stabilizing effect of the psychological law according to which the propensity to save increases as income increases and vice versa. The marginal efficiency of capital, on which investment depends, is instead liable to violent and sudden fluctuations. It depends, in fact, on the entrepreneurs' expectations, which are guided not by Bentamite calculus but by some arbitrary conventions driving them to abrupt losses of confidence whenever the prevalent state of opinion changes. The suddenness and violence of the crisis is a necessary feature of the intrinsically nondeterministic way in which expectations are formed (for a detailed discussion, see De Vecchi 1983, pp. 281–290).

The example of Keynes is helpful to stress that the main distinction between "cycles" and "recurring crises" approaches does not lie much in the usage of metaphors, or in the conception of time, or in the relationship between physiological and pathological, or again in the morphological characterization of the cycle. It concerns the order of priority, in the explanatory process, of crises and cycles. Although in the trade cycle chapter of the *General theory*, Keynes *writes* using cycle terminology, he *reasons* otherwise. This is not only because he stresses the asymmetry of the cycle and the suddenness and violence of the crisis,[149] and because he places it at the outset of his description of the cycle (Keynes, [1936]1973, p. 315), but also because the entire explanation of the cycle is constructed starting from the abrupt drop in the marginal efficiency of capital. Starting from the premise that investment is the driving force of economic systems, the engine of the cycle must lie with what determines investment, that is, interest rates and expectations. Keynes explicitly denies that fluctuations in interest rates are the main causes of crises (although they can "play an aggravating and, occasionally perhaps, an initiating part"), while the "sudden and even catastrophic" "collapse" of the marginal efficiency of capital is "of the nature of organised investment markets," where expectations are formed on the basis of fragile conventions. The abrupt crumbling of the marginal efficiency of capital is at the core of the trade cycle: the remainder of the movement is described as the recovery of the marginal efficiency from the changes the crisis brought in the stock of materials and working capital, taking into account the changes in the rate of interest on the one hand and the reaction of the marginal propensity to consume on the other. Keynes's explanation of the cycle is thus based on his explanation of the crisis, a feature that he shares (in spite of the theoretical differences and the aims of the analysis) with writers such as Juglar and also Marx, making it a distinctive mark of the "recurring crises" approach.[150]

5. CONCLUSION

The history of the birth of business cycle theory is much more complicated than Mitchell and Aftalion thought, and also more intricate than illustrated by the few existing accounts supplied in the twentieth century. It is a history that has no linear unfolding, in which analytical, methodological, and epistemic shifts interacted with the historical course of events that induced commentators to recognize some features of crises and discard some others. The phenomenon of economic crises presents many facets, making it possible to have different perspectives depending on the angle chosen to examine it. Each crisis has its own peculiarities, takes place in a specific historical, political, economic, and financial context. It was perhaps natural that at first writers on the subject focused precisely on the specific features of the events they were witnessing. But crises also share some common traits, and as these events repeated with a certain regularity, an ever growing number of observers started to shift the emphasis from the individual character of each crisis to their common aspects.

Juglar's writings, from his first contribution on the subject in 1856 till the end of the century, came in this context. Almost all ingredients of his contribution had several antecedents in the writings of his contemporaries and forebearers. His characterization of the phenomenon came at a time when the periodicity of crises (intended not in terms of absolutely isochronous phenomenon but of a semiregularly recurrent one) was a widely recognized fact. Moreover, a number of writers had already pointed out that the course of events followed a regular pattern and had began to describe its morphology (Sections 3.2 and 3.3). Juglar's interpretation of the role of crises in the working of the economic system was shared by a number of writers who had come before him to the conclusion that crises are essential for the liquidation of the bad debts that hinder the accumulation process (Section 3.7). Juglar's explanation of the phenomenon belongs to a family of theories, which had started to thrive more than half a century earlier, based on the overtrading made possible by the existence of a credit system and degenerating into speculation (Section 3.5). A number of writers belonging to this tradition also anticipated Juglar's specific mechanism based on the instability of credit (Section 3.10). His analogical frame of reference was shared with a number of writers, although Juglar's medical background gave him a better understanding of the analog than his contemporary had (Section 3.6).

Juglar's interesting reflections on causality were also not new: several writers anticipated him in recognizing that the common features of crises required, by the causal principle, that they be generated by the same cause. Similarly to Juglar, those writers also rejected as inadequate the previous approach to crises interpreted as individual and disconnected events, using a rhetorical argument very similar to Juglar's (Section 3.8). Juglar also shared the theoretical limits of most (but by no means all) of his contemporaries. Having taken for granted the progress of accumulation as the "natural" state of the system, they failed to adequately characterize it and often fell into the trap of defining it in a circular way in terms of the absence of perturbations and failed to supply a mechanism capable of explaining the recovery (Sections 3.5 and 3.9).

This is not to disparage Juglar's contribution. He was the first to elaborate on these arguments at length, while they were previously scattered in pamphlets and short articles (some of which, one must say, were very much to the point, while Juglar was rather verbose in his exposition), and has the undoubted merit of having amply corroborated his argument with data and some statistical analysis, primitive as it was (Section 3.1). His most important contribution was probably the explicit setting of some of the *problems* of business cycle theory: in particular, the necessity of identifying causal links between successive phases. The same problems were indeed discussed by others before him, and some had even provided better articulated and more complete answers than he did, but had not always expounded the problem as clearly as Juglar. He began his treatment with a discussion of the epistemic requisite for a good theory (see Section 2.1.2) and carefully laid the principle that the explanation of the recurrence of crises should be based on the chaining of the different phases of the cycle (Section 2.2.1). He was not himself capable of solving this problem, but he has the merit of having clearly posed it. This was a fundamental step for the development of the first theories of crises, concerned with the causes of each individual instance, into theories of *recurring* crises, concerned instead with crises as a *class* of related phenomena. Juglar thus gave an important contribution by channeling the efforts of a multitude of writers into a new and fruitful direction.

Schumpeter wrote that Juglar was the discoverer of the continent of business cycles, while some of the islands around had been discovered before

(1954, pp. 1123–1124). This characterization is surely hyperbolic. In most respects, Juglar came very late and did not add much new to what was already taken for granted (Sections 3.2, 3.3, 3.7, 3.8, and 3.10). Moreover, his explanation of the cycle was incomplete: it failed to account for the lover turning point, and even his description of the speculative phase relied (in the first edition of his book, 1862) on some "speculative furor" rather than on a precise mechanism stimulating the process (Sections 2.1.4, 2.2.1, and 3.9). If a prize for discovering the continent should be assigned at all, I would rather award it to John Mills for his characterization of crises in their recurrence as "facts of a new order" (Section 3.8.7).

Whereas Schumpeter (and many before and after him) thought of Juglar as the first of business cycle theorists and one of the greatest economists of all times, I see him in a different light (see Besomi, 2010c). He was not the first of a new era of "cycle" theorists but a representative of the current of thought that saw in economic crises the essential feature of the capitalist accumulation process. He placed crises at the center of their theoretical construction and understood the "cycle" through which trade passes in terms of the properties of crises, rather than seeing crises as one of the phases of the cycle (Section 4). Chronologically, such an approach may appear to be a stage in the passage from the theories of crises to the theories of cycles. Indeed, in some respects, it was. But this approach to the problem is not without merits. While the "cycles'" approach either disregards crises or treats them as anomalies with the respect to the normal and smooth oscillations through which business runs its course, the emphasis on crises enables one to interpret such recurring catastrophes in terms of a specific set of concepts. Those developed by Juglar are behind our times (and largely also behind his own), but the perspectives developed in this light by Marx and Keynes, if suitably elaborated, still have something to say in the face of the sudden and violent reversals that still affect our financial markets and productive system.

NOTES

* The Notes are divided into two parts. The first lists the author's notes; the second provides the original texts of translated quotations. In the main body of the text, notes that begin with the letter "F" refer to the second set of notes. All translations, unless otherwise indicated, are mine; Cécile Dangel-Hagnauer and Philippe Le Gall have helped with the translations from French. As Juglar's language is sometimes loose and not always consistent, I have chosen to pay more attention to the sense than to the precise wording.

1. Most of these are little known nowadays, and some wanted to remain unknown at their time by publishing anonymously. In this chapter, a number of these writings are cited, with the purpose of illustrating that most of the ideas to which Juglar resorted were already circulating, sometimes even widely. My emphasis is on the ideas rather than their authors, and I will thus refrain from supplying biographical information on these writers.

2. To some observers, it was already clear not only that crises were coming in waves but were also followed by surges of diagnoses of each event. Marx, for instance, wrote to Lassalle that the time of crises, in England, is also the time of theoretical research (letter of January 23, 1855, in Marx & Engels, 1967). Mills (1868, p. 11) noted that "It is scarcely a matter for surprise, and still less for regret, that every commercial crisis occurring in this country is promptly followed by a literature of pamphlets, discussing the phenomena and their supposed causes, while they are yet a matter of painful interest to the public mind."

3. It should be noted that Schumpeter's assessment of Juglar's status is based on the second edition of his book (1889), not on the first (1862), which Schumpeter does not seem to have read. Not only did he misdate it as having been published in 1860, a mistake suggested by Juglar's own misquoting of the publication date in his revised version (1889, p. xv) and only quoted verbatim from the second edition, but attributed to the first some ingredients that were only present in the second, such as the emphasis on prices.

4. "One could hesitate before choosing the starting point of the inquiry. But when one takes into account that the Bank of France is the main intermediary of commerce and that the movement of discounts represents rather well the movement of trade, it becomes natural to take it as the reference point" ("On pouvait hésiter sur le point de départ de ce travail; mais quand on réfléchit que la Banque de France est le grand intermédiaire du commerce, et que le mouvement des escomptes représente assez bien le mouvement commercial, il était naturel de s'en servir comme point de comparaison": Juglar, 1857, p. 37). This explanation is a bit flimsy; however, at the time of Juglar's first inquiries, examinations of the relationship of financial crises and the banking system were quite common and did not call for any special justification. Recent examples for France were H. Say (1847, 1855) and Coquelin (1848, 1852a).

5. In 1852, Juglar wrote an article on population in France from 1725 to 1849. In the introduction to his book on crises, Juglar (1862, pp. i–ii) indicates that after having recorded the influence of epidemics, wars, and famines, he wanted to examine how the state of trade affects population dynamics. A short chapter of the book is dedicated to this problem.

6. Rather unwarrantedly, see note 31.

7. At this point, however, Juglar's emphasis is fully on speculation (see, e.g., 1862, p. 199); credit will conquer the center of the stage in the second edition of Juglar's book, where the explanatory mechanism will be considerably amplified and centered on the relationship of credit, prices, and speculation. See Section 2.2.

8. Niehans (1992, p. 549) stresses that in Juglar "very little economic analysis" is to be found.

9. Gide later pointed out that such competitions, of which the Academy promoted 30 annually, were part of a self-perpetuating régime of academic power and of transmission of the Liberal ideological framework. There were only a few

competitors for each prize (about two or three), and the winner's *mémoire* was published with the indication "crowned by the Academy" (Gide, 1890, in particular, pp. 618–622; on the role of the Academy in the teaching of political economy, see Le Van-Lemesle, 2004, in particular Ch. 3).

10. The plural should be noted. As it will be argued below (Section 3.2), the idea that crises recur and are part and parcel of capitalistic development was already widely shared at the time of Juglar's first writings on the subject.

11. Juglar's original wording may suggest that he was referring to the law of large numbers in some statistically relevant sense: "En nous appuyant non seulement sur des relevés statistiques, mais sur des grands nombres, sur des longues périodes, et dans trois grand pays, nous pensons avoir rempli beaucoup mieux que par des assertions toujours discutables les principales conditions d'une démonstration scientifique" (Juglar, 1862, p. xiii). However, he meant that he relied not simply on data but on a large amount of data. His actual usage of statistical analysis did not go far beyond the simple listing of tables and picking maxima and minima from his series (with some occasional cheating). For a discussion, see Section 3.1. With such a statement, Juglar probably aimed at distinguishing himself from a number of other writers in the field who used to support their arguments with the occasional illustrative reference to historical data.

12. "A proof by boredom!" (Morgan, 1990, p. 41). We find a similar argument in Tugan-Baranowsky: "there is evident an extraordinary resemblance between [crises] in all their essential characteristics ... This makes the history of crises very monotonous and serves as the best evidence of the uniformity of the phenomenon under investigation" (Tugan-Baranowsky, [1914] 1954, p. 745). Della Bona (1888, p. 76) also took up this argument; he left, however, the boring pieces to de Laveleye, Juglar and Max Wirth.

13. The passages cited in these paragraphs also appeared in the second edition, but as the second chapter (Juglar, 1889, pp. 27–29).

14. For a discussion of the medical literature on this issue and for further examples, see Carter (2003, Ch. 1).

15. Respectively "causes occasionelles" and "prédisposition" (Juglar, 1862, pp. 1–3).

16. The chronology is interesting. According to Carter, the first appearance in the literature of the etiological approach can be precisely pinned down to a lecture on puerperal fever delivered by Ignaz Semmelweis on May 15, 1850. Semmelweis's claim, however, do not seem to have been taken up by anyone before 1862 (Carter, 2003, pp. 44–47) – that is, the year of publication of Juglar's book. For a more detailed discussion of this point, see Besomi (2011).

17. Another definition of predisposing cause found in the same Medical dictionary runs as follows: "They are the causes whose action is often uncertain, always obscure. Sometimes they act by gradually affecting the constitution, at other times by gradually disrupting the equilibrium in which health consists. In a word, they prepare the body for such or such disease" ("ce sont les causes dont l'action est souvent incertaine, toujours obscure, qui agissent tantôt en modifiant peu-à-peu la constitution, tantôt en rompant par degrés l'équilibre qui constitue la santé, préparant en un mot le corps à telle ou telle affection": Beaude, 1849, p. xxxix). This wording describes very effectively (as will be seen in the sequel of this section) Juglar's view of the cause of crises for its reference to the gradual action and to the

idea of health as equilibrium and the crisis as a disease suddenly exploding as a consequence of the progressive distancing from equilibrium.

18. Groenewegen (2001, pp. 122–123) emphasized the medical origin of Juglar's notion of predisposition and caught well its meaning and implication without, however, noticing that the concept was counterpoised to the "occasional cause," which also plays a part in the methodology and the rhetoric of Juglar's construction. Frobert and Hamouda, in their essay on the medical metaphor in Juglar, altogether failed to take up the point (Frobert & Hamouda, 2008). It should be noted that the distinctions similar to Juglar's one between occasional and predisposing causes were also advanced by other writers starting from different backgrounds: see Section 3.8.

19. Juglar (1857, p. 38, 1889, p. xvii) went so far as claiming that wars and revolutions are actually a consequence, not a cause of crises.

20. In truth, he did not insist on this point in the first edition, but he specifically tackled it in the second: see Section 2.2. For a discussion of this aspect, see Section 3.4.

21. Juglar (1862, p. 202), however, indicates the approximate average length of the cycle: the crisis is sudden and short, liquidation takes one to two years, prosperity about six to seven years.

22. Beaude's *Dictionnaire de Médecine Usuelle* (1849, p. 621): "Period: refers to the different phases of a disease. A period implies a certain number of days during which one of the cycles of the diseases comes to a full circle" ("Période: se dit des différentes phases d'une maladie; une période suppose un certain nombre de jours pendant lequel s'est accomplie une des révolutions de la maladie"). See for instance, the *Dictionnaire de l'Académie Française*, sixth and seventh editions (1835 and 1878, respectively) for a comparison of the different connotations of the substantive.

23. Curiously, in his early writings, Juglar treated the liquidations as the cause of the crisis, then conceived on the crisis as consisting in the general liquidation, and only later, he thought of the liquidation as following the explosion of the crisis. In 1856 and 1857, in fact, he wrote that liquidations *produce* crises ("Ce sont ces liquidations qui produisent les crises": 1856, p. 560, 1857, p. 38). In the *mémoire* presented to the Académie des Sciences Morales et Politiques in 1860, he wrote that during crises, everything comes to a halt for some time: "it is a general liquidation" ("Dans les crises, tout s'arrête pour un temps, le corps social parait paralysé; mais ce n'est qu'une torpeur passagère, prélude de plus belles destinées. En un mot, c'est une liquidation générale." The original text does not seem to have survived; this passage is cited by de Molinari, the Rapporteur for the economic section of the Académie, incorporated in Juglar, 1862, p. xiv). In the 1862 book, Juglar repeats throughout that liquidation follows the outburst of the crisis (see, e.g., pp. xii, 7–9); on one occasion, however, the notion of crisis as general liquidation is cited again (p. 176).

24. Juglar's emphasis on abuses and exaggerations is likely to reflect the medical emphasis on excesses as the cause of most diseases, a view still prevalent at the time of Juglar's first writings (Carter, 2003, pp. 20–21). The discovery of pathogenic agents, in fact, was taking place in those years and was far from being a generally accepted theory; some specific instances were known, but a general perception of disease in these terms was still lacking. Pasteur's discovery of bacteria was more or less contemporary with Juglar's book. On the contrary, the idea that men are prone to excesses fits well with Juglar's Jansenism, which could therefore have played a role in the formation of Juglar's view on crises.

25. All citations are from the first edition of Juglar's (1862) book, but the list could easily be expanded with a number of similar citations from other of his writings, such as 1863, p. 623, English translation in this volume, p. 135 and passim; similar quotes from the second edition and other late writings are given in Section 2.2.

26. Niehans (1992, pp. 546–547) thus considers Juglar's conception as belonging to the family of relaxation oscillation theories of fluctuations.

27. "Solid houses seldom go bankrupt" ("Il est rare de voir de bonnes maisons succomber": 1862, p. 14). This view, however, was not universally shared: the editor of *The Bankers' Magazine* appended a note to Lawson (1848b) observing he overlooked the fact that a crisis, "ruins not only the speculator but the prudent man of business also; for the latter is invariably involved with the former. The large number of solvent houses who were forced to suspend payments last year is a melancholy proof of this fact" (*Bankers' Magazine*, 1848).

28. Health: "state in which all the functions [of the organism] are performed freely and easily; it is the normal state" ("État dans lequel toutes les fonctions s'exécutent librement et facilement: c'est l'état normal": Beaude's *Dictionnaire de Médecine Usuelle*, 1849, Vol. 2, p. 780).

29. Intrinsic; not, as stated by Frobert and Hamouda (2008), "normal." Juglar reserved the term "normal" to prosperity, the equilibrium state free of the exaggerations of credit and speculation (the passages relating to the first edition are given in the text, while the references to the later writings will be given in Section 2.2), and indeed, there is nothing normal in a diseased organism. The normality of the entire cycle is an issue that arose later, as seen in Section 4.2. Frobert and Hamouda, however, have rightly stressed that Juglar's analogy of crisis as illness was rooted in the medical conception of his time. Their argument that this metaphor has played a heuristic role in the development of Juglar's thought, rather than a purely illustrative one, is of interest. In the present contribution, further instances are supplied to this effect.

30. Juglar is adamant – it is also part of his rhetorical apparatus – that the periodicity of crises is a universal and synchronous phenomenon (1862, e.g., pp. 4, 13, 15, and passim), but only relative to countries where commerce, industry, and especially credit are developed (e.g., p. 5).

31. One may also note that the passage cited at the opening of this section, where Juglar "chose his side" and inferred from the regularity of the recurrence of crises that at its origin there must be excesses of speculation, was left unexplained. If he identified the culprit before starting his inquiry, his argument was bound to bring precisely that result!

32. There is an asymmetry here, which reflects in the asymmetry in the division in three phases: while what happens during the prosperity provides the "cause prédisposante" of the crisis, liquidation *prepares the way* for the prosperous phase (this appropriate wording is suggested by Hutchison, 1953, p. 371). In Juglar's view, however, prosperity does not seem to need a specific cause; prosperity is simply in the nature of things.

33. Juglar seems to have become aware of such issues while translating into French large excerpts of the British Parliamentary commissions on banks, money, and credit (Juglar & Cullet, 1865), and later writing his treatise on exchanges and freedom of issue (Juglar, 1868). This is apparent in the changes he introduced when

revising, in 1873, his entry on commercial crises for Block's *Dictionnaire général de la politique* (Juglar, 1863, 1873). Translations of these two dictionary entries are available in this volume, along with an introduction by the translator, Cécile Dangel-Hagnauer.

34. Although the book is still centered, also terminologically, on crises, the terms "circle" (p. 10) and "cycle" (p. 17, 97, 162, 166, 554 – the list is due to Niehans, 1992, p. 550) are occasionally used. It should be noted, however, that Juglar's use of the term refers either to a period of years or to a round of course of the three phases, not to the (causal) succession of such cycles (see, for details of the meanings of the word "cycle," note 122). The term has been in use long since: some instances are cited in Section 3.2.

35. In Niehans's view, Juglar's focus on prices – as well as that of most of the literature on cycles up to the interwar years, when prices were substituted by output – reflects the fact that statistics were more readily available (Niehans, 1992, p. 552). This explanation, however, fails to account for the shift of emphasis between the first and the second editions: some statistics on prices were available by 1862 (in particular those collected by Tooke), but Juglar chose instead to inquire into banking data, in spite of the difficulties in gathering some of them. The reference to prices as a link between credit and speculation enabled Juglar to give a better formulation of the cumulative process in the upswing and give some intuitive kind of characterization of the prosperity phase in terms of equilibrium in prices (not a static one, but an equilibrium of raising prices reflecting the joint acceleration of credit and production), which was entirely lacking in the first edition. One may thus conjecture (pending historical research into the development of Juglar's thought) that Juglar was aware that his first edition lacked an adequate theoretical basis and that his intuition needed a more precise analytical setup. He would have easily found the missing ingredient in the literature of the time: see Section 3.5.

36. Although Juglar used the term "equilibrium," he did not supply any precise definition of it. See Section 3.9.

37. The medical metaphor also reappears in other of Juglar's late writings: "La crise commerciale, comme dans les maladies, est un moment critique à passer" (1891, p. 641). Crises "are not accidents, a fortuitous disease that one cannot forecast; they are a true illness, perfectly determined, that takes place at almost fixed times always announcing its arrival" (les crises "ne sont pas des accidents, un malaise fortuit impossible à prévoir, mais bien une véritable maladie parfaitement déterminée, qui survient à époques presque fixes et qui annonce toujours son arrivée": Juglar & Des Essart, 1889, p. 1355).

38. This (as we already had in the first edition: see Section 2.1) is occasionally expressed in terms of a comparison of the public's habits as to savings and the use of capital, as mediated by credit (p. xix).

39. "It is the very nature of business to do forward operations in order to give the buyer enough time to sell the goods" ("Il est de l'essence même des affaires d'opérer à terme pour laisser à l'acheteur le temps de placer la marchandise," Juglar, 1889, p. 47). "The prosperity of a country depends on the development of business, and ... there is no business without credit" ("la prospérité d'une nation dépend du développement des affaires, et ... il n'y a pas d'affaires sans crédit," p. 48). As a consequence, the more a country is advanced the more credit is widespread, and crises

are therefore more intense: "One could even claim that the depth of crises is related to the development of a country's wealth" ("On peut même dire que la gravité des crises est en rapport avec le développement de la richesse du pays," p. 255).

40. On the abuses of credit as cause of crises, see also Juglar (1900a, p. 10).

41. Juglar used the expression "l'équilibre instable du marché" or "du crédit," with reference to the last phase of the prosperity when speculation prevails (1889, pp. 34, 165). Emphasis on instability recurs in several of Juglar's writings: crises "éclatent d'abord sur une place quand la situation est déjà très tendue, ébranlent et renversent cet équilibre instable, s'étendent sur tout le monde des affaires, puis se liquident dans les mêmes conditions pour reparaître après avoir parcouru le même cycle" (1882, p. 5). "Cette prospérité repose sur une base essentiellement fragile" (Juglar & Des Essart, 1889, p. 1349).

42. Juglar stresses that credit permits increasing demand and thereby leads to raising prices. It is clear, however, that he is not referring to consumers' credits but to credits for production. Yet, Juglar does not seem to account for the increase in production this should entail, which should to some extent compensate for the increase in demand. Tugan-Baranowsky (1913, pp. 243–244) actually criticizes Juglar for not having realized that if demand increases, so does supply: he inverts Juglar's perspective, asserting that it is not demand preceding supply, but the other way around.

43. "In spite of the distress they lead to, the losses and even the ruin they bring about, crises have their silver lining. They clear the market of all doubtful credits ... Everything that had already lost its equilibrium has succumbed" ("Les crises, malgré le malaise qu'elles occasionnent, malgré les pertes, les ruines même qui en sont la conséquence, ont au moins cet avantage de débarrasser le marché de tous les crédits douteux ... tout ce qui avait déjà perdu son équilibre a succombé," p. 46). Similarly, Juglar states that speculation develops "the unhealthy elements that have to be wiped out by the storm" ("les éléments malsains qui doivent être balayés par la tempête," p. 165) and that crises and liquidations "rid the market of all impure elements, enabling it to stand again on its feet" ("débarrassent le marché de tous ses éléments impurs, lui permettant de reprendre pied," p. 186).

In his later writings, he insisted even more on the healing character of crises. In the dictionary entry written with Des Essars, he described the crisis as a brake capable of channeling the frantic movement taking place in the prosperity (1889, p. 1349). In 1900, he wrote of "crises of progress in production" ("crises de progrès dans la production"), referring to the necessary adaptation to the "general progress of production" altering the customary proportions between supply and demand. He commented, "in fact, crises lead to a positive result. Humankind will be better capable, and with less effort, of getting hold of the multitude of things it needs. Neverhteless, this will happen via a painful phase of adaptation" ("Au fond, ces crises aboutissent à un résultat bienfaisant, l'humanité sera mieux pourvue et avec moins d'efforts de la généralité des objets dont elle a besoin; mais il y a une phase pénible d'adaptation à subir," Juglar, 1900a, pp. 13–17). See also Juglar (1891, 1900b, pp. 648–649, translated in this volume, Chapter 6, Section 4).

44. Occasionally, Juglar seems to throw out, almost parenthetically, reflections on the interest and discount rates, whose importance lies in maintaining "in equilibrium the entire system of credit" ("en équilibre tout le système du crédit": p. 138; see also

pp. 126–127, 148, 170, 252, 271). These are not, however, really playing a part in his theory of crises except for the point discussed in the text and for a "golden break" deriving from foreign trade (Niehans, 1992, p. 556). The question of how, in spite of this equilibrating force, credit can go out of hand is not even asked. At any rate, Juglar admits that a rise in the discount rate before the situation degenerates could help prevent crises (1889, pp. 170–171), but this is all the more puzzling, as there is no discussion of how the equilibrating effect of interest interacts with the disequilibrating effect of credit (see, for some early reflections on this point by Mills (1868); Section 3.7 in this chapter; the point was taken up by Bagehot, 1873a). Nevertheless, Commons, McCracken and Zeuch (1922, p. 261) highly evaluated this part of Juglar's contribution: "For the first time in the theory of cycles, the volume of credit becomes a dependent variable, depending on the one hand, on the transactions and expectations of businessmen and, on the other hand, on the state of the bank reserves, with its connecting link, the rate of discount, or 'value of money.' Out of this relationship of time value to exchange value Juglar develops his recurring cycle of prosperity, crisis, and depression. It is the introduction of the definite use of the discount rate to contract credit expansion and its inherent effect upon the movement of the price level that gives us the cleancut contribution of Juglar."

45. It may be noted that this mechanism is similar to the one later propounded by Tugan-Baranowsky (see Besomi, 2006a), although Tugan himself found Juglar's discussion "très maladroit" (Tugan-Baranowsky, 1913, p. 243). A mechanism based on the cumulation of loanable funds during depression, however, was meanwhile expounded by Bagehot (1873b, pp. 149–150) (Bagehot was also probably the author of the anonymous piece in *The Economist* of January 4, 1873, purporting the same principle) and similarly by de Laveleye (1885).

46. The point is also stressed by Niehans (1992, pp. 553–555) and by von Bergmann (1895, pp. 256–257). Hutchison (1953, p. 425) listed Juglar among the workers in the field of crises and cycles "sceptical or ignorant" of the theoretical developments in the analysis of normal equilibrium of prices, value, production, and distribution.

47. It is an asymmetrical role: while Juglar (p. 138) mentions (without, in truth, insisting particularly on the point) the role of the accumulation of unused capital during liquidation, he explicitly denies that scarcity of capital at the end of prosperity may play a role in causing the crisis.

48. This account of Juglar's revised edition is far from complete. In particular, his description of the credit mechanism, including its international implication on specie and other transactions, is ignored here as not relevant for the topic of this chapter. For a summary see, for example, Niehans (1992, pp. 555–558).

49. After having stressed that prosperity is characterized by rising prices, that the crisis approaches when the increase slows down, and finally bursts out when the movement ceases altogether, in a dangerous passage, Juglar adds, "In a word, the main cause of crises – and one could even say the only one – is the cessation of the *price rise*" ("En un mot, la principale, on pourrait dire l'unique cause des crises, c'est l'arrêt de la *hausse des prix*," p. 33). Having defined crisis as the moment of stoppage of the raise of prices, Juglar is running in circles, thereby giving room to the criticisms of Tugan-Baranowsky (1913, pp. 241–244) and Minnie England (1913, p. 346), and is laying the premises for eliminating as altogether redundant the very

notion of crisis. He did not, however, take such a step (which came about two decades later at the hand of another Frenchman, Lescure: see Section 4.2, and in particular note 139.

50. Juglar was one of the founding members (and at some point was the President) of the Société de Statistique de Paris in 1860 and a member of the International Institute of Statistics and of the Royal Statistical Society.

51. Similar statements can surely be found elsewhere in the literature (e.g., in Briaune, 1857, p. 68, where it is argued that to ascertain whether the price of corn is limited by demand, one should start "not from hypotheses and abstractions, but from the facts as presented by history and the practice of life"), although at the time it was uncommon to see such a principle elevated to a methodological premise to a systematic study.

52. Similarly, a few years later, West also discussed fluctuations of the price of corn and wages of labor and produced a diagram with average price fluctuations from 1743 to 1821 (West [1826] 1993); see also note 56.

53. Evans's book counts over 200 pages of text and 250 pages of appendices, mainly consisting in balance sheets.

54. Wirth's book ran through over 470 pages, almost twice as many as Juglar's first edition.

55. Jevons (1862, p. 4) indicates only two articles attempting to separate periodic from occasional variations. Jevons's paper, offering a further contribution to this task, was published only in 1884, but the results were taken up in his 1863 tract on the fall of the value of gold. By 1879, Jevons had communicated to de Foville that he had a copy of Juglar's book for some time but had "not read the whole of it with the care which it deserves" (letter of February 1, 1879, in Jevons, 1977, letter 578).

56. The history of graphical representations of time series is discussed at length in Funkhouser, 1937, and more briefly in Beniger and Robyn (1978); with specific reference to economics, see Klein (1995, 1997, 2001) and Maas and Morgan (2002). To the writers cited in these essays of relevance to the early studies of economic change (in particular Playfair, Langton, and Jevons), the following should be added: West's fold-out chart of the yearly average price of wheat, 1774–1821 (curiously, the 1993 reprint by Routledge/Thoemmes mistakenly included the chart with another of the essays included in the collection); John and Charles Walker's (1840) "Mercantile Chart, exhibiting the fluctuations of the prices of Consols, Exchequer Bills, Foreign Exchanges, and the principal articles of commerce in London, during the last seven years"; Anonymous, (1862, 1863), Ellison (1862), Howard (1863), Stansfeld (1864); Meyer (1865), Duncan (1867), and Baker (1876). Mills's abstract charts illustrating the "general characteristics of a credit cycle," showing the ups and downs of several variables (bullion, bank reserves, bills, rate of discount, number of bankruptcies, general prices, prices of metals, savings of the working classes, expenses in railways, and pauperism) in the course of the four-phase cycle are particularly noteworthy (Mills, 1868). Finally, the publication date of Cooke's *Statistical Charts showing the Fluctuations in Quantity and Value of the Products of the Soil* should be moved back from 1844 to 1827 or 1828.

57. The extensive display of all types of graphic works held at the Exposition universelle in Paris in 1878 (see Funkhouser, 1937, p. 331; Cheysson, 1878, p. 324)

may have contributed to making Juglar aware of the potentialities of this kind of instrument.

58. Only the lines connecting these points were missing but were so obviously hinted at which de Foville (1879, p. 192) explicitly mentioned "the curves traced by the author" and their remarkable symmetry.

59. The intermediate passage without zigzag line supports the conclusion by Maas and Morgan (2002, p. 121n) according to whom Juglar's "tabular-graphs" of 1889 can be interpreted "as a 'natural' move to turn tables into graphs."

60. The diagram (Fig. 1) was printed as a stand-alone in 1900 (Juglar, 1900c); it is similar to the one appended to Juglar (1900a), which does not include the yearly maxima and minima.

61. It is worth noting that Mitchell's inductivist approach and specific statistical methodology to some extent resembles Juglar's. See Niehans (1992, pp. 552–553) and Pellissier (2000, p. 275).

62. On Petty's usage of the term "cycle," see note 122.

63. On Briaune, see Le Gall (2006) and Simonin (2006). On the 1847 crisis, among French authors, see, for example, de Molinari (1847, p. 274) and Horace Say – who pointed out that "everybody acknowledges" that crises had origin in the scarcity of crops (H. Say, 1847, p. 194). For a nice sample of authors attributing the main cause of the 1857 crisis to the agricultural factors (Lavergne, Bénard, and Hippolite Dussard), see the proceedings of the meeting of December 5, 1857 of the Société d'Économie Politique.

64. Tooke (1823, Part I, section VII): "Explanation of the causes of extension and contraction of private paper and credit." For a discussion, see Arnon (1991, pp. 74–77).

65. For a discussion, see Link (1959, pp. 127–147); for Schumpeter's appreciation of the endogenous character of Tooke's account, see his 1954 (pp. 744–745) study. Precisely for this reason, Spiethoff considered Tooke as Juglar's predecessor: in Persons's summary, "Juglar's forerunner, says Spiethoff, was not Sismondi, Malthus, J.-B. Say, or Marx, but Thomas Tooke (1774–1858). In support of this view, Spiethoff says that Tooke (1) used expressions for commercial expansion, crisis, and depression, (2) placed these phenomena in the nineteenth century, describing their features, and (3) pointed out their cyclical character" (Spiethoff, 1925, p. 61, quoted in Persons, 1926, p. 98).

66. A similar mechanism was suggested by J. R. McCulloch, to explain the fall of prices of corn for 1804 and 1812–1813: "high prices ... attracted so much additional capital to the land, and occasioned such an extension of tillage, that we grew ... an adequate supply of corn for our own consumption. And it is certain, that, under such circumstances, the price of corn must inevitably have fallen" (in 1814 as a consequence of an abundant crop, in 1804 simply as a consequence of the application of new capital). McCulloch brings as "uniform and striking" evidence the fluctuations in the number of enclosure acts (*J.R. McCulloch, 1826a, pp. 72–73).

67. On the theories of crises in France among socialist writers (including some maintaining that they recur periodically), see Marcy (1946).

68. This is not, of course, the first instance of the word "crises" in the plural in the title of writings on the subject: see a list in note 72.

69. Lawson added, anticipating Juglar, the observation that crises "are diseases which exhibit themselves only in a very civilized state of society, where trade and commerce flourish, where there is commercial enterprise and spirit; they occur in

England, France, Holland, and the United States of America; but I do not find any account of such in Spain or Portugal" (Lawson, 1848a, p. 2). For a discussion, see Besomi (2008b).

70. Summaries of the main positions after the 1820s are given in Jevons ([1878] 1884, pp. 222–224) and Miller (1927, pp. 192–193). The most detailed account is Bergmann's (1895, pp. 235–260). For a survey of some less known contributions from the 1780s to the 1840s, see Besomi (2010b).

71. The word "crises" (in the plural) was more frequently used in French than in English, often in association with the attribute "commercial." In English, it was often used in the singular since the late eighteenth century, while in the plural, only a few instances are recorded before the 1860s.

72. See for instance McCulloch (1819, 1826a, 1826b), Anonymous (1819a), Anonymous (1819b), Anonymous (1826), Guéroult (1831), Lemonnier (1835; the first dictionary entries on commercial crises), Millot (1837), Anonymous (1837), Chitti (1839), Briaune (1840), T. Joplin (1841), Duncan (1842), Cargill (1845), Engels (1847), Lawson (1848a), Coquelin (1848, 1849, 1850), Stansfeld (1849, 1854), Anonymous (1850), Francis (1853), W. Joplin (1854), Swiney (1855), Société d'Économie Politique (1857), Obert and Van Langenhove (1857), Anonymous (1858), Clément (1858), Sampson (1858), Van Hall (1858), Williams (1858), Bonnet (1859), and Garnier (1859). This list could be considerably lengthened if the appearance of "crises" and similar words in the text is considered.

73. During a session of the House of Lords in 1811, Lauderdale had already recognized that "no country had ever experienced commercial distress without exhibiting the phenomena which had been witnessed in this country" in 1809 (Anonymous, 1811).

74. Colquhoun (1793, p. 6) went so far as stating that "there seems to be no medium between the two extremes of great prosperity and national utility, and that species of extended adversity, which deprives the country not only of the labour of the immense body of people, most beneficially employed; but adds to the calamity by subjecting the public to the expense of maintaining them."

75. On the meaning of the term "cycle" as used in Overstone's passage, see sense (2) note 122.

76. Such a division, in contrast to Juglar's, stresses the revival rather than the liquidation. The ingredients for a four-phase synthesis were thus already present.

77. A nice example of disparate causes of crises advocated by Juglar's learned colleagues at the time he was beginning to write is the summary of a discussion having taken place in December 1857 at the Société d'Économie Politique (1857, p. 473): "Mr. Ch. Renouard, adviser to the Court de Cassation, summarized as follows the main causes of the crise: the famine, first cause independent of people; – the war, which has occasioned direct and indirect losses and thrown the social economy in disarray; – the excessive development of public works; – the spirit of speculation, which always tends by its nature to go to extremes; – the moral state of the country, which has abandoned (it must be admitted) the noble concerns of art, science, politics, and broad ideas to focus almost exclusively on business, physical enjoyment and luxury" ("M. Ch. Renouard, conseiller à la Cour de Cassation, résume les principales causes de la crise: dans la disette, première cause indépendante des hommes; – dans la guerre, qui a occasionné des pertes directes et indirectes et jeté

le trouble dans l'économie sociale; – dans le développement excessif des travaux publics; – dans l'esprit de spéculation qui, de sa nature, tend à aller toujours à l'extrême; – dans la situation morale du pays, qui abandonnant beaucoup trop, il faut le dire, les nobles préoccupations des arts, des sciences, de la politique, des grandes idées, enfin, s'est beaucoup trop exclusivement jeté dans les préoccupations d'affaires, de jouissance physiques et de luxe."

78. As the leading example of the attitude of those who rejected the possibility of finding a unifying explanation, Miller cites Roscher. An anonymous "political economist" writing to the editor of the *Economist* against the "Alleged commercial decades or cycles" (*Leslie, 1864) indicates that such an interpretation was widespread. However, when the Commissioner of Labor inquired into the causes of depressions, his agents reported, along with some of the usual suspects, also a number of bizarre ones, such as the abolition of the apprentice system, the reckless legislation in Congress, depressions and mental diseases, and too much and indiscriminate education, immorality, and extravagant living (Wright, 1886). In his *Geschichte der Nationalökonomischen Krisentheorieen*, Bergmann (1895) collected and classified in eight categories 230 different opinions on the origin and nature of crises. These were counted by Lescure (1907, p. 13), who, however, in a later edition revised the total to 280 (Lescure, 1932; quoted by Robertson, 1915, p. 1). A further list of extravagant opinions is given by Wells (1899, pp. 20–26).

79. Later, some writers resorted to oceanic metaphors to describe the phenomenon. Langton (1857, p. 11) wrote that "These disturbances [quarterly and seasonal fluctuations] are the accompaniment of another wave, which appears to have a decennial period, and in the generation of which, moral causes have no doubt an important share." Mills, who cites Langton approvingly, specifies, "They are indeed 'waves', as distinguished from the current or tide" (1868, p. 13). Other early occurrences of the oceanic metaphor are cited by Miller (1927, p. 192): a speaker in the Massachusetts House of Representatives attributed to "periodical revulsions," occurring "about every three years" "as much regularity as the billow from the ocean" (Rantoul, 1836, p. 14 – as cited by Miller, 1826, p. 192), and Balfour (1848, p. 477) commented on the "apparently tidal regularity" with which crises recur.

80. For some time at the turn of the century, these two contrasting views on periodicity were actually taken as representing the field. Later, as Jevons's view on cycles and sunspots was quickly relegated to the domain of theoretical curiosa, and his own view of exceptional events being capable of affecting the duration of the cycle was incorporated anyway in the subsequent theoretical approaches, the expediency of contrasting his views with Juglar's also disappeared. The only interwar reference I have found is in Kuznets (1930, pp. 383–384). The issue of periodicity, without comparison with Jevons, is discussed by Mitchell, who correctly stressed that Juglar did not identify any strict period but only aimed at pointing out the regularity in the alternation of phases (1927, pp. 453–454).

81. This theory was welcomed with a mix of ridicule and respect, as it was not unfounded in the contemporary literature on agricultural cycles (see Besomi, 2008a).

82. Jevons himself recognized that, in his collection and interpretation of data concerning the cycle phenomenon, he was at first guided by a theoretical bias in favor of a strict periodicity (Jevons, 1878b, in 1884, p. 228). Keynes ([1936] 1972, p. 126) remarked that Jevons had "passed over with surprising levity" the discrepancies with

strict periodicity he had himself pointed out and that "the details of the inductive argument are decidedly flimsy." On Jevons's quest for a time unit of a fluctuating economic activity, see Maas (2005, pp. 243–248).

83. This mechanical principle was also advocated by Danson (1848, p. 101): "The commercial distress which has so strongly marked the year just closed would appear to be, in the main, only a recurrence of a state of things which has become, in some degree, periodical. Effects occurring repeatedly, at intervals having some appearance of regularity, seem to indicate a corresponding regularity in the recurrence of their causes."

84. Juglar does not supply references; he may be referring to Cobden's introduction to the English translation of Chevalier's *Probable Fall in the Price of Gold*, who wrote of crises "visiting the commercial world once in each decade" (Cobden, 1859, p. x).

85. Jevons himself, of course, admitted that other events, besides fluctuations in agricultural production following sunspots, could also affect the period.

86. The biblical image had been previously evoked to reject not only the strict periodicity of crises but their recurrence tout court: an anonymous political Economist, in a letter to the *Economist* dated November 15, 1864, claimed that if the alternation of seven years of abundance and seven years of famine was not an extraordinary circumstance, Joseph's prediction would have been unnecessary (*Leslie, 1864, p. 1428). Interestingly, Briaune appealed to the biblical image to argue, in the name of the universality of the laws of nature, that the period of the agricultural cycle must be 14 years: "If such a periodicity existed in Egypt, it exists everywhere; for the very nature of the law is to be general, regardless of the initial conditions regarding the climate" (Briaune,1857, p. 122).

87. Later, a fourth issue became prominent in the debate on economic fluctuations, namely, the simultaneous presence of cycles of various lengths and their mutual relationships. We do not need to be concerned with this here.

88. Previously, Bastiat (1860, p. 55) had argued that crises were disappearing altogether, and an anonymous author of an article on "Credit and banking" had denied that crises are periodical, without, however, elaborating (Anonymous, 1860). Ferrara also "doubted that there is any principle in the science [of political economy] from which the periodicity of crises can be deduced as an economic dogma, and even less that it is a mathematical law." He admitted that Juglar's tables showed that they had recurred with some periodicity but claimed that his series were too short to deduce a theory or law (Ferrara, [1864] 1890, p. 278).

89. Niehans (1992, p. 552) conjectured that the relative ease of gathering statistics on prices rather than, for example, production, surely favored emphasizing this factor (see note 35). One, however, should also consider that a number of equilibrating mechanisms in classical economics (and, later, also neoclassical economics) were based on prices (whether of goods or of capital), and there was therefore also a theoretical interest in examining this factor.

90. Besides Tooke's writings already cited, the explicit reference to "The connection of the Currency with Prices" in Tooke (1844) also has to be mentioned.

91. Such generic usages of the medical metaphor are innocuous if only used to give some color to the argument but may become dangerous if any kind of conclusion is drawn from them. As correctly pointed out by Bernhard with reference

to the usage of medical and other metaphors to account for business cycles in the early decades of the twentieth century, "The objection to these metaphorical words and phrases is not that they are picturesque – that would be a point in their favor – but one must object when such words are used without an adequate conception of their meaning and connotation. Around such words has grown a mystic aura which seems to satisfy inquiry by suggesting something universally true and strangely profound, but what they suggest is totally inadequate either as a statement of an economic problem or as a causal explanation ... [The] fact that there are tides in the ocean or seasons during the year gives no ground for arguing that there *must* be cycles, uncontrollable cycles, in economic activity, unless it is shown either that the same forces produce tides and economic cycles or that there are other forces which act in similar fashion on economic activity to those forces exerted on the ocean waters" (Bernhard, 1943, p. 57).

More specific analogies, however, can perform useful functions, in particular, as a heuristic device; accordingly, the study of the metaphorical transfers is illuminating both in terms of the general understanding of the object to which it is applied and in terms of some specific analytical mechanisms used in the explanatory process. Some examples are discussed in this section; for a more thorough analysis, see Besomi (2011).

92. Hardy (1849, p. 388): "The disease is not the lesion itself; it is its continuation, its repercussion on vitality" ("La maladie n'est pas la lésion elle-même, elle est plutôt la suite, le retentissement vital de cette lésion").

93. Yet, there are precedents of usage of the medical metaphor in the same sense as Juglar. Innes (1848, p. 380), for instance, wrote that "Scotland has been subject to the periodical revulsions which attend all commercial enterprise, where the very prosperity and success tempt to overtrading, and out of the superabundance of health comes the malady."

94. See note 91.

95. According to Schumpeter, Hare "was one of the earliest of the few writers who attributed to cycles the function of speeding up economic advance" (Schumpeter, 1954, p. 743n). Schumpeter's opinion on the scarcity of such writers contrasts with Ferrara's and Hoyle's, cited below in the text.

96. "This opinion is nowadays spread far and wide" ("Quest'ultima opinione è oggi assai divulgata," Ferrara, [1864] 1890, p. 274).

97. Ferrara ([1864] 1890) recognized the impact of Juglar's book but referred to him rather diminishingly as "a writer, author of a booklet that drew much attention from economists. It was written with the aim of demonstrating, with abundance of data, the periodicity of crises, which he denotes – using a language I find somewhat cynical – as simple *liquidations*. In his view, their return is 'one of the conditions on which the progress of industry depends'" ("uno scrittore, autore di un'operetta che molto eccitò l'attenzione degli Economisti e scritta di proposito per provare con ricca copia di cifre la periodicità delle crisi, le chiama sovventi, in un linguaggio che mi permetterò di trovare un poco troppo cinico, semplici *liquidazioni*; ed il loro frequente ritorno sarebbe, secondo lui, 'una delle condizioni, a cui è vincolato il progresso della grande industria'"; Ferrara, [1864] 1890, p. 274).

98. A passage by Overstone was reported by Ernest Jones at a meeting in Halifax in January 1848 as follows: "Jones Loyd, the banker, has summed up our financial

policy in a few words, when he said: 'Perodical panics were necessary to keep our commercial system going.' What a system that must be that requires periodical ruin to make it live. What a clock, of which you must break the mainspring every time you wind it up" (Anonymous, 1848).

99. This distinction is based on the separation of essential phenomena and accidents, which is at the heart of Galileo's epistemology. See, for example, Koertge (1977) or Ducheyne (2006).

100. "Not an immediate one" ("Pas immédiate").

101. "Protecting or aggravaring cause" ("Cause preservatrice ou aggravante").

102. Briaune thus went almost as far as Juglar in claiming that wars can be a consequence, rather than a cause, of crises (compare Section 2.1, note 19).

103. In these writings, Lawson directly tackles the problem of periodical panics. The foundations of this distinction, however, were laid a few years before in his *Lectures on Political Economy* (1844). For a more detailed discussion, see Besomi (2008c).

104. This, however, does not necessarily mean Juglar had read Lawson's article, as the magazine had published a number of pieces on crises and panics.

105. Lawson also stressed a few other elements later to be found in Juglar's writings: his emphasis on periodicity, credit, speculation, and psychological causes have already been pointed out in Sections 3.2 and 3.5; to this, it should be added that the mechanism that he envisaged – following Tooke – to explain the explosion of credit was based on price changes: the scarcity of most articles gives rise to speculation, which brings price rises, thereby inducing the creation of the most extravagant enterprises (Lawson, 1848c, p. 282); he also stressed that credit is not necessarily banking credit, but credit traders raise to one another, and even concluded with an analogy anticipating the passage from Juglar 1862, p. 14, cited in p. 177: "when the prices begin to rise under its [the spirit of speculation's] influence, the early purchasers are sure to realize a profit, they sell to another who sells again, producing additional rise of price, and so the torch, passed from hand to hand, is sure to burn the last holder" (1848b, p. 285). Finally, like Juglar (1862, p. iv), he rejected the theories blaming crises upon the banking system, observing that banks are victims of the crises, compelled to act as they do, not their originators (Lawson, 1848a, p. 7); incidentally, such statements could be found in France as well. Chevalier, for instance, is reported having said before a meeting of the Société d'Économie Politique in 1854 that "the Banks do not cause the movement; they follow it" ("ce ne sont pas les Banques qui provoquent le mouvement; elles le suivent" – Société d'Économie Politique, 1854, p. 429).

106. The expression "almost periodical" recurs three times in the article on "Crises commerciales" (Coquelin, 1852a, pp. 526, 528, 530) and also occurs in previous writings (e.g., Coquelin, 1850, p. 219; in 1849, p. 374, Coquelin dropped the adverb).

107. The last two words of the French original, "Le mal se propage rapidement comme une trainée de poudre," literally translate as "line of gunpowder." The analogy is interesting, as it takes an explosive charge (implicitly at the end of the line) as a metaphor for instability in a similar way as Juglar and Jevons later did (see Section 3.10).

108. This part of Coquelin's argument was taken up and translated into Italian a few years later by Boccardo, who began his discussion of the causes of crises by

distinguishing between external and internal ones, the former being those susceptible of scientific inquiry. Boccardo also agreed with Coquelin's conclusion that the monopoly of central banks is the ultimate cause of crises and their periodical recurring (Boccardo, 1857).

109. Mills's paper had a follow-up, as it was taken up by Jevons (see below and Peart, 1996, pp. 46–49), was fully discussed by Bergmann and cited for instance by Pigou (1927), Hutchison (1953), and Schumpeter (1954), and recently reprinted in Hagemann (2002).

110. This expression is quite interesting, as it clearly defines the cycle as a new phenomenon, to be explained in itself ("dictating the search of cause at a deeper level," p. 13) and not as the result of a mere sequence of crises.

111. Such conditions are the same for both authors. In Mills's words, "exaggeration of healthy functional action," "diseased overgrowth of credit," intervening gradually but eventually inducing the "degeneration" of the stable "healthy confidence" of the prosperity "into the disease of too facile a faith" in the highly speculative and unstable time preceding the panic (Mills, 1868, pp. 27, 36).

112. See also Jevons (1878a, in 1884, p. 206), "No accidental cause, however, is sufficient to explain so widespread and recurrent a state of trade." For a discussion of Jevons's reinterpretation of secondary causes as disturbing factors, see Peart (1995) and Maas (2005, Ch. 9). In the light of the present section, Maas's claim that Jevons was the first writer to take such a step (Maas, 2005, p. 220) is surely not accurate.

113. Besides the learned writers cited in this section, a similar argument was advanced in the press by an anonymous correspondent of *Reynold's Newspaper* on November 15, 1857. After noting that "as for the causes of the panic, [the theories are] as various, incomprehensible, and contradictory as those on the cholera itself," he ridiculed the variety of explanations offered, "whether it be owing to Canning or to crinoline, – to female extravagance or to Indian disasters, – to the recklessness of trader or the bounty of Providence, – the abundant harvest being (not for the first time) one of the alleged causes of the starvation of the people," and observed that the periodic recurrence of financial panics, the interval between which being of 10 years on average, suggests a unique cause common to all such events: "when such regularity as this is observed, one cannot help suspecting that panics occur in obedience to some intelligent cause. The idea of these periodically-recurring events being the children of chance, is not for a moment to be entertained. There must be a fixed cause; but what that cause is, the 'wise men of Gotham' have not yet succeeded in deciding" (Anonymous, 1857b). Although the argument is only outlined, a piece like this being submitted to the press indicates that similar approaches were in the air.

114. "On the one side are those who believe that the existing economic system is, in the long-run, a self-adjusting system, though with creaks and groans and jerks, and interrupted by time lags, outside interference and mistakes ... These authorities do not, of course, believe that the system is automatically or immediately self-adjusting. But they do believe that it has an inherent tendency towards self-adjustment, if it is not interfered with and if the action of change is not too rapid. On the other side of the gulf are those who reject the idea that the existing economic system is, in any significant sense, self-adjusting. They believe that the failure of effective demand to reach the full potentialities of supply, in spite of human psychological demand being

immensely far from satisfied for the vast majority of individuals, is due to much more fundamental causes" (Keynes, [1934] 1973, pp. 486–487).

115. Marx's starting point, both logical and chronological, were the conditions that make the systematic recurrence of crises possible without reducing them to the result of mere accidents. This was first discussed, in its most abstract form, in *A Contribution to the Critique of Political Economy* and in the *Grundrisse* (Marx [1859] 1971, pp. 96–98; [1857–1858] 1973, pp. 148–149), then taken up again in increasingly concrete forms, first in the *Theories of Surplus Value*, where Marx explicitly attacked Ricardo's acceptance of Say's law of markets, which made it impossible for crises to occur and its rejection by Malthus and Sismondi (Marx, [1862–1863] 1969, Vol. 2, pp. 492–535), then in *Capital* (Marx, [1867–1894] 1974).

116. J. S. Mill, "On the influence of consumption on production," in Mill ([1844] 1967). As it was immediately clear that Say's law presupposes a barter-like system, with money only acting as an intermediary in the exchanges, quite naturally a number of authors attributed violations of Say's Law to some or other peculiarity of the working of the monetary system – from the currency issues to the working of the banking system, from credit to the abolition of £1 notes (see, e.g., Glasner, 1989, pp. 219–221). This explains the emphasis of most early crisis theorists on this kind of issues, while focus on real causes remained in a minority – although, of course, there were approaches based, for instance, on underconsumption or on the provision of capital.

117. Auguste Ott also attempted to construct some reproduction schemes to establish the equilibrium conditions that would maintain consistency between consumption and production, but limited his analysis to a cooperative society (Ott, 1851, 1854, pp. 516–523). For a discussion, see Besomi and Colacchio (2010).

118. Precedents of the awareness of the relation of crises to a breach in equilibrium must not be rare. The following anonymous author, for instance, so described in 1816 the premises of the "present embarrassments": "The ordinary channels through which the various produce of art and industry was formerly distributed, are completely obstructed; the natural communication between the producer and consumer is interrupted; the supply by the former is not adjusted either in kind or proportion to the demands of the latter; and the dissolution of a connexion, which the prosperity of the national trade and manufactures requires to be steadily maintained, carries with it, too surely, their decay" (Anonymous, 1816, p. 373).

119. For a discussion of Wilson's work on fluctuations, see Link (1959) (on this issue, see in particular pp. 108–114).

120. "We have, in fact, one of those cases to which the axiom of Mr. Mill is applicable, – 'the joint effect of causes is the sum of their separate effects'" (Mills, 1868, p. 32).

121. At this junction, Mitchell still accepted the division of the cycle in three phases; he later changed his mind – see note 137.

122. To avoid misunderstandings, a note on terminology is in place at this point. The term "cycle" has several meanings, of which three recur in the nineteenth-century literature on the issues we are discussing here. The most common usage, occurring fairly frequently at least from the 1820s to the end of the century is that of "cycle" as (1) "an interval of time during which a characteristic, often regularly repeated event or sequence of events occurs" (*American Heritage*: 1). For example, Petty's reference to the average duration of the "Cycle within which Dearths and

Plenties make their revolution" (Petty, 1662, p. 43; the full passage is cited in Section 3.2). More commonly, the word was loosely used to indicate an interval in time in expressions such as "cycle of prosperity," or "cycle of depression," as for instance in this passage: "cycles of abundance which are supposed to alternate with cycles of dearth every five years" (Anonymous, 1849b, p. 573). The other two notions of cycle both refer to recurring events following the same pattern. One of them, however, focuses on what happens within a *single* cycle, whereas the other refers to the *succession* of cycles. The former of these is defined as follows: (2) "A single complete execution of a periodically repeated phenomenon" (*American Heritage*: 2a; see also *Oxford English Dictionary*: 4 or *Grand Robert*: 2). This usage of the term "cycle" stresses the order in which events occur within each cycle; as an example, one may consider the cycle of a washing machine, which goes through a number of phases, from prewashing to spinning, following a constant order, but which stops after the last one, and only resumes when the button is pushed again. The other notion focuses more on the repetition of the sequence than on the sequence itself within a single course; this is somehow taken for granted. It is defined as follows: (3) "A recurrent round or course (of successive events, phenomena, etc.); a regular order or succession in which things recur; a round or series which returns upon itself" (*Oxford English Dictionary*: 3a; see also *American Heritage*: 2b or *Grand Robert*: 2). An example is the working of a piston in a combustion engine.

When I refer to the "cycles" approach, the word is used in the latter sense. It should be noted that the use of the word "cycle" by a writer does not immediately classify him in the "cycles" approach: when "cycle" is used in the first of the senses defined above, it has no intrinsic relation with the way of approaching the problem of crises or economic fluctuations. When used in the second sense, it is compatible with the "recurring crises" approach, but it is not sufficient to characterize the "cycles" approach. Only when used in the third sense, it is fully compatible with both the "recurring crises" and the "cycles" approaches.

123. Here, I focus on the recurring crises and cycles approaches to clarify the position of Juglar and other writers too lightly considered as forerunners of the "cycles" approach but really discussing crises in terms of recurring events. A full comparison of the four approaches shall therefore be postponed to another occasion.

124. As an example of the "crises" approach on this point consider for example Ferrara's ([1864] 1890, pp. 256–269) view: "Crises originate, as we have seen, from abnormal production. If production constantly followed the line of its natural development, it would cut at the root all the ills lamented by mankind, and our world would offer the view of a continuous ascension, from the state of misery from which we began, to an unlimited and indefinable perfection."

125. Marx noted that Ricardo, who "did not actually know anything of crises, of general crises of the world market" could indeed explain them in terms of the rise of the price of corn due to poor harvest and due to the transition from war to peace. But "Later historical phenomena, especially the almost regular periodicity of crises on the world market, no longer permitted Ricardo's successors to deny the facts or to interpret them as accidental" (Marx [1862–1863] 1969, Ch. 17, p. 7).

126. There naturally were some exceptions: de Laveleye (1865, p. 290), for instance, maintained that crises recur with increasing frequency because the specific cause of each of them tend to cluster more and more often.

127. The word "cycle" can be used in this connection, in the second meaning of the term described in note 122.

128. Juglar's phases reflect the disease-centered medical distinction between a period of growth of the disease, when the disease invades the body; its acme; and its decline, after which either the patient dies or is healed (Hardy, 1849, p. 389). If the patient survives, his normal functions resume their regular course; this does not need a specific explanation.

129. Accordingly, the prevalent terminology to the 1820s stresses the *consequences* of crises, rather than characterizing the events themselves by means of words like "distress" or "embarrassment."

130. As in the case of the medical metaphor, the atmospheric one was also used in general terms, with the storm indicating the trouble itself rather than the consequence of a previous condition. See for instance Tooke's (1823, p. 53) reference to "succession of hurricanes which swept away so many banking and mercantile establishments," or Blanqui's (1836, p. 257) reference to crises as "storms that disrupt momentarily the serenity of the industrial horizon, and after which, except some devastation, business resumes its accustomed course."

131. The principle has been misunderstood by Frobert and Hamouda (2008, Section 4), who argue instead that the pathological is one and the same as the physiological (for an extended criticism, see Besomi, 2011).

132. See the passage by Lawson (1848a, p. 1) cited on p. 123 above.

133. On the distinction of "normal" and "pathological" in medical thought, see Canguilhem ([1966] 1991).

134. Oppenheimer's reflections are relevant to this issue. He pointed out that crises have always been understood as a disturbance to the normal economic process and qualified as diseases, in contrast to the healthy state of the economy. Yet, this "normal" state has not been well defined, if not negatively as the lack of crises, so that economists did not really have a "normal" state with which to compare the abnormal ones. Oppenheimer reviews some preceding discussions of the relationship of normality and crisis, with special reference to W. Fischer (1911), Pinkus (1906), and Sombart (1904). His remarks on Sombart are particularly interesting. Sombart raised the issue but believed the problem not to be solvable: he maintained that the normal capitalistic process inevitably leads to crises, which are thus understood as its normal consequence precisely as a hangover is the ordinary aftereffect of alcohol poisoning. But this leaves the problem of whether alcohol intoxications are normal, revealing that Sombart mixes up two notions of "normal": the regular operational sequence and repetition of features of the same kind, and on the contrary, a "correct," ideal process. Fischer is also guilty of the same confusion, and his methodological conclusion that the determination of the "normal" can only be a result of a theory of crisis, but never its condition (Fischer, 1911, p. 12), is, in Oppenheimer's view, untenable. Oppenheimer argues that this would be analogous to the case of an isolated island, where everyone including the only physician suffers of malaria: the physician's determination of the "normal" state would reflect the island's condition. He thus concludes that inquiries on crises need an accurate picture of the normal, healthy state as a basis for comparison (Oppenheimer, 1911).

135. At the time he wrote the second edition of his book, Juglar was aware of the problem, although he was not able to solve it satisfactorily; see Section 2.2.

136. Interestingly, no particular term appears to have come into common usage between the 1820s and the 1870s to mirror, for business activity after a recovery, what the term "re-action" indicated about the change in business direction after the speculative phase.

137. The early divisions in three phases was criticized, for instance, by Mitchell (who, however, had accepted it up to 1913: see the quotation at the beginning of Section 4.1, p. 226): "if the transition from prosperity to depression is recognized as a separate phase, it seems logical to give similar recognition to the transition from depression to prosperity" (Mitchell, 1927, p. 378).

138. The first division in four phases may be due to Mills (not surprisingly, in the light of what was said in Section 3.7 on his discussion of the lower turning point). He did not actually list four phases, but three phases *plus* the panic, the departing and arriving point of the whole movement:

> Through the normal cycle of credit we have now worked our way again to a point corresponding to that where I started that Panic was 'the destruction of a bundle of beliefs.' The road we traversed was found clearly enough divided into three stages:
>
> 1. The Post-panic period, marked by plethora of reserve Capital, and dormancy of speculation.
>
> 2. The Middle, or Revival period, marked by increasing trade, moderate speculation, and a sound state of Credit.
>
> 3. The Speculative period, showing inflation of Credit, high range of prices, unproductive investment, and excessive commitments; and leading to Crisis and the end of the cycle.
>
> With each of these stages there appears to be a concurrent change in the mental mood of the trading public; and these changes are the same in each decade, and follow the same relative order. (Mills, 1868, p. 29)

139. For a discussion of this notion, as compared to the alternative interpretation held by other authors (e.g., Bouniatian and Tugan-Baranowsky), emphasizing the violence and the ruin caused by crises, see Mitchell (1927, pp. 378–381; [1927] 1969). It may be noted that Lescure's definition of crisis as the interruption of the period of prosperity is fully compatible with Juglar's 1889 definition of crisis as the time when prices cease to grow, thereby interrupting prosperity (p. 16; Guitton actually confuses them: 1951, p. 90n). Perhaps, Lescure did even develop his own definition elaborating upon Juglar's. Yet the implications are quite different: Lescure stresses the *transition* from prosperity to depression ("the general overproduction crisis is the point of intersection between a period of expansion ... and a period of depression" – "la crise générale de surproduction est le point d'intersection d'une période d'essor ... avec une période de dépression"), while Juglar is interested in stressing the crisis as a special state of the system, where equilibrium breaks down. Moreover, while for Lescure the crisis is a *point* of transition between phases, for Juglar it is a *period*, a phase (brief as it may be, pp. 16–17). Such a conception deprived the crisis of any function, thereby preparing its complete euthanasia, while for Juglar, the crisis was an all important phase in the capitalistic process.

140. Although mechanical metaphors largely substituted the reference to disease, the medical diagnostic approach kept competing with deterministic forecasting of cycles. Research in the history of the so-called business barometers has emphasized that economic forecast was guided by two paradigms originating in the late nineteenth century and dividing economic statistics up to the 1920s. On the one hand, there was a "semiological" approach derived from medicine, which based its diagnostic on the identification of a number of "symptoms" treated as indicators. It originated from Juglar's late writings and was adopted among others by Neumann-Spallart and de Foville and later formed the basis of Mitchell's descriptive method. The second approach, at the basis of, for example, the Harvard Barometer, privileged instead the recognition of causal chains, in a Newtonian fashion eventually leading to the application of correlation methods (Armatte, 1992, pp. 99–123; 2003). Deblock (2000, pp. 36–41) added that the opposition between mechnical and organicist conceptions guided not only the methodology of business forecasting but also the forecasters' general view on economic theory, its place is society, and the nature of society itself.

141. In 1913, Mitchell had written that "the strains relax as gradually as they gather and the crisis merges into a depression in the same unobtrusive fashion that it emerges from prosperity," so that "Expansion gives place to contraction, though without a violent wrench" and that "The very condition that make business profitable gradually evolve conditions that threaten a reduction of profits" (Mitchell, [1913] 1941, pp. 122, 158, 61 respectively). Mitchell, of course, recognized that sometimes crises are sudden and violent, but ascribed such facts to "unreasonable alarm" on the part of the public, degenerating into the unreasonable behavior characterizing panics.

142. Guitton, having defined crises as "discontinuous and catastrophic moments of a continuous cyclical evolution" (Guitton, 1956, p. 365), wondered whether after 1929 and World War II the idea of cycle would not be questioned and the idea of crisis (possibly in a revised form) would conquer the field again (Guitton, 1956, p. 350).

143. Not, however, of the distant past, as commercial crises are a feature of the advanced state of economies where exchanges and credit are highly developed.

144. In the (linear) dynamic approach, the unification of cycles and trend has been an analytical problem that deeply troubled most writers. In Kalecki's approach, in particular, the trend even needed a specific explanation to be superimposed from the outside onto the cyclical one (Kalecki, 1968; for a discussion, see Besomi, 2006c).

145. Interestingly, in an earlier part of his book, Cassel called for a "sharp distinction between the periods of normal development, including what is usually called Business Cycles, and the periods denoting essential interruptions of this normal development," with reference to the world slump and the crisis generated by the War (Cassel, 1932, p. 40).

146. It should be remembered that a large number of explanations of recurring crises pointed at some specific circumstances, normally some institutional factors such as the banking policy, the presence of trade regulations or tariffs, and so on, the elimination of which would have solved the problem and eliminated crises. Some writers, however, were shamelessly deterministic. An anonymous correspondent (calling himself "Pactolus") of the *Liverpool Mercury*, for instance, started from

Overstone's list of 10 phases of the overtrading cycle, identified the current state of trade within that list, and went as far as boldly predicting the timing of the next two stages (Anonymous, 1849c, 1949d). Another writer pushed so far as claiming that the seeming conclusion of the 1873 crisis in the United States authorized optimism for several years to come: "Every ten years we have been taught by the past to expect some such financial convulsion. If the present storm has spent its force, and if it be really the periodical panic itself, and not a mere harbinger and forerunner of that decennial event, then we may look forward to eight or ten years of prosperous activity, industrial growth, and commercial success" (Anonymous, 1875, p. 2). Similarly, another writer wrote, "The hope of an ultimate improvement in the more solid evidence of the state of trade was ... entertained; it was throughout the year remembered that trade is subject to cycles, that the depression of prices and languor of business could not last indefinitely, that the lane had been long, and a turning was every month approached more nearly" (Anonymous, 1879a, p. 291).

147. Besides the writers cited at the end of Section 3.4, a statement by Sir William Harcourt before the Oxford Liberal Associations is illustrative of this attitude: "I do not share the fatalism of those who attribute the recurrence of distress to some fortuitous cycle. These disturbances have their origin in one great cause, and that cause is war" (Anonymous, 1879b). A comment in *The Economist*, presumably by Bagehot, is particularly interesing: he rubutted the idea that crises recur with determinate periodicity, but only to substitute it with the idea of a regular cycle in economic activity driven by fluctuations in the amount of loanable funds: "We have often had to confute the common notion that by some fixed fate we must have a panic every ten years. If our commerce is well managed, as, on the whole, it generally is, and if an adequate cash reserve is kept against bank liabilities payable on demand, we may believe ourselves safe against such catastrophes. But there is nevertheless a great truth at the bottom of the common notion. Though there is no reason to fear periodical panics, there is every reason to expect periodical cycles – in one part of which the rate of interest is exceptionally low, and in another part of which it is exceptionally high" (*Bagehot, 1874, p. 1).

148. This also applies to the semiexogenous approaches, such as Frisch's and Kalecki's, which consisted in superimposing random shocks onto deterministic systems. The nature of the resulting fluctuations is fully deterministic, also in its appearance. Firstly, the period of the fluctuations entirely depends on the structural part; secondly, the system's response to the shocks is fully defined by the system's structure. The situation changed in the 1980s, when chaotic dynamics appeared on the scene. The movement they describe is fully deterministic as to its structure but is so sensitive to initial conditions that any neighboring initial state gives rise to completely different results, thereby appearing nondeterministic.

149. The terms "sudden," "violence," and "catastrophic" recur several times in the opening pages of the chapter (Keynes, [1936] 1973, pp. 314–316).

150. Marx also stressed the human factor, as opposed to a mechanistic interpretation of crises. In his view, the *possibility of crises* depends on a number of features intrinsic in the capitalistic mode of production and exchange: money, by separating purchases from sales in distinct and independent acts, makes it possible to sell without immediately spending the money received in return, thereby opening the prospect of a shortening of demand; money, moreover, being a general representative

of wealth can be hoarded; and the credit system is always open to the possibility that some debtor defaults, interrupting the chain of payments. These possibilities eventually become a *necessity* not in virtue of some automatic iron law but only when social classes actively intervene in the production process. During prosperity, more and more workers are employed, reducing the reserve army of the unemployed. Workers can therefore obtain higher wages, thereby reducing profit rates. After some time, this becomes unsustainable, as capitalist will sooner or later be faced with difficulties in facing their debts, starting off a chain of insolvency which quickly and violently stalls the entire system. Halting production is the means for restoring profit rates; the crisis is therefore necessary for the capitalistic production process to go back on tracks and recommence. Although each capitalist perceives the crisis as an external event, it is the result of their collective behavior, coupled with the action of workers. (For a discussion along these lines, see De Vecchi, 1983, pp. 234–252.)

F1. "Depuis longtemps, les crises apparaissent à des époques plus ou moins éloignées, sans qu'aucune des théories qui on été proposées pour les expliquer ait été acceptée."

F2. "Les crises se renouvellent avec un telle constance, une telle régularité, qu'il faut bien en prendre son parti et y voir le résultat des écarts de la spéculation et d'un développement inconsidéré de l'industrie et des grandes entreprises commerciales."

F3. "tout paraît conspirer pour donner un essor sans pareil aux affaires; toutes les entreprises qui se fondent trouvent les capitaux nécessaires; on s'arrache les titres, on les achète avec une confiance sans réserve dans l'avenir."

F4. "Loi des crises et de leur périodicité."

F5. "sans faire intervenir aucune théorie, aucune hypothèse."

F6. "l'observation seule des faits."

F7. "Quoique l'examen des documents statistiques qui vont suivre puisse engager à conclure et à reconnaître une loi économique, la prudence conseille de ne pas trop se hâter."

F8. "Le renouvellement et la succession des mêmes faits, dans des *circonstances spéciales*, dans tous les *temps*, dans tous les *pays* et sous tous les *régimes*, voilà ce qu'il fallait faire remarquer."

F9. "Rechercherles causes et signaler les effets des crises commerciales survenues en Europe et dans l'Amérique du Nord durant le cours du dix-neuvième siècle. Ces crises ont été fréquentes à toutes les époques; mais, à mesureque les relations commerciale sont acquis de nouveaux développements, leur action perturbatrice s'est étendue de proche en proche sur un plus grand nombre de points."

F10. "La répétition constante des mêmes accidents donne une monotonie réelle à notre histoire: nous sommes forcés de passer successivement et toujours par les mêmes phases, non sans causer un certain ennui à l'esprit qui aime la variété et toujours avide de nouveautés; n'est-ce pas cependant la meilleure confirmation de ce que nous voulions démontrer?".

F11. "Nous nous bornerons donc aux divisions principales ou à la classification des causes morbides. Il en est qui préparent les maladies; elles sont pour la plupart dans l'organisation elle même: on les nomme *prédisposantes*; d'autres, presque toutes extérieures, font éclater la prédisposition et produisent la maladie, et l'on appelle celles-là *déterminantes* ou *occasionnelles*. Prenons un exemple: cet homme a le cœur volumineux, le sang abondant, le cou court, cette complexion est la cause prédisposante à l'apoplexie; que, maintenant, dans un accès de colère, il soit foudroyé, l'émotion sera la cause occasionnelle. Sans la prédisposition, les influences maladives sont impuissantes, mais les signes qui la révèlent sont souvent cachés. Ce ne serait pas une mince difficulté que d'annoncer *a priori* quelle serait la part de chacun de quatre imprudents qui, couchés en sueur sur de la terre humide, devraient se relever l'un avec un rhumatisme, l'autre avec un catarrhe pulmonaire, le troisième avec une diarrhée, le quatrième en santé parfaite. L'examen préalable de l'organisation de chacun aiderait sans doute à la solution du problème, mais avant l'épreuve le résultat resterait souvent incertain."

F12. "Les disettes, les guerres, les révolutions, les changements de tarif, les emprunts, les variations de la mode, de nouvelles voies ouvertes au commerce, voilà les principales causes invoquées tour à tour. Mais le véritable critérium des causes, c'est de les voir, dans des circonstances semblables, reproduire les mêmes effets, particularité malheureusement assez rare dans les phénomènes sociaux et dans tout ce qui touche à la vie. Dans cette incertitude, on invoque tour à tour les causes les plus contraires pour se rendre compte des mêmes effets. On est surpris de la légèreté, de la facilité avec laquelle l'esprit humain accepte tout ce qu'on lui propose; tellement il est avide de savoir, de se rendre compte, et, quand il ne trouve rien de mieux, combien facilement il se paye de mots. La multiplicité même des causes que l'on invoque le plus souvent suffit, il nous semble, pour prouver leur peu d'efficacité, puisque, alors qu'une seule devrait suffire, on en accumule un grand nombre, sorte que, comme elles ne sont pas toujours réunies pour produire le même effet, on peut aussi rigoureusement, conclure, en les éliminant une à une, qu'aucune n'est cause déterminante, pas même secondaire, puisque sa présence n'est pas indispensable pour produire le résultat attendu." [Translation by C. Dangel-Hagnauer in this volume, p. 118]

F13. "État antérieur ... en l'absence duquel les causes que l'on croirait les plus puissantes sont sans action. C'est ce qu'en médecine on appelle la prédisposition."

F14. "les conditions indispensables à leur existence, sur les phénomènes constants que l'on observe alors en dehors des causes si diverses, si variées, que l'on invoque selon le besoin du moment."

F15. "une grande guerre ne saurait arrêter le movement."

F16. "Les mauvaises récoltes, la cherté des céréales, les disettes, par leur retour périodique se rencontrent assez souvent dans notre pays avec l'engorgement du portefeuille des banques, et apportent une nouvelle complication à une situation déjà mauvaise: leur présence n'est cependant pas indispensable pour produire une crise commerciale."

F17. "Il est dans la nature humaine de ne se tenir jamais dans des justes limites."

F18. "extravagante application du capital flottant," "écarts de la spéculation," "spéculation insensée" (p. 25) or "imprudente," "au delà de leurs moyens."

F19. "développement exagéré des escomptes," "abus du crédit," "overtrading," "crédit fictif," "douteux" or "artificial," "prix exagéré," "développement inconsidéré de l'industrie."

F20. "souvent aussi l'emploi et l'immobilisation d'un capital supérieur à celui qui pouvait fournir les ressources ordinaires du pays, autrement dit l'épargne."

F21. "tant que la hausse persiste, on échange les produits, personne ne perd, mais malheur au dernier détenteur!"

F22. "Un crédit trop tendu que les charges accumulées finissent par rompre."

F23. "perturbations sérieuses pour des causes peu graves."

F24. "tout à coup tous les canaux paraissent remplis, il n'y a plus d'écoulement possible, toute circulation cesse et une crise éclate. Toutes les spéculations s'arrêtent; l'argent, si abondant quelque mois auparavent, diminue, se resserre, disparaît même."

F25. "comme dans les maladies [les crises] préparent un état meilleur en rejetant au dehors tout ce qui était impur." [Translation by C. Dangel-Hagnauer in this volume, p. 132]

F26. "et débarrassent le marché d'une cause incessante de trouble et de ruine."

F27. "une crise n'est qu'une liquidation générale pour permettre aux affaires de reprendre sur une base plus solide."

F28. "développement régulier de la richesse des nations."

F29. "un dérangement dans la marche des affaires." [Translation by C. Dangel-Hagnauer in this volume, p. 116]

F30. "Les crises, comme les maladies, paraissent une des conditions de l'existence des sociétés où le commerce et l'industrie dominent. On peut les prévoir, les adoucir, s'en préserver jusqu'à un certain point, faciliter la reprise des affaires; mais les supprimer, c'est ce qui jusqu'à ici, malgré les combinaisons les plus diverses, n'a été donné à personne. Proposer un remède à notre tour, quand nous reconnaissons le peu d'efficacité de ceux des autres, n'était pas possible, d'autant que leur évolution naturelle rétablit l'équilibre et prépare un sol ferme sur lequel on peut s'appuyer sans crainte pour parcourir une nouvelle période." [Translation by C. Dangel-Hagnauer in this volume, p. 143]

F31. "Fureur," "élan," "engouement, frénésie."

F32. "une fois le *mouvement commencé* dans un sens ou dans l'autre, *croissant* ou *décroissant*, il continue sans interruption jusqu'au moment où un revirement complet a lieu." [Translation by C. Dangel-Hagnauer in this volume, p. 122]

F33. "Nous voudrions montrer ici qu'on peut en suivre le *développement pas à pas*, presque mois par mois, au moins, d'une manière très claire, *année par année*."

F34. "les périodes s'enchaînent, se suivent avec une régularité qui étonne toujours."

F35. "ces trois périodes reconnues, il fallait chercher les rapports qu'elles pouvaient avoir entre elles et sous l'influence de quelles causes elles se succédaient."

F36. "la réaction qui se succède à l'action."

F37. "Dans le langage vulgaire, la période prospère n'a pas de nom; c'est ce que l'on regarde comme l'état normal, on n'en parle même pas; il en est de la prospérité comme la santé, rien ne paraît plus naturel": "c'est l'état normal du marché, la période prospère."

F38. "L'équilibre des prix est rompu."

F39. "le mot crise indique un état de malaise ou de souffrance."

F40. "des inconvénients sous quelques rapports," but are "à d'autres points de vue extrêmement salutaires et avantageuses."

F41. "Esprit d'entreprise."

F42. "La crise serait donc l'*arrêt* de la *hausse* des *prix*, c'est-à-dire le moment ou l'on ne *trouve* plus de *nouveaux preneurs*."

F43. "les crises ne se reproduisent pas à des époques fixes."

F44. "cela ne veut pas dire ... qu'il y a des cycles d'abondance et de disette réguliers; la prédiction de Joseph des sept ans de prospérité [et de sept ans] de misère prouve même que c'était un fait exceptionnel."

F45. "Prophète des crises."

F46. "Je crois que le retour des crises industrielles est une maladie endémique chez les nations démocratiques de nos jours. On peut la rendre moins dangereuse, mais non la guérir, parce qu'elle ne tient pas à un accident, mais au tempérament même de ces peuples."

F47. "Le corps social est, comme le corps humain, sujet à des maladies dont les unes tiennent à des accidents extérieurs et n'apportent qu'un trouble momentané dans les fonctions vitales, tandis que les autres, causés par des vices organiques et passant à l'état chronique, influent sur la constitution et sur le développement des individus et des societés."

F48. "infermità del mondo sociale moderno. Non è solo fisiologia, l'economia politica, ma è eziando patologia e clinica."

F49. "une réaction salutaire de l'économie opposée à la maladie et en lutte contre ses mauvais résultats. Cette puissance qu'on désigne sous le nom de force médicatrice de la nature, est, comme l'antidote, à côté du poison; elle tend sans cesse à rétablir le calme et l'équilibre dans l'organisation." The translation of this passage is a bit tricky. The term "économie" is translated as "organism" following the definition of "économie animale" given in the same dictionary: "On désige sous ce nom l'ensemble des fonctions du corps humain. (v. Organisme.)" (This name designates the whole of the functions of the human body. See "Organism"). "Force" and "puissance" have been inverted in the translation, on the ground that the expression "force médicatrice de la nature" (the "vis medicatrix naturae") is normally translated into English as "healing power of nature"; the author of the entry seem to treat "force" and "power" as equivalent in his sentence.

F50. "Elles son inévitables; mais les inconvénients ne peuvent, à beaucoup près, balancer les immenses avantages que leur peuples retirent des développements immenses de leur affaires. Les crises de cette nature [les crises commerciales] sont des crises de croissance; et mieux vaut l'activité et la richesse avec les crises commerciales (celles-ci dussent-elle être dans la nature permanente des choses) que l'inaction et la pauvreté. Les pays riches et prospères sont quelque fois en crise; les pays pauvres y sont d'une manière permanente. Au surplus, les crises commerciales sont passagères de leur nature. Les baisses soudaines dans la valeur des choses amènent des acheteurs, facilitent la consommation, font cesser l'engorgement et provoquent la liquidation des affaires mal engagées. Dans ces évolutions, les producteurs ou les détenteurs de marchandises ont perdu; mais les acheteurs ou détenteurs de capitaux circulant ont gagné; certaines fortunes particulières ont été détruites, d'autres se sont élevées; il y a eu des souffrances individuelles, mais, au point de vue social, il n'y a pas le même appauvrissement, et l'inconvénient de la crise est racheté par la disparition des entreprises véreuses. C'est ainsi qu'après un temps assez limité on voit souvent, après la crise, les affaires reprendre avec plus de vigueur et plus d'activité que jamais."

F51. "Il faudrait prétendre que la prospérité de 1820 à 1827 été due au changement de la loi des élections, à la suspension de la liberté de la presse, à celle de la liberté individuelle; aux émeutes des écoles, aux conspirations de Paris, de Saumur, de Bedfort, de la Rochelle, qui en on été la conséquence; à la guerre d'Espagne, aux lois de l'indemnité, du droit d'ainesse, du sacrilège, qui en ont été la suite et le complement."

F52. "Si ces causes sont les véritables, elles doivent avoir influé sur les crises de 1811, de 1817, de 1827: car ce retour périodique d'un même mal entraîne nécessairement l'existence de causes identiques et permanentes. Or personne n'oserait assigner à ces crises antérieures la prétendue origine de la crise actuelle; et c'est déjà quelque chose de peu logique que d'attribuer des effets pareils, et dont la liaison est évidente, à des accidents toujours différents. Contre le principe général qui recherche une même cause dans une série de mêmes effets, il faudrait apporter des preuves irrécusables, et ces preuves sont encore à donner."

F53. "Le mal s'augmente dans une proportion géométrique."

F54. "Une commotion quelconque."

F55. Respectively "cause première" and "cause originaire."

F56. "Les premiers investigateurs du phénomène, frappés des désastres qui accompagnent la crise, ne considéraient que la crise elle-même, la rupture violente de l'équilibre économique qui s'observe pendant un temps assez court. Ils négligeaient ce qui précède et ce qui suit. On sait aujourd'hui, grâce surtout à Juglar, que la crise est seulement un des moments d'un cycle entier qui se déroule périodiquement, le moment il est vrai le plus douloureux ... La crise est le point d'intersection [entre] la prospérité [et] la dépression. Elle marque l'achèvement de l'une des phases et le début de l'autre ... Aussi ne saurait-on comprendre et expliquer ce qui a lieu à la minute même de la crise sans avoir examiné l'ensemble du cycle: la prospérité qui prépare la crise, la dépression qui se traîne ensuite et qui achemine vers un retour des bonnes années. Quand la matière sera plus connue, on parlera moins des *crises de surproduction* et davantage des *cycles économiques*. Dans les travaux scientifiques, cette seconde expression tendra à se substituer à la première."

F57. "Le cycle est un phénomène collectif, physiologique, vital, situé hors de l'action monétaire; la crise est un phénomène pathologique de dissociation de l'économie, dissociation favorisée par la violence des oscillations cycliques et plus ou moins étroitement liée aux phénomènes monétaires."

F58. "N'y veulent voir qu'une de ces secousses périodiques, une des maladies de croissance qui sont comme l'accompagnement et la rançon de tous les progrès et qui, amenées par le cours naturel des choses, ayant un caractère en quelque sorte fatal, disparaissent d'elles-mêmes."

F59. "La crise doit se terminer en telle année à moins que ce ne soit en telle autre, cela dépend de ce qui va surgir. Une nouvelle crise reviendra à telle époque à moins que ce soit à telle autre; cela résultera de faits à venire."

ACKNOWLEDGMENTS

I am grateful to Cécile Dangel-Hagnauer, Giorgio Colacchio, Pascal Bridel, Philippe Le Gall, Denis O'Brien and to a referee for comments and suggestions on preliminary drafts of this paper and for discussing thoroughly and at length its main thesis. Any remaining mistakes and obscurities are my responsibility.

REFERENCES

References with asterisk indicate attribution of anonymous or initialled writings.

Académie des Sciences Morales et Politiques. (1860). [Prix Bordin. Section d'économie politique et statistique]. *Académie des Sciences Morales et Politiques, Séances et Travaux*, p. 186.
Aftalion, A. (1913). *Les crises périodiques de surproduction, Essai d'une théorie* (2 volumes). Paris: Marcel Rivière.
Åkerman, J. (1932). *Economic progress and economic crises*. London: Macmillan.
American Beacon and Commercial Diary. (1816). Short chapters of hints and advisements on the subject of hard times. *The American Beacon and Commercial Diary*, September 26.
Anderson, A. (1789). *An historical and chronological deduction of the origin of commerce: From the earliest accounts* (Vol. 4, Rev. ed.). London: J. Walter.
*Anderson, W. (1797). *The iniquity of banking, or, bank notes proved to be injurious to the public, and the real cause of the present exorbitant price of provisions*. London: J. S. Jordan.
Anonymous. (1796). *A few reflections upon the present state of commerce and public credit: With some remarks upon the late conduct of the bank of England.* by an old merchant. London: J. Sewell.
Anonymous. (1811). United Parliament of Great Britain and Ireland. *The Morning Chronicle*, February 29, Issue 13358.
Anonymous. (1816). Commercial distress of the country. *Edinburgh Review, 27*(24), 373–391.
Anonymous. (1819a). *An enquiry into the causes of the present commercial embarrassments in the United States with a plan of reform of the circulating medium*, s.n.
Anonymous. (1819b). Commercial fluctuations and embarrassments. *Orleans Gazette and Commercial Advertiser (New Orleans, LA)*, July 27, col. E.
Anonymous. (1825). History of Europe. In: *The annual register, or, a view of the history, politics, and literature for the year 1824*. London: J. Dodsley.
Anonymous. (1826). Commercial embarrassments. *The Times*, January 26, p. 3C.
Anonymous. (1837). Reflections on the causes of commercial embarrassments in the United States. *New-York Spectator*, April 13, col. A.
Anonymous. (1848). Great meeting at Halifax. *The Northern Star and National Trades' Journal (Leeds, England)*, February 5, Issue 537.
Anonymous. (1849a). Handelskrisis. In: *Das grosse Conversations-Lexikon für die gebildeten Stände (Meyers Konversations-Lexikon)* (Vol. 14, p. 1030). Hildburghausen: Bibliographisches Institut.
Anonymous. (1849b). Marriages and abundance. *The Economist, 7*(300, May 26), pp. 573–547.
Anonymous. (1849c). The great question for discussion – The currency. *Liverpool Mercury*, January 9.

Anonymous. (1849d). Jones Loyd's cycle again. *Liverpool Mercury*, December 18.

Anonymous. (1850). The causes of commercial crises. Causes of commercial embarrassments; speculations; California trade; money market, etc. *The Bankers' Magazine and Statistical Register*, 5(1), 1–4.

Anonymous. (1857a). *A brief popular account of all financial panics and commercial revulsions in the United States from 1690 to 1857*. New York: Haney.

Anonymous. (1857b). Concerning the panic. *Reynolds's Newspaper (London)*, November 15, Issue 379.

Anonymous. (1858). *Cause première de toutes les crises sociales, financières, alimentaires, industrielles, etc.*, Paris: Dentu.

Anonymous. (1860). Credit and banking. *The Independent: Devoted to the Consideration of Politics, Social and Economic Tendencies, History, Literature, and the Arts (New York)*, 12(615), p. 8.

Anonymous. (1862). Diagram showing the fluctuations in the imperial average price of wheat, weekly, during the year 1861. *Estates Gazette*, London.

Anonymous. (1863). Diagram showing the fluctuations in the imperial average price of wheat, weekly, during the year 1862. *Estates Gazette*, London.

Anonymous. (1875). Monetary panics and the board of trade. *The Bankers' Magazine and Statistical Register*, 10(1), 1–3.

Anonymous. (1879a). Financial and commercial history of 1878. *Journal of the Statistical Society of London*, 42(1), 276–305.

Anonymous. (1879b). Dinner at the Oxford liberal associations. *Jackson's Oxford Journal*, (656).

Anonymous. (1886). Depression of trade and prices of commodities. *Bankers' Magazine (London)*, 46, 465–471

Armatte, M. (1992). Conjonctions, conjoncture, et conjecture. Les baromètres économiques (1885–1930). *Histoire & Mesure*, 7(1), 99–149.

Armatte, M. (2003). Cycles and barometers: Historical insights into the relationship between an object and its measurement. *Papers and proceedings of the colloquium on the history of business-cycle analysis*, Office for Official Publications of the European Community, Luxemburg (pp. 45–74).

Arnon, A. (1991). *Thomas Tooke: Pioneer on monetary theory*. Aldershot, UK: Edward Elgar.

Ashton, T. S. ([1934] 1977). *Economic and social investigations in Manchester, 1833–1933: A centenary history of the Manchester Statistical Society*. Hassocks: Harvester Press.

Attwood, M. (1817). *Observations concerning the distress of the country: January 1816 and 1817*. London: Thomas Wilson.

*Bagehot, W. (1873a). The very peculiar position of the year 1873. *The Economist*, 31(January 4), pp. 1–3.

Bagehot, W. (1873b). *Lombard street: A description of the money market*. London: King.

*Bagehot, W. (1874). The probable money market of 1874. *The Economist*, 32(January 3), 1–3.

Baker, H. (1876). Observations on a continuation table and chart, shewing the 'balance of accounts between the mercantile public and the bank of England, 1844–75, with special reference to its course in the years 1866–75'. *Transactions of the Manchester Statistical Society*, session 1875–76, pp. 203–221.

Balfour, D. M. (1848). The present commercial crisis. *Hunt's Merchants' Magazine*, 18(5), 477–488.

Bankers' Magazine. (1848). [Note appended to Lawson 1848b]. *Bankers' Magazine (London)*, 8, p. 420.

Baring, F. (1801). *Observations on the publication of Walter Boyd, Esq. M.P.* London: Lane.

Bastiat, F. (1860). *Harmonies of political economy.* P. J. Stirling (Trans.). London: Murray.

Baudin, L. (1936). La crise et le pouvoir d'achat. *Revue des deux mondes,* May 1, CVI(33), 180–192.

Beaude, J. P. (1849). "Introduction" to Beaude. *Dictionnaire de Médecine Usuelle,* Didier, Paris.

Bell, G. M. (1850). History of English panics. *Hunt's Merchants' Magazine, 23*(6), pp. 604–610.

Beniger, J. R., & Robyn, D. L. (1978). Quantitative graphics in statistics: A brief history. *The American Statitsician, 32*(1), 1–11.

Bernhard, R. C. (1943). Myths and illogic in popular notions about business cycles. *Journal of Political Economy, 51*(1), 53–60.

Besomi, D. (2006a). 'Marxism gone mad': Tugan-Baranovsky on crises, their possibility and periodicity. *Review of Political Economy, 18*(2), 147–171.

Besomi, D. (2006b). Tendency to equilibrium, the possibility of crisis, and the history of business cycle theories. *History of Economic Ideas, 14*(2), 53–104.

Besomi, D. (2006c). Formal modelling vs. insight in Kalecki's theory of the business cycle. *Research in the History of Economic Thought and Methodology, 24A,* 1–48.

Besomi, D. (2008a). 'Hath rain a father?' Sunspots and the periodicity of panics: Jevons, his critics, and an harbinger in the press. *Storia del Pensiero Economico, 5*(1), 169–179.

Besomi, D. (2008b). James Anthony Lawson on commercial panics and their periodical recurrence. *Structural Change and Economic Dynamics, 19*(4), 330–341.

Besomi, D. (2008c). John Wade's early endogenous dynamic model: 'Commercial cycle' and theories of crises. *European Journal of the History of Economic Thought, 15*(4), 611–639.

Besomi, D. (2010a). Paper money and national distress: William Huskisson and the early theories of credit, speculation and crises. *European Journal of the History of Economic Thought, 17*(1), 49–85.

Besomi, D. (2010b). The periodicity of crises: A perusal of the early literature. *Journal of the History of Economic Thought, 32*(1), 85–132.

Besomi, D. (2010c). *The fabrication of a myth: Clément Juglar's commercial crises in the secondary literature.* Unpublished manuscript.

Besomi, D. (2011). Disease of the body politick. A metaphor for crises in the history of nineteenth century economics. *Journal of the History of Economic Thought, 33*(1).

Besomi, D., & Colacchio, G. (2010). Auguste Ott on commercial crises and distributive justice: An early input-output scheme. *Review of Political Economy, 22*(1), 75–96.

Black, R. D. C. (1992). Dr. Kondratieff and Mr. Hyde Clarke. *Research in the History of Economic Thought and Methodology, 9,* 35–58.

Blanqui, A. (1836). Crise commerciale. In: *Encyclopédie des gents du monde* (Vol. 7, pp. 257–259). Paris: Librairie de Treuttel et Würtz.

Boccardo, G. (1857). Crisi. In: G. Boccardo (Ed.), *Dizionario della economia politica e del commercio così teorico come pratico: utile non solo allo scienziato ed al pubblico amministratore ma eziandio al commerciante, al banchiere, all'agricoltore ed al capitalista* (Vol. 1, pp. 731–738). Torino: Sebastiano Franco e figli.

Boccardo, G. (1879). *Trattato teoretico-pratico di Economia Politica* (6th ed.). Torino: Roux and Favale.

Bonnet, V. (1859). *Questions économiques et financières à propos des crises.* Paris: Guillaumin.

Bonnet, V. (1865). Enquête sur le crédit et la crise de 1863–64. *Revue des Deux Mondes,* November 15 and December 1, XCVI, 682–698.

Boston Board of Trade. (1858). Causes of the commercial crisis: Report of the Boston board of trade. *The Bankers' Magazine and Statistical Register, 7*(11), 849–853.

Boyd, W. (1801). *A letter to the right honourable William Pitt: On the influence of the stoppage of issues in specie at the Bank of England, on the prices of provisions, and other commodities.* London: J. Wright.

Brand, F. (1800). *A determination of the average depression of the price of wheat in war, below that of the preceding peace and of its readvance in the following; according to its yearly rates from the Revolution to the end of the last peace: With remarks on their greater variations in that period.* London: Rivington.

*Bray, J. F. (1836), Association of all classes of all nations, Sunday, February 21. *New Moral World*, February 27, pp. 137–138.

Briaune, J.-E. (1840). *Des crises commerciales. De leur causes et de leur remèdes.* Paris: Bouchard-Huzard.

Briaune, J.-E. (1857). *Du prix du grain, du libre échange et des réserves.* Paris: Didot.

Bouniatian, M. (1922). *Les crises économiques: Essai de morphologie et théorie des crises économiques périodiques et de théorie de la conjoncture économique.* Paris: Giard.

Canguilhem, G. ([1966] 1991). *The normal and the pathological.* New York: Zone Books.

Carey, M. (1823). *The crisis.* Philadelphia, PA: Carey and Lea.

Cargill, W. (1845). *The currency, showing how a fixed gold standard places England in permanent disadvantage and produces periodical domestic convulsion.* London: Olliver.

Carter, K. C. (2003). *The rise of causal concepts of disease: Case histories.* Burlington, VT: Ashgate.

Cassel, G. (1932). *Crisis in the world's monetary system.* Oxford: Oxford University Press.

Cheysson, É. (1878). Les méthodes de la statistique graphique à l'exposition universelle de 1878. *Journal de la Société de Statistique de Paris, 19,* 323–333.

Chitti, L. (1839). *Des Crises Financières et de le Réforme du Système Monétaire.* Brussels: Meline.

Clarke, H. (1838). On the mathematical law of the cycle. *The Railway Magazine and the Annals of Science, 5*(November), 378–380.

Clarke, H. ([1847] 1999). Physical economy – A preliminary inquiry into the physical laws governing the periods of famine and panic. In: F. Louçã & J. Reijnders (Eds), *The foundations of long wave theory: Models and methodology* (Vol. 1, pp. 3–20). Cheltenham, UK: Elgar.

Clément, A. (1858). Des crises commerciales. *Journal des Économistes, 17*(February), 161–191.

Cobden, R. (1859). Translator's preface. In: M. Chevalier (Ed.), *On the probable fall in the value of gold, the commercial and social consequences which May ensue, and the measures which it invites.* Manchester: Alexr Ireland.

Cock, S. (1810). *An examination of the report of the bullion committee: Shewing that the present high price of bullion, together with the scarcity of gold coin, and also the low rate of the foreign exchanges, are not attributable to the issue of bank paper; and explaining what are the true causes by which these effects have been produced.* London: Richardson and Hatchard.

*Cockburn, R. (1840). *Remarks suggested by the present state of trade and credit.* London: E. Wilson.

*Colquhoun, P. (1793). *Reflections on the causes which have produced the present distress in commercial credit.* London: J. Sewell, J. Debrett and J. Downes.

Commons, J. R., McCracken, H. L., & Zeuch, W. E. (1922). Secular trends and business cycles: A classification of theories. *Review of Economic Statistics, 4*(4), 244–263.

Cooke, L. (1827). *A series of statistical charts shewing the fluctuations in quantity and value of the products of the Soil, with various ascertainments obviously influential on the husbandry of the British Empire, founded on official and other authentic documents.* London: The Author.

Coquelin, C. (1848). Les Crises Commerciales et la Liberté des Banques. *Revue des Deux Mondes*, 26(November 1), 445–470.

Coquelin, C. (1849). The causes of commercial crises. *Hunt's Merchants' Magazine*, 21(October), pp. 371–388.

Coquelin, C. (1850). Restrictions on banking the cause of commercial crises. *Bankers' Magazine (London)*, 10, pp. 219–227, 308–313 [Abridged translation of Coquelin (1848)].

Coquelin, C. (1852a). Crises commerciales. In: C. Coquelin & G.-U. Guillaumin (Eds), *Dictionnaire de l'Économie Politique*. Paris: Guillaumin.

Coquelin, C. (1852b). Crédit. In: C. Coquelin & G.-U. Guillaumin (Eds), *Dictionnaire de l'Économie Politique*. Paris: Guillaumin.

Corbet, T. (1841). *An inquiry into the causes and modes of the wealth of individuals, or, the principles of trade and speculation explained*. London: Smith, Elder & Co.

Cory, I. P. (1842). *Competition: Its abuse one of the chief causes of the present distress among the trading, manufacturing, and commercial classes: With suggestions for remedying it*. London: Painter.

Courcelle-Seneuil, J. G. (1858). *Traité théorique et pratique d'économie politique*. Paris: Amyot.

*Courcelle-Seneuil, J. G. (1860). Crise. In: L.-A. Garnier-Pagès (Ed.), *Dictionnaire politique: encyclopédie du langage et de la science politique*. Paris: E. Duclerc et Pagnerre.

*Currie, J. (1793). *A letter, commercial and political, addressed to the Rt. Hon. William Pitt: In which the real interests of Britain in the present crisis are considered and some observations are offered on the general state of Europe*, by Jasper Wilson (pseudonym), Printed for P. Byrne and J. Moore, Dublin.

Daily Herald. (1837). Speculation and overtrading. *Daily Herald and Gazette (Cleveland, OH)*, May 2, Issue 282, col. C.

Danson, J. T. (1848). A contribution towards an investigation of the changes which have taken place in the condition of the people of the United Kingdom during the eight years extending from the harvest of 1889 to the harvest of 1847; and an attempt to develop the connexion (if any), between the changes observed and the variations occurring during the same period in the prices of the most necessary articles of food. *Journal of the Statistical Society of London*, 11(2), 101–140.

Deblock, C. (2000). *Le cycle des affaires et la prévision économique. Les instituts de conjoncture et la méthode des 'baromètres' dans l'entre-deux-guerres*. Working paper, Groupe de recherche, sur l'intégration continentale, Université du Québec à Montréal, Département de science politique, Notes et études en EPI, January.

Defoe, D. (1726). *The complete English tradesman, in familiar letters; directing him in all the several parts and progressions of trade. ... Calculated for the instruction of our inland tradesmen; and especially of young beginners*. London: Charles Rivington.

Della Bona, G. (1888). *Delle crisi economiche*. Torino: Bocca.

Ducheyne, S. (2006). Galileo's interventionist notion of 'cause'. *Journal of the History of Ideas*, 67(3), 443–464.

Duncan, W. B. (1842). *Mercantile embarrassments, and the present state of the banking system*. Edinburgh: John Johnstone.

Duncan, W. J. (1867). *Notes on the rate of discount in London from January 1856 to August 1866: With sketch since the crises of 1847*. Edinburgh: Muir and Paterson.

Dupin, C. (1846). Crise commerciale. In: *Encyclopédie du dix-neuvième siècle* (Vol. 9, pp. 308–311). Paris: Bureau de l'Encyclopédie du dix-neuvième siècle.

Dupont de Nemours, P. S. ([1806] 1811). Sur la Banque de France, les causes de la crise qu'elle a éprouvé. London: J. Hatchard.

Duthy, J. (1801). *The different effects of peace and war on the price of bread corn, considered, in an examination of principles attempted to be established, from the yearly rates of the market, by J. Brand, etc.*, Winchester.

Ellison, T. (1962). *Diagram showing the fluctuations in the prices of 'Fair' Pernam, 'Middling' New Orleans & 'Fair' Surat Cotton from 1820 to 1862, etc.*, London.

Engels, F. (1847). The commercial crises in England. – The Chartist Movement. – Ireland. *La Réforme*, October 26.

England, M. T. (1913). Economic crises. *Journal of Political Economy, 21*(4), 345–354.

Evans, D. M. (1848). *The commercial crisis 1847–48*. London: Lett.

Evans, D. M. (1859). *The history of commercial crises, 1857–58 and the stock exchange panic of 1859*. London: Groombridge.

Ferrara, F. ([1864] 1890). Delle crisi economiche. In: *Esame storico-critico di economisti e dottrine economiche del secolo XVIIIe prima metà del XIX. Raccolta delle prefazioni dettate dal Professore Francesco Ferrara* (Vol. 2). Torino: UTET.

Fischer, W. (1911). *Das Problem der Wirtschaftskrisen im Lichte der neuesten nationalökonomischen Forschung*. Karlsruhe: Braun.

Foville, A. de (1879). Les tâches du soleil et les crises commerciales. *L'Économiste Français, 7*, February 15, pp. 191–193, and March 1, pp. 257–259.

Foville, A. de (1888). Essai de météorologic economique et sociale. *Journal de la Societé de Statistique de Paris, 29*, 243–249.

Foville, A. de (1905). Clément Juglar. *Economic Journal, 15*(58), 293–298.

Foxwell, H. S. (1884). Appendix on the theory of cycles. In: W. S. Jevons & H. S. Foxwell (Eds), *Investigations in currency and finance* (pp. 361–362). London: Macmillan.

Foxwell, H. S. (1886). *Irregularity of employment and fluctuations of prices*. Edinburgh: Co-operative Printing Company.

*Francis, J. (1853). Commercial excitements and crises. *The Eclectic Magazine of Foreign Literature, 28*(4), 471–477.

Frend, W. (1801). *The effect of paper money on the price of provisions: Or, the point in dispute between Mr. Boyd and Sir Francis Baring examined: The bank paper money proved to be an adequate cause for the high price of provisions: Constitutional remedies recommended*. London: J. Ridway.

Frisch, R. (1933). Propagation problems and impulse problems in dynamic economics. In: *Economic essays in honour of Gustav Cassel* (pp. 171–205). London: Allen & Unwin.

Frobert, L., & Hamouda, O. (2008). The influence of medicine on Juglar's first take on the economic cycle 1846–1862. *Journal of the History of Economic Thought, 30*(2), 173–198.

Funkhouser, H. G. (1937). Historical development of the graphical representation of statistical data. *Osiris, 3*, 269–404.

Gallatin, A. (1831). *Considerations on the currency and banking system of the United States*. Philadelphia, PA: Carey & Lea.

Ganilh, C. (1826). Spéculation. *Dictionnaire Analytique d'Économie Politique*. Paris: Ladvocat.

Garnier, J. (1845). *Elements de l'économie politique. Exposé des notions fondamentales de cette science et de l'organisation économique de la société*. Paris: Garnier/Guillaumin.

Garnier, J. (1859). Crises commerciales. In: G.-U. Guillaumin (Ed.), *Dictionnaire universel théorique et pratique du commerce et de la navigation*. Paris: Guillaumin.

Gide, C. (1890). The economic schools and the teaching of political economy in France. *Political Science Quarterly, 5*(4), 603–635.

Giffen, R. (1885). Trade depression and low prices. *Contemporary Review, 47*(June), 800–822.

Glasner, D. (1989). On some classical monetary controversies. *History of Political Economy, 21*(2), 201–229.

Great Britain Parliament, House of Commons. (1793). *Jordan's Parliamentary Journal for the year MDCCXCIII being an accurate and impartial history of the debates and proceedings of both Houses of Parliament, from the opening of the Session on the Thirteenth day of December, 1792* (Vol. 3). London: J. S. Jordan.

Groenewegen, P. (2001). Joseph Clément Juglar (1819–1905): From physician to analyst of business cycles. In: P. Groenewegen (Ed.), *Physicians and political economy: Six studies of the work of doctor-economists*. London: Routledge.

Guéroult. (1831). *De la Banque de France et du Crédit considéré comme moyen de soustraire le pays aux crises commerciales*. Paris: s.n.

Guitton, H. (1951). *Les fluctuations économiques*. Paris: Recuiel Sirey.

Guitton, H. (1956). Cycles. In: J. Romeuf (Ed.), *Dictionnaire des sciences économiques* (pp. 365–366). Paris: Presse Universitaires de France.

Guthrie, W. (1864). Introduction. In: G. Guthrie (Ed.), *Bank monopoly the cause of commercial crises*. Edinburgh: Blackwood.

Hagemann, H. (2002). *Business cycle theory: Selected texts, 1860–1939* (Vols. 1–4). London: Pickering & Chatto.

Hardy, A. (1849). Maladie. In: J.-P. Beaude (Ed.), *Dictionnaire de Médecine Usuelle*. Paris: Didier.

Hare, R. (1852). Do banks increase loanable capital? *Hunt's Merchants' Magazine, 26*(6), pp. 702–706.

Hawtrey, R. G. (1913). *Good and bad trade: An inquiry into the causes of trade fluctuations*. London: Constable.

Henderson, J. P. (1992). Astronomy, astrology, and business cycles: Hyde Clarke's contribution. *Research in the History of Economic Thought and Methodology, 9*, 1–34.

Howard, J. P. (1863). *Howard's gold chart; showing at a glance all the fluctuations in the price of gold from January 1, 1862, to the present date, and arranged so that any one can continue it from day to day*. Compiled by Joseph P. Howard. New York: Andrews & Co.

Hoyle, W. (1877). *On the causes of bad trade*. London: Simpkin, Marshall, and Co.; Manchester: John Heywood.

Huskisson, W. (1810). *The question concerning the depreciation of our currency stated and examined* (4th ed.). London: John Murray.

Huskisson, W. (1826). Free trade: Speech of the Right Hon. W. Huskisson in the House of Commons, Thursday, the 23d of February, 1826, on Mr. Ellice's motion for a select committee to inquire into and examine the statements contained in the various petitions from persons engaged in the silk manufacture. In: *Hansard, The Parliamentary debates*, New Series, Vol. 14, 2 February–17 March (pp. 763–809).

*Huskisson, W. (1830). *Essays in political economy: In which are illustrated the principal causes of the present national distress; with appropriate remedies*. London: Longman, Rees, Orme, Brown, & Green.

Hutchison, T. W. (1953). *A review of economic doctrines 1870–1929*. Oxford: Clarendon Press.

*Innes, C. N. (1848). Review of *The statistical account of Scotland; drawn up from the communications of the ministers of the different Parishes*; and *The new statistical account of Scotland. Quarterly Review, 82*(164), 342–390.

Jamieson, A. (1829). Medicine. In: A. Jamieson (Ed.), *A dictionary of mechanical science, arts, manufactures, and miscellaneous knowledge* (Vol. 2, pp. 649–650). London: Henry Fisher & Sons.

Jevon, W. S. (1977). Papers and correspondence of William Stanley Jevons (Vol. 4), Correspondence, 1873–1878, and Correspondence, 1879–1882 (Vol. 5). R. D. C. Black (Ed.). London: Macmillan.

Jevons, W. S. ([1862] 1884). On the study of periodical commercial fluctuations. In: H. S. Foxwell (Ed.), *Investigations in currency and finance* (pp. 3–11). London: Macmillan.

Jevons, W. S. ([1863] 1884). A serious fall in the value of gold ascertained, and its social effects set forth. In: H. S. Foxwell (Ed.), *Investigations in currency and finance* (pp. 13–118). London: Macmillan.

Jevons, W. S. ([1869] 1883). Inaugural address as president of the Manchester statistical society on the work of the society in connection with the questions of the day, read November 10th, 1869. In: W. S. Jevons (Ed.), *Methods of social reform, and other papers*. London: Macmillan.

Jevons, W. S. (1874). *The principles of science: A treatise on logic and scientific method*. London: Macmillan.

Jevons, W. S. ([1875] 1884). The solar period and the price of corn. In: H. S. Foxwell (Ed.), *Investigations in currency and finance* (pp. 194–205). London: Macmillan.

Jevons, W. S. ([1878a] 1884). The periodicity of comemrcial crises and its physical explanation. In: H. S. Foxwell (Ed.), *Investigations in currency and finance* (pp. 206–220). London: Macmillan.

Jevons, W. S. ([1878b] 1884). Commercial crises and sun-spots. In: H. S. Foxwell (Ed.), *Investigations in currency and finance* (pp. 221–235). London: Macmillan.

Jevons, W. S. (1879). Sun-spots and commercial crises. *The Times*, April 19.

Jevons, W. S. (1884). In: H. S. Foxwell (Ed.), *Investigations in currency and finance*. London: Macmillan.

Jones, E. D. (1900). *Economic crises*. London: Macmillan.

Joplin, T. (1841). *The cause and cure of our commercial embarrassments*. London: Ridgway.

Joplin, W. (1854). *A letter on fluctuations in the money market chiefly with the view of explaining the nature of those violent pressures termed panics, addressed to the Bank of England* (2nd ed.). London: Hamilton, Adams.

Juglar, C. (1852). De la population en France de 1725 à nos jours (1849). *Journal des Économistes*, *31*(129), 75–80 and *32*(133–134), 54–77.

Juglar, C. (1856). Des crises commerciales en France de l'an VIII à 1855. *Annuaire de l'économie politique et de la statistique*, *13*, 555–581.

Juglar, C. (1857). Des crises commerciales et monetaires de 1800 à 1857. *Journal des Économistes*, 2nd series, No. 40, pp. 35–60, and No. 41, pp. 255–267.

Juglar, C. (1862). *Des Crises Commerciales et de leur retour périodique en France, en Angleterre et aux États-Unis*. Paris: Guillaumin.

Juglar, C. (1863). Crises commerciales. In: M. Block (Ed.), *Dictionnaire général de la Politique* (pp. 615–627). Paris: O. Lorenz. (Translated in this volume as Chapter 5).

Juglar, C. (1868). *Du change et de la liberté d'émission*. Paris: Guillaumin.

Juglar, C. (1873). Crises commerciales. In: M. Block (Ed.), *Dictionnaire général de la Politique* (2nd ed., Vol. 1, pp. 586–598). Paris: O. Lorenz. (Translated in this volume as Chapter 5).

Juglar, C. (1877). La liquidation de la crise de 1873 et la reprise des affaires. *Journal des Économistes*, 3rd series, No. 141, pp. 372–382. (Translated in this volume as Chapter 6).

Juglar, C. (1882). Tableaux graphiques des crises commerciales et de leurs retours périodiques d'après les bilans de la Banque de France. *Académie des Sciences Morales et Politiques, Séances et travaux*, New series, No. 17, Vol. 42, 1st sem., pp. 698–718.

Juglar, C. (1886). Des Retours périodiques des crises commeriales et de leurs liquidations. In: *Le 25e Anniversaire de la Société de Statistique de Paris. Compte Rendu des Séances* (pp. 74–84). Paris: Berger-Levrault.

Juglar, C. (1889). *Des Crises Commerciales et de leur retour périodique en France, en Angleterre et aux États-Unis* (2nd ed.). Paris: Alcan.

Juglar, C. (1891). Crises commerciales. In: L. Say & J. Chailley (Eds), *Nouveau Dictionnaire d'Économie Politique*. Paris: Guillaumin.

Juglar, C. (1893). A brief history of panics and their periodical occurrence in the United States. Edited and Englished by D. W. Thom. New York: Putnam.

Juglar, C. (1900a). Les crises commerciales et financières et les crises économiques générales. Paper read before the Congrès International des Valeurs Mobilières, Imprimerie Paul Dupont, Paris.

Juglar, C. (1900b). Crises commerciales. In: L. Say & J. Chailley (Eds), *Nouveau Dictionnaire d'Économie Politique* (2nd ed., pp. 641–651). Paris: Guillaumin. (Translated in this volume as Chapter 6).

Juglar, C. (1900c). *Retours périodiques des crises commerciales (diagram)*, Imprimerie Dufrinoy, Paris.

Juglar, C., & Cullet, P.-J. (Eds). (1865). *Extraits des Enquêtes parlementaires anglaises sur les questions de banque, de circulation monétaire et de crédit*. Volumes 8, Furne, Paris.

Juglar, C., & des Essart, P. (1889). Crises financières et commerciales. In: L. Say (Ed.), *Dictionnaire des Finances* (pp. 1348–1355). Paris, Nancy: Berger-levrault.

Kalecki, M. (1935). A macrodynamic theory of the business cycle. *Econometrica*, 3(3), 327–344.

Kalecki, M. (1968). Trend and business cycles reconsidered. *Economic Journal*, 78(310), 263–276.

Keynes, J. M. ([1934] 1973). Poverty in plenty: Is the economic system self-adjusting. In: D. E. Moggridge (Ed.), *The collected writings of John Maynard Keynes, Vol. 13, The general theory and after, Part 1* (pp. 485–492). London: Macmillan.

Keynes, J. M. ([1936] 1972). William Stanley Jevons. In: D. E. Moggridge (Ed.), *The collected writings of J. M. Keynes* (Vol. 10, pp. 109–160). London: Macmillan.

Keynes, J. M. ([1936] 1973). The general theory of employment, interest and money. In: *The collected writings of J. M. Keynes* (Vol. 7). London: Macmillan.

Kinnear, J. G. (1847). *The crisis and currency: With a comparison between the English and Scottish systems of banking* (2nd ed.). London: Murray.

Klein, J. L. (1995). The method of diagrams and the black art of inductive economics. In: I. H. Rima (Ed.), *Measurement, quantification and economic analysis: Numeracy in economics* (pp. 98–139). London: Routledge.

Klein, J. L. (1997). *Statistical visions in time: A history of time series analysis 1662–1938*. Cambridge: Cambridge University Press.

Klein, J. L. (2001). Reflections from the age of economic measurement. In: J. L. Klein & M. S. Morgan (Eds), *The age of economic measurement* (pp. 111–136). Durham, NC: Duke University Press.

Koertge, N. (1977). Galileo and the problem of accidents. *Journal of the History of Ideas*, 38(3), 389–408.

Kuznets, S. (1930). Equilibrium economics and business cycles theory. *Quarterly Journal of Economics*, 44(3), 381–415.

Lagasquie, A. (1849). Causes. In: J.-P. Beaude (Ed.), *Dictionnaire de Médecine Usuelle* (p. 313). Paris: Didier.

Laidler, D. (1987). The bullionist controversy. In: J. Eatwell, M. Milgate & P. Newman (Eds), *The new Palgrave: A dictionary of economics*. London: Macmillan.

Langton, W. (1857). Observations on a table shewing the balance of accounts between the mercantile public and the Bank of England. *Transactions of the Manchester Statistical Society*, Session 1857–1858, pp. 9–22.

Laveleye, E. de (1865). *Le marché monétaire et ses crises depuis cinquante ans*. Paris: Guillaumin.

Laveleye, E. de (1885). Crise. In: H. D. Berthelot, F.-C. Dreyfus, et al. (Eds.), *La grande encyclopédie: inventaire raisonné des sciences, des lettres et des arts* (Vol. 13, pp. 380–385). Paris: H. Lamirault.

Lawson, J. A. (1844). *Five lectures on political economy: Delivered before the University of Dublin, in Michaelmas Term, 1843*. London: Parker.

Lawson, J. A. (1848a). *On commercial panics: a paper read before the Dublin Statistical Society*, Dublin.

Lawson, J. A. (1848b). The cause of commercial panics. *Bankers' Magazine (London)*, 8, pp. 415–420.

Lawson, J. A. (1848c). The cause of commercial panics. *Hunt's Merchants' Magazine*, 19, p. 282.

Le Gall, P. (2006). L'*astronomie sociale* de Jean-Edmond Briaune. In: J. P. Simonin (Ed.), *Jean Edmond Briaune (1798–1885): Cultivateur, agronome, économiste*. Angers: Presses Universitaires d'Angers.

Le Van-Lemesle, L. (2004). *Le juste ou le riche. L'einsegnement de l'économie politique 1815–1950*. Paris: Comité pour l'histoire économique det financière de la France.

Ledru-Rollin, A. A. (1850). *The decline of England* (2nd ed.). London: Churton.

Leroy-Beaulieu, P. (1886). La Baisse des Prix et la Crise Commerciale dans le Monde; Causes Alléguées, remèdes proposés. *Revue des Deux Mondes*, 56(3), 383–418.

Lemonnier, C. (1835). Crises commerciales. In: *Dictionnaire de la conversation et de la lecture* (Vol. 18, p. 218). Paris: Belin-Mandar.

Lescure, J. (1907). *Des crises générales et périodiques de surproduction*. Paris: Domat-Montchrestien.

Lescure, J. (1932). *Des crises générales et périodiques de surproduction* (4th ed.). Paris: Domat-Montchrestien.

*Leslie, C. (1864). Alleged commercial decades or cycles (by 'A Political Economist'). *The Economist*, November 19, pp. 1428–1429, and December 24, pp. 1577–1578.

Link, R. G. (1959). *English theories of economic fluctuations 1815–1848*. New York: Columbia University Press.

Long, C. (1800). *A temperate discussion of the causes which have led to the present high price of bread: addressed to the plain sense of the people*. London: J. Wright.

Longfield, S. M. (1840). Banking and currency. *Dublin University Magazine*, 15(85), pp. 1–15; 15(86), pp. 218–233; 16(94), pp. 371–389; and 16(96), pp. 611–620.

Louçã, F. (2001). Intriguing pendula: Founding metaphors in the analysis of economic fluctuations. *Cambridge Journal of Economics*, 25(1), 25–55.

Maas, H. (2005). *William Stanley Jevons and the making of modern economics*. Cambridge: Cambridge University Press.

Maas, H., & Morgan, M. S. (2002). Timing history: The introduction of graphical analysis in 19th century British economics. *Revue d'Histoire des Sciences Humaines* (7), 97–127.

Macleod, H. D. (1863). Crisis, commercial. In: *Dictionary of political economy: Biographical, bibliographical, historical, and practical.* London: Longmans.

Malthus, T. R. (1815). *Observations on the effects of the corn laws and of a rise or fall in the price of corn on the agriculture and general wealth of the country* (3rd ed.). London: Murray.

*Malthus, T. R. (1800). *An investigation of the cause of the present high price of provisions.* London: J. Johnson.

*Malthus, T. R. (1826). Review of *Thoughts and details on the high and low prices of the last thrity years,* by T. Tooke. *Quarterly Review, 29*(April), 214–239.

Marcy, G. (1946). La théorie des crises chez les socialistes français au XIXe siècle. In: *Mélanges économiques dédiés à M. le Professeur Gonnard* (pp. 261–274). Paris: Librairie Générale de Droit et de Jurisprudence.

Marshall, A. ([1887] 1925). Remedies for fluctuations of general prices. In: A. C. Pigou (Ed.), *Memorials of Alfred Marshall* (pp. 188–211). London: Macmillan.

Marx, K. ([1857–58] 1973). *Grundrisse: Foundations of the critique of political economy.* M. Nicolaus (Trans.). Harmondsworth, UK: Penguin.

Marx, K. ([1859] 1971). *A contribution to the critique of political economy.* London: Lawrence and Wishart.

Marx, K. ([1862–63] 1969). *Theories of surplus value.* London: Lawrence and Wishart.

Marx, K. ([1867–94] 1974). *Capital: A critique of political economy.* London: Lawrence and Wishart.

Marx, K., & Engels, F. (1967). *Werke* (vol. 29). Berlin: Dietz.

*McCulloch, J. R. (1819). Commercial embarrassments and trade with France. *Edinburgh Review, 32*(63), 48–74.

*McCulloch, J. R. (1822). Agricultural distress: Causes-remedies. *Edinburgh Review, 36*(72), 452–482.

*McCulloch, J. R. (1826a). Thoughts on banking. Fluctuations in the supply and value of money, banking system of England. *Edinburgh Review, 43*(86), 263–298.

*McCulloch, J. R. (1826b). Commercial revulsions [review of *The Late Crisis in the Money Market Impartially Considered*]. *Edinburgh Review, 44*(87), 70–93.

McCulloch, H. (1867). Letter of the Hon. Hugh McCulloch to Gray. *The North American Review, 105*(216), 275–280.

Meyer, E. L. (1865). *Chart of the fluctuations of the price of gold. With the important events, financial measures, rumors, etc.,* New York.

Mill, J. S. ([1826] 1967). Paper currency and commercial distress. In: J. M. Robson (Ed.), *The collected works of J.S. Mill* (Vol. 4, pp. 71–123). Toronto: University of Toronto Press.

Mill, J. S. ([1844] 1967). Essays on some unsettled questions of political economy. In: J. M. Robson (Ed.), *The collected works of J.S. Mill* (Vol. 4). Toronto: University of Toronto Press.

Mill, J. S. ([1848] 1965). Principles of political economy, with some of the their applications to social philosophy. In: V. W. Bladen & J. M. Robson (Eds.), *The collected works of J.S. Mill* (Vols. 2 and 3). Toronto: University of Toronto Press.

Mills, J. (1868). On credit cycles and the origin of commercial panics. *Transactions of the Manchester Statistical Society,* Session 1867–1868, pp. 5–40.

Miller, H. E. (1927). *Banking theories in the United States Before 1860.* Cambridge: Harvard University Press.

Millot, L. (1837). *Études sur les principales causes des crises commerciales et périodiques.* Paris: E. Legrand et Descauriet.

Mitchell, W. C. ([1913] 1941). *Business cycles.* Berkeley: University of California Press.

Mitchell, W. C. (1927). *Business cycles: The problem and its settings.* New York: National Bureau of Economic Research.

Mitchell, W. C. ([1927] 1969). The inter-relation of monetary practices, economic theory and business cycles. In: J. Dorfman (Ed.), *Types of economic theory: From mercantilism to institutionalism* (Vol. II, pp. 831–836). New York: Kelly.

Molinari, G. de (1847). La Crise financière et commerciale en Angleterre. *Journal des Économistes, 17*(1st Series), 274–284.

Moore, H. L. (1908). The statistical complement of pure economics. *Quarterly Journal of Economics, 23*(1), 1–33.

Morgan, M. S. (1990). *The history of econometric ideas.* Cambridge: Cambridge University Press.

Myrdal, G. (1939). *Monetary equilibrium.* London: Hodges.

Numann-Spallart, F. X. de (1886). Mesure des variations de l'état économique et social des peuples. *Bulletin de l'Institut international de statistique (Rome), 2*(1), 150–159.

New York Herald. (1857). Financial panics. Causes of these periodical disturbances. Chronological account of the great monetary revulsions in England and in the United States. The great railway schemes. Over-trading, over-banking, over-dressing, and over-building. Corn and cotton speculations. Extravagance and bankruptcy, &c. *New York Herald,* November 9, pp. 1 and 4.

New-York Spectator. (1826). Commercial revulsions. *New-York Spectator,* September 29, col. A. [Article composed of extracts from *McCulloch (1826b)].

New-York Spectator. (1840). Overtrading and speculation. *New-York Spectator,* August 26, col. D.

Niehans, J. (1992). Juglar's credit cycles. *History of Political Economy, 24*(3), 545–569.

Noyes, A. D. (1908). The cycle of prosperity. *Century, 75*(4), 629–633.

Obert, H., & Van Langenhove. (1857). *Des crises financières et de leur extinction.* Paris: Firmin-Didot.

Oppenheimer, F. (1911). Normalität und Krise. *Archiv für Rechts- und Wirtschaftsphilosophie, 5*(1), 144–161.

Ott, A. (1851). *Traité d'économie Sociale ou l'économie politique coordonnée au point de vue du progrès.* Paris: Renou.

Ott, A. (1854). Crise. In: A. Ott (Ed.), *Dictionnaire des sciences politiques et sociales comprenant la politique, la diplomatie, le droit naturel, le droit ds gens, les rapports de l'Eglise et de l'Etat, l'administration, les finances, la police, la force armée, l'économie politique et la statistique: avec le texte ou le résumé des traités les plus importants, des constitutions et lois fondamentales des peuples anciens et modernes, et l'analyse des principaux ouvrages sur la politique et les autres sciences sociales.* Paris: Migne.

Overstone, *Loyd, S. J. (1837). *Reflections suggested by a perusal of Mr. John Palmer's pamphlet on the causes and consequences of the pressure on the money market.* London: Richardson.

Owen, R. (1836). Address to the imperial parliament of Great Britain. *New Moral World* (February 27), 138–139.

Passy, F. (1905). [Obituary of Juglar]. *Journal des économistes, 64*(Series 6), 420–421.

Peart, S. J. (1995). 'Disturbing causes,' 'noxious errors,' and the theory-practice distinction in the economics of J.S. Mill and W.S. Jevons. *Canadian Journal of Economics/Revue canadienne d'Economique, 28*(4b), 1194–1211.

Peart, S. J. (1996). *The economics of W. S. Jevons.* London: Routledge.

Persons, W. M. (1926). Theories of business fluctuations. *The Quarterly Journal of Economics, 41*(1), 94–128.

Petty, W. ([1662] 1899). Treatise of taxes & contributions. In: C. H. Hull (Ed.), *The economic writings of Sir William Petty* (Vol. 1, pp. 1–97). Cambridge: Cambridge University Press.

Petty, W. (1690). *Political arithmetick*. London: Clavel and Mortlock.

Pigou, A. C. (1927). *Industrial fluctuations*. London: Macmillan.

Pinkus, N. (1906). *Das Problem des Normalen in der Nationalökonomie*. Leipzig: Duncker & Humblot.

Playfair, W. (1821). *A letter on our agricultural distresses, their causes and remedies: Accompanied with tables and copper-plate charts, shewing and comparing the prices of wheat, bread, and labour, from 1565 to 1821*. London: W. Sams.

Pomian, K. (1977). Ciclo. *Enciclopedia Einaudi*, *2*, 1141–1199.

Pomian, K. (1978). *L'ordre du temps*. Paris: Gallimard.

*Raguet, C. (1829a). Untitled report from "Philadelphia, May 9, 1829". *The Free Trade Advocate and Journal of Political Economy*, *1*(9), 303–304.

Raguet, C. (1829b). On the principles of banking. *Free Trade Advocate*, *2*(1), 1–8.

Raithby, J. (1811). *The law and principle of money considered, in a letter to W. Huskisson, Esq., M.P.* London: T. Cadell and W. Davies.

Rantoul. (1836). [Speech in the Massachussetts House of Representatives], March 22.

Rey, J. A. (1862). *Les Crises et le Crédit*. Paris: Guillaumin.

Richmond Enquirer. (1837). The commercial crisis. *Richmond Enquirer*, *33* (114, 18 April), p. 4.

Robertson, D. H. (1915). *A study of industrial fluctuation: An enquiry into the character and causes of the so-called cyclical movement of trade*. London: King.

Robertson, D. H. (1926). *Banking policy and the price level*. London: King.

Rogers, J. E. T. (1879). Causes of commercial depression. *Princeton Review* (January–June), 211–238.

Roscher, W. (1849). Die Produktionkrisen mit besonderer Rücksicht auf die letzten Jahrzehn. In: *Die Gegenwart. Eine Encyclopädische Darstellung der neuesten Zeitgeschichte für alle Stände* (Vol. 3, pp. 721–758). Leipzig: Brockhaus.

Roscher, W. ([1877] 1882). *Principles of political economy*. Chicago: Callaghan.

Roscoe, W. (1793). *Thoughts on the causes of the present failures* (2nd ed.). London: J. Johnson.

*Sampson, M. B. (1858). *The currency under the Act of 1844. Together with observations on joint-stock banks and the causes and results of commercial convulsions. From the City articles of the "Times"*. London: John van Voorst.

Say, H. (1847). La crise financière et la Banque de France. *Journal des Économistes*, *16*(January), 193–207.

Say, H. (1855). La crise financière. *Journal des Économistes*, *8*(2nd series, November), 215–222.

Say, J.-B. (1803). *Traité d'économie politique ou Simple exposition de la manière dont se forment, se distribuent et se consomment les richesses*. Paris: De Chapelet.

Schäffle, A. (1859). Handelspolitik. In: J. C. Bluntschli & K. Brater (Eds), *Deutsches Staats-Wörterbuch* (Vol. 4, pp. 634–656). Stuttgart: Expedition des Staats-Wörterbuchs.

Schumpeter, J. A. (1934). Preface to the English edition. In: *The theory of economic development: an inquiry into profits, capital, credit, interest, and the business cycle*. Cambridge: Harvard University Press.

Schumpeter, J. A. (1954). *History of economic analysis*. London: Allen & Unwin.

Scott, A. (1827). *Proposed measures for the removal of national distress and establishment of permanent prosperity: To which are added, notes in illustration and proof of their expediency and necessity*. London: Ridgway.

Secret Committee on Commercial Distress. (1848a). *First Report from the Secret Committee on Commercial Distress; with the minutes of evidence,* June 8. House of Commons, London.

Secret Committee on Commercial Distress. (1848b). *Report from the Secret Committee of the House of Lords appointed to inquire into the causes of the distress which has for some time prevailed among the commercial classes, and how far it has been affected by the laws for regulating the issue of bank notes payable on demand,* July 28. House of Commons, London.

Siegfried, J. (1886). *Les crises commerciales et la reprise des affaires: possibilité de les prévoir par la corrélation entre l'encaisse et le portefeuille de la Banque de France,* Paris: s.n.

Simonin, J.-P. (2006). La théorie des crises commerciales de Briaune et sa place dans la théorie française des crises en France au XIXe siècle. In: J.-P. Simonin (Ed.), *Jean Edmond Briaune (1798–1885): Cultivateur, agronome, économiste.* Angers: Presses Universitaires d'Angers.

Sinclair, J. (1810). *Observations on the report of the bullion committee.* London: T. Cadell and W. Davies.

Smith, A. ([1776]1979). *An inquiry into the nature and causes of the wealth of nations.* London: Stahan and Cadell (critical edition: R. H. Campbell, A. S. Skinner, W. B. Todd, Oxford: Clarendon Press).

Société d'Économie Politique. (1854). Influence des banques sur l'entrainement des capitaux et sur les crises. Réunion du 6 juin 1854. *Journal des Économistes, 11*(2nd Series, June), 429–432.

Société d'Économie Politique. (1857). Origine et causes de la crise actuelle. *Réunion du 5 décembre 1857.* Journal des Économistes,, *16*(2nd Series, December), 465–473.

Société d'Économie Politique. (1893). Y a-t-il loi ou accident dans la périodicité des crises? Séance du 5 Janvier 1893. *Journal des Économistes, 51*(5th Series, January—March), 1–13.

Sombart, W. (1904). Versuch einer Systematik der Wirtschaftskrisen. *Archiv für Sozialwissenschaft und Sozialpolitik, 19,* 1–21.

Spiethoff, A. (1925). Krisen. In: L. Elster (Ed.), *Handwörterbuch der Staatswissenschaften* (4th ed.). Jena: Fischer.

Spiethoff, A. (1953). Business cycles. *International Economic Papers, 3,* 75–171.

Stansfeld, H. (1849). *A remedy for monetary panics and free trade in currency, suggested in a brief view of the currency questions.* Bonn: C. Georgi.

Stansfeld, H. (1854). *The Currency Act of 1844, the cause of the panic of October 1847, and the generator of monetary panics periodically.* London: Effingham Wilson.

Stansfeld, H. (1864). *Diagram, showing the striking contrast between the fluctuations in the bank rate of discount, during a period of 140 years of unrestricted issues, or free trade in currency, and one of 14 years of restricted issues and monopoly in money.* London: Yorkshire Joint-Stock Pub.

Surr, T. S. (1801). *Refutation of certain Misrepresentations relative to the Nature and Influence of Bank Notes.* London: T. Hurst; W. J. & J. Richardson.

Swiney, W. (1855). *Notes on monetary panics and convulsions, and the effects of the Currency Acts of 1819 and 1844, etc.* London: Richardson.

Targe, G. (1902). *Psychologie économique* (Vol. 2). Paris: F. Alcan.

Thompson, W. ([1827] 1971). *Labor rewarded: The claims of labor and capital conciliated; or, how to secure to labor the whole products of its exertions.* New York: Burt Franklin.

The Atlas (1837). Are banks the causes of speculation and overtrading? *The Atlas (Boston, MA),* September 21, Issue 69, col. B.

The Times. (1826). [Untitled leader]. *The Times,* February 20, p. 2, col. E.

Tocqueville, A. de (1840). *De la démocratie en Amérique.* Brussels: Hauman.

Tooke, T. (1823). *Thoughts and details on the high and low prices of the last thirty years.* London: Murray.

Tooke, T. (1838–57). *A history of prices and of the state of the circulation from 1792 to 1856.* London: Longman.

Tooke, T. (1844). *An inquiry into the currency principle: The connection of the currency with prices and the expediency of a separation of issue from banking.* London: Longman.

Torrens, R. (1816). *A letter to the right honourable the earl of liverpool, on the state of the agriculture of the United Kingdom, and on the means of relieving the present distress of the farmer, and of securing him against the recurrence of similar embarrassment.* London: J. Hatchard.

Tugan-Baranowsky, M. I. (1901). *Studien zur Theorie und Geschichte der Handelskrisen in England.* Jena: Fischer.

Tugan-Baranowsky, M. I. (1913). *Les crises industrielles en Angleterre.* Paris: Giard & Brière.

Tugan-Baranowsky, M. I. ([1914] 1954). Periodic industrial crises: A history of British crises. *Annals of the Ukranian Academy of Arts and Sciences in the United States,* 3(3), 745–802.

*Turner, J. B. (1844). Banking. *New Englander,* 2(5), 48–58.

Van Hall, F. A. (1858). *Considérations sur les Crises Financières et sur la Législation Anglaise Concernant les Banques de Circulation.* The Hague: Belinfante.

Veblen, T. ([1904] 1958). *The theory of business enterprise.* New York: Mentor Books.

Vecchi, N. De (1983). Crisi. In: G. Lunghini (Ed.), *Dizionario di economia politica* (Vol. 7, pp. 221–305). Torino: Boringhieri.

von Bergmann, E. (1895). *Die Wirtschaftskrisen: Geschichte der nationalökonomischen Krisentheorien.* Stuttgart: W. Kohlhammer.

Wade, J. (1826). *Digest of facts and principles on banking and commerce: With a plan for preventing future re-actions.* London: Thomas Ward.

Wade, J. (1833). *History of the middle and working classes.* London: Effingham Wilson.

Walker, A., & Stansfield, H. (1860). Monetary panics. Correspondence between Hon Amasa Walker, of Massachussets, and Homer Stansfield, Esq., of Burley, England. *Bankers' Magazine (New York), New Series,* 14(7), pp. 497–509.

Walker, J., & Walker, C. (1840). *Mercantile Chart, exhibiting the fluctuations of the prices of Consols, Exchequer Bills, Foreign Exchanges, and the principal articles of commerce in London, during the last seven years.* London.

Wallerstein, I. (1991). A theory of economic history in place of economic theory? *Revue économique,* 42(2), 173–180.

Wasserrab, K. (1889). *Preise und Krisen.* Stuttgard: Gottaschen.

Wells, A. D. (1899). *Recent economic changes, and their effect on the production and distribution of wealth and the well-being of society.* New York: D. Appleton.

West, E. ([1826] 1993). *Price of corn and wages of labour.* London: Routledge/Thoemmes Press.

Western, C. C. (1826). A letter to the Earl of Liverpool on the cause of our present embarrassment and distress, and the remedy. *The Pamphleteer,* 27, pp. 219–238.

Williams, J. H. (1919). The role of prices in the business cycle. *Review of Economic Statistics,* 1(2), 206–210.

Williams, T. H. (1858). Observations on money, credit, and panics. *Transactions of the Manchester Statistical Society,* Session 1857–1858, pp. 49–66.

Wilson, J. (1839). *Influences of the corn laws as affecting all classes of the community and particularly the landed interests.* London: Longman, Orme, Brown, Green and Longmans.

Wilson, J. (1840). *Fluctuations of currency, commerce, and manufactures.* London: Longman, Orme, Brown, Green and Longmans.

Wilson, J. (1859). *Capital, currency and banking.* London: AIRD (Economist).

Wirth, M. (1858). *Geschichte der Handelskrisen.* Frankfurt: Sauerländer.

Wolowsky, L. (1862). Rapport verbal sur un ouvrage de M. le docteur Clément Juglar intitulé: 'Des crises commerciales et de leur retour périodique en France, en Angleterre et aux Etats-Unis'. *Académie des Sciences Morales et Politiques, Séances et travaux,* Series 4, (12), p. 481.

Wright, C. D. (1886). *Industrial Depressions,* Report of the Commissioner of Labor. Government Printing Office, Washington, DC.

REVIEW ESSAYS

WENNERLIND & SCHABAS' DAVID HUME'S POLITICAL ECONOMY

HUME'S PHILOSOPHICAL POLITICAL ECONOMY

Willie Henderson

Review essay on Wennerlind, C. and Schabas, M. (Eds). (2008). *David Hume's Political Economy*. London: Routledge. xiii + 378 pp. ISBN 9780415320016. $160.

David Hume's image, as produced by his fellow Scot, Allan Ramsey, is printed large on the hardback cover of *David Hume's political economy*. This handsome portrait captures Hume's confidence and intelligence and displays, in its scarlet cloth, fine lace and elaborately worked, golden trim, Hume as a successful *philosophe*, a man of knowledge and also of commercial success (a success of considerable psychological importance for Hume, and a source of pride) founded upon the literary works on which his left arm rests. Indeed, without the significant reference to the books, this could as well be the portrait of a Scottish merchant or affluent banker, both types ranked among his Edinburgh friends. Hume with no University post and no inherited income worth speaking of made the most of the commercial possibilities open to authorship. This is a refined, even luxurious painting, and brings together in one enduring image, at least for those in the know, Hume's notion of "luxury" or of "Refinement in the Arts" and the idea of virtue in commercial society. This is a fitting cover for a work that

A Research Annual
Research in the History of Economic Thought and Methodology, Volume 28-A, 287–296
Copyright © 2010 by Emerald Group Publishing Limited
All rights of reproduction in any form reserved
ISSN: 0743-4154/doi:10.1108/S0743-4154(2010)000028A011

places Hume's political economy firmly in the contexts of his notion of a science of human nature and of the role of virtue in commercial society.

Hume did not write much in the way of "pure" political economy. His writing is integrated methodologically and thematically in his concerns that led to the production, in his twenties, of his *Treatise of human nature*. It is as well to remember that Hume's concerns, set out in the "Advertisement" to that work, were not narrowly defined. Hume treats of the "Understanding" and "Passions" and then declares his ambition to expand the work and to treat of "Morals, politics *and* criticism." By "Politics," Hume refers to "men united in society," a definition that allows, as it does extensively in the *Treatise*, for the examination of economic cooperation. In a sense Hume never abandoned this set of connected ideas, which is why Le Blanc could link Hume with Montesquieu under the appellation of *Philosophes Politiques* (p. 237) though it is true to say that the political economy of money (for which he is most noted by historians of economic thought) is hardly directly mentioned in the *Treatise*. The development of his political economy, even in later works, is bound up within the earlier context. This volume and the contributions that it presents make every effort to ensure that Hume is understood as a *philosophe* pursuing an analytical agenda that incorporates economic ideas. The list of topics covered in 13 contributions illustrates this very well. The volume is devoted to re-position Hume's economic ideas within the context of his empirical philosophy. It also deals with the reception of his economics writing in Britain and especially in France where *le bon David* and the circulation of his ideas became, in fashionable salons, a "cause célèbre." In Hont's words, Hume became, after the translation of his *Political discourses* in 1754, "an instant and influential intellectual presence" (p. 248).

There is, for review, an *embarrass de choix*. It is possible though hardly rhetorically convenient to attempt to review each individual and highly specialized contribution *in great detail*. The review will consist in a synopsis of themes rather than textual detail as this ought to bring the work of reviewing into something that is more manageable from the point of view of production and perhaps more helpful to the potential reader. Such themes are loosely set out (their judgment) in the introduction by Wennerlind and Schabas: Hume's "life and times"; "the broader dimensions of human motivation"; Hume on "money"; "Hume's political economy in France"; and the "seminal" significance of the "rich country–poor country debate." The fact that they are loosely set out means that there is some original work to be done in shaping the review in this way.

Context is significant for the study of Hume's writing. Context is usually significant but it is all the more so for Hume whose thought drew on and furthered international discussion. He was one of the Edinburgh *literati* and by this very fact had Scottish concerns. His work, in that enlightenment context has implications for the development of Smith's thinking. His fame in France provides a different setting for the interpretation and development of his ideas. Ian Simpson Ross chooses, not surprisingly, to provide a detailed biographical approach to Hume's policy, and practical, development. Ross' contribution is focused on what "early" and later "impressions" contributed to Hume's economic concerns as revealed by his correspondence and potential reading. The context there is, for example, radical financial changes in Hume's adolescence or observations of economic life in Bristol. Ross sees Hume's interest in matters commercial as starting very early in his life and he charts Hume's observation and reading in the context of Great Britain and, later, France. Some mention is made of the *Treatise* and of Hume's economic interests at the time of its writing. More could have been made of this as this is the literary work in which Hume's thinking in economic terms first emerges.

Emerson's chapter provides some Scottish context of Hume's thinking. Like other members of what we call the Scottish Enlightenment, Hume was interested in practical matters relating to the development of Scotland, matter discussed in public in various improving societies. Like Smith, who discussed trade with the Glasgow merchants, Hume had access through his friendships to the views of merchants and bankers even if such people did not automatically share his progressive views on free trade. Empiricism for Hume meant just that: observing and conversing human beings engaged in political and economic activities and subjecting the results to critical consideration and reflection. According to Emerson "Hume's advocacy of peace was also rooted in economic realities" as was his understanding of the consequences of war (p. 14). Hume closely observed the realities in the fortunes of those whom he knew while backing his observations with extensive reading.

Hume was engaged in the discussion concerning the fate of the Highlands after 1745. Rather than see wholesale (and punitive) British government intervention, Emerson argues that Hume can be read (for few of his ideas make explicit reference to Highland conditions – characteristically Hume keeps his arguments at a general level) as favoring a policy toward the Highlands in which governments take "mankind as they find them" and hence adopt polices that look to gradual rather than "violent" change (pp. 22–23). Emerson also sees a Scottish context for Hume's thinking in the intellectual continuity of questions of population and of the nature of ideal government, themes discussed in pre-Union Scotland. What emerges from

Hume's "Idea of a perfect commonwealth" (an essay influential in the formation of the American constitution) is a world, according to Emerson, in which economic policy would still be influenced by government concerns. Emerson relates Hume's general ideas to particular sets of economic and political concerns and so provides a richer reading of Hume's essays. Hume never wrote in a vacuum and was usually arguing against a prevailing or cenventional idea.

Motivation, based on the passions and served by reason, is a fundamental issue in Hume's philosophical analyses. Interest (personal, familial, public, and factional), institutions, customs, and manners are central to Book three of the *Treatise* and to his political and economic essays. Hume, in the words of the introductory essay in this volume, "sought to illuminate the behavioral dynamics of commercial society" (p. 4). In a sense this theme is generic – it could sum up all of Hume's economic and social concerns – but one that is specifically developed by the contributions to the volume by Berry, by Boyd and in the joint paper by Grün-Yanoff and McClennen. The essays pose interesting questions and answer them insightfully.

"Luxury" is a word, Berry argues, that carried many meanings (and this insight is essential to understanding Hume's reception in France with respect to the notion of "luxury") and around its use gathered many anxieties generated by the emergence of commercial society. Berry makes a very fine analysis of Hume's challenging contribution to the debate making use of the concept, located in Hume, that Berry calls "superfluous value." Berry neatly illustrates the issues in classical and in Christian reasoning ("voluntary poverty" is recommended by Aquinas for those who can sustain a spiritual life – though we ought to recall that Aquinas held that poverty was otherwise an "evil") and in Hume's contrasting reasoning about commercial society by using the device of the "embroidered slipper." "Pleasurable pride" is relatively innocent in Hume's account, according to Berry, when it brings in its train employment, productivity, and growth. "Luxury" as a concern in French life did not end with the 18th century so Berry's contribution is on an enduring theme.

Boyd pursues the notion of the improvement of morals and manners through commercial development. He poses many useful questions. The most general, and this follows neatly from Berry's contribution, is: "How, specifically, will the instrumental reason and self-interest of the market-place polish away the "barbarity" and "ignorance" of premodern societies and the "superstition" and "enthusiasm" that have arisen with modern Christianity?" (p. 66). Such a question necessarily requires investigation of changes in customs and manners and the replacement of feudal and aristocratic values with Hume's essentially democratic and indeed, complex notion of "civility," founded upon "mutual deference" (Hume's term; p. 66). Boyd in developing this theme exploits the 18th century notion of "commerce" as trade and as social intercourse. Both require a sense of equality and reciprocity if they are to be sustained over time. "Good manners" rather than aristocratic manners are called for and "civility" as developed by Hume implies, for Boyd, "democratic ideals of social mobility, inclusivity, equal respect, and mutual recognition" (p. 83).

Hume is, as Rostow recognized many years ago, a development economist and Grüne-Yanoff and McClennen, in recognizing this, put the "primary role of the passions" served by reason as central to Hume's "account of economic development" and associated policy (p. 86). Human passions allow for predictable behavior. Action is the result of a passion interacting with reason though the authors conclude that Hume in the details of his writing allocates to reason "a greater role" than appears at first sight (p. 101). A passion is normally constrained only by another passion but reflection, based on the understanding, too has a role – indeed a central role on the emergence of society and justice in the *Treatise*. Legislators need "to comply with the common bent of mankind" when working toward social improvement. The process of refinement has already been touched on in looking at Berry and Boyd. This chapter is more closely woven around motivational issues developed in the *Treatise*. New tastes, made possible by economic change, refine the mind and "counterbalance" violent passions by strengthening the calmer passions. These new refinements "men from their indolence" and creates through the consumption of "objects of luxury" a sustained desire for economic improvement. Passion changes, developed within what the authors call a "natural history of the passions," explain changed economic behaviors and institutions.

Hume is noted for his discussion of money. Wennerlind's chapter attempts to bring together Hume's views on money as developed in the *Treatise* and in the *Political discourses*. "Money" does not feature in the index of editions of the *Treatise*. Wennerlind is using Hume's notion of "promises" as a direct reference to money. Certainly promissory notes must fall under the institutional arrangements though my own view is that Hume was not simply explaining the emergence of commercial society but also of earlier forms of economic cooperation. "Contracts" as the general sense is still valid. What is important is that "money" in all its forms is part of the conventions based on interest. Wennerlind is correct when he argues that we should not focus on the "novelty" of Hume's theoretical contributions specified in terms of (say) "the quantity theory of money" but rather on "how he theorized money as a social relation embedded in a larger societal and political context" (p. 123). In this case any over-extended supply of paper money offends, I would have thought, against "interests" as defined in the *Treatise*. Without the buttress of further rules concerning liquidity, the common conditional statements cannot be met. Hume, as we can see in this chapter, did not abandon his "science of human nature" even when writing on economic topics.

Schabas starts with Hume's practical concern to challenge aspects of mercantilist notions of money and commerce. Hume was in Schabas' account more concerned with production, with the real things of economic life than he was with money. Nonetheless he recognized not only the significance of money for the circulation of goods but also the variety of forms that money took in the commercial society of his day and the liquidity attached to various kinds of financial assets. Hume's discussion of monetary adjustments and time periods is essentially long-run even if he does not use such a term. Hume was inconsistent, there are gaps in his treatment, according to Schabas, of the "specie-flow mechanism, and in his real-growth account" (p. 143) but there was a method ("a thought experiment") behind his approach. What counted for Hume, as it did for Smith, was production and economic wellbeing. Money was however, in line with the demands of economic society set out in the *Treatise*, a form of promise keeping and so is "woven right into the social condition" (p. 143). Hume shares with Smith the notion that the emulation of wealth as money holds out more promises of happiness than it cannot sustain.

Hume, according to Caffentzis, in a difficult paper, has a "complex" attitude with respect to money, seeing it as "a product" of commercial change and "its nemesis" (p. 148). Caffentzis focuses on Hume's notion that gold is "*fictitious* value" stemming from "convention" (like other economic institutions) and paper "counterfeit" (p. 149). The question is "why"? Hume is engaged with the "not true" ("belief") in his notion of human psychology and perception. In illustrating Hume's use of "fictions" Caffentzis quotes with approval Baier: "Fictions are plausible stories we tell ourselves to organize experience" (p. 153). *Natural fictions*, in Caffentzis' account of Hume, are involuntary and these can be contrasted with *artificial and consciously orchestrated ones*. Caffentzis contrasts the features of the two and applies the elements to metallic money and paper money. The question is that of a capacity for "universal belief." Even debased money sustains this capacity but paper money does not. Gold is located in a "weight-versus-tale dialectic" in this interpretation of Hume whereas paper money is a symbol of the "absent and general" and so requires regulation (p. 159). Where the two circulate together to the system is likely to be under strain. Paper money has the disadvantage of being subject to "wild imagination" (p. 160, quoting Chetwynd, the "master of the mint"). The conventions with respect to paper money are specific and not the general conventions that give rise to language or gold as money. Paper money is based on "opinion" and so suspect. The underlying distinction that Hume is making, according to this chapter, is philosophical rather than technical. Any challenge to this paper will require a sophisticated investigation of the *Treatise*.

The final paper in the series of money is one that alters us to the practical possibility of Hume's thinking. Hume was not merely a philosopher, he was also, for parts of his life, what we would call a civil servant or administrator. As *chargé d' affaires* in Paris, Dimand shows that Hume had to deal with the problem of negotiating a settlement to the problem of the currency ("playing cards," endorsed by the political authorities) of New France through the late summer and autumn of 1765, with earlier involvement from his date of joining the mission and later involvement through his post as under-secretary to in London to General Conway. Hume's involvement with this international settlement has been very usefully surfaced by Dimand. It had "long been hidden in plain view" (p. 171). Dimand shows that his experience with the paper money of New France may have changed Hume's views on the "usefulness of bank notes, in the 1764 edition of his essays." Hume loved games of chance (see for example *Treatise*, 2.3.10.9) and his intellectual curiosity is certainly to have been aroused by this monetary phenomenon.

France continues in all the following chapters to be a significant location for Hume, a place where his works met with instant success and in contexts that differed greatly for the context in Great Britain. Charles focuses on the translation of the *Political discourses* by Jean-Bernard Le Blanc, who heightened the influence of French thinkers such as Melon and Montesquieu on Hume's thought. This translation drew Hume's work into the context of "the new politics of the nations," concerns pushed by Vincent de Gourney (p. 182). Its British context was therefore broadened to enable Hume's voice to be heard in a wider French and even European context. The focus was on the views on luxury and commerce in general rather than on Hume's monetary theory. Gourney's "science of commerce" became as the result of the adaptations made by Le Blanc the context for reading Hume's *Political discourses*.

That changed context change significance is the theme too of Shovlin's chapter on the Hume's reception within the French debate on luxury. The issue of luxury in France was tied up heavily with the wasteful luxury of the court life and of the methods and profits available to those "tax farmers" who financed the absolute monarchy and married into the aristocratic class. Hume's argument is that where industry, knowledge, and humanity work together society a "more polished" and life progressively lived beyond the basic needs. In his *Theory of moral sentiments*, Smith also recognized that motivation from necessities was soon left behind as a form of economic motivation. For Hume government and economy improve in refined ages and military power increases rather than declines. Thinkers such as Mirabeau "decried the luxury that Hume defended" (p. 210) and saw the tendency of luxury to disrupt the social order. Wealth competes with honor for social approval. Other thinkers produced what Shovlin calls a "dualistic conception" of luxury in which commerce and industry leads to good outcomes but in which the aristocratic classes are debauched by it. Good societies have little or nothing to fear.

Cheney's chapter examines the relationship between "constitution" and "economy." Hume is seen as part of a wider group of enlightenment thinkers trying to match the expansion of trade with reflections on constitutional issues. Hume, while concerned with British political life, "spoke to a common social and political evolution" in Europe (p. 224). Hume saw an evolutionary progression form a situation in which constitution was significant to one in which government coexisted with market forms and institutions, including new commercial institutions, of "civil society, peopled by the middling classes" (a class that Smith thought could unite commerce with virtue). Hume, Cheney argues, thought that the laws of commerce "constituted a universal and universalizing force" leading to similar changes throughout Europe (p. 228). This meant that French reformers could be hopeful in the face of Hume's general argument. However, the fiscal problems in France (bound up with the method of state financing) and general economic performance seemed to imply the deliberate reform along English lines was needed. Contemporary England was seen as the product of violent change and unstable conditions in the past. Reformers did not wish to trade "the stability of monarchy for commercial prosperity" if this meant a period of chaos. Once again the debate on French conditions "shaped" the way in which his works were read. The French did not perceive the possibility of change to the absolutist regime in the way envisaged by Hume, there were in their eyes "limits to the convergence" (p. 239). Was Hume so certain that the English model based on factional interest was entirely stable?

The rich country–poor country debate has its origins in discussions about Ireland. Hume develops the debate, according to Hont, in the specific context of Scotland and England (movements within a state) but its "reception" in France becomes yet again significant. The issue is one of the longer-term economic developments in the context of international trade and competition. Hont's chapter is long, perhaps inordinately so, and indeed complex. I cannot hope to do other than point out some key features of the argument. According to Hont, "the rich-country–poor country argument became a fashionable topic in French international relations theory." This is a concern about relations between states, in particular with respect to any suggestion that English commercial dominance would be challenged in the longer-run (pp. 247, 261). The French debate had competing models. Melon argued, according to Hont, for a "three-stage theory of the natural progress of commerce." Agriculture was the first stage, then food surpluses reading to local trade and industry and then a final stage of foreign trade (a pattern that has some similarities to Smith's notion, in the *Wealth of nations*, of a natural growth path) with rivalry and the prospect of hegemony for the successful nation. War is the alternative open to lesser nations. Montesquieu thought, in contrast, that any "lasting military superiority" was an unlikely proposition. Economic life was always in a state of flux, monopolies could not endure because they could be undercut by states with lesser wage-rates. Hume was received as putting out mixed signals though it was clear that he was correct in pointing to the centrality of commerce to politics. Many different voices were heard in the debate with positions ranging from the nationalism of Forbonnais, that was capable of contemplating autarchy in the fullness of time, perhaps, as Hont may be construed as saying, like China and Japan at the time, to Hume seen by the French participants as a "supra-national" and "cosmopolitan" (pp. 317, 273). Hont's conclusion is that looking at Hume through French eyes helps us to clarify Hume's thought and establish his modern-day relevance.

This is an admirable set of papers. It had added hugely to my (developing) understanding of Hume, particularly in the relationship between his economic and philosophical thinking and his reception in France. It correctly locates Hume's political economy in a wider set of intellectual concerns in Great Britain and France. There is a degree of overlap among the papers. This *tends* to be cumulatively useful rather than distracting. I would have liked to see more emphasis on the general economics understanding that Hume develops in the *Treatise* as a significant personal and methodological context for his later writing, including his approach to literary topics such as the development of models for criticism. The significance of analogy for Hume's economic reasoning is not addressed. Certainly the significance of the

Treatise is acknowledged within Grüne-Yanoff and McClennen's very interesting joint chapter and in Caffentzis' paper, and in others as well, so my comments are to be taken only as a very minor criticism. The economics understanding demonstrated by Hume in the *Treatise* is of considerable sophistication and of surprising breadth of coverage. Apart from the obvious methodological issues, recognized in various chapters here, Hume deals with economic motivation, deferred gratification, specialization, and the division of labor (with an economy in the writing that is every bit as good as Smith), trade-offs between "needs" and "wants," the significance of scarcity, the possibility of economic development and change, the issue and significance of relative scarcity, the free-rider problem, substitution, the institutional conditions for economic stability, and other issues.

I would also like to have seen some reflection on "how," rather than simply on "what" and "why," Hume wrote. He may have rejected the *Treatise* but most scholars accept, including those published in this work, that it is fundamental to his intellectual development. Given his literary reflections on its lack of success, the experience of the *Treatise*'s reception also led to his growing awareness of the capacities and limitations of his target readers and hence contributed to the rhetorical success of his later essays. The *Treatise* made huge demands on his readers. He never made the same mistake again. This awareness, this refinement in his art of writing gave rise to the fortune that allowed him to be pained by Ramsey. His literary refinement allowed him to create, within the notion of "polite discourse," a drawing-room audience, both constrained and liberated by civility, for potentially difficult policy topics. Hume in a very real sense domesticated "political economy" and in so doing helped create an audience for Smith's *Wealth of nations*.

STIGUM'S ECONOMETRICS AND THE PHILOSOPHY OF ECONOMICS

WORLDS APART?

Kevin D. Hoover

Review essay on Stigum, B. (2003), *Econometrics and the philosophy of economics: Theory-data confrontations in economics*. Princeton, NJ: Princeton University Press. xxii + 768 pp. ISBN: 9780691113005. $105.

The long delay between the publication of Bernt Stigum's *magnum opus* and this review owes not only in part to personal reasons of no interest to anyone but the reviewer, but also to the sheer heft and density of the book itself. It is a long (768 pages) and difficult book. In fact, it is really two books: the first is Stigum's treatise on the philosophy of econometrics and the second is an anthology of contributions, constituting 8 of its 27 chapters, from a distinguished group of 16 econometricians, including two Nobel Prize winners (Granger and McFadden). The anthology sits somewhat uneasily alongside the treatise. The inclusion criteria seem to be either that the topic is one that Stigum thought ought to be covered or one that illustrates his larger points. Yet, it is unclear that the contributors fully subscribe to Stigum's analysis or that their contributions do not rather obscure than clarify his own position. The work would have been stronger and more readable had Stigum chosen to publish the treatise and the anthology separately. Even broken up in this way, Stigum's own 329 page contribution would be a formidable and erudite work. Although it is rare enough to find a scholar who is comfortable in mixing such disparate thinkers as Aristotle, Carol Gilligan, and E.E. Evans-Pritchard in the same

A Research Annual

Research in the History of Economic Thought and Methodology, Volume 28-A, 297–303

Copyright © 2010 by Emerald Group Publishing Limited

All rights of reproduction in any form reserved

ISSN: 0743-4154/doi:10.1108/S0743-4154(2010)000028A012

work, it is, I am sure, unprecedented when that work is principally concerned with econometrics.

According to Stigum, his book is about a riddle: "How is it possible to gain insight into the social reality with data concerning a socially constructed world of ideas?" (p. 3). He gives this riddle a philosophical gloss, explicitly drawing the parallel with Kant's question: "How is pure natural science possible?" (p. 4). Kant turned this into a more abstract question: How is the synthetic a priori possible? Although Stigum says that he differs from Kant in important ways, the Kantian influence is a genuine one. Stigum believes that there is no substantial economic knowledge without an a priori interpretive framework and that there are real gulfs between theory and data that are bridgeable only through a priori assumptions. The *Ding an sich* of economic reality is truly unknowable.

It is, therefore, somewhat surprising to find Stigum claiming in "a final remark on the riddle" that "I have tried to write a book that gives an econometrician the idea that he or she should 'get on with the job' while keeping" the problem of the gulfs between theory and data and data and the world in mind (p. 7). Had he not said it, I do not believe any reader would have taken such a pragmatic attitude to be a central one in the book. Pragmatism requires a different approach. Just before beginning to compose this chapter, I happened to be glancing through a wonderfully succinct, deeply insightful, and unfortunately neglected econometrics textbook from the late 1950s. In discussing how hypotheses are chosen, its author, Stefan Valavanis (1959), writes:

> The economist, geneticist, or other investigator usually begins with (1) prejudices instilled from previous study, (2) vague impressions, (3) data, (4) some vague hypotheses.
>
> He then casts a preliminary look at the data and informally rejects some ... He uses the remaining data informally to throw out some of his hypotheses, from among those that are relatively vague and not too firmly grounded in prejudice.
>
> At this stage he may prefer to scan the data mechanically ... rather than impressionistically ... Logically, of course, any mechanical method is an implicit blend of theory and estimating criteria; but, psychologically, it has the appearance of objectivity. The good researcher know this, but he is too overwhelmed by the illusion that mechanisms are objective.
>
> Having done all this, the investigator at long last comes to specification ... he then estimates, accepts, rejects, or samples again.
>
> This stage-by-stage procedure is logically wrong, but economically efficient, psychologically appealing, and practically harmless in the hands of a skilled researcher with a feel for his area of study. (pp. 154–155)

Valavanis has truly described "getting on with the job." Nothing in Stigum's book compares to such a robust pragmatism, and it is difficult to see how Stigum's highly formal, axiomatized approach could actually aid in the practice of work-a-day econometrics.

Yet, there are other goals than furthering practical econometrics. Stigum's book might be seen as a case study in the philosophical analysis of an applied discipline. Much of the philosophy of science has traditionally been somewhat abstracted from the sciences that are supposed to be its subject. Though highly formalized approaches have become less popular in the philosophy of science in recent years, even in their heyday, there were few attempts to move beyond the schematic to a concrete implementation. Stigum does just that, and it is hard not to admire the intellectual scope and energy that allows him to write confidently about economic theory, econometrics, and philosophy. Practical economists often act as if the line between theory and data were direct; Stigum's *tour de force* brilliantly characterizes the structure of the relationships between economic theory, data, and the world in a way that makes clear that the connection is very indirect indeed.

The puzzle posed in Stigum's riddle arises from his view that economic theory is not really about the economic world that we live in. Rather he regards all theoretical models as toys – models that are true about a separate theoretical world that cannot, in principle, directly attach to the data. The data themselves also belong to a realm that is separate from the real world and are equally characterized by models. In a move that goes back to the logical positivists, Stigum invokes bridge principles as a means of connecting theory to data to the world. The worlds of theory and of data, and the bridge principles as well, are presented as axiomatized systems. Philosophers have distinguished between the syntactic view and the semantic view of theories. The syntactic view treats theories as formal systems, whose terms are uninterpreted and whose important properties are logical deductions. On the syntactic view, theories attach to the world by being assigned a relevant interpretation. On the semantic view theories are instead collections of models, where in the classic (strong) interpretation a "model" means a consistent interpretation of a formal system. Stigum rightly recognizes that the difference between the syntactic and the strong semantic view of theories is vanishingly small. Both trade in axiomatized formal systems, and Stigum sees no reason to commit to one view over the other. His rhetoric may, to some extent, favor the semantic view, since he recognizes a great deal of flexibility about the contents of the worlds addressed by economic theories, so that it is convenient to stress the multiplicity of models.

The most characteristic point is not any preference for one view over the other, but a clear preference for formal systems. This has the practical implication that Stigum's approach appears to be top-down: we start with axioms and work out implications. "Top-down" should not be thought to imply a priority of theory over data, since for Stigum even data is characterized axiomatically. Stigum's vision of the theory–data confrontation is one in which theory, data, and bridge principles are all characterized as formal systems, which are tested by asking whether the different systems are logically consistent. This vision shortchanges the observational and investigative aspects of science and gives no real account of how loose insights get refined into theory. Though Stigum does not believe that the work-a-day econometrician must actually employ an axiomatic approach to get on with his research, he nevertheless manages to step on that message through his own relentless formalism, which is poles apart from Valavanis's messy pragmatism.

Stigum could have adopted a weaker semantic approach – one in which a theory is seen as a group of interpreted models linked by Wittgensteinian family resemblance, a view familiar from Paul Teller (2001) and Ronald Giere (2006) among others. A scientific architecture in which theory and data are worlds apart is quite consistent with the weaker semantic view. Nancy Cartwright (1999, chap. 2) has, for instance, argued in a manner parallel to Stigum that the truths of models are exact in their own world. On her view, models are fables as interpreted by the German romantic dramatist and critic Georg Lessing. A fable tells a genuine truth about its subject; but our interest in a fable is in its positive analogy with something that we want to understand in the world. This fits nicely with Stigum's understanding of theoretical models as having positive and negative analogies with data and the world. The application of models draws on the positive analogies while steering clear of the negative ones.

Stigum maintains that (1) when we claim that, say, an economic agent maximizes utility, we mean that literally about the theoretical world in which people are economic agents; (2) despite negative analogies, we should not think of the application of positive analogies as approximations; and (3) "[o]ne's understanding of the theory and the data one possesses determine [sic] what kind of questions about social reality one can answer in a theory–data confrontation" (p. 11; see also p. 118). Points (1) and (3) together rule out an instrumentalism (which Stigum attributes to Milton Friedman) in which theories are successful if the world acts as if they were true; for Stigum maintains that there is no "as if" – theories are literally true in their world.[1]

He takes points (2) and (3) as distancing himself from John Stuart Mill's notion that economic theories express tendency laws. He does not further amplify this position. Whether it is reasonable depends largely on how one reads the notion of a tendency law. Stigum seems to read it as an approximation. But Mill, who was an *apriorist* with respect to economic theory, is open to another reading, one that is consistent with Cartwright's (1989) notion of causal capacities. A capacity for Cartwright always acts to express itself appropriately and fully in the circumstances. But different capacities combine together in various ways; so that what we see in the world is a complex interaction that may quite obscure the unimpeded action of the capacity. A *tendency* then would be the product of the interaction of some set of capacities without the interference of other capacities. Just as for Stigum, this is not an approximation, but a truth (for Mill a deductive truth) about a world that we do not actually observe. If interfering causes (that is, the actions of capacities that are not in the set that defines the world of the model) are not too potent, a regularity (of various degrees of exactness) might be produced. We might even say that such a regularity is approximately true, but the *law* is not this regularity but the outcome of the interaction of the capacities in a world without interference.

Stigum rejects scientific realism on the ground that the terms in economic theories "pertain to matters of fact in a toy economy and nothing else." This position is closely related to his notion that that theory and data occupy separate worlds and that the standard of resolution for confrontations – both theory–data and theory–theory – is consistency of complete formal axiomatizations of these worlds. "Toy" is a pejorative – or, at the least, distancing – adjective. Toy models are not models of the world, it would seem, because the world is vastly more complex than any model, which must be simple enough to analyze formally if logical consistency is to be the principal virtue. But there are other sorts of realism. Cartwright, for instance, is a realist about capacities. Stigum cannot follow her because, in effect, he subscribes to what Teller (2001) refers to as the "perfect model model" – the idea that a realistic model of the actual world must be *complete* and *consistent*. Here again, Stigum's adherence to the strong semantic approach does not serve him well. A weak semantic approach allows a realism, like Cartwright's, in which realistic models are less than universal in scope.

As I have already observed, Stigum pays lip service to data analysis, but even his treatment of actual data is top-down and axiomatic, driven by the view that data do not speak for themselves. His vision of scientific investigation is explicitly anti-Popperian. The goal of the scientist is not to propose strong hypotheses and to let data falsify them. It is rather more like solving a complex crossword puzzle, where some parts are known and others have to be filled in a consistent manner. It is an attractively constructive view. But it puts a great deal of weight on what the investigator himself brings to the table (Kantianism again) with little attention to how one might reasonably modify these prior commitments. The result is arbitrariness and an extraordinary view of investigatorial privilege

> It is quite clear that two researchers can have different opinions about the meaning of a given set of observations. It is equally clear that the same two researchers may differ in the ways they relate the given observations to variables in a particular theory universe. Be that as it may, for the purposes of this book, it is important that there be agreement that in any given theory-data confrontation, *it is the opinion of the researcher in charge that counts.* (p. 255; emphasis added)

Without some sort of privileged view, there are so many degrees of slippage among the different levels of modeling that it a single, unequivocal understanding of a theory–data confrontation seems unlikely – the Duhem-Quine problem. Yet, Stigum offers a procedure that "may enable the econometrician to circumvent the Duhem trap" (p. 256 and chapters 10, 11, and 17). Try as I might have not been able to grasp Stigum's solution to the Duhem-Quine problem.

I have dwelled perhaps too much on the shortcomings of a remarkably ambitious and largely unprecedented analysis of the philosophical foundations of econometrics. Econometrics as defined in the founding documents of the Econometrics Society was the field that considered "economic theory in its relation to statistics and mathematics" and whose object was the "unification of the theoretical-quantitative and the empirical-quantitative approach to economic problems" (Frisch, 1933, p. 1). Most econometrics texts today are long on statistics and rather short on economic theory. Stigum has made a bold attempt to understand the enterprise of econometrics in its original formulation. It is not only a difficult book, but also a rich and provocative one. No other such work exists. It sets the standard against which any future contribution to the philosophical foundations of econometrics will be judged.

NOTE

1. That Friedman is actually an instrumentalist is widely but not universally accepted (see Mäki, 1992; Hoover, 2009).

REFERENCES

Cartwright, N. (1989). *Nature's capacities and their measurement.* Oxford: Clarendon Press.

Cartwright, N. (1999). *The dappled world: A study in the boundaries of science.* Cambridge: Cambridge University Press.

Frisch, R. (Ed.) (1933). Editor's note. *Econometrica, 1*(1), 1–4.

Giere, R. N. (2006). *Scientific pespectivism.* Chicago: University of Chicago Press.

Hoover, K. D. (2009). Milton Friedman's stance: The methodology of causal realism. In: U. Mäki (Ed.), *The methodology of positive economics: Milton Friedman's essay fifty years later.* Cambridge: Cambridge University Press.

Mäki, U. (1992). Friedman and realism. *Research in the History of Economic Thought and Methodology, 10*, 171–195.

Teller, P. (2001). Twilight of the perfect model model. *Erkenntnis, 55*(3), 393–415.

Valavanis, S. (1959). *Econometrics: An introduction to maximum likelihood methods.* New York: McGraw-Hill.

HUNT'S MARX'S GENERAL

FRIEDRICH ENGELS RESUSCITATED

John F. Henry

Review essay on Hunt, T. (2009). *Marx's general*. New York: Metropolitan Books. 430 pp. ISBN 9780805080254. $32.

Let me begin this essay with some propositions found in the preface to this study. "(A) dynamic of contradiction ... stands at the heart of Marxist theory" (p. 8). And (quoting Engels) while "men make their own history ... in that each person follows his own consciously desired end, and it is precisely the result of these many wills operating in different directions and of their manifold effect upon the world outside that constitute history." "What driving forces in turn stand behind these motives? What are the historical causes which transform themselves into these motives in the minds of actors?" (p. 9). Hunt's study demonstrates that Engels was certainly a most contradictory figure, alternating and sometimes conjoining a life of womanizing and carousing to one of the serious and dedicated political work to one of the capitalist manager. As to the second issue, while Hunt shows the various influences that prompted Engels to move toward, indeed, facilitate the development of what is termed Marxism, the question of motivation that caused him to honor those influences is left unanswered. That is, while many were subject to the same influences, the same historical forces, why did Engels "allow" these forces to pull him in a particular direction?

What are the strengths of this account? First, Hunt has a most appealing writing style. Clearly, this book was written for mainly a popular audience

A Research Annual
Research in the History of Economic Thought and Methodology, Volume 28-A, 305–318
Copyright © 2010 by Emerald Group Publishing Limited
All rights of reproduction in any form reserved
ISSN: 0743-4154/doi:10.1108/S0743-4154(2010)000028A013

though there's certainly enough "meat" here for academics in various disciplines to chew on. Hunt himself is an academic, associated with Queen Mary, University of London where he lectures on modern British history and specializes in urban history. But he's also an active participant in BBC radio and television programs and writes a regular column in *The Observer*. As well, he's an activist in New Labour. Although my general impression is that historians demonstrate a higher standard of quality in their writings than do economists, it is probable that in this case, Hunt's non-academic work brings him into direct relation with an audience that requires (or demands) a clear, fluid style of presentation, free of academic cant: an outcome is a book such as this. I would, though, recommend reading Hunt's book in tandem with *Frederick Engels: A Biography* (Ilyichov et al., 1974) an account that, though a bit hagiographic, fleshes out in much greater detail the political and theoretical details of Engels' life.

Beyond his dexterous writing style, Hunt is always mindful to develop a context within which Engels' theoretical and political development is portrayed. Indeed, in examining Engels' political trajectory against the backdrop of the development of capitalism, the social movements induced by that development, and the various ideological contests within various socialist organizations, Engels himself becomes alive, a man both buffeted about by historic forces, but also one who aids in molding history itself. And, in the process of telling Engels' story, Hunt introduces the reader to a veritable honors list of characters with whom Engels (and Marx) came into contact and who were influential in shaping the 19th century socialist (and anarchist) movements.

Before moving on to Engels proper, it seems reasonable to discuss one important aspect of the milieu within which Engels matured politically and which Hunt captures reasonably well. One tends to forget the vitality of European and British working class life in the first half of the 19th century. This vitality was not limited to organizing for a better life, raising wages, improving working conditions and the like, but extended to what can only be termed a working-class culture (on which for the British case, see Claeys, 1987). In England, the Owenites were especially active, and when Engels arrived in Manchester in 1842, he began regularly attending meetings at the Owenite Hall of Science, one of the several such institutions established throughout the country. Here, workers attended lectures – some 3,000 convening at the Sunday gatherings – and participated in high-level discussions on a wide range of topics. Here, Engels heard "working men, whose fustian jackets scarcely held together, speak on geological, astronomical, and other subjects with more knowledge than most 'cultivated' bourgeois in Germany possess" (p. 87, quoting Engels).

Engels' first foray into political economy, "Outlines of a Critique of Political Economy" (or *Umrisse*) (1843), drew heavily on Owenite thinking (coupled to Fourier), though went beyond both theoretical streams in its early application of the dialectical method to economic theory, its criticism of competition, of Malthus, the distinction between value and price, and analyses of property and alienation. It must be noted that Engels came to an understanding of the importance of political economy in the socialist movement earlier than did Marx, and it was this essay that prompted Marx to undertake his own engagement with economics.

Essentially, in France, Belgium, Germany, and England there was great working-class ferment, encompassing all facets of social existence. The whole post-Industrial Revolution period in Europe was one fraught with political discord and socialist/communist activities – a veritable laboratory within which Engels' ideas developed. Bakunin, Fourier, Saint-Simon, Owen, Blanqui, and so on were the topics of intense political debate. It can be said that in the post-Industrial Revolution period, this class was attempting to forge its own identity and trying to come to grips with its own, newly formed, existence. Hunt's account should, at a minimum, cause one to ask, what happened? What were the forces, the mechanisms, the institutional processes at work to bring this development under control and tame it?

Let me attempt a truncated overview of Hunt's narrative before moving on to some criticisms of Hunt's account. Born to Friedrich and Elise Engels in 1820 in the Wupper Valley town of Barmen (Prussia), Engels was raised in a strongly Pietist family environment. This form of Lutheranism, while condemnatory of the future lifestyle of the young Engels in its renunciation of worldly pleasures, did promote industriousness and discipline, two hallmarks of the mature Friedrich. His father was a successful businessman, and Engels' later apprenticeship in and eventual co-manager of the family firm, Ermen and Engels in Manchester, would not only influence his political development – *The Condition of the Working Class in England* (1845) was written as a result of his first stay in that city – but also provided him the income to not only subsidize Marx among others, but to live quite comfortably. Hunt estimates that in current U.S. dollars, Engels left an estate valued at $4,000,000.

Following a youthful flirtation with European romanticism, which in Germany saw the development of a literature seeking to "invent" a Germanic tradition that would allow the identification of a "*Volk*," Engels came into contact with the party *Das Junge Deutschland* when his father removed him from the *Gymnasium* in 1837 and sent him to Bremen to begin his apprenticeship as a businessman. Young Germany, whose members included the notable Heinrich Heine, the poet who would remain in touch with Marx and Engels over the years, promoted an activist political program, rejecting the romanticized medievalism of Schiller and others. The party would represent Engels' first relationship with an organized effort to effect political change in Germany. This led to his first political writing – "The Bedouin," a poem attacking "western" colonization and the destruction of the "noble savage" way of life – his rejection of religion, influenced in this regard by his reading of David Friedrich Strauss' *Life of Jesus Critically Examined* (1835), and his early exposure to the philosophy of Hegel.

In 1841, Engels fulfilled his military obligations to the Prussian state by signing on with the Royal Prussian Guards Artillery, stationed in Berlin. Straying as often as possible from his official duties, Engels attended the lectures of Friedrich von Schelling at the new University of Berlin. Sharing lecture hall space with Engels were Jacob Burckhardt, Michael Bakunin, Søren Kierkegaard – a not inconsiderable set of students, one of whom, of course, who would figure prominently in a later theoretical battle with Marx.

The significance of this episode in the life of young Engels cannot be overstated. An aged Schelling had been brought to Berlin specifically to counter the growing – and politically dangerous – trend of "left" Hegelianism. Although Hegel's *system* can be read as lending support to the *status quo ante*, specifically support of "the state" and religion, his *method* was dialectical, where all was in a process of change, of coming into being and passing away. Thus, the method was in contradiction to the system, calling the supposed permanence and ideal nature of the (Prussian) state into question. The "left Hegelians," following the intellectual leadership of Ludwig Feuerbach, emphasized Hegel's method.

In his *Essence of Christianity* (1841), Feuerbach carried the criticism of religion, begun by Strauss and deepened by Bruno Bauer to its conclusion. Feuerbach's contention was that religion was not only created by people, but represented their "self-alienation," their separation from their very (material) humanity. It was not sufficient to criticize religion but to destroy it – along with Hegel's idealist philosophical system. "In place of God or the Idea, he wanted Man: anthropology not theology" (p. 54). And, if religion is to be displaced, could the Prussian state, largely resting its justification on Christianity, could be far behind? It was this line of thinking that Schelling was to attack, and it was Schelling's criticism of Hegel's philosophy that sharpened Engels' own thinking and brought him into contact with the "Young Hegelians," those who carried a nascent dialectical materialism into their ideological forays. And it was in connection with these critics – in particular the brothers Bauer – that Engels made the acquaintance of Karl Marx.

Their first meeting, at the offices of *Rheinische Zeitung* in November 1842, resulted in something of a dispute over the political orientation of the Bauer brothers. At the time, Engels was in friendly correspondence with Edgar and Bruno, whereas Marx had already developed a position critical of their political orientation. Later, of course, Engels would join Marx in criticizing the Bauers in *The Holy Family*, but at that point Engels viewed Marx's objections "with suspicion" (p. 63).

Engels would not have the occasion to further his relationship with Marx at this point, as his disapproving father, always anxious to direct his son toward the straight-and-narrow path of religion and commercial industriousness, sent him to Manchester to serve his apprenticeship in the family firm. Before departing, Engels sought an audience with Moses Hess, the communist rabbi, "among the first to introduce (the) 'social question' – the human costs of industrial capitalism – into the political dynamic" (p. 73). Hess was largely responsible for the next step in Engels' political development; Engels now became a communist, accepting the position that only with a social revolution based on common ownership of the means of production could humanity be liberated and reach its existential potential.

Manchester, of course, was the industrial laboratory that provided the material for Engels' first major work, *The Condition of the Working Class in England*, a book that would provide much material that Marx would incorporate in *Capital* and which had a major impact in German radical circles in particular. (*The Condition* was published in German, an English edition not appearing until 1885.) Indeed, Marx was indebted to Engels, practical businessman as he was, for information as to the actual operations of a capitalist enterprise. In contrast to more typical criticisms of *The Condition*, Hunt gives this work high marks, as did Marx himself, arguing that its purpose "was to confirm, not create the theory" learned from Moses Hess (p. 107), and that the main point was to argue that social class was economically determined. Engels had now reached the conclusion that it was only through the liberation of this class that a decent society could be constructed. At this stage, then, Engels was ahead of Marx in the intellectual process that would lead to mature Marxism.

It was in Manchester that Engels met Mary Burns, the woman who probably was the one love of his life and with whom he lived, somewhat sporadically to be sure and never in wedlock, until her death in 1863. Burns, an illiterate Irish woman, not only provided Engels human companionship, but introduced him to the poorest, most brutalized section of Manchester's workers, Irish immigrants who provided much fodder for Engels' scathing account. It should be mentioned that at the time Engels did display typical

"English" disdain for the Irish, a disdain much akin to racism. This attitude, that extended to Slavs, Africans, and other non-Western Europeans (pp. 165–167), would later dissipate as he and Marx improved their understanding of colonization (pp. 225–227, 230–231).

Engels renewed his acquaintanceship with Marx in the summer of 1844 in Paris, and here, over "ten beer-soaked days" (p. 115), they formed the relationship that would last the rest of their lives. Out of their discussions over the next several years came their first joint publication, the pamphlet *A Critique of Critical Criticism: Against Bruno Bauer and Co.* (1845) (extended by Marx, drawing on his "Economic and Philosophical Manuscripts" and appearing as *The Holy Family* with the original title now the subtitle). This was followed by *The German Ideology* (which was not published in their lifetime). This work represents their break with the Young Hegelians, and while retaining traces of idealism and mechanical materialism (the hand-mill, steam-mill correlation with feudalism and capitalism), can be said to be the first work where their general position was laid out in which class struggle was the driving force of history.

In addition to theoretical work, and Engels, while always claiming to play second-fiddle to Marx should be seen as an equal contributor to the developing doctrine, Engels was active politically, particularly in his connection with the League of the Just (later renamed the Communist League with its slogan, "Working Men of All Countries, Unite!"), the conflicts with Wilhelm Weitling (an advocate of immediate proletarian revolution) and, more importantly, Pierre Proudhon (attacked by Marx in *The Poverty of Philosophy*). In connection with these ideological struggles, Engels was not above employing dubious tactics ("a little patience and some terrorism") to push the incipient theoretical and political program he and Marx were developing.

This period of Engels' life well displays his seemingly contradictory nature. Even though he was immersed in both theoretical and political work, even though he was in a relationship with Mary Burns in Manchester, he allocated time to enjoy the more earthy aspects of Parisian life. In addition to consume large quantities of wine and beer, he became well acquainted with the city's "grisettes" – working class women who, while not exactly prostitutes, were apparently quite willing to have money spent on them in return for sexual favors. As Hunt shows, such behavior was characteristic. He was a drinker, a womanizer, and later, when assuming his role as co-manager of the family textile works, an avid fox-hunter, consorting socially with the class enemy. But it was also the period in which he and (mainly) Marx wrote *The Communist Manifesto* (a work that Hunt reminds us was little read in its time).

A most fascinating portion of the book lies in Hunt's account of the relation of Marx and Engels to the Continental revolutions of 1848. At this time, both believed that it was possible to forge an alliance between workers and capitalists in promoting "bourgeois democracy" against the feudal reactionaries who dominated politics in most European countries. The uprisings of 1848, particularly that in Paris in June, were now seen as embodying a new stage in the progress of socialism, that of a "war between labor and capital" (p. 159, quoting Marx from *Class Struggles in France*). In Germany, Engels played an active role in the renewed conflicts occurring in 1849. Indeed, he was on the barricades and he seemed to enjoy this role, apparently, one of the very last to give up the good fight. Hunt informs us that Engels had a great affinity for military heroes such as Wellington, Napoleon, Cromwell and studied military tactics. Perhaps Engels was more optimistic than Marx regarding the possibility of socialist revolution and was preparing accordingly? Various jubilant expressions of such a possibility associated with specific events are scattered throughout this account. Certainly his study of *The Peasant War in Germany* (1850), his attempt to secure a journalist's position with the *Daily News* analyzing military operations in the Crimean War, his work as a columnist for the *Pall Mall Gazette* reporting on the Franco-Prussian War are indicative of such a possibility. It was this interest in and acute analysis of military affairs that earned him the Marx family nickname, "The General."

With the collapse of these revolutionary movements, Engels and Marx began to rethink their position on the proletarian-bourgeois alliance. In all areas where fighting occurred, the capitalist elements retreated in the face of the armed onslaught of the reactionary forces. Given this experience, our two protagonists began abandoning their previous position and focused on working-class revolution as the only possibly solution to "the social question." Again, we see the social forces at work informing the theoretical stance of Marx and Engels as they continued to develop that body of doctrine known as Marxism.

On his return to England, where he spent the rest of his life, Engels threw himself into the work of Ermen and Engels, dividing his time in co-managing the family firm, fox hunting (becoming a member of the Cheshire Hounds), and socializing with his fellow bourgeoisie, while continuing his political work – though this was given short shrift as Engels essentially sacrificed his own interests to earn an income to support Marx and a host of others. Engels was exceptionally generous and one can say that he was abused in this regard by many, including Marx on occasion. He was also generous in other ways. The story of his assumption of the parentage and financial support of Freddy

Demuth, Marx's illegitimate son by Helene Demuth, is well known (though Demuth was not well treated personally by Engels).

Manchester provided a rude reception for Engels. The home of the militant workers' movement in England had been swamped by the free trade, minimal government intervention, and (propertied) democracy program of the Manchester School. The Chartist leadership had largely adopted the Manchester program, and the workers had become increasingly "bourgeois" in their orientation. The Free Trade Hall, built on the site of the Peterloo Massacre, had replaced the Owenite Hall of Science (sold by the Chartist John Watts) as the symbol of the new Manchester, now a "community based upon the orderly, sober and peaceful industry of the middle classes" (p. 185, quoting the *Manchester Guardian*).

At the personal level, during this period Engels not only suffered significant physical and mental ailments caused most probably by overwork, but also connected to the strain associated with living the double life of capitalist boss and socialist revolutionary. Hunt here reminds us that while Marx's boils receive a great deal of attention, his partner and benefactor's health issues have been generally ignored. Then, in 1863, Mary Burns died. This was a calamitous event in Engels' life and Marx's somewhat callous response to this news caused the one major breach in their long association. At the same time, Burns' death did not hinder Engels' private life for long: shortly thereafter, he took up with Burns' sister Lizzy and eventually did marry her – on her own deathbed.

The next major event in Engels' political life was the publication – finally! – of *Das Kapital* (1867). Engels had been prodding Marx to finish this work for some time, and Marx finally overcame his tendency to go madly off in all directions, and grind out the final version. Engels then wrote review after review, adjusting both style and content to accommodate different readerships (and ownerships) of various periodicals. He even wrote reviews critical of the book to stimulate controversy and to draw attention to the work. In addition to the nickname "The General," one might also affix the moniker, "Marx's Publicist."

In 1869, at the age of 49, Engels ended his association with Ermen and Engels, and, following a lengthy battle over a final settlement (Hunt estimates this at $2.4 million), left for London where he lived the rest of his life. "The General was once more ready for action" (p. 238).

In London, Engels was in his element. Freed of his business duties, he threw himself into political work. Elected to the General Council of the First International and named corresponding secretary for Belgium (then, other countries), Engels' discipline, strong work ethic, and facility at languages, served him well as he more or less established himself as the center of the European socialist movement and his new home at 122 Regent's Park Road became, according to Edward Aveling, the "Mecca" for revolutionaries – and was under constant police surveillance. August Bebel, Karl Kautsky, William Morris, Wilhelm Liebknecht, and Keir Hardie – the list is very long – all used the weekly Sunday visitation time to discuss socialist politics and drink beer.

From this point forward, Hunt's book takes us through the Paris Commune, the conflict with Bakunin and the anarchists in the International, the struggles with Lassalle and the Eisenachers and shows the relationship between these events and political contests on the theoretical work of Marx and Engels (*Class Struggles in France, Critique of the Gotha Program*, etc.). The reader is also given an exposure to the influence of non-socialist authorities in Engels' theoretical development, in particular Charles Darwin and Lewis Henry Morgan. It is well known that Marx and Engels had high regard for Darwin (though Marx thought him too "bourgeois" in his underlying perspective given his emphasis on the competitive struggle in the theory of natural selection), and Engels' study of Darwin and scientific developments in general are captured in his *Dialectics of Nature* – first published in 1927 and seen in manuscript form by Einstein who "judged the science confused ... (but) worthy of a broader readership" (p. 283). The most striking essay in this collection of somewhat disjointed papers and fragments is "The Part Played by Labour in the Transition from Ape to Man," and Hunt notes that this piece was given high marks by the evolutionary biologist, Stephen Jay Gould (p. 285). It was Morgan's *Ancient Society* that provided the scholarship for Engels' own "popularized" version of that account in his *The Origin of the Family, Private Property, and the State* ... (1884). As Hunt demonstrates, the nature of the family and related issues was a hot topic in the socialist circles of the 1880s. Bebel's *Women and Socialism* had been published in 1879, Kautsky had addressed primitive sexual relations in the early 1880s, Marx and Engels had an ongoing discussion – and debates; Engels was clearly not Marx's toady – on these matters and both had undertaken a fairly significant reading program in then-current anthropological research. Engels' own book was prompted by his discovery of Marx's "Ethnological Notebooks" in which "the Moor" had written extensive commentaries on his own forays into this literature. And Engels book continues to have an impact, "rediscovered" at various junctures in recent political history, in particular in connection with the feminist movement of recent years, though not without sometimes severe criticism (pp. 309–310).

The other major work contributed by Engels during this period was the 1878 *Herr Eugen Dühring's Revolution in Science* (*Anti-Dühring*). Though this work was clearly an aspect of the ideological contests waged by Marx and Engels against those proposing alternate theories to that of dialectical materialism, there was a very clear immediate purpose in countering the blind philosopher's argument: Dühring's "revisionist" approach was increasingly looked on as a substitute for that of Marxism by the very social democrats who had previously been swayed by Marx. Among these, and the one household name that will strike a chord among historians of economic thought, was Eduard Bernstein of *Evolutionary Socialism* (1907) fame. Engels' criticism thus was in part designed to bring the theoretical deviants back into the Marxist camp. Although Hunt does not pick up on this point, *Anti-Dühring* contains a fair bit of economic theorizing (largely contributed by Marx), in particular a criticism of the utility theory of value, then becoming the central unifying principle of the emergent neoclassical approach in economics. As well, it was out of this work that *Socialism: Utopian and Scientific* was extracted – and this was a major seller in that time.

At this point, Hunt briefly takes up the charge, leveled by Lukás, Althusser, and others that Anti-Dühring represents a deviation from, a revision of Marxism and is responsible for a host of misunderstandings as well as leading to the "materialistic idealism of Stalin" (p. 295, quoting Norman Levine). Hunt argues against such an interpretation, showing Marx's own approval of the book and his affinity to the explication of dialectical materialism put forward by Engels.

With Marx's death in 1883, Engels, as is well known, undertook the responsibility of gathering Marx's (rather jumbled) notes for the remaining volumes of *Kapital*. A question is raised as to whether Engels modified Marx's position at several points, in particular changing the "shaking" of capitalism to its "collapse" in the discussion surrounding the tendency for the rate of profit to fall, ostensibly leading later Marxists to search for a systemic breakdown of the system. But, on the whole, Engels' massive effort in developing Marx's theoretical analysis is seen as most commendable by Hunt.

His main theoretical work behind him, Engels continued to be active politically. He contributed articles on trade unionism to *The Labour Standard*, attempting to revive (unsuccessfully) the spirit of militant Chartism. He marched with 200,000 in the 1890 London May Day parade where socialists of all stripes – except Marxists! – celebrated the supposed dawn of a new age. A participant in the 1889 Paris Congress that led to the formation of the Second Socialist International, he was the principal figure that brought a modicum of unity to the competing parties and factions and guided the German Social Democratic Party back toward a Marxist path (at least for the time). And, though having his moment of despair regarding the revival of a militant British (and Continental) working class, he remained generally optimistic. In particular, the successful 1889 Dock Workers' strike revitalized his hopes for a revolutionary working class alternative to capitalism.

Throughout this last period of his life, Engels continued to display those personal and political characteristics that defined his life. Generous to a fault (and accordingly taken advantage of by, among others, the Burns sisters' niece, Mary Ellen [or "Pumps"] and her husband, Percy Rosher, and Paul Lafargue, Marx's son-in-law), Engels continued to entertain visitors, both political and social in nature. And, while age had certainly slowed down his appetite for drinking and womanizing, he continued to have close female companionship (though apparently not sexual), first with Helene Demuth, who moved into the Regent's Park home after the death of Lizzie Burns. Then, following Demuth's death, Engels invited Louise Kautsky (nee Freyberger), recently divorced by Karl, to share his abode. (She was then 30 years of age.) There are also reports of fairly prodigious drinking bouts that would occur when celebrating various events such as his birthday.

In August 1895, Engels succumbed to cancer of the esophagus and larynx. Following the ceremony honoring his life, attended by many leading socialists of the period, his body was cremated and his ashes scattered in the English Channel. No Highgate memorial next to his comrade Marx, no tombstone in the family plot in Germany: "After his brief years as first fiddle, Engels returned to the orchestra" (p. 351).

So, beyond a good read, how does Hunt's account strike one from the vantage point of history of economic thought? Given that this biography was written for a general audience, I give it fairly high marks, in particular in the development of the social and political background that laid the basis for the theoretical work of Marx and Engels. However, if one is interested in a critical account of the unfolding theory itself, one will be disappointed. For the most part, the seminal works – such as the *Umrisse* – are given short shrift. But, this is understandable. Hunt is not writing for an audience of historians of economics, and, assuming he were up to the task, an extended excursion into such pamphlets, articles, and monographs would detract from the purpose of the book.

There are more substantial issues, however. At several points, Hunt passes questionable judgment on important issues. For example, in his account of the relationship between Engels and William Morris – whom

Engels eventually dismissed as a "sentimental dreamer" (p. 324) – Hunt repeats the typical position that Morris' most important work, *News From Nowhere*, "advocated a return to the preindustrial past" in which "London would be rid of industry altogether" (p. 323). In his introduction to the 1968 edition of that work, A. L. Morton, a close student of Morris and other socialist writers, expressly deals with this misconception (Morton, in Morris, 1968, pp. 24–32). Morris wrote *News* in response to Edward Bellamy's 1888 utopian novel *Looking Backward*. Here, factories and machinery take center stage; the story is largely bereft of the life of workers. Morris' focus is precisely this life. Although it is certainly true that craft production, useful and enjoyable, is the dominant form of production (for Bellamy, work is repugnant), factories are still in operation – "(a)ll work which would be irksome to do by hand is done by immensely improved machinery ... " (Morris, 1968, p. 280). This point was important in the socialist circles of the period, and remains so today. When speculating on the nature of a future society, the issues surrounding both the working and social lives of people were and are of paramount concern. I, for one, would much rather live in Morris' utopia than that of Bellamy's.

More important perhaps than issues such as this, is Hunt's insistence that Engels is to be held responsible for both the failure of a communist movement to take root in England as well as various problems (or crimes or errors, depending on how one looks at it) in the Soviet Union. On the first issue, Engels is taken to task for promoting Edward Aveling to the leadership position in the British socialist movement. Aveling, then engaged in a liaison with Marx's daughter "Tussy" while still married, was, by all accounts, a brilliant scientist (though he lost his position at University College London due to his outspoken secularism), but was viewed with repugnance by socialists of all stripes. Hunt quotes Kautsky, Bernstein, and George Bernard Shaw to this effect (p. 325). And, while politically active and ideologically straight-arrow, Aveling's abrasive personality, his womanizing, his carelessness with money (Engels had to bail him out on more than one occasion), made him anathema to the very people with whom it was necessary to build relationships to advance the cause of Marx and Engels. This charge was recently advanced in a *Guardian* online piece in which Hunt also claims that, in addition to his misplaced loyalty to the Marx clan in "appointing" Aveling to the leadership position, "The General" ... (couldn't) get on with anyone" (Hunt, 2009).

Now, after many references in the biography to Engels' affability, his entertaining socialists of somewhat differing positions, this is a rather strange position to hold. To be sure, Engels did take a strong position in various political battles, but this is something to be expected. More important is the notion that British communism failed due to the personality quirks of a single individual. Throughout this work, Hunt, as noted earlier, usually places specific developments in a much broader social and political context. Here we find something of a "great man" approach to an attempted explanation for a development that surely cries out for a much deeper, nuanced, balanced argument.

Regarding the Soviet Union, Hunt lays many issues confronting that confederation at Engels' feet. From the treatment of the Volga Germans with the invasion of the fascist armies, to the "liquidation" of the kulaks (misidentified by Hunt (p. 353) as "smallholders"), to the biology of Lysenko (learned from Engels' *Dialectics of Nature* apparently) – the list goes on. Without question, Engels' works, more accessible than those of Marx, were studied in the U.S.S.R. The issue here, again, is reducing a very complex set of issues to a single cause, in this case Engels' supposed distortions of Marxism. My own suspicion is that the history of the Soviet Union, in particular the specifics with which Hunt deals in his epilogue, will not be properly written for another 50 years (if that) when political passions have had sufficient time to be tempered. In fact, there are recent works that have begun to cast doubt on the usual understanding of what actually occurred in the Soviet Union, an understanding that Hunt shares (see Thurston, 1996 for one example). I would suggest that Hunt's biography would have been better served had he not tread on such politically volatile ground.

Independent of my reservations concerning the last sections of the work, I found this to be not only a generally fair and most interesting biography, but also one that casts Engels in a somewhat different light than is usually the case. Engels emerges as something of a co-equal to Marx, though clearly their specific contributions to this canon are different. One can debate the extent to which Engels "revised" Marx, and whether such revisions alter, reinforce, or supplement the work of Marx himself. And this issue cannot be resolved through a reading of this work. But, again, in a popular account, this is not to be expected. Where I do believe Hunt leaves the reader a bit adrift is in answering a question I posed at the beginning of this essay: why did Engels respond to the social and political forces surrounding him by moving, unlike so many others, in the direction of what we call "Marxism"?

REFERENCES

Bernstein, E. (1907). *Evolutionary socialism: A criticism and affirmation*. London: International Labour Party.

Claeys, G. (1987). *Machinery, money and the millennium*. Princeton, NJ: Princeton University Press.

Hunt, T. (2009). The Marxist misanthrope. Available at http://www.guardian.co.uk/commentisfree/2009/may/01/may-day-communism-marx, May.

Ilyichov, L. F., Kandel, Y. P., Kolpinsky, N. Y., Malysh, A. I., Obichkin, G. D., Platkovsky, V. V., Stepanova, Y., & Tartakovsky, B. G. (1974). *Frederick Engels: A biography (V. Schneierson, Trans.)*. Moscow: Progress Publishers.

Morris, W. (1968). *Three works by William Morris*. New York: International Publishers.

Thurston, R. (1996). *Life and terror in Stalin's Russia, 1934–1941*. New Haven, CT: Yale University Press.

FREY'S AMERICA'S ECONOMIC MORALISTS

TWO SCHOOLS, ONE THESIS, STILL NO CLEAR ANSWER

Stewart Davenport

Review essay on Frey, D.E. (2009). *America's economic moralists: A history of rival ethics and economics* (vii + 239 pp). Albany: State University of New York Press. ISBN: 9780791493519. $75.

Do not be deceived by the apparent thinness of this book. The mere 216 pages are dense, the subject is weighty, and the print a little small. In other words, even someone already familiar with the material at hand is going to have to slow down to take in everything that Frey has to offer here. Speaking of which – and before we get to the proper review – there is probably no one out there except for Frey who brings to the subject of economics and ethics the impressive historical breadth of this book. Beginning with the Puritans and continuing all the way through Michael Novak and Amartya Sen, *America's Economic Moralists* is a truly encyclopedic historical treatment of this crucial and often confusing topic.

In the face of the conceptual challenges any author would confront when dealing with a subject as unwieldy as ethics and economics, Frey is admirably clear without risking oversimplification. His main thesis and organizing principle is that "Two major economic moralities have existed as rivals in America since the colonial era" – "autonomy morality" and "relational morality" as he calls them. Each is still "an individualistic ethic" (p. 1) but, as

A Research Annual
Research in the History of Economic Thought and Methodology, Volume 28-A, 319–327
Copyright © 2010 by Emerald Group Publishing Limited
All rights of reproduction in any form reserved
ISSN: 0743-4154/doi:10.1108/S0743-4154(2010)000028A014

the names clearly imply, the former prizes the autonomy of the economic actor, whereas the latter sees him as being a part of a web of interdependent human relationships, including but not limited to economic relationships. In addition, Frey informs us, autonomy moralists have gloomily assumed "pervasive natural scarcity," whereas relational moralists have not. Instead, relational moralists see scarcity as originating "with imperfect human institutions" (p. 3). Predictably, autonomy moralists and relational moralists also differ over the role of government in economic activity, as well as the inevitability versus preventability of poverty in the world.

But Frey's most illustrative distinction between autonomy moralists and relational moralists has to do with the nature of limits and the tendency of a capitalist economy to encourage excess. In my humble opinion, capitalism's inherent boundlessness (morally, geographically, and institutionally) is its greatest weakness. If the free exercise of competitive self-interest is the engine that drives personal and institutional economic activity, what precisely are the brakes? For better or for worse, a capitalist economy does not have the resources within itself to provide them. I agree with Frey on this point and appreciate his obvious preference for the relational moralist tradition, although I would also like to do the reviewer's job and play devil's advocate a little by sticking up for the autonomy moralists and their ilk.

Frey praises the relational moralists for their perspicacity and their consistency. Throughout the centuries, they have warned against capitalism's dangerous limitlessness, and have sought to establish clear boundaries to economic activity – limits that make "human dignity, as perfected in community, [the] highest good" (p. 8). In other words, the problem is clear, the solution is clear, and the principles by which the whole economic system is evaluated in the first place (prioritizing human dignity) are likewise clear. And whether the specific target of relational moralists has been racial slavery, child labor, social Darwinism, inexcusable inequality, or conspicuous consumption, they have always upheld the same general principle of human dignity, and the need to secure it by imposing constraints on unbridled economic activity. "Autonomy morality," however, "historically has demanded the improbable: asking the free self to restrain the self" (p. 7). As mentioned already, in what follows I would like to defend the priorities and prescriptions of autonomy moralists, but I do also think that Frey's general critique hits its mark.

Frey's admirable clarity extends also to the book's organization. With 16 chapters, the book is nicely broken up into three main chronological chunks: the time from the Puritans to the Civil War (chapters 2–4), the heart of industrialization between the Civil War and World War II (chapters 8–11), and the Cold War to the present (chapters 12–15). Chapters 5–7 are more topical than chronological in nature, and frankly stick out a little. Although informative as usual, they are a way for Frey to deal with loose ends and topics apparently close to his heart (public education, the Moravians, and the abolitionists), but they do not add as much to the work's overall argument or narrative flow. It is fine that they are there, but if a reader is wishing to move a bit more quickly through this complicated story, I would suggest skipping them. In what follows, I am going to take one chronological chunk at a time.

Chapters 2–4, on the seventeenth, eighteenth, and early nineteenth centuries, respectively, are some of the best in the book. The narrative arc of this section, one could say, is the evolution in American thought regarding the centrality of the self, with the obvious ethical question being the role of self-interest in economic life. At the very beginning of this strange and tension-filled story, Frey informs us, were the Puritans who simultaneously and paradoxically both valued and feared the self. Explicitly, the Puritans thought of the self as a sinful idol factory and a potential rival to God. Implicitly, however, "Puritan thought ... was highly individualistic" (p. 14), requiring a deeply personal conversion experience for all church members, and upholding the idea of an even more personal calling to an economic "vocation [that] served to glorify God by serving others in worldly activity" (p. 14). But as this quote makes clear, all of this potentially neurotic self-focus was still subordinate to the Puritan community and the glory of God. Thus, while establishing a culture of self-absorption that would endure in American history down to the present, the Puritans were really the first relational moralists, citing the common good as a way to restrain individuals' self-interested economic activity. Such a healthy and balanced economic order, however, was only as strong as the community that was enforcing it, and sure enough, as the seventeenth century turned into the eighteenth, the Puritan world inevitably changed, and so did the place of the self in economic life.

Although much contributed to these changes, Frey rightly focuses on the role of the enlightenment tradition of thought that unabashedly exalted the individual, and militantly sought to preserve autonomy against all encroachments. As he puts it "A certain tone of utilitarianism and individualism had crept into this Puritan's outlook" (p. 26). Frey is here referring to Cotton Mather (1663–1728) who subtly "accommodated" (p. 27) to the rising individualism of his time by downplaying moral obligation to God and community, and emphasizing instead the benefits of right action to the actor himself. In other words, it paid to be ethical. Thus, even if the consequences of an action were not blatantly self-interested, its motive still could be, and

Mather said that there was nothing wrong with that. Later in the eighteenth century, Benjamin Franklin (1706–1790), the quintessential secularized Puritan, took this line of thinking to its next level by illustrating and praising the way in which sowing to a virtuous character (via industry, frugality, sobriety, delayed gratification, etc.) would reap material benefits. And at the very end of the century, the natural theologian William Paley (1743–1805), expanded the consequences of this consequentialist logic beyond earthly punishments and rewards to include heavenly ones as well. Believing that the scales of justice must always be balanced, Paley reasoned that if an individual's actions did not reap their rightful consequences in this world, they most definitely would reap them in the next. But as Frey points out "Gone was any unselfish rationale, such as a duty to glorify God or to serve others in one's actions, or even pure love of the good" (p. 31). People were moral only – and selfishly – because of what it would eventually get them.

In the new American republic, this elevation of the self "reached its fullest form as nineteenth-century laissez-faire, which viewed self-interest [positively] as the engine of the economy and source of economic good for society" (p. 35). One key difference here, although unacknowledged by Frey, is that these economic moralists were now trying to consider what was good for whole societies, and not just for individuals. Franklin's and Paley's utilitarianism, in other words, was individualistic: personal actions reap personal consequences. In the nineteenth century, economic moralists brought in whole economic systems. As a result, they could not possibly avoid consequentialist thinking – even if they protested against it – but it was real utilitarian thinking (the greatest good for the greatest number), and not mere personal actions and just desserts. This is where Adam Smith enters the picture. Divorcing ethical motivations from ethical consequences almost entirely, Smith claimed that "self-seeking *unintentionally* produces social good" (p. 37, emphasis in the original) through the happy but mysterious guidance of the "invisible hand." Although wanting to eschew as much as possible the "private vices, public virtues" of Bernard Mandeville, Smith nevertheless clearly championed the good social consequences of economic actions, whose origin and motivation was not benevolence but self-love.

But this elevation of self-interest to a positive good reached its apotheosis in America in the paradoxical figure of the Baptist minister Francis Wayland (1796–1865). In a pivotal passage that is worth quoting in full, Frey writes that

Wayland exploited the fact that Protestant morality had never condemned self, as such, but only exclusively selfishness. Wayland, thus, defined an ethical realm of "innocent" self-interest in which he let laissez-faire principles have full play. ... In this neutral realm, evangelical ethics and Enlightenment economics would converge (p. 43).

Standing between the past and the future, "Wayland repeated the forms of Protestant orthodoxy while neglecting much of its substance" (p. 46). In other words, he reached back into the past to draw what he could from Protestantism, namely individualism, to legitimize and sanctify a developing economic order that was actually highly problematic to the central tenets of the Christian ethical tradition. In the end, and pointing toward the future, he was the first in a long line of American autonomy moralists – thinkers who believed that in this newly carved out "neutral, or innocent, [economic] realm" there was room for unabashed self-interested activity. The only real boundary to economic activity, as Frey describes it, was the *"duty of reciprocity*, namely, that each person should respect in neighbors the same rights he claimed for himself" (p. 44, emphasis in the original). This minimalist ethical formula, ironically first codified by a devout evangelical Christian, was far from the Puritans' more robust concern for the common good, and would form the ethical foundation of autonomy morality down to our very own twenty-first century.

In the next chronological chunk of the book (chapters 8–11, covering the years 1865–1940), we see this autonomy morality reach its most distasteful conclusions, and a more robust relational morality rise in opposition. This was the era of social Darwinism, when theorists like Herbert Spencer (1820–1903) and William Graham Sumner (1840–1910) described economic competition in terms of "survival of the fittest," with the winners rightfully taking their prizes, and the losers doomed either to extinction or lives of inescapable poverty. Clearly, the "neutral, or innocent, realm" (p. 44) of self-interested economic activity as Wayland had described it, has become a free-for-all war of natural selection. Ostensibly, some good still emerged from this way of conceiving of the economy, but it is obviously hard to see a benevolent "invisible hand" anymore, and instead see only "nature red in tooth and claw." Andrew Carnegie's "Gospel of Wealth" softened this harsh rhetoric a little, and called upon the rich to give back to their communities, but he had no consistent philosophical rationale for brutal competition on the one hand and a life of philanthropy on the other.

In contrast, this era's growing cadre of Christian relational moralists did articulate a more consistent, if still inchoate, philosophy of economic life in community. On the Protestant side were Richard T. Ely (1854–1943) and Walter Rauschenbusch (1861–1918), the architects of the Social Gospel movement. Moved by their personal experiences in urban churches, these theorists were appalled by both the moral indifference of more otherworldly Christians, and the ethical poverty of the entire discipline of economics, which "subordinated people to dehumanized abstract principles" (p. 108). "Set against these false absolutes" of individual autonomy and the so-called "laws" of economics, Frey informs us, "the true standard by which to judge an economy was human dignity – the 'personality and manhood of men'" (p. 122). For Catholics, it was virtually the same. Both Pope Leo XIII and the American moralist John Augustine Ryan (1869–1945) agreed that human beings were ends in themselves, and not mere means to the end of greater economic efficiency or conformity to economic laws. They, therefore, advocated for reforms and reconceptualizations that would give human dignity its proper due, including a living wage, the just treatment of labor, and a right understanding of property as a tool "to meet real human needs" (p. 124), and not an end in itself. Incidentally, Frey rightly points out that these relational moralists stood in a tradition previously founded by the Quakers, Moravians, and abolitionists, but it is really in this era, when capitalism began reaping its bitter fruit, that the relational moralist position picks up steam and becomes a consistent and more widespread alternative to autonomy morality.

The era from the end of World War II to the present is the time when these two rival moralities – now fully mature and coherent – really clashed with one another. On the autonomy morality side are the welfare economists, the Chicago school, the Austrian school, Milton Friedman, and Michael Novak. On the relational morality side, the list is much longer: Amatai Etzioni, John Kenneth Galbraith, John Rawls, Arthur Okun, Amartya Sen, Abraham Heschel, the U.S. Catholic Bishops in 1986, Robert Bellah, Philip Wogaman, and Sallie McFague. By this point in the book, frankly, Frey has done such a good job describing the two camps that this final clash of the titans risks being a bit repetitive, but obviously several important factors have changed the game. For starters, obviously, this ideological exchange is more relevant because of its closeness to our own time. Also, with the Chicago and Austrian schools, we get such a stark articulation of the "self-interest as science" (p. 153) position, and such an inflexible advocacy for free markets and personal utility maximization that it actually makes for a somewhat easy target. And finally, as the long list of relational moralists indicates, it seems that this side of the debate is finally having its day.

After decades and centuries of being the still, small voice of conscience in a discourse (and an economy) dominated by autonomy morality, it seems as if the relational moralists have tipped the balance. This is due largely to the fact that the harshness and rigidity of the Chicago and Austrian schools made them not only morally and ethically vulnerable, but intellectually vulnerable as well. As Frey describes it "Chicago economists ... named egoism as the key to virtually all human activity" (p. 153). Against this claim the relational moralists waged a long and, according to Frey, ultimately successful war, not only critiquing the implausibility of this position, but also recommending something (many things) in its place. For one, John Kenneth Galbraith's "writings on advertising" severely problematized "autonomy morality's central assumption – the self-defined individual with innate preferences." "It is a major problem for autonomy ethics," Frey adds, "if the individual's definition of his or her highest good can be manipulated by advertisers or other outsiders" (p. 178). Good point.

But the real destroyer of autonomy morality's claims is Amartya Sen. Taking on the intellectual assumptions of neoclassical economics one by one, Sen systematically dismantled "the assumption of egoism," "the dictum that the rational goal is utility or welfare maximization," and the idea "that every choice 'is guided immediately by the pursuit of one's own goal'." Sen argued that even game situations reveal a certain level of cooperation among the players rather than self-interest alone. There is, therefore, no such thing as "the utility maximizing 'economic man' of neoclassical economic theory" (p. 187). Rather, "human beings do not restrict their notion of goodness to assessments of their utility (or well-being) alone. The ethical person also understands himself or herself in terms of 'goals, commitments, values,' what Sen called a person's 'agency'" (p. 186). "Ultimately," as Frey concludes, "such a one-dimensional version of humanity demeaned human dignity" (p. 189), the sine qua non of relational morality. On this point, Sen is in perfect harmony with the values of more explicitly religious thinkers such as the U.S. Catholic Bishops in their 1986 pastoral letter, *Economic Justice for All*, Philip Wogaman in his *Economics and Ethics: A Christian Inquiry* (1986), and Sallie McFague's environmentalism.

Both the narrative thrust and the concluding chapter of the book leave no question as to which ethical school Frey prefers – although to his credit Frey was also clear about his bias at the very beginning and throughout the book as well. "When guided by autonomy ethics," he writes, "economic life lacks internalized moral boundaries" (p. 212), which invariably leads to excesses that can be both immoral and fiscally hazardous, in that (as with our recent real-estate and financial meltdown) they threaten to destroy the very structure of the economic mechanism. "In contrast," Frey argues, "the great strength of relational morality is that moral boundaries are inherent in the maintenance of relationships. Within relationships, the dignity of the other is recognized, and respect, not excess, is the normal response" (p. 213). Enough said.

In conclusion, although I agree with Frey as to the obvious virtues of relational morality and the internal inconsistencies and potential amorality of autonomy morality, I feel the reviewer's responsibility to argue the contrary. But again, to his credit, Frey is aware of all sides of the debate, and does a laudable job himself of pointing out the real virtues of the autonomy morality position. The problem, however, is that this praise is buried right smack in the middle of the book where it risks being either minimized or overlooked completely by a reader. As Frey himself makes the case, autonomy morality has at its foundation an admirable and defensible concept of human dignity that (as with many such concepts) is best understood historically. In medieval Europe, people were severely constrained religiously, politically, legally, and economically. "Enlightenment thought," Frey writes, "was in large measure a protest against premodern society's lack of respect for the individual," and thus can be conceived as a "movement for individual rights." At the heart of the Enlightenment discipline of economics, therefore, was an understanding that people "are the best judges of their own interests," and that "human dignity meant self-definition" (p. 130), as opposed to having oneself defined coercively by whatever powers that be. To this reviewer anyway, this kind of self-definition is not only obviously liberating, but also precious and thoroughly defensible ethically.

It is true that the self has the power to make itself the center of the universe at the expense of all others, God, or any concept of the common good. The self, therefore, clearly needs restraints for the good of others, and less clearly (and potentially dangerously) for its own good. The problem comes in the setting of those restraints because then we are subject to the world of power, and forced limitations that may not only be unwelcome to some individuals, but harmful to everyone except those who set and agree to them. And if this all sounds a little too much like Friedrich Hayek, I do not intend it. Actually, I hope that this sounds more like Frank Knight, whom Frey describes as "an inside critic" of the Chicago school. "[A]cutely aware of the moral weaknesses of markets," Knight nevertheless embraced laissez-faire because he disliked the "authoritarian social alternatives" (p. 157) even more. There is still, I believe, a great deal of truth in this lesser-of-two-evils argument. On the autonomy morality side, we do definitely have excess and egocentrism; but on the relational morality side we have not only the relationships into which people enter freely and by which they are bound lovingly, but also those in which raw power can play an unwelcome role. If we are to seriously consider the ethical flaws of the nearly unrestrained "economic man," in other words, let us also think seriously about the obvious ethical dangers of binding him too tightly – and who precisely will be doing the binding.

REFERENCES

National Conference of Catholic Bishops (1986). *Economic justice for all: Pastoral letter on catholic social teaching and the U.S. economy.* National Conference of Catholic Bishops, Washington, DC.

Wogaman, P. (1986). *Economics and ethics: A Christian inquiry.* Philadelphia, PA: Fortress Press.

STABILE'S THE LIVING WAGE

THE LIVING WAGE AND THE HISTORY OF ECONOMICS

Thomas A. Stapleford

Review essay on D. R. Stabile's *The Living Wage: Lessons from the History of Economic Thought*. Cheltenham, UK: Edward Elgar, 2008. 176 pp. ISBN 978184844197.

In 2006, a group of students at St. Mary's College of Maryland held a sit-in within the president's office, demanding that the college grant its workers a "living wage." Donald Stabile, an economist at St. Mary's, found himself deeply ambivalent about the students' campaign, sympathizing with their motivations ("wanting to see the workers gain a better life") but objecting to their methods. As an accomplished historian of economics, he responded by turning to history, studying "what leading economists [have] said both for and against the idea of a living wage" (p. vii). The result was *The Living Wage: Lessons from the History of Economic Thought*, an account that ranges from Aristotle to Milton Friedman, with most attention going to economists from Adam Smith onwards.

Given the broad chronological sweep of Stabile's coverage and the short length of the book (150 pages, plus a short bibliography and index), he has little time for historical context or detailed engagement with secondary literature. Rather, Stabile offers a series of carefully constructed summaries (supplemented by key quotations) from the published writings of various economists. It is an eclectic, though useful, mix, including canonical figures (such as Smith, Alfred Marshall, and Joseph Schumpeter), equally prominent

A Research Annual
Research in the History of Economic Thought and Methodology, Volume 28-A, 329–338
Copyright © 2010 by Emerald Group Publishing Limited
All rights of reproduction in any form reserved
ISSN: 0743-4154/doi:10.1108/S0743-4154(2010)000028A015

critics and outsiders (such as Karl Marx or Thorstein Veblen), and less well-known figures (such as Herbert Davenport and Solomon Barkin) who offer important perspectives that complement those of their more famous colleagues.

Using published work from long-dead authors as a guide to current policy debates is a dangerous enterprise, as Stabile is aware. The "lessons" from this survey of the past, he warns, should not be applied "in the spirit of asking, 'What would Jesus do?'" (or, perhaps more appropriately, "What would Adam Smith do?"). Such questions are impossible to answer definitively, since the economists who figure most heavily in his analysis (notably Smith, John Stuart Mill, Marx, and Marshall) confronted a social, political, and economic world very different from our own. Some of the principles drawn from Smith's writings, for example, would suggest his sympathy with the aims of the contemporary living wage movement, but other passages could be cited against that interpretation. How Smith himself would have reconciled the matter, we cannot say (p. viii).

As this problem indicates, the lessons that Stabile offers in *The Living Wage* are of an indirect sort, less answers than questions and less the resolution of old issues that the raising of new ones. In general, Stabile wants to "move the debate over the living wage away from a debate over the definition of 'social justice' towards a consideration of the economic issues involved in that debate" (p. vii). That quotation may seem to echo the common desire of many contemporary economists to dismiss moral reasoning about wages in favor of allegedly non-normative, scientific analysis, but Stabile has something more complicated in mind. As the book makes clear, leading economists through the early twentieth century had explicitly normative goals for society – including the belief that low-wage workers should receive an adequate basic income – and they sought to devise policies that would help to realize those objectives. Nonetheless, these economists also gave hard-nosed attention to the methods that might be used to reach such a goal and their likely consequences. Here are the "economic issues" that Stabile finds missing in too much of the contemporary living wage movement.

Rather than approaching his topic through a strict chronological survey, Stabile takes a thematic approach organized around three related arguments for a living wage: sustainability, capability, and externality. Arguments from sustainability emphasize the need to maintain an effective workforce, whereas those from capability highlight the desirable traits and rights of workers as citizens and productive members of a community. Arguments derived from externalities take a different tack, insisting that a given industry's failure to sustain its workforce or to provide the wages necessary for capable citizenship thereby creates externalities – that is, problems that affect a third party (in this case, the community as a whole) that is not a direct participant in the relevant labor negotiations.

Stabile's exploration of these arguments as they were proposed, developed, and challenged by various economists makes for enlightening reading. The living wage, a seemingly basic idea, soon draws Stabile and his protagonists into discussing an impressive range of important concepts in the history of economics, such as wage theory, marginalism, unions, the alienation of labor, Pareto optimality, creative destruction, human capital, conspicuous consumption, and the Coase Theorem, among others. No one, I suspect, can read the book without learning something valuable; likewise, no reviewer can summarize the diversity of positions that it aptly and succinctly elucidates while still reserving adequate space for a broader commentary on the book.

Instead of offering a detailed summary, therefore, I propose to address two more general questions: First, what are the main lessons that Stabile intends his readers to draw from this parade of exemplars, and second, who is his intended audience? The latter question will lead us – fruitfully, I hope – into an issue that has occasioned much commentary among historians of economics in recent years, namely wherein lies the future for the field? For Stabile's work is a superb example (in both senses of that phrase) of a particular style of writing the history of economics, and in considering its very real merits and what I fear may be the limitations on its reception, we may be led to some useful conclusions.

STABILE'S LESSONS

As I suggested earlier, Stabile's "lessons" typically take the form of questions. For example, what is the conceptual basis for defining a minimum income sufficient to sustain a labor force (what Stabile dubs the argument from sustainability)? Is there an absolute standard based strictly on basic biological needs, as Rose Friedman argued (p. 53)? Or do the necessities of life also include "whatever the custom of the country renders it indecent for creditable people, even of the lowest order, to be without," as Adam Smith declared (quoted in Stabile, p. 17)? Introducing Amartya Sen's notion of capability broadens our scope even further, for now we are concerned about developing the traits, abilities, and opportunities that can make workers more productive, effective, and valuable citizens (a concern that Stabile finds implicitly in numerous authors, including Aristotle, Smith, Marshall, and Richard Ely).

Even a sympathetic observer, I think, would thus recognize that the notion of an adequate income inherently requires normative judgments. How, then, are these judgments made? How might a living wage be determined and implemented? The contemporary living wage movement often relies on some form of expert calculation, such as the "Family Budget Calculator" created by the Economic Policy Institute.[1] Activists then rally community members to press local governments or institutions (typically universities) to mandate a minimum wage based upon those figures.

Surprisingly, in one of the most significant conclusions of the book, Stabile demonstrates that none of his chosen economists recommended government legislation or third-party activism as a means to procure a living wage. Instead, those who worried that a free labor market based on individual negotiation might not produce sufficient incomes for low-skill workers looked toward unions as the solution (p. 146). Nineteenth-century economists such as Mill and Marshall believed that unions could overcome the asymmetries of bargaining power between workers and employers and thereby produce a more effective negotiation that would allocate to workers the true value of their labor. Moreover, Mill believed that unions would foster a "broader social outlook" among workers and prevent a debilitating dependence on the state because laborers had earned their wages through voluntary collective bargaining rather than legal mandates (p. 68). By the twentieth century, many economists – including generally pro-labor economists such as Thorstein Veblen, John R. Commons, and Ben Seligman – had grown more skeptical of Mill's idealized vision of unions' power and moral beneficence, but even they continued to view collective bargaining as the best hope for achieving an appropriate wage.

Closely tied to the determination of a living wage is an equally complex set of questions about the consequences of implementing any given scheme. If creating a living wage will transfer money to lower-income workers, where will that money come from? Who, ultimately, will bear the costs? Furthermore, how will establishing a living wage affect the labor market in a community and, ultimately, the economy as a whole? As Stabile's account illustrates, even economists who strongly believed in the moral and social necessity of ensuring adequate incomes for workers and their families wrestled mightily with these difficult questions. Indeed, it was partially for these reasons that they favored collective bargaining over universal government mandates (which might distort labor markets and thereby hinder the efficient allocation of labor). In a related vein, economists who viewed unions themselves as distorting influences but nonetheless recognized a social need for a minimum income sought to move the problem outside of labor markets altogether, a solution exemplified by Milton Friedman's proposal for a negative income tax (p. 52).

In general, then, the book forms a sympathetic critique of the contemporary living wage movement, for as Stabile repeatedly notes, most current activists have ignored these important and complex questions in favor of a heavy emphasis on the serious ethical and social problems raised by low incomes among the working class. Still, those who dismiss ethical norms such as a living wage as inappropriate subject matter for economics (the "market economists," in Stabile's terminology) are also brought to task, since the decision to treat efficiency as the only and ultimate value in economic analysis is itself a normative judgment, and one that would have startled many of the greatest minds in the history of the discipline. As Stabile concludes, "fairness matters even if it cannot be defined with precision" (p. 149).

THE MISSING AUDIENCE

Having witnessed living wage campaigns at two institutions (Harvard University and the University of Notre Dame), I have no doubt that participants on both sides of these struggles could learn much from Stabile's account. Moreover, the book's benefits extend beyond its coverage of the living wage itself, since in examining that issue, Stabile is drawn into a basic introduction to wage theory and a series of important reflections (from Smith, Marx, Veblen, Hayek, von Mises, Commons, and others) on the economic and social effects of the free market, industrial economy. Yet the very strengths of the book lead us to an important question: who is going to read it?

A similar question has plagued the history of economics more generally, as the field continues to be marginalized within the economics profession (e.g., Weintraub, 2002; Tubaro & Anger, 2008). One solution has been to move the history of economics toward intellectual history and toward the history of science in particular (e.g., Schabas, 1992). That is clearly not the direction that Stabile is heading in this book, however. Not only does he eschew detailed consideration of the historical context for the authors whom he examines, but his thematic approach (organized around the concepts of sustainability, capability, and externality) relies on an anachronistic re-reading of texts that has become (rightly or not) anathema in intellectual history. Stabile's three basic concepts were not clearly delineated until the late-eighteenth century (in the case of sustainability) or even the twentieth (for capability and externality). Thus, in analyzing earlier texts, Stabile is forced to rely upon roughly analogous themes, precursors, or inchoate principles that encompass some aspect of these ideas. The trouble extends to the very notion of the living wage itself, since that phrase did not become common until the nineteenth century and was not always used in a consistent manner (see Stapleford, 2008). In short, Stabile is taking a colonial approach to the past, mining historical texts for excerpts or ideas that might be relevant to the debates and intellectual framework of his homeland, that is, the present.

This impression is strengthened by the choices Stabile has made in selecting economists for inclusion in his account. Although we learn that Marshall, for example, ignored the living wage movement in late nineteenth-century Britain (p. 146), we hear nothing about how numerous turn-of-the-century economists (including Henry Seager, Sidney and Beatrice Webb, John R. Commons, and Richard Ely) did support minimum-wage legislation, in part because they believed that the resulting disemployment would primarily affect marginal classes of low-skill workers (immigrants and women) who lacked adequate bargaining power and thus needed to be protected or excluded from the labor force (Power, 1999; Leonard, 2005). More generally, Stabile makes no attempt to justify his particular selections as representative of political economists more broadly during specific periods, nor does he delve deeply into the extensive literature on the history of the living wage ideal or minimum-wage legislation, in which economists were closely involved (as both supporters and critics) from the late-nineteenth century onwards (e.g., Paulsen, 1996; Glickman, 1997; Mutari, 2000).

All these objections would be nearly fatal had Stabile set out to write a balanced survey of the history of economists' views on the living wage and its close cousin, the minimum wage. Yet that was not his intent. As the subtitle makes clear, this is a book of "lessons from the history of economic thought" (or better, "from certain past economists"), and not a contribution to history *per se*. Furthermore, as I noted earlier, these lessons are worthwhile. Still, the puzzle remains: who will be learning them, if not historians?

Economists (at least those outside the history of economics) are an unlikely choice. As Stabile rightly indicates in his introduction, most contemporary economists have little interest in discussing the living wage since it is fundamentally grounded in the kinds of ethical judgments that they believe should be excluded from economic analysis. Most economists try to side-step these questions by talking about minimum-wage legislation (not the living wage ideal) and focusing entirely on empirical estimates of its effects on employment, prices, incomes, and so forth (e.g., Card & Krueger, 1995; Neumark & Wascher, 2008). Given economists' similar inclination to ignore the history of economics, a book that combines the two will hardly be attractive.

Instead, given the tenor of the book and its emphases, Stabile's primary audience seems to be the activists and students who support the current living wage movement. Indeed, knowing the origins of the book, it is not hard to believe that Stabile wrote the book while envisioning the student activists at St. Mary's College or their peers at numerous institutions across the United States. Moreover, because Stabile's treatment leads him into broader theoretical discussions, the book serves as an excellent introduction to basic concepts in the economics of wages while also acquainting students with other important topics (e.g., externalities) and major figures in economics. All told, in fact, it would make an admirable complement or core text for an undergraduate course that aimed to give students a basic grasp on the economic analysis of labor.

Here, though, abstract virtues come crashing into practical realities, since the publisher (Edward Elgar) has set a price for the book ($100) that precludes its adoption at the undergraduate level. It is hard to blame Edward Elgar for this decision, given the minor place of the history of economics within undergraduate economics curricula. Stabile's book thus exemplifies the conundrums facing the history of economics: the field has a real relevance to contemporary economic problems but has not attracted sufficient student or administrative interest within economics to make specialized texts (as opposed to general histories) financially viable.

Nonetheless, I think Stabile is on the right track, at least for those historians of economics who wish to see their work contribute to contemporary political economy rather than to debates among intellectual historians. By choosing to focus his book on a major, current public policy issue instead of the more general, abstract theory that lies behind it (wage theory), Stabile created a much larger potential readership. If economists are uninterested in learning from their past, there are plenty of other academics (and their undergraduates) who could benefit from a richer understanding of how a historically-informed economic analysis might shed light on salient topics in their own disciplines, whether political history, political science, law, sociology, or the myriad of interdisciplinary fields that cluster around public policy issues such as poverty, health care, and labor. Moreover, these groups (who have made the study of politics a central part of their disciplines) are generally more open to examining topics with obvious normative aspects. Those who wish to keep the history of economics directly relevant to contemporary political and economic life have, I suspect, cast their nets far too narrowly by choosing to emphasize academic economics and high economic theory (e.g. Moscati, 2008; Palma, 2008) to the detriment of major public policy questions with rich and complex economic dimensions. Health care, welfare programs, trade policy, international finance, government regulation, monetary and fiscal policy: perhaps the future of the history of economics lies in its relevance to these issues more broadly and not in recapturing the field's previous status as a handmaiden to academic economic theory.

By organizing his book around the living wage, Stabile has moved partially in this direction, but not far enough, I fear. As his subtitle indicates, Stabile ultimately remains with a traditional conception of the history of economics as a history of the "thought" of the great theorists of the past. Missing from his account are the practical political and social efforts to wrestle with the economic problems that sparked these theoretical reflections, efforts that (by the turn of the twentieth century) involved many intelligent economists. The old version of the history of economics (the history of theory) is entirely appropriate if one wishes primarily to engage theoretically inclined economists. But if one wishes, like Stabile, to inform a debate about public policy (where participants may have limited interest in economic theory per se), then a correspondingly broader focus is needed.

Ironically, attention to the history of the living wage movement might have helped to sharpen Stabile's account. For example, the previous high-point of the living wage concept in U.S. political economy occurred in the wake of the First World War (Glickman, 1997; Stapleford, 2008). At that moment, however, perceptive and sympathetic economists (such as the University of Chicago's Paul Douglas) recognized a basic problem. An "adequate" income – the living wage, however that might be defined – surely depended on the number of dependents supported by a given worker. But of course, these numbers varied from worker to worker; thus a uniform living wage would undercompensate some workers and overcompensate others. The latter outcome was a serious danger, as Paul Douglas realized to his great chagrin, since supplying the most-commonly cited value of a living wage in the early 1920s to every American employee would require a sum greater than the entire U.S. national income at the time (Douglas, 1925, pp. 11–25). In short, "adequate" incomes could only be defined on an individualized basis.

A little thought, though, suggests that such individualized calculations could have numerous pernicious consequences if they were allowed to determine wages directly. (Surely, for instance, employers would avoid workers with greater number of dependents, who would require correspondingly higher "living" wages.) Small wonder, then, that Douglas looked beyond wages for his solution. Following the path of like-minded European reformers in the 1920s, Douglas advocated a system of "family allowances" administered by the state or industrial associations in which money would be collected from firms (or potentially all citizens) and redistributed to families based on their individual circumstances (Douglas, 1925, pp. 41–190). Milton Friedman's proposal for a negative income tax, though implemented differently, shares a similar logic: a uniform tax that is used to meet individualized needs without distorting the labor market. Douglas (who later became a Democratic senator) and Friedman had very different political views, hence, it is telling that they came to similar conclusions about the problems of the living wage and the structure of a more viable alternative. Likewise, Stabile notes (but does not emphasize sufficiently) that Friedman's proposal drew support from left-wing economists such as Ben Seligman (Stabile, p. 145). Ultimately, the great lesson from a history of the living wage ideal may be that though low wages are a proximal cause of inadequate incomes, the solution to that social problem may lie outside the wage system itself.

NOTE

1. The Family Budget Calculator can be found online at: http://www.epi.org/pages/budget_calculator_intro/. The Economic Policy Institute's formula was recommended by the Association of Community Organizations for Reform Now in its living wage campaign (http://www.livingwagecampaign.org) and has been further developed into a fine-grained, living wage calculator by the Poverty in America project at Penn State University: http://www.povertyinamerica.psu.edu/projects/living_wage/

REFERENCES

Card, D. E., & Krueger, A. B. (1995). *Myth and measurement: The new economics of the minimum wage*. Princeton, NJ: Princeton University Press.

Douglas, P. H. (1925). *Wages and the family*. Chicago: University of Chicago Press.

Glickman, L. B. (1997). *A living wage: American workers and the making of consumer society*. Ithaca, NY: Cornell University Press.

Leonard, T. C. (2005). Protecting family and race: The progressive case for regulating women's work. *American Journal of Economics and Sociology, 64*(3), 757–791.

Moscati, I. (2008). More economics, please: We're historians of economics. *Journal of the History of Economic Thought, 30*(1), 85–91.

Mutari, E. (2000). The fair labor standards act of 1938 and competing visions of the living wage. *Review of Radical Political Economics, 32*(3), 408–416.

Neumark, D., & Wascher, W. L. (2008). *Minimum wages*. Cambridge, MA: MIT Press.

Palma, N. P. G. (2008). History of economics or a selected history of economics? *Journal of the History of Economic Thought, 30*(1), 93–104.

Paulsen, G. E. (1996). *A living wage for the forgotten man: The quest for fair labor standards, 1933–1941*. Selinsgrove, PA: Susquehanna University Press.

Power, M. (1999). Parasitic-industries analysis and arguments for a living wage for women in the early twentieth-century United States. *Feminist Economics, 5*(1), 61–78.

Schabas, M. (1992). Breaking away: History of economics as history of science. *History of Political Economy, 24*(1), 187–203.

Stapleford, T. A. (2008). Defining a "living wage" in America: Transformations in union wage theories, 1870–1930. *Labor History, 49*(1), 1–22.

Tubaro, P., & Anger, E. (2008). Introduction: mini-symposium on the future of history of economics: Young-scholar's perspective. *Journal of the History of Economic Thought, 30*(1), 81–84.

Weintraub, E. R. (Ed.) (2002). *The future of the history of economics*. Durham, NC: Duke University Press.

HUNT AND MCNAMARA'S LIBERALISM, CONSERVATISM, AND HAYEK'S IDEA OF SPONTANEOUS ORDER

SPONTANEOUS ORDER AND THE LIMITS OF REASON AND TRADITION

Steven Horwitz

Review essay on L. Hunt and P. McNamara's (Eds)*Liberalism, Conservatism, and Hayek's Idea of Spontaneous Order*. New York: Palgrave Macmillan, 2007. viii + 232 pp., ISBN 9781403984255.

Over the past decade or two, the Hayek Studies industry has been in a period of significant growth. A whole variety of books about Hayek, both his life and his thought, have appeared, with each trying to differentiate its product sufficiently to make a mark on both scholarship and sales. Into this fairly crowded marketplace comes a volume edited by two political scientists, neither of whom is known for contributions to the Hayek literature. The volume grew out of a lecture series at Utah State University, and the group of scholars that they assembled is notable as well for not being a cast of the "usual Hayekian suspects," nor exclusively economists. In fact, there is only one economist contributing to the volume, with a couple of philosophers and one historian, and the rest being political

A Research Annual
Research in the History of Economic Thought and Methodology, Volume 28-A, 339–347
Copyright © 2010 by Emerald Group Publishing Limited
All rights of reproduction in any form reserved
ISSN: 0743-4154/doi:10.1108/S0743-4154(2010)000028A016

scientists. In addition, all the essays address the concept of "spontaneous order," which is central to Hayek's intellectual framework. More specifically, each essay approaches that topic in light of its relationship to "liberalism" and "conservatism." The result is a largely excellent set of papers that offer critical and constructive explorations of the idea of spontaneous order and its place in Hayek's thought and in understanding the social world.

Peter McNamara usefully introduces the volume by contrasting Hayek's conceptions of the "tribal society" and the "Great Society." The former is the world that humans inhabited for the centuries before modernity, and industrialization and capitalism more specifically. It is a world where the fundamental social groups were small, kinship-based, face-to-face, and characterized by members having "closely shared ideals and interests" (p. 3). Such groups were also notable for their "internal" peace but great discomfort with out-group strangers. The tribal society is the one in which humans have evolved to survive, which implies, for Hayek, that the adjustment to the larger, anonymous, "ends-independent" world of the Great Society will involve overcoming deeply ingrained customs and traditions and, if evolutionary psychology is right, the structure of the human mind itself. As McNamara points out, Hayek's description of that transition process is more "conjectural history" than finely detailed anthropology. Nonetheless, it does point to important differences between the kinds of society.

For the volume at hand, the important difference worth noting is the way in which the Great Society is characterized by individual action and spontaneous order, rather than collective decision-making and a more intentional form of social order. Such a society requires, according to Hayek, that individuals agree to obey sets of abstract rules that enable them to pursue their separate purposes with the indirect cooperation of numerous anonymous others. However, as Hayek argued in *The Fatal Conceit*, even in the Great Society, we must learn to "live in two sorts of worlds at once" (Hayek, 1988). We still maintain connections with our family and friends that, in McNamara's words, "resemble those of the tribal society" (p. 10). Modernity requires that we recognize that each of these "worlds" exist and that different moral rules apply in each. Furthermore, the Great Society requires that we not succumb to the temptation to apply the moral rules of the tribal society, which are deeply ingrained in our biological and social inheritance, to our interactions in this very different world. That need to "check our emotions" necessitates, according to McNamara, a kind of "stoicism" that co-exists uneasily with Hayek's simultaneous belief that checking those emotions in favor of the abstract rules of the Great Society is the path toward a liberal, progressive future. McNamara rightly notes that this is a difficult balancing act to pull off.

It is also one of the volume's recurring themes, namely the never-ending debate over whether Hayek was "really" a conservative or a liberal. Conservatives reading Hayek are likely to pay more selective attention to those moments of stoicism and his highly respectful attitude toward long-standing human social traditions. Liberals, by contrast, will focus on his more liberatory themes, especially the way in which the spread of the abstract rules of the Great Society brings more and more of humanity out of poverty, as well has his belief in the power of ideas to change the world and his cosmopolitanism and internationalism. Each of these readings has implications for how the concept of spontaneous order fits into Hayek's thinking. McNamara's introduction sets this up nicely by distinguishing between the operation of the market (and by extension much of the Great Society) and the "framework" that makes the society possible. He then notes that even if the concept of spontaneous order explains well the operation of markets, "it is less obvious that it is adequate for explaining just how the framework that makes the market possible comes into being" (p. 13). Most of the essays in the collection explore the questions raised by the degree to which Hayek's powerful belief in the social evolutionary forces of spontaneous order requires and/or is compatible with any role for human reason in consciously creating the framework of rules within which that evolution takes place.

The first two essays, by James Otteson and Louis Hunt, are grouped under the heading of "Fundamental Themes" and both address the history of spontaneous order thinking. Otteson provides a clear and concise overview of the role of the Scottish Enlightenment and Adam Smith specifically in developing the concept of spontaneous order. Otteson focuses on Smith's "market model" of the evolution of morality, by which we come to "shared moral standards" (p. 28). He compares these moral and economic standards to John Searle's concept of "institutional facts," which are features of the world that are factual by virtue of being the product of "human agreement." Otteson then explores the question of whether Smith's "market model" can really explain the evolution of morality in the face of modern game-theoretic concerns with Prisoner's Dilemma problems and the like. He argues that a renewed look at Smith's claim that we have a "desire for mutual sympathy of sentiments," a claim bolstered by contemporary work in evolutionary psychology, pushes us to find "social situations of reciprocal exchange" (pp. 36–37). The result is that our desire to avoid the disapproval of others might well help us overcome the problems to the spontaneous emergence of the moral rules that frame the liberal social order.

Hunt's essay, which is one of the best in the collection, looks at the way in which the concept of spontaneous order finds its origins and scope within Hayek's work. The first part of the essay locates Hayek's spontaneous order theorizing in his contributions to the socialist calculation debate of the interwar years. Hunt offers a very nice reading of the debate that stresses the ways in which Hayek's engagement with the arguments for planning led him to reconsider not just the narrow arguments for the market, but the entire edifice of neoclassical economics and the philosophic framework of the defense of the liberal order. In "The use of knowledge in society" Hayek (1948), argues Hunt, makes the transition from the narrowly economic to the broader social and cultural application of spontaneous order by identifying the emergence of unplanned order as the "central theoretical problem of all social science." Hunt also quite appropriately mentions the role that Hayek's work in psychology (e.g., Hayek, 1952) plays in his broader use of spontaneous order. His theory of cognition portrays the human brain/mind as a spontaneous order that is rooted in nature but critical to our understanding of the spontaneous order of society. Specifically, Hunt points toward the need for a better understanding of Hayek's "social epistemology" as a species of spontaneous order.

Hunt also has an excellent discussion of the roles of reason and tradition in Hayek's concept of spontaneous order. He rightly points out that although Hayek is respectful of tradition, he allows scope to challenge traditions, just not all traditions at once. Hunt likens his position here to those of Burke and Gadamer, though without their strong sympathy toward conservatism. There is a difference between reverence for tradition and respect; for Hayek, tradition has a status not unlike a "rebuttable presumption" in the law, a view also adopted by Gerald Gaus in a later essay. Hunt also points out that, in turn, this suggests that although Hayek rejects "rationalism," he does not reject "reason." Individual traditions can be subject to the use of reason, including elements of rules that frame spontaneous ordering processes. It is possible, Hunt argues, for a Hayekian to argue consistently for conscious change in the legal or institutional structure. If not, how else to explain Hayek's trenchant criticisms of conservatism in the postscript to *The Constitution of Liberty* (Hayek, 1960) or the various places where he argues that problems of the mixed economy have resulted from poorly defined property rights that could be improved upon? Although Hunt clearly takes one side on the question of Hayek's liberalism/conservatism, he does understand why others would come down differently and the issues he raises are ones that recur in the remaining essays.

The remaining seven essays are grouped as "critical reflections." The first of these is Ross Emmett's overview of Frank Knight's challenge to Hayek that spontaneous order is "not enough to govern a liberal society." Hayek and Knight of course tangled over other issues during the early part of the century, but Emmett focuses in on Knight's argument that Hayek's account of the liberal tradition assumes that "spontaneous order emerges without *discussion*" (p. 72, emphasis in original). More specifically, Knight argued that liberal democracies "require...a moral vision of what they want their societies to become" and implementing a vision requires discussion and conscious action, rather than just adopting "institutions via natural selection." For Knight, Emmett argues, the key aspect of liberalism was that it "endogenized law making," putting in the hands of humans the ability to "make" the law and thus create the framework within which the spontaneous order of the market could play itself out. Knight's criticisms are echoed in Buchanan's later work, with its distinction between the pre- and post-constitutional levels of analysis. Like Knight, Buchanan argued that Hayek under-appreciated both the need for, and our ability to engage in, conscious construction of the rules of the game based on ideas and moral visions. For Knight, Hayek's reliance on spontaneous order to generate the rules of the game is misplaced and ultimately commits him to a form of conservatism that Knight sees as antithetical to the more substantive notion of freedom promised by liberalism's commitment to discussion as the basis for law making.

As evidence of the inkblot that is Hayek's thought, the very next essay by Richard Boyd and James Ashley Morrison fruitfully compares Hayek's thinking on spontaneous order to that of Michael Oakeshott, who found Hayek's "liberal optimism about the progressive and cumulative benefits of the competitive market order" to be unwarranted. Where Knight saw Hayek as a conservative for believing that spontaneous order could and should generate the rules of the game, Oakeshott saw him as a liberal for believing that spontaneous ordering processes would "secure an unambiguously superior future" (p. 89). The core of Oakeshott's disagreement, they argue, is his view that the value of tradition comes not from "any innate superiority or efficiency" as Hayek argued, but from the connections it gives us with others who have done things that way. Tradition's value is in the social cohesion it creates, regardless of its propensity to promote human survival and flourishing. Oakeshott places more emphasis on the disruptive nature of social change, whereas Hayek would see ongoing social evolution as superior responses to new circumstances. Hayek's belief that institutions and practices would, and must, evolve as new human problems arose makes him too much of an enemy of tradition to be a conservative in Oakeshott's view.

Boyd and Morrison lay out this argument clearly; however, they do not always give Hayek's argument the most charitable reading possible. In particular, they seem to offer (pp. 100–102) a reading of Hayek that paints him as overly attached to a *homo economicus* conception of human action and as not sufficiently recognizing that the gains of progress come with costs as well. The former is clearly false, though perhaps is understandable coming from Oakeshott's perspective of not wishing to evaluate tradition and change in terms of efficiency considerations. Hayek does, however, recognize that the loss of traditions comes at a cost. Much of his social anthropology of our move from the tribal to the anonymous society is offered in terms of a struggle between the gains from challenging tradition and cost of resisting the powerful hold that long-standing ways of doing things have on us. Even our contemporary struggle to live in two worlds at once is understood in terms of costs and benefits. Boyd and Morrison (and Oakeshott) are clearly right that Hayek believes the gains outweigh the costs, but a liberal reading of Hayek's theory of spontaneous order does not deny that there are such costs.

Scott Yenor addresses the role of religion in the history of liberalism and Hayek's spontaneous order theory of the rise of the West by offering a comparison to Hume. Yenor explores some scattered remarks of Hayek about the role that religious belief plays in convincing people to adhere to the abstract moral rules of the Great Society in the absence of our ability to articulate completely why such rules are beneficial. In these passages, Hayek offers a sort of "noble lie" defense of religion's role in supporting the spontaneous ordering of society: those who are unable to understand the social science behind the need to obey the moral rules of the Great Society can be "duped" into doing so through religious beliefs (e.g., most of the Ten Commandments and the versions of the Golden Rule that exist in almost every faith tradition) that create incentives to obey them. God is a useful fiction in this view. Yenor uses Hume's more critical view of religion to argue that it has more often been a barrier to the development of commercial morality. Yenor also points out, echoing the themes of McCloskey's (2006) recent work, that the commercial world is often "the place where humane virtues are most at home" (p. 121). He concludes with a call for a role for philosophy and history in making judgments about the roles played by institutions such as religion in the evolution of the liberal order against what he sees as Hayek's attempt to "sanitize" religion's role. A more thorough treatment of the dual role of religion in both limiting and supporting different elements of the liberal order would be a welcome addition to the Hayek literature, and Yenor has provided a useful starting point, especially when seen alongside McCloskey's work.

Larry Arnhart's and Gerald Gaus's chapters each develop evolutionary themes in Hayek. Arnhart explores the ways in which Darwinian biology undergirds Hayek's conservatism, and conservatism more generally. Arnhart, notably, includes modern libertarians within the broad notion of conservatism he uses. He nicely traces the way in which our understanding of our biological heritage can be used to defend the core conservative notions of private property, family life, and limited government. However, he also recognizes that biology is simply a set of constraints and that it does not strictly determine our behavior. This gives, in his view, scope for rational deliberation and changes in rules and traditions. Legislators can, at the margins, tweak the rules of property when new circumstances arise, and changes in the nature of heterosexual marriage make the calls of same-sex marriage an understandable evolution in the institution (pp. 139–142). Arnhart's analysis in this section is, I believe, very faithful to Hayek's own views. I would only add that the ways in which a "Darwinian" approach to the social world such as Arnhart lays out can allow for the sorts of adaptations of tradition he notes suggest that it is more properly understood as a variety of liberalism rather than conservatism.

Gaus's chapter looks at Hayek argument that governments should "follow abstract general principles" rather than pursue more expedient policies that would seem to make people better off, at least in the short run. He offers an excellent and novel philosophical defense of Hayek's position, focusing on the knowledge problems facing attempts to be "expedient" in a complex social order. Gaus also defends a more liberal reading of Hayek by offering a defense of our "evolved morality that grounds an attitude of qualified rational deferral to our current evolved moral rules" (p. 170). Such a defense, he argues, is less deferential to evolved norms than Hayek himself was as it allows us to challenge those evolved norms by invoking the qualifiers and/or rational arguments for challenging them. Gaus also, rightly in my view, notes that a reading of Hayek that is overly deferential to evolved norms seem to "not fit well with his liberalism and faith in the dynamic and self-regulating character of the Great Society" (p. 170).

In "Culture, Order, and Virtue," Michael Munger looks at culture as a spontaneous order and the ways in which culture enables us to cooperate in strategic situations such as the Prisoner's Dilemma. With the inability to communicate directly, players in a prisoner's dilemma game may well be able to reach the cooperative solution by relying on Hayekian "learnt rules" deep in the culture rather than any rational calculation of the costs and benefits. Munger points out that this is precisely, on a Hayekian account, why these sorts of cultural norms have survived the evolutionary test: they promoted the social cooperation that is at the core of a growing civilization.

Jerry Muller's thoughts on the limits of spontaneous order close the volume. Unfortunately, his reading of Hayek is both uncharitable and mistaken in places. He takes the most conservative reading of Hayek, claiming that he gives no scope for legislators guided by social science to foresee negative unintended consequences of social developments (p. 202). Hayek, to the contrary, did believe legislators could do precisely this, especially when evolutionary paths reached apparent dead ends or when expedient policies violating general principles were proposed. Muller could have used a good reading of Gaus's chapter on this point. Muller also charges Hayek with ignoring the market's shortcomings and not trying to develop remedies for them (p. 204). Again, Hayek acknowledged those shortcomings and defended more of a government safety net than most of his modern-day libertarian followers. He also proposed positive legislation to deal with certain weaknesses in how markets functioned in the contemporary world, as well as what some consider an inappropriately constructivist redesign of democratic political institutions. Muller also lays blame on Hayekian ideas for the failures of post-Soviet Russia because the "limited government" crowd supposedly did not understand that one needed a government "strong enough to enforce the rule of law, protect property," and so on. He makes a similar claim about post-Saddam Iraq.

Unfortunately, he offers no citations of anyone invoking Hayek to make such arguments, and I would claim that it is because no such citations exist, mostly because Hayekians have always recognized the need for institutions able to enforce the rule of law and property rights, and no Hayek-influenced Sovietologist I am aware of argued otherwise. And I know of no Hayekian making the claim that post-Saddam Iraq would magically produce order out of chaos in the absence of certain underlying cultural values and legal institutions. In fact, one Hayekian observer of Iraq has made this point explicitly (Coyne, 2006). Muller has constructed a very flimsy straw man that he easily knocks over. Doing so, however, adds little to our understanding of Hayek and his ideas. The overall high quality, intellectual fairness, and lack of ideological tone of the preceding essays makes Muller's contribution especially striking and disappointing.

This volume's attempt to both explore Hayek's work on spontaneous order and evaluate its relationship to liberalism and conservatism has produced a largely excellent collection of essays that show the richness and complexity of Hayek's thought. It contains several effective defenses of both the liberal and conservative readings of Hayek, and scholars interested in those issues will find much to chew on here. Historians of economics and methodologists will find it of value as well, despite only one chapter by an economist. The concept of spontaneous order has been part of our history from at least Adam Smith, and evolutionary explanations of economic phenomena have been part of our theoretical framework for much of our history as well. Various perspectives and breadth of thinking that Hunt and McNamara have collected in this volume will enhance economists' understanding of spontaneous order and Hayek's social and economic thought.

REFERENCES

Coyne, C. (2006). *After war*. Stanford, CA: Stanford University Press.

Hayek, F. A. (1948). The use of knowledge in society. In: *Individualism and economic order* (pp. 77–91). Chicago: University of Chicago Press.

Hayek, F. A. (1952). *The sensory order*. Chicago: University of Chicago Press.

Hayek, F. A. (1960). *The constitution of liberty*. Chicago: University of Chicago Press.

Hayek, F. A. (1988). *The fatal conceit*. Chicago: University of Chicago Press.

McCloskey, D. N. (2006). *The bourgeois virtues*. Chicago: University of Chicago Press.

YU'S FIRMS, STRATEGIES AND ECONOMIC CHANGE

AUSTRIAN ECONOMICS MEETS COMPARATIVE INSTITUTIONAL ANALYSIS BY WAY OF FRANK KNIGHT

Giampaolo Garzarelli

Review essay on F.-L. T. Yu's *Firms, Strategies and Economic Change: Explorations in Austrian Economics.* Cheltenham, UK: Edward Elgar, 2005. xii + 177 pp. ISBN 1843768941.

We have come a long way since O'Driscoll and Rizzo (1996, p. 123) noted in 1985 that the Austrian School of economics had no theory of the firm. Since then, we have witnessed an increasing number of works in both economics and management that rely on the insights of the Austrian School for the analysis of the firm and of corporate strategy. To be sure, the Austrian approach is particularly suited for these analyses because of its emphasis on the knowledge dispersion problem, on the nature of entrepreneurship, and on economic change more generally. Tony Yu is one of the most active scholars who take the Austrian approach seriously. His new book – *Firms, Strategies and Economic Change: Explorations in Austrian Economics* – collects nine of his works over the past years on the firm and on corporate strategy, and more.

A Research Annual
Research in the History of Economic Thought and Methodology, Volume 28-A, 349–360
Copyright © 2010 by Emerald Group Publishing Limited
All rights of reproduction in any form reserved
ISSN: 0743-4154/doi:10.1108/S0743-4154(2010)000028A017

We may sum up the general message of Yu's new book as follows. The economic theory that addresses problems of industrial and economic organization – which has also filtered into other disciplines, most notably business studies – is not equipped with a complete analytical toolbox. What is missing from its analytical toolbox is an understanding of the implications of subjectivism and of incomplete knowledge. Without this understanding, it is not possible, Yu continues, to properly study various issues, from demand dynamics to institutional evolution more generally.

Firms, Strategies and Economic Change is extremely eclectic, drawing on economic, philosophical, and sociological contributions to a considerable extent. Moreover, it deals with a great variety of topics (business cycles, the economics of Frank H. Knight, entrepreneurship, innovation, institutions, organizations, and preferences, among others). The outcome is a work that is not always easy to follow. For this reason, here I focus on the big picture rather than on the details.[1] My primary purpose is to concisely place what I understand to be Yu's main contribution within a narrower framework. To do so, I proceed in four sections, and, on balance, dedicate more attention to theory than to methodology, although my most substantive comments are ultimately methodological. In next three sections, I succinctly spell out the three theoretical vectors upon which I infer Yu's approach to rest on, namely, (Austrian School) subjectivism, Knightian uncertainty and comparative institutional analysis. The final section wraps up by presenting some methodological considerations having to do with the way Yu approaches the issues, that is, with the stance of Yu's various musings grounded on the three vectors.

The pages that follow basically point out that the merit of Yu's book is that of attempting to bridge Austrian economics and comparative institutional analysis through Frank Knight. As I suggest, however, this bridging attempt is not unique to Yu. Per se, this is obviously not a shortcoming, as *Firms, Strategies and Economic Change* can easily be interpreted as a "normal science" contribution to a now fairly recognizable research program in the economics of organization and management. But the way in which the discussion is carried out renders Yu's effort less incisive than it could be.

SUBJECTIVISM MAKES A DIFFERENCE

Like its predecessor – *Firms, Governments and Economic Change* (Yu, 2001) – this new book originates from Yu's dissatisfaction with the axiomatic optimization-and-equilibrium framework, which he sees as dominating the theory of industrial and economic organization as well as the theory and practice of business strategy. The most succinct statement of the framework that I think Yu takes issue with probably remains that of Vilfredo Pareto: "[A] full representation of the individual's preferences ... is sufficient to determine economic equilibrium. The individual can disappear as long as he leaves us a photograph of his preferences" (Pareto, 1927, p. 170, my translation).[2] But whereas in the previous book Yu mostly studied the role of governments vis-à-vis firms and innovation, in this new book Yu mostly studies the role of long run business planning vis-à-vis firms and innovation.

Yet even though the two books have different if related objects of inquiry they share the same "preanalytic vision" (Schumpeter, e.g., 1949). Analogously to the previous book, Yu considers subjectivism crucial to pursue his objective. At the same time, Yu does not offer a clear definition of what he means by subjectivism; what is clear, however, is that his subjectivism is mostly inspired by the Austrian School, especially by the more "radical subjectivist" one of Ludwig Lachmann (1976).[3] Be that as it may, my inference is that in Yu's hands subjectivism should be understood as an economic approach that not only places the individual at the center of value theory, but that places an error making and learning individual at the center of value theory. Differently put, unlike the Paretian mechanical approach where the individual is superfluous, subjectivism stresses the importance of purposeful human action in an uncertain world (more on the latter in the next section).

Yu's suggested subjectivist approach highlights how purposeful human action matters in the domain of demand just as it matters in the domain of supply: we cannot, in short, do away with the individual, no matter the context of analysis. Yu emphasizes how we should not assume agents having the same characteristics and then sum up these characteristics to obtain the representative agent. He suggests, rather, that we should assume agents with different characteristics and build up from that.[4]

Now, Yu's individual ideal type is important on the demand side because it illustrates that consumers are not passive but can communicate their needs to the market if need be. On the supply side, it illustrates how firms are not black boxes, but entities composed of individuals capable of strategic thinking: it illustrates how tastes can be created and influenced by "alert" (Kirzner, 1973) entrepreneurs and managers. Thus, it does not make sense to forget the individual in exchange theory, *and* it does not make sense to forget the individual in production theory.

KNIGHTIAN UNCERTAINTY MAKES A DIFFERENCE

In *Firms, Strategies and Economic Change* Yu's subjectivist ideal type is therefore central to both sides of the Marshallian scissors. Still, what kind of society does Yu's ideal type live in? As emerges most clearly in Parts I and II, Yu's ideal type populates a society characterized by Knightian uncertainty (Knight, 1946). Since in his approach Yu grants central importance to Knightian uncertainty, it seems useful to unpack this notion.

For Knight, as for Yu, measurable uncertainty refers to risk, and immeasurable uncertainty to *true* uncertainty (Knight, 1946, pp. 19–20, 233). Risk allows the categorization of possible states of nature: fire/no fire, accident/no accident, win/loss, black ball/white ball, lemon/no lemon, and so on. Thus, under risk one's decision can be aided by attaching probability distributions to possible outcomes. For example, even though there may be asymmetric information as concerns the quality of a product, under risk all concerned parties still know that the product could be of quality q_1 or q_2 – even if the relationship $q_2 > q_1$ is only known to a few, under risk one can always attach some probability to the likelihood of buying or not buying a lemon. True uncertainty conversely regards situations posing the "greatest logical difficulties of all" because "*there is no valid basis of any kind* for classifying instances" (Knight, 1946, p. 225, original emphasis). Under true uncertainty we are not able to classify a set of outcomes according to probability distributions, for we are uncertain not about which state will occur, but actually about which states are even possible. To continue with our lemon example, one does not know about the relationships among the quality descriptors $\{q_i\} \in Q, i = 1, ..., n$, of some product; and one does not even know about the set of descriptors Q. True uncertainty, in essence, derives from incomplete knowledge; and incomplete knowledge ultimately leads to specialization (Knight, 1946, p. 245). In this way, true uncertainty raises the most interesting economic problems (Knight, 1946, p. 268) – rationalizing, for Knight as well as for Yu, the existence of the firm as well.

True uncertainty necessitates what Knight calls *judgment*. Judgment is the ability to exercise action without making use of ratiocination – by inference or, as it were, by instinct (Knight, 1946, p. 233).[5] The entrepreneur is the economic actor whose special judgment leads him to found a firm. More specifically, the entrepreneur is that special individual who, to paraphrase Buchanan and di Pierro (1980, pp. 699–700), in the presence of an urn containing balls of different color has the *intuition* or *hunch* about the color of the ball that will be extracted next: he acts because he *judges* that he can win (see Knight, 1946, pp. 281–282).

One implication of this is that the firm itself becomes a manifestation of judgment, a sort of inference or intuition. The firm is a means to deal with uncertainty for the market cannot always do so: its purpose is to transform situations of uncertainty into those of risk or, if you prefer, to make speculative action insurable (Knight, 1946, p. 245). A firm is that entrepreneurial organ that coordinates specialization of labor to achieve a more-or-less well-defined end, which has profit generation as its core. Because strategic planning is centralized and routine operations are not, it itself possesses judgment. The centralization of the judging function allows the firm to have that forward-looking characteristic that is proper only of organic life. It allows, additionally, for trial-and-error learning and adaptation. A firm does not necessarily plan – or necessarily survive, if you wish – according to ratiocination or to maximization of expected profit. Rather, it adapts according to contingency (Knight, 1946, pp. 268–269).

COMPARATIVE INSTITUTIONAL ANALYSIS MAKES A DIFFERENCE

Yu then follows Knight to explain the existence of the firm and embraces its basic Knightian coordinative and flexible nature as well. But at the same time he adds that the firm itself does not exist in a vacuum. The socioeconomic system, to which the firm belongs to, is institutionally embedded. There are constitutions, laws, conventions, and so on that constraint and enable firm and other behavior. And, like the firm, these institutions also have the role to decrease uncertainty. But whereas the firm is an organization that has the role to decrease uncertainty for a more or less well defined objective, an institution has the role to decrease uncertainty at a more general level so that, for example, entrepreneurial activity can take place, contracts can be stipulated, and firms themselves may be founded.

In this regard Yu more or less explicitly adheres to the method of comparative institutional analysis typically employed by the New Institutional Economics (NIE).[6] This method attempts to evaluate the relative efficiency properties of *feasible* alternative organizational and institutional arrangements. The comparison is never among ideal and feasible alternatives, but always among feasible alternatives. As a result, "there is no guarantee whatsoever that" the "outcome is the most efficient one," such as in, say, the case of a "Walrasian equilibrium or…a Nash equilibrium" (Aoki, 2007, p. 10).[7]

Yet, unlike more familiar approaches to the study of institutions, Yu directs attention to the dynamic rather than to the static role of institutions. That is, he emphasizes an approach where innovation, knowledge, trial-and-error learning, and option creation and discovery are important. This is different from more familiar approaches to comparative institutional analysis (Williamson, e.g., 2005) where the main role of institutions is to decrease a type of uncertainty tied to well-defined problems mostly dealing with misaligned incentives (what Knight would rather call "risk"). But, Yu implies, if all relevant economic problems boil down to *structured* incentive compatibility issues, then there's little scope for dynamic considerations. It thus turns out that in Yu's contribution institutions have not only the function to decrease uncertainty tied to the infringement of generally followed rules but also the function to decrease uncertainty in order to stimulate the search for novelty. A citation from one of Yu's main inspiring scholars seems warranted.

> An institution provides a means of orientation to a large number of actors. It enables them to coordinate their actions by means of orientation to a common signpost. If the plan is a mental scheme in which the conditions of action are coordinated, we may regard institutions, as it were, as orientation schemes of the second order, to which planners orientate their actions to a plan. ... The existence of such institutions is fundamental to civilized society. They enable us to rely on the actions of thousands of anonymous others about whose individual purposes and plans we know nothing. They are nodal points of society, coordinating the actions of millions whom they relieve of the need to acquire and digest detailed knowledge about others and form detailed expectations about their future action. (Lachmann, 1971, pp. 49–50)

By emphasizing the "coordination-and-orientation" nature of institutions that sees expectation formation as central Yu is trying to underscore that a comparative institutional analysis of institutions should employ two criteria. The first, and more familiar criterion, is the one concerning incentive alignment, rent seeking reduction, opportunism elimination and the like. That is, one dimension along which to evaluate feasible, alternative institutional arrangement hinges on the relative ability of these arrangements to obviate negative externalities. Is "organizational arrangement A" relatively better than "organizational arrangement B" at avoiding dead-weight losses from delegation? The second criterion concerns the ability of alternative arrangements to create value. Is "business plan J" relatively better than "business plan K" in making "strategy Z" more successful? Is "division of labor arrangement X" relatively more likely to generate profit than "division of labor arrangement Y"? As such, we may think of this second criterion as in many cases being logically before the first. Though, once an arrangement is in place, it is not inconceivable for the two criteria to actually serve as concurrent discriminants for comparative institutional "efficiency" assessment. Be that as it may, the bottom line is that in any point in time it may be useful to carry both the productive (e.g., entrepreneurial and innovative) and unproductive criteria in our comparative institutional analysis toolbox.[8]

DOES YU MAKE A DIFFERENCE?

Yu's argument arguably will prove familiar to a number of scholars interested in the theory of the firm and management who, in one fashion or another, consider the subjectivist theory of the Austrian School, Knightian uncertainty and the NIE method of comparative institutional analysis as valuable. It seems to me, in fact, that at its core Yu's work can be interpreted as an attempt to tie the Austrians to the NIE by means of Knight.

Consequently, Yu's work squarely falls within the so-called capability approach of the economics of organization, of which, *inter alia*, Richardson, Teece, and Langlois are major exponents. The capability approach suggests that the problem of economic organization is not just about technological relationships among factors of production, but also about the different division of labor arrangements among the different factors of production. More precisely, what matters for the capability approach is not just production "blueprints" à la Robinson (1956), but especially how diverse "knowledge, experience and skills" (Richardson, 1972, p. 888) influence the existence, internal organization, and, above all, the scope of firms. In capability theory, the firm is about the creation, internalization, organization, and use of specific knowledge that is germane to its production objective: firms coordinate different plans and resources that are not necessarily given in every point in time.

Observed through the lens of capability theory, then, the problem of economic organization becomes not just quantitatively interesting but qualitatively so as well, because disparate knowledge, learning, problem solving, and task partitioning all become crucial objects of analysis. They become crucial in that these objects of analysis all regard expectation alignment; the firm is nothing more than judgment, a coherent guess held together by a thin glue of speculative confidence. As a result, ensuring that everyone is on the same page means also, for example, that if communication of expectations is better defined about production objectives, shirking may not obtain. So, it is possible to face a capabilities alignment question that is logically before (but clearly does not necessarily exclude) that of incentive alignment. In line with Yu's outlook, hence, the ultimate primitive of economic organization here is the coordination of idiosyncratic knowledge. To the capability theorist, in sum, organization is more than the attempt to solve transaction-cost, agency, and ownership problems. For these problems are found to be a subset of the knowledge coordination issue.

The attempt to combine the ideas of the Austrians, Knight, and NIE is accordingly in line with the research program of capability theory. Yet, notwithstanding the connection to an existing research program, *Firms, Strategies and Economic Change* does not nail as accurately as possible its objective to offer a broader analytical toolbox to study firm and management issues. For it does not simultaneously precisely relate its objective with the dominant theory in economics that it sees as inadequate. Such inadequate economic theory – which we hypothesized could be traced back as far back as Pareto,[9] and apparently dominates management too – is what Yu calls the "orthodox neoclassical approach."

Yu's analysis could have been more persuasive if it did not fail what we may call the rhetorical test (see McCloskey, 1983).[10] That is to say that *Firms, Strategies and Economic Change* does not readily invite the fruitful exchange of ideas among different theories – especially from the one it challenges. For example, at the outset Yu quickly dismisses the "orthodox neoclassical approach" as inadequate, because it is missing a number of elements he sees as scientifically important. The "neoclassical approach ignores knowledge and learning.... Accordingly, nothing can be discovered regarding new ways of using given resources or regarding the existence of hitherto unnoticed resources" (p. 3). But at the same time he does not genuinely prove why the absence of these elements renders the "orthodox neoclassical approach" inadequate. Instead, he simply introduces the elements he believes are missing.[11]

We know at least since Polanyi (1962) that science is also a sociological enterprise with its explicit and implicit rules of interaction. An important aspect of this sociological enterprise is the appropriate use of rhetoric: sufficiently letting one's proposed ideas be open to already accepted ones by conversation. Such use of rhetoric broadens and hones the logic of reasoning, and invites further research and dialogue. Improper rhetorical use on the contrary does not invite intellectual engagement, and hence isolates. In science, the last thing one wants is isolation, for isolation is tantamount to the death of a research program. This is something that the contemporary Austrian School of economics, to which Yu's contribution owes quite a lot and justly wants to fit in, is very much aware of. Mises, for instance, did not always invite conversation, even from his fellow Austrians and students (Caldwell, 2004, pp. 143–149), and this did not benefit the Austrian School.[12] We owe it most of all to the work of Kirzner, Rizzo, and Boettke if today the Austrians are beginning to return on a dialogical plane with the mainstream, and vice versa.[13] At the sociological level, therefore, the objective of scientific enterprise resides in the attempt to create incentives to stimulate others to inquire into one's own area, approach or subject of inquiry through constructive interaction.

> The invitation to rhetoric ... is not an invitation to irrationality in argument. Quite the contrary. It is an invitation to leave the irrationality of an artificially narrowed range of arguments and to move to the rationality of arguing like human beings. It brings out into the open the arguing that economists do anyway – in the dark, for they must do it somewhere and the various official rhetorics leave them benighted. (McCloskey, 1983, p. 509)

Relatedly, Yu's rhetoric encloses an additional slip: a static notion of science. Science is a complex undertaking that is always forward looking. As such, "orthodox" should always be seen as a mere label employed to attempt to better understand the past – and not the current – status of a certain intellectual approach. That is, orthodoxy is but a heuristic expedient to aid our analytical reasoning when we need to freeze frame an otherwise unfreezable enterprise, such as when we refer to a particular school of thought to help drive our point home. Furthermore, what may be the mainstream today – the dominant ideas and research programs of the economics profession – may not be the mainstream tomorrow. The mainstream is always changing. Nowadays, for example, there is an increasing number of mainstream economists interested in what yesterday would be considered non-mainstream ideas, such as the role of institutions, endogenous technological change, and dynamic rather than static analysis. This entails that classifications in science should be seen as ephemeral, and not, as Yu appears to believe, as permanent. The dominant economic paradigm may hence very well still be mostly neoclassical with its emphasis on mathematical formalism, but the objects of analysis of this paradigm are certainly of wider scope than Yu assumes. Today's mainstream is more catholic than it has been in a long time (Colander, Holt, & Rosser, 2004).

The methodological level of science – to which rhetoric belongs – has implications for the substantive level of science. And, more generally, teaches (among other things) how eclecticism is not a sufficient condition to contribute to knowledge. The eclectic *Firms, Strategies and Economic Change* does make a difference, but not as much of a difference as it could have made.

NOTES

1. By doing so, I will also not consider other issues that may actually frustrate the reader, like poor proofreading, redundancy in contents, and the presence of some bold, questionable and unarticulated claims (one for all: "Hayek's contribution can only be described as neoclassical Austrian" [p. 32].)

2. In the French version of Pareto's classic text: "[Une] représentation complète des goût de l'individu ... et cela nous suffit pour déterminer l'équilibre économique. L'individu peuit disparaître, pourvu qu'il nouse cette photographie de ses goùts."

3. For an elaboration of Lachmann's thought more generally, see Foss and Garzarelli (2007).

4. Cf. the Marshallian population thinking versus Pigovian representative firm thinking discussion of industry composition in, e.g., O'Brien (1984).

5. Knight (1946, p. 211, p. 223) also calls judgment "common sense" and "intuition."

6. The early Frey (1984) still remains in my view a fairly accurate concise description of this method.

7. This is not to say that comparative institutional analysis does completely away with any notion of equilibrium. Strictly speaking, the approach is a comparative static one between known alternatives.

8. For a recent attempt to use both criteria in the context of local public finance, see Garzarelli (2006).

9. Like it could have been traced back to Ricardo, Jevons, Walras, the early Arrow, the early Sargent, and others.

10. A test not alien to the Austrian School, which actually has more stringent prescriptions than McCloskey on the matter, see Machlup (1963) and compare Langlois (1985, pp. 229–232).

11. And at times he does so rather hastily. To take one case, his theory of institutional change hinges on the role of the entrepreneur as a driver of change, in both its Schumpeterian and Kirznerian incarnations; but very little is said about the moments of complementarity and substitutability between these two incarnations (pp. 133–153).

12. And yet, in his pathbreaking critique of socialism that same Mises underscored the pragmatic value of dealing with different ideas (Mises, 1981, p. 460).

13. As we owe it to the recent work of the emerging "eighth Austrian generation" (Coyne, Lesson, etc). For a quick summary of the relationship between the Austrians

and the mainstream, as well as among the Austrian themselves, over 1950–2000, see Boettke and Leeson (2003) and see also Rizzo (2009).

REFERENCES

Aoki, M. (2007). Endogenizing institutions and institutional changes. *Journal of Institutional Economics*, *3*(1), 1–31.

Boettke, P., & Leeson, P. (2003). The Austrian school of economics: 1950–2000. In: W. Samuels, J. Biddle & J. Davis (Eds), *A companion to the history of economic thought* (pp. 445–453). Oxford: Blackwell.

Buchanan, J. M., & di Pierro, A. (1980). Cognition, choice, and entrepreneurship. *Southern Economic Journal*, *46*(3), 693–701.

Caldwell, B. (2004). *Hayek's challenge. An intellectual biography of F. A. Hayek.* Chicago, IL: University of Chicago Press.

Colander, D., Holt, R., & Rosser, B., Jr. (2004). The changing face of mainstream economics. *Review of Political Economy*, *16*(4), 485–499.

Foss, N. J., & Garzarelli, G. (2007). Institutions as knowledge capital: Ludwig M. Lachmann's interpretative institutionalism. *Cambridge Journal of Economics*, *31*(5), 789–804.

Frey, B. S. (1984). A new view of economics: Comparative analysis of institutions. *Economia delle scelte pubbliche/Journal of Public Finance and Public Choice*, *2*(1), 3–16.

Garzarelli, G. (2006). Cognition, incentives, and public governance: Laboratory federalism from the organizational viewpoint. *Public Finance Review*, *34*(3), 235–257.

Kirzner, I. M. (1973). *Competition and entrepreneurship.* Chicago: University of Chicago Press.

Knight, F. H. (1946). *Risk, uncertainty, and profit.* London: London School of Economics and Political Science (First published 1921).

Lachmann, L. M. (1971). *The legacy of Max Weber.* Berkeley: The Glendessary Press.

Lachmann, L. M. (1976). From Mises to Shackle: An essay on Austrian economics and the kaleidic society. *Journal of Economic Literature*, *14*(1), 54–62.

Langlois, R. N. (1985). From the knowledge of economics to the economics of knowledge: Fritz Machlup on methodology and on the 'knowledge society'. *Research in the History of Economic Thought and Methodology*, *3*, 225–235.

Machlup, F. (1963). *Essays on economic semantics.* Englewood Cliffs, NJ: Prentice-Hall.

McCloskey, D. N. (1983). The rhetoric of economics. *Journal of Economic Literature*, *21*(2), 481–517.

Mises, L. (1981). *Socialism: An economic and sociological analysis* (2nd ed.). Indianapolis, IN: Liberty Press (This edition originally published 1932; first edition 1922).

O'Brien, D. P. (1984). The evolution of the theory of the firm. In: F. H. Stephen (Ed.), *Firms, organization and labor* (pp. 25–62). London: Macmillan.

O'Driscoll, G. P., & Rizzo, M. J. (1996). *The economics of time and ignorance (with a new "Introduction").* London and New York: Routledge (First published 1985).

Pareto, V. (1927). *Manuel d'économie politique* (2nd ed.). Paris: Marcel Giard (Translation, revised by Pareto, from the original Italian by Alfred Bonnet.).

Polanyi, M. (1962). The republic of science: Its political and economic theory. *Minerva*, *1*(1), 54–73.

Richardson, G. B. (1972). The organization of industry. *Economic Journal*, *82*(327), 883–896.

Rizzo, M. (2009). Austrian economics: Recent work. In: S. N. Durlauf & L. E. Blume (Eds), *The new Palgrave dictionary of economics online*. New York: Palgrave Macmillan. Accessed 28 February 2010, DOI:10.1057/9780230226203.1915.

Robinson, J. (1956). *The accumulation of capital*. London: Macmillan.

Schumpeter, J. A. (1949). Science and ideology. *American Economic Review, 39*(2), 345–359.

Williamson, O. E. (2005). The economics of governance. *American Economic Review, 95*(2) (Papers and Proceedings), 1–18.

Yu, F.-L. T. (2001). *Firms, governments and economic change: An entrepreneurial perspective*. Cheltenham, UK: Edward Elgar.

DE SOTO'S THE AUSTRIAN SCHOOL

HISTORICAL PERSPECTIVE AND THE ROLE OF ENTREPRENEURSHIP IN AUSTRIAN ECONOMICS

Subbu Kumarappan

Review essay on De Soto, J.H. (2008), *The Austrian School: Market Order and Entrepreneurial Creativity*, Edward Elgar, Cheltenham, UK. x + 129 pp. ISBN 978-1847207685. $95.00.

Jesús Huerta De Soto's book *The Austrian School: Market order and entrepreneurial creativity* – published in association with the Institute of Economic Affairs – is an English translation of his Spanish first edition book '*Escuela Austriaca, La-Mercado y Creatividad*.' The book's aim is to provide an introduction to the Austrian economic thought by discussing the ideas and characteristics that differentiate the school from other paradigms. Austrian economic theories are discussed through the lens of leading scholars in the school to show how Austrian economic theories are superior to that of neo-classical economics. My objectives in reading this book were: (i) to understand how Austrian economic theories can help conceptualize the importance of knowledge and entrepreneurship in the field of agricultural economics; (ii) to become aware of the shortcomings of

A Research Annual
Research in the History of Economic Thought and Methodology, Volume 28-A, 361–368
Copyright © 2010 by Emerald Group Publishing Limited
All rights of reproduction in any form reserved
ISSN: 0743-4154/doi:10.1108/S0743-4154(2010)000028A018

neo-classical tradition with a logical positivist empirical analytic approach that is common in agricultural economics; and (iii) to gain an Austrian economic perspective with regard to emerging problems in agriculture and natural resource management. My comments are based on how well these objectives were served from reading this book.

SUMMARY OF CONTENT

For the most part, the book presents a comparative assessment of Austrian economic theories with the predominant neo-classical economic theories. One fundamental theme is that Austrian economic theories are significantly better than that of neo-classical economics and the author provides a variety of reasons to support that conclusion. The author starts with a direct comparison of these two schools in chapter 1. The comparison of the neo-classical economic principles and methodology with Austrian thinking is done in a commendable manner and the summary table in chapter 1 is excellent.

The dimensions of knowledge and definition of entrepreneurship (chapter 2) offer a different and stimulating perspective. The author's effort to understand the Spanish language roots of the word 'entrepreneurship' captures its essence. His classification of the 'two different types of knowledge' (table 2.1) depends on the reader's orientation and is debatable.

The historical perspective of Austrian economists starting with the School of Salamanca (16 th century) and Carl Menger (19 th century, chapter 3) seems to be one of the brightest spots in the entire book. The author has captured the essence of libertarian principles in this chapter which forms a cornerstone in Austrian thinking; but the discussion could have proven much better if they were explicitly stated and discussed. The book concedes the general ignorance of the public about Austrian economic ideas and that the school has been relegated to a status of being an alternative to the dominant paradigm of neo-classical tradition. Thus, chapter 3 singlehandedly provides a different flavor to the book – which is not surprising since the author has already written on that subject matter (De Soto, 1999).

The discussion of Bohm Baverk's capital theory (chapter 4), and its differences from that of others – Marshall (section 4.5), Marx (4.6), John Bates Clark (4.7) and Friedrich von Wieser (4.8) – is useful from the beginner's viewpoint. The Ludwig von Mises quote (pp. 58–59) shows the early origins of what constitutes Austrian economic theory and what does not; in spite of this brief mention, the book generally ignores the modern day arguments of which branches of the school are truly (classical) Austrian. The discussion of Mises (chapter 5) and Friedrich A Hayek (chapter 6) focuses on the impossibility of socialism and the importance of entrepreneurship; it serves as a concise introduction to the two leading thinkers in the Austrian school. The discussion on socialism and its downfall is a good review of Mises contributions in the form of subjective values and the resultant "human action" are highlighted Mises' dynamic market processes and Hayek's spontaneous order – but the criticisms on Hayek by other contemporaries (within the Austrian school) are not elaborated. The author recognizes the importance of Hayek's work by stating that the "upcoming years could be described as the 'Hayek era.'" A quote from Keynes (p. 65) shows the respect and recognition that Austrian economists received from other schools. The brief biographies of both Mises and Hayek help the reader understand and appreciate the social and personal circumstances that influenced their thinking and economic contributions. The personal tidbits about Hayek's orientation towards religion (p. 78) provide a glimpse into author's attempt to understand how the giants of the school might have formulated and possibly changed their ideas later. It would have been more useful, had the evolution of ideas within the Austrian school were discussed.

The author's review of Hayek's theory of economic cycles (which led to Hayek's Nobel Prize) provides a cursory summary for beginners; the dynamics of economic (dis)coordination has been discussed in a commendable manner since it is one of the key contributions of Austrian school. The debates between Austrians and other schools (socialists, Keynes, Frank Knight and the Chicago School) form the basic theme of the entire book. Table 6.1 supplements table 1.1 by providing an additional comparison between Austrians and the Chicago school.

De Soto's discussion of the success and predominance of neo-classical approach (section 4.9) and its crisis (section 7.1) complement each other; if any instructor chooses to use sections of this book for class readings or discussions, such specific combinations of this book can greatly serve that purpose. The reader's wish to know more about the works of recent scholars is appeased only with a cursory mention of their names and works in section 7.2. The book's lack of focus on how the Austrian principles evolved over time is a key reason why the book is not a sufficient introduction to the School. Although various names are given, the reader has no idea if that list is complete. A better way would have been to refer to some bibliographical work on the writings of contemporary Austrian economists, which are only implicitly mentioned by reference to journals dedicated to Austrian economics.

The current themes of the Austrian School and how entrepreneurship affects multiple aspects (competition, monopoly, institutional coercion, and welfare economics) are well described in section 7.3. The authoritative replies to the comments and criticisms against the Austrian school in section 7.4 show the author's expertise in the field. The focus of this section reverberates with the rest of the book with an ultimate message that Austrian perspective is better than the predominant neo-classical approach.

ANALYSIS AND EVALUATION

Branches within the Austrian school: Although there are various branches within Austrian economics, the author seems not to take any single particular view (his website – www.jesushuertadesoto.com – features photos with scholars supposedly from the different branches!). But recognition of these alternative ideas and what constitutes the 'Austrian' way of thinking would have added much more value to this book. The comparison of schools could have been supplemented with a comparison of branches within the Austrian school. While a plethora of Austrian ideas are presented, information on how they had evolved (within various branches of Austrian school) would have been interesting (see Rothbard, 1997).

Entrepreneurship: Since the book is presented as a comparison of two schools, I expected a comparison of modern treatment of entrepreneurship in neo-classical school with that of Austrian school. Exclusion of the modern developments makes this book incomplete in its coverage even in its main focus area of entrepreneurship (see Adaman and Devine, 2002). There is also no discussion of Austrian theory of the firm and the role of entrepreneurship that other Austrian economists have covered (see Foss & Klein, 2002). While De Soto addresses some criticisms leveled against the school, he fails to give the areas where improvements are needed within the Austrian school or its branches.

Competition: The discussion of competition and entrepreneurship is unfortunately limited to less than two pages (pp. 25–26). Their relationship and how government plays a role in limiting their interaction would be very important for any new reader in Austrian economics (see Kirzner, 1982); unfortunately, the book falls woefully short of that mark. The abject rejection of neo-classical economic models with mathematical basis even seems contradictory, since the author seems to accept the mathematically derived results regarding the "limit on knowledge" (p. 26).

Schumpeter's Entrepreneur: Even though the focus of the book is on entrepreneurial creativity, there is no mention of the theory of creative destruction advanced by Joseph Schumpeter. Except for a couple of references to Schumpeter's work (pp. 60, 63), there is little discussion of Schumpeter's (1949) innovative entrepreneur. Schumpeter's work on entrepreneurship is considered to contain some basic elements of Austrian economics and leaving them out in a book that focuses on entrepreneurship seems odd.

Alternative concepts: Hayek also wrote in considerable detail about the "coordination of plans," which is not explained much in the book. Coordination of plans is markedly different from the "coordination of prices" which Misesians (a branch that focus on von Mises ideas) consider to be the only valid Austrian concept (Rothbard, 2005, p. 18). By leaving out all these discussions on alternative view points, the reader seems to lose out on the intellectual richness of Austrian school. It seems that there is more room to write a series of papers or even a book on the 'alternative economic thoughts among the various branches of Austrian school' itself. But that should not belittle this book, since this book adopts a similar approach by comparing Austrian economic thought with that of other major schools such as neo-classical, and social design theorists.

Even though there have been two Hayek's (Hayek I and Hayek II – see Caldwell, 2004; Rothbard, 2005), there is no mention of these different writing phases of such a major scholar's work (similarly, Schumpeter had two phases as well – see Langlois, 2003). A beginning reader should be adequately warned about these differences – which would enable him (or her) to understand the opposing strands in the same author's writings. It can also help readers take a stand and either accept or question these opposing Austrian economic ideas.

The Hayek era: The resurgence since the late 1970s could have been discussed in more detail. Failure to do so leaves out two important aspects or contributions of the Austrian school. First, it fails to show how the branches are evolving currently and who are the leading researchers. Secondly, it also fails to recognize how other schools have accepted and incorporated the theoretical findings of Austrian school in recent times.

Empiricism: I agree with many of the observations made in defense of the Austrian School in section 7.4. One disagreement would be with the author's observation about empiricists – if the Austrian ideas are ratified by the empirical studies, then the methodology adopted in those empirical studies would be correct since data and analysis support the theory predicted by the Austrian school economists. If the same method offers counter evidence to any of the Austrian concepts then those 'anomalies' should be adequately explained by alternative theorizing (Shane, 2008). It would seem illogical to reject all the counter-evidence to Austrian economic theory.

I find myself in a position that accepts both the economic ideas of Austrian theories and the rigor and elegance of neo-classical theories; such a position is simply brushed away by the author who takes an unsympathetic position to readers who accept more than that of Austrian economics (p. 106). Some Austrian economists themselves see the need to incorporate concepts and methods from other fields such as bounded rationality, rule following, institutions, cognition, and evolution (see Koppl, 2006 on BRICE economics). The book could have acknowledged and evaluated such claims. But such perspectives were largely omitted, offering little help to the readers. As a book trying to provide an introduction to Austrian economic theory, *The Austrian School* should have examined in more detail the claims of other Austrian economists and ideas incorporated from other schools, methodologies and approaches within economics.

Organization: The role of entrepreneurial creativity on the economic system is weaved well throughout the book by including a discussion of entrepreneurship in all chapters. This approach seems acceptable since entrepreneurship is one of the primary focus areas of the book. But for other ideas such as the methodologies of neo-classical economics (discussed in sections 1.8, 3.6, 4.9, 5.6, and 7.4) and the role of macroeconomics (discussed in sections 1.6, 5.3, 6.3, 6.4, and 7.1), the concepts reach the reader only in a diluted manner since they are dispersed throughout the book. As is, the book is only a tribute to major figures in the School. Differently organized, De Soto's book could have shown the evolution of the main Austrian economics concepts and how their positions are vindicated today.

Philosophical Origins: The book relies heavily on criticizing the neo-classical approach and mathematical formalism instead of concentrating on the philosophical origins of the school. The relevance of "libertarian principles" and "how the social conditions of early 20 th century could have helped solidify the philosophical roots of Austrian school" are not mentioned in the beginning but only in the later discussions. I would have liked additional focus on the "non-economic" origins and implications of Austrian economic thinking. A undergraduate student might even mistake that the Austrian school became prominent only for being 'a superior alternative' to the neo-classical school. Although the neo-classical approach is criticized throughout the book, the author seems to redeem those theories in the conclusions of chapter 1 (p. 15); interestingly, he rejects the proposition that these schools can be complementary to each other (p. 106).

New fields within economics: The book does not provide an answer to how Austrian economics analyzes emerging fields such as environmental & ecosystem economics, and natural resource management. Neither 'the role of government' nor 'the importance of entrepreneurship in tackling these emerging issues' that hinges on sustainable production of goods and services is discussed in the book. I specifically pick out this area since it offers an intellectual challenge to the disequilibrium concepts purported within the Austrian theory. The lack of equilibrium (steady state) in an ecosystem can be highly detrimental to human race, since the disequilibrium concepts of social systems can be devastating in the context of an ecosystem. Climate change and global warming will affect human beings' actions considerably in the foreseeable future (see Cordato, 2004). There is considerable scope to discussing how the knowledge generated by a group of scientists (however uncertain) will be perceived and used by the society. Using Austrian theories on knowledge creation and innovation can yield valuable insights in the context of ecosystem management.

Globalization: One prominent area for future research would be to explain how the asymmetrically distributed entrepreneurship and knowledge would engage and form economic entities (companies and corporations) and what role would they play in a globalized world. It is always within the purview of a prominent school such as that of Austrian economists to explore and theorize how the unfettered trade among nation-states would affect economic well being of peoples who are separated by geography, culture and other social factors.

References: The author provides a list of publications with a list which he considers important; the book readers are suggested to follow up with some of the seminal articles and books contained therein. For the uninitiated readers in economics, best-seller books like Henry Hazlitt's *Economics in one lesson* (2008), which embody the core of Austrian ideas, can be prescribed as they offer a simple introduction to Austrian economic thought; unfortunately, Hazlitt's book is not even mentioned.

The Austrian School offers a clear historical perspective to Austrian ideas. However, my goal of getting a comprehensive introduction to Austrian economics was only partly served since the discussion on knowledge and entrepreneurship is incomplete. I did learn the problems Austrians associate with a pure neo-classical approach. But I did not gain any useful perspective on the future problems that concern environmental and natural resource economics. The readers are encouraged to supplement this text with other readings from the Austrian school. As stated in the preface, it is not a complete introduction to all different Austrian economic ideas. In the back cover review comments, Israel M. Kirzner had expressed his reservations about "the author's treatment(s)" of certain conclusions and themes – I could not agree more.

REFERENCES

Adaman, F., & Devine, P. (2002). A reconsideration of the theory of entrepreneurship: A participatory approach. *Review of Political Economy, 14*(3), 329–355.

Caldwell, B. (2004). *Hayek's challenge: An intellectual biography of F. A. Hayek.* Chicago, IL: University of Chicago Press.

Cordato, R. (2004). An Austrian theory of environmental economics. *Quarterly Journal of Austrian Economics, 7*(1), 3–16.

De Soto, J. H. (1999). Juan de Mariana: The influence of the Spanish scholastics. In: R. G. Holcombe (Ed.), *15 Great Austrian Economists* (pp. 1–12). Auburn, AL: Ludwig von Mises Institute.

Foss, N. J., & Klein, P. G. (2002). *Entrepreneurship and the Firm: Austrian perspectives on economic organization.* Aldershot, UK: Edward Elgar.

Hazlitt, H. (2008). *Economics in one lesson: 50 th anniversary edition.* Gilbert, AZ: Laissez Faire Books.

Kirzner, I. (1982). Competition, regulation, and the market process: An 'Austrian' perspective. *Cato Policy Analysis*, No. 18, September 30.

Koppl, R. (2006). Austrian economics at the cutting edge. *Review of Austrian Economics, 19*(4), 231–241.

Langlois, R. N. (2003). Schumpeter and the obsolescence of the entrepreneur. *Advances in Austrian Economics, 6,* 287–302.

Rothbard, M. N. (1997). The present state of Austrian economics. In: *The Logic of Action One: Method, Money, and the Austrian School* (pp. 111–172). Aldershot, UK: Edward Elgar.

Schumpeter, J. A. (1949). *Economic theory and entrepreneurial history.* Cambridge, MA: Harvard University Press.

Shane, S. A. (2008). *The illusions of entrepreneurship: The costly myths that entrepreneurs, investors, and policy makers live by.* New Haven, CT: Yale University Press.

HEYNE'S ARE ECONOMISTS BASICALLY IMMORAL?

A DEFENSE OF ETHICAL ECONOMICS

Joe Blosser

Review essay on Paul Heyne, P. (2008). In: Brennan, G. & Waterman, A.M.C. (Eds), *"Are economists basically immoral?" and other essays on economics, ethics, and religion* (xxv + 483 pp.). Indianapolis, IN: Liberty Fund. ISBN 9780865977136. $30 (hdbk), $18 (pbk).

As an expanding market facilitates the increased specialization of academic fields, fields like economics, ethics, and theology find it increasingly possible – and indeed often preferable – to have little to do with each other. When an errant economist dares to make an ethical or theological claim, he/she finds himself or herself an unwanted visitor in a foreign land and a traitor not easily welcomed home. When an errant ethicist or theologian wanders into the specialized territory of economics, he/she is quickly shunned and urged to move along. Indeed economic kings like Lionel Robbins and Milton Friedman have warned their subjects that engagement with subjective disciplines like ethics or theology will yield at least a loss of rigor and at worst violence ("thy blood or mine" as Robbins put it). With such warnings and deepening disciplinary boundaries, economics, ethics, and theology have all developed their own dogmas – their own claims to the truth, the good, or righteousness – that have long gone unchallenged by each other.

A Research Annual
Research in the History of Economic Thought and Methodology, Volume 28-A, 369–379
Copyright © 2010 by Emerald Group Publishing Limited
All rights of reproduction in any form reserved
ISSN: 0743-4154/doi:10.1108/S0743-4154(2010)000028A019

That is until Paul Heyne – a University of Chicago–trained ethicist and a Concordia Seminary–trained theologian – snuck his way into the field of economics and started a critical interdisciplinary inquiry. Although a graduate of the Religion and Society program (now known as the Religious Ethics program) at the University of Chicago Divinity School, Heyne put himself through school by teaching economics at Valparaiso University. So convincing did his economist disguise become that the biographical statement on the back of his first book, *The Christian Encounters the World of Economics,* states that he "received his Ph.D. in economics from the University of Chicago." The myth became reality as Heyne himself "gradually became an economist with an interest in ethics rather than an ethicist with an interest in economics" (p. vii).

Although Heyne passed away in 2000, his great legacy to the academy – and the central theme of this posthumously published collection of his essays – is the warning that no single perspective has a lock on the truth. Said otherwise, Heyne's legacy can be seen as a thoroughgoing attack on dogmatism in all its forms, or as he put it, "The thesis of this entire essay is that the enemy is dogmatism" (p. 28). The biggest problem Heyne perceives with theologians, ethicists, and economists alike is that they all in some way deny the limits of human nature and claim that at least some people can have a unique God-like knowledge. As I argue in this review, Heyne's critiques of these three forms of dogmatism help him cast a constructive social vision in the tradition of Adam Smith that urges a realistic assessment of human life and a deeply interdisciplinary conversation.

A CRITIQUE OF ETHICISTS

In the title essay of the volume, Heyne wonders why ethicists get so bothered by economists who make claims like, "polluting activities ought to be shifted from developed to less developed countries."[1] And in a keen rhetorical move – one that Heyne employs throughout the volume – he shows how all of the usual answers to this question merely hide a deeper problem. Heyne suggests the real issue is that most ethicists assume "a social system that's completely known and completely controllable" (p. 5). Consequently, the problem most ethicists have with economics is that "economic analysis is rooted," according to Heyne, "in the fact that economists specialize in the analysis of social systems that no one controls and that produce results that no one intended" (p. 5). Heyne sees that ethicists dogmatically hold to an ideal of the good in which people act so as to intend the good of others.

Such a view demands that people act only in social systems where they personally know other people's needs or else that people are assumed to have a God-like omniscience that will allow them to know everyone's needs.

Heyne perceives that most ethicists focus on intention rather than outcomes. Thus, their ethics are geared more for "face-to-face" interactions.[2] Heyne shows, however, that commercial society is fundamentally an impersonal society and that the ethics of an impersonal system must differ from those of personal life. Although "the moral principles that most people learned in their youth" may help them know how to treat family, friends, and neighbors, such benevolent actions can have harmful consequences in a large impersonal system such as the market. Heyne at this point turns to Adam Smith's famous dictum that in a commercial society the public interest is best served when people pursue their own interests, not those they believe will help others (p. 5).

But ethicists make an additional error in their understanding of economics. Not only do they falsely attempt to ascribe personal morality to an impersonal system, but they also wrongly confuse the claim of economists that the public interest is best served when people pursue their self-interest with an endorsement of selfishness. To illustrate his point, Heyne turns to the metaphor of traffic – he frequently invokes such commonplace examples to help explain complex ideas, offering the reader a glimpse into what it might have been like to hear Heyne teach his introduction course to economics:

> Meanwhile, let's note in the traffic situation what harm is likely to be done by people who decide to insert 'morality' into their decisions. What will a driver accomplish if he refrains from advancing when the light turns green, perhaps because he's running early and suspects that some in the cross-traffic are running late? He will almost certainly not persuade the cross-traffic to go on red; he will delay people behind him, who could well be on much more urgent missions than his own; and he will increase the likelihood of an accident by introducing substantial new uncertainties into the calculations of drivers who are observing and trying to anticipate his erratic behavior. And, of course, if everyone decided to be "unselfish" in this manner, traffic would come to a halt, as drivers regularly got out of their vehicles to discuss the relative urgency of their current goals and to insist that the welfare of others be advanced before their own. (p. 33)

Heyne's traffic example goes to show that self-interested behavior in the market is really "purposive behavior" or "focused responsibility" (p. 39). To drive safely is to drive with focused responsibility and purpose. So too, to act morally in the impersonal system of the market is to act with self-interested purpose, and those purposes can be to make money, to give to your church, or to work less and spend more time with the family.

The free market is in Heyne's words, "a social system in which individuals pursue their own interests on the basis of the situation they perceive, obeying a few clear and stable rules of the game" (p. 35).

Three main questions need to be raised though about Heyne's own treatment of ethics. First, though Heyne posits "two kinds of societies," the "Face-to-Face v. Commercial Society," we cannot be deluded into believing the separation between them is so pure and complete. Rather than two kinds of societies, should we not recognize that these are two poles on a spectrum of social forms? Although commercial interactions may not typically occur between friends, they also are not always completely anonymous. Plenty of us still use dentists who sit behind us at church and dry cleaners we talk to in the grocery store. Loyalty and friendliness still permeate the market and are engendered by personalized interactions. The point of seeing the forms of social interaction on a scale rather than as completely different is that the morality we learned in our youth still applies in different degrees to the various forms of commercial life. Commercial society can never be wholly disembodied from personal relations.

Second, Heyne argues the free market deserves moral accolades because its outcomes are better than any other economic system. Just as some accidents occur during rush hour, some market failures do occur, but by and large, both systems function rather well. But when he argues at the end of the first chapter that hunger is not an injustice, he bases the claim on the fact that "no one intends the hunger of other people" (p. 9). How are we to reconcile Heyne's insistence that the morality of the market be judged by its outcomes with his claim that one outcome of the market, that is, hunger, is not a moral issue because it was not part of anyone's intention? That is, Heyne appears to want it both ways. The market should be judged good because of its good outcomes, and it cannot be held accountable for bad outcomes because no one intends them.

Such confusion leads to a third question about Heyne's moral position. If the free market is a social system in which individuals pursue their interests in accordance with the rules of the game, then the incentives in the market and the laws that structure it have a large influence on people's actions. Hunger can indeed be a moral problem if the laws and incentives that contextualize the way people act in the market are devised by politicians and businesspeople to benefit some at the expense of others. Although the market may be on the far impersonal end of the spectrum of social forms, it is nevertheless bounded and shaped by human decisions, and such decisions are most certainly suited for moral judgment. If economics both studies and suggests incentive structures that induce humans to act, then it must attend to the outcomes such incentives produce. Although I perceive some murkiness in Heyne's ethical position at this point, he certainly would have advocated for this kind of more ethically attuned economics.

A CRITIQUE OF THEOLOGIANS

Like ethicists, Heyne sees that theologians object to the impersonal nature of commercial society and the lack of "dignity" with which it treats people. Theologians want "people to be treated 'as individuals, not as commodities'" (p. 106). Such a desire illustrates many theologians' preference for the kind of personal relations ethicists endorse, but it also points to a deeper problem that plagues theological statements about the economy. Theologians construct social visions of the economy that Heyne believes "[deny] our humanity by insisting that we be gods" because they proclaim a universal ethic in which a particular group of people (typically those in the church) is believed to be able to perceive and correct social ills (p. 108).

One of the main problems theologians have with economics is that *homo economicus* has "limited knowledge" (p. 80). Theologians – and much of Heyne's criticism in this volume is targeted toward the Bishops who drafted the *U.S. Bishops' Pastoral Letter on Catholic Social Teaching and the U.S. Economy* in the 1980s – believe "some vantage point exists above the fray, a vantage point from which, once it is attained, all social ills can be corrected" (p. 77). Because they do not recognize the limits that finitude places on human knowledge, theologians often falsely believe government programs and legislation can know enough to correct the problems left by the market. Too many theologians believe the government – guided by the church – is "always equal to the task at hand" (p. 79).

But the problem runs even deeper than just the desire for a perspective that exists beyond the rough and tumble of finite life. Heyne is troubled by the fact that theologians want to make universal claims about ethical matters. Here he launches not an economic critique but a theological one against universalism. He contends that such a "Constantinian" perspective on Christianity ignores the teachings of the New Testament. For Heyne, the Christian social vision is defined wholly and completely by the New Testament. And since Christian ethics in the beginning was "an ethics for a community" and not the whole world, Christians today should not attempt such universal moral claims (p. 209). Furthermore, since "[t]he New Testament provides no agenda for government," theologians who want to say something about politics must in all honesty "give up the authority of the New Testament as support for what they are doing" (pp. 189–190). The point of his theological critique is to urge theologians to keep their religious arguments out of the public sphere (p. 210). In a theological message that stretches from these later works all the way back to the preface of his first book, Heyne (1965, p. 8) believes "Christianity has very little to say about the economic order." Although he acknowledges that faith commitments will inform public policy positions, he says that invoking religion in public discourse only creates divides too deep to bridge.

Heyne's critique of theologians should not be taken just as an economist deriding the ignorance of another field; it should be seen as one theologian cautioning others to recognize the depths of human sin in their own social visions. Rather than dismissing economics for treating humans as commodities, theologians should see the accuracy of much contemporary economics as a commentary on the fallenness of human life. To be true to Heyne's Lutheran theological training, we could say that economics functions as the theological use of the law. The truth about human limitations conveyed through economics should teach people, in Luther's (1962, p. 90) words, "to recognize sin in order that it may make them humble unto grace and unto faith in Christ." Economics works because humans really are self-interested most of the time. Theologians may not want to admit it, but it appears to be the reality of the fallen human condition.

Before leaving Heyne's critique of theology, a few questions have to be raised of Heyne's own theological position, which drives his attacks.[3] Heyne's strong rhetoric comes out of a minority position in the theological world. Although Catholic and Protestant theologians alike use the New Testament as a source for theological and ethical thought, few claim it as their sole source. Furthermore, few would say that real Christianity ended with Constantine and neglect the entire history and tradition of Christian experience. And still fewer theologians set up the stark church verses world dichotomy Heyne develops under the influence of the Mennonite John Howard Yoder. Heyne sees a world in which good and evil are defined by and apply only within the confines of a particular religious community. His particularist theological stance is why he attacks theologians who believe the moral standards of their particular church communities apply to others. Heyne's particularist theology, however, leads him to make the troubling universal claim that all other universal claims are invalid. Without any universal standards or moral processes, Heyne offers no way to judge between good norms and bad ones across communities. If everyone's morality is limited to their own community, the United States, as a nation of multiple communities, is left with no way to adjudicate between the ends sought by an Episcopalian church and those sought by a terrorist cell. The only guidance Heyne provides is that the "good" of a pluralist society is achieved when it helps everyone best attain their own self-interest, whatever that self-interest may be.

With a better understanding of Heyne's theology, we can see that the ethical divide he draws between face-to-face society and commercial society reflects the theological divide he sees between the church and world. The morality of the church cannot change the sinfulness of the world, just as the morality of personal relations cannot change the impersonal nature of commercial life. Heyne, however, seems at times unclear on his own position. Often he argues that religious arguments should be discouraged from public discourse – should not be allowed to affect economics: "Religious stories and economic stories will continue to influence one another. That cannot be prevented. But it does not have to be encouraged" (p. 130). And he quotes Friedman to support the idea that religion must be kept out of economic debates because religion relies on people's fundamental values, which raise "differences about which men [and women too] can ultimately only fight" (p. 82). Like Friedman, Heyne argues that economic debates proceed more smoothly if they deal with economic arguments alone and do not get mired down in theology.

But in other articles Heyne critiques Friedman – and himself by implication – saying that it simply is not true that people "can ultimately only fight" if they have basic value differences (p. 344). Although at times he wants to ban religious language from public discourse because it only creates dogmatic divides, Heyne also at times contends that people more often than not will discuss their differences instead of fighting over them. He says, "Economics and ethics do not in fact inhabit completely separate realms of discourse, and keeping them rigorously apart will not help us to resolve our political differences" (p. 411). It seems that if economics and ethics can be discussed together, so too can economics and theology. Does ethics not make just as basic of value claims as theology? Those of us who accept Heyne's basic argument that at root economics cannot be seen as a value-free inquiry set apart from other aspects of life must push beyond Heyne's own sometimes dichotomous thinking and pursue his line of thought that puts both the personal and the theological in conversation with the impersonal and commercial.

A CRITIQUE OF ECONOMISTS

Although Heyne made his home among economists, he spares them no criticism, and he insists that they have much to learn from their colleagues in ethics and theology. If ethicists want a God-like world in which everyone benevolently treats everyone else and theologians want to solve the problems of the world from a God-like vantage point, then the problem with economists is that they think they have attained something reserved for God alone – the Truth. All three claims produce dogmatic certainty, and Heyne cannot countenance any of them.

Although economists insist that humans have limited knowledge and thus the price system is needed to organize vast amounts of information, they see themselves exempt from such limits. The demands for "rigor" among economists amount to the claim that no one has "real authority to speak until they have transcended the human condition" and can speak objective Truth (p. 112). Heyne refers to such economists as "foundationalists," who "believe that economic science can and should consist of clear and unambiguous axioms and hypothesis that jointly generate implications that can be checked against equally clear and unambiguous observations" (p. 118). Heyne, however, decries such an approach to economics. Not only does it create for boring introductory courses, but it also neglects the reality of the human condition. Fact and value are not separate things in human life; the positive–normative distinction is a myth. Economists must recognize that "[s]o-called factual or scientific judgments are formulated on the basis of particular preconceptions and addressed to others who appropriate them on the basis of their own preconceptions" (p. 109).

As Heyne sees it, science after Thomas Kuhn must acknowledge itself as a value-laden project, and this is not a bad thing (p. 83). In fact, Heyne believes theologians, ethicists, and politicians would pay more attention to economics if economists acknowledged that they were not in pursuit of objective truth, but in the business of persuasion (p. 108). Here Heyne acknowledges his debt to Deirdre McCloskey as he argues that the task of economists is to persuade others to see the world as they do, and the best way to do this, both as scholars and teachers, is to tell stories. Although economists have much to teach theologians, Heyne believes they need to learn from theologians how to use stories to shape people's views of world.[4]

For Heyne, one fulfills the economists' task when one persuasively "[explains] market processes, interpersonal transactions, and patterns of exchange" (p. 309). Economists no longer need to bore introductory students with basic principles abstracted from reality, but rather, students should be challenged to think through the implications of real world economic activities. Students should develop "plausible stories" about economic exchanges, not just run formulas. "A story will not be plausible," in Heyne's mind, "if it is inconsistent with the basic assumptions of economic theory, which is that all social phenomena emerge from the choices individuals make in response to expected benefits and costs to themselves" (p. 311). There remains much to be taught in an introductory course, both about economizing and exchange, but what gets taught no longer pretends to be separate from moral, social, and political forces.

Outside the classroom, Heyne challenges economists to learn some ethics and stop surrendering the realm of values and morality to people who know little about the actual workings of the economy (p. 334). In fact, he asserts that "[b]y claiming that their analysis is independent of all ethical or political judgments, economists have succeeded only in convincing opponents that they are naïve, philistine, and possibly even dishonest" (p. 110). In Heyne's mind the reason economists lack public influence is because they have claimed a God-like knowledge of objective truth that others find to be both condescending and impossible. If economists would admit the limits of their knowledge, they might realize that they must begin to tell persuasive stories that exemplify the economic way of thinking. Only such passionate stories will persuade people of the moral value of the market and the moral dangers that arise when we pretend to be God-like and fix it ourselves.

HEYNE'S RETURN TO ADAM SMITH

Heyne fortunately never stops with critique – he uses it to develop a constructive position that draws on the social vision of Adam Smith to chart a new direction for economics. Heyne's vision, like Smith's own, is both humble in its claims and humbling in its descriptive power. Smith saw humans as mostly motivated by self-interest (not to be confused with greed or selfishness), though with some room for benevolent action. He, furthermore, believed the specific interest that drives most humans is the opportunity to "better their condition," which can include monetary accumulation, but "[o]ur ultimate concern, according to Smith, is for our reputation" (pp. 60–61). Self-interested action for Smith and Heyne reaches far beyond just economic means and ends but encompasses one's whole life. Heyne insists we remember that for Smith there was no "'economic' system that could be distinguished from the total social system and that was governed by laws of its own" (p. 63). Similarly, Heyne's own social vision extends far beyond the narrow reaches of blackboard economics.

Through Smith's influence, Heyne develops a realistic picture of human life as deeply limited and partial to itself. For Heyne economics is not about objective truth and social physics but about explaining how limited and self-interested people work together in an impersonal market to meet their needs and those of others. As Heyne (1963, p. 227) wrote in his dissertation, "It follows that economics must in large part confine itself to the task of facilitating discussion. The primary responsibility of the economist is to reveal the relations among events, so that those who participate in these events can more effectively discern and discuss the implications of their activity. The economist is first of all an educator and not a social engineer." And Heyne was above all an educator. His early words here reflect the integrity of his lifelong vocation to understand and share the "economic way of thinking."

To be sure, Geoffrey Brennan and Anthony Waterman edit an out-standing volume and representative testament of Heyne's work. *Are Economists Basically Immoral (AEBI)* includes a helpful and interesting biographical introduction before moving to 26 pieces of Heyne's work, mostly written during his tenure at the University of Washington (1976–2000). I have focused on the first 13 chapters, which include Heyne's writings on economics, ethics, and theology. They are followed by six exemplary chapters on teaching that reveal how Heyne made his economic way of thinking come alive in the classroom. And the volume ends with three pieces on economic methodology and four in which Heyne applies the theory discussed throughout the text to a number of policy issues, namely corporate responsibility, labor unions, illegal drugs, and the environment.

Although a number of the chapters deal with rather specific and complex issues, Heyne's way with words makes the entire volume accessible to well-guided undergraduates as well as scholars in theology, ethics, and economics. Heyne's lively style of writing evokes visions of a most engaging undergraduate instructor. His frequent practice of moving from the obvious sources of problems to their more deeply seated origins demonstrates his skill at telling persuasive plausible stories. And his sometimes heated language – like calling the *Bishops' Letter* a "hodgepodge of citations from the Bible, papal encyclicals, and other church documents, mixed with ringing assertions about dignity and justice" – reveals his passion for his vocation (p. 99). Although one can take issue with Heyne's particular moral positions or his theological stance, he offers a social vision that calls all of us to lay down our dogmas, recognize the limits of our finite nature, and engage one another in fruitful dialogue. This volume represents a necessary read for all engaged in the good work of economic analysis and others who want to understand it.

NOTES

1. Heyne cites this claim since it was one that got Lawrence Summers in such trouble (p. 2).
2. Heyne here seems to ignore the prevalent forms of Kantian ethics, which are both concerned with intention and formulated for vast, impersonal, and pluralistic societies.
3. And they are attacks. Heyne does not mince words in his contempt for some theologians. For instance, he quips of the ignorance of the Bishops that "[o]ne of the great advantages possessed by those who enter a discussion without knowing its context is that they can employ weak arguments with a clear conscience" (p. 127).
4. Heyne's debt to the narrative theology of Stanley Hauerwas also informs this position.

REFERENCES

Heyne, P. (1963). *The presuppositions of economic thought: A study in the philosophical and theological sources of economic controversy.* Ph.D. thesis, University of Chicago, Chicago, IL.
Heyne, P. (1965). *The Christian encounters the world of economics.* St. Louis, MO: Concordia Publishing.
Luther, M. (1962). The Christian in society II. In: W. I. Brand (Ed.), *Luther's works* (Vol. 45). Philadelphia, PA: Fortress Press.

CARTWRIGHT'S HUNTING CAUSES AND USING THEM

CAUSAL PLURALISM AND THE LIMITS OF CAUSAL ANALYSIS ☆

Kevin D. Hoover

Review essay on Cartwright, N. (2007), *Hunting Causes and Using Them: Approaches in Philosophy and Economics*. Cambridge, UK: Cambridge University Press. x + 270pp. IBSN 978-0-521-86081-9 $85.

For the past 30 years, Nancy Cartwright has been one of the most significant philosophers of science. Beginning with a focus on physics, she was at the forefront of the movement to use philosophy to help to understand the practices of physics as seen from the working physicists' point of view rather than simply to pronounce on those practices from an Olympian, but perhaps irrelevant, perspective. Starting with her *Nature's Capacities and Their Measurement* (Cartwright, 1989), she has steadily taken in a wider scope of sciences, including social sciences.

In Cartwright's view, economics is not some poor stepchild to physics but a significant part of a complex world in which the sciences are not (as so often thought by philosophers, physical scientists, and economists alike) arranged in a clear hierarchy in which each of the "special" sciences is reducible to the more basic sciences – physics forming the bedrock.

☆This chapter is a substantially expanded version of the review of the same book that appeared in the *Journal of Economic Literature* 47(2) (2009) 493–495.

A Research Annual
Research in the History of Economic Thought and Methodology, Volume 28-A, 381–395
Copyright © 2010 by Emerald Group Publishing Limited
ISSN: 0743-4154/doi:10.1108/S0743-4154(2010)000028A020

Cartwright has also been a major player in the philosophical analysis of causation, a role that suits her turn toward economics, which has been undergoing a causal revival in, for example, the work of Granger in time-series econometrics, Heckman in microeconomic policy analysis, and the program of natural experiments in applied microeconomics. Given this background a new book by Nancy Cartwright – particularly one that singles out economics in its subtitle – is surely a welcome event.

Hunting Causes and Using Them unfortunately represents a missed opportunity. It is not a systematic treatise but a compilation of occasional papers written with various particular – and mainly philosophical – targets in view. The papers have been too lightly edited to form coherent chapters in a unified volume. They are frequently repetitive, and notation shifts from chapter to chapter. It is often difficult to appreciate fully the point of the chapter without the full context of the debates to which they originally contributed. They are heavy sledding for an *economist* not already immersed in those debates.

Despite professing to seeing useful insights in various approaches, Cartwright's method is more critical than constructive. And she sometimes misunderstands the approaches that she criticizes. This is unfortunate, as she is a deeply insightful philosopher with a rare connection to actual practice and, even here, her discussion is full of genuine insights about causation and the problems of modeling it. A constructive treatise that tempered her criticism with a lucid exposition of its objects would have been exceedingly helpful.

To take an example that cuts close to the bone, I do not recognize my own position in her account of my analysis of causal order (chapter 14). She attributes causal judgments to me that straightforward applications of the formal definitions in chapter 3 of my *Causality in Macroeconomics* (2001) contradict. At the risk of appearing to give a greater importance to my own work in *Hunting Causes* than it deserves, later in this review I try to correct, what I believe to me misunderstandings of my own views.

THE VARIETY OF CAUSAL CONCEPTS AND THEIR USES

Three themes dominate *Hunting Causes*. The first is that *cause* is a plural concept. The methods and metaphysics of causation, Cartwright believes, are context dependent. Different causal accounts seem to be at odds with one another only because the same word means different things in different contexts. Every formal approach to causality uses a conceptual framework that is "thinner" than causal reality. She lists a bewildering variety of approaches to causation: probabilistic and Bayes-net accounts (of, for example, Patrick Suppes, Clive Granger, Wolfgang Spohn, Judea Pearl, and Clark Glymour), modularity accounts (Pearl, James Woodward, and Stephen LeRoy), invariance accounts (Woodward, David Hendry, and Kevin Hoover), natural experiments (Herbert Simon, James Hamilton, and Cartwright), causal process accounts (Wesley Salmon and Philip Dowe), efficacy accounts (Hoover), counterfactual accounts (David Lewis, Hendry, Paul Holland, and Donald Rubin), manipulationist accounts (Peter Menzies and Huw Price), and others. The lists of advocates of various accounts overlap. Nevertheless, she sometimes treats these accounts as if they were so different that it is not clear why they should be the subject of a single book. And she fails to explain what they have in common. If, as she apparently believes, they do not have a common essence, do they have a Wittgensteinian family resemblance? She fails to explore in any systematic way the complementarities among the different approaches – for example, between invariance accounts, Bayes-nets, and natural experiments – that frequently make their advocates allies rather than opponents.

The second theme is her distinction between schemes that deductively *clinch* causal inferences and those that inductively *vouch* for them. Her idea is that certain schemes of causal inference work by making such strong background assumptions that inductive arguments are turned into deductive arguments. She is surely right that many arguments take the form of clinchers, conditional on background assumptions. But she is wrong to imply that advocates of these forms of argument are insensitive to the tentativeness and the fallibility of those strong background assumptions. Such sensitivity means that arguments that take the form of clinchers are, in reality, always practically vouchers.

For example, with Bayes-net approaches a statistical model describes data from which probabilities are inferred, and causal order, in turn, is inferred deductively from those probabilities. The inferences are based on strong assumptions. For instance, analysts frequently assume *causal sufficiency* (i.e., there are no omitted variables of a type that would confuse causal inference), the *acylicality* of causal structure, and the *linearity* of functional relationships. Serious users of Bayes-net approaches are deeply aware of the fragility of the statistics – both the quality of the data and the modeling assumptions (e.g., stationarity and homogeneity). And they are aware that the assumptions about causal structure may fail in practical cases, which is why they have investigated the implications of alternative assumptions – for example, latent variables (relaxing causal sufficiency), nonlinearity, and cyclical models.

And what is the alternative? Absent the strategy of embedding clinchers within maintained, but criticizable, assumptions, Cartwright provides no account of how evidence vouches for causal claims.

The final theme is the distinction between hunting and using causes highlighted in the title. The distinction gets it bite in Cartwright's belief that the strategies that successfully allow the identification of casual mechanisms frequently serve policy applications ill. Building on a longstanding theme of her work, real world processes are seen as the complex composition of a variety of deeper tendencies. The function of scientific experiments is to isolate those tendencies through stringent controls so that they can be exhibited in pure form. The application of scientific knowledge in practice is frequently complicated – if not thwarted altogether – because the real world is open and, unlike in the laboratory, the complicating tendencies are uncontrolled. In such cases, it is not necessarily reliable to infer that effects found under stringent controls will play out similarly in the world.

Her insight trades on the old distinction between *internal* and *external* validity. For example, we may discover in a randomized controlled trial that a drug is effective against the malaria parasite; and, yet, for a variety of social and biological reasons, the drug may prove to be practically ineffective in patients. One lesson, perhaps, is that randomized controlled trials need to be supplemented with epidemiological studies. The exact same issues can arise with respect to natural experiments in economics: can the mechanism that they isolate be carried over to other policy contexts?

The theme of hunting versus using causes is elaborated in the final chapter on the use of counterfactuals in economics. Cartwright argues that the relevant counterfactuals isolate a cause from its own causes and set it to some value come what may. Using the same *implementation-neutral* strategies counterfactually to evaluate policies typically results in "imposters" – the wrong counterfactual for the issue at hand. Genuine policy analysis typically, though not always, requires *implementation-specific* counterfactuals. (Not always because some policies need to be robust across different implementations if they are to be useful, since, in some cases, targeting is practically restricted.)

Cartwright is clearly correct that good policy requires the right counterfactuals and that, naturally, economists sometimes get it wrong. Yet, as a generic criticism, her case is not persuasive. For example, a straightforward reading of the Lucas critique, which Cartwright cites in other parts of the book with other purposes, is precisely as a plea for understanding counterfactuals in a causally structured, implementation-specific manner. Implementation of policy requires the specification of conditional rules and not a come-what-may setting of particular variables.

PRODUCTION- VERSUS STRATEGY-CAUSATION: A MISATTRIBUTION

I now turn to a quite specific disagreement with Cartwright. In chapter 14 (Hoover on Simon on Causation) Cartwright draws a distinction between a *production* account and a *strategy* account of causation:

> A production account of causation focuses on the relation between x and y: x produces y; x makes y happen or is responsible for y; y comes out of x. Hoover's strategy account by contrast focuses on the relation between us and x, y: we affect y by/in affecting x. So for strategy causation we do not consider what happens to y by virtue of what x does but rather what happens to y by virtue of what we do to ensure that x happens. Roughly, x strategy-causes y if and only if what we do that is sufficient for the value of x to be fixed is "partially sufficient" for y to be fixed. (p. 204)

Cartwright presents the account of strategy-causation that she attributes to me in a positive light; yet it is simply not a position that I hold.

I see the roots of my own views on causation in the work of Herbert Simon (1957). Cartwright argues that Simon's views are quite different from mine (in chapter 13, as well as chapter 14). And she claims that my approach is fundamentally different from other approaches that she characterizes as production-causation, including those of Woodward (2003), Pearl (2000), and Spirtes, Glymour, and Scheines (2001). There are, of course, differences in our approaches, but the distinction that Cartwright is drawing here – whatever its merits in its own right – is not a distinction that separates me from these other authors.

A policymaker is, of course, interested in strategy: what can we do to make something happen? But in common with those authors to whom Cartwright attributes a production-causation account, I believe that it is only by understanding the fundamental connections between x and y that we can know "if what we do that is sufficient for the value of x to be fixed is 'partially sufficient' for y to be fixed." In that respect, my account is not significantly different from, say, Woodward's manipulationist account that Cartwright classifies as a production-causation account.

The source of at least some of the disagreement between Cartwright and me is over how to represent causal relationships in equations and diagrams. Simon presents a schema for representing causal relationships in equations. So, let us start there. My own interpretation of Simon's account of causal order has been extensively developed elsewhere and need not be defended here (Hoover, 1990, 2001 [Chapters 2–3], 2009a, 2009b). The essence of Simon's approach is that causal order is expressed in a hierarchy of self-contained subsystems of equations.

Consider the simplest example

$$x = a \tag{1}$$

$$y = bx + c \tag{2}$$

where x and y are variables and a, b, and c coefficients expressing the way in which those variables are functionally related.

Simon says that x causes y because x is determined in the subsystem (Eq. (1) only) independently of the value of y, whereas y cannot similarly be determined independently of x. Simon realizes, of course, that different linear combinations of Eqs. (1) and (2) could produce equations with the same solutions for x and y but different coefficients and, therefore, possibly different apparent causal orders. To block such "observational equivalence," Simon argues that the true causal structure corresponds to a particular set of these coefficients that may be chosen independently by "experimenters," including nature among them (Simon, 1957, p. 26). Thus, if we know which set of coefficient has that property, the causal order is determined uniquely – independently of the way in which the equations are written. This is not a syntactic property, but semantic property that requires that we know something about the world. The reference to "experimenters" is a suggestion of the kind of epistemological strategies that would allow us to come by that knowledge.

I call Simon's privileged coefficients *parameters*. The distinctive feature is that a parameter may take any value in its range without restricting what values other parameters may take. This is not generally true of the coefficients of any arbitrary linear combination of equations.

I think of causal diagrams in a way closely related to Pearl (2000) or Spirtes et al. (2000). Causal arrows connect variables. I do not draw arrows from parameters to variables. The reason for this is that it is part of the notion of direct control, invoked by Simon in his discussion of experimenters. The parameter represents how the experimenter sets a variable that is controllable, and the link between the parameter and the variable it influences is a tight and unmediated one. For me a parameter serves a dual function of saying whether a causal connection exists and, if it is one that can exist in multiple (or continuous states), saying which state (or strength of connection) obtains. Given the role that parameters play for Simon in identifying which of the set of observationally equivalent systems of equations corresponds to the true causal order, one way to think about the parameterization of a system of equations is that it determines on which end of the shaft to place each of the arrowheads in a causal graph.

My account can be clarified by considering one of the Cartwright's examples in which she provides an explicit, independent description of the structure. A good one is the lemonade/biscuit machine (Model 2.1, pp. 209–210), which she claims illustrates how strategy and production accounts diverge. Cartwright tells a personal anecdote:

> There was a lovely machine in my residence in Bologna that dispensed lemonade and biscuits. When it dispensed lemonade it made clack-clack noises – by a pump, I was told; for biscuits, a whirring noise by a motor. Most often it made both kinds of noises and gave out both lemonade and biscuits. I never knew if the motor tripped the pump or the reverse or neither, though I was told that the whole thing was made of bicycle parts by local students so I knew that whatever connections there were, were all mechanical. There were levers on the machine to push in order to get the lemonade and biscuits but my Italian was not good enough to read the instructions. So whichever I wanted, I just pulled all the levers and I always got both. (p. 209)

Cartwright offers a hypothesis about the structure of the machine in which the motor causes the pump represented in Fig. 1:

Fig. 1. Cartwright's Figure 14(2.1).

where α and β represent the motion of the two levers and the variables M, the action of the motor and P the rate of the pump. The figure corresponds to the system of equations

$$M = a$$
$$P = M + \beta \qquad (2.1)$$

Cartwright considers an alternative hypothesis in which the pump causes the motor, represented by a graph shown in Fig 2:

Fig. 2. Cartwright's Figure 14(2.2).

and a set of equations "which keep the same functional relationships but with a different causal order" (p. 210):

$$P = \alpha + \beta$$
$$M = P - \beta$$

(2.2)

The builders of the machine later tell Cartwright that the second hypothesis was correct.

She then goes on to ask:

What are the strategy-causal relations for the machine? α and β are parameters sufficient to fix both M and P and

$$Par_M = \{\alpha\} \subset \{\alpha, \beta\} = Par_P$$

so on Hoover's account M strategy-causes P. And that is reasonable. Anything I could do to set P set [sic] M as well, but not the reverse, even though the production relations are just the opposite of the strategy ones. (p. 209)

Here Cartwright appeals to a parameter-nesting condition found in my formal account of causal structure in *Causality in Macroeconomics* (Hoover, 2001, Chapter 3). Since Cartwright does not want to believe that the students were lying about the construction of the machine, she believes that strategy and production causation must not be the same.

The problem is that I agree with the students. In the second hypothesis, P causes M. So if Cartwright gives me the same presumption of honesty as she gives to the students, something is wrong in her analysis. What is it?

It is literally a case misrepresentation – i.e., a case in which Cartwright's representation does not correspond to the representation on which I base my analysis. Cartwright interprets α and β as levers. To me this is a category mistake. Levers are elements of the machine. The state of the levers can be represented by variables that take the values of, say, *on* and *off* or *up* and *down*. The machine in which M causes P might therefore be represented as in Fig. 3.

Fig. 3.   Hoover's Representation of the Machine in which the Motor causes the Pump.

Now this may appear to be a trivial amendment, since it looks like I have simply renamed α and β. But that is not quite right, because there is a substantive difference between the Ls and α and β. A parameter might, on Cartwright's interpretation, simply govern the setting (or partial setting of a variable) – e.g., whether the lever is up or down. But it may also govern the existence and strength of connection between the variables. (It is common in linear path diagrams to indicate a causal strength for each arrow.) Implicitly, Cartwright has normalized all causal strengths to unity, so that she fails to make explicit at least one parameter, namely the one that governs the relationship between M and P. So, in place of Model (2.1) we could more clearly write the first hypothesized structure of the machine as

$$L_1 = \alpha$$
$$L_2 = \beta$$
$$M = aL_1 \tag{2.1'}$$
$$P = bM + cL_2$$

where when the levers are connected, a and c represent the rate *ceteris paribus* at which the motor and the pump operate when L_1 or L_2 is in the *on* position, and where b represents the rate at which the pump responds to the motor. Cartwright's original parameters, α and β, indicate the state of the levers (*on* or *off*). (Of course, this is an easy case; nothing prevents us from having more complicated interactions among the levers and the motor-pump linkage.) The parameters are α, β, a, b, and c. In Cartwright's models a, b, and c have been in effect normalized to unity, so that they are invisible in Model (2.1).

Normalization is not necessarily a problem, but I think that it leads to confusion, when Cartwright considers the second hypothesis in which she imagines that the pump causes the motor and the motor slows down when the pump is on, because the pump lever is connected to a damping mechanism, which she represents as an arrow running from β to M. I would diagram the structure of the model that Cartwright describes as in Fig. 4

Fig. 4. Hoover's Representation of the Machine in which the Pump Causes the Motor with a Damping Mechanism.

which might be represented by a model such as

$$L_1 = \alpha$$
$$L_2 = \beta$$
$$M = dP + eL_2 \tag{2.2'}$$
$$P = fL_1 + gL_2$$

where α, β, d, e, f, and g are the parameters, with α, β as before and d representing the rate at which the motor responds to the pump and e, f, and g the rates *ceteris paribus* at which the motor or pump responds to the levers being on. In particular, $e < 0$, as it is supposed to damp the motor. (Note, however, that this stretches the linearity assumption a bit, since damping is a negative influence that operates only when other positive influences are operating. Nonetheless, that could easily be fixed; so I ignore it for simplicity.)

Under this description, which I think exactly captures Cartwright's physical description of the machine, contrary to Cartwright's claim about what I should conclude, the definitions in chapter 3 of my book imply P causes M (Hoover, 2001, Chapter 3). What is the source of Cartwright's confusion?

She is, I think, misled by failing to follow my usage with respect to parameters. She thinks that the second, quite different machine, can be represented with exactly the same functional forms as the first machine, because she fails to make explicit the parameters implicit on the variables of the system and elides the variables that represent the state of the levers by including only the parameters that govern their setting (α and β) and not the parameters that govern the strength of their influence (e and g) in the causal diagram. Had she been explicit about the full parameterization, she would see that, in general, there is no reason for the parameters of the second model to be algebraic transformations of those of the first model (generally d, e, f, and g, need not be algebraic transformations of a, b, and c).

Cartwright wants us to read Model (2.2) as taking β to represent the damping of one of the levers on the motor. But because Model (2.2) merely rewrites Model (2.1), the value of β is necessarily exactly the value needed to offset the putative effect of P on M. That is not damping, since M runs exactly the same speed for the same α and β in Model (2.2) as it does under Model (2.1). Model (2.2) cannot be the generic representation of the second machine as she describes it, but a quite particular representation that ensures that it will be observationally equivalent Model (2.1) in terms of the values of the variables it generates.

This is exactly the problem that Simon warned us about. Systems of linear equations with undirected equalities do not wear their causal orders on their faces. I pin down the causal order by saying which things are parameters as I have defined them. Pearl and Spirtes et al. pin it down by saying which variables are connected by causal arrows. I conjecture – and I have yet to see a counter-example – that any causal graph under their rules can be represented by a system of equations under my rules in which the parameterization determines exactly the same causal orderings among the variables. In this respect, Cartwright's attempt to drive a wedge between Pearl and Spirtes et al. and me is misguided. Consider another of Cartwright's causal graphs shown in Fig. 5:

Fig. 5. Cartwright's Figure 14(1.1).

(We need not interpret this graph as involving motors and pumps; it can just as well involve money and prices.) The graph violates my standard conventions. That would pose no problem – Cartwright is not obligated to adopt my representational conventions – except that she writes as if she were respecting my conventions. Consider a model corresponding to Fig. 5:

$$M = \alpha$$
$$P = \alpha + \beta \tag{1.1}$$

A diagram, such as Fig. 5 is not, according to my conventions, a proper representation of Model (1.1) for the simple reason that, if α and β are truly parameters and not structural variables, then by the definitions of causal order in my chapter 3, the only diagram compatible with Model (1.1) is $M \to P$. And this does not change, when the model is transformed algebraically. Thus, Model (1.1) is, to my mind, written more perspicaciously as Cartwright's Model (2.1), which I take to be exactly the same model, with exactly the same causal diagram $(M \to P)$:

$$M = \alpha$$
$$P = M + \beta \tag{2.1}$$

Its advantage follows only because we have an implicit convention that interprets the equal signs causally as running right to left, and that allows us to read the causal diagram directly off the equations. (This is why, in my book, I use $\Leftarrow$ as a causally directed equal sign. Elsewhere Cartwright uses $c^=$ with the same intent.) Applying my definitions to Model (1.1) or (2.1) generates exactly the same causal relations. Cartwright's notation misleads her, as she makes trivial algebraic transformations and treats them as if they represent new causal orders. This seems to me to be the problem that Simon exposed perfectly clearly. If we always wrote models in a canonical form with causal equal signs ($\Leftarrow$) and the convention that every causal equal sign has one causally structural variable on the pointed side and at least one on the non-pointed side, it would be hard to be misled by such transformations.

Rather than starting with the algebra, start with Fig. 5. Then, Cartwright appears to say that it something like the lemonade/biscuit machine but with the linkage between the motor and the pump omitted – there really is no structural connection between M and P. Yet she believes that I am committed to identify M as causing P. Again, this is clarified if we are careful about diagrammatic conventions. Cartwright continues to view α and β as levers or switches; so let me propose the following as a diagram that suits my conventions but gets to her major point as shown in Fig. 6:

Fig. 6.

One model that corresponds to this diagram is:

$$L_1 = \alpha$$
$$L_2 = \beta$$
$$M = aL_1$$
$$P = bL_1 + cL_2$$

System(C″)

Using the definitions of my *Causality* (pp. 61–63), M does not cause P. Let one subsystem be:

$$L_1 = \alpha$$
$$M = aL_1$$

Subsystem(C′)

Cartwright is tempted to say that my definitions would imply that M causes P, since the parameters of this subsystem are $P^1 = \{\alpha, a\} \subset \{\alpha, \beta, a, b, c\} = P^2$, the parameters of the full model (System C″). But while that would get the conclusion that she wants – namely, that strategy-causation is different from production-causation – it does so only by ignoring an essential element of my definitions. Parameter subset relationships are not everything. In fact, there exist another subsystem (C^*), defined by

$$L_1 = \alpha$$
$$L_2 = \beta \qquad \text{Subsystem } (C^*)$$
$$M = aL_1$$

that intervenes between C′ and C″ – that is, C′ determines L_1 and M; and C^* determines L_1, L_2, and M, whereas C″ determines P in addition to the other three variables, so that the subsystems are arranged in hierarchy. The existence of the intervening subsystem rules out (for Simon as well as for me) M being a direct cause of P. At best, it could be an indirect cause (e.g., M causes X and X causes P), but in fact there is no intermediating variable (i.e., no X) in C″, and so there is no causal connection between M and P at all. This is a very formal way of making the point that, despite the fact that the same parameters influence M and P, the actual value taken by M does not really matter – independently of the parameter α itself to the value of P. My definitions, then, point to exactly the same conclusions about the causal relation between M and P as those that Cartwright attributes to the production-causal account. The distinction between a strategy-causal and a production-causal account, insofar as it rests on my own position collapses.

How is it that Cartwright misreads my account to the point that she concludes that I would identify exactly the opposite causal order than the ones I believe that my definitions imply? One possibility, which I take seriously, is that the representation scheme in chapter 3 of *Causality* uses unfamiliar mathematics and is explained less clearly than it could have been. Two recent papers try to present a clearer account in more familiar notation and actually widen the class of causal information that can be encoded into the bargain (Hoover, 2009a, 2009b).

Whatever the source, one consequence of reading me as unconcerned with what Cartwright calls "internal production relations" is that Cartwright claims that I define causal relations in a framework of *reduced forms* in the econometricians' sense of that term. This is baffling, as the entire point of my account is to provide a structural understanding of causation. One source of the confusion may be that, when talking about inference from data, I am often using what are clearly reduced forms (in the econometrician's sense). But when characterizing and discussing causal relations – that is through most of the first seven chapters of my book – I am always talking about structural and not reduced form equations. I see the characterization of causal order – conceptually and ontologically – as distinct from the epistemological problem of how to infer it from data. My methods of conducting causal inference (see chapter 8 of *Causality*) involve structural-break testing of reduced forms. Similarly, the Bayes-net methods of Spirtes et al. involve the construction of correlation matrices, which are essentially a byproduct of reduced-form estimation. But in both cases, the reduced forms are treated as a source of information, whereas object of the investigation is to find out what sort of internal production relations must lie behind them. I believe that this involves a problem of digging, and that one will gain coarser knowledge (for instance, through an unknown mechanism, pulling lever 1 delivers lemonade) which may with luck be refined later (for instance, by providing an accurate mechanical description of the mechanism that connects the lever to the lemonade). Cartwright's discussion of my account does not, however, have anything to do with these inferential issues; rather it considers how to characterize what causal relations are. At this level, there is not a reduced form in sight in my work.

The account that Cartwright attributes to me is actually quite similar to that of Stephen LeRoy (1995). LeRoy believes that internal causal relations are often hopelessly ambiguous. Some clear causal relations run from *exogenous* to *endogenous* variables. Exogenous variables in LeRoy's schema are similar to variables such as L_1 and L_2 in the models of the lemonade/biscuit machine – variables that cause, but are not caused by, other variables in the system. For LeRoy, the only unambiguous internal causal relations occur when a variable, say, x is determined by a subset of the exogenous variables that determine another variable, y. This is a nesting criterion similar to the parameter nesting criterion in my representation schema. Unlike Simon's or my schemas, however, LeRoy does not have a hierarchical account of systems of equations nor an identity criterion for those systems based in a notion of a unique parameterization. These are precisely the features of my account that Cartwright fails to respect, which suggests that LeRoy provides a better example of her notion of strategy-causation.

THE MISSED OPPORTUNITY

Nancy Cartwright has once again written an intellectually challenging book, full of insights. It is too bad that the presentation is not well adapted to an audience of econometricians and applied economists, for whom the issues that she considers are important and not always clearly thought through.

ACKNOWLEDGMENT

The American Economic Association's permission to use material from that review is gratefully acknowledged.

REFERENCES

Cartwright, N. (1989). *Nature's capacities and their measurement*. Oxford University Press: New York.

Hoover, K. D. (1990). The logic of causal inference: Econometrics and the conditional analysis of causality. *Economics and Philosophy, 6*(2), 207–234.

Hoover, K. D. (2001). *Causality in macroeconomics*. Cambridge, UK: Cambridge University Press.

Hoover, K. D. (2009a). *Identity, structure, and causation*. unpublished typescript. Duke University. Available at http://www.econ.duke.edu/~kdh9/research.html

Hoover, K. D. (2009b). *Counterfactuals and causal structure*. Unpublished typescript. Duke University. Available at http://www.econ.duke.edu/~kdh9/research.html

LeRoy, S. F. (1995). On policy regimes. In: K. D. Hoover (Ed.), *Macroeconometrics: Developments, tensions and prospects* (pp. 235–252). Boston: Kluwer.

Pearl, J. (2000). *Causality: Models, reasoning, and inference*. Cambridge, UK: Cambridge University Press.

Simon, H. A. (1957). Causal order and identifiability. In: *Models of man: Social and rational* (pp. 10–36). New York: Wiley.

Spirtes, P., Glymour, C., & Scheines, R. (2001). *Causation, prediction, and search* (2nd ed). Cambridge, MA: MIT Press.

Woodward, J. B. (2003). *Making things happen: A theory of causal explanation*. Oxford, UK: Oxford University Press.

MEDEMA'S THE HESITANT HAND

SWINGING TO AND FRO: GOVERNMENT AND MARKET, PIGOU AND COASE

Humberto Barreto

Review essay on Medema, S.G. (2009), *The Hesitant Hand: Taming Self-Interest in the History of Economic Ideas*. Princeton, NJ: Princeton University Press. xiii + 230 pp. ISBN 9780691122960. $35

In 1995, I wrote a paper titled "Pigou, Coase, and efficiency applied to Pennsylvania Coal Mining Law" (Barreto, 1995). My discussant at the History of Economics Society conference that year, Warren Samuels, was kind and encouraging (as usual). I decided to send the paper to Ronald Coase. In my cover letter, I said

> Although I know you must be extremely busy, I would greatly appreciate any comments or criticisms. In the paper, I try to guess how a Pigovian and a Coasian might view the conflicting-use problem contained in the case of Pennsylvania coal mining. Even though you won't like my conclusion (that Pigou and Coase are in many ways really quite similar), the obvious question is, How close to your position am I?

The ensuing exchange troubled me so much that I never attempted to publish the paper. I simply was not confident that I was right. In The *Hesitant Hand*, Steven Medema covers more than externalities and how best to handle them, but he has a lot to say about Coase and Pigou. It was a pleasure to learn much more about the complicated relationship involving

A Research Annual
Research in the History of Economic Thought and Methodology, Volume 28-A, 397–404
Copyright © 2010 by Emerald Group Publishing Limited
All rights of reproduction in any form reserved
ISSN: 0743-4154/doi:10.1108/S0743-4154(2010)000028A021

these two great economists. It is certainly not Medema's fault, but I remain unsure of my position. After reviewing Medema's book, I will explain why.

MANAGING SELF-INTEREST

The Hesitant Hand is a book about the struggle between market and state control of human behavior. Medema tells a convincing story of the evolution of the management of self-interest, which has fluctuated over time from more government control to less and back again. Adam Smith's lack of confidence in government and his explanation that the invisible hand of the market could harness self-interest led to the rejection of reliance on state regulation. The book's cover illustration is a human hand. I grant the obvious connection with the title of the book, but I would offer Fig. 1 as a picture that conveys the essence of the argument.

The book itself is a compilation of previous papers (listed in the acknowledgements). This gives a bit of disjointed, cut-and-paste feel. Some ideas are repeated (especially on the Coase Theorem), whereas others seemed artificially separated (e.g., the public choice sequence). I found the last chapter on the development of law and economics to be somewhat off point – it was not clear to me how this contributed to the taming of

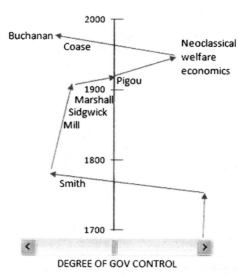

Fig. 1. Major Players Driving the Swinging Pendulum.

self-interest. Overall, however, Medema is a good editor and the unifying arc makes sense.

It begins, of course, with Adam Smith. Medema mentions a few precursors, but finds that "Nearly all of the economic literature prior to the eighteenth century expressed significant qualms about the effects of self-interested behavior on social welfare and held out state intervention as the only means to mitigate these problems" (p. 2). It was Smith who "launched" the debate, Smith who argued the "reverse," and "turned the tables," effectively convincing his reader not just that the market can manage self-interest, but that "it does it *better* than the state" (p. 22). Medema concludes the chapter, however, by rejecting naïve, proto-modern characterizations of Smith.

The next two chapters, as depicted in Fig. 1, describe a long slide back toward state regulation. "The tide began to turn back in the mid-1800s, as political economists became increasingly concerned about the ability of the invisible hand to channel self-interested behavior to society's benefit, though there was still great pessimism about the degree to which the state could improve on market performance" (p. 2). John Stuart Mill and Henry Sidgwick were part of a two-stage process. The former advanced the idea that markets were not perfect and the latter that government was not as bad as everyone thought. In addition, Sidgwick played an important role through his influence on Pigou.

In the third chapter, "Marginalizing the market," Medema covers Alfred Marshall and Arthur Cecil Pigou. Marshall established a theoretical case for market failure – a matter of "great philosophical importance" in the words of John Maynard Keynes (p. 56). But Marshall's deep distrust of government prevented him from embracing government control. Medema offers this statement from Marshall, who sympathized with the need to help the poor, to help explain Marshall's reluctance

> Government creates scarcely anything. If Governmental control had supplanted that of private enterprise a hundred years ago, there is good reason to suppose that our methods of manufacture now would be about as effective as they were fifty years ago, instead of being perhaps four or even six times as efficient as they were then. (p. 57)

Marshall did, however, see cause for optimism as government improved and corruption waned. Unfortunately, even as government got better, the problems it faced got even more complicated. For Marshall, government management of self-interest was only a futuristic fantasy.

In 1908, Pigou succeeded Marshall as Professor of Political Economy at Cambridge University and promptly devoted himself to further Marshall's legacy and economics. In 1912, Pigou published *Wealth and Welfare*, which became, in 1920, *The Economics of Welfare*, a book that would be the foundation of neoclassical welfare economics. By focusing on divergences between private and social product, Pigou established a *prima facie* case for government intervention via corrective taxes and subsidies familiar to every modern economist.

Fig. 1 captures Medema's story in that Pigou does give a larger role for government involvement, but it is other neoclassical economists (e.g., James Meade) who run much farther with the ball. Medema uses Pigou's 1935 essay, "State action and laisser-faire" to support the claim that Pigou was pragmatic and cautious about the role of government. Medema is convinced that "Pigou's practical approach falls squarely within the larger Cambridge tradition" (p. 72). It is a combination of neoclassical followers and Pigou's opponents, especially Coase, who will create a caricature of Pigou.

In the fourth chapter, Medema shifts focus to forerunners of public choice theory, reviewing various works in Italian *scienza delle finanze* and Knut Wicksell. Just like Marshall and Pigou had chipped away at the idea of perfect markets, these authors cast doubt on government's ability to handle self-interested behavior. Instead of market failure, we have government failure.

This leads to the best chapter of the book, "Coase's challenge." By 1960, when Coase published "The problem of social cost," Pigovian orthodoxy was firmly entrenched. The need for government correction of externality-induced market failure was undisputed. Coase would shake the foundations of neoclassical welfare analysis and the pendulum would swing once again. Medema provides a brief biography and dives into the issue. He reviews the familiar basics, the reciprocal nature of the problem and the Coase Theorem. Then he turns to Coase's handling of Pigou, which "can hardly be considered charitable, and he treated the Pigovian tradition with no more kindness than he treated Pigou himself, labeling the tradition 'inadequate' and 'incorrect,' both in analysis and in policy conclusions" (p. 117).

Medema believes that Coase's claim that "Pigou considered government the solution to all problems of harmful effects" (p. 119) is incorrect and unfair. Medema thinks that Coase, like Meade and other neoclassicals, spend too much time on *The Economics of Welfare*, a book devoted to theory, with almost no consideration given to issues of practice. For Medema, the neoclassical emphasis on formalism easily explains their blindness; Coase, however, has no such excuse.

The penultimate chapter is devoted to the rise of public choice theory. Medema reviews the invasion of political science by economic imperialists.

Led by James Buchanan, the anti-government swing started by Coase is given more momentum. By casting legislators, regulators, and voters as rational agents who respond to incentives, the idea of perfect government is soundly trashed.

In the final chapter, Medema returns to Coase and the rise of the new law and economics. He points out the irony in that Coase, who has explicitly rejected any interest in using economic analysis to explain legal rules and behavior, unintentionally triggered an economics invasion of the law. It was the legal cases cited by Coase in "The Problem of Social Cost," along with the suggestion that judges recognize, perhaps unconsciously, the economic implications of their decisions, which stimulated Richard Posner and others to apply economic reasoning to legal rules.

As Fig. 1 shows, Medema sees Coase and Buchanan as the vanguard of a movement fighting neoclassical welfare theory. Coase offered evidence that the market works better than commonly thought and Buchanan argued that government is deeply flawed. Where is the pendulum today? Medema devotes a three page (too brief) epilogue to this question, with the last paragraph explaining the title of the book. The swing toward less government that marked the last quarter of the 20th century may be receding as we hear calls for regulatory checks of the financial system. There are true believers on each extreme, "but for the moment at least, the debate seems to have settled at an intermediate point, with the majority of economists, like Coase, seeing neither the invisible hand nor the visible one as a panacea. The past two centuries of theoretical debate has suggested that the hand is hesitant – and increasingly, of late, so too is the economist" (p. 199).

COASE AND PIGOU

Having provided an overall summary of *The Hesitant Hand*, the remainder of this chapter will focus on Coase and Pigou. In my unpublished paper on Pennsylvania coal mining law, I expressed views that mirrored Medema's quite closely. I argued that Coase and Pigou are actually quite similar. They are perceived as opposites for several reasons. DeSerpa (1993) argues that the explanation lies in the default position: "Whereas *Welfare* was developed as a criticism of doctrinaire laissez-faire, Coase (1959, 1960) was a criticism of doctrinaire government regulation" (DeSerpa, 1993, p. 34). Perhaps, however, a different process was at work: the loss of subtlety and meaning as the master's words are translated by disciples and critics.

Like Medema, I saw Coase's "uncharitable treatment" playing a major role in how Pigou was perceived.

> Coase has often complained of being misunderstood, but it was really Pigou who was grossly caricatured when rendered by Coase in "The problem of social cost." By painting Pigou as a wild-eyed socialist, eager to step in and regulate at the drop of a hat with absurdly incalculable tax/subsidy/regulatory schemes, Coase effectively destroyed the true Pigovian view of the conflicting resource use problem, in particular, and of markets, in general. In doing so, Coase seemed to take the middle ground, but even a cursory reading of *The Economics of Welfare* immediately reveals Pigou's respect for market forces. (Barreto, pp. 42–43)

In his reply, Coase questioned my depiction of his treatment of Pigou, "What has charity to do with it? What matters is whether it is correct." Coase rejected my claim that he had misunderstood or mischaracterized Pigou. He explained that he had studied Pigou's work since 1930 and closed by saying, "This is a very hasty note. But as Marshall would say, there is constructive work to be done and life is short."

I immediately wrote him back. I tried to explain how I was surprised when I first read Pigou: "I expected – naively perhaps – to find a pure, textbook, chalkboard economist. Instead, I discovered a Pigou that appreciated the self-organizing character of a market system ... He didn't come across as I thought you and others had described him. He seemed much more aware of the power of the market system in generating good solutions to resource allocation problems."

I was delighted to hear back from Coase. He said, "I don't think you are right about Pigou. Read Pigou's *Socialism versus Capitalism* particularly the final chapter and then ask yourself whether there is any significant difference between Pigou's views and mine." Coase was referring to Pigou's "confession of faith" in the last chapter, where Pigou supports a gradual, but clear domination of government control over the economy. In these few pages, one can plainly see a chasm between Pigou and Coase.

The thoughts Coase expressed in my correspondence were repeated in a public reply to Simpson (1996a). Coase quoted Simpson's view of Pigou (which are similar to Medema's, DeSerpa's, and mine in 1995)

> It is hardly an exaggeration to say that Pigou demonstrated that self-interest operating through the market is unlikely to lead to an optimal use of resources but that he had no developed idea as to what, if anything, should be done about this ... . By 1937, when he published his *Socialism versus Capitalism*, he had come to have grave doubts even about the use of bounties and taxes in either a capitalist or a communist system ... . Ignorance of the facts militated against the use of these possible remedies ... Pigou's view was thus

much the same as that of Coase, though he was marginally less skeptical about the merits of state action. (Simpson in Coase, 1996, p. 113)

Coase (1996) was amazed by Simpson's reading of Pigou

I am completely baffled by these statements and cannot understand how Simpson came to make them. How was it possible for someone to go through *Socialism versus Capitalism* to find the one passage (of approximately two pages) in which Pigou expressed the same thought that I had without reading the rest of the book? (p. 114)

Coase went on to quote extensively from Pigou's *Socialism versus Capitalism* and made his case that Pigou is neither pragmatic nor balanced in his view of markets versus government. When interviewed by Richard Epstein in 2002, Coase offered this definition of a socialist: "a believer in the possibility that a socialist system could reproduce the results of perfect competition" (Coase, 2002, 9 min-45 sec). In *Socialism versus Capitalism*, Pigou explains exactly how accounting wages and interest rates could be used to mimic the market. In a reply to Coase, Simpson remained unconvinced, granting merely that Pigou held "mildly left-wing views" (Simpson, 1996b, p. 101).

So here is the question: Are Coase and Pigou intellectual friends or foes? Certainly mainstream economics paints a picture of Pigou as championing government intervention through taxes and subsidies, whereas Coase is portrayed as solving externality-induced misallocation via creation of property rights and the market system. But is this an accurate statement of their original positions?

In *The Hesitant Hand*, Medema says it is not. He argues that Coase himself has played a role in portraying Pigou as wedded to government intervention. "At the heart of Coase's criticism of Pigou's analysis, though, is his sense that Pigou considered government the solution to all problems of harmful effects" (p. 119). It was Coase, argues Medema, who tarred Pigou with the "nirvana fallacy," a simplistic algorithm that utilizes government intervention to repair any deviation from an optimal allocation of resources.

Years ago, I would have wholeheartedly agreed with Medema, but I may be swinging back to Coase's view. I am swayed by Coase's argument and it is true that Pigou's *Socialism and Capitalism* makes quite clear his sympathy for central planning, but why is it that so many see fairness and impartiality in Pigou's analysis of markets versus government? I reject straw man arguments – Coase really believes Pigou was a socialist. I believe there is neither malice nor strategic calculation in Coase's position. As he said to me, Coase spent a lot of time studying Pigou and it is obvious that Coase's considered opinion should be heavily weighted. Thus, the caricature of Coase versus Pigou, locked in a battle over the proper role of government may not be as far-fetched as I used to believe. In fact, viewing Pigou and Coase as advocates for government and markets, respectively, may offer a convenient vehicle to express the central idea of Medema's thought-provoking *Hesitant Hand* – a pendulum has swung from government to market throughout the history of economic thought.

REFERENCES

Barreto, H. (1995). *Pigou, Coase, and efficiency applied to Pennsylvania Coal Mining Law.* Unpublished manuscript. URL: http://fs6.depauw.edu/~hbarreto/working/

Coase, R. H. (1996). Law and economics and A. W. Brian Simpson. *Journal of Legal Studies,* 25(1), 103–119.

Coase, R. H. (2002). The intellectual portrait series: A conversation with Ronald H. Coase. Available at oll.libertyfund.org/title/979. Accessed on 28 December 2009.

DeSerpa, A. C. (1993). Pigou and Coase in retrospect. *Cambridge Journal of Economics, 17*(1), 27–50.

Pigou, A. C. (1937). *Socialism versus capitalism.* London: Macmillan.

Simpson, A. W. B. (1996a). 'Coase v. Pigou' reexamined. *Journal of Legal Studies, 25*(1), 53–97.

Simpson, A. W. B. (1996b). An addendum. *Journal of Legal Studies, 25*(1), 99–101.

PITOFSKY'S HOW THE CHICAGO SCHOOL OVERSHOT THE MARK

ANTITRUST LAW & POLICY IN TERMS OF THE LEGAL-ECONOMIC NEXUS

Nicholas Mercuro

Review essay on Pitofsky, R. (Ed.) (2008). *How the Chicago school overshot the mark: The effects of conservative economic analysis on U.S. antitrust.* New York: Oxford University Press. 328pp. ISBN: 9780195339765. $99.

The focus of Robert Pitofsky's book is on the impact (or alleged impact) that the Chicago school of economics has had on U.S. antitrust law and policy. The contention of Pitofsky's book is that, given the impact that adherents to the Chicago school have had on antitrust law and policy, the result has been (1) an attenuation of the U.S. Supreme Court's application and interpretation of antitrust doctrine, as well as (2) a diminution of federal enforcement of the antitrust laws (p. 3). It is that trend that is of concern and being assessed by the contributors to this volume.

The book is divided into six categories.

1. Conservative Economic Analysis and its Effects
2. Is Efficiency All that Counts?
3. Chicago School and Dominant Firm Behavior

A Research Annual
Research in the History of Economic Thought and Methodology, Volume 28-A, 405–438
Copyright © 2010 by Emerald Group Publishing Limited
All rights of reproduction in any form reserved
ISSN: 0743-4154/doi:10.1108/S0743-4154(2010)000028A022

4. Are Conservatives Correct that Vertical Arrangements (Merger and Distribution) can very Rarely Injure Consumer Welfare?
5. Has the Free Rider Explanation for Vertical Arrangements been Unrealistically Expanded?
6. Reinvigorating Merger Enforcement that has Declined as a Result of Conservative Economic Analysis

As the publisher's description states: "[the book] was written by academics, former law enforcers, private sector defense lawyers, Republicans and Democrats, representatives of the left, right and center. Virtually all agree that antitrust enforcement today is better as a result of conservative analysis, but virtually all also agree that there have been examples of extreme interpretations and misinterpretations of conservative economic theory that have led American antitrust in the wrong direction" (Oxford University Press).

Previous reviewers of this book (mainly for law reviews) have focused (as would be natural) on the many legal issues and questions raised in antitrust law and policy (see Crane, 2009; Wright, 2009; Kolasky, 2009). The purpose of this essay is not to revisit each of the antitrust issues from their perspective, but rather, given the readership of the research annual, to approach the subject from a different vantage point. In the tradition of Institutional law and economics, the emphasis here will be on the nexus between economics (the market) and the law (antitrust law). Given the space limitations, I will focus on the several essays in the first two sections of the book inasmuch as they, more than the latter essays, raise some very interesting economic issues and more general questions regarding the relationship between economics and the law. This in no way is intended to denigrate the scholarship of the other contributors to the book. Most of the other essays are very well done and focus on specific areas of antitrust policy exploring, more narrowly, the legal issues and cases involving: (i) predatory pricing, (ii) unilateral refusal-to-deal, (iii) vertical restraints (including analysis of leveraging, foreclosure and free riding issues), (iv) tying and exclusive dealing, and (v) mergers. Those interested in the specific evaluations made are encouraged to consult the essays in the last four sections of Pitofsky's book.

So as not confuse some who may find it objectionable,[1] throughout this chapter I am using the phrase "antitrust law and policy" to include the statutes, administrative rulings, the court's interpretations of said statutes and administrative rulings, policy, and alternative approaches to and teachings of antitrust. This broad definition is, in part, necessary due to the fact that the Sherman Act (and other antitrust statutes) were written sufficiently vague so as to: (a) at a minimum, effectively delegate their meaning to common law interpretation and resolution and (b) more broadly, open the door to alternative interpretations and formulations.

Before proceeding with substance, some general structural remarks are in order. I found the use of endnotes for each subsection of the book awkward. The structure of the book was not even. Some subsections had more contributors than others, indeed, one subsection had only one contributor while another had five contributors; one subsection had an essay and a commentator. There were also certain redundancies, particularly with the overlapping reviews of past antitrust law and policy.

Antitrust law has been identified as part of "old law and economics," a label given to those fields of law that were, by their very nature, inherently concerned with both economics and the law (for example, public utility regulation, corporate law, federal taxation, labor law, and, of course, the subject of this book – antitrust).[2] Given the inherent linkages between economics and antitrust law, it was only natural for the then "new" (circa, late 1940s and 1950s) Chicago school of law and economics to delve into the field of antitrust law, and so they did.[3] Indeed, the Chicago approach to antitrust was, in fact, a precursor to what we know today as the Chicago approach to law and economics. This was not a serendipitous event. As Steven M. Teles describes those events, it was a conscious political and ideological maneuver pulled off by Henry Simons, Henry Manne, and Aaron Director, aided and abetted by the monied interests inside the Volker Fund.[4] Antitrust was the first area of legal policy that the Chicagoans sold to corporations and foundations, in particular those at the Volker Fund. And of course, it makes sense. If one was to select one area of law to (re)shape the economy, what area of law would be more appropriate to capture than antitrust? Thus, it was only natural for the early Chicago law and economics movement to concentrate exclusively on antitrust, and nothing more. The focus was on Aaron Director and his work on challenging antitrust and building a young cadre of believers (including the likes of Robert Bork) who could go out and capture antitrust law and policy and reshape it to advance their own agenda.

Today, much of the conventional study of law is organized around modern doctrinal principles and concepts drawn from legal theory and political theory. The target of this collection is the Chicago approach to law and economics which attempts to place economic theory alongside of (or in place of ?) the legal and political theory that presently informs law; to place efficiency alongside of (or in place of ?) the concepts of justice and/or fairness that presently help fashion legal rules and doctrines. The Chicago school is but one school of thought or one way to think about the law – one way to think about antitrust law. With respect to antitrust law and policy, there are other schools of thought that explore the interrelationship between the nation's economy and its laws – between the market and government. These include the Harvard school, the new Harvard school, the new institutional economics, and Public Choice Theory (Mercuro & Medema, 2006; Mercuro, 2007).

Each school of thought has its own unique perspective – each looks into the room that houses our nation's economy and our legal system through a different window. Their respective views of what is in that room (even *within* a particular school of thought) are by no means homogeneous; these schools of thought are in some ways competing and in other ways complementary approaches to the study of the development and the reformulation of law. Each school of thought, in its own way, helps us come to grips with the implications of legal-economic policy in general and, for present purposes – antitrust policy in particular – ultimately by stating: (i) what the law (antitrust law) is, (ii) to discern a basis for law's (antitrust law's) legitimacy, and (iii) to say what the law (antitrust law) should be.

I will proceed as follows: the next section will review and briefly comment on the seven essays contained in the first two parts of the book; the following section will provide a brief description of the various schools of thought "at play" in antitrust policy; and the last major section will explain antitrust from vantage point of Institutional law and economics with a focus on the legal-economic nexus – the inherent interrelationship between the economy (the market) and law (the government) as previously set forth by Warren J. Samuels (1989) in his article "The legal-economic nexus" (see also Mercuro & Medema, 2006, pp. 208–240).

BRIEF REVIEW OF THE ESSAYS IN SECTIONS I & II

Conservative Economic Analysis and Its Effects

The first contribution to this section is by Richard Schmalensee titled "Thoughts on the Chicago school legacy in U.S. antitrust." It appears the purpose of this essay is to set up a target for the rest of the contributors to shoot at – a target that is emphatically pro-Chicago. In his essay, Schmalensee reviews some of the aspects of U.S. antitrust policy that outraged Chicago school lawyers and economists in the 1970s. He takes a brief look at some of Chicago's subsequent victories that he claims are now generally accepted as positive changes. And finally, he argues that some of Chicago's lost battles also constitute positive aspects of its legacy. His discussion is focused on four broad issues: the objectives of antitrust, the past policy toward "no-fault" concentration, the treatment of productive efficiency, and the evaluation of non-standard business conduct (pp. 11–12).

On the whole, the essay does accomplish what it sets out to do. In the "Economic Welfare" section he recounts Chicago's purported victory in establishing one single objective – economic welfare – for antitrust policy, leading him to conclude that "the choice between total welfare and consumer welfare ... is rarely critical in practice," and that "economic welfare or efficiency is the only worthy objective" (p. 13). He goes on to argue that Chicago economic analysis (basically deductive price theory) which advocates for a single objective in antitrust policy, namely efficiency, allows for consistency and predictability to make antitrust policy more effective. All stroke patients should thank God the field of neurology did not follow this line of logic, as stroke patients would take little solace knowing their temperature (another single objective) was normal while suffering the debilitating effects of a stroke. In a latter essay, Kauper makes a similar point more directly. He wrote: "Chicagoans have traditionally urged that antitrust be confined to economic efficiency concerns in part because a more multivalued approach improperly would require courts to make political decisions, a perversion of their role" (p. 49) – as if invoking the sole use of efficiency is *not* political.

The next section, entitled "Deconcentration," describes Chicago's effort to reverse some of the Warren court's decisions, the prevailing antitrust theories of that time, as well as to undermine the support for the then prevailing "no-fault" deconcentration movement (in particular, proposed legislation to deconcentrate American industry). The thrust of that deconcentration movement was to argue that the leading firms in highly concentrated industries should be broken up to deconcentrate the industries and thereby enhance competition. Schmalensee recounts the two-prong attack on the deconcentration movement based on Chicago empirical work that purportedly demonstrated: first, a relatively weak relationship between high concentration and profitability together with the contention that concentration which arises by internal growth due to sources of internal efficiency should be applauded and second, the existence of a wide variety of other factors leading to firm-specific productive efficiency (beyond the well-accepted traditional scale-determined efficiency). All these allowing him to conclude that Chicago was victorious in putting an end to the "no-fault" deconcentration movement (p. 16).

The third section, "Productive Efficiency" argues the Chicago case that productive efficiency should be counted as a virtue and be considered at least as an important concern as allocative efficiency. Proponents of the Chicago school were attacking the pre-Chicago antitrust court decisions (1940s–early 1970s) that took the position that it was generally undesirable to make a leading firm more efficient and thus a more formidable competitor. He notes that by attaching a positive weight to productive efficiency in antitrust law (while theoretically sound), has proven to be a Chicago defeat (p. 18) due in part to the scholarship of Oliver Williamson and Richard Posner where they demonstrated that an assessment of merger-specific economies simply could not be done in a reliable manner.

The fourth section is titled "Inhospitality." Chicago argued that various practices traditionally accorded an "inhospitable" treatment in law could, in fact, enhance efficiency. The theoretical argument put forth by Chicago is that with respect to firms without market power, non-standard/unfamiliar contracting practices are always pro-competitive; when market power is present, the courts should adopt the rule of reason. He believes that while Chicago has won the academic argument, generally the courts continue to adhere to their inhospitable-treatment precedents in deciding cases (p. 18). The remainder of the section briefly explored Chicago's attempts to move from "form-based" to "effects-based" analysis of (i) horizontal restraints, (ii) vertical mergers, (iii) vertical restraints, and (iv) tying arrangements.

The second essay in this section, "Some practical thoughts about entry" by Irwin M. Stelzer, is one of the shorter but one of the more insightful essays. Although it mainly (and briefly) focuses on (1) assessing predatory pricing policies, (2) policies related to pricing strategies by multiproduct firms, and (3) arguments to resurrect structural remedies in antitrust, it is the introductory remarks that raise some very fundamental questions. He argues that "the free market system can be defended in the long run only if it provides fair and open opportunity to all comers"; and that "the greatest threats to the capitalist free market system ... are anticompetitive practices by dominant firms ... and managerial abuses by managers pursuing their own enrichment" (p. 24). Hence, he disagrees with the Chicago proposition that government intervention is always efficiency reducing and comes to agree with Herbert Hovenkamp who argued that when it comes to antitrust policy, the risks of underdeterrence of anticompetitive acts are greater than the risks of overdeterrence. In addition, Stelzer argues that the Chicago school's success in promoting the idea that efficiency should be the sole goal of antitrust policy liberates them from the necessity of considering other possible social objectives, and this he thinks is wrong. He believes that good policy should come to grips with all aspects of antitrust laws including social goals. He concludes with a warning that Washington think tanks are far more influential [in effective rent seeking] than the legal and economic scholars housed in universities.

Of course, as we know, the proponents of the Chicago school try to reveal themselves as well-intentioned guardians of the market as if the government is an all-to-often annoying intruder. In fact, what they became was a kind of intellectual protection racket for big business. The Chicago school (in all of its manifestations) set the stage for 2008 housing, financial, and economic meltdown. As Eleanor M. Fox has written in her essay "modern [read Chicago] U.S. antitrust protects monopoly and oligopoly, suppressers innovative challenges, and stifles efficiency" (p. 77). But there is more to it.

The Chicago school, by act of commission, goes to great lengths – often through the keepers of the faith at the Cato Institute and Heritage Foundation (two of the more prominent homes for conservative rent seekers) – to defend the risky, profit maximizing behavior of dominant firms. Up until 2008 the scheme worked; the Chicago school, it seemed, could do no wrong. However, their beliefs, teachings, policies, and politics ultimately set the stage for the financial and economic meltdown. At the same time, by act of omission, the proponents of the Chicago school of course neglected to articulate that which they learned from their Public Choice colleagues; indeed, perhaps even by some of the most highly regarded members of the Chicago school itself, beginning with George Stigler and the other "masters of deregulation."[5] That is, the behavior of dominant firms – whose positions in the market were rationally set in place and then intellectually protected by proponents of the Chicago school – was such that the firms could safely afford to engage in the riskiest types of ventures and schemes including fraud. Scholars in the field of Public Choice over the previous two decades had made clear to both the proponents of the Chicago school and the high rollers of the biggest financial firms that the firm's massive losses would be covered by others (namely the U.S. tax payers) and this would be accomplished through various forms of rent seeking.

This has been recently documented. We now know that U.S. banks that spent more money on lobbying were more likely to get government bailout money; banks whose executives served on Federal Reserve boards were more likely to receive government bailout funds from the Troubled Asset Relief Program; banks with headquarters in the district of the U.S. House of

Representatives member who serves on a committee or subcommittee relating to TARP also received more funds; and that political connections played an important role in a firm's access to capital, indeed political influence was most helpful for poorly performing banks (see Duchin & Sosyura, 2009). The only surprise for the proponents of the Chicago school was the Lehman Brothers Inc. was not saved. What transpired in the publically funded "resolution" of the 2008 housing, financial, and economic meltdown (1) may have surprised the public, (2) was largely expected in Public Choice circles, and (3) was probably greeted with a wink and a smile at Chicago – their protection racket worked! But in retrospect, in many respects Chicago did not overshoot its mark ... it shot itself in its foot. Their high priests were shaken and their acolytes went running in circles when they read Richard A. Posner's recent article in *The New Republic* entitled "How I Became a Keynesian" (Posner, 2009a).

"Conservative economics and antitrust: a variety of influences" is the title of F.M. Scherer's contribution. It opens with an interesting (but unclear) discussion of the relation among economics, conservative economics, and Chicago economics. One can only wonder why he chose to muddy this otherwise clear body of water. He writes that "there are conflicting economic analyses" and praises the fact that "there are alternative theories" (p. 31). But he goes on to say that "we should be thankful for the existence of the Chicago school of economics (which is incorrectly associated with conservative economics)" (p. 31), while asserting "that virtually all professional economists plying their trade in the United States are conservatives," and "that there widely varying degrees of conservativism in the economics practiced within the U.S." (p. 31). He then goes on to emphasize geographic locales in economics, thereby conflating Chicago economics (the "ideas") with Chicago (the "place"). I would contend that when those working in the field of antitrust policy in all of its manifestations refer to "Chicago" – whether in reference to antitrust statutes, administrative rulings, the court's interpretations of said statutes and administrative rulings, or alternative approaches to and teachings of antitrust – they are typically referring to a brand of economics (indeed, of law and economics), not the geographic "locale." There are a variety of universities outside Chicago at which Chicago economists reside. These economists largely share the same paradigm, not the same place.

In his section titled "The Influence of Chicago Economics," Scherer attempts to argue that Chicago economists and antitrust scholars have been far from monolithic in advocating a retrenchment of antitrust enforcement. In a rambling account of antitrust policy and court decisions, he documents his interpretation of which cases were impacted by members of the Chicago school as well as which case were driven by those outside it. The section is a useful compilation of "the facts," but reveals little by way of insight as to why a field of law so integral to the performance of the U.S. economy has treated, and continues to treat, antitrust law as a jurisprudential buffet.

The section on "Other Influences" opens with a "killer" sentence: "[The causes of backtracking in antitrust enforcement] can be identified with conservativism per se, even if not with conservative scholarship and especially economic scholarship." Let's just leave it at that! He goes on to castigate, on two different counts, those Chicago or conservative economists who were appointed to key antitrust positions by the Reagan and Bush II administrations. On the one hand, he asserts they were wrong for adopting a "do nothing" approach to their jobs (p. 37), and on the other hand, for buying into John McGee's policy position regarding mergers and monopolization policy describing it as merely "a Panglossian diagnosis that asserts everything that is, is good" (p. 37). Before closing this section, Scherer adds one wonderful observation. He points out that Chicago conservative economists "are fervent in their beliefs" and "when there is a clash of [policy] views, fervor tends to trump ambivalence"; this is what really "explains the ascendance of conservative thinking in antitrust law and economics" (p. 37). One can interpret this as saying that the Chicago message – "government is the problem" and "unregulated markets can resolve all problems" – was so simple that they not only believed it, they actually became fervently excited over it, and hence prevailed!

Thomas Kauper's "Influence of conservative economic analysis on the development of the law of antitrust" provides an historical account of antitrust law and policy in the United States that reveals an uneasiness as to where we have been and where we presently are. I will not recount the history here, but will highlight a few points made in his essay. Kauper makes the point that the legislative history of the Sherman Act is not consistent with Robert Bork's account of the statute's alleged single-minded focus on efficiency. This debunking of Bork's improbable account of history is a common theme throughout several of the essays in this volume (see especially the Kirkwood and Lande essay discussed below, which lays Bork to rest). Kauper's essay demonstrates that over the past two decades Chicago has not carried the day in the courts concluding that "we do not find in decided cases anything like a complete acceptance of Chicago's views" (p. 45; see also Elhauge, 2007). Nonetheless, Kauper's essay makes the important point that Chicago's main impact has been on how those involved in antitrust policy think, observing that "it is difficult today to find academic pieces, court decisions, and commentaries that do not, first begin by accepting certain basic premises that are central to Chicago thinking, second, use at least some part of Chicago's methodology, and third, deal directly, even if by rejection, [with] Chicago's results" (p. 46).

Daniel L. Rubinfeld's essay "On the foundations of antitrust law and economics" reviews the evolution of antitrust policy. After taking a brief look at the extent to which conservative economics has influenced the development of antitrust law, he then moves on to a more extensive analysis, exploring its impact on the enforcement of antitrust law. As to the former, he reminds us that it was the development of the economics of industrial organization – from the 1950s which had a liberal bent, through the Chicago school's conservative approach of the 1970s, on to the more mature, improved, and recent understanding of industrial organization economics that has focused on the implications of strategic behavior typically using game theory. I believe he does make an error in referencing an article by Einer Elhauge in the context of his discussion of the post-Chicago school. In fact, Elhauge's article focused on the New Harvard approach (versus Chicago school) which Rubinfeld neglects to mention. That aside, his discussion as to why there are a variety of economic perspectives on antitrust law is illuminating. He suggests that the key differences include: (1) the issue as to whether efficiency should be the sole goal of antitrust; (2) the question as to whether the courts and antitrust agencies are capable of sorting out complex legal-economic questions and facts (the informational question); (3) on the emphasis given to economic theory in contrast to empirical regularities; (4) the question as to whether the antitrust enforcement agencies are capable of enforcing the law in complex cases (the enforcement question); and (5) associated with (4), the balance between enforcement's concern over false positives versus false negatives (pp. 56–57), concluding that the nature of antitrust enforcement may well be dictated by the political business cycle.

Is Efficiency All that Counts?

The second section of the book opens with an essay by Elinor M. Fox titled "The efficiency paradox." It is very good. She explains the shift in antitrust thinking; from "antitrust is for competition" to the Borkian-propagated notion embraced by Chicago that "antitrust is for efficiency." In an effort to debunk the Borkian notion, Fox first asks the question: "What is efficiency?" and then goes on to map allocative efficiency, productive efficiency, and dynamic efficiency. She then explores the question "Can antitrust law produce efficiency?" To that, her response is "no" inasmuch as the law is proscriptive not prescriptive (p. 79). She then explores the paradox of the Chicago school and the reasons for it. In doing so, she compares the conservative-Chicago "outcomes approach" that focuses solely on efficiency with the more robust "rivalry/process approach," an approach that stresses the importance of maintaining an environment conducive to enhancing welfare (broadly conceived) and preserving a dynamic process to prevent inefficient outcomes. Fox argues that the presumptions of the Chicago school together with their "output perspective," that is, asking only, "Will the outcome of a particular merger or conduct be inefficient in the sense of reducing output?" ends up with minimizing the scope of antitrust by condemning only inefficient outcomes. She is thus able to explain the paradox Chicago finds itself ... By shrinking antitrust law to its smallest possible scope, in harms efficiency by undermining rivalry and forestalling dynamic changes that lead to more efficient outcomes (pp. 79–80).

In the last section of her essay, Fox reviews four U.S. Supreme Court cases and one European Union case (the latter is not discussed here). She reviews the facts of *Brooke Group, California Dental Association, Trinko,* and *Leegin.* Upon a review of each she poses two simple questions: Did efficiency drive the Supreme Court's outcome? ... And if not, what did? Consistent with the theme of this book, Fox found that while the decisions of each of the four rulings all maintained some ambiguities regarding efficiency, they all placed a "heavy thumb on the scale in favor of the autonomy of the dominant firms" (p. 86) a thumb print that revealed an imprint of conservative economics-based theory rather than facts.

The second essay in this section is titled "The Chicago School's foundation is flawed: antitrust protects consumers, Not efficiency" by John B. Kirkwood and Robert Lande. This essay is important for several reasons. First, Kirkwood and Lande (p. 89) expose Bork's contention that "the legislative history of the Sherman Act established that Congress had only one concern – economic efficiency" as a train wreck of the actual facts (see Kauper's essay in the volume, p. 42; also, Hofstadter, 1996; Hovenkamp, 1985, p. 249; Lande, 1982; Pitofsky, 1979, pp. 1051–1066). Of course, we know the Chicago school "anti-antitrusters" hopped aboard that feeble train and went along for the ride transforming and elevating the bogus efficiency assertion as Chicago school gospel. In fact, as Kirkwood and Lande (and other contributors to this volume) so ably recount, the facts are otherwise both with respect to the congressional intent with regard to passage of the Act and recent case law.

The first section of the essay focuses on the legislative history of the Sherman Act and demonstrates that the wealth transfer concern (the unfair transfer of consumer surplus away from consumers) is a far more plausible explanation for the passage of the Act than Bork's fabricated contention. With respect to that legislative history, Kirkwood and Lande provide quote after quote in recounting the real history that supports their position, leading one to wonder how anyone with any modern understanding of the English language could come up with Bork's efficiency conclusion. In the second section of the essay, Kirkwood and Lande provide an extended discussion U.S. Supreme Court and Federal Appellate Court decisions as well as an illuminating analysis of merger cases (the latter being the type of cases where there often is a conflict between consumer welfare and economic efficiency). This case analysis allows them to conclude (1) that "the recent case law has largely adopted the view that the ultimate goal of the antitrust laws is to protect consumers, not increase efficiency" (p. 92) and (2) that "the normative foundation [the strict pursuit of economic efficiency] of the Chicago school is flawed" (p. 97).

A BRIEF HISTORY OF RECENT ANTITRUST THINKING

Before exploring antitrust law and policy from the vantage point of the legal-economic nexus, I will provide a brief description of the various approaches and schools of thought that presently inform antitrust law and policy, especially in their relation to the Chicago school. The impact of the Chicago school on antitrust began to be felt in the mid-1970s as the legal community, in all of its manifestations – the courts, the administrative agencies, the antitrust bar, and academic scholarship and teachings in antitrust – began to respond to the cases litigated over the previous 40 years. The Chicago school was responding, not only to what many have termed the populist inclinations and decisions of the U.S. Supreme Court (the Warren Court), but also to a brand of antitrust scholarship prevailing at Harvard (circa 1950s, 1960s, and early 1970s).[6]

Early Harvard School

Largely influenced by industrial organization economics of the day (i.e., the structure-conduct-performance paradigm) and a suspiciousness of unregulated markets, the Harvard school focused primarily on the structural manifestations of markets (in particular with the fewness of firms, entry barriers, vertical integration, degree of product differentiation along with technology).[7] In an effort to develop a sound basis for antitrust policy, Joe Bain, Leonard Weiss, and others focused their research on the nexus between the structure and performance of firms in various markets ultimately concluding that concentrated oligopolies did, in fact, earn above normal profits (see Bain, 1951; Kaysen & Turner, 1959; Mason, 1964; Weiss, 1974). These antitrust scholars believed that fashioning antitrust remedies so as to modify firm behavior or conduct was pointless because, based on their studies, the ultimate source of the firm's market power was predicated by market structure. When markets sufficiently diverged from the model of perfect competition, they were viewed suspiciously under the Harvard approach and these industries quickly became a focus of concern and subject to close scrutiny and possible prosecution. In short, business practices that were shown to be either predatory or exclusionary, as well as mergers that would increase concentration or foreclose on competition, were to be prevented; for those industries that were concentrated, policies aimed at their deconcentration were set forth (hence the moniker "the structuralists"). During much of those four decades, particularly under the Warren Court, the populist approach to antitrust, aided and abetted by the structure-conduct-performance approach of the Harvard school, was highly interventionist and concerned with the well being of small entrepreneurs, occasionally to the detriment of consumers (Hovenkamp, 2005, p. 2). Antitrust jurisprudence of that time has been described as an almost randomized mix of economic, social, and political values. (p. 43).

Chicago School

During the 1970s, at the same time the Harvard school was evolving (see below), the Chicago school had matured sufficiently to begin to challenge and uproot the interventionist case precedents (of the populist Warren Court and the early Harvard structuralists) and replace them with more permissive rules. The impetus for this came from those forming the Chicago approach to law and economics, virtually indistinguishable from the Chicago school of economics with its defining characteristic being the straightforward application of microeconomic (or price-theoretic) now applied to law. Chicago economists, buttressed by their empirical research, emphasized the efficacy of the competitive market system, arguing for less government intervention, fewer wealth redistribution policies, reliance on voluntary exchange with a concomitant reliance on the common law for mediating conflicts (as opposed to direct regulation), and an across-the-board promotion of more private enterprise which, based on the evidence provided by their empirical research, would facilitate a more efficient allocation of resources.

With respect to antitrust, for the Chicago school, competition came to mean lower prices, maximum output, and room (more freedom) to innovate and grow. More specifically, their view of the economy to be "regulated" is one characterized by a wide range of opportunities for efficiencies associated with economies of scale and scope. It is an economy where most markets are competitive even when there were only a few firms competing; barriers to entry were said to be exaggerated by previous theories and enforcement agencies; monopoly leveraging was not seen as an issue as it would not enhance profits; and, antitrust enforcement was thought to be appropriate only if it would enhance efficiency (a slightly modified version of the list provided by Rubinfeld on p. 54 of the volume). For those firms that are able to position themselves as near monopolies, the belief was that they are likely to succumb due to firm entry induced by the existence of above normal profits. In short, the extent to which monopoly-like problems do develop, they tend to be both anomalous and ultimately, self-correcting. Alan Greenspan (1966a) became a leading propagator of this assertion:

> The entire structure of antitrust statutes in this country is a jumble of economic irrationality and ignorance. It is the product: (a) of a gross misinterpretation of history, and (b) of rather naive, and certainly unrealistic, economic theories ... The churning of a nation's capital, in a fully free economy, would be continuously pushing capital into profitable areas – and this would effectively control the competitive price and production policies of business firms, making a coercive monopoly impossible to maintain .... [T]he very existence of those undefinable statutes and contradictory case law inhibits businessmen from undertaking what would otherwise be sound productive ventures. No one will ever know what new products, processes, machines, and cost-saving mergers failed to come into existence, killed by the Sherman Act before they were born. No one can ever compute the price that all of us have paid for that Act which, by inducing less effective use of capital, has kept our standard of living lower than would otherwise have been possible. (p. 71)

Unique for American jurisprudence, the courts have recognized that in deciding antitrust cases, two types of errors should be considered. The first is a Type I error which refers to a false positive. In a legal context, this amounts to mistakenly imposing liability on an innocent defender. For example, if a court were to find (mistakenly) that a firm held a monopoly and proceeded to force divestiture of some of its assets to de-concentrate the industry, that enforcement action (in error) could place substantial costs on society. However, there is the possibility of a Type II error, namely a false negative, or failing to punish a guilty party; that is, incorrectly not finding that a firm amounts to being a monopolist. This error also imposes costs on society. Given the need to consider Type I and Type II errors, the Chicago school inherently (by advocating for less enforcement and asserting that monopoly-like problems tend to both anomalous and self-correcting) favors an enforcement regime that allows for the commission of Type II errors. Thus, Chicago argues against the per se approach (favoring the rule of reason) to antitrust enforcement asserting that it (the per se approach) greatly enhances the commission of Type I errors and all the sundry costs. The extent to which the courts have followed this policy approach, (focusing on Type II and its policy implications and thereby relying more heavily on the rule of reason) is celebrated by Chicago. Their common response typically goes something like this: "the second development of the past generation of antitrust is the demise of the per se rules of illegality and the concomitant rise of the rule of reason as the dominant mode of antitrust analysis" (McChesney, 2004, p. 49).

Under the Reagan administration that commonly asserted "government was the problem," the Chicago approach to law and economics was embraced. Both within the antitrust agencies (appointments within the Justice Department and the Federal Trade Commission) and the courts (through the appointment of conservative federal judges), the immediate impact was to draw back from the interventionist positions taken with respect to vertical restraints, strategic pricing, and mergers. Advocates of Chicago argued that markets were sufficiently robust to correct themselves and that government interference was apt to cause more harm (enhance inefficiency) than good. The scope of antitrust policy was reduced to concern over cartel activity (price fixing) and large horizontal mergers with some concern over the behavior of dominant firms and some tying arrangements.[8] But, by and large most tie-ins, vertical integration, restricted distribution, predatory pricing, and other assorted practices rarely, if ever, were thought to lead to an increase in monopoly (Meehan & Lerner, 1989, p. 190). Although many proponents of the Chicago school argue that all of the other antitrust law should be repealed, some extremists argue for an across-the-board repeal of all antitrust laws (among the latter, see Armentano, 2007; Rockefeller, 2007). As Stelzer (p. 28) described them in his essay in this volume, they are "anti-antitrusters." The Chicago school imparted a persuasive message to the students of antitrust – a strong skepticism about the efficiency of government intervention into markets (Welch & Greaney, 2005, p. 93) and that regulation was the proper function of markets, not government. This message was one that often resulted in legal reasoning losing out to economic analysis and was, to the students of law, "a message which was at once both unfamiliar and yet quite understandable" (Duxbury, 1995, p. 344).[9]

The "New" Harvard School

By the late 1970s, with the structuralists largely in decline (due in part to the emergence of the new empirical industrial organization literature), a new Harvard school began to take shape – one that moved away from the more populist inclinations of the Warren court and a reliance on structuralist remedies. The main architects of this recent Harvard school include Donald Turner, Phillip Areeda, Stephen Breyer, and Herbert Hovenkamp. Initially, as compared to their Chicago school contemporaries, they retained a more interventionist stance. But over time, they too have evolved and now are guided by the following principles (see Kovacic, 2007, pp. 31–43; Hovenkamp, 1996, pp. 822–826):

(1) They embrace economic efficiency (with some disagreement over which definition to employ; see Fox, 1981, pp. 1176–1179) along with a reliance on economic theory in the formulation of antitrust rules.
(2) They discourage consideration of non-efficiency objectives such as dispersion of political power and the preservation of opportunities for smaller enterprise to compete.
(3) They believe that the social costs of enforcing antitrust rules governing dominate firm conduct too aggressively are likely to exceed the costs of enforcing them too weakly.
(4) With respect to merger policy, they have moved away from condemning mergers on the basis of economic efficiency now advocating a much more qualified structuralist approach.
(5) Related to the latter, they regard potential efficiencies as a reason for justifying a merger rather than a priori condemnation – as a consequence, they have a "diluted concern with entry barriers, they began to dismiss most of the claims that vertical integration was inherently anti-competitive, and proposed greatly relaxed merger standards" (Hovenkamp, 2005, p. 37).

(6) In addition, over time, they became increasingly "concerned over the administratabilty of various antitrust rules and the costs of likely errors by generalist judges and juries trying to implement them" and thus admonished enforcement agencies to pay close attention institutional design and institutional capacity in formulating and applying antitrust rules.[10]

This latter Harvard school has been able to benefit from new insights and to draw from alternative ideologies (including Chicago). In doing so, it is argued that it has yielded a reasoned approach to produce balanced and practical solutions to today's challenges to antitrust (see Gavil, Kovacic, & Baker, 2008, p. 68).[11]

Post-Chicago School

In response to Chicago, in the mid-1980s a post-Chicago school (hereafter, P-C-S) began to emerge. Generally, as compared to the Chicago school, proponents of P-C-S developed a renewed belief in the efficacy of government intervention, in part, brought on by their having less confidence in markets and their purported ability to self-correct. Much of the earlier economic literature that tried to describe the behavior of non-cooperative oligopolists relied on conjectural variation models that originated in the work of Antoine Augustin Cournot, Joseph Bertrand, and Heinrich Freiherr von Stackelberg. These models assumed firms confronted each other in a single competitive episode (i.e., they were static, single-period models); hence they were unable to predict how firms would adjust price and/or output over time. Drawing from the new empirical industrial organization literature, and given their concern over strategic conduct, proponents of P-C-S rely more heavily on game theory (using multi-period repeated games models) to examine the strategic behavior among established firms and their actual or potential rival firms and how these competitive interactions will unfold over time.[12] Advocates of the P-C-S believe markets are more varied and complex than the Chicago school characterization and hence the need for more careful governmental scrutiny. The call is for antitrust enforcement agencies and the courts to conduct full-scale rule of reason inquires on a case-by-case basis. P-C-S has become the approach to antitrust that is most favored in economics departments with articles reflecting their ideas now being published in many top economic journals. It is an approach that has led some to ponder whether the Robert's Court will lean more heavily toward the Chicago school or become influenced by the more game theoretic P-C-S (Wright, 2010). On the one hand, some "Post-Chicago commentators generally propose qualifying rather than supplanting Chicago views" (Gavil et al., 2008, p. 70)." Other proponents of P-C-S conclude that the government should have a much greater concern with the strategic, anticompetitive behavior by large dominate firms and argue that certain market structures lead to types of collaborative behavior that make anticompetitive outcomes more plausible. As aptly summarized by Ernest Gellhorn, William E. Kovacic, and Stephen Calkins (1994, p. 97, emphasis added): "If Chicago school economics helped observers understand why puzzling conduct might *not lessen* competition, post-Chicago economics helped observers understand why conduct thought benign in light of Chicago school teaching might in fact *lessen* competition."

New Institutional Economics

In the 1980s under the leadership of Oliver Williamson (1974, 1975, 1979, 1989, 1996), transaction cost economics (part of the new institutional economics-NIE) began to identify alternative reasons or rationales to curtail antitrust enforcement (see also Joskow, 1991; Wright, 2010). Within NIE the focus was on how both organizational structure and contractual design affect the cost of organizing activity within the firm and among firms. NIE – transaction cost economics' attention has consistently been on the alternative modes of organizing transactions, with the objective of identifying those modes that economize on transaction costs. Their analysis has centered on the incentive, adaptive, and contractual expenses associated with alternative governance structures with a special attention given to past vertical market restrictions. With respect to antitrust, the thrust of this approach was to advance the proposition that certain business practices can be explained as an effort to economize on transaction costs. More generally, in a world of uncertainty and asymmetric information, parties to a transaction may, in an effort to enhance their profits, act opportunistically. That is, efforts by individual firms who are parties to a contract, so as to curb the negative impact of other firm's opportunistic behavior, may be forced to engage in wasteful protective expenditures thereby incurring high transaction costs. As a consequence, the parties may try to economize on transaction costs by entering into joint ventures, tying arrangements, restrictive redistribution contracts or vertically integrate which (while in the past were treated as strategies undertaken to enhance market power) are interpreted by NIE to be devices which are efficiency enhancing (enabling firms to make transactions less risky and thereby reduce costs). Accordingly, NIE antitrust argues for a policy (a policy consistent with, but for different reasons than Chicago) that allows for a variety of coordinated arrangements (arrangements more suspect under New Harvard and P-C-S) and thus minimizes scrutiny and possible prosecution by antitrust enforcement agencies.

Public Choice

To understand Public Choice's approach to antitrust, it must be clear from the outset that Public Choice's emphasis is on "government failure," leading some to describe it as having "a jaundiced view of legislative motivation" and leading to almost inevitably to normative conclusions "that are generally not happy ones" (see Farber & Frickey, 1999, p. 22).[13] Thus, unlike some of the other approaches to antitrust, proponents of Public Choice reject the assumption that the antitrust enforcement agencies and/or the courts are populated by benevolent maximizers of the public interest. From their vantage point the government is not motivated by the goal of serving the public interest.[14] They argue instead that antitrust policy (like other public policies) emerges from political bargains in which special interest groups purchase protection from the forces of unfettered competition. In short, Public Choice theory has explored and believes to have demonstrated that over time, antitrust laws were passed by "special interest" legislation and administered and (un)enforced accordingly (see McChesney & Shughart, 1995; Shughart & Tollison, 1985; DiLorenzo, 1985; Baxter, 1980). As a consequence, proponents of Public Choice reject the idea that whenever antitrust policy "fails," the failures are attributable to one or more correctable errors that can be remedied by: (1) demanding agencies do a better job, or (2) having judges and lawyers learn more (and more of the "right") economics, or (3) have the present set of antitrust bureaucrats to be replaced by public servants better able to promote the public interest. In fact, in their view it is the interactions of a large number of self-interest-seeking demanders, suppliers, and political brokers of wealth transfers in political markets that determine public policies in general, and antitrust policies in particular. It would come as little surprise to any of them that (as described above) U.S. banks that spent more money on lobbying were more likely to get government bailout money. The most important point to be made regarding Public Choice versus the other approaches outlined earlier is that what many of the latter approaches identify and treat as antitrust policy "failures" are in fact very predictable consequences of the interplay of self-interested demanders of wealth transfers and suppliers of regulation that ultimately imposes deadweight loses on society. And further, whenever the government intervenes in antitrust cases (whether through legislation, regulation, or the courts), it, in fact, fosters a pattern and opens up the opportunity of rent-seeking behavior.

THE LEGAL-ECONOMIC NEXUS WITHIN ANTITRUST

As stated earlier, this chapter will not attempt to follow the previous reviewers of this book (mainly for law reviews) who have focused on the many legal issues and questions raised in antitrust law and policy. This chapter will come at the collection of articles from a particular vantage point – that of the *legal-economic nexus* – the inherent interrelationship between the economy (the market) and law (the government) previously explored by Warren Samuels (1989) in his article on "The Legal-Economic Nexus."

Before proceeding with a critique and analysis it is helpful to establish the present-day "folklore" as to the Chicago school's impact on U.S. antitrust law. As proponents of Chicago claim, this has been their grandest victory. Thus, it is not at all unusual to read comments such as: "Since the 1980s, the Chicago school model of antitrust has reigned as the predominant approach of both the courts and the agencies" (Jacobs, 1995, p. 219).[15] Similarly, Neil Duxbury (1995, p. 349) observed that "there exists very little in the way of contemporary antitrust theory which has not been inspired to some degree by Chicago economic analysis," which led Robert Lande (1990, p. 258) to conclude that "the dominant paradigm today is that the only goal of the existing antitrust laws is to increase economic efficiency."[16] Others predict it will continue "as part of the largely uninterrupted march by the Chicago school on antitrust analysis ... the antitrust jurisprudence of the [Roberts] Court will increasingly reflect the influence of the Chicago school" (Wright, 2007).

Apparently, many contributors to this collection (for the most part) believe that much of the above characterization is factual and indeed, may well have been part of the inspiration for the volume. Most of the contributors also contend that the Chicago school did, indeed, overshoot its mark. As will be analyzed below, this belief implies that there was a "different" mark or a "clear" mark, a "blissful state of law" if you will, that antitrust almost achieved, and would have done so had it not been for some "overshooting" by Chicago types. I will contend in the context of the legal-economic nexus, there is no final globally efficient resting place for antitrust law. Given antitrust's intricate interrelations with an evolving economy, there can be no settled antitrust law however disquieting that may be to policy makers.

Although many of the contributors to this edited collection come at antitrust from somewhat different vantage points, for the most part, though nuanced, I contend that they share in the common belief that there is a self-subsistent economy and a self-subsistent government – that the economy and the law are separate and distinct. It is a view that suggests that the economy is the sphere of production, consumption and exchange, while the government (law) is the sphere of the courts, the political parties, elections, and thus politics; the economy is the sphere of cooperation and opportunity (movements from "off to on" contract curves) whereas the polity is the sphere of coercion and constraint (about who gets to trade and where one starts trading in the Edgeworth box). Virtually all of the contributors expressed misgivings regarding antitrust law and policy are based on descriptive models that assume or perceive (at least to some extent) the self-subsistent distinct spheres of the economy and government – distinct spheres of economics and the law. It is from that mind set (and hence economic models that reflect that mind set) that they then (with respect to motive, commendably), all go on to (re)fashion antitrust law and policy to enhance the performance of the nation's economy (as they perceive it).

As an aside, before proceeding with an explanation of antitrust as part of the legal-economic nexus, this book was published before the fall 2008 housing, financial, and economic meltdown – and event which caused many of the Chicago school acolytes to return to their knees and ask forgiveness for propagating economic models that describe a reality that may exist on some parallel universe. The meltdown required some of their more prominent advocates, such as Alan Greenspan and Richard Posner to admit the crisis was brought on by insufficient regulation. As Posner observed recently, "the movement to deregulate the financial industry went too far by exaggerating the resilience – the self-healing powers – of laissez-faire capitalism" (Posner, 2009b, p. xii). In the case of Greenspan, while he recently conceded in testimony before a committee of the U.S. Congress that he had put too much faith in the self-correcting power of free markets, he seems to have neither an inclination nor a capacity to offer any clear-cut substantive remedies (Andrews, 2008). In addition, we still await to hear if he has jettisoned his belief that the laws pertaining to corporate fraud need not be enforced under his contention (along with a diminishing cadre of other prominent and embarrassed Chicago economists) that markets would be sufficient to regulate even fraudulent conduct.[17] Greenspan and some of his colleagues have been peddling this idea for years. In the early 1960s, he wrote:

> Protection of the consumer against "dishonest and unscrupulous business practices" has become a cardinal ingredient of welfare statism. Left to their own devices, it is alleged, businessmen would attempt to sell unsafe food and drugs, fraudulent securities, and shoddy buildings. Thus, it is argued, the Pure Food and Drug Administration, the Securities and Exchange Commission and the numerous building regulatory agencies are indispensable if the consumer is to be protected from the "greed" of the businessman. ... Capitalism is based on self-interest and self-esteem; it holds integrity and trustworthiness as cardinal virtues and makes them pay off in the marketplace, thus demanding that men survive by means of virtues, not of vices. It is this superlatively moral system that the welfare statists propose to improve upon by means of preventative law, snooping bureaucrats, and the chronic goad of fear ... But it is precisely the "greed" of the businessman or, more appropriately, his profit-seeking, which is the unexcelled protector of the consumer ... The incentive to scrupulous performance operates on all levels of a given field of production. It is a built-in safeguard of a free enterprise system and the only real protection of consumers against business dishonesty. (Greenspan, 1966b, pp. 126–127, 130)

As evidenced in all of the approaches to antitrust outlined earlier, antitrust law and policy are at the heart of the interrelationship between the nation's laws and its economic performance; it is one field of law that speaks directing to the interrelationship between the market and government – between economics and the law. At issue then is how does one perceive that relationship. In contrast to models that assume the self-subsistent spheres of economics and the law, the organizing concept of the legal-economic nexus, as described by Samuels argues that "the law is a function of the economy, and the economy (especially its structure), is a function of law. The point is that these seemingly distinct spheres commonly originate. ... [The law and economy] are jointly produced, not independently given and not merely interacting" (Samuels, 1989, pp. 1558, 1567). Both the law and the economy are continuously and simultaneously (re)formed in a manner that negates any conception of their independent self-subsistence. Through the legal-economic nexus, the structure of the law and the economic system are simultaneously worked out, where each serves as both dependent and independent variable in the construction of legal-economic reality.

In the context of the legal-economic nexus, antitrust – including the statutes, administrative rulings, the court's interpretations of said statutes and administrative rulings, the teachings in antitrust, including the several schools of thought (the ways we think about antitrust) from which we then try to fashion antitrust policy (including those who want to abolish it altogether) – becomes the arena in which the government operates to (re)define and (re)create the economy (market). But at the same time, nominally private and group economic interests operate to (re)define and (re)create the law (government). The seemingly distinct spheres of the economy and law commonly originate in a social location where, on the basis of differing ideologies, private individuals, group interests, consumers, and producers influence the political and social agenda through the exercise of government – including antitrust law and policy – thereby determining the scope and performance of the market. Thus, the economy and the law are jointly produced, *not* independently given and *not* merely interacting. The legal-economic nexus suggests antitrust law and policy are a function of the economy, while, at the same time, the economy is, in part, a function of antitrust law and policy (Samuels, 1989, pp. 1566–1567). It is an ongoing contest over political power and ideology. It is field of law that does not wait to be discovered, like the economy. Antitrust is always in the process of becoming – as an evolving entity, it cannot be overshot, undershot, or hit.

It must be underscored here that this descriptive Institutional approach to law and economics is avowedly positive; it does not have a normative component comparable to the alternative normative policy approaches described earlier: "Our principal goal," Warren Samuels and Allan Schmid (1981) tell us in the introduction to their book on Institutional law and economics:

> is quite simply to understand what is going on – to identify the instrumental variables and fundamental issues and processes – in the operation of legal institutions of economic significance, [and to promote] the development of skills with which to analyze and predict the performance consequences of alternative institutional designs. (p. 1)

The positive approach is of course disquieting to those engaged in trying to fashion antitrust policy – policy that, from their particular approach or vantage point, seems comprehensive, substantive, and responsible. No one expresses that frustration (which I share) more clearly than Daniel A. Crane in his review of this same book where he called for "the articulation and defense of a unified, comprehensive normative vision to contend with the

implicit ideological assumptions of Chicago" (Crane, 2009, p. 20). He goes
on to say:

> What is needed is an expression of a strong normative position on why antitrust law
> should exist and what its limits are, who its intended beneficiaries are, how conflicts
> between different stakeholders should be mediated, how more vigorous enforcement is
> consistent with broader political values, and how antitrust should be implemented given
> political and institutional constraints. (*ibid.*)

For proponents of Chicago they have already answered those questions
(for themselves). For most of the contributors to this book, they remain
unsatisfied. For Crane, he thinks he has found a way forward. But all of
these efforts seem to be efforts to "hit the mark." They maintain a mind set
of self-subsistence and separation of economics and the law that allows them
to think unidirectionally that there changed antitrust law and/or policy will
systematically alter economic performance. But, as proponents of Institutional law and economics argue "failure to appreciate the legal-economic
nexus can only result in partial attenuated comprehension of what actually
goes on at the most fundamental levels of legal-economic life" (Samuels,
1989, p. 1572). In short, policy makers end up looking for marks to shoot at
when, in fact, the mark exists only in the mind of the analyst.

In the contest over fashioning antitrust (statutes, regulations, judicial
treatment, and ideas) – the Chicago school is but one ideology – an ideology
that operates under the cover of science, in this case, the science of
neoclassical economics (see Hackney, 2007). But, as briefly described earlier,
there are other approaches. The structure-conduct-performance paradigm
of the early Harvard school, the Chicago school, the recent Harvard
school, the P-C-S, new institutional antitrust economics, Public Choice,
perhaps even the contributions of New Legal Realism (Nourse & Shaffer,
2009), may now compete for the soul of antitrust. That there is a
competition of ideas over antitrust policy is nothing new. But now the
ideas are more closely intertwined: "The formative intellectual DNA of U.S.
competition law and policy today toward dominant firms is a double helix
that intertwines the contributions of scholars from the Chicago school
and the [new] Harvard School" (Kovacic, 2007, p. 33). Kovacic's view is
shared by others. In a recent article, Einer Elhauge (2007, p. 60) looks
back on seven recent antitrust cases decided by the U.S. Supreme Court
and describes the decisions as ones that generally "embrace the moderate
Harvard school approach ... rather than embrace the Chicago school
principles" (see also Hovenkamp, 2007). On this, F.M. Scherer's (1989)
perspective is illuminating.

Antitrust is accomplished through enforcement, and what gets done depends in significant measure on the laws Congress passes and how the courts, especially the higher courts, interpret statutes whose implications and intent are often not precisely stated. What gets written into the statutes and how the courts interpret the statutes depends in part upon economic analysis, although to be sure, much else is thrown into the stew. (p. 30)

In terms of the legal-economic nexus what goes into the "stew of antitrust" is far more complex. It must never be forgotten that the courts, in deciding cases, have not eliminated non-economic concerns. As Hovenkamp (1994, p. 69) has observed, "one must doubt whether such concerns can ever be eliminated from policy making in a democratic society. The public purpose of economics is not to eliminate political concerns from policy making." And given the interests at stake as to what gets into that "stew," debate would (should) be expected as parties of interest attempt to reposition themselves within the larger legal-economic arena. As the way we think about U.S. competition policy continues to evolve, it will continue to raise fundamental questions that underlie the formation and enforcement of antitrust laws. The question is not just simply one of the "more or less government interventions into the market" as much of the past nonsensical debate seems to suggest. When it comes to such issues as – Too big to fail? – the direction of antitrust in answering the many questions raised will undoubtedly come down to policies provided by the school(s) of thought that guide and impact the Congress, the enforcement agencies, and the courts. More specifically, in confronting the question – Too big to fail? – the issues are: (1) How do the proponents of any one school of thought characterize the mechanism (i.e. the real mechanism) that is at work to allocate our nation's scarce resources? (2) Who wins and who loses as one school or the other comes to dominate? (3) What is their perspective on the linkages between our nation's laws and our nation's economy? Can any substantive antitrust law be passed or antitrust policy enforced if one is only casually interested in how our nation's scarce resources are actually allocated; if one maintains a distorted view as to the fundamental linkage between the market and government; or if one does not really care about who wins and who loses as antitrust policy is played out?

As described earlier, from the vantage point of the legal-economic nexus, the structure of the law and the economic system are simultaneously worked out. The legal-economic nexus is founded on several interrelated premises. One premise was articulated by many American institutional economists some 50 or 60 years ago, and stated explicitly by Clarence Ayres. Recognizing that in the United States the organizational structure of society – its constitution, its judiciary, its legislature, and its bureaucracy – ultimately determines the allocation and distribution of resources through its public sector, its market sector, and through its non-profits. He argued:

> The object of dissent is the conception of the market as the guiding mechanism of the economy, or more broadly, the conception of the economy as organized and guided by the market. *It simply is not true that scarce resources are allocated among alterative uses by the market.* The real determinant of whatever allocation occurs in any society is the organizational structure of that society – in short, its institutions ... By focusing attention on the market mechanism, economists have ignored the real allocation mechanism. (Ayres, 1957, p. 26; emphasis added)[18]

Thus, one contention here is that you cannot fashion effective antitrust laws if you have not identified the "real allocation mechanism." In the 21st century, any school of thought that believes that the market is allocating our nation's resources is starting from a position that serves as a predicate for misguided antitrust law and policy. The shout of "unintended consequences" cannot be far off. Indeed, in response to the banking industry's 2008/2009 collapse, while contemplating its causes and consequences, Posner (2009a, p. 2) concluded that "that the present generation of economists has not figured out how the economy works."

The second point to be made (directly related to the point described above) is that many antitrust policy makers (particularly those more sympathetic to the Chicago school) continue to advance a false dichotomy – the notion that the market is the premier regulator of resources as *opposed* to government. In short "that government is the problem" (p. 36). Nothing could be further from the truth – the narrative that the market is an alternative to government in allocating resources is simply wrong and the cause of much mischief. That narrative serves to narrow, in most cases distort, legal-economic reality and thus channels policy (antitrust) debates toward a preferred normative outcome rather than a positive analytical outcome. In fact, the truth is quite the contrary. The state (government) in all of its manifestations stands as an essential complement to the market – the latter is not a superior substitute for the former. As the conservative columnist George Will (2002) (someone I believe maintains a realistic understanding of conservative economic doctrine) has counseled his fellow conservative travelers:

> [I] will remind everyone – some conservatives, painfully – that a mature capitalist economy is a government project. A properly functioning free market system does not spring spontaneously from society's soils as dandelions spring from suburban lawns. Rather *it is a complex creation of laws and mores.* (p. 3; emphasis added)

Thus, for Chicagoans to speak of the market (or market remedies) as if devoid of government or as government as an intruder is misleading when, in fact, the government is the predicate for the market sector allocation of resources and hence, any market remedy. The assertion that the market is an alternative to government is a fabrication. The market is not part of a parallel universe; it does not stand above and apart from the activities of human law makers; it does not have a "natural" legitimacy that rests with either reason or divine inspiration. The constant assertion that the market is an alternative to government asks one to believe that market is much like Will's spontaneous dandelions. We are asked to believe that markets somehow predate human activity or are spontaneous phenomena – with beaver pelts in the Labrador Peninsula often used as their prototype for the 21st century (Demsetz, 1967). Even Posner, the doyen of the market-oriented Chicago law and economics movement, was led to conclude that "we are learning that we need a more active and more intelligent government to keep our model of a capitalist economy from running off the rails" (Posner, 2009b, p. xii). The ploy Chicago has advanced is that if only the government stepped aside, if it stayed out of our lives (never quite getting to "if only there was no government"), the market would be unharnessed and the dandelions would sprout.

In the legal-economic nexus, it is the government-selected, government-sanctioned, and government-enforced structure of private property rights that gives rise to markets – the market sector is *niched within* a nation's political and legal institutions (its government) not an alternative to them (to it). Since markets exist through the active role of government and *not* by government forbearance, the government is the means by which the market gains its status and legitimacy. Indeed, if a market for certain product should spontaneously arise (e.g., the free market for heroin or the free market of nuclear weapons) they are named "black' and relentlessly prosecuted. It is those markets that have the state's sanction, those that are aided, abetted and fostered by government; it is those markets that are ultimately embraced by capitalism. In short, markets are a function of the nation's political-legal institutions – its constitution, its judiciary, its legislature, and its bureaucracy – and the power structures which form and operate through them.

A simple (and timely) example makes the point ... the market for automobiles. First, in the market for automobiles, on the product side, what constitutes an automobile includes, among other things, the rights governing: (i) the very definition of an automobile (now including seat belts, air bags, and a catalytic converter together with severe legal sanctions for disconnecting any of the items); (ii) the government mandated standards and tests that govern automobile production and performance; and (iii) the terms, conditions, and the enforcement of warranties. It is the government-structured definition, assignment and enforcement of rights that shape the market for automobiles; it is not a question of an automobile market with government or without government. In a like manner, on the input side, what constitutes labor in an automobile plant includes, among other things, (i) the rights governing child labor laws; (ii) occupational health and safety laws governing the plant environment; (iii) labor and union law; and (iv) the quality of the materials and various factors of production. Again, it is not a question of an auto-worker labor market with government or without government. The market for automobiles, including the market for auto workers, indeed all of the related markets, are a manifestation of the legal-economic nexus; markets complemented by government and governments constantly being reshaped as market performance unfolds. And, as we now know, further manifestations of the legal-economic nexus within the U.S. automobile industry was at center stage in the wake of the 2008 housing, financial, and economic meltdown as the U.S. government took a partial ownership position in both General Motors and Chrysler.

Thus, like it or not, we must come to understand that law (including antitrust law) is not something that is given or to be discovered by either reason or divine inspiration but is instead a human artifact marked by deliberative and non-deliberative human choice where specific political-legal-economic outcomes are seen as an expression of the values of those who have participated and prevailed in the political-legal-economic arena. Prevailing laws (especially antitrust laws) and the interpretation of those laws, together with the way we think (and are taught to think) about antitrust law,[19] are an expression of those who were able to most effectively use government and institutions to further their own ends. And as stated earlier, it is with respect to antitrust law that Chicago claims its greatest victory. But in fact, Chicago is only one ingredient in the making of the "stew." Kauper captured the essence of what has transpired in antitrust:

> Change has come not from a single source, but from many including Phillip Areeda, Bob Pitofsky, and Herbert Hovenkamp, whose views are not always easily pigeonholed, but who have exerted a considerable influence along with those from Chicago. Change has come in the best of legal methods, taking from one source, shaping it in the light of another, and so on. (p. 42)

The real world in which public policy (including antitrust) is worked out was clearly described by Ralph Miliband:

> More that ever before men now live in the shadow of the state. What they want to achieve, individually or in groups now mainly depends on the state's sanction and support. But since that sanction and support are not bestowed indiscriminately, they must, ever more directly, seek to influence and shape it altogether. It is for the state's attention, or for its control, that men compete. (Miliband, 1969, p. 1)

NOTES

1. Using the general term "antitrust" inclusively runs contrary to Rockefeller (2007).
2. The use of the "old" and "new" terminology was recognized early on in Posner (1975, p. 759; see also Kitch, 1983).
3. The history of antitrust teachings at the University of Chicago Law School by Aaron Director, Edward Levi and others is recounted in chapter 8 of Van Overtveldt (2007) and chapter 5 of Duxbury (1995).
4. The ideological nature and the political machinations to establish law and economics at Chicago is recounted by Teles (2008, chapter 4). Many at Chicago have tried to claim this movement was void of ideological content. For instance, read Edmund Kitch (1983):

> [t]he interest ... in economics did not come out of any anti-interventionist thinking. It essentially came out of the idea that the legal system is going to [impacting the economic system] now and that means we need to learn how to do it right and maybe economists know something about how to do it right ... There is a great legitimacy given to the idea that government is going to be doing these things and we in the law schools should try to help the government do it right. (pp. 175–176).

5. See Turgeon (2009, pp. 151–157) for the warnings that public choice theory provided in anticipation of the financial crisis. As to whether the theories of regulation belong to the Chicago school or to Public Choice is sometimes confusing. The major contours of the literature are captured in Stigler (1971), Posner (1974), Peltzman (1976), Becker (1983, 1985), and Whitman (1995).
6. F. M. Scherer (1989) contends that structuralism reached it zenith during the three years of Michael Mann's tenure and head of the FTC (early 1971 to mid-1973); see also a balanced and scholarly description and assessment of the Harvard structural approach by Meehan and Lerner (1989).
7. According to Hovenkamp (2005, p. 36), their approach was largely attributable to the Harvard school's belief in the Cournot theory of oligopoly.
8. According to Easterbrook (1986, p. 1701), the Chicago school generally advocated an antitrust policy that consisted of "little other than prosecuting plain

vanilla cartels and mergers to monopoly." Posner characterized the Chicago school's focus and impact on antitrust as follows:

> [T]he focus of the antitrust laws ... should instead be on: (1) cartels and (2) horizontal mergers large enough either to create monopoly directly, as in the classic trust cases, or to facilitate cartelization by drastically reducing the number of significant sellers in the market .... [T]his implied a breathtaking contraction in the scope of antitrust policy." (Posner, 1979, p. 928)

9. Herbert Hovenkamp (2001, p. 336) aptly described it: "The Chicago school gave antitrust an elegant and simple set of models that emphasized the robustness of markets and the frequent futility of government intervention."

10. The focus on institutional factors and to make certain that antitrust rules should not outrun the capabilities of implementing institutions is a recurring theme in the New Harvard literature (see, for example, Kovacic, 2007, p. 37).

11. The following question still remains in dispute: did the Chicago school and the Harvard school's views converge because the Chicago school successfully pulled leading Harvard school researchers into their orbit? See Kovacic (2007).

12. The new empirical industrial organization describes techniques for estimating the degree of competitiveness in an industry, relying more on prices rather than data as to costs or profits. The studies use comparative statics of equilibria and typically focus on a single industry to deal better with product heterogeneity and institutional details.

13. Judge Abner Mikva, a U.S. Circuit Court Judge, U.S. Court of Appeals for the District of Columbia and former Illinois state legislator, offered an even more stinging assessment: "Not even five terms in the Illinois state legislature – the last vestige of democracy in the 'raw' – nor my terms in the U.S. Congress, prepared me for the villainy of the public choice literature" (Mikva, 1988, p. 167).

14. Depending on the wider context of the particular public policy under scrutiny, in Public Choice theory the goal of the self-interested legislators and bureaucrats is that of maximizing the probability of (re)election to political office; maximizing the probability of (re)appointment to an administrative position; and/or the maximization of their wealth (broadly defined to include, salary, perquisites of office, and expected income from post-government employment).

15. See also Hovenkamp's (1986, p. 1020) observation that "the Chicago School has done more for antitrust policy than any other coherent economic theory since the New Deal. No one ... can escape [its] influence on antitrust analysis."

16. Baker (1988, p. 655) wrote that "Antitrust has accepted the Chicago school's conclusions about the effect of business practices."

17. Alan Greenspan's perspective regarding fraud was commented on by a staff writer for the online news magazine *The Seminal*: "During an introduction lunch as guest of guru Greenspan, Chairman of the Federal Reserve, Born was stunned to discover his 'absolutist' (Brooksley Born's word) disdain for 'regulation'. In so many words, Greenspan advised her not to fret about any occurrences of fraud since, after all, the market would take care of the 'fraudsters' by self-regulating itself" (The Seminal, 2009).

18. From his Public Choice perspective, James Buchanan (1986, p. 20) described the implication of using (expanding) the notion of methodological individualism for contractarian public choice theory forming what he termed a "genuine theory of law" where "there are no lines to be drawn at the edges of 'the economy' and the 'polity,' or between 'markets' and 'governments,' between 'the private sector' and the 'public sector.'"

19. Kauper correctly observed in his entry for Pitofsky's volume (p. 46): "[W]hile we have not seen total acceptance of the Chicago program, its real influence is found in how we think."

ACKNOWLEDGMENT

The author wishes to thank David Schweikhardt for comments and suggestions on earlier drafts of this chapter.

REFERENCES

Andrews, E. L. (2008). Greenspan concedes error on regulation. *New York Times*, October 24, p. B1.

Armentano, D. T. (2007). *Antitrust: The case for repeal*. Auburn, AL: Ludwig von Mises Institute.

Ayres, C. E. (1957). Institutional economics: Discussion. *American Economic Review, 47*(2), 13–27.

Bain, J. (1951). Relation of profit rate to industry concentration: American manufacturing, 1936–1940. *Quarterly Journal of Economics, 65*(2), 293–324.

Baker, J. B. (1988). Recent developments in economics that challenge Chicago school views. *Antitrust Law Journal, 58*(3), 645–655.

Baxter, W. (1980). The political economy of antitrust: Principal paper. In: R. D. Tollison (Ed.), *The political economy of antitrust* (pp. 3–49). Lexington, MA: D.C. Heath.

Becker, G. (1983). A theory of competition among pressure groups for political influence. *Quarterly Journal of Economics, 98*(2), 371–400.

Becker, G. (1985). Public policies, pressure groups, and dead weight costs. *Journal of Public Economics, 28*(3), 329–347.

Buchanan, J. M. (1986). *Liberty, market and state*. New York: New York University Press.

Crane, D. (2009). Chicago, post-Chicago, and neo-Chicago. *University of Chicago Law Review, 76*(4), 1911–1933.

Demsetz, H. (1967). Toward a theory of property rights. *American Economic Review, 57*(2), 347–359.

DiLorenzo, T. J. (1985). The origins of antitrust: An interest-group perspective. *International Review of Law and Economics, 5*(1), 73–90.

Duchin, R. & Sosyura, D. (2009). TARP investments: Financials and politics. Ross School of Business Paper No. 1127. Available at SSRN: http://ssrn.com/abstract = 1426219

Duxbury, N. (1995). *Patterns of American jurisprudence*. Oxford: Oxford University Press.

Easterbrook, F. H. (1986). Workable antitrust policy. *Michigan Law Review, 84*(8), 1696–1713.

Elhauge, E. (2007). Harvard, not Chicago: Which antitrust school drives recent supreme court decisions? *Competition Policy International, 3*(2), 59–77.

Farber, D. A., & Frickey, P. P. (1999). *Law and public choice.* Chicago, IL: University of Chicago Press.

Fox, E. M. (1981). The modernization of antitrust: A new equilibrium. *Cornell Law Review, 66*(6), 1140–1191.

Gavil, A. I., Kovacic, W. E., & Baker, J. B. (2008). *Antitrust law in perspective: Cases, concepts and problems in competition policy* (2nd ed). St. Paul, MN: American Casebook Series.

Gellhorn, E., Kovacic, W. E., & Calkins, S. (1994). *Antitrust law and economics.* St. Paul, MN: Thomson-West.

Greenspan, A. (1966a). Antitrust. In: A. Rand (Ed.), *Capitalism: The unknown ideal* (pp. 63–72). London: New American Library.

Greenspan, A. (1966b). The assault on integrity. In: A. Rand (Ed.), *Capitalism: The unknown ideal* (pp. 126–130). London: New American Library.

Hackney, J. R., Jr. (2007). *Under the cover of science: American legal-economic theory and the quest for objectivity.* Durham, NC: Duke University Press.

Hofstadter, R. (1996). What happened to the antitrust movement? In: *The paranoid style in American politics and other essays* (pp. 188–237). Cambridge, MA: Harvard University Press.

Hovenkamp, H. (1985). Antitrust policy after Chicago. *Michigan Law Review, 84*(2), 213–284.

Hovenkamp, H. (1986). Chicago and its alternatives. *Duke Law Journal, 1986*(6), 1014–1029.

Hovenkamp, H. (1994). *Federal antitrust policy: The law of competition and its practice.* St. Paul, MN: Thomson-West.

Hovenkamp, H. (1996). The Areeda-Turner treatise in antitrust analysis. *Antitrust Bulletin, 41*(4), 815–842.

Hovenkamp, H. (2001). Post-Chicago antitrust: A review and critique. *Columbia Business Law Review, 2001*(2), 257–337.

Hovenkamp, H. (2005). *The American enterprise.* Cambridge, MA: Harvard University Press.

Hovenkamp, H. (2007). The Harvard and Chicago schools and the dominant firm. University of Iowa Legal Studies Research Paper No. 07-19. Available at ssrn.com/ abstract = 1014153

Jacobs, M. S. (1995). An essay on the normative foundations of antitrust economics. *North Carolina Law Review, 74*(1), 219–265.

Joskow, P. L. (1991). The role of transaction cost economics in antitrust and public utility regulatory policies. *Journal of Law, Economics & Organization, 7*(special issue), 53–83.

Kaysen, C., & Turner, D. F. (1959). *Antitrust policy: An economic and legal analysis.* Cambridge, MA: Harvard University Press.

Kitch, E. W. (1983). The fire of truth: A remembrance of law and economics at Chicago, 1932–1970. *Journal of Law and Economics, 26*(1), 163–233.

Kolasky, W. H. (2009). Book review: How the Chicago school overshot the mark, competition. *Competition Policy International, 5*(1), 173–178.

Kovacic, W. E. (2007). Intellectual DNA of modern U.S. competition law for dominant firm conduct: The Chicago/Harvard double helix. *Columbia Business Law Review, 2007*(1), 1–80.

Lande, R. H. (1982). Wealth transfers as the original and primary concern of antitrust: The efficiency interpretation challenged. *Hastings Law Journal, 34*(1), 65–151.

Lande, R. H. (1990). Commentary: Implications of professor Scherer's research for the failure of antitrust. *Washburn Law Journal, 29*(2), 256–269.

Mason, E. S. (1964). *Economic concentration and the monopoly problem.* Cambridge, MA: Harvard University Press.

McChesney, F. (2004). Talking 'bout my antitrust generation. *Regulation, 27*(3), 48–51.

McChesney, F. S., & Shughart, W. F., II (Eds). (1995). *The causes and consequences of antitrust: The public-choice perspective.* Chicago, IL: University of Chicago Press.

Meehan, J. W., Jr., & Lerner, R. J. (1989). In: *Economics and antitrust policy* (pp. 179–208). Westport, CT: Quorum Books.

Mercuro, N. (2007). *Law and economics. Vol. 5, critical concepts in law.* London, UK: Routledge.

Mercuro, N., & Medema, S. G. (2006). *Economics and the law: From Posner to post-modernism and beyond.* Princeton, NJ: Princeton University Press.

Mikva, A. J. (1988). Foreword: Symposium on the theory of public choice. *Virginia Law Review, 74*(2), 167–177.

Miliband, R. (1969). *The state and the capitalist society.* London: Weidenfeld and Nicolson.

Nourse, V., & Shaffer, G. (2009). Varieties of new legal realism: Can a new world order prompt a new legal theory? *Cornell Law Review, 95*(1), 61–137.

Van Overtveldt, J. (2007). *The Chicago school: How the University of Chicago assembled the thinkers who revolutionized economics and business.* Chicago, IL: Agate.

Oxford University Press. Catalog description: *How the Chicago school overshot the Mark.* Available at www.oup.com/us/catalog/general/subject/Economics/Policy/?view = usa& ci = 9780195339765

Peltzman, S. (1976). Toward a more general theory of regulation. *Journal of Law and Economics, 19*(2), 211–240.

Pitofsky, R. (1979). The political content of antitrust. *University of Pennsylvania Law Review, 127*(4), 1051–1075.

Posner, R. A. (1974). Theories of economic regulation. *Bell Journal of Economics and Management Science, 5*(2), 335–358.

Posner, R. A. (1975). The economic approach to law. *Texas Law Review, 53*(4), 757–782.

Posner, R. A. (1979). The Chicago school of antitrust analysis. *University of Pennsylvania Law Review, 127*(4), 925–948.

Posner, R. A. (2009a). How I became a Keynesian: Second thoughts in the middle of a crisis. *The New Republic,* September 23, pp. 1–16. Available at www.tnr.com/article/how-i-became-keynesian

Posner, R. A. (2009b). *Capitalism's fault lines.* Cambridge, MA: Harvard University Press.

Rockefeller, E. S. (2007). *The antitrust religion.* Washington, DC: Cato Institute.

Samuels, W. J. (1989). The legal-economic nexus. *George Washington Law Review, 57*(6), 1556–1578.

Samuels, W. J., & Schmid, A. A. (1981). *Law and economics: An institutional perspective.* Boston, MA: Kluwer-Nijhoff Publishing.

Scherer, F. M. (1989). Merger policy in the 70s and 80s. In: J. W. Meehan, Jr. & R. J. Lerner (Eds), *Economics and antitrust policy* (pp. 83–101). Westport, CT: Quorum Books.

Shughart, W. F., II., & Tollison, R. D. (1985). The positive economics of antitrust policy: A survey article. *International Review of Law and Economics, 5*(1), 39–57.

Stigler, G. (1971). The theory of economic regulation. *Bell Journal of Economics and Management Science, 2*(1), 137–146.

Teles, S. M. (2008). *The rise of the conservative legal movement: The battle for control of the law.* Princeton, NJ: Princeton University Press.

The Seminal. (2009). No foes to Fraud – Greenspan, Rubin, Summers – Owe Brooksley Born and the American Taxpayer a Big Fat Apology and a Ton of Money. *The Seminal*, October 24. Available at seminal.firedoglake.com/diary/11000

Turgeon, E. (2009). Boom and bust for whom? The economic philosophy behind the 2008 financial crisis. *Virginia Law and Business Review*, 4(1), 139–186.

Weiss, L. W. (1974). The concentration-profits relationship and antitrust. In: H. J. Goldschmid, H. M. Mann & J. F. Weston (Eds), *Industrial concentration: The new learning* (pp. 184–232). Boston, MA: Little Brown.

Welch, P. J., & Greaney, T. L. (2005). Alternative economic approaches to antitrust enforcement. In: M. Oppenheimer & N. Mercuro (Eds), *Law & economics: Alternative economic approaches to legal and regulatory issues* (pp. 77–98). Armonk, NY: M.E. Sharpe.

Whitman, D. (1995). *The myth of democratic failure: Why political institutions are efficient.* Chicago, IL: University of Chicago Press.

Will, G. (2002). It's time Bush showed anger over Enron. *Jewish World Review*, January 16, p. 3. Available at http://www.jewishworldreview.com/cols/will011602.asp

Williamson, O. E. (1974). The economics of antitrust: Transaction cost considerations. *University of Pennsylvania Law Review*, 122(6), 1439–1496.

Williamson, O. E. (1975). *Markets and hierarchies: Analysis and antitrust implications.* New York: Macmillan.

Williamson, O. E. (1979). Assessing vertical market restrictions: Antitrust ramifications of the transaction cost approach. *University of Pennsylvania Law Review*, 127(4), 953–993.

Williamson, O. E. (1989). Transaction cost economics. In: R. Schmalensee & R. D. Willig (Eds), *Handbook of industrial organization* (pp. 136–184). Amsterdam: North-Holland.

Williamson, O. E. (1996). Revisiting legal realism: The law, economics, and organization perspective. *Industrial and Corporate Change*, 5(2), 383–420.

Wright, J. D. (2007). The Roberts' court and the Chicago school of antitrust: The 2006 term and beyond. *Competition Policy International*, 3(2), 24–57.

Wright, J. D. (2009). Overshot the mark? A simple explanation of the Chicago school's influence on antitrust. *Competition Policy International*, 5(1), 179–213.

Wright, J. D. (2010). Antitrust and merger policy. In: P.G. Klein & M.E. Sykuta (Eds), *The elgar companion to transaction cost economics.* Cheltenham, UK: Edward Elgar, forthcoming.